COMPUTER PERFORMANCE

IFIP Working Group 7.3 Conference on
Computer system Modeling
Yorktown Heights, USA August 16 - 18, 1977

NORTH-HOLLAND PUBLISHING COMPANY
AMSTERDAM • NEW YORK • OXFORD

COMPUTER PERFORMANCE

Proceedings of the International Symposium on
Computer Performance Modeling, Measurement and Evaluation,
IBM Thomas J. Watson Research Center,
Yorktown Heights, New York August 16 - 18, 1977

edited by

K. Mani Chandy
University of Texas, Austin

and

Martin Reiser
Thomas J. Watson Research Center

PREPRINTS

1977

NORTH-HOLLAND PUBLISHING COMPANY
AMSTERDAM • NEW YORK • OXFORD

North-Holland ISBN: 0444 85038 4

Proceedings will be published by:
NORTH-HOLLAND PUBLISHING COMPANY
AMSTERDAM • NEW YORK • OXFORD

Distributors for the U.S.A. and Canada:
Elsevier/North-Holland, Inc.
52 Vanderbilt Avenue
New York, N.Y. 10017

PRINTED IN THE USA

TABLE OF CONTENTS

FOREWORD

The area of central computer and computer communication system
analysis has come a long way from the early attempts about a decade
ago to the present state-of-the-art as represented in this volume.
The most outstanding difference of this conference compared with
previous ones lies, in my opinion, in its emphasis on case studies
and careful validation of results. Models, brushed over as grossly
unrealistic not long ago have gained a lot of credibility in the
process. Subsequently I take the opportunity to comment on where
I think we stand today. These comments are strictly my own and I
realize that other people might distribute the weights differently.

(1)   "First generation" analytical models such as cyclic
        queues [Gaver] and central server model [Buzen]
        are now widely used in practice. Validation of
        results is taken more seriously and a consistent
        picture is emerging. In this volume, we find an
        excellent set of validated case studies. Modeling
        approaches which go beyond the early models are
        described in chapters by Bard, Guillon, Abell and
        Rosen, Hamilton, Diethelm and Kraemer. The lack
        of model validation, so obvious in many earlier
        conferences, stems largely from the logistical
        difficulty and costs of data collection. I think
        that much progress could be made by architected
        performance monitoring functions and by the use of
        combined hardware/software monitors. Development
        of such measurement tools seems a promising topic for
        future research. Also needed is a better data
        gathering methodology. Some statistical aspects of
        this problem are described here by Hempy, Chouinard,
        Lazowska and Gomaa, but I think more remains to be
        done.

(2)   The multiclass queuing network model with generalized
        servers has been a breakthrough. The development of
        efficient numerical algorithms [Buzen, Reiser and
        Kobayashi] for the first time made queuing theory

a powerful tool for the non-mathematically oriented
analyst. To me, the real significance of the
generalized servers (e.g. servers with processor
sharing, last-come first-served and no-queuing
disciplines) is the realization that in many instances
the form of the distribution function does not matter.
Therefore, one often need not worry about the
"Exponential assumption" of the models. It is obviously
the robustness of real systems, i.e. their relative
insensitivity with respect to distributional forms
which is largely responsible for the success of early
models (such as the central server model with
exponential servers). Yet there are of course systems
which are not robust (communication networks, for
example). I think that further study is required to
more clearly delineate robust systems from non-robust
ones. One chapter addresses this problem in some
detail [Sevcik et. al.] .

(3)   Despite my calling the multiclass network model a
breakthrough, it is still seriously deficient in
system structure and workload features exhibited by
real systems. To mind come priority queuing disciplines
and blocking phemomena (i.e. the existence of limited
capacity subsystems). There seems no easy analytical
solution. Therefore a lot of work went into the study
of approximate solutions, good enough for practical
purposes. Most of these methods are based on some
decomposition heuristic, often paired with approximations
to the G/G/I queuing problem (such as the diffusion
approximation) or with numerical solutions of Markov
chains. The high interest is manifest in various
chapters on the subject [Labetoulle and Pujolle,
Kraemer, Sevcik et. al., Foschini, Brandwajn] . An
alternative approach is to get numerical solutions to
the continuous time Markov chains into which many of the
more general queuing network problems can be mapped.
One chapter Stewart explores in detail the numerical
properties of the resulting linear equations. Use of

Markov chain solutions is made in various other papers
in this volume. Unfortunately, this approach is
severly computationally limited. Nevertheless, I feel
that the limit can be further pushed and that the Markov
chain solution could become a practical tool utilized
best in conjunction with the other methods such as
approximation methods and separable network solutions
see for example the chapter by Bux and Herzog .
Besides the queuing network problem, the single resource
system is still a challenge when it comes to correlated
inputs [Gopinath and Morrison, Wolff] or other
deviations from classical queuing theory.

(4)   I already mentioned the satisfactory results obtained
      with various queuing models. However, their application
      requires prior knowledge of workload parameters on the
      level of execution intervals of the central processors.
      This is not an intrinsic workload parameter and is not
      even easy to measure. Clearly a more basic program
      behaviour model which could generate execution intervals
      from individual program parameters is of paramount
      interest. A lot of work has been done and the subject
      is represented by various chapters by Chow and Chiu,
      Schroeder, Graham and Denning and Marcus and Cerino.
      Despite the impressing progress reported, I feel that
      the modeling of the workload is still the weakest side
      in a total system model (especially when it comes to
      multithread workloads).

(5)   Simulation has always been a powerful model solution
      technique. In contrast with analytical models which
      bring to bear advanced mathematical theories,
      simulation is of almost trivial simplicity. Every
      programmer can master it in a short time. Yet I think
      this simplicity is also a great problem since too
      often enough attention is not paid to proper modeling
      (i.e. abstraction) and to the analysis of simulation
      output. A considerable effort is now made to improve
      the situation by developing appropriate modeling

languages and by providing automation of output analysis.
Several papers address the topics of modeling
languages which force the user to think in suitable
abstractions [Parent et. al., Schwandt] and of
confidence interval generation [Lavenberg et. al.] .
Simulation run time is also a perennial problem As a
radical cure, a special purpose simulation computer is
suggested in one of the chapters [Parent et. al.]   .
Whether this proves a commercially viable alternative
remains to be seen.

(6)   The analyst of computer communication networks faces
in many respects a problem more formidable than his
colleague who is concerned with host performance.
Nodal blocking and sensitivity to the distributional
form make an analytical solution very difficult. The
trick which was so successful in the central server
model, namely to represent the limited capacity system
by a closed queuing model does not take care of the
mutual blocking of store-and-forward nodes. Other
heuristics are called for. I don't think a satisfactory
solution has yet been found but some progress is
reported by [Labetoulle and Pujolle] . Another important area in network resource management (e.g. routing
and flow control). I think that the flow control
problem, i.e. the regulation of admittance to the
network is among the most important but least understood
problems. Hopefully, analytical studies will supplant
brute force simulation in the future. Contributions
to these topics are found in the chapters by Foschini,
Chu and Chen and Holtzmann. Besides management of a
transmission network the access methods used to enter
the network still pose problems, despite a lot of analysis.
I don't think this book is fully representative of this
field. To mention is the chapter by Eckberg.

I have tried to organize my overview along the lines of modeling
methodology and solution techniques. Two major uses for models are
as configuration or planning tolls and for system design and

optimization. While I think that in the first category, a quite
satisfactory state is reached, it is still difficult to analyze
algorithms such as schedulers or storage managers other than by
simulation models. There are several papers in this volume which
do show important progress in this latter area [see Kraemer,
Chow and Kohler, Graham and Denning, Coffmann et. al., Mendelson
and Yechiali, Noetzel].

I am deeply grateful to Hisashi Kobayashi, who made this Symposium
possible and who appointed me as Proceeding editor and to Mani K.
Chandy who compiled a program of such impressive technical
excellence.

COMPUTER PERFORMANCE, K.M. CHANDY AND M. REISER (EDS.)
NORTH HOLLAND PUBLISHING COMPANY, 1977

IMPROVING APPROXIMATIONS OF AGGREGATED QUEUING NETWORK SUBSYSTEMS

K. C. Sevcik, A. I. Levy, S. K. Tripathi and J. L. Zahorjan
Computer Systems Research Group
University of Toronto
Toronto, Canada

Queueing network models become more difficult
to analyze as they include more detail of the
computer systems they represent. Only those
models that satisfy local balance are currently
susceptible to analysis by computationally
efficient algorithms. Other models can be treated
by simulation, or, if small enough, by the
solution of global balance equations. A third
alternative is to use an approximate solution
technique. Such techniques involve altering the
structure, parameters, or assumptions of the model
in order to permit efficient analysis. Analysis
of the approximate model yields answers close to
those that would result from exact analysis of the
original model, but with far less computational
effort. One important approximation technique is
the aggregation of subnetworks. After analysing
the subnetwork, a composite server replaces it in
a reduced model. In this paper, we examine some
improved methods of establishing the
characteristics of composite servers. Because the
variance of interarrival times is known to affect
the queueing properties at a single server, we
examine the influence of transition processes, by
which customers circulate among the service
centers of a queueing network model.

1. Introduction

Queueing network models have attained acceptance as useful tools in assessing and predicting the performance of computing systems. Efficient computational techniques for analyzing these models have been developed for queueing networks satisfying certain restrictive conditions. While these conditions have been substantially weakened in the recent years, models directly solvable with the efficient computational algorithms still cannot fully represent the complexity of the actual computer systems that we would like to study [BCBKTD].

Models for which efficient computational analysis algorithms are not known must be treated using other techniques. One approach is to decompose the model [CHW1,Cou]. For example, a subnetwork can be independently analyzed, then replaced by a single composite service center, selected to represent the interaction of the subnetwork with the rest of the system. Relative to direct analysis of the entire network, far less computational effort is required by analyzing first the subnetwork, then the network in which the subnetwork is represented by a single service center. Although some parts of the analysis involve approximations, under certain conditions the estimations of performance measures are sufficiently accurate to be useful [Cou]. An additional motivation for aggregating subnetworks is to increase the efficiency of repeated experiments in which a portion of a queueing network stays fixed while parameters are altered elsewhere in the network. Representing the fixed subnetwork by a single service center substantially reduces the computational effort required in each trial.

In this paper, we will discuss and extend techniques that have been proposed for establishing the characteristics of a composite service center intended to represent an entire subsystem to the rest of the network. In section 2, we define our terminology and establish the context of this work by surveying relevant literature. In section 3, we establish some approximations for characterizing activities that occur in queueing networks. The approximations are intended to permit a more detailed representation of the patterns in which programs use computer system resources. The relationship of the approximations to the aggregation of subnetworks and the analysis of entire networks is presented in section 4, and examples are discussed in section 5. Section 6 contains a summary of our conclusions.

2. Terminology and Previous Work

A queueing network model of a computer system consists of service centers representing such computer system resources as processing units, channels, peripheral devices and terminals, and customers, whose usage of system resources is represented by a sequence of visits to the corresponding service centers. Customers are completely characterized by their class. With each class of customers and each service center are associated service time distributions and transition probabilities. Samples from the service time distribution determine the duration of a customer's use of a service center, and the transition probabilities govern the movements of customers among the service centers. In this paper, we treat only closed networks, in which the total number of customers in the network is constant.

A special form of queueing network model that has proven to be particularly useful in modelling computer systems is the closed central server model with a single class of customers [Buz]. Customers alternately visit a central server and one of several peripheral servers. Typically, the central server represents the central processor of a computer system, while each peripheral server represents a group of peripheral devices and their channel. Figure 1 shows a closed central server model. Pi is the probability that a customer leaving the central server next visits service center i. If P1 is not zero, the transition of a customer back to the central server can be interpreted as the completion of one program and its instantaneous replacement by a statistically identical program. Mi denotes the mean service time required by a customer at each visit to service center i.

When service time distributions are characterized completely by their mean (Mi), they are assumed to have an exponential form. This assumption facilitates mathematical analysis. When their variance (VARi) or squared coefficient of variation (CVi^2=VARi/(Mi)^2) is also used, many of the analytical benefits of the exponential distribution can be retained by assuming one of the three distributional forms shown in figure 2 and defined below:

HE2: Hyperexponential (2-stage)   (CVi^2>1)

$$f(t) = are^{-rt} + (1-a)se^{-st}$$

where
$$a = (1/2)(1-\sqrt{(CVi^2-1)/(CVi^2+1)})$$
$$r = 2a/Mi$$
$$s = 2(1-a)/Mi$$

Exp: Exponential   (CVi^2=1)

$$f(t) = re^{-rt}$$
where $r = 1/Mi$

GEr: Generalized Erlang (k-stage)   (CVi^2<1)

$$f(t) = \frac{(rt)^{k-2}}{(k-2)!}(1-a+(art/(k-1))re^{-rt}$$

where $k = \lceil 1/CVi^2 \rceil$
$$a = T + \sqrt{kT}/(CVi^2+1)$$
where $T = 1-(k-1)CVi^2$
$$r = (k-1+a)/Mi$$

The formulae for specifying the distribution parameters determine a unique distribution within the family of distributions that have the required mean and coefficient of variation.

For the HE2 distribution, the values of a, r and s are established as by Sauer and Chandy [SC]. The GEr distribution of figure 2 differs from the generalized Erlang structure used previously by others. With this GEr structure, all customers pass through either k-1 or k stages, while structures used previously

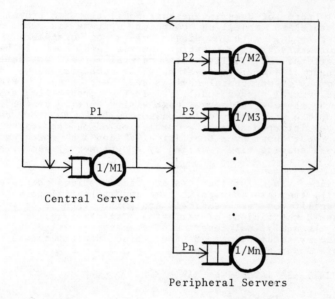

Figure 1: Central Server Model

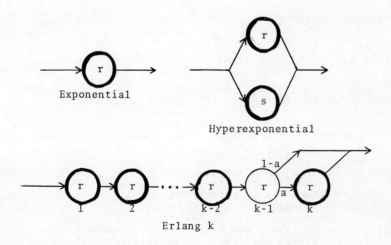

Figure 2: Distributional Forms

permit some customers to pass through only one or even zero stages. The advantage of the GEr structure used here is that its density function has only one relative maximum, so that it resembles empirically observed service time distributions of low variance.

In single class models with exponentially distributed service times, most performance measures of interest are independent of the service disciplines used. However, in multiple class models or models including non-exponential service time distributions, the service disciplines must be considered. The two disciplines that we will use are first-come-first-served (FCFS), where customers are served in the order of their arrival to the service center, and processor-sharing (PS), where all customers at the service center share the processor's power equally. A server is said to be load dependent if its service rate changes depending on the customer mix at the server.

Queueing networks that obey certain constraints are known to satisfy local balance and to have product form state probabilities [CHT,GN,BCMP]. The product form can be exploited by efficient computational algorithms for calculating performance measures of interest [Buz,CHW1,RK2]. Unfortunately, local balance is precluded by the presence of a FCFS service center with either a non-exponential service time distribution or non-identical exponential service time distributions for different classes.

Analysis of queueing networks that do not satisfy local balance typically requires several steps. Either some simplifying assumptions are employed to modify the network to satisfy local balance, or a decomposition approach is used. In the latter case, a composite server replaces a subnetwork in order to facilitate analysis. It is feasible to solve the set of global balance equations only for very simple networks.

A central theme of this paper will be the role of transition processes in queueing network analysis. A transition process is a stream of events that mark the movement of customers from one place to another. Each service center has an arrival (or input) process of arriving jobs and a departure (or output) process of completed jobs. Note that the departure process at one center is split up according to transition probabilities, and each part contributes to the arrival process of some other service center. We will characterize a transition process by only the mean and the coefficient of variation of the distribution of interevent times in the stream. We will ignore the higher moments of the interevent time distributions, and also the fact that transition processes are not necessarily renewal processes, that is, successive interevent times are not independent samples from the overall interevent time distribution. The most well-understood transition process is the Poisson process, in which interevent times are exponentially distributed.

The initial work on the use of a composite server to represent a subsystem in a queueing network model was reported by Chandy, Herzog and Woo [CHW1]. They defined Norton's theorem for queueing network models, which is analogous to Norton's theorem of electrical circuit theory. A Norton's theorem reduction in a queueing network model involves replacing a subnetwork that has a single input stream and a single output stream with a composite server. The composite server is intended to behave, with respect to the rest of the queueing network, exactly as did the original subnetwork. By studying the

subsystem to be replaced in isolation under each possible customer
mix, mean throughput rates conditioned on the customer mix are
obtained. To do this, all service centers outside the subsystem are
short-circuited by either removing them or, equivalently, by giving
them extremely high service rates. The scheduling discipline at the
composite server is conceptualized as "composite queueing" (CQ)
[Tow]. CQ can be thought of as providing each customer class with a
processor whose service rate depends on the current mix of customers
in the subsystem. For each class and customer mix, the rate of the
processor is set to be the throughput of the subsystem. The
customers of each class are served at their processor according to a
PS discipline. For example, if a particular customer mix in the
subsystem includes three class A customers and causes the class A
throughput in the subsystem to be 1/2, then class A's CQ processor
with that customer mix has rate 1/2, and each of the three class A
customers is served at rate 1/6.

When a queueing network satisfies local balance, a Norton's
theorem reduction of a subsystem is exact in that the joint
probability distribution of queue lengths at servers not in the
subsystem is identical in the original and reduced systems. For each
class, the service time distribution at the composite server can be
assumed exponential with the required mean to assure the appropriate
throughput. In locally balanced networks, the choice of service
discipline within each class is irrelevant since it does not alter
the probability distribution of system state.

Sauer and Chandy have investigated the direct application of
Norton's theorem reductions to queueing networks that do not satisfy
local balance [SC]. In this case, the network containing the
composite server provides only an approximation to the original
network. The step in which the subsystem is examined in isolation
involves an implicit assumption that the input process to the
subsystem is identical to its output process. This assumption is not
valid in networks that do not satisfy local balance (generally, only
mean input and output rates are identical) and causes the reduction
to be inexact. Thus, there is a motive to give closer consideration
to transition processes into and out of the subsystem, treating
characteristics other than the first moment. Specifically, in the
following sections, we will study the benefits of involving the
second moments of interevent times in representing a subsystem.

Since direct application of Norton's theorem reductions in non-
locally-balanced networks can result in unacceptable error in the
estimation of performance measures [CHW2]. Sauer and Chandy have
incorporated the reduction into several higher level approximation
algorithms, each designed to be applicable to a specific class of
non-locally-balanced networks [SC]. One class of networks they treat
is the class of central server models in which one or more FCFS
service centers have non-exponentially distributed service times.
Their approach starts by assuming exponentially distributed service
times at each service center in the subnetwork to be reduced. A
Norton's theorem reduction is applied to reduce all the peripheral
servers to a composite server. Next, the non-exponential nature of
service time distributions is accounted for by computing an estimate
of the coefficient of variation to be reflected in the service
structure of the composite server. Then both the central server and
the composite server are represented by HE2, Exp, or GEr service
structures according to the estimated coefficients of variation. The
method of determining the coefficient of variation to be used for the

composite server is important and will be discussed in detail later. Having reduced the system to two servers, it can be solved by global balance or other techniques that are not contingent on the presence of local balance [HWC].

Three potential sources of error can be distinguished in the direct application of a Norton's theorem reduction in a network that does not satisfy local balance.

(1) Exponential Assumption -- Because all service time distributions are assumed exponential when analyzing the subsystem, errors in the estimation of throughput rates may result.

(2) CV Omission -- The coefficient of variation of the composite server is set to one, regardless of the characteristics of the service processes at the individual service centers.

(3) Input/Output Assumption -- By ignoring the rest of the network while analyzing the subsystem, an implicit assumption is made that the input process and the output process of the subsystem are identical.

The tools to be developed in section 3 will permit us, in section 4, to treat each of these sources of error individually.

3. Transformations of Transition Processes.

Because much is known about queueing systems to which the arrival process is Poisson, most approximations made in simplifying queueing networks assume that certain transition processes are Poisson, when they actually may not be. In this section, we will develop some approximations that indicate how the first two moments of the interevent times of a transition process are affected when the event stream is split, merged with other streams, or routed through a service center with a general service time distribution. In the next section, we will show how the inclusion of additional information about transition processes can be incorporated to avoid some of the potential errors in methods of aggregating subnetworks.

For service centers satisfying the characteristics of local balance, Muntz has shown that a Poisson arrival process will guarantee a Poisson departure process [Mun]. In general, however, the departure process depends on the arrival process as well as the service discipline and the service time distribution at the service center. In a queueing network, the departure process from a service center may indirectly affect its own arrival process. In fact, the arrival process to any service center may depend on the entire network.

Rather than characterize each transition process by a single parameter, its mean rate, we will involve a second parameter, namely, the variance (or, equivalently, the coefficient of variation) of the interevent times. One danger to keep in mind is that, in general, successive interevent times will not be independent selections from the overall distribution of interevent times. Some results are available on the serial correlation of interevent times [Dal, Mar], however, for mathematical convenience, we follow the tradition of assuming that transition processes are renewal processes [DC, GP].

As a first step, we examine a single server in isolation, and try to specify the mean and coefficient of variation of interdeparture times in terms of the means and coefficients of variation of the interarrival and service times. We assume that the service discipline is FCFS. Clearly, unless the queue is saturated, the mean interdeparture time and the mean interarrival time are equal, so we only need to seek the coefficient of variation of the departure process.

While our ultimate goal is to determine the departure process that results from a general arrival process and a general service time distribution, it is useful to examine special cases in which either the interarrival times or the service times are exponentially distributed. When both interarrival times and service times are exponentially distributed, it is known that the interdeparture times are also exponentially distributed [Bur,Mun]. When the arrival process is Poisson but the service times have a general distribution, CV_d^2 is given by [DC]

$$CV_d^2 = 1 + r^2(CV_s^2-1) \tag{1}$$
where $r = M_s/M_a$, and a,s, and d denote, respectively, the arrival, service, and departure processes.

Since $r=M_s/M_a$ is the loading or utilization of the server, the higher the utilization, the more the variation in service times governs the variation in the departure process. Equation (1) is consistent with the intuition that as the utilization approaches zero, the departure process becomes identical to the arrival process, and as the utilization approaches one, the departure process becomes identical to the service process. Finally, note that CV_d^2 is never farther from one than is CV_s^2.

When service times are exponentially distributed but the arrival process is not Poisson, CV_d^2 is again approximately proportional to CV_a^2. Simulation experiments involving HE2 and GEr interarrival time distributions indicate an approximation for CV_d^2 that is symmetric to (1):

$$CV_d^2 = 1 + (1-r^2)(CV_a^2-1) \tag{2}$$
where $r = M_s/M_a$.

Again the limiting cases of utilization at zero and one cause the departure process to approach the arrival process or the service process respectively, and again CV_d^2 is no farther from 1 than is CV_a^2.

When both CV_a^2 and CV_s^2 differ from 1, the relationship to CV_d^2 is less intuitive. The asymptotic dependence of the departure process on the arrival process at low load and on the service process at high load still holds. The simplest generalization of formulae (1) and (2) is:

$$CV_d^2 = 1 + r^2(CV_s^2-1) + (1-r^2)(CV_a^2-1) \tag{3}$$

Simulation experiments indicate that (3) yields good predictions of CV_d^2 for a range of CV_s^2 and CV_a^2 values. Figure 3 compares predicted and simulated values of CV_d as a function of CV_a with $CV_s=4$. (The third curve is based on [GP] and will be discussed in section 6.) Note that formula (3) guarantees that

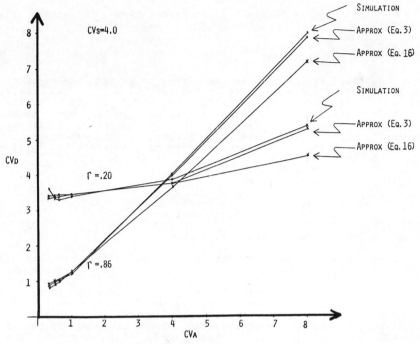

FIGURE 3: DEPARTURE PROCESSES

$$|CVd^2-1| \leq \max(|CVa^2-1|, \ |CVs^2-1|)$$

Having obtained a basic understanding of how the departure
process depends on the arrival and service processes in studying a
single queue, we can proceed to investigate how transition processes
interact when a number of service centers are interconnected in a
closed queueing network model. In a network of queues, departures
from one service center flow to other service centers according to
fixed transition probabilities. This involves splitting the stream
of departures into substreams with different destinations.
Similarly, the stream of arrivals to each service center is formed by
merging substreams of arrivals from various other service centers.

Very useful properties of Poisson streams are that splitting them
(choosing a substream by a Bernoulli trial) and merging them both
result in Poisson streams. In the current context, we need analogous
results for splitting and merging non-Poisson streams. We cannot
hope for such aesthetic results as arise in the Poisson case, but we
can attempt to determine the mean and coefficient of variation of the
split or merged streams in terms of the same characteristics of the
contributing stream(s). We will discuss only two-way splitting and
two-way merging. N-way splits and merges can be treated as sequences
of two-way operations.

We first consider splitting a non-Poisson stream (x) into two
substreams (y1 and y2) according to Bernoulli trials where the
probability of being directed to y1 is p, and to y2, 1-p. The mean

and coefficient of variation of interevent times in stream y1 are given by:

$$M_{y1} = M_x/p \qquad (4)$$
$$CV_{y1}^2 = 1 + p(CV_x^2 - 1) \qquad (5)$$

The equation for the mean is easy to derive from the fact that proportion p of the events are routed to stream y1. The derivation of the coefficient of variation is based on the fact that each interevent time in stream y1 is made up of one or more interevent times from stream x. Because routing is based on independent Bernoulli trials, the number of stream x interevent times that composes each stream y1 interevent time is geometrically distributed. Thus, the interevent time distribution of stream y1 is

$$f(t) = \sum_{k=1}^{\infty} p(1-p)^{k-1} g(k,t)$$

where $g(k,t)$ is the k-fold convolution of the stream x interevent time distribution.

Equation (5) can be derived from $f(t)$.

Equation (5) guarantees that CV_{y1}^2 is no further from one than is CV_x^2. Intuitively, the basis for this is the presence of the geometric distribution mentioned above. The coefficient of variation of the geometric distribution is one. Note that a substream selected with probability p becomes asymptotically Poisson as p approaches zero. Kobayashi presents a formula of identical form to that of the equation (5) as an approximation of one component of the arrival process to a given service center [Kob]. His equation uses the squared coefficient of variation of service times where we use CV_x^2, and thus he requires that the server at which the arrival process component originates be heavily loaded. By using the coefficient of variation of the output process instead of the service process, the heavy load assumption is avoided and the equation is exact.

A pleasing feature of equations (4) and (5) is that the first two moments of the original stream fully determine the first two moments of each substream resulting from the splitting. This holds for all distributional forms assuming no serial correlation of interevent times.

The merging of non-Poisson streams is somewhat more complex [DC]. Even if two contributing streams each have no serial correlation of interevent times, the stream that they form when merged may have substantial correlation. Fortunately, the situations in which this effect is most serious occur either when the interevent time distributions are discrete or when they have extremely low coefficients of variation. Neither of these situations occurs commonly in the contexts in which we wish to use the results, so we proceed as in the case of splitting. We wish to express the first two moments of the interevent times in the merged stream (y) in terms of the known characteristics of the contributing streams (x1 and x2). Since the rate of the merged stream is the sum of the rates of the contributing streams,

$$M_y = (M_{x1} * M_{x2})/(M_{x1} + M_{x2}) \qquad (6)$$

Unfortunately, CV_y^2 cannot be expressed in terms of only M_{x1}, M_{x2}, CV_{x1}^2, and CV_{x2}^2. For example, consider merging two streams whose

interevent time distributions are respectively exponential and one of
the family of hyperexponentials with a given mean and variance.   The
coefficient of variation of the interevent times in the merged stream
depends on which member of the hyperexponential distribution family
is chosen, even though all members have the same mean and coefficient
of variation [Sev].

One way to determine the characteristics of the merged stream is
to express its interevent time distribution in terms of the
characterstics of the contributing streams. Each event in stream x1
starts a stream y interevent time drawn from the cumulative
distribution

$Fy1(t) = Fx1(t) + (1-Fx1(t))RMx2(t)$

where $RMx2(t) = \dfrac{1}{E[x2]} \int_{v=0}^{t} (1-Fx2(v))dv$

is the cumulative distribution function of a "random
modification" of the stream x2 interevent time distribution
[CMM, p.146].

Intuitively, this reflects the fact that the next stream y event
can occur within time t in one of two ways: either the next event in
x1 occurs within time t or, otherwise, the next event in x2 occurs
within time t. The independence of the x1 and x2 streams justifies
the assumption that the time from an x1 event to the next x2 event
has the distribution RMx2(t).   Symmetrically,   the   cumulative
distribution of interevent times initiated by stream x2 events is

$Fy2(t) = Fx2(t) + (1-Fx2(t))RMx1(t)$

Since the proportion of x1 events in stream y is
$(1/Mx1)/(1/Mx1+1/Mx2)$, the cumulative distribution of interevent
times in stream y is

$Fy(t) = [Mx2(Fy1(t))+Mx1(Fy2(t))]/(Mx1+Mx2)$

The mean and coefficient of variation of the interevent times in
stream y can be determined from Fy(t).   However, the symbolic
integration required is lengthy for all but the simplest
distributional forms of Fx1(t) and Fx2(t) [Sev]. Even for HE2 and
GEr distributions, the expression for the CV of the merged stream
contains so many terms that it is useful only for numerical
evaluation.

In related investigations, the following approximation has been
proposed:

$$CVy^2 = \sum_i (My/Mxi)CVxi^2 \qquad\qquad (7)$$

Kobayashi expresses the arrival process at one center in terms of the
transition probabilities and the service processes at other centers
[Kob].   Gelenbe and Pujolle refine the expression by giving the
departure process at a service center in terms of its service process
and the departure processes at other centers, thus removing the need
for a heavy-load assumption [GP]. When distilled to an expression
for aggregating non-Poisson substreams, each of the above expressions
reduces to equation (7). Sauer and Chandy use a closely related
formula in which CVy and CVxi replace their squared counterparts.

The coefficient of variation of the composite server resulting from a Norton's theorem reduction is set to be the weighted sum of the coefficients of variation of the service processes at the service centers being aggregated [SC].

While equation (7) is exact when all substreams are Poisson, there are other special cases in which it is not realistic. For example, if all the substreams being merged have the same CV^2, equation (7) causes the merged stream to have that CV^2 also. Actually, merging two streams with CV's less than one will yield a stream with somewhat larger CV. Similarly, merging two streams with CV greater than one yield one with somewhat lower CV. Finally, it is known that merging a large number of independent streams of arbitrary characteristics yields a nearly Poisson stream.

A slight modification of equation (7) avoids the problems indicated above:

$$CVy^2 = 1 + \sum_i (My/Mxi)^2 (CVxi^2-1) \tag{8}$$

The exponent of the (My/Mxi) term was chosen rather arbitrarily based on a few specific cases. Any choice in the range 1.5 to about 3 seems to make equation (8) more realistic than equation (7). Note that equation (8) reduces to equation (7) when the exponent is set to one. We will use equation (8) for estimating the CV that results from merging non-Poisson streams.

In this section, we have developed tools for approximating how a transition process can be split, how each substream is affected by passing through a service center with a general service time distribution, and how the streams can be merged. With these tools, we are able to suggest some improved techniques for aggregating subnetworks and for analyzing entire queueing network models.

4. Approximate Analysis Techniques Using Transition Processes

In this section, we describe a sequence of successively more complex, more accurate, and more expensive approximate analysis techniques based on the transition process transformations developed in section 3. Each will be aimed at reducing the error resulting from one or more of the three potential sources of error in using a direct Norton's reduction on a central server network with a single customer class, non-exponential service times and FCFS service discipline at each service center. These three potential sources of error were named Exponential Assumption, CV Omission, and Input/Output Assumption at the end of section 2.

4.1 Improved CV Estimation

Direct application of Norton's theorem reduction to central server models with non-exponential service times and FCFS service disciplines can lead to unacceptable errors in performance measure estimates even when the CV's of service time distributions differ from one by factors of five or less [CHW1]. (Empirically observed CV's frequently differ from one by factors far larger than five.) Sauer and Chandy try to remedy the CV Omission error of direct

Norton's theorem reductions by estimating a coefficient of variation to be used in the composite server. As was mentioned in the previous section, their estimate is calculated from the formula:

$$CVc = \sum_i Pi(CVi) \qquad (9)$$

where Pi is the probability of transition from the central server to the ith peripheral service center,

and CVi is the coefficient of variation of the service time distribution at the ith peripheral server.

Then, depending on CVc, a distributional form is chosen for the composite server. If CVc is significantly greater than one, HE2 is chosen, if it is significantly less than one, GEr is chosen, and otherwise Exp is chosen. A unique distribution is determined by setting parameters according to formulae similar to those given in section 2.

Experiments with this refined form of aggregate server show it to give good results over a wide range of models [SC]. Thus, simply representing the variance in service times at the peripheral servers by giving the composite server a non-exponential distributional form seems to be helpful.

It is not difficult, however, to identify reasonable models for which the approach involving CVc does not yield acceptable results. For example, when the coefficients of variation of service times at the peripheral devices differ from one by a factor of five or more, errors in utilization and mean queue length predictions can reach twenty percent or more.

There is little intuitive basis for choosing CVc according to equation (9), although it is exact for the special case in which all service time distributions are exponential so that the system satisfies local balance. In a central server model, strict modelling of the aggregate service process leads us to calculate CVc² from

$$CVc^2 = \frac{\sum_i Pi(CVi^2 Mi^2) + \sum_i PiMi^2 - \sum_i (PiMi)^2}{[\sum_i (PiMi)]^2} \qquad (10)$$

This formula yields a coefficient of variation that is exactly the coefficient of variation of the overall distribution of service times in the subsystem. The parallelism of service in the subsystem is represented by adjusting the service rate, with a higher rate indicating greater parallelism.

Experimentation has shown that in some queueing networks, calculating CVc² according to equation (10) yields significantly better results than using equation (9), while in other cases, the opposite is true [TL]. Thus, only having the composite server reflect the variance in the aggregate service time distribution does not help consistently.

When replacing a subsystem with a composite server, the goal is to make the composite server resemble the entire subsystem as observed by the rest of the system. The only way that the rest of the network sees the composite server is as a stream of customers leaving it. Thus, the task is to select a composite server that as much as possible duplicates the output process from the subsystem. The fact that an exact representation of the aggregate service process (such as equation (10)) does not do consistently well is a strong argument that it is not appropriate to attempt to represent the service process. Instead, we must attempt to represent the output process.

The composite server may have any one of a number of service disciplines. Its mean service rate must be load dependent so that the required throughput rate for each multiprogramming level can be achieved. While any service discipline may be chosen, we will give special attention to FCFS and PS. (A load dependent version of PS is simply the single class special case of CQ.) In a locally-balanced queueing network model, PS eliminates the effect of variance in the service time distribution, making the state probability distribution identical to that with FCFS service and an exponential service time distribution. When the system does not satisfy local balance, however, the variance of service time distribution at PS service centers does affect the system state probability distribution. We conjecture that either FCFS or PS at the composite server can yield equally effective representations of the subsystem's output process, as long as the service time variance is adjusted appropriately.

Based on the developments of section 3, Sauer and Chandy's algorithm can be improved by simply replacing the estimation of CVc^2. The simplest generalization of the Sauer and Chandy formula is

$$CVc^2 = 1 + \sum_i Pi^2 (CVsi^2 - 1) \qquad (11)$$

This is equation (8) for aggregating substreams, where the substreams are the service processes. It is only accurate when all the service centers are heavily loaded.

If a good estimate of the throughput (or mean interarrival time) of the subsystem is available, a more sophisticated formula can be used:

$$CVc^2 = 1 + \sum_i Pi^4 (Msi/Mc)^2 (CVsi^2 - 1) \qquad (12)$$

Equation (12) is derived from equations (1) and (8) assuming Poisson input to the peripheral service centers. It does not assume the service centers to be heavily loaded. The results of using various ways of estimating CVc^2 will be discussed in section 5.

4.2 Improved Throughput Estimation

In order to reduce the error in throughput rate calculation, it is necessary to avoid the Exponential Assumption. This eliminates the possibility of using the efficient computational techniques that require local balance in order to analyse the subsystem. An alternative approach has been developed by Zahorjan [Zah]. He proposes an approximate solution technique based on the global balance method to obtain load dependent throughput rates appropriate to the actual service time distributions of the subnetwork. The problem with using global balance to solve for the throughputs exactly is that the number of simultaneous linear equations which must be solved grows combinatorially with the number of service centers, stages of service at each center, and customers in the system. Even for subnetworks of moderate complexity, a global balance solution would be infeasible.

The computational complexity of the global balance technique can be greatly reduced by repeated applications of Norton's theorem reductions aggregating only a small number of service centers (probably two) at each step but using global balance equations to determine the subnetwork throughput. The load dependent server formed at each step then replaces the corresponding service centers in the original network, and the series of reductions continues until there is only a single load dependent server. In this way the total amount of work required to solve the system grows only linearly with the number of service centers, and the total storage requirement at any point of the computation is much smaller than it would be if the entire network consisting of all the centers were solved using global balance equations. The tradeoff involved in deciding how many service centers to aggregate at each step is that the complexity of the solution increases greatly as the number of centers grows, but the error of the approximation decreases because fewer applications of the approximation technique are required.

A program capable of solving a restricted class of single class queueing networks, including the central server model, has been implemented [Zah]. The errors in performance measure predictions are significantly smaller than those obtained by treating only the CV Omission error as was done in section 4.1. The error which does occur is due to the Input/Output Assumption. The accuracy of this approximation will be illustrated with an example in section 5.

4.3 Improved Input/Output Process Characterization

Once the Exponential Assumption is avoided, the most significant remaining error source is the Input/Output Assumption where the input process and output process of a subsystem are presumed to be identical. In order to remove this assumption, we must consider the subsystem's environment. In a central server models, this involves extending equation (12) to include the effect of the central server. Assuming Poisson input to the central server, equations (3), (5), and (8) can be composed to express the coefficient of variation of the subsystem's departure process (see figure 4):

$$CVa4^2 = 1 + \sum_i Pi^2\{(\frac{PiMsi}{Ma0})^2 (CVsi^2-1)$$

$$(13)$$

$$+ Pi[1-(\frac{PiMsi}{Ma0})^2][(\frac{Ms0}{Ma0})^2 (CVs0^2-1)+(1-(\frac{Ms0}{Ma0})^2)(CVa0^2-1)]\}$$

By assuming some value for $CVa0^2$, equation (13) allows us to calculate $CVa4^2$. In a closed central server model, however, since the departure process from the subsystem (a4) is the arrival process at the central server (i.e., $CVa0^2 = CVa4^2$), equation (13) reduces to:

$$CVa0^2 = 1 + \frac{\sum\limits_i Pi^2\{(\frac{PiMsi}{Ma0})^2(CVsi^2-1)+Pi[1-(\frac{PiMsi}{Ma0})^2][(\frac{Ms0}{Ma0})^2(CVs0^2-1)]\}}{1 - \sum\limits_i Pi^3\{[1-(\frac{PiMsi}{Ma0})^2][1-(\frac{Ms0}{Ma0})^2]\}}$$

$$(14)$$

To use the coefficient of variation obtained from equation (14), we modify the load dependent composite server specified by Zahorjan by giving it a structure dependent on this estimate of coefficient of variation.

5. Examples

In this section, we examine two examples and compare the accuracy achieved by the proposed techniques. The exact answers are obtained by using QSOLVE, a global balance solution system [Lev].

The parameters and results of example 1 are shown in figure 5. The methods that employ the Exponential Assumption all produce similar answers even though they deal differently with the CV Omission error. Since the exact answer and Zahorjan's answer lie substantially below the others, it appears that the Exponential Assumption is more critical than the CV Omission. Once throughput is estimated, the manner of setting CVc^2 is not critical. Thus, seeking less arbitrary formulae for CVc^2 does not seem to be, by itself, worthwhile. Moreover, in this case, even direct Norton's theorem reduction does better than the more detailed approaches.

Zahorjan's approach, which corrects for the Exponential Assumption, gives consistently good approximations. Over a wide range of examples, the largest utilization and mean queue length errors observed were approximately five percent.

The structure and results for example 2 are shown in figure 6. Having seen the importance of accurate estimation of throughput in example 1, we select here exponential servers at the peripheral service centers, thus avoiding any throughput error due to the Exponential Assumption. In this situation, most of the approaches

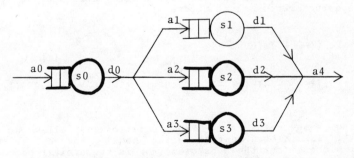

Figure 4: Transition Processes

that we have discussed are equivalent since they all treat the special case of exponential peripheral service times identically.

If the arrival process at the central server is Poisson, however, then the departure process has the coefficient of variation given by equation (13). Further, since the network is of the central server form, the subsystem's departure process is identically the arrival process at the central server. Hence, equation (14) can be used to establish the coefficient of variation of the transition process between the subsystem and the central server.

The use of equation (14), after establishing throughput rates by Zahorjan's pair-wise aggregation technique, gives a good estimation of the coefficient of variation of the arrival process at the central server. This CV^2 can then be used with the composite server's load dependent throughput rates to improve the accuracy of Zahorjan's approximation.

6. Summary and Conclusions

In section 3, we established formulae for approximating the coefficient of variation of transition processes in queueing network models. In terms of figure 4, the formulae are summarized below:

Splitting: For $i=1,2,3,$
$$Mai = MaO/Pi$$
$$CVai^2 = 1 + Pi(CVdO^2-1)$$

Queueing: For $i=0,1,2,3,$
$$Mdi = Mai$$
$$CVdi^2 = 1 + (Msi/Mai)^2(CVsi^2-1) + [1-(Msi/Mai)^2](CVai^2-1)$$

Merging:
$$MaO = [\sum_i (1/Mdi)]^{-1}$$
$$CVaO^2 = 1 + \sum_i [(MaO/Mdi)^2(CVdi^2-1)]$$

In the context of diffusion approximations, others have obtained results related to ours [Gel, Kob]. We state them here with the notation of figure 4.

(a) If $CVai^2 = 1$ for a single queue,
$$CVdi^2 = 1 + (Msi/Mai)^2(CVsi^2-1) \qquad [DC]$$

(b) If $MsO/MaO = 1$ in a central server model,
$$CVai^2 = 1 + Pi(CVsO^2-1) \qquad [Kob]$$

(c) If QjO is the transition probability between center j and center O in a general queueing network,
$$CVaO^2 = 1 + MaO\sum_j (\frac{QjO^2}{Mdj})(CVsj^2-1) \qquad [RK1]$$

(d) With QjO defined as above,
$$CVdO^2 = 1 + (\frac{MsO}{MaO})^2 + (1-\frac{MsO}{MaO})\sum_j (\frac{MaO}{Mdj})QjO^2(CVdj^2-1) \qquad [GP]$$

Result (a) is the special case of equation (3) with Poisson arrivals, and result (b) is the special case of equation (5) in which the central server is heavily loaded. In the case of a central server model, result (c) (with $Qj0=1$) specializes to equation (7) rather than to equation (8), which, as we have seen, represents merging more accurately. When all customers at service center zero come directly from a single service center (say j), result (c) further specializes to:

$$CVa0^2 = CVsj^2 \qquad (15)$$

This makes the heavy load assumption obvious.

Result (d) has numerous special cases of interest. It specializes to equation (5) for splitting, and, like result (c), it specializes to equation (7), rather than equation (8), for central server models. When all center zero customers come from center j, result (d) specializes to:

$$CVd0^2 = 1 + r^2(CVs0^2-1) + (1-r)(CVdj^2-1) \qquad (16)$$
$$\text{where } r = Ms0/Ma0$$

Note that equation (16) differ from equation (3) only in that $(1-r^2)$ is replaced by $(1-r)$.

Substantial evidence indicates equation (3) to be the more accurate approximation. Figure 3 compares both equation (3) and equation (16) with simulation results for a range of $CVdj$ and $CVsC$ values. The simulation program used HE2 and GEr distributional forms to obtain various values for $CVdj$ and $CVs0$. Equation (3)'s predictions are significantly closer to the simulation results. Additionally, table I compares equations (15), (16) and (3) in four specific cases involving only exponential and deterministic distributions. For the M/M/1 case, all three agree and are exact. For the M/D/1 case, equations (16) and (3) agree and are correct [Pac], while equation (15) is correct only when the queue utilization is near one. For the D/M/1 case, equation (15) again gives the answer for very high utilization. Equation (16) and (3) differ although they approach one another as utilization approaches either one or zero. For intermediate utilizations, simulation verifies that equation (3) makes more accurate predictions of $CVd0^2$ than does equation (16). Finally, for the D/D/1 case, equations (3) and (15) agree and are correct, while equation (16) is correct only as utilization approaches either zero or one. Because equation (3) makes better predictions than does equation (16), it is possible that the more general formula of Gelenbe and Pujolle [GP eq.(13)] would be improved by using $(1-r^2)$ in place of $(1-r)$.

All the results in section 3 lead to the conclusion that transition processes in closed queueing networks tend toward being Poisson. High or low variance service time processes may introduce transition processes of high or low variance but splitting and merging tend to direct the coefficient of variation of the resulting process toward one.

Somewhat contrary to intuition, splitting then immediately remerging an event stream according to equations (5) and (8) does not result in a stream with the same coefficient of variation as the original stream. This situation can be explained as follows. While equation (5) is exact, equation (8) is not. Equation (8) is an approximation that characterizes stochastic processes entirely by their first two moments, even though higher moments do influence the

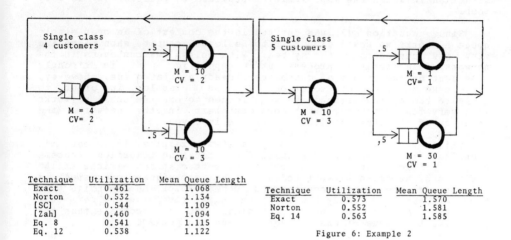

Technique   Utilization   Mean Queue Length
Exact   0.461   1.068
Norton   0.532   1.134
[SC]   0.544   1.109
[Zah]   0.460   1.094
Eq. 8   0.541   1.115
Eq. 12   0.538   1.122

Figure 5: Example 1

Technique   Utilization   Mean Queue Length
Exact   0.573   1.570
Norton   0.552   1.581
Eq. 14   0.563   1.585

Figure 6: Example 2

Case	CV_{dj}^2	CV_{s0}^2	CV_{d0}^2		
			Eq. 15 [RK1]	Eq. 16 [GP]	Eq. 3
M/M/1	1	1	1	1	1
M/D/1	1	0	0	$1-r^2$	$1-r^2$
D/M/1	0	1	1	r	r^2
D/D/1	0	0	0	$r(1-r)$	0

Table I: Comparison of CV_{d0}^2 predicting methods.

result of aggregating streams. When we remerge a stream that has
just been split, we happen to be systematically choosing one
situation in which the approximation provided by equation (8) is very
poor.

Since equation (3) was derived in the context of an open single
queue network, we would expect it to be least accurate when there are
very few customers in the system. With only a few customers in the
network, the arrival process at a specific queue is strongly
dependent on the number of customers already at that queue. However,
because we sought exact solutions for our examples in order to
evaluate the approximations, we were forced to examine small networks
with very few customers. With more customers in the network, the
accuracy of the approximations should be improved.

While we have examined only a few examples, it appears the
techniques that have been discussed for estimating transiton process
characteristics can aid in obtaining better approximations in the
analysis of queueing network models. The techniques suggested in
this paper are more accurate, but more complex and expensive than
those of Sauer and Chandy [SC]. At the same time, we belief that
they are simpler and more economical, but less accurate than the
iterative technique of Chandy, Herzog, and Woo [CHW2].

Acknowledgements

The authors are grateful for many fruitful discussions with and
helpful comments from G.S. Graham, M. Kienzle, and E.D. Lazowska.
Very useful comments were also received from K.M. Chandy and J. Wong.
This research has been partially supported by the National Research
Council of Canada.

References

[BCBKTD] J.C. Browne, K.M. Chandy, R.M. Brown, T.W. Keller, D.F.
    Towsley and C.W. Dissley, Hierarchical techniques for   the
    development of realistic models of complex computer systems,
    Proc. IEEE 63, 6 (June 1975), 966-75.

[BCMP] F. Baskett, K.M. Chandy, R.R. Muntz, and F.G. Palacios, Open,
    closed and mixed network of queues with different classes of
    customers, JACM 22, 2 (April 1975), 248-60.

[Bur] P.J. Burke, Output processes and tandem queues, Proc. Symp. on
    Computer-Communications Networks and Teletraffic, Polytechnic
    Institute of Brooklyn (April 1972), 419-28.

[Buz] J.P. Buzen, Computational algorithms for closed queueing
    networks with exponential servers, CACM 16, 9 (September 1973),
    527-31.

[CHT] K.M. Chandy, J.H. Howard, and D.F. Towsley, Product form and
    local balance in queueing networks, JACM 24, 2 (April 1977), 250-
    63.

[CHW1] K.M. Chandy, U. Herzog, and L. Woo, Parametric analysis of
    queueing networks, IBM J. Res. and Dev. 19, 1 (January 1975), 36-
    42.

[CHW2] K.M. Chandy, U. Herzog, and L. Woo, Approximate analysis of general queueing networks, IBM J. Res. and Dev. 19, 1 (January 1975), 43-49.

[CMM] R.W. Conway, W.L. Maxwell, and L.W. Miller, Theory of Scheduling, Addison-Wesley (1967).

[Cou] P.J. Courtois, Decomposability, instabilities, and saturation in multiprogramming systems, CACM 18, 7 (July 1975), 371-77.

[Dal] D.J. Daley, Notes on queueing output processes, in Mathematical Methods in Queueing Theory, A.B. Clarke (ed.), Springer-Verlag, Berlin (1974).

[DC] R.L. Disney and W.P. Cherry, Some topics in queueing network theory, in Mathematical Methods in Queueing Theory, A.B. Clarke (ed.), Springer-Verlag, Berlin (1974).

[Gel] E. Gelenbe, On approximate computer system models, JACM 22, 2 (April 1975), 261-69.

[GN] W.J. Gordon and G.F. Newell, Closed queueing systems with exponential servers, Oper. Res. 15, 2 (1967), 252-67.

[GP] E. Gelenbe and G. Pujolle, The Behaviour of a single queue in a general queueing network, Acta Informatica 7 (1976), 123-36.

[HWC] U. Herzog, L. Woo, and K.M. Chandy, Solution of queueing problems by a recursive technique, IBM J. Res. and Dev. 19, 3 (May 1975), 295-300.

[Kob] H. Kobayashi, Application of the diffusion approximation to queueing networks: Part I Equilibrium queue distributions, JACM 21, 2 (April 1974), 316-28.

[Lev] A.I. Levy, QSOLVE: A queueing network solution system, M.Sc. thesis, technical note TN-6, Computer Systems Research Group, University of Toronto (January 1977).

[Mar] K.T. Marshall, Some relationships between the distributions of waiting time, idle time and inter-output time in a GI/G/1 queue, SIAM J. Appl. Math. 16 (1968), 324-27.

[Mun] R.R. Muntz, Poisson departure processes and queueing networks, Proc. 7th Annual Princeton Conf. (March 1973), 435-40.

[Pac] C.D. Pack, The output of an M/D/1 queue, Op.Res. 23 (1975), 750-60.

[RK1] M. Reiser and H. Kobayashi, Accuracy of the diffusion approximation for some queueing systems, IBM J. Res. and Dev. 18, 2 (1974), 110-24.

[RK2] M. Reiser and H. Kobayashi, Queueing networks with multiple closed chains: theory and computational algorithms, IBM J.Res. and Dev. 19, 3 (May 1975), 283-94.

[SC] C.H. Sauer and K.M. Chandy, Approximate analysis of central server models, IBM J. Res. and Dev. 19, 3 (May 1975), 301-13.

[Sev] K.C. Sevcik, Merging and splitting non-Poisson streams, Project SAM notes, Computer Systems Research Group, University of Toronto (March 1977).

[TL] S.K. Tripathi and A.I. Levy, When does Norton reduction fail? Project SAM notes, E.D. Lazowska(ed.), Computer Systems Research Group, University of Toronto (September 1976).

[Tow] D.F. Towsley, Local Balance models of computer systems, Ph.D. thesis, University of Texas at Austin, (December 1975).

[Zah] J.L. Zahorjan, Iterative aggregation with global balance, Project SAM notes, Computer Systems Research Group, University of Toronto (February 1977).

COMPUTER PERFORMANCE, K.M. CHANDY AND M. REISER (EDS.)
NORTH HOLLAND PUBLISHING COMPANY, 1977

THE PHASE CONCEPT: APPROXIMATION OF MEASURED DATA AND PERFORMANCE ANALYSIS

W. Bux
Institute of Switching and Data Techniques
University of Stuttgart
Stuttgart, Germany

U. Herzog
Institute of Mathematical Machines
and Data Processing
Friedrich-Alexander University
Erlangen, Germany

Distribution functions (d.f.) for interarrival and service times are described by means of a simplified Cox model with a uniform service rate for all phases but different branching probabilities.

We first present an efficient algorithm to determine a phase-type d.f. which fits actual measured data with a prescribed accuracy. Investigating queueing models with that type of d.f. it is shown how to reduce the complexity of state spaces.

The paper contains the following sections:

1. Introduction
2. Modeling with measured data
3. Analysis by means of the special phase concept
4. Numerical results
5. Conclusion and outlook

1. INTRODUCTION

One of the most famous methods for the exact or approximate analysis of queueing systems is the phase concept (method of stages), introduced by Erlang [1]. It is based on the idea of representing generally distributed interarrival or service times by sums of convolutions of exponentially distributed random variables, the so-called "phases".

Due to the memoryless property of the exponential distribution, the stochastic processes, described at the phase level, are of the Markovian type, so that the well-known method of analysis can be applied.

Typical and successfully treated examples are queueing systems with Erlangian or hyperexponentially distributed interarrival and service times, respectively [2].

1.1 GENERAL COX MODEL

Cox [3] generalized the concept in showing that any distribution function (d.f.) having a rational Laplace transform can be represented by a simple sequence of exponentially distributed phases, as shown in Figure 1.

Figure 1 should be interpreted in the following way:

23

With probability α_0 the service time is equal to zero*. With probability $\beta_0 = 1-\alpha_0$ a request enters the first exponentially distributed phase with mean μ_1^{-1}. After leaving this phase it enters the second phase (mean μ_2^{-1}) with probability β_1 or leaves the server with probability $\alpha_1 = 1-\beta_1$, etc.

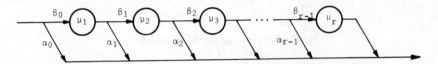

Fig.1. Representation of d.f. with rational Laplace transform by exponentially distributed phases, according to Cox ("general Cox model")

The Laplace transform of the probability density function, generated in this way, is given by

$$\Phi(s) = \alpha_o + \sum_{i=1}^{r} \beta_o \beta_1 \cdots \beta_{i-1} \alpha_i \prod_{j=1}^{i} \frac{\mu_j}{s + \mu_j} \tag{1}$$

Since any d.f. may be approximated arbitrarily closely by rational functions the phase concept can in principle be used in very general cases.

However, two main problems arise in applying this general concept:

1) No effective method is known to determine all parameters of the d.f. (1), if actual measured values are given. (The approach which is mostly proposed for approximation [2,3] , namely Prony's method [4] , has several severe disadvantages [5] .)

2) The complexity of state spaces and transitions increases remarkably in most cases. Hence, the evaluation of the state probabilities may become an extremely difficult numerical problem.

In the following it is shown how to overcome both problems for a wide range of application.

1.2 COX MODEL WITH UNIFORM SERVICE RATE

The key to the solution is to simplify the general Cox model by assuming a uniform, real service rate for all phases:

$$\mu_1 = \mu_2 = \ldots = \mu_r = \mu \tag{2}$$

This leads to the following d.f.**:

$$F(t) = \sum_{i=1}^{r} q_i (1 - e^{-\mu t} \sum_{j=0}^{i-1} \frac{(\mu t)^j}{j!}) \qquad t \overset{\geq}{=} 0 \tag{3}$$

$$q_i = \beta_1 \beta_2 \cdots \beta_{i-1} \alpha_i \qquad i \in \{1,2,\ldots,r\}$$

Despite the simplification the class of functions in (3) still possesses the following important property:

---

* We refer to service times here. Of course, Fig.1 may stand for interarrival times, too.

** For the sake of a simplified description, only d.f.s F(t) with F(O) = O are considered, i.e. $\beta_o = 1$.

For any probability d.f. F(t) with F(t) = 0 for t<0, there exists a series of
functions (3) which converges weakly to F(t) [6] .

This means that measured data still may be approximated with any required accuracy.

We investigated the phase concept with this type of model. Although the number of
phases may increase, we found the advantage of this approach to be twofold:

1) An efficient algorithm can be formulated to determine a d.f. of the type given
   in (3) which fits measured data with a prescribed accuracy (c.f. chapter 2).

2) The complexity of state spaces can often be drasticly reduced, so that frequently a large amount of computing time and memory is saved in evaluating characteristic traffic values (c.f. chapter 3).

2. MODELING WITH MEASURED DATA

In this chapter we present an algorithm that allows to determine an approximating
d.f. of the phase-type with uniform service rates, if a set of measured data is
given.

2.1 APPROXIMATION TASK

The problem to be solved may be stated as follows:

Be given n discrete values $F(t_\nu)$ of a d.f. F(t) at points t_ν, $\nu \in \{1,2,...,n\}$,
as well as the values for the first moment M_1 and the second moment M_2 of F(t)*.

Find a d.f. A(t) so that the following four conditions are fulfilled ($\delta_\nu^u, \delta_\nu^o$ are
prescribed values):

$$A(t_\nu) \leq F(t_\nu) + \delta_\nu^o \qquad \qquad (4)$$

$$A(t_\nu) \geq F(t_\nu) - \delta_\nu^u \qquad \qquad (5)$$

$$\int_0^\infty t \, dA = M_1 \qquad \nu \in \{1,...,n\} \qquad (6)$$

$$\int_0^\infty t^2 \, dA = M_2 \qquad \qquad (7)$$

2.2 MOTIVATION

Compared to standard approximation criteria our approach possesses two special
features:

1) Mixed conditions: Experience shows that even if a (standard) approximation fits
   well the form of a given d.f. the moments of both functions may differ significantly. The use of such approximations is unsatisfactory (e.g. in a pure delay
   system even the value for the server utilization might be incorrect).

   Therefore we use a mixture of conditions which prescribe the form of the d.f.
   within a certain tolerance scheme as well as the values of the moments of low
   order.

2) Limited deviations: After the approximating d.f. has been found, a goodness-of-
   fit test may be performed to determine whether the measured data can be considered as being obtained from the hypothesized distribution. The most suitable
   procedure, the Kolmogorov-Smirnov test [7] , uses as a criterion for rejection
   the maximum deviation between the hypothesized d.f. and the sample d.f.

   By an appropriate choice of the maximum deviations $\delta_\nu^u, \delta_\nu^o$ in (4) and (5), we may
   achieve that the approximation is not rejected when this test is applied.

---

*The proposed method is not restricted to two moments, as described here for rea-
sons of convenience.

2.3 APPROXIMATION PROCEDURE

For the reasons described above the class of functions defined in (3) is taken for approximation.

To fulfill the relations (4) to (7) the approximation task can be formulated as the following optimization problem:

Find the minimum number r of phases and the values of the parameters $q_1, \ldots, q_r$ and μ under the following restrictions:

$$\sum_{i=1}^{r} q_i (1 - e^{-\mu t_\nu} \sum_{j=0}^{i-1} \frac{(\mu t_\nu)^j}{j!}) \leqq F(t_\nu) + \delta_\nu^o \tag{8}$$

$$\nu \in \{1, \ldots, n\}$$

$$\sum_{i=1}^{r} q_i (1 - e^{-\mu t_\nu} \sum_{j=0}^{i-1} \frac{(\mu t_\nu)^j}{j!}) \geqq F(t_\nu) - \delta_\nu^u \tag{9}$$

$$\mu^{-1} \sum_{i=1}^{r} i q_i = M_1 \tag{10}$$

$$\mu^{-2} \sum_{i=1}^{r} i(i+1) q_i = M_2 \tag{11}$$

$$\sum_{i=1}^{r} q_i = 1 \tag{12}$$

$$q_1, \ldots, q_r \geqq 0 \tag{13}$$

$$\mu \geqq 0 \tag{14}$$

Our algorithm for the solution of this problem is described in the following.

- To fulfill equations (10) and (11) the range of the parameter r has a lower boundary, dependent on the values of M_1 and M_2 [8] :

$$r \geqq \frac{1}{c^2} \qquad \text{if } c^2 \leqq 1 \tag{15}$$

$$r \geqq 2c^2 + 2\sqrt{c^4 - 1} \qquad \text{if } c^2 > 1 \qquad c^2 = \frac{M_2 - M_1^2}{M_1^2} \tag{16}$$

- r is set to the lowest possible value and a solution is searched as described below. In case of non success search, r is incremented by one and again a solution is searched, etc.

- Searching values $\mu, q_1, \ldots, q_r$ for a given r that fulfill conditions (8) to (14) is performed in the following way:

In each of the 2n+3 relations (8) to (12) a nonnegative auxiliary variable h_k is introduced, and their sum is defined as a new variable z

$$z = \sum_{k=1}^{2n+3} h_k \tag{17}$$

The problem is to find a zero of z. Since z is nonnegative this problem is equivalent to finding out whether the minimum of z is zero or not. This is done in two separate parts:

- For a given μ we are faced with a linear optimization problem with variables $q_1, \ldots, q_r$. This problem is solved using the well-known simplex algorithm [9]. The minimum value found is a (nonlinear) function of μ:

$$z_{min} = z_{min}(\mu) \tag{18}$$

- It remains to determine a minimum of z_{min}; this can be performed with the aid of known algorithms for the optimization of a nonlinear function of one variable [10]. The latter problem can be simplified, because boundaries for the location of a zero of z_{min} can be derived, dependent on r, M_1 and M_2. The interval I, which may contain a zero of z_{min}, if any, is given by [8]:

$$I = \begin{cases} \left[\dfrac{1}{c^2 M_1} , \dfrac{1}{M_1} \sqrt{\dfrac{r(r+1)}{1+c^2}} \right] & \text{if } c^2 \overset{\le}{=} 1 \\[4mm] \left[\dfrac{1}{M_1} , \dfrac{1}{M_1} \sqrt{\dfrac{r(r+1)}{1+c^2}} \right] & \text{if } c^2 > 1 \end{cases} \qquad c^2 = \frac{M_2 - M_1^2}{M_1^2} \tag{19}$$

- As mentioned above, r is incremented by one, if the minimum of z is found to be greater than zero. This is repeated until a prescribed maximum value r_{max} is reached.

2.4 EXAMPLES

Figures 2,3 show two examples for our method of approximation [8]. In both examples five values of the d.f. were prescribed with different deviations δ. In all cases the first and second moment were kept exactly at the prescribed values.

It is interesting to see how the approximation approaches the prescribed values when the allowed tolerance δ becomes smaller and smaller. At the same time the corresponding number of phases increases.

Another example, demonstrating the applicability of phase-type d.f.s is presented in chapter 4.

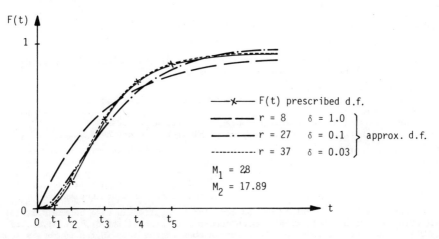

Fig.2. Approximation of a distribution function.
    The first two moments of the approximation are exactly equal to the
    prescribed values M_1 and M_2, respectively. The form of the d.f. is
    kept within the prescribed tolerance scheme, defined by the maximum
    deviation δ (cf. text).

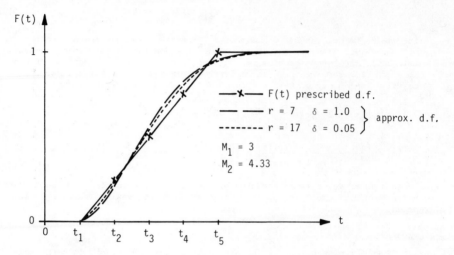

Fig.3. Second example for the approximation of a distribution function.
For comments see Fig.2.

3. ANALYSIS BY MEANS OF THE SPECIAL PHASE CONCEPT

This chapter describes how the phase concept with uniform service rates of all
phases is effectively used in the analysis of queueing systems. After some general
considerations two examples are considered.

3.1 GENERAL CONSIDERATIONS

3.1.1 STATE DESCRIPTION

If the general Cox model is used to describe interarrival or service times, then
the state description of a queueing system usually includes:

- the number of requests in the system
- a variable describing the instantaneous phase of service for the
  request being processed
- a corresponding variable for the phase-type arrival process
- additional variables depending on the particular type of the system.

In case of an Erlangian distributed service time a well-known trick to reduce the
complexity of the state description is to use a state variable defined as the total
number of "unfinished" service phases (phases not yet completed by all requests in
the system) [2,11]. A newly arriving request is equivalent to a bulk arrival of
phases with fixed bulk size k, the order of the Erlangian distribution.

The concept of bulk arrival of phases can also be applied in case of the d.f. (3)
but here with random bulk size i which occurs with probability q_i, $i \in \{1,...,r\}$
[6]. Although the knowledge of the actual number of requests in the system is lost
in this case, the interesting performance values of most systems can be determined,
as shown in the succeeding sections.

In describing the arrival process by means of a phase-type model there is no great
difference regarding the complexity of the state space between the general Cox
model and the simplified model with uniform service rates.

3.1.2 NUMERICAL EVALUATION

The "normal" way of solution for a system of equilibrium equations is to use generating functions. Usually, this leads to the problem of determining the roots of
a polynomial equation, if a closed form solution for the generating function of
the state probabilities can be found, at all. Since often numerical problems arise
with this solution another approach is more favourable in many cases, namely a recursive technique [12] .

3.2 EXAMPLE M/G/1

The usefulness of the special phase concept is demonstrated most evidently by analyzing the queueing system M/G/1.

3.2.1 STATE DESCRIPTION AND EQUILIBRIUM EQUATIONS

We assume that the d.f. of service times be represented by a phase-type function
with uniform service rate μ and branching probabilities q_i, $i \in \{1,\ldots,r\}$, according to equation (3).

The system state is described by means of a random variable X defined as the total
number of service phases yet to be completed by all requests in the system. The
corresponding state-transition diagram is shown in Fig. 4 .

Fig.4. State-transition
       diagram for the
       queueing system
       M/G/1 (here r=3)

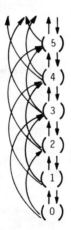

Herewith the equilibrium equations are as follows, if the mean arrival rate of the
Poisson process is denoted by λ and for convenience q_i is set to zero, if $i > r$:

$$p(0) \lambda = p(1) \mu$$
$$p(x)(\lambda+\mu) = \sum_{i=0}^{x-1} p(i)\lambda q_{x-i} + p(x+1)\mu \qquad x>0 \tag{20}$$

3.2.2 SOLUTION BY MEANS OF GENERATING FUNCTIONS

The generating function of the state probabilities is defined as:

$$F(z) = \sum_{x=0}^{\infty} z^x p(x) \tag{21}$$

The solution of equations (20) is derived in a straightforward manner by multiplying the k-th equation by z^k and summing all equations. This leads to:

$$F(z) = \frac{\mu(z-1)}{(\lambda+\mu)z - \lambda z Q(z) - \mu} \, p(0) \tag{22}$$

$Q(z)$ is the generating function of the branching probabilities q_i:

$$Q(z) = \sum_{i=0}^{\infty} z^i q_i = \sum_{i=0}^{r} z^i q_i \tag{23}$$

The probability $p(0)$ is given by:

$$p(0) = 1 - \frac{\lambda}{\mu} \sum_{i=1}^{r} i q_i \tag{24}$$

From equation (22) the moments of the distribution $p(x)$ can be derived; this leads for example to the Pollaczek-Khintchine formula of the mean waiting time in the system M/G/1.

If we are interested in the explicit values of the probabilities $p(x)$, the generating function $F(z)$ has to be retransformed. Then we are faced with the problem of determining the zeroes for the polynomial in the denominator. According to the degree r of $Q(z)$ this may become a difficult numerical problem.

3.2.3 SOLUTION BY MEANS OF A RECURSIVE EVALUATION

An alternative approach to the use of generating functions is to evaluate the state probabilities recursively. It follows immediately from equations (20):

$$p(1) = \frac{\lambda}{\mu} \, p(0)$$
$$p(x+1) = \frac{\lambda+\mu}{\mu} \, p(x) - \frac{\lambda}{\mu} \sum_{i=0}^{x-1} p(i) q_{x-i} \qquad x > 0 \tag{25}$$

In practice, the computation of the probabilities $p(x)$ is carried out for all x with $p(x)$ greater than a prescribed boundary.

3.2.4 CHARACTERISTIC PERFORMANCE VALUES

Once the state probabilities are known the interesting performance values can be determined (first-come-first-served is assumed):

 - Moments of the waiting time d.f.:

$$E\left[T_w^m\right] = \frac{1}{\mu^m} \sum_{i=1}^{\infty} \frac{(i+m-1)!}{(i-1)!} \, p(i) \tag{26}$$

 - Waiting time d.f.:

$$P(T_w \overset{<}{=} t) = \sum_{i=0}^{\infty} p(i)(1 - e^{-\mu t} \sum_{j=0}^{i-1} \frac{(\mu t)^j}{j!}) \qquad t \overset{\geq}{=} 0 \tag{27}$$

Of course, there is no gain in evaluating the mean time in queue by means of equation (26), whereas in many cases the numerical evaluation of the waiting time d.f. is much easier and faster to carry out in the described way than by retransforming its well-known Laplace-transform, as usually done.

Numerical examples are given in chapter 4.

3.3 EXAMPLE $G/E_k/1,s$

This chapter demonstrates the application of the special phase concept to systems with a general input process. To our knowledge, there is no exact method available for the direct solution (via generating functions, etc.) which allows an efficient evaluation [14]. However, a recursive solution is possible and outlined in the following sections.

3.3.1 STATE DESCRIPTION AND EQUILIBRIUM EQUATIONS

It is assumed that the d.f. of interarrival times is represented by a phase-type d.f. with uniform rates . (Our way of solution is also applicable for nonuniform service rates; however, no method is available to fit measured data by that type of d.f., cf. chapter 1.1 .) For the service process we assume the well-known Erlangian d.f.

The following abbreviations will be used:

λ :   uniform rate for all phases in the interarrival time model
q_i :   branching probabilities of the interarrival time model, $i \in \{1,...,r\}$
μ :   uniform rate for all k phases in the Erlangian service time model
s :   number of waiting places .

The system state is described by means of a two-dimensional vector (X_1,X_2), where

X_1 :   number of phases yet to be completed within the interarrival time model
        until arrival of the next request ($X_1 \in \{1,2,...,r\}$)
X_2 :   total number of service phases yet to be completed by all requests in
        the system ($X_2 \in \{0,1,...,x_{2max}\}$)

Figure 5 shows an example for the corresponding state-transition diagram.

Fig.5. State-transition
       diagram for the
       queueing system
       $G/E_k/1,s$ (here
       r=3, k=2, s=3,
       x_{2max}=k(s+1)=8)

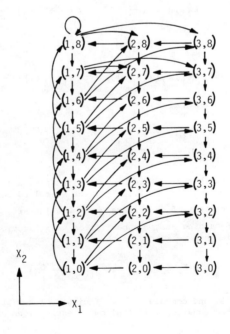

The equilibrium equations for the state probabilities are as follows:

$x_2 = 0$:

$$p(x_1, 0) \cdot \lambda \quad = p(x_1, 1) \cdot \mu + p(x_1+1, 0) \cdot \lambda$$

$1 \leq x_2 \leq x_{2max} - k$:

$$p(x_1, x_2) \ (\lambda + \mu) = p(x_1, x_2+1) \mu + p(x_1+1, x_2) \cdot \lambda + p(1, x_2-k) \lambda q_{x_1} \qquad (28)$$

$x_2 > x_{2max} - k$:

$$p(x_1, x_2)(\lambda + \mu) = p(x_1, x_2+1) \mu + p(x_1+1, x_2) \cdot \lambda$$
$$+ p(1, x_2-k) \cdot \lambda q_{x_1} + p(1, x_2) \cdot \lambda q_{x_1}$$

3.3.2 SOLUTION BY MEANS OF A RECURSIVE EVALUATION

To solve equations (28) a recursive technique is applied [12,13]. From equations (28) it follows immediately:

$$p(x_1, 1) \quad = p(x_1, 0) \cdot \frac{\lambda}{\mu} - p(x_1+1, 0) \frac{\lambda}{\mu}$$

$$p(x_1, x_2+1) = p(x_1, x_2) \cdot (\frac{\lambda}{\mu} + 1) - p(x_1+1, x_2) \cdot \frac{\lambda}{\mu}$$
$$- p(1, x_2-k) \cdot \frac{\lambda}{\mu} \cdot q_{x_1} \qquad \text{if } 1 \leq x_2 \leq x_{2max} - k \qquad (29)$$

$$p(x_1, x_2+1) = p(x_1, x_2) \cdot (\frac{\lambda}{\mu} + 1) - p(x_1+1, x_2) \cdot \frac{\lambda}{\mu}$$
$$- p(1, x_2-k) \cdot \frac{\lambda}{\mu} \cdot q_{x_1}$$
$$- p(1, x_2) \cdot \frac{\lambda}{\mu} \cdot q_{x_1} \qquad \text{if } x_{2max} - k < x_2 \leq x_{2max}$$

These equations show that all state probabilities $p(x_1, x_2)$ could be determined if the probabilities $p(x_1, 0)$, $x_1 \in \{1, \ldots, r\}$, the so-called boundaries were known.

Therefore, the main steps of our recursive evaluation are [12,13]:

- Determine all remaining state probabilities as a function of the boundary values. This is possible when we introduce the substitution

$$p(x_1, x_2) = \sum_{\gamma=1}^{r} c_{x_1, x_2}^{\gamma} \ p(\gamma, 0) \qquad (30)$$

in equations (29) and compare the coefficients of the probabilities $p(\gamma, 0)$ on both sides of the equations. The following expressions are obtained immediately ($\gamma \in \{1, \ldots, r\}$):

$$c^{\gamma}_{x_1,1} = c^{\gamma}_{x_1,o} \cdot \frac{\lambda}{\mu} - c^{\gamma}_{x_1+1,o} \cdot \frac{\lambda}{\mu}$$

$$c^{\gamma}_{x_1,x_2+1} = c^{\gamma}_{x_1,x_2} \cdot (\frac{\lambda}{\mu}+1) - c^{\gamma}_{x_1+1,x_2} \cdot \frac{\lambda}{\mu}$$

$$-c^{\gamma}_{1,x_2-k} \cdot \frac{\lambda}{\mu} \cdot q_{x_1} \qquad \text{if } 1 \le x_2 \le x_{2max} - k \tag{31}$$

$$c^{\gamma}_{x_1,x_2+1} = c^{\gamma}_{x_1,x_2} \cdot (\frac{\lambda}{\mu}+1) - c^{\gamma}_{x_1+1,x_2} \cdot \frac{\lambda}{\mu}$$

$$-c^{\gamma}_{1,x_2-k} \cdot \frac{\lambda}{\mu} \cdot q_{x_1}$$

$$-c^{\gamma}_{1,x_2} \cdot \frac{\lambda}{\mu} \cdot q_{x_1} \qquad \text{if } x_{2max}-k < x_2 < x_{2max}$$

Since the coefficients

$$c^{\gamma}_{x_1,o} = \begin{cases} 1 & \text{if } \gamma = x_1 \\ 0 & \text{if } \gamma \neq x_1 \end{cases} \tag{32}$$

are known by definition (cf. equation (30)), all remaining coefficients can be determined recursively by equations (31).

- Solve a reduced system of only r equations for the unknown boundaries. This reduced system of equations is obtained by making substitution (30) to the remaining (r-1) independent equations of (29) as well as to the normalizing condition:

$$O = \sum_{\gamma=1}^{r} c^{\gamma}_{x_1,x_{2max}} \cdot p(\gamma,o) \cdot (\frac{\lambda}{\mu}+1)$$

$$-\sum_{\gamma=1}^{r} c^{\gamma}_{x_1+1,x_{2max}} \cdot p(\gamma,o) \cdot \frac{\lambda}{\mu}$$

$$-\sum_{\gamma=1}^{r} c^{\gamma}_{1,x_{2max}-k} \cdot p(\gamma,o) \cdot \frac{\lambda}{\mu} \cdot q_{x_1} \tag{33}$$

$$-\sum_{\gamma=1}^{r} c^{\gamma}_{1,x_{2max}} \cdot p(\gamma,o) \cdot \frac{\lambda}{\mu} \cdot q_{x_1} \qquad x_1 \in \{1,\ldots,r-1\}$$

$$1 = \sum_{x_1=1}^{r} \sum_{x_2=o}^{x_{2max}} \sum_{\gamma=1}^{r} c^{\gamma}_{x_1,x_2} \cdot p(\gamma,o)$$

- Determine all interesting state probabilities by means of the (now known) boundaries and equations (29).

3.3.3 CHARACTERISTIC PERFORMANCE VALUES

Due to the non-Markovian input process, an important value is the probability $\pi(x_2)$, the probability that x_2 phases are in the system at the arrival instants. This conditional probability is given by:

$$\pi(x_2) = \frac{p(1,x_2)}{\sum\limits_{x_2=0}^{x_{2max}} p(1,x_2)} = p(1,x_2) \sum_{i=1}^{r} iq_i \qquad (34)$$

These probabilities allow to find the following expressions for the interesting performance values:

- Probability of waiting:

$$W = \sum_{x_2=1}^{x_{2max}-k} \pi(x_2) \qquad (35)$$

- Moments of the waiting time d.f. (first-come-first-served):

$$E\left[T_w^m\right] = \mu^{-m} \sum_{i=1}^{x_{2max}-k} \frac{(i+m-1)!}{(i-1)!} \pi(i) \qquad (36)$$

- Waiting time d.f. (first-come-first-served):

$$P(T_w \overset{<}{=} t) = \pi(0) + \sum_{i=x_{2max}-k+1}^{x_{2max}} \pi(i) +$$

$$+ \sum_{i=1}^{x_{2max}-k} \pi(i)(1 - e^{-\mu t} \sum_{j=0}^{i-1} \frac{(\mu t)^j}{j!}) \qquad t \overset{\geq}{=} 0 \qquad (37)$$

Numerical examples are given in chapter 4.

4. NUMERICAL RESULTS

We presented in Figure 3 a special d.f. suitable for the modeling of access and transfer times for fixed head disks or drums. The corresponding results for the waiting time d.f. are shown in Figure 6.

Fig.6. Waiting time d.f.
       for a fixed head
       disk or drum model
       (M/G/1 ; service
       times acc. to Fig.3
       A: offered traffic
       in Erlangs)

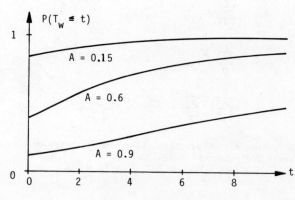

Figure 7 shows another example for a service time d.f. approximated by a phase-type d.f. with uniform service rates. Again, Figure 8 presents results for the corresponding waiting time d.f.

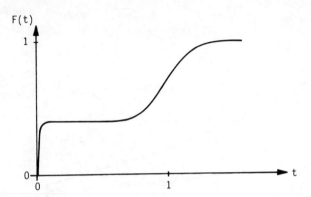

Fig.7. Third example for the approximation of a service time d.f. by a
phase-type d.f. with uniform service rates.
(μ=40, r=40, q_1=0.4, q_{40}=0.6, E[T]=0.61, Var[T]=0.24)

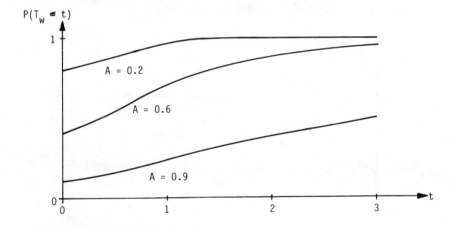

Fig.8. Waiting time d.f. for the above presented service time model.
(M/G/1 ; A: offered traffic in Erlangs)

Finally, Figures 9 and 10 summarize results for state probabilities and the waiting time d.f. in case of a $G/E_k/1$,s queueing system (the corresponding state transition diagram is sketched in Figure 5).

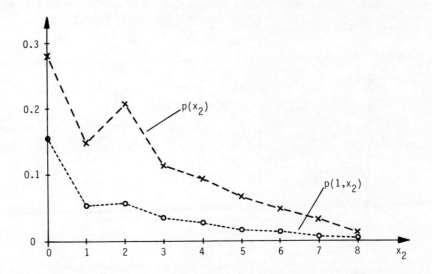

Fig.9. State probabilities for the queueing system $G/E_k/1,s$.
(corresponding state-transition diagram cf. Fig.5 ;
$r=3$, $k=2$, $s=3$, $x_{2max}=k(s+1)=8$, $\lambda=1$, $q_1=0.1$, $q_2=0.1$,
$q_3=0.8$, $\mu=1$; mean arrival rate $\lambda_m=0.37$)

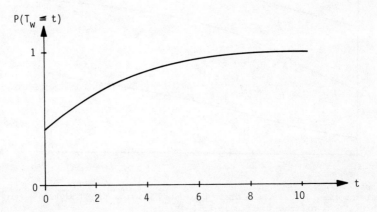

Fig.10. Waiting time d.f. for the queueing system $G/E_k/1,s$.
(parameters cf. Fig.9)

5. CONCLUSION AND OUTLOOK

We investigated the classical phase concept and found that there are two main problems:

1) No efficient method is known to determine the type of general d.f.s when measured values are given.

2) The evaluation of the state probabilities for queueing systems with phase-type arrival and service processes may be extremely difficult.

Using the special phase concept with uniform rates of the phases, the number of phases may increase remarkably. However, we found the advantage of this approach to be twofold:

1) An efficient algorithm can be formulated for the approximation of measured data with a prescribed accuracy.

2) A large amount of computing time and memory can be saved in evaluating the state probabilities and other important performance values.

In this paper we first outlined the approximation procedure. Secondly, we presented results on the performance analysis of $M/G/1$ and $G/E_k/1$,s queueing systems.

Current and future work concentrates on the area of analysis, where we try to apply the special phase concept to more complex systems with and without priorities.

ACKNOWLEDGEMENT

The authors are grateful to Professor Dr.-Ing. A. Lotze, director of the Institute of Switching and Data Techniques, University of Stuttgart, for supporting the above investigations. We thank also Mr. P. Reutter and Mr. W. Hummel for their valuable contributions.

REFERENCES

[1] Brockmeyer,E., Halstrøm,H.L., Jensen,A.: The Life and Works of A.K. Erlang. Acta Polytechnica Scandinavia (1960).

[2] Kleinrock,L.: Queueing Systems. Vol. I: Theory. John Wiley & Sons. New York/London/Sydney/Toronto, 1975.

[3] Cox,D.R.: A Use of Complex Probabilities in the Theory of Stochastic Processes. Proc. Camb. Phil. Soc. 51 (1955), pp. 313-319.

[4] Whittaker,E.T., Robinson,G.: The Calculus of Observations. Blackie & Son, London/Glasgow/Bombay, 1926.

[5] Bux,W., Herzog,U.: Approximation von Verteilungsfunktionen, ein wichtiger Schritt bei der Modellbildung für Rechensysteme. Workshop über Modelle für Rechensysteme, Bonn, 31.3.-1.4.1977. Informatik-Fachberichte 9, Springer-Verlag, Berlin/Heidelberg/New York, 1977.

[6] Schaßberger,R.: Warteschlangen. Springer-Verlag, Wien/New York, 1973.

[7] White,J.A., Schmidt,J.W., Bennett,G.K.: Analysis of Queueing Systems. Academic Press, New York/San Francisco/London, 1975.

[8] Bux,W., Herzog,U., Reutter,P.: Analyse von Wartesystemen mit Hilfe der Phasenmethode. Monograph. Institute of Switching and Data Techniques, University of Stuttgart, Stuttgart, 1976.

[9] Neumann,K.: Operations Research Verfahren. Hanser-Verlag, München/Wien, 1975.

[10] Himmelblau,D.M.: Applied Nonlinear Programming. McGraw-Hill, New York, 1972.

[11] Morse,P.M., Garber,H.N., Ernst,M.L.: A Family of Queueing Problems. Operations
      Research 2 (1954), pp. 444-445.

[12] Herzog,U., Woo,L., Chandy,K.M.: Solution of Queueing Problems by a Recursive
      Technique. IBM J. Res. Dev. 19 (1975), pp. 295-300.

[13] Bux,W., Hummel,W.: Anwendung der Phasenmethode auf Wartesysteme mit allgemei-
      nen Ankunfts- und Bedienungsprozessen. Monograph. Institute of Switching and
      Data Techniques, University of Stuttgart, Stuttgart, 1977.

[14] Krämer,W., Langenbach-Belz,M.: Approximate Formulae for the Delay in the queue-
      ing System GI/G/1. Proc. 8th International Teletraffic Congress, Melbourne,
      1976, pp. 235/1-8.

[15] Neuts,M.F.: Computational Uses of the Method of Phases in the Theory of Queues.
      Comp. and Maths. with Appls. 1 (1975), pp. 151-166.

[16] Revelle,R.: An Interactive Graphically Oriented Program Package for Analysis
      of Computer System Data. IBM Research Report RJ 1782, San José, 1976.

COMPUTER PERFORMANCE, K.M. CHANDY AND M. REISER (EDS.)
NORTH HOLLAND PUBLISHING COMPANY, 1977

DYNAMIC LOAD BALANCING IN HOMOGENEOUS TWO-PROCESSOR DISTRIBUTED SYSTEMS

Y. C. Chow and W. H. Kohler

Department of Electrical and Computer Engineering
University of Massachusetts
Amherst, Massachusetts, USA

The performance of homogeneous two-processor distributed
computer systems under several dynamic load balancing
strategies is analyzed and compared. The analysis is based
on a recursive method for solving queueing models with
state-dependent routing probabilities. The results indicate that simple load balancing policies can significantly
improve system performance.

I. INTRODUCTION

In recent years much attention has been focused on the development of distributed
computer systems [FARB73, MANN76, MICH76]. Among the many factors that motivate
this interest are the desire to share resources and the need to achieve higher
system performance and reliability. Queueing models have been widely used for
analyzing the performance of such multiple processor systems [BROW75, BUCC76,
CHOW76, MANN76]. One of the problems that must be faced when designing distributed computer systems is the scheduling of jobs among processors in the system.
Current research in this area is directed to the study of automatic load balancing methods for systems that support distributed processing. The objective is to
achieve system balance, with a resultant performance increase, by automatically
shifting jobs from heavily loaded processors to lightly loaded processors in the
system.

Load balancing can be done statically at system configuration time by preassign-
ing certain jobs or classes of jobs to specific processors, or dynamically as the
load and state of the system changes by automatically transferring jobs from one
processor to another. Recent theoretical studies of how to implement dynamic
load balancing have taken two different approaches. One approach is to formulate
the problem of assigning jobs to processors as a combinatorial optimization problem [STON77]. Jobs are reassigned dynamically by monitoring the state of the
system and recomputing the optimal assignment as the state changes. The other
approach, which will be presented in this paper, is to develop queueing models
to analyze the performance of systems incorporating simple job routing policies
that automatically shift jobs from heavily loaded processors to lightly loaded
processors.

A queueing model for load balancing in a simple distributed computer system consisting of two identical central processors is presented in Section II. The
queueing model captures the behavior of the system as a function of component
characteristics, job routing policy, and workload characteristics. Routing at
the time of job arrival is controlled by a job dispatcher, and routing after the
initial assignment is controlled by an interprocessor communication channel. The
state of the system is defined as a snapshot of the workload distribution among

---

*
Work reported herein was supported in part by National Science Foundation Grant
MCS 76-03667.

system components. We are interested in the use of state-dependent job routing
policies for dynamic load balancing in distributed systems. In this case the
transfer of a job between processors is dependent upon the workload distribution
of the system.

In Section IV we compare the performance of various configurations of the two-
processor distributed system under different load sharing policies. The measure
of performance used in the comparisons is mean job turnaround time, which is the
average time between a new job arrival and its departure from the system. An
efficient recursive method for analyzing the models with state-dependent job
routing policies is developed in Section III. Some approximate models with known
closed form analytical solutions are used to compare and validate the performance
of the state-dependent models. Our results indicate that the mean turnaround
time of the system decreases as the degree of load balancing increases. A high
degree of load balancing decreases the mean turnaround time by 40-45%.

II. DISTRIBUTED SYSTEM MODELS

In this section we consider a model for a simple distributed computer system
formed by interconnecting two independent multiprogramming systems for the purpose of higher performance and reliability through load sharing. Figure 1 is a

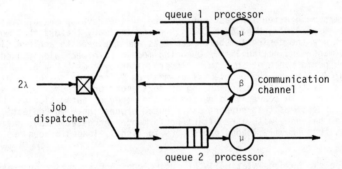

Figure 1: A Two-Processor Distributed Computer System
with Load Balancing.

queueing model of the system. Two identical processors, each with average processing rate μ, are connected through a channel of mean transfer rate β. The
service time distributions of the processors and the transfer time distribution
of the channel are assumed exponential. The job arrival is a Poisson process
with mean rate 2λ and the queueing disciplines are first-come-first-served. Load
balancing is done by the dispatcher at the time of job arrival or by the communication channel after jobs have joined the queues. The job routing rules are
defined as follows:

  1) The dispatcher assigns an arriving job to the shorter queue;

  2) If both queues have an equal number of jobs (including empty), the
      arriving job is dispatched randomly to one of the two queues with
      equal probability;

  3) The communication channel initiates a job transfer from queue i to
      queue j whenever the number of jobs in queue i is two or more greater
      than the number of jobs in queue j. The channel can only service one
      job at a time.

  4) The transfer of a job is discontinued if the imbalance condition in 3)
      changes before the channel completes the transfer.

The communication channel can be viewed as an input/output processor. If jobs waiting in queue i are interpreted as being resident in the memory system of central processor i, then the model ignores the effect of memory contention between the input/output and central processors. This is a reasonable approximation for systems with multi-port memory.

We can describe the state of the system at time t by the variables $X(t)$ and $Y(t)$, which denote respectively the number of jobs in queue 1 and queue 2 at time t. The state probabilities are defined as

$$P_{ij}(t) \stackrel{\Delta}{=} Pr[X(t) = i, Y(t) = j].$$

This discrete-state-continuous-time process forms a Markov process since the future states of the system depend only on the current state and the time distributions are assumed exponential. Following the queueing disciplines and routing strategies of this system, we can obtain the transition equations

$$\frac{dP_{00}(t)}{dt} = -2\lambda P_{00}(t) + \mu P_{10}(t) + \mu P_{01}(t)$$

$$\frac{dP_{ij}(t)}{dt} = -(2\lambda + 2\mu)P_{ij}(t) + 2\lambda(P_{i-1,j}(t) + P_{i,j-1}(t))$$

$$+ \mu(P_{i+1,j}(t) + P_{i,j+1}(t)) + \beta(P_{i+1,j-1}(t) + P_{i-1,j+1}(t))$$

$$i > 0, j > 0,$$
$$i = j$$

$$\frac{dP_{ij}(t)}{dt} = -(2\lambda + 2\mu_{ij} + \beta_{ij})P_{ij}(t) + 2\lambda P_{i,j-1}(t)$$

$$+ \mu(P_{i+1,j}(t) + P_{i,j+1}(t)) + \beta P_{i+1,j-1}(t) \qquad i > 0, i > j$$

$$\frac{dP_{ij}(t)}{dt} = -(2\lambda + 2\mu_{ij} + \beta_{ij})P_{ij}(t) + 2\lambda P_{i-1,j}(t)$$

$$+ \mu(P_{i+1,j}(t) + P_{i,j+1}(t)) + \beta P_{i-1,j+1}(t) \qquad j > 0, j > i$$

where $P_{ij}(t) = 0$ if $i < 0$ or $j < 0$,

and

$$\mu_{ij} = \begin{cases} 0 & i,j \leq 0 \\ \mu & i = 0, j > 0 \text{ or } i > 0, j = 0 \\ 2\mu & i,j > 0 \end{cases} \qquad \beta_{ij} = \begin{cases} 0 & |i-j| \leq 1 \\ \beta & |i-j| > 1 \end{cases}$$

We are only interested in the steady-state equilibrium equations which can be obtained from the above equations by setting $\frac{d}{dt} P_{ij}(t) = 0$ and by defining $P_{ij} \stackrel{\Delta}{=} \lim_{t \to \infty} P_{ij}(t)$. The behavior of the system can be equivalently described by means of the state-transition-rate diagram shown in Figure 2. Here the (i,j)th node represents the state $X(t) = i$, $Y(t) = j$. The branches identify the allowable state transitions and the branch labels specify the rate at which the transitions proceed. The state transition equations can be written immediately by

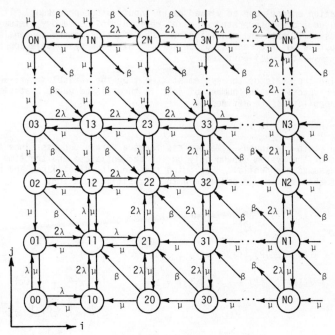

Figure 2:   State-Transition-Rate Diagram.

noting that the rate of change of flow into state (i,j), i.e. $\frac{d}{dt} P_{ij}(t)$, must be equal to the difference between the rate at which the system enters state (i,j) and the rate at which the system leaves state (i,j). The state equilibrium equation obtained by equating the total flow out of the state to the total flow into the state is called the global balance equation (GBE) for the state. Characteristics such as utilization of the processors and the mean turnaround time for the system can be computed if the state equilibrium probabilities are known. The recursive technique described in the next section allows us to compute efficiently the state equilibrium probabilities in Figure 2.

Interesting special cases of the general model in Figure 1 are obtained by choosing different job arrival and transfer policies. The analysis of these models (Figure 3 - Figure 8) allows us to compare the impact of various load balancing strategies. Model A (Figure 3) represents a system without load balancing. Incoming jobs are dispatched randomly to either queue, causing an arrival rate of λ to each queue, and there is no channel transfer between the two queues, i.e. $\beta = 0$. The model is equivalent to two independent M/M/1 systems. In Model B (Figure 4) arriving jobs are dispatched to the shorter queue with ties broken randomly, but again there is no channel to transfer jobs between queues. Model C (Figure 5) is the general model discussed earlier. Model D (Figure 6) has a random job arrival policy like Model A but loads are balanced by the communication channel with $\beta > 0$. We get Model E (Figure 7) when the job transfer rate β approaches infinity. This is equivalent to an M/M/2 system in which two processors share the same queue. We again ignore the memory contention between the two processors. The arrival policy becomes irrelevant since we may assume the system has a common queue due to $\beta = \infty$. The transfer of jobs between queues is sometimes called jockeying. Instantaneous jockeying ($\beta = \infty$) between heterogeneous or homogeneous queues (as in Model E) has been studied by [KOEN66, DISN76]

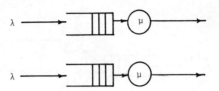

Figure 3: Model A - Join Random Queue without Channel Transfer.
(Two independent M/M/1 systems)

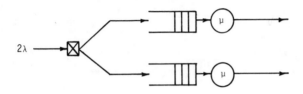

Figure 4: Model B - Join Shorter Queue without Channel Transfer
($\beta=0$).

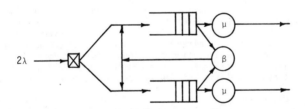

Figure 5: Model C - Join Shorter Queue with Channel Transfer.

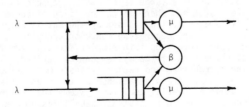

Figure 6: Model D - Join Random Queue with Channel Transfer.

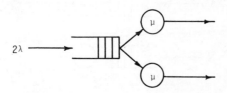

Figure 7: Model E - Instantaneous Channel Transfer.
           ($\beta=\infty$, M/M/2)

Figure 8: Model F - Single Fast Processor System.

and they have derived closed form solutions for P_{ij}. In Model F (Figure 8) the
system is reduced to a single processor of twice the individual processing rate.
This model is introduced for comparison with the others since it has the lowest
mean turnaround time that can be achieved by a system of total processing rate
2μ. All models except Model D are analyzed in Section III and compared in
Section IV. There is no efficient solution technique known for Model D, but the
infinite system of simultaneous state equations can be truncated and in principle
solved directly or a direct simulation of the system can be done if necessary.

III. RECURSIVE SOLUTION TECHNIQUE

Various analytical, numerical, and simulation techniques are available for obtaining the exact or approximate solutions of queueing models. Notable among them
are the power iteration method [WALL66], generating function approach [KLEI75],
product form solution [GORD67, BASK75], and recursive solution technique [HERZ75].
The power iteration method can be used to numerically solve the set of simultaneous equations for P_{ij} by iteration. The difficulties with this approach are that
it involves the manipulation of a large matrix which represents the state equilibrium equations of the system and there is the question of convergence of the
iteration process. It is also tedious to set up the matrix automatically for an
arbitrary queueing network. The generating function approach is a mapping method
which transforms the system equations into simpler forms. From the simplified
generating functions, properties of the system can be derived. The widely used
transforms include the z-transform and Laplace transform. Most complex systems
usually require multi-variable transformations for their analysis. The product
form solution technique is a powerful tool for systems that exhibit the local
balance property [CHAN72]. The joint state probabilities of a system that obeys
local balance can be expressed as a product of the marginal state probabilities
of individual queues. Unfortunately, the general model that we are considering

in this paper does not satisfy the local balance property. The recursive solution technique was first suggested by [HERZ75] for single queue models with other than exponential arrival or service distributions. This technique uses the fact that the state probabilities of a system can sometimes be expressed in terms of other state probabilities to reduce the number of unknowns in the system equations. The computation will be further simplified if the unknowns can be evaluated without solving all states in the system simultaneously.

The recursive solution technique can be applied to queueing models with more than one queue. In the case of Model B and Model C, the systems can be described by the two dimensional state diagram in Figure 2. If the system is ergodic, P_{ij} will approach zero for large i and j. It is therefore reasonable to truncate the infinite state diagram by assuming that the maximum queue length is N. This will introduce a negligible error if N is properly chosen. The total number of states is then $(N + 1)^2$. Let $P_{N,j} = X_j$, where the X's are unknown variables for j = 0, 1, ..., N. Using the GBE for $P_{N,j}$ we can express $P_{N-1,j}$ as a function of the X's. In turn all the P_{ij}'s, for i = N-1 down to 0, can be expressed in terms of the X's. This process reduces the unknowns from $(N + 1)^2$ to N + 1. Finally, we can use the GBE for P_{0j}, j = 0, 1, ..., N, to obtain a set of N independent linear homogeneous equations in the X's. Together with the conservation equation $\sum_{i=0}^{N} \sum_{j=0}^{N} P_{ij} = 1$, the set of N + 1 simultaneous equations can be solved for the X's.

Additional properties exhibited by Model B and Model C enable us to further simplify the method. First, we recognize that the state diagrams (Figure 2) are symmetric about the diagonal elements (i,i) and therefore can be folded over to obtain a triangle (Figure 9). From Figure 9 we now notice that if state probabilities $P_{N,N}$ and $P_{N-1,N-1}$ were known, then $P_{N,j}$, for j = N-1 down to 0, could be calculated recursively by using the GBE for state (N,j+1). This property allows us to efficiently calculate all the state equilibrium probabilities by proceeding recursively from top to bottom and right to left in the state diagram. We may

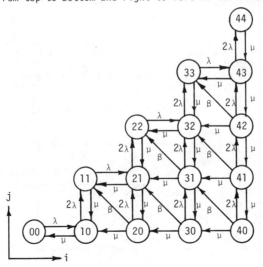

Figure 9: A Folded State Diagram for N = 4.

initially set $P_{N,N}$ to an arbitrary constant, since the P_{ij}'s will be computed
iteratively and normalized at the end of the process. $P_{N-1,N-1}$ is initially unknown and represented by the variable X, but can be found by solving the GBE for
state (N,0). The general method is described by the following algorithm and
illustrated in the Appendix for the sample system of Figure 9.

1. Set i = N, CONST = 1.
2. Set $P_{i,i}$ = CONST, $P_{i-1,i-1}$ = X (an unknown variable).
3. For j = 1 down to 1, use GBE for state (i,j) to determine
   an expression for $P_{i,j-1}$ as a function of X.
4. Use the GBE for state (i,0) to solve for X.
5. With X known, compute P_{ij} for j = 0, ..., i-1.
6. Set i = i-1, CONST = X.
7. Repeat Step 2 through Step 6 until i = 0.
8. Set P_{00} = CONST.
9. Normalize all P_{ij}.

X is the only unknown variable at any time during the iterations. It can be seen
that each P_{ij} is expressed as a + bX, where a and b are known numerical values and
X is the unknown variable whose value is subjected to change after each iteration.
The algorithm can be implemented by using complex numbers to temporarily represent
the P_{ij}, with the real part and imaginary part of each complex number denoting a
and b respectively. Since the P_{ij} are relative to one another, they must be normalized at the end to satisfy the conservation relation $\sum_{i=0}^{N} \sum_{j=0}^{N} P_{ij} = 1$. The
algorithm is not applicable to Model D, for in the state diagram of Model D the
GBE for state (i,j) involves two unknown states, state (i-1,j) from the left and
state (i,j-1) from below. Thus, $P_{i,j-1}$ cannot be expressed as a function of X as
described in Step 3 of the algorithm. However, the general recursive method can
still be used to reduce the number of unknown states from $(N + 1)^2$ to N + 1.

The algorithm applies similarly to closed queueing models with load balancing
policies like those of Model B and Model C. Figure 10 shows a closed queueing
model which can be interpreted as representing a distributed multiprogramming
system with fixed degree of multiprogramming 2N, or a demand paging system in
which the I/O subsystem represents the activities of the paging system [CHOW76].
The definition of a state and the state-transition-rate diagram are the same as
in the open model except that the P_{ij} are by definition identically zero whenever
i > N or j > N.

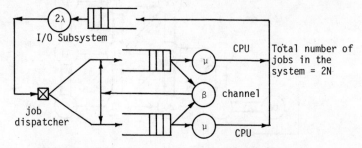

Figure 10: Closed Queueing Model with Load Balancing Policies.

IV. COMPARISON OF PERFORMANCE

Performance measures obtained by analyzing the queueing models include the utilization of the processors (U), the average queue length (L), and the mean job turnaround time (T). By definition the utilization of the processors in each of the open models is $U = \lambda/\mu$ for any given λ and μ. The average queue length is directly related to mean response time by Little's law, $\lambda T = L$. Our comparisons are based on an analysis of the mean turnaround time T of each model. Models A, E, and F are standard queueing models and have the simple closed form solutions [KLEI75]

$$T_A = \frac{1}{\mu - \lambda} \, ,$$

$$T_E = \frac{\mu}{(\mu - \lambda)(\mu + \lambda)} \, ,$$

and $T_F = \frac{1}{2(\mu - \lambda)}$ respectively.

Model B was studied by [FLAT76] using the generating function approach and it was shown that P_{ij} has a rather complicated closed form solution. The algorithm described in the previous section provides an effective way to compute the P_{ij}'s for Model B and Model C. The average queue length L can then be computed using

$L \stackrel{\Delta}{=} \sum_{i=1}^{N} \sum_{j=1}^{N} i \, P_{ij} \stackrel{\Delta}{=} \sum_{i=1}^{N} \sum_{j=1}^{N} j \, P_{ij}$. The mean turnaround time is calculated directly from the relation $T = \frac{L}{\lambda}$.

Table 1 and Figure 11 show comparisons of the mean turnaround time T for the five models A, B, C, E, and F as a function of λ. In each case $\mu = 1.0$ and λ varies from 0.1 to 0.9. The channel rate in Model C is $\beta = 1.0$. The results indicate that for each choice of parameter λ

$$T_A \geq T_B \geq T_C \geq T_E \geq T_F \, .$$

Model	Description of Model	λ	.1	.2	.3	.4	.5	.6	.7	.8	.9
A	two independent M/M/1	T_A	1.11	1.25	1.43	1.67	2.00	2.50	3.33	5.00	10.00
B	join the shorter queue without jockeying	T_B	1.02	1.06	1.14	1.26	1.42	1.68	2.10	2.95	5.47
C	join the shorter queue with jockeying, $\beta = 1.0$	T_C	1.01	1.05	1.12	1.23	1.39	1.63	2.05	2.88	5.35
E	M/M/2, $\beta = \infty$	T_E	1.01	1.04	1.09	1.19	1.33	1.56	1.96	2.78	5.26
F	processor with twice the speed	T_F	0.56	0.63	0.71	0.83	1.00	1.25	1.67	2.50	5.00

Table 1: Comparison of Mean Turnaround Time for Models A, B, C, E, F.

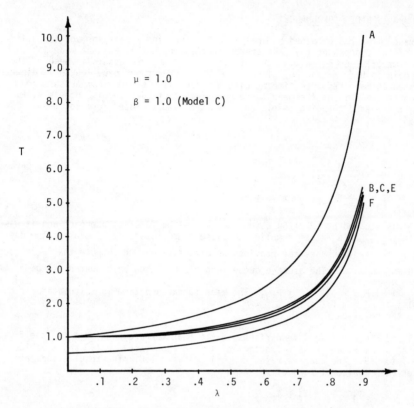

Figure 11: Comparison of Mean Turnaround Time (T) as a Function of
           Arrival Rate (λ) for Models A, B, C, E, F.

We also notice that under heavy load conditions, the performance of the distributed models with load balancing (Models B, C, E) is significantly better than the
system of two independent processors. Furthermore, the performance rapidly
approaches that of Model F, which is the best that can be achieved. Although the
method developed in Section III cannot be used to solve Model D, Models A and E
represent the limiting cases $\beta=0$ and $\beta=\infty$ respectively. By changing the channel
rate any intermediate mean turnaround time can be obtained. Model E is also the
limiting case of Model C as $\beta \to \infty$. Simulation was used to determine the mean
turnaround time of Model D for $\beta=0.5$ and 1.0. Figure 12 compares these results
with the limiting cases. Figures 11 and 12 show that the shorter queue dispatching and channel transfer load balancing strategies achieve almost the same effect.

V. CONCLUSION

The results of our analysis suggest that the performance of distributed systems
under heavy load can be improved significantly with simple load balancing strategies. Two characteristics make it possible to apply the simple recursive algorithm to solve Model B and Model C. First, since the systems are homogeneous we
can fold the state-transition-rate diagram into a triangle. Second, since the
models have a join-the-shorter-queue arrival policy, each state in the state diagram has at most one transition from states to its left and one transition from
states below. In this case the recursive algorithm is shown to be efficient and

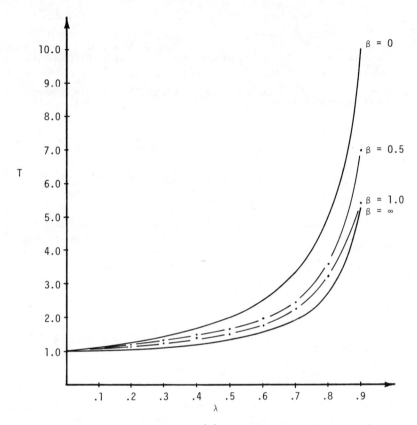

Figure 12: Mean Turnaround Time (T) of Model D as a Function of
Arrival Rate (λ) for Several Channel Rates (β).

easy to implement. A similar method can be applied to analyze nonhomogeneous two-
processor systems. The overall system performance was improved by dynamic load
balancing, although the average arrival rate and service rate remained unchanged.
This is due to the fact that the state-dependent-job-routing policy has changed
the inter-arrival distribution from exponential to hypoexponential with the same
mean. The hypoexponential distribution has a lower coefficient of variation than
the exponential distribution, resulting in more consistent inter-arrival times.
The load of the system is thus better balanced. This coincides with our intuition
about the join-the-shorter-queue load balancing policy. Unfortunately, we cannot
find an analytical solution for Model D. We have tried to use the generating
function approach, but the approach was only partially successful. One interesting question is: What channel rate β in Model D is required to give the same
performance as the join-the-shorter-queue policy of Model B? We are currently
working to extend the analysis to nonhomogeneous distributed systems with various
load balancing policies and systems with more than two processors.

REFERENCES

[BASK75] Baskett, F., K.M. Chandy, R.R. Muntz, and F.G. Palacios, "Open, Closed, and Mixed Networks of Queues with Different Classes of Customers," J.ACM, Vol. 22, No. 2, April 1975, pp. 248-260.

[BROW75] Browne, J.C. et al., "Hierarchical Techniques for the Development of Realistic Models of Complex Computer Systems," Proceedings of the IEEE, Vol. 63, No. 6, June 1975.

[BUCC76] Bucci, G. and Streeter, D.N., "A User-Oriented Approach to the Design of Distributed Information Systems," IBM Technical Report RC 5887, March 1976.

[CHAN72] Chandy, K.M., "The Analysis and Solutions for General Queueing Networks," Proceedings of the Sixth Annual Princeton Conference, 1972, pp. 224-228.

[CHOW76] Chow, Y. and W.H. Kohler, "Analysis and Comparison of Several Queueing Models for Multiprocessor Multiprogramming Systems," Technical Report ECE-CS-76-2, Dept. of Electrical and Computer Engineering, University of Massachusetts, Amherst, July 1976.

[DISN70] Disney, R.L. and W.E. Mitchell, "A Solution for Queues with Instantaneous Jockeying and Other Customer Selection Rules," Naval Research Logistics Quarterly, Vol. 17, No. 1, March 1970, pp. 315-325.

[FARB73] Farber, D.J., et al., "The Distributed Computer System," Proc. 7th Annual IEEE Computer Society International Conference, Feb. 1973, pp. 31-34.

[FLAT76] Flatto, L., and H. McKean, "Two Parallel Queues with Equal Serving Rates," IBM Research, RC 5916, March 1976.

[GORD67] Gordon, W.J. and G.F. Newell, "Closed Queueing Systems with Exponential Servers," Operations Research, Vol. 15, 1967, pp. 254-265.

[HERZ75] Herzog, U., L. Woo, and K.M. Chandy, "Solution of Queueing Problems by a Recursive Technique," IBM J. Res. Develop., Vol. 19, No. 3, May 1975, pp. 295-300.

[KLEI75] Kleinrock, L., Queueing Systems, Vol. I: Theory, Wiley Interscience, New York, 1975.

[KOEN66] Koenigsberg, E., "On Jockeying in Queues," Management Science, Vol. 12, No. 5, January 1966, pp. 412-436.

[MANN76] Manning, E.G. and Peebles, R.W., "A Homogeneous Network for Data Sharing - Communications," Computer Communications Network Group, Report E-12, University of Waterloo, July 1976.

[MICH76] Michael, J. and A. Van Dam, "Experience with Distributed Graphics Processing on a Host/Satellite System," Technical Report, Division of Applied Mathematics, Brown University, 1976.

[STON77] Stone, H.S., "Multiprocessor Scheduling with the Aid of Network Flow Algorithms," IEEE Transactions on Software Engineering, Vol. SE-3, No. 1, January 1977, pp. 85-93.

[WALL66] Wallace, V.L., R.S. Rosenburg, "Markovian Models and Numerical Analysis of Computer System Behavior," SJCC, Vol. 28, 1966, pp. 141-148.

APPENDIX

Solution steps for the system in Figure 9.

1. Set $P_{44} = 1$.

2. Set $P_{33} = X$.

3. Use the GBE for state (4,4) to determine P_{43}.

$$\mu P_{44} = 2\lambda P_{43}$$

$$P_{43} = \frac{\mu}{2\lambda}$$

4. Use the GBE for state (4,3) to determine P_{42}.

$$(2\lambda + 2\mu)P_{43} = \mu P_{44} + \lambda P_{33} + 2\lambda P_{42}$$

$$P_{42} = \frac{1}{2\lambda} \left[(2\lambda + 2\mu) \frac{\mu}{2\lambda} - \mu - \lambda x \right]$$

$$= \frac{1}{2\lambda} \left[\frac{\mu^2}{\lambda} - \lambda x \right]$$

5. Use the GBE for state (4,2) to determine P_{41}.

$$(2\lambda + 2\mu + \beta)P_{42} = \mu P_{43} + 2\lambda P_{41}$$

$$P_{41} = \frac{1}{2\lambda} \left[(2\lambda + 2\mu + \beta) \frac{1}{2\lambda} (\frac{\mu^2}{\lambda} - \lambda x) - \frac{\mu^2}{2\lambda} \right]$$

$$= \frac{1}{4\lambda^2} \left[(2\lambda + 2\mu + \beta)(\frac{\mu^2}{\lambda} - \lambda x) - \mu^2 \right]$$

$$= \frac{1}{4\lambda^2} \left[\mu^2(1 + \frac{2\mu}{\lambda} + \frac{\beta}{\lambda}) - \lambda(2\lambda + 2\mu + \beta)x \right]$$

6. Use the GBE for state (4,1) to determine P_{40}.

$$(2\lambda + 2\mu + \beta)P_{41} = \mu P_{42} + 2\lambda P_{40}$$

$$P_{40} = \frac{1}{2\lambda} \left[(2\lambda+2\mu+\beta) \frac{1}{4\lambda^2} [(2\lambda+2\mu+\beta)(\frac{\mu^2}{\lambda} - \lambda x) - \mu^2] - \frac{\mu}{2\lambda}(\frac{\mu^2}{2\lambda} - \lambda x) \right]$$

$$= \frac{1}{8\lambda^3} \left[(2\lambda+2\mu+\beta)^2(\frac{\mu^2}{\lambda} - \lambda x) - \mu^2(2\lambda+2\mu+\beta) - 2\lambda\mu(\frac{\mu^2}{\lambda} - \lambda x) \right]$$

$$= \frac{1}{8\lambda^3} \left[(2\lambda+2\mu+\beta)^2 \frac{\mu^2}{\lambda} - (2\lambda+2\mu+\beta)\mu^2 - 2\mu^3 - (2\lambda+2\mu+\beta)^2 \lambda x + 2\lambda^2\mu x \right].$$

7. Use the GBE for state (4,0) to solve for X.

$$(2\lambda + \mu + \beta)P_{40} = \mu P_{41}$$

$$\frac{(2\lambda+\mu+\beta)}{8\lambda^3} \left[(2\lambda+2\mu+\beta)^2 \frac{\mu^2}{\lambda} - (2\lambda+2\mu+\beta)\mu^2 - 2\mu^3 - (2\lambda+2\mu+\beta)^2 \lambda x + 2\lambda^2\mu x \right]$$

$$= \frac{\mu}{4\lambda^2} \left[\mu^2(1 + \frac{2\mu}{\lambda} + \frac{\beta}{\lambda}) - \lambda(2\lambda + 2\mu + \beta)x \right]$$

$$X = \frac{(2\lambda+\mu+\beta)[(2\lambda+2\mu+\beta)^2 \frac{\mu^2}{\lambda} - (2\lambda+2\mu+\beta)\mu^2 - 2\mu^3] - 2\mu^3(\lambda+2\mu+\beta)}{(2\lambda+\mu+\beta)[\lambda(2\lambda+2\mu+\beta)^2 - 2\lambda^2\mu] - 2\lambda^2\mu(2\lambda+2\mu+\beta)}$$

8. Substitute the value of X into equations in Steps 2, 4, 5, 6 to obtain numerical values for P_{33}, P_{42}, P_{41}, and P_{40}.

9. Since P_{33} and the state equilibrium probabilities in column 4 are now known, the same process may be repeated for column 3 to obtain P_{22} and all P_{3j}'s. This is repeated in turn for columns 2 and 1.

10. Use the relation $P_{ji} = P_{ij}$ to find the state progabilities for the other half of the state diagram.

11. Normalize all P_{ij} by setting

$$P_{ij} \longleftarrow \frac{P_{ij}}{\sum\limits_{k=0}^{N} \sum\limits_{l=0}^{N} P_{kl}}$$

COMPUTER PERFORMANCE, K.M. CHANDY AND M. REISER (EDS.)
NORTH HOLLAND PUBLISHING COMPANY, 1977

THE USE OF PERCENTILES IN MODELING CPU SERVICE TIME DISTRIBUTIONS

E. D. Lazowska

Computer Systems Research Group
University of Toronto
Toronto, Canada

Success stories and "doesn't matter" results to the contrary, there are times when representing the CPU as an exponential server in a queueing network model results in unacceptable error in matching or predicting various performance measures. Should this occur, the modeller will usually turn to a first-come-first-served service discipline with a two-stage hyperexponential server that matches the mean and variance of the observed service time distribution. The third constraint required for unique parameter selection is chosen arbitrarily, typically for algebraic convenience.

This paper develops a new technique for matching general service time distributions in central server queueing network models. I will show that attempting to match several higher moments of these distributions is not only insufficient, but also unnecessary and frequently misleading. The magnitude of the error will be demonstrated using a model of the IBM System/370 Model 165 at the University of Toronto Computer Centre. I will show that attempting to match the empirical probability density function of the service time distribution is a superior approach. I will introduce a three-stage server whose inherent density function resembles that of empirically observed service time distributions, and describe my experiences in using a heuristic that selects parameters for this server based upon the location of certain percentiles of the observed distribution.

Simple queueing network models using exponential servers have demonstrated a remarkable ability to predict computer system performance accurately. It is an unfortunate fact of life, though, that significant errors sometimes occur in using them to model even seemingly straightforward computer systems. An insufficiently accurate characterization of the CPU service time distribution is frequently the principal cause of this error.

Throughout this paper I shall make reference to a queueing network model of the IBM System/370 Model 165 at the University of Toronto Computer Centre. We shall study the predictions of this model when various server structures are used to represent the CPU service time distribution. The basic model was constructed with considerable care. It is of the central server type, with eight exponential servers representing the major I/O devices of the actual system. Its parameters were determined using a combination of hardware and software monitor data and accounting data. Particular attention was paid to the effect of parallelism in the I/O subsystem [Zahorjan 1976]. This subsystem model, once developed, was reduced to a single load-dependent server via Norton's theorem [Chandy et al. 1975]. The structure of the model is illustrated in Figure 1 on the following page.

Our standard of comparison will not be the actual system, but a detailed
simulation model in which the CPU service time distribution was obtained by
processing full interrupt traces of the actual system in operation. Since this
distribution includes CPU activity attributable to the operating system, overhead
is implicitly represented. The performance measure used throughout is CPU
utilization, typically the most robust metric.

The departure point for this study is the observation that with a
multiprogramming level of 5, the CPU utilization of the Toronto system is .74.
Using an exponential CPU server matching the observed mean, the queueing network
model predicts a utilization of .83, an unacceptably large error.

The Failure of HE-2 Moment Matching

The Pollaczek-Khinchin equation demonstrates that the mean time in system for
an M/G/1 queue is fully determined by the first two moments of the service time
distribution [Kleinrock 1975]. In applying queueing network models to computer
systems, it seems reasonable to generalize this intuition, characterizing the CPU
service time distribution in terms of its moments and representing the CPU by the
simplest Cox-type server that can match the observed mean and coefficient of
variation (the coefficient of variation is equal to the square root of the
variance, divided by the mean). Since the coefficient of variation of
empirically observed CPU service time distributions is greater than one, this
server is the two-stage hyperexponential (HE-2), illustrated in Figure 2.

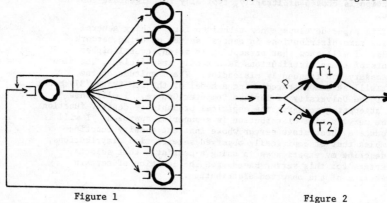

Figure 1   Figure 2

In attempting to match the mean and variance of an observed distribution with
a two-stage hyperexponential server, we arrive not at a single set of parameters,
but at a family of parameter values constrained by the following two equations:

$$\text{mean} = (P)T1 + (1-P)T2$$
$$\text{variance} = 2((P)T1^2 + (1-P)T2^2) - \text{mean}^2$$

where T1 is the mean service time of stage 1, P is the selection probability of
that stage, and T2 is the mean service time of stage 2.

Given the Pollaczek-Khinchin intuition, it is surprising that when the
various members of this family are used in a queueing network model they yield
dramatically different predictions for CPU utilization. For example, when the
family having a mean of 8.7 and a coefficient of variation of 12.7 (the observed
characteristics of the Toronto CPU service time distribution) is used in our
model, the approximate range of predicted CPU utilizations is:

P	T1	T2	Utilization
.0005	3454.06	6.95	.79
::::	::::	::::	::::
::::	::::	::::+	::::
.0124	701.16	0.00	.56

The range of values that P can assume is constrained by the variance of the distribution. P was not pushed to the absolute extreme in the above example, nor, of course, was the example artificially constructed to achieve maximum effect.

There is a convincing intuitive explanation for this phenomenon. For arbitrary but fixed mean and variance, Figure 3 illustrates the behaviour of T1 and T2 as P is varied over its feasible range. (Note that the y-axis scales for T1 and T2 differ.) The value of T2 varies almost linearly from the mean of the server (asymptotically, when P is extremely small) to zero (again asymptotically, as P approaches its upper feasible limit). The value of T1 asymptotes towards the mean of the server as P approaches its upper feasible limit.

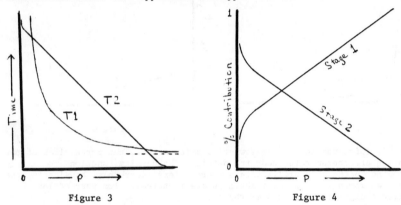

Figure 3   Figure 4

Figure 4 illustrates the relative contribution of each stage to the overall mean of the server as P is varied over its feasible range. The relative contribution of stage 1 is (P)T1 divided by the mean of the server; for stage 2, the numerator is (1-P)T2. Notice that for P near the upper feasible limit, the contribution of stage 2 to the overall mean is negligible. In other words, essentially the entire utilization of the CPU is attributable to a stage whose selection probability is .01. With a probability of .99, a customer will have a negligible service time at the CPU server and will proceed immediately to the I/O servers. I/O queue lengths will grow, and this congestion will decrease system throughput and CPU utilization.

As P decreases, the relative contributions of the two stages first become equal, then stage 2 dominates until finally, as P approaches zero, almost all of the CPU activity is attributable to stage 2. But this stage now has a selection probability of nearly 1, so CPU utilization is nearly as high as for an exponential server.

This observation explains another phenomenon of the HE-2 CPU server: as its coefficient of variation decreases, so does the range of CPU utilizations that can be attained. For instance, using the same model with a coefficient of variation of 2 instead of 12.7 results in the following range of utilizations:

P	T1	T2	Utilization
.0005	465.97	8.45	.83
::::	::::	::::	::::
::::	::::	::::+	::::
.4000	21.75	0.00	.74

With this lower coefficient of variation, stage 1 does not account for all of the CPU activity until its selection probability reaches .4. There is greater inherent balance in this server, so queue lengths at the I/O servers do not become excessive, and CPU utilization is not as severely affected. Note, incidentally, that the actual CPU utilization of the system is barely included in the range of this server.

The two extremes of an HE-2 family may be distinguished more formally by considering their probability density functions. Figures 5 and 6 display the general forms of the density functions corresponding to HE-2 servers at the low and high extremes of predicted CPU utilization, respectively:

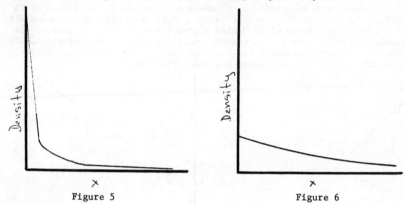

Figure 5   Figure 6

In Figure 5, corresponding to the low utilization server, the percentiles of the distribution are concentrated near the origin. The density function corresponding to the high utilization server differs remarkably, considering that the first two moments of the distributions are identical. Its percentiles are spread over a significantly greater range.

Since the actual CPU utilization is included in the range predicted by the HE-2 family matching the observed mean and variance, it is natural to seek a third constraint that will allow us to select the appropriate set of parameters. Two approaches have been used in practice. The more common [Sauer & Chandy 1975] attempts to achieve a balanced server, in the sense of Figure 4, by setting $(P)T1 = (1-P)T2$. This constraint is somewhat arbitrary, and when the HE-2 server satisfying it is used in the model, predicted CPU utilization is .69.

The more conscientious approach attempts to match the third moment of the observed CPU service time distribution, in addition to the first two. Although it is not always possible to achieve this match with an HE-2 server, the observed distribution of the Toronto system can be matched quite well. Unfortunately, though, predicted CPU utilization is .64. It is worth noting that for an HE-2 server with fixed mean and variance, predicted CPU utilization is proportional to skewness; the distribution illustrated in Figure 6 has a higher skewness than the one illustrated in Figure 5.

The following table summarizes our rather discouraging results to this point:

server	utilization	percent error
system	.74	
exponential	.83	+12
HE-2		
low extreme of the family	.56	−24
high extreme of the family	.79	+ 7
matching coef. of skewness	.64	−13
equal relative contribution	.69	− 7

(The coefficient of skewness equals the cube root of the skewness, divided by the square root of the variance.) In short, matching the first few moments of the observed CPU service time distribution using a two-stage hyperexponential server does not seem to be a fruitful approach, unless the modeller is willing to resort to calibration of the model via arbitrary parameter modification.

Price's Observation

In a recent article, Price [1976] discusses a result of Jaiswal's [1968] concerning the M/G/1 queueing system with fixed number of customers, N. This queueing system is of interest to us because it is equivalent to a closed queueing network with N customers in which the central server has a general service time distribution with FCFS scheduling, and the N I/O servers have identical exponential service time distributions with no queueing delays. (Although the equivalence of these two systems may not be immediately obvious, their state transition representations are identical.)

Jaiswal derives an expression for server utilization in the M/G/1 queueing system with fixed number of customers which shows that utilization is inversely proportional to the Laplace transform of the CPU service time distribution. (In Jaiswal's result, the transform function is evaluated at several fixed values.) Price notes that since the Laplace transform encodes all moments of a distribution, there is no reason to believe that the first few moments restrict the range of the value of the transform sufficiently to ensure accuracy. He provides an HE-2 example illustrating this point.

The implication of Price's observation is important and has not received the attention it deserves: to ensure accuracy in the M/G/1 system with fixed number of customers, it is sufficient that the server have the same Laplace transform as the observed service time distribution.

The Laplace transform of a service time distribution is the integral of the product of its probability density function and the negative exponential function:

$$B^*(s) = \int_0^\infty e^{-sx} f(x) \, dx$$

Price's observation rings true, for we have already noted the dramatically different density functions of the HE-2 servers corresponding to opposite ends of the range of predicted CPU utilizations.

Robustness

Before this observation can be used in building queueing network models, we must assess its robustness by answering two questions: (1) Does the Laplace transform result hold for queueing systems other than the M/G/1 with fixed number of customers? (2) As a practical matter, is it any easier to characterize a distribution accurately in terms of its Laplace transform than in terms of its moments? I shall address each of these questions in turn:

● Applicability to Other Queueing Network Configurations

The M/G/1 queueing system with fixed number of customers is a reasonable high-level model of a time sharing system: the central server represents the computer system itself, and the N I/O servers represent interactive terminals. For more detailed studies, though, the model is not sufficiently realistic. For instance, should we desire to represent a CPU and its I/O servers, we are forced to assume that all I/O servers have the same service time and that each I/O server is uniquely assigned to a single customer.

In observing the behaviour of this queueing network, it is apparent that the magnitude of the Laplace transform effect (i.e., the width of the range of CPU utilizations predicted by the various members of an HE-2 family) is dependent upon the relative load of the CPU and the I/O devices. This makes sense; the greater the extent to which the CPU is the bottleneck device, the greater the degree to which its service time distribution affects performance.

It is reasonable to expect that I/O queueing may substantially diminish the magnitude of the effect. In order to establish the generality of the result, I will now consider the other extreme of the queueing network spectrum: a system with a CPU and a single I/O server.

Consider the M/G/1 queueing system with bounded queue size, N-1. In this queueing system, customers arrive at a fixed rate that is independent of the number of customers already in the system. If an arriving customer finds N customers already in the system, however, it balks and vanishes. This queueing system is equivalent to a queueing network having N customers, a FCFS CPU with general service time distribution, and a single, exponentially distributed I/O server. (As with Price's observation, the equivalence of these two systems may not be immediately obvious. Once again, though, their state transition representations are identical. Although the open system always has a Poisson arrival process, new arrivals are rejected if there are already N customers in the system, so the "effective" arrival rate is zero during these periods. This behaviour is identical to that of the closed system.)

Of course, most computer systems lie somewhere between the extremes delimited by the two M/G/1 queueing systems we have described: there is more than one I/O server, but there are not so many that queueing never occurs. A proof of the Laplace transform result for the M/G/1 queueing system with bounded queue size would argue convincingly that the result is valid over the entire spectrum.

This proof, along with some motivational material, is included as an appendix to this paper. In the remainder of this section I shall emphasize the magnitude of the effect. Figure 7 illustrates the range of CPU utilizations yielded by the HE-2 family with a mean of 8.7 and a coefficient of variation of 12.7 used in the two-server queueing network model equivalent to the M/G/1 queueing system with bounded queue size. The range is graphed against relative I/O power, expressed as the ratio of CPU service time to I/O service time. (Again, it is not surprising that both the CPU utilization and the range decrease as the I/O server becomes the bottleneck device.)

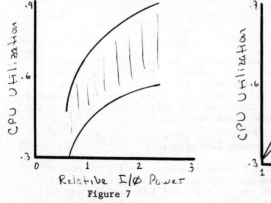

Figure 7

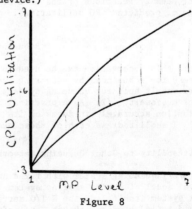

Figure 8

Figure 8 illustrates another interesting phenomenon. It shows the range of predicted utilizations as a function of multiprogramming level (N) for fixed I/O service time. This graph is similar to one that Price plots for the queueing network equivalent to the M/G/1 queueing system with fixed number of customers. This phenomenon is well supported intuitively.

Results similar to those shown in Figures 7 and 8 can be demonstrated for queueing network models in the middle of the spectrum: those with a fixed number of non-identical I/O devices at which queueing occurs. Given the existence of these phenomena throughout the spectrum, along with proofs of the Laplace transform result at either extreme, we confidently assert that the Laplace transform result applies throughout.

● Characterizing Distributions in Terms of Laplace Transforms

We have demonstrated that the Laplace transform result for certain M/G/1 queues can be applied to queueing networks, and that it applies not only to networks in which I/O queueing does not occur, but to more realistic networks as well.

We have yet to demonstrate that the result is of any practical value, however. We know that by using a sufficiently complex Cox-type server, enough moments of an observed service time distribution can be matched to ensure accurate predicted utilization. It is not at all obvious that accurately characterizing a distribution in terms of its Laplace transform is any less complex.

Let us return to Figures 5 and 6 and to the definition of the Laplace transform. Consider s to be fixed, so that the transform specifies a value rather than a function. Because the mass of the Figure 5 density function is concentrated near the origin, the area under the product curve of this function and the negative exponential will be quite large, and predicted CPU utilization will be quite low. The percentiles of the Figure 6 density function are spread over a wider range, and the area under the corresponding product curve will be quite small, leading to higher predicted utilization.

The key to the usefulness of the Laplace transform result lies in the negative exponential. Just as values of the density function are multiplied by factors whose values decrease exponentially with distance from the origin, so the significance of any error in the specification of the density function decreases exponentially with distance form the origin. In other words, we can tolerate large errors in the specification of the density function, f(x), for large x, and still arrive at a Laplace transform value extremely close to that of the observed distribution.

Matching Percentiles

In characterizing an observed service time distribution in terms of its Laplace transform, we are concerned more with identifying the area in which its mass is concentrated than with the specific density at a few selected points. For this reason, the cumulative distribution function, $F(x)$, which expresses the location of the various percentiles of the distribution, is a more appropriate measure than the probability density function, $f(x)$. The characteristics of the Toronto CPU service time distribution (expressed in milliseconds) are:

mean	coefficient of variation	coefficient of skewness	percentiles				
			10th	25th	50th	75th	90th
8.70	12.7	3.0	1.2	1.9	3.8	6.8	10.9

Despite its relatively high coefficient of variation, the observed distribution has a median (we shall use the 50th percentile for comparative purposes) that lies quite far from the origin. The value of its Laplace transform is therefore fairly low, and the CPU utilization fairly high. This statement is supported by the observation that using the HE-2 server at the high utilization extreme of the family matching the first two moments of the observed distribution (the HE-2 server with a density function resembling that of Figure 6) results in a utilization only slightly greater than the observed value.

To understand the errors that result when various HE-2 servers are used in the model, notice that the observed distribution has a relatively low coefficient of skewness. Within an HE-2 family, skewness is proportional to the location of the median (and thus inversely proportional to P). For the family with the observed mean and variance, the attainable range for the coefficient of skewness runs from 2.7 to 4.5, and binding the parameters by matching skewness commits us to a distribution with a relatively low median, high Laplace transform value, and low predicted utilization.

It is worth mentioning that the observed service time distribution could just as easily have occupied the other end of the spectrum: low median, high skewness, and low utilization. In this case, both methods of binding the HE-2 parameters would have resulted in predicted utilizations that were substantially too high.

Figure 9 roughly illustrates the density function of the Toronto distribution. Its most distinctive characteristic is that the density is zero at the origin. Clearly an HE-2 server, which has its greatest density at the origin, will not be able to provide a close match in this critical area. For this reason, I turn my initial efforts towards a three-stage Cox-type server with more suitable inherent characteristics. This server is illustrated in Figure 10.

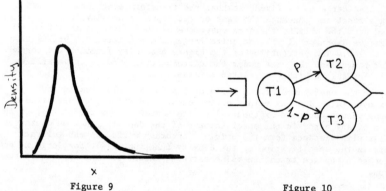

Figure 9   Figure 10

(In the next section, we return to the HE-2 server and attempt to match percentiles using it. We discover that the error in predicted utilization is surprisingly small.)

I have developed a simple heuristic that attempts to match the mean and several percentiles of an observed distribution by varying the parameters of the server illustrated in Figure 10. There are thus three free parameters; the fourth parameter is adjusted to maintain the mean. The heuristic biases in favour of percentiles located near the origin, both in selecting those percentiles to be matched and in setting the error tolerance. Although approximating a density function by means of percentiles generally requires that a large number of percentiles be specified where the slope of the density function differs most from zero, the fact that we are working with a server whose distribution has certain inherent nice properties (e.g., continuity) minimizes the impact of this requirement.

The heuristic used to match $F(x)$ is not interesting enough to describe in detail. (More sophisticated approaches, which attempt to match the Laplace transform of the observed distribution directly, are presently under study.) The value of x at which a particular cumulative percentage occurs is monotone in each free parameter except at one extreme. It is important to realize that we are not solving a linear system; the existence of three free parameters does not imply that three cumulative percentages can be matched. For some observed distributions, five points can be matched, each to within 5%; for others, the best fit to three points has a maximum error in excess of 15%. For a particular cumulative percentage of the observed distribution, $F(x)$, the error is measured as the difference between $F(x)$ and the cumulative percentage that results when the cumulative distribution function of the server is evaluated at x.

The observed distribution of the Toronto system can be matched quite well by the server. When a three-percentile fit is attempted, the x-values corresponding to the 25th, 50th and 75th percentiles yield cumulative percentages of .25, .52 and .72, respectively. At the expense of some accuracy at these percentiles, we can achieve a five-percentile fit that includes the 15th and 90th.

When the model is evaluated using either of these servers, the predicted utilization of the CPU is .75, an error of roughly 1%.

Further Experiments

A number of experiments have been performed that add weight to the success and potential of this new approach to characterizing service time distributions:

● Matching the Percentiles of Other Observed Distributions

In describing the Toronto CPU service time distribution we described a contrasting distribution: one with low median, high skewness, and low utilization. Such a distribution was constructed, with mean and variance reasonably close to those of the observed distribution. Its characteristics are:

mean	coefficient of variation	coefficient of skewness	percentiles 10th 25th 50th 75th 90th
8.73	11.3	4.5	0.5 0.6 0.9 1.2 1.7

I shall refer to this distribution as D2, and to the observed distribution as D1.

When D2 is employed in the simulation model, CPU utilization is .61. The mean and variance of D2 are sufficiently close to those of D1 that the utilizations predicted by the various HE-2 servers can be taken from the table that appeared earlier. No HE-2 server is able to match all of the first three moments of this distribution; the high extreme of the family matching the first two moments comes closest, and results in an error of 30% in predicted CPU utilization.

The heuristic is not able to find a particularly close match to D2. Using a four-percentile fit, the x-values corresponding to the 25th, 50th, 75th and 90th percentiles yield cumulative percentages of .30, .42, .60 and .78, respectively. Nonetheless, when the analytic model is evaluated using this server, predicted CPU utilization is .60, an error of less than 2%.

Although further work must be done to determine tolerable error bounds, the general robustness of the technique is evident.

● Matching Percentiles Using an HE-2 Server

Because the density function of an HE-2 server has its greatest value at the origin, it is impossible to obtain a close fit to typical CPU service time distributions, which have zero density there. Nonetheless, I have attempted to match the mean and three percentiles of both D1 and D2 using HE-2 servers.

For the HE-2 matching D1, the x-values corresponding to the 10th, 25th and 50th percentiles yield cumulative percentages of .17, .25 and .44, respectively. Surprisingly, when the model is evaluated using this server, CPU utilization is .77, an error of only 4%.

For the HE-2 matching D2, the respective cumulative percentages are .28, .33 and .45. Predicted CPU utilization using this server is .60, an error of less than 2%.

These two experiments strongly support the robustness of the technique. Note, incidentally, that the error in matching D2 is not as severe as it appears at first glance. The slope of the cumulative distribution function is so great in this range that the x-value of each percentile and the value of the density function there are only slightly in error.

● The Apparent Unimportance of Variance

There is only a limited correlation between the variance of the observed CPU service time distribution and the variance of the servers that yield the correct CPU utilization.

First consider D1, which has a coefficient of variation of 12.7. The three-stage server matching three percentiles has a coefficient of variation of 2.0, while the one matching five percentiles has a coefficient of variation of 2.4. The HE-2 that yields a 4% error has a coefficient of variation of 35.7.

D2 has a coefficient of variation of 11.3. The three-stage server matching it has a coefficient of variation of 110, while the HE-2 matching it has a coefficient of variation of 117.

Further evidence comes from experiments with the three-stage server matching D2. By varying P (and maintaining the mean by varying T3 as well), it is possible to radically alter the coefficient of variation of the server without affecting its percentiles substantially. As the coefficient of variation is varied from 12 to 400, CPU utilization drops from .592 to .583, a truly insignificant change.

I do not mean to imply that predicted CPU utilization is unrelated to the coefficient of variation of the CPU server. The two are inversely proportional in the following limited sense:

Consider a queueing network model in which the CPU is represented by an HE-2 server with mean M and coefficient of variation V. Let the predicted CPU utilization of this model by U. There exists an HE-2 server with mean $M' = M$ and coefficient of variation $V' < V$ that, when used in the model, results in a predicted CPU utilization $U' > U$.

● A "Limited Damage" Argument for Closed Queueing Networks

One might deduce from the previous subsection that for the models we have been considering, the tail of the service time distribution does not play an important role in the determination of system performance. This is a correct inference, and it deserves further comment since it serves to highlight an important theme: finite and infinite population systems have decidedly different characteristics.

Buzen [1977] has explained this phenomenon in terms of a "limited damage" argument: In a closed queueing network, the performance degradation resulting from a customer with an extremely long service time is bounded, because at most N-1 customers (where N is the multiprogramming level) will queue behind that customer. Thus the transient behaviour of such a system is much less volatile than that of a similar open system.

This observation lies at the heart of the results in this paper. In essence, the moments of a distribution are strongly influenced by its tail, while the Laplace transform of a distribution emphasizes its form near the origin. Thus in a closed queueing network, the Laplace transform provides a superior characterization of the service time distribution.

Conclusions

The need in analytic modelling for non-exponential service time distributions with FCFS queueing is well established. There are occasions, illustrated by my own attempts to model the University of Toronto Computer Centre system, when other service centre representations simply are not accurate enough.

In this paper I demonstrate that the intuition derived from the Pollaczek-Khinchin equation for the M/G/1 queue is not applicable in a queueing network context. Matching the second or even third moment of the observed service time distribution is not only insufficient, but also unnecessary and frequently misleading. Of course, such models can be calibrated by arbitrarily adjusting the parameters of the CPU or the I/O servers, but such tampering can only diminish our confidence in the predictive ability of the model.

I have presented an alternative approach to parameter selection: matching the percentiles of the observed distribution. The intuitive and mathematical bases for this approach are presented, and I describe a number of successful modelling experiments.

Of course, if an observed service time distribution is represented by a server that matches a large number of moments then the percentiles of the observed distribution will also be matched. Similarly, if a large number of percentiles are matched, then the moments will also be correct. Approximations are necessary in modelling, though, and the results in this paper demonstrate that percentile matching is the more fruitful approach.

Although the model does not satisfy the local balance assumptions, computational requirements still can be kept to a minimum by using Norton's theorem to reduce the I/O subsystem to a single, load-dependent server. The model of the Toronto system, for instance, was solved in less than a tenth of a second of CPU time.

In short, we feel that the technique presented here is accurate, robust and practical. It has contributed substantially to our understanding of the behaviour of our models and to our confidence in their predictions.

Acknowledgements

Each of the members of Project SAM, the Systems Analysis and Modelling Group of the Computer Systems Research Group, has contributed either directly or indirectly to this research. Special thanks go to John Zahorjan for computational tools, to Satish Tripathi for countless hours of discussion, and, most importantly, to Ken Sevcik for his guidance throughout my graduate years. David Elliott provided a number of helpful organizational suggestions, and Cliff Addison verified my differentiations.

References

Buzen, Jeffrey P. (1977). Private communication.
Chandy, K.M., Herzog, U., and Woo, L. (1975). "Approximate Analysis of General Queueing Networks", IBM J. Res. Develop. 19,1.
Cohen, J.W. (1969). The Single Server Queue, North-Holland.
Cooper, R.B. (1972). Introduction to Queueing Theory, Macmillan.
Jaiswal, N.K. (1968). Priority Queues, Academic Press.
Kleinrock, Leonard (1975). Queueing Systems, Volume I: Theory, John Wiley & Sons.
Price, T.G. (1976). "A Note on the Effect of the Central Processor Service Time Distribution on Processor Utilization in Multiprogrammed Computer Systems", JACM 23,2.
Sauer, C.H., and Chandy, K.M. (1975). "Approximate Analysis of Central Server Models", IBM J. Res. Develop. 19,3.

Zahorjan, John (1976). "A Queueing Model of Rotational Position Sensing Disk Storage", M.Sc. Thesis, Department of Computer Science, University of Toronto.

Appendix: The Laplace Transform Result for the
M/G/1 System With Bounded Queue Size, N

We seek an expression for PO, the equilibrium probability that an M/G/1 system with bounded queue size, N, is idle.

In this system, as with most variants of the M/G/1 system, Pj, the equilibrium probability that there are j customers in the system, equals PAj, the probability that an arriving customer finds j customers already in the system.

In an M/G/1 system with unbounded queue size, PAj equals PDj, the probability that a departing customer leaves behind j customers. This relationship does not hold in the M/G/1 system with bounded queue size, however, since customers are sometimes rejected. For this latter system, PDj, 0≤j≤N, equals PAj | j≤N, the probability that an arriving customer finds j customers already in the system, conditioned on the fact that this arriving customer is not rejected.

The two sets of probabilities are proportional, and we can express the PAj in terms of the PDj by considering PAj for j equal to N+1, the probability that an arriving customer is rejected. (This is observed by Cohen [1969], among others.) Once this probability is determined, the constant of proportionality, s, can be computed by solving

$$(1) \qquad PA_{N+1} + s \sum_{j=0}^{N} PD_j = 1$$

The probability that an arriving customer is rejected is equal to $(\rho - (1-PO))/\rho$, or $1 - 1/\rho + PO/\rho$, where ρ is the load factor (the mean arrival rate divided by the mean service rate). Intuitively, the numerator of this expression equals the difference between the presented load (ρ) and the accepted load (1-PO). Since PO equals sPDO, (1) becomes

$$(2) \qquad 1 - 1/\rho + sPDO/\rho + s \sum_{j=0}^{N} PDj = 1$$

and we find

$$(3) \qquad s = \frac{1}{PDO + \rho \sum_{j=0}^{N} PDj}$$

I stated earlier that PO, the equilibrium probability that an M/G/1 system with bounded queue size, N, is idle, equals PAO, which in turn equals sPDO. So from (3), we have

$$(4) \qquad PO = \frac{PDO}{PDO + \rho \sum_{j=0}^{N} PDj}$$

Cooper [1972] shows that the PDj are proportional to the corresponding quantities for an M/G/1 system with unbounded queue size. These latter probabilities, which we denote by P'j, are easily obtained. The constant of proportionality, t, can be found by solving

$$(5) \qquad t \sum_{j=0}^{N} P'j = 1$$

So from (4) and (5), we have

(6) $P0 = \dfrac{tP'0}{tP'0 + \rho t \sum\limits_{j=0}^{N} P'j}$

$= \dfrac{P'0}{P'0 + \rho \sum\limits_{j=0}^{N} P'j}$

But $P'0$ equals $1-\rho$, so

(7) $P0 = \dfrac{(1-\rho)}{(1-\rho) + \rho \sum\limits_{j=0}^{N} P'j}$

This is the expression we have been seeking. It shows that server utilization in the M/G/1 system with bounded queue size, N, is a function both of the load factor and of the proportion of time that there would be N or fewer customers in the corresponding M/G/1 system with unbounded queue. Knowing this latter quantity is equivalent to knowing the full equilibrium distribution of the number of customers in the unbounded M/G/1 system, P'.

It is obvious that the $P'j$ are dependent on certain characteristics of the service time distribution. In fact, to determine the $P'j$ we must fully specify the service time distribution, since the Pollaczek-Khinchin mean value equation yields exactly M-1 moments of the equilibrium distribution, given M moments of the service time distribution [Kleinrock 1975]. Thus no finite number of moments will suffice, and nothing short of the Laplace transform of the service time distribution is adequate.

Before continuing with the proof, consider (7) in a more intuitive light. It shows that for a fixed load facgor, i.e., for a fixed mean service time and mean interarrival time (or I/O service time, in the equivalent network model), a range of server utilizations may be attained. This range depends upon three factors: the service time distribution, the load factor, and the size of the queue, N (the multiprogramming level, N+1, in the equivalent network model).

As the load factor increases, the effect of the service time distribution becomes more pronounced. This makes sense; the CPU (in the equivalent network model) is becoming the bottleneck device. The role played by the multiprogramming level is more complex to analyze. Clearly, as N goes to infinity the effect of the service time distribution diminishes. It is less obvious (but equally correct) that the effect is also minimal for extremely small values of N, principally because the $P'0$ term of the summation is determined solely by the load factor, which is held constant. Neither of these extreme cases is of practical interest.

In (7), we established the dependence of server utilization upon the Laplace transform of the service time distribution. To complete the proof we must demonstrate that the relationship is an inverse one. We must show that for arbitrary but fixed load factor and N, the probability that an M/G/1 system with unbounded queue contains N or fewer customers is inversely proportional to the Laplace transform of the service time distribution.

We denote the Laplace transform by $B*[s]$. We say that the Laplace transform corresponding to a particular service time distribution is greater than some other Laplace transform if the value of the first transform evaluated at some point s' exceeds the value of the second transform evaluated at that point, for all s'.

Note that the moments of a distribution can be recovered from its Laplace transform by applying

(8) $E[X^j] = (-1)^j \{B*[0]\}^{(j)}$

where the parenthesized superscript denotes differentiation. Thus the Laplace transform of all service time distributions with identical means will have the same slope at the origin, although their values there, $B*[0]$, may differ. The load factor in (7), ρ, can be expressed in terms of the transform by

(9) $\rho = -\lambda \{B*[0]\}^{(1)}$

where λ is the arrival rate.

Jaiswal [1968] derives the generating function of the equilibrium state residence probabilities for the M/G/1 system in terms of the Laplace transform of the service time distribution, as follows

(10) $Q[\alpha] = \dfrac{(\alpha-1)(1-\rho) B*[\lambda(1-\alpha)]}{\alpha - B*[\lambda(1-\alpha)]}$

The probabilities themselves can be recovered from the generating function by repeated differentiation according to

(11) $P'j = \dfrac{\{Q[0]\}^{(j)}}{j!}$

Proceeding in this manner, we obtain

(12) $P'0 = (1-\rho)$

(13) $P'1 = (1-\rho) \dfrac{1 - B*[\lambda]}{B*[\lambda]}$

(14) $P'2 = (1-\rho) \dfrac{1 + \lambda\{B*[\lambda]\}^{(1)} - B*[\lambda]}{\{B*[\lambda]\}^2}$

The differentiations become increasingly complex, and each successive expression involves an additional derivative of the transform.

To complete the proof, we rely on intuition regarding the equilibrium queue length distribution of an unbounded M/G/1 system (i.e., the probability density function of the $P'j$). We note that this function has a single maximum, and no local maxima or minima. Thus if $P'0$ remains constant and $P'1$ decreases, for example, the residual probability will be distributed among the remaining $P'j$, and the probability that the system contains N or fewer customers will decrease.

We note that $P'1$ is inversely proportional to the value of the Laplace transform evaluated at λ. For $P'2$, this inverse relationship is more pronounced (because of the squared term in the denominator), but is modulated by a term involving the first derivative of the transform. For large j, of course, the $P'j$ will increase slightly with increasing Laplace transform value.

From (14) and the discussion following it, we note that the moments of the service time distribution do, in fact, play an explicit role. They are λ-moments rather than central moments, however, and the value of the Laplace transform evaluated at λ is dominant term.

COMPUTER PERFORMANCE, K.M. CHANDY AND M. REISER (EDS.)
NORTH HOLLAND PUBLISHING COMPANY, 1977

THROUGHPUT IN LOCALLY BALANCED COMPUTER SYSTEM MODELS

A. S. Noetzel

Applied Mathematics Department
Brookhaven National Laboratory
Upton, New York, USA

The optimization of throughput in locally balanced queueing
network models is investigated. A general result, useful in
the design of computer system models, shows that throughput is
a nondecreasing function of the number of customers contained
in any subnetwork. Then processor allocation algorithms that
maximize throughput are shown for the case where processing
power can be switched between queues, as when several queues
are served at a single multiprocessor system. The maximization
of throughput is shown first in the case that processing power
allocations to a queue depend on the queue state only, and then,
in an extension of known locally balanced queue, the case in
which processing power is allocated on the basis of an entire
subnetwork state. The latter case provides a simple and optimum
rule for processor allocations that maximize throughput in networks containing multiprocessor systems.

1. INTRODUCTION

The complete solution of queueing networks of arbitrary configuration is possible
only for the class of networks that have been variously described as separable,
locally balanced or admitting a product form solution [13,3,8]. Recently, this
class of networks has been shown to include queues with general service time distributions under several different scheduling disciplines, and multiple classes of
customers. As a result, the local balance model has found wide utility in the
analysis of computer systems and networks [1,3]. It has been implemented as the
basis of several interactive systems that yield quick analyses of computer systems
and configurations [7,12]. Because of its unique tractability in general network
configurations, this network model has also been studied as an approximation to
networks whose queues do not meet the local balance requirement [5].

Some studies of locally balanced queueing models have assumed a limited variation
of the processing rate of the queue with the number of customers contained therein.
For example, in Gordon and Newells classical work, a queue was considered to have a
fixed number R of processors [6]. If the mean processing time of a single customer
is $1/u$, then when the queue contains n customers, the mean processing rate of the
queue is nu for $n \leq R$, and Ru for $n > R$. However, it is not difficult to show that
the local balance property will be retained if the number of processors in use at a
queue is any general function $r(n)$ of the number n of customers at the queue. We
investigate the implications of this and a more general form of processing power

---

*Work performed under the auspices of the ERDA.

allocation for the optimization of throughput.

Throughput is a central consideration in network models of computer systems. In open network models, it is fully specified by the assumed rates of the external sources. In closed networks, however, it is determined by the combined effects of congestion at the various queues. The question of processing power allocation to maximize throughput is important in the realistic case when processing power is limited, but can be traded off between queues.

Consider, for example, the several possible interpretations of the subnetwork of a closed queueing system, as shown in Figure 1. The queues might represent the sequential phases or steps of programs, with the parallel paths reflecting the differing requirements of identified special classes of programs, and the class of general user programs. The processing units would then be the individual computers at a computer center.

Alternatively, the queues may represent the phases of programs, either system functions or user-written routines, loaded into the executable memory of a multiprocessor system. Under either interpretation, the customers at the queues may be served by any of the processors. If time-sharing with a small time slice is used, it will be reasonable to speak of allocating a fractional number of processors to a queue. Throughout, we assume that the processing rate of a customer is linearly related to the processing power allocated him; the processing rate u on a single processor becomes rate ru when processing power r is allocated. The physical interpretations impose only the following constraints on the queueing model: since not more than n processors can be useful in serving a queue that contains n customers, $r(n) \leq n$; and not more than the fixed number R of processors may be in use by the subnetwork at any time.

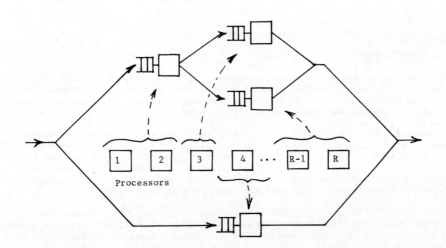

Figure 1:   Processor Assignments in Subnetwork
            with Processing Power Tradeoffs

In order to establish the policies for maximization of throughput via processing-power tradeoffs, several general properties of throughput in locally balanced queueing networks must first be established. These general properties are discussed in Section 3.

The question of processing power allocation is examined in two fundamental cases. First, using the known model of locally balanced queues, queue-state dependent processing rates are considered. This is the case in which processing power $r_i(n_i)$ is allocated to queue i when it contains n_i customers. The processor allocation decisions can be made locally to the queue by the software processor in control, without considering the distribution $\{n_j: j \neq i\}$, of customers at the other queues of the subnetwork. It will be seen in Section 4 that optimization strategies under this form of processor allocation are severely constrained.

Then the case of subnetwork-state dependent processing rates is considered. The processing power allocations at queue i of the subnetwork take the form $r_i(n_1 \ldots n_j \ldots n_M)$, when there are n_j customers at queue j, for each of the M queues of the subnetwork. The strategy for processor allocation in this case is global to the subnetwork. Processing power allocations of this form require an extension of the known local balance queue model. The state probability solutions for cases of n-queue parallel and two-queue series subnetworks with this form of processing power allocation are shown in Section 5. The policy for allocating processing power for maximum throughput within the local balance constraint is demonstrated.

2. LOCALLY BALANCED NETWORKS AND NORTON'S THEOREM

The separable or locally balanced networks to be considered have fixed topology. After leaving queue i, a customer will go to queue j with fixed probability p_{ij}. Let P be the matrix of transition probabilities p_{ij}, $1 \leq i, j \leq M$, for a network of M queues. Let λ_i be the mean flow rate into queue i. If $L = \overline{\lambda_1 \lambda_2 \ldots \lambda_M}$ is a vector of relative flow rates or throughputs for the network, then LP=L. If the network is open, L is determined by the absolute input rate to the network. For closed networks, the above relation determines L to within a constant. Then, if the network contains N customers, the actual throughput at queue i is given by $\tau_i(N) = \lambda_i \frac{G(N-1)}{G(N)}$, where G(n), n = 1, ..., N, is the normalization factor computed when the network contains n customers. G(n) is computed by the convolution algorithm using the flow vector L [2,11,13]. Since the throughputs at the branches of the network remain fixed relative to each other as N and the processing rates at the queues are varied, the network throughput, or total processing rate, is optimized as throughput in any branch of the network is optimized.

The throughput characteristics of two queue networks are of considerable importance because of the reduction of arbitrary closed networks to an equivalent two queue network made possible by Norton's theorem for computer networks [4]. The behavior of a particular queue Q within a closed network η is the same as that of Q in a network with one other queue Q_e, which serves as the equivalent of all the queues of η except for Q (see Figure 2). The processing rate U(n) of the equivalent queue, when it contains n customers, is determined by constructing network η', which is the same as η except for a short circuit in place of Q. U(n) is simply the mean throughput in the link replacing Q, when η' contains n customers. To study via the equivalent network, the effects of Q in η when η contains N customers, the rates U(1),...,U(N) must be measured in the link in η', when η' contains 1,...,N customers.

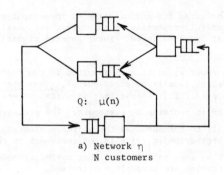

a) Network η
N customers

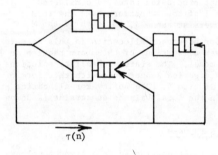

b) Network η′
n customers

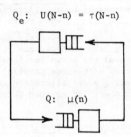

c) Equivalent network
N customers

Figure 2: Nortons Equivalent Queue

It is possible to analyze in the same manner as Q the behavior of any subnetwork σ
that can be isolated by a single pair of input and output terminals. Network η
may be therefore reduced to a two queue network; an equivalent queue for σ, and an
equivalent for the complement of σ in η. Study of throughput in the two queue network is straightforward, since the normalization constant $G(n)$ is expressed as a
single convolution.

3. THROUGHPUT AS A FUNCTION OF LOAD

An important characteristic of separable queueing networks that can be determined
with the aid of Norton's Theorem is that the throughput, or output rate, of any
subnetwork is a nondecreasing function of the load, or the number of customers in
the subnetwork. It is first shown that this holds for the equivalent two queue
network.

> Theorem 1. Let $u(m)$ and $U(n)$ be the processing rates of the queues in a
> closed locally balanced two queue network, when the queues contain m and
> n customers, respectively. Let $\tau(N)$ be the mean throughput of the closed
> network when it contains N customers. Then if $u(n+1) \geq u(n)$ and $U(n+1)$
> $\geq U(n)$ for all $0 < n \leq N$, then $\tau(N+1) \geq \tau(N)$.

The proof follows from the form of $\tau(N) = \dfrac{G(N-1)}{G(N)}$. The details are in Appendix A.

Through the use of Norton's theorem, the characteristic of nondecreasing throughput with increasing load may now be proven for all locally balanced networks.

Theorem 2. Let $\tau(n)$ be the mean throughput in some branch of a closed locally balanced network that contains n customers. If the processing rate of each queue in the network is a nondecreasing function of the number of customers at the queue, then for all $n > 0$, $\tau(n+1) \geq \tau(n)$.

Proof. The proof is by induction on M, the number of queues in the network. Let $\tau_M(n)$ be the mean throughput in some branch b of a network of M queues that contains n customers. Let $\mu(n)$ be the processing rate of an arbitrary queue when it contains n customers, and let $\mu(n+1) \geq \mu(n)$. For M = 1, the network has only one queue, but may have a number of probabilistically selected branches from the queue back to itself. Let p be the probability that a customer takes branch b in returning to the queue. Then $\tau_1(n+1) = p\mu(n+1) \geq p\mu(n) = \tau_1(n)$.

Let U(n) be the processing rate of the equivalent queue for an M - 1 queue network with respect to branch b. Then by Norton's Theorem and the inductive hypothesis, $U(n+1) = \tau_{M-1}(n+1) \geq \tau_{M-1}(n) = U(n)$. And if the equivalent queue is placed in series with a queue with processing rate $\mu(n+1) \geq \mu(n)$, $1 \leq n \leq N$, and there are N customers in this network, then the throughput of the closed two queue network is $\tau_M(N)$. But then $\tau_M(N+1) \geq \tau_M(N)$ by Theorem 1. This completes the proof.

Queues that have a fixed number of processors available meet the conditions of this theorem. But $\mu(n+1) \geq \mu(n)$ may not hold if processing power is traded off between queues.

4. THROUGHPUT WITH QUEUE-STATE DEPENDENT PROCESSING RATES

A queue may have the local balance property if each customer has an exponential processing time, or else if the queueing discipline is processor sharing or pre-emptive last-come-first-served. The total processing rate of the queue may be any function of the number of customers in the queue. We assume that $1/\mu$ is the mean processing time of one customer on one processor, and that the queue state is simply the number n of customers at the queue. If the number of processors assigned the queue is an arbitrary function r(n) of the queue state, then $\mu(n) = r(n)\mu$. We will call processing rates of this form queue-state dependent.

There are several instances in which increased throughput can be obtained by dynamically switching processors from one queue to another. For example, two queues may represent two different processes or programs to be executed in one multiprocessor system. Then any or all of the processors may be available for either queue when they are not required for the other. However, with the developed model of a locally balanced queue (that is, with queue-state dependent processing rates), the analysis of processing power tradeoffs is severely constrained. When the network state changes by means of a customer moving from one queue to another, processing power exchanges may take place only between the two queues involved in the transition.

Throughput with processing power tradeoffs between a single queue and the remainder of the network can be analyzed in the network consisting of the selected queue and the Norton's equivalent queue. But first, the relationship of throughput to processing rates in a two queue network will be established when the rates at each of the queues are independent of each other. This is expressed in the following theorem.

Theorem 3. Let $\mu(m)$ and U(n) be the processing rates at the queues of a locally balanced two queue network, when the queues contain m and n customers, respectively, and suppose all the U(n) and the $\mu(m)$ are mutually independent for $0 < m, n \leq N$. Let $\tau(N)$ be the throughput when the network contains N customers. Then

a) $\tau(N)$, as a function of $U(n)$, $0 < n \leq N$, has no extrema.

b) $\tau(N)$ is a nondecreasing function of $U(n)$ if $\mu(i) \geq \mu(j)$ for all $j \leq N - n$ and $N - n < i \leq N$.

c) If $\tau(N)$ is a nonincreasing function of $U(n)$, then it is a strictly increasing function of $\mu(N-n)$.

The theorem is proved by differentiating $\tau(N) = \dfrac{G(N-1)}{G(N)}$ with respect to $U(n)$, for $1 \leq n \leq N$. The details are in Appendix B.

As a simple example, consider optimizing a two-queue network, containing three customers in an environment where processing power tradeoffs between the queues might be possible. By Theorem 3b, both $\mu(3)$ and $U(3)$ can be maximized without decreasing throughput $\tau(3)$. Suppose $\mu(1) \leq \mu(2)$, $\mu(3)$. Then by 3b, $U(2)$ can be maximized without decreasing $\tau(3)$. Likewise, $U(1)$ can be maximized if $\mu(1)$, $\mu(2)$ $\leq \mu(3)$. But suppose the condition $\mu(2) > \mu(3)$ holds. Then, it is possible that $\tau(3)$ will decrease as $U(1)$ increases. By 3c, $\tau(3)$ will then be a strictly increasing function of $\mu(2)$. Although independence of the rates was assumed in the theorem, switching processing power to minimize $U(1)$ and maximize $\mu(2)$ causes no conflict, and will be the optimal solution. But then, if the processing rate U varies linearly with the processing power, as in the assumption of queue-state dependency, $U(1)$ will be reduced to zero. The network will effectively contain two customers; which leads to a refutation of the $\mu(2) > \mu(3)$ assumption. Similar reasoning is employed in proof of the following theorems.

The optimum allocation of $R(N)$ available processors to a network that contains N customers will now be considered. Suppose $r_i(n_i)$ processors are allocated to queue i, when it contains n_i customers. A possible allocation strategy may be to hold some processing power in reserve, that is, $\Sigma r_i(n_i) < R(N)$ for some network state $(n_1 \ldots n_M)$; the reason for doing this may be to ensure that more processing power is available for $r_i(n_i+1)$, or even $r_i(n_i-1)$ if throughput might be more sensitive to those rates. But it can be shown that throughput cannot be optimized by such strategies.

Theorem 4. Let $R(N)$ be the processing power available to be allocated to the M queues of a closed locally balanced network that contains $N > 0$ customers. Let $r_i(n)$ be the processing power allocated queue i, when there are n customers at queue i, for $1 \leq i \leq M$. Let $\tau_M(N)$ be the mean throughput at some branch of the network.

a) Then for maximum $\tau_M(N)$, the available processing power must always be fully utilized; that is, $\displaystyle\sum_{i=1}^{M} r_i(n_i) = R(N)$ for all $\displaystyle\sum_{i=1}^{M} n_i = N$,

and $r_i(0) = 0$ for $1 \leq i \leq M$.

b) And any processing power distribution meeting the above constraints provides the maximum throughput, and when $\tau_M(N)$ is maximum,

$\tau_M(N) = kR(N)$, where k is a constant.

The proof is again by induction on the number of queues in the network. The M queue network is reduced to a two queue network by Norton's Theorem. Then

Theorem 3 is used to show that for maximum throughput, each processing rate of the two queue network must be maximized. The details of the proof are in Appendix C.

Therefore, for maximum throughput with queue-state dependent rate assignments, the processing power added to one queue must be exactly that taken from another whenever there is a transition between the queues. But for closed networks with more than two queues, it can be seen that this determines the processing power uniquely.

Theorem 5. Consider any network of $M > 2$ locally balanced queues, containing N customers, in which any fraction of the processing power of $R(N)$ processors may be assigned to any queue. If $r_i(n)$ is the processing power assigned queue i when it contains n customers, for $1 \leq i \leq M$, then throughput is maximized by the assignment $r_i(n) = \frac{n}{N}R(N)$.

Proof. From Theorem 4, for maximum throughput, one must consider processing power allocations such that

$$\sum_{i=1}^{M} r_i(n_i) = R(N) \text{ for each network state } (n_1 \ldots n_M).$$ When there are N - k

customers at queue one, the processing rate at queue one remains constant and independent of the distribution of the remaining k customers. Therefore, for $1 < i \leq n$, $r_i(k) = R(N) - r_1(N-k)$. Similarly, when there are N - k customers at queue two, for $2 < i \leq M$, $r_1(k) = r_i(k) = R(N) - r_2(N-k)$. Hence, $r_i(k) = r_j(k)$ for $1 \leq i, j \leq M$, as long as $M > 2$. Consider the case k = 2. With N - 2 customers at queue one, the remaining two customers may both be at queue i, or may be at queues i and j, $1 < i < j \leq M$, while the processing rate at queue one remains constant. Hence, $r_i(2) = r_i(1) + r_j(1) = 2r_i(1)$. Similarly, considering k = 3, 4...N it is seen that $r_i(k) = kr_i(1)$. And, since $r_i(N) = Nr_i(1)$, $r_i(k) = \frac{k}{N}$ for $1 \leq i \leq M$ and $1 \leq k \leq N$. The proof is complete.

It is seen that there is a simple rule for optimally allocating processing power if queue-state dependencies are assumed. But, it applies only if all processors may be freely switched to any queue in the network. This limits the applicability of the model to networks of logical processes entirely within a single multiprocessor system, in which any processor may execute any logical function. But in such case there is little scheduling difficulty. In a model of a computer network, the capability of processing power tradeoffs must be limited to subnetworks representing processes that can be served by compatible devices located at the same processing center.

But in this case, it can be seen that queue-state dependencies cannot yield an efficient solution. Maximum throughput requires full utilization of the available processors. Since the number of customers in a subnetwork does not remain constant, either processing power must be held in reserve when the number of customers in the subnetwork is less than N, or else there is the possibility of an arrival to the subnetwork when all of the processors are busy. If the arriving customer joins a queue that is idle, a processor must be taken from another subnetwork queue, even though there is no change in the number of customers at that queue. This violates the assumption of queue-state rate dependency.

5. THROUGHPUT WITH SUBNETWORK-STATE DEPENDENT PROCESSING RATES

Dynamic processing power allocations in a subnetwork can be useful to optimize throughput only if they are subnetwork-state dependent; in this case, the processing power at queue i of an M-queue subnetwork is determined by the function $r_i(n_1 \ldots n_M)$ of the subnetwork state. We assume as before that a total processing power R(N) is available to a subnetwork when it contains N customers, and that the subnetwork retains the local balance property. Consider, for example, the parallel and series subnetworks of Figure 3. For either case, when there are m and n customers at queues one and two, respectively, the processing rates are $u_1(m,n)$ and $u_2(m,n)$, respectively. Each of these two-queue subnetworks will have the local balance property if and only if

$$\frac{\mu_1(m,n-1)}{u_1(m,n)} = \frac{u_2(m-1,n)}{u_2(m,n)} \quad , \text{ for all } m, n > 0. \tag{5-1}$$

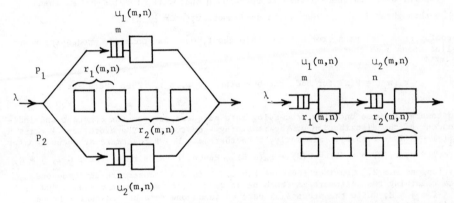

Figure 3: Parallel and Series Subnetworks

A generalization for more than two queues is straightforward for the parallel case, but not for the series subnetwork case. The state probabilities for either subnetwork are expressed by

$$P(m,n) = \frac{\lambda_1^m}{\prod\limits_{i=1}^{m} \mu_1(i,n)} \cdot \frac{\lambda_2^n}{\prod\limits_{i=1}^{n} u_2(0,i)} P(0,0), \tag{5-2}$$

where $\lambda_1 = p_1\lambda$, $\lambda_2 = p_2\lambda$ for the parallel case, and $\lambda_1 = \lambda_2 = \lambda$ for the series case.

According to Norton's Theorem, the processing rate of a subnetwork that contains n customers is the same as the throughput of the subnetwork when it stands alone as a closed network containing n customers. This is because the distribution of the n customers in the subnetwork is the same in either case. For both the series and parallel subnetworks, then, maximization of network throughput apparently entails maximization of each processing rate $\tau(1)$, $\tau(2)$ ... $\tau(N)$, which are the throughputs of the two queue network (i.e., the isolated subnetwork) containing n = 1, 2, ... N customers. By Theorem 4, these rates may be achieved by any processing power distribution such that no processing power is wasted; i.e., for maximum $\tau(n)$, $r_1(n,0) = r_2(0,n) = R(n)$. But notice that if the local balance condition (5-1) holds, $\tau(n)$ cannot be maximized independently of $\tau(n-1)$, for $1 < n \leq N$. The optimization procedure is, therefore, not as straightforward as indicated above; the details can be found in [10]. The result is that the optimal processing rate assignments are consistent with full processing power utilization, and are only further constrained by (5-1). For maximum network throughput, when processing-power tradeoffs in either subnetwork are possible,

$$r_1(m,n) = \frac{m}{N} R(N), \text{ and } r_2(m,n) = \frac{n}{N} R(N),$$

where m and n are the number of customers at queues one and two, respectively, and N = m + n.

The state probabilities for the subnetwork with this processing power assignment are

$$P(m,n) = \binom{m+n}{n} \frac{1}{\alpha(m+n)} \rho_1^m \rho_2^n P(0,0),$$

where $\rho_i = \frac{\lambda_i}{\mu_i}$, and $\alpha(n) = \prod_{i=1}^{n} R(i)$. If R processors are available to the subnet-

work,

$$\alpha(n) = \begin{cases} n! & , \text{ for } n \leq R \\ n! R^{n-R}, & \text{ for } n > R. \end{cases}$$

The state probability of this form will be a component of the product form solution of any locally balanced network containing the subnetwork.

The result, that maximum throughput is achieved by sharing the processing power proportionately based on the load at each queue, can be generalized for the case of any fixed number of queues in parallel. This will serve as a local balance model of a multiprocessor system handling parallel queues in a computer network.

ACKNOWLEDGEMENT

The author would like to thank the session chairman, Ken Sevcik, and the referees, particularly Tom Giammo, for their helpful suggestions.

REFERENCES

1. Baskett, F., K. M. Chandy, R. R. Muntz and F. Palacios-Gomez, "Open, Closed and Mixed Networks of Queues with Different Classes of Customers", JACM 22 2 (1975), pp. 248-260.

2. Buzen, J. P., "Computational Algorithms for Closed Queueing Networks with Exponential Servers" CACM 16, September 1973.

3. Chandy, K. M., "The Analysis and Solutions for General Queueing Networks", Proc. Sixth Annual Princeton Conf. on Information Sciences and Systems, Princeton Univ., Princeton, N. J., (March 1972), pp. 219-224.

4. Chandy, K. M., U. Herzog, and L. Woo, "Parametric Analysis of Queueing Network Models" IBM Journal of Research and Development, 19,1 (January 1975), pp. 36-42.

5. Chandy, K. M., U. Herzog, and L. Woo, "Approximate Analysis of General Queueing Networks" IBM Journal of Research and Development, 19, 1 (January 1975).

6. Gordon, W. J. and G. F. Newell, "Closed Queueing Systems with Exponential Servers", Oper. Res. 15, 2 (1967), pp. 252-267.

7. Keller, T. W., "ASQ Manual" Dept. of Computer Sciences Report TR-27, University of Texas, Austin, Texas, 1973.

8. Kleinrock, L., Queueing Systems, Vol. 1: Theory. John Wiley and Sons, N. Y., 1975.

9. Noetzel, A. S., "Analysis of Discrete-Time Queues for Random Output Processes and Network Solutions" Proc. 1977 Conf. on Information Sciences and Systems, The Johns Hopkins University, March 1977.

10. Noetzel, A. S., "Product-Form Queueing Networks with Processing-Rate and Arrival-Rate Tradeoffs" Technical Report 53, Department of Computer Sciences, The University of Texas at Austin, December 1975.

11. Reiser, M., and H. Kobayashi, "Recursive Algorithms for General Queueing Networks with Exponential Servers" IBM Res. Report. RC-4254, March 1973.

12. Reiser, M., "QNET4 User's Guide". IBM Research Report RA71, June 1975.

13. Reiser, M. and H. Kobayashi, "On the Convolution Algorithm for Separable Queueing Networks" Proceedings, 1976 International Symposium on Computer Performance Modeling, Measurement, and Evaluation, Harvard University, Cambridge, Mass.

Appendix A: Proof of Theorem 1.

The throughput $\tau(N)$ of the locally balanced two queue network can be expressed as the ratio of the normalization constants with $N - 1$ and N customers in the network. Hence, the theorem is proved if

$$\tau(N+1) = \frac{G(N)}{G(N+1)} \geq \frac{G(N-1)}{G(N)} = \tau(N), \tag{A-1}$$

where

$$G(n) = \sum_{i=0}^{n} X(n-i)Y(i), \text{ and } X(n) = \prod_{i=1}^{n} \frac{1}{u(i)} \text{ and } Y(n) = \prod_{i=1}^{n} \frac{1}{U(i)}$$

for $n = 0, 1 \dots N$.

The inequality (A-1) can be written

$$G^2(N) \geq G(N+1)G(N-1) \tag{A-2}$$

The terms of $G^2(N)$ contain the factors $Y(i)Y(j)$ for $0 \leq i, j \leq N$. The terms of $G(N+1)G(N-1)$ contain the factors $Y(i)Y(j)$ for $0 \leq i \leq N - 1$, $0 \leq j \leq N + 1$. In both cases $0 \leq i + j \leq 2N$. The inequality (A-2) is demonstrated by grouping the terms into $2N + 1$ inequalities. Inequality k, $0 \leq k \leq 2N$, will have all the terms with factors $Y(i)Y(j)$ such that $i + j = k$.

First, consider the case $0 \leq k < N$. Collecting terms from (A-2),

$$\sum_{i=0}^{k} X(N-i)Y(i)X(N-k+i)Y(k-i) \geq \sum_{i=0}^{k} X(N+1-i)Y(i)X(N-1-k+i)Y(k-i). \quad (A-3)$$

Grouping coefficients of $Y(i)Y(k-i)$,

$$\sum_{i=0}^{k} [X(N-i)X(N-k+i) - X(N+1-i)X(N-1-k+i)]Y(i)Y(k-i) \geq 0. \quad (A-4)$$

This sum can be rewritten as two summations; first for index $i = 0$ to $[\frac{k}{2}]$, and then for $i = k - [\frac{k}{2}] + 1$ to k. If k is even, these two ranges obviously cover the range 0 to k. If k is odd, the term for $i = [\frac{k}{2}] + 1$ is missing. But the term in the summation for this value of i is zero. Hence, rewriting (A-4) in two summations, and letting $j = k + 1 - i$ replace i as the index of the second summation, one has

$$\sum_{i=0}^{[\frac{k}{2}]} [X(N-i)X(N-k+i) - X(N+1-i)X(N-1-k+i)]Y(i)Y(k-i)$$

$$+ \sum_{j=1}^{[\frac{k}{2}]} [X(N-k-1+j)X(N+1-j) - X(N-k+j)X(N-j)]Y(k+1-j)Y(j-1) \geq 0. \quad (A-5)$$

Note that for each $X(m)X(n)$ in (A-5), $m + n = 2N - k$. Also, note that for any m,n with $m \geq n$ and any $j \leq n$,

$$X(m)X(n) - X(m+j)X(n-j)$$

$$= X(m)X(n-j) \left[\prod_{i=n-j+1}^{n} \frac{1}{u(i)} - \prod_{i=m+1}^{m+j} \frac{1}{u(i)} \right] \geq 0, \quad (A-6)$$

since all of the indices i, and hence rates $u(i)$ in the second product are greater than those of the first product. Therefore, the products $X(m)X(n)$ for all $m + n = 2N - k$ are ordered inversely as $|m-n|$, or directly as $\min(m,n)$. If $i = \min(m,n)$ let $\overline{X}(i) = X(m)X(n)$ and let $\overline{Y}(i) = Y(m)Y(n)$. Then the inequality (A-5) can be rewritten by selecting the smaller index of each product, as follows:

$$\sum_{i=0}^{[\frac{k}{2}]} (\overline{X}(N-k+i) - \overline{X}(N-k+i-1))\overline{Y}(i) + \sum_{j=1}^{[\frac{k}{2}]} (\overline{X}(N-k+j-1) - \overline{X}(N-k+j))\overline{Y}(j-1) \geq 0.$$

$$(A-7)$$

The summations of (A-7) can be combined and terms rearranged to obtain

$$(\overline{X}(N-k) - \overline{X}(N-k-1))\overline{Y}(0) + \sum_{i=1}^{[\frac{k}{2}]} [\overline{X}(N-k+i) - \overline{X}(N-k+i-1)][\overline{Y}(i) - \overline{Y}(i-1)] \geq 0.$$

$$(A-8)$$

It is seen that each factor of every term of the summation is nonnegative. Hence, the inequality is demonstrated.

Now consider the case $k = N$. In collecting all terms of (A-2) with factors
$Y(i)Y(j)$ where $i + j = N$, $G(N-1)$ contributes terms with factors $Y(i)$ for
$0 \leq i \leq N - 1$. Hence, $G(N+1)$ contributes terms with factors $Y(j)$ for $1 \leq j \leq N$.
The inequality corresponding to (A-3) is

$$\sum_{i=0}^{N} X(N-i)Y(i)X(i)Y(N-i) \geq \sum_{i=0}^{N-1} X(i+1)Y(N-i)X(N-1-i)Y(i). \qquad (A-9)$$

Collecting terms, and then adjusting the index of the summation to range from 1 to
N, this inequality is written as follows:

$$X(0)X(N)Y(0)Y(N) + \sum_{i=1}^{N} [X(N+1-i)X(i-1) - X(i)X(N-i)]Y(N-i+1)Y(i-1) \geq 0.$$

$$(A-10)$$

The summation can be expressed as two summations, first with index $i = 1$ to $[\frac{N}{2}]$,
then with $i = N - [\frac{N}{2}] + 1$ to N, noting that if N is odd, the term for $i = [\frac{N}{2}] + 1$
disappears. Then rewriting the second summation with index $j = N + 1 - i$, one
obtains

$$X(0)X(N)Y(0)Y(N) + \sum_{i=1}^{[\frac{N}{2}]} [X(N+1-i)X(i-1) - X(i)X(N-i)]Y(N+1-i)Y(i-1)$$

$$+ \sum_{j=1}^{[\frac{N}{2}]} [X(j)X(N-j) - X(N+1-j)X(j-1)]Y(j)Y(N-j) \geq 0. \qquad (A-11)$$

Then, if $i = \min(m,n)$, let $\overline{X}(i) = X(m)X(n)$, and $\overline{Y}(i) = Y(m)Y(n)$.

The summations of (A-11) can be combined and terms rearranged to obtain

$$\overline{X}(0)\overline{Y}(0) + \sum_{i=1}^{[\frac{N}{2}]} [\overline{X}(i) - \overline{X}(i-1)][\overline{Y}(i) - \overline{Y}(i-1)] \geq 0. \qquad (A-12)$$

Since each term in the summation is (A-12) nonnegative, the inequality is demonstrated.

Last, the case for $N < k \leq 2N$ must be considered. But from the symmetry of X
and Y in the definition of the function G, inequality k of A-2 is exactly inequality 2N - k with the roles of X and Y interchanged. Hence, it has been demonstrated
in the first case. The theorem is proved.

Appendix B: Proof of Theorem 3

Let $Y(n) = \prod_{i=1}^{n} \frac{1}{U(i)}$ and $X(n) = \prod_{i=1}^{n} \frac{1}{u(i)}$ for $0 < n \leq N$. Let

$G(N) = \sum_{i=0}^{N} Y(i)X(N-i)$ be the normalization constant for the state probabilities of the two queue network with N customers. Then for all $N > 0$,

$$\tau(N) = \frac{G(N-1)}{G(N)} .$$ (B-1)

For $0 < n \leq N$ let $G_n^+(N)$ be all of the terms of $G(N)$ that have the factor $U^{-1}(n)$.

$$G_n^+(N) = \sum_{i=n}^{N} Y(i)X(N-i),$$ (B-2)

and $G_n^-(N) = G(N) - G_n^+(N)$.

Then, differentiating $G(N)$ with respect to $U(n)$,

$$\frac{\partial G(N)}{\partial U(n)} = -\frac{1}{U(n)} G_n^+(N),$$

and differentiating $\tau(N)$ with respect to $U(n)$,

$$
\begin{aligned}
\frac{\partial \tau(N)}{\partial U(n)} &= \left[G(N) \frac{\partial G(N-1)}{\partial U(n)} - G(N-1) \frac{\partial G(N)}{\partial U(n)} \right] \frac{1}{G^2(N)} \\
&= \left[-(G_n^-(N) + G_n^+(N)) G_n^+(N-1) U(n)^{-1} \right. \\
&\quad \left. + (G_n^-(N-1) + G_n^+(N-1)) G_n^+(N) U(n)^{-1} \right] \frac{1}{G^2(N)} \\
&= \left[-G_n^-(N) G_n^+(N-1) + G_n^-(N-1) G_n^+(N) \right] \frac{1}{U(n) G^2(N)}
\end{aligned}
$$ (B-3)

The derivative will be **nonnegative** if

$$G_n^-(N-1) G_n^+(N) \geq G_n^-(N) G_n^+(N-1) .$$ (B-4)

But each term of this inequality has exactly one factor $U^{-1}(n)$. Hence, it may be cancelled out of the inequality. As a function of $U(n)$, $\tau(N)$ is, therefore, either always increasing, always decreasing, or is constant. This proves part a) of the theorem.

The terms on the right of the inequality (B-4) have factors $Y(k)Y(i)$, $0 \leq k < n$, $n \leq i < N$, and the terms on the left have factors $Y(k)Y(i)$, $0 \leq k < n$, $n \leq i \leq N$. The coefficient of each $Y(k)Y(i)$ that appears on the right is $X(N-k)X(N-1-i)$, and the coefficient of that term on the left is $X(N-1-k)X(N-i)$. Hence, if $X(N-1-k)X(N-i) \geq X(N-k)X(N-1-i)$, the inequality holds. But since $i > k$, $X(N-1-i)X(N-1-k)$ can be factored out of this inequality, leaving $\frac{1}{u(N-i)} \geq \frac{1}{u(N-k)}$. Therefore, if $\mu(N-k) \geq \mu(N-i)$ for all $0 < k < n \leq i \leq N$, $\tau(N)$ is a nondecreasing function of $U(n)$. This proves part b) of the theorem.

In particular, it should be noted that if $u(i) \geq u(j)$ for all $i > j$, which is the usual case, then $\tau(N)$ is a nondecreasing function of $U(n)$, for all n.

Now let $H_m^+(N)$ be the sum of all of the terms of $G(N)$ that have the factor $u^{-1}(m)$.

$$H_m^+(N) = \sum_{i=m}^{N} Y(N-i)X(i) \tag{B-5}$$

and

$$H_m^-(N) = G(N) - H_m^+(N).$$

Then, from the definition of $H_m^+(N)$, the following relationships are noted:

$$H_{N-n}^+(N) = G_{n+1}^-(N) \tag{B-6}$$

and

$$H_{N-n}^+(N-1) = G_n^-(N-1). \tag{B-7}$$

By the steps leading to (B-4) the condition for $\dfrac{\partial \tau(N)}{\partial u(N-n)} > 0$ is determined to be

$$H_{N-n}^-(N-1)H_{N-n}^+(N) > H_{N-n}^-(N)H_{N-n}^+(N-1). \tag{B-8}$$

Using (B-6) and (B-7) this can be expressed as

$$G_n^+(N-1)G_{n+1}^-(N) > G_{n+1}^+(N)G_n^-(N-1). \tag{B-9}$$

And then $G_{n+1}^+(N)$ can be related to $G_n^+(N)$,

$$G_n^+(N-1)[G_n^-(N) + Y(N-n)X(n)] > [G_n^+(N) - Y(N-n)X(n)]G_n^-(N-1), \tag{B-10}$$

which can be written

$$[G_n^+(N-1)G_n^-(N) - G_n^+(N)G_n^-(N-1)] + Y(N-n)X(n)G(N-1) > 0 \tag{B-11}$$

The inequality (B-11) must be satisfied if the term in brackets is nonnegative. But, this term expresses the condition (B-4); it will be nonnegative of $\tau(N)$ is a nonincreasing function of $U(n)$. This proves part c) of the theorem.

Appendix C: Proof of Theorem 4

The proof is by induction on M. First, consider any network with M = 1. Let p be the probability that a customer leaving the queue uses a particular branch b in returning to the queue. Let the processing rate at the queue be u when a single processor is assigned the queue. If r(N) processors are assigned the queue when the network contains N customers, the throughput in branch b is $\tau_1(N) = pr(N)u$. The throughput is maximum when r(N) = R(N). Then $\tau_1(N) = puR(N)$, which satisfies the theorem.

Suppose the theorem holds for all networks of M - 1 queues. Let $\tau_{M-1}(n)$ be the throughput at some branch b of an M - 1 queue network when there are n customers in the network. Then by Norton's Theorem, the M - 1 queue network may be represented by an equivalent queue with respect to branch b. If U(n) is the processing rate of the equivalent queue when it contains n customers, then $U(n) = \tau_{M-1}(n)$. Let $R_1(n)$ be the processing power available to the M - 1 queue network. By the inductive hypothesis, the maximum throughput at branch b is $\tau_{M-1}(n) = UR_1(n)$, where U is a constant, and is achieved when processing power $R_1(n)$ is fully utilized.

This is also the maximum processing rate of the equivalent queue when it contains n customers and has available processing power $R_1(n)$.

Let $\tau_M(N)$ be the throughput in the two queue network consisting of the equivalent queue in series with queue M; this will be the same as the throughput in branch b of the M - 1 queue network with queue M inserted in branch b. Assuming the processing rate at queue M is $\mu(n) = r(n)\mu$ when it contains n customers and is using processing power $r(n)$, the throughput of the equivalent two queue network is determined as follows.

Let $G(n)$, $X(n)$ and $Y(n)$ be as defined in (A-1).

Then $\tau_M(N) = \dfrac{G(N-1)}{G(N)}$ $\qquad\qquad\qquad\qquad\qquad\qquad$ (C-1)

Let $R(N)$ be the processing power available to the M queue network when it contains N customers. And let $\rho(n) = \dfrac{r(n)}{R(N)}$ be the optimum fraction of the available processing power to be used by queue M when it contains $n \leq N$ customers, in order to maximize $\tau_M(N)$. Then $\mu(n) = \rho(n)R(N)\mu$ are the processing rates at queue M that maximize $\tau_M(N)$.

Let $\overline{\rho}(n) = 1 - \rho(n)$. Then, for maximum $\tau_M(N)$, processing power $R_1(n) = \overline{\rho}(n)R(N)$ is available to be allocated to the equivalent queue when it contains N - n customers.

Examining (C-1) shows that for maximum $\tau_M(N)$, $U(N)$ and $\mu(N)$ are to be maximized. Clearly, all available processing power is used for these rates, so that $\rho(N) = \overline{\rho}(0) = 1$.

Note that $\rho(n) > 0$ for all $n > 0$ may be assumed. For if this is not the case, let m be the largest integer for which $\rho(m) = 0$. Then at least m customers will always be at queue M. Let $N' = N - m$ and $\mu'(n) = \mu(n+m)$. Maximization of $\tau_M(N)$ is accomplished in this case by considering only the rates $U(N'-n)$ and $\mu'(n)$, for $n \leq N'$. The result will be the same as maximization with $\rho(n) > 0$ for $n \leq N$, if it is shown that processing power is fully utilized when there are m customers in queue M. But note that $\rho(m) = 0$ only if $\tau_M(N)$ is a nonincreasing function of $\mu'(0)$. By Theorem 3C, then, $\tau_M(N)$ is an increasing function of $U(N')$, and hence, $\overline{\rho}(m) = 1$.

With the rates $\rho(n)R(N)$ for queue M fixed at the values required for maximum $\tau_M(N)$, the rates $U(n)$ may be selected within the range $0 \leq U(n) \leq U\overline{\rho}(N-n)R(N)$ to maximize $\tau_M(N)$.

Suppose $\tau_M(N)$ is not an increasing function of $U(n)$, for some $n < N$. Then, by Theorem 3C, it must be an increasing function of $\mu(N-n)$. Then $\rho(N-m) = 1$, and, therefore, $U(m) = 0$. If m is the largest integer for which $\tau_M(N)$ is not an increasing function of $U(m)$, then there will never be less than m customers at the equivalent queue. Hence, letting $N' = N - m$ and $U'(n) = U(n+m)$, only rates $U'(n)$ for $0 \leq n \leq N'$ must be considered in maximizing $\tau_M(N)$. And this maximization will yield the same result as maximization with $\tau_M(N)$ an increasing function of $U(n)$ for all $n > 0$. Therefore, the maximum value $U(n) = U\overline{\rho}(N-n)R(N)$ must be chosen for $U(n)$, $n \leq N$ in order to maximize $\tau_M(N)$. This proves part a) of the theorem. Then each term $X(j)Y(k)$ of $G(N-1)$, where $j + k = N - 1$, can be written

$$X(j)Y(k) = \mu^j U^k R^{j+k}(N) \prod_{i=1}^{j} \rho(i) \prod_{i=1}^{k} \rho(N-1)^{-1} . \qquad (C-2)$$

The terms of $G(N)$ have the same form, but $j + k = N$. Each term $X(j)Y(k)$ of $G(N)$ with $j, k > 0$ contains the product

$$\frac{1}{\rho(j)} \cdot \frac{1}{\bar{\rho}(j)} = \frac{1}{\bar{\rho}(j)} + \frac{1}{\rho(j)} . \quad \text{Hence, it can be written}$$

$$X(j)Y(k) = \frac{1}{\mu R(N)} \left[\mu^{j-1} U^k R^{N-1}(N) \prod_{i=1}^{j-1} \rho(i) \prod_{i=1}^{k} \bar{\rho}(N-i) \right]^{-1}$$

$$+ \frac{1}{U R(N)} \left[\mu^j U^{k-1} R^{N-1}(N) \prod_{i=1}^{j} \rho(i) \prod_{i=1}^{k-1} \bar{\rho}(N-i) \right]^{-1}$$

$$= \frac{1}{\mu R(N)} X(j-1)Y(k) + \frac{1}{U R(N)} X(j)Y(k-1). \qquad (C-3)$$

$G(N)$ also includes the terms

$$X(N)Y(0) = \left[\mu^N R^N(N) \prod_{i=1}^{N-1} \rho(i) \right]^{-1} = \frac{1}{\mu R(N)} X(N-1)Y(0) \qquad (C-4a)$$

and

$$X(0)Y(N) = \left[U^N R^N(N) \prod_{i=1}^{N-1} \bar{\rho}(N-i) \right]^{-1} = \frac{1}{U R(N)} X(0)Y(N-1). \qquad (C-4b)$$

$G(N)$ may then be expressed as follows:

$$G(N) = X(N)Y(0) + \sum_{\substack{j+k=N \\ j,k>0}} X(j)Y(k) + X(0)Y(N)$$

$$= \frac{1}{\mu R(N)} X(N-1)Y(0) + \sum_{\substack{j+k=N \\ j,k>0}} \frac{1}{\mu R(N)} X(j-1)Y(k)$$

$$+ \frac{1}{U R(N)} X(0)Y(N-1) + \sum_{\substack{j+k=N \\ j,k>0}} \frac{1}{U R(N)} X(j)Y(k-1)$$

$$= \frac{1}{\mu R(N)} \sum_{j+k=N-1} X(j)Y(k) + \frac{1}{U R(N)} \sum_{j+k=N-1} X(j)Y(k)$$

$$= \left(\frac{1}{\mu} + \frac{1}{U} \right) \frac{1}{R(N)} G(N-1). \qquad (C-5)$$

Therefore, when $\tau_M(N)$ is maximum, $\tau_M(N) = \dfrac{G(N-1)}{G(N)} = \left(\dfrac{1}{\mu} + \dfrac{1}{U} \right)^{-1} R(N). \qquad (C-6)$

Then part b) of the theorem is proved.

COMPUTER PERFORMANCE, K.M. CHANDY AND M. REISER (EDS.)
NORTH HOLLAND PUBLISHING COMPANY, 1977

AN APPROACH TO THE NUMERICAL SOLUTION OF SOME QUEUEING PROBLEMS

A. Brandwajn
Ecole National Superieure Des
Telecommunications
Paris, France

This paper presents an approach (believed to be
novel) to the efficient numerical solution of
balance equations for a broad class of queueing
problems. The approach is based on a systematic
use of the notion of equivalence, and in most
cases, though not always, implies an iterative
scheme of computation. Sufficient convergence
conditions are derived for this scheme. Several
examples of queueing systems related to computer
models illustrate the use of our approach.

INTRODUCTION

We shall present an approach (believed to be novel) to the numerical solution of
many queueing problems. This approach is based on a systematic use of the notion
of equivalence, and, hence, of conditional probability distributions. We shall
start by introducing the method on a simple two-dimensional example so as to
get an intuitive feeling on how and why it works. Then, in the next section, we
shall generalize the approach to more than two state variables, and we shall
derive sufficient convergence conditions for the iterative scheme which is in most
cases involved in our approach. The last section is devoted to several examples
illustrating the use of our approach.

Let us now consider the queueing network represented in Figure 1. It is a finite-
source network with two service centers, labelled 1 and 2. The arrivals to each
center form a Poisson process with parameters λ_1 and λ_2, respectively. The service
at each center is exponential with rates $\alpha(n_1,n_2)\mu_1$ and $\beta(n_1,n_2)\mu_2$, where

$$\alpha(n_1,n_2) = \begin{cases} \alpha, & \text{if } n_1 = 1,\ldots,N_1 \text{ and } n_2 \neq 0 \text{ ;} \\ 1, & \text{if } n_1 = 1,\ldots,N_1 \text{ and } n_2 = 0 \text{ ;} \\ 0, & \text{otherwise,} \end{cases} \qquad (1.1)$$

and

$$\beta(n_1,n_2) = \begin{cases} 1-\alpha, & \text{if } n_2 = 1,\dots,N_2 \text{ and } n_1 \neq 0 ; \\ 1 , & \text{if } n_2 = 1,\dots,N_2 \text{ and } n_1 = 0 ; \\ 0 , & \text{otherwise.} \end{cases} \qquad (1.2)$$

The interpretation of this network is quite straightforward : it represents a service station with two classes of customers, where a fraction of the processing power is allocated to each class. This fraction becomes 1 whenever there are customers of one class only.

Let

$$\lambda_1(n_1) = \begin{cases} \lambda_1, & \text{if } n_1 = 0,\dots,N_1-1 ; \\ 0 , & \text{otherwise} ; \end{cases} \qquad \lambda_2(n_2) = \begin{cases} \lambda_2, & \text{if } n_2 = 0,\dots,N_2-1 ; \\ 0 , & \text{otherwise.} \end{cases}$$

Denote by $p(n_1,n_2)$ the stationary joint probability distribution (assuming it exists) for the numbers of customers at each service center. The balance equations for our system are easily obtained as

$$-\left[\lambda_1(n_1) + \lambda_2(n_2) + \alpha(n_1,n_2)\mu_1 + \beta(n_1,n_2)\mu_2 \right] p(n_1,n_2)$$
$$+ \lambda_2(n_2-1)p(n_1,n_2-1) + \beta(n_1,n_2+1)\mu_2 \, p(n_1,n_2+1) \qquad (1.3)$$
$$+ \lambda_1(n_1-1)p(n_1-1,n_2) + \alpha(n_1+1,n_2)\mu_1 \, p(n_1+1,n_2) = 0,$$

$$n_1 = 0,\dots,N_1 ; \; n_2 = 0,\dots,N_2.$$

Let $p(n_1)$ $(n_1 = 0,\dots,N_1)$ be the stationary probability of having n_1 customers at center 1, and $p(n_2|n_1)$ the stationary conditional probability that there are n_2 customers at service center 2 given that there are n_1 customers at center 1. We have, of course,

$$p(n_1,n_2) = p(n_1)p(n_2|n_1) , \text{ for all } n_1,n_2. \qquad (1.4)$$

It is not difficult to show, either after some algebra on (1.3) or by a direct reasoning on $p(n_1)$, that our system of Figure 1 has the same stationary probability distribution of n_1, $p(n_1)$, as a simple finite-source, state-dependent M/M/1 queue with arrival rate $\lambda_1(n_1)$, and service rate

$$u(n_1) \triangleq \sum_{n_2=0}^{N_2} p(n_2|n_1)\alpha(n_1,n_2)\mu_1. \qquad (1.5)$$

We shall also say that our system is equivalent with respect to n_1 to the M/M/1 queue just defined.

Using (1.4) in (1.3) and the equivalence property we can replace (1.3) by the following set of equations

$$\{-\left[\lambda_1(n_1) + \lambda_2(n_2) + \alpha(n_1,n_2)\mu_1 + \beta(n_1,n_2)\mu_2\right] p(n_2|n_1)$$
$$+ \lambda_2(n_2-1)p(n_2-1|n_1) + \beta(n_1,n_2+1)\mu_2 p(n_2+1|n_1)\} \, p(n_1) \qquad (1.6)$$
$$+ \lambda_1(n_1-1)p(n_2|n_1-1)p(n_1-1) + \alpha(n_1+1,n_2)\mu_1 p(n_2|n_1+1)p(n_1+1) = 0,$$

$$n_1 = 0,\ldots,N_1 \; ; \quad n_2 = 0,\ldots,N_2 \; ;$$

$$-\left[\lambda_1(n_1) + u(n_1)\right]p(n_1) + \lambda_1(n_1-1)p(n_1-1) + u(n_1+1)p(n_1+1) = 0, \qquad (1.7)$$

$$n_1 = 0,\ldots,N_1$$

with $\displaystyle\sum_{n_1=0}^{N_1} p(n_1) = 1.$

This set of equations is equivalent to (1.3), and it enjoys some interesting properties which were not apparent in (1.3). Notice that the probabilities $p(n_2|n_1)$ are normalized with respect to unity independently for each n_1, so that, if we neglect terms involving n_1-1 and n_1+1, (1.3) becomes a very simple recurrence relation for the $p(n_2|n_1)$. This suggests to use an iterative scheme to solve (1.6), (1.7). The scheme may be as follows : starting from $n_1 = 0$, for successive n_1's, at iteration $t(t = 1, 2,\ldots)$ solve first

$$-\left[\lambda_1(n_1) + u^{t-1}(n_1)\right]p^t(n_1) + \lambda_1(n_1-1)p^t(n_1-1) + u^{t-1}(n_1+1)p^t(n_1+1) = 0,$$

$$n_1 = 0,\ldots,N_1 \; ; \qquad\qquad (1.8)$$

with $\displaystyle\sum_{n_1=0}^{N} p^t(n_1) = 1 \; ;$ $\quad u^t(n_1)$ is obtained by using $p^t(n_2|n_1)$ in (1.5) ;

then

$$\{-\left[\lambda_1(n_1) + \lambda_2(n_2) + \alpha(n_1,n_2)\mu_1 + \beta(n_1,n_2)\mu_2\right]p^t(n_2|n_1)$$
$$+ \lambda_2(n_2-1)p^t(n_2-1|n_1) + \beta(n_1,n_2+1)\mu_2 \, p^t(n_2+1|n_1)\} \, p^t(n_1)$$
$$+ \lambda_1(n_1-1)p^t(n_2|n_1-1)p^t(n_1-1) + \alpha(n_1+1,n_2)\mu_1 \, p^{t-1}(n_2|n_1+1) \, p^t(n_1+1) = 0,$$

$$n_2 = 0, 1,\ldots,N_2 \; ; n_1 = 0, 1,\ldots,N_1.$$

$p^t(n_1)$, $p^t(n_2|n_1)$ are the approximations to $p(n_1)$, $p(n_2|n_1)$ computed at iteration t. The iteration starts with some initial set of distributions $p^0(n_2|n_1)$ ($p^0(n_2|n_1)$ should preferably be such that $u^0(n_1) \neq 0$, $n_1 = 1,\ldots,N_1$). Note that the computation involved at each iteration is very simple ; no matrix operation is needed. The storage requirements are moderate : essentially an array for the $p(n_1)$ and $p(n_2|n_1)$. In the latter, every just computed distribution $p^t(n_2|n_1)$ replaces the corresponding $p^{t-1}(n_2|n_1)$ successively for each $n_1 = 0, 1,\ldots$

The important questions to answer now are : when and how fast does this scheme converge, and how to choose the initial distributions $p^0(n_2|n_1)$. Before tackling this problem formally, let us note that on an intuitive basis one would expect this scheme to converge if $\lambda_1(n_1-1)$ and $\alpha(n_1+1,n_2)\mu_1$ are not important as compared to $\lambda_2(n_2)$ and $\beta(n_1,n_2)\mu_2$. This is because the $\lambda_1(n_1-1)$ and $\alpha(n_1+1,n_2)\mu_1$ are the coefficients of the "neglected" terms.

We shall now attempt to answer rigorously the convergence question. If one considers an iterative scheme of the form (in vector notation)

$$x^t = f(x^{t-1})$$

(1.10)

(X is the vector of unknowns $X_1,\ldots, X_p$, and f is the set of equations $f_1,\ldots,f_p$), it is well known from the theory of iterative methods in numerical analysis (see [1] , for example) that (1.10) converges if and only if f(X) satisfies a Lipschitz condition

$$||f(X') - f(X'')|| \leq L \, ||X' - X''||,$$

(1.11)

with L (the Lipschitz constant) L < 1, for any X', X" in the convergence domain. An upper bound for L can be obtained as the norm of the Jacobi matrix for f. In our case the iteration is of the form

$$F(x^t, x^{t-1}) = 0,$$

so that the elements of the Jacobi matrix, J, are given by

$$j_{m,n} = - \frac{\partial F_m}{\partial x_n^{t-1}} \; / \; \frac{\partial F_m}{\partial x_m^t} \quad , \quad m,n = 1,\ldots, p,$$

(1.12)

p being the number of equations (and unknowns). Before applying this result to (1.8), (1.9) we will transform slightly this system of equations, so as to ease the computation of the elements of J, and the subsequent evaluation of its norm.

Let us introduce explicitly the equations for $u(n_1)$

$$u^t(n_1) = \sum_{n_2=0}^{N_2} \alpha(n_1,n_2)\mu_1 \; p^t(n_2|n_1),$$

(1.13)

$$n_1 = 1, \, 2,\ldots,N_1 \; ;$$

and use $u(n_1)$ as another variable in the vector X. The elements of the corresponding Jacobi matrix are

$$
j_{m,n} = \begin{cases}
\dfrac{\alpha(n_1+1,n_2)\mu_1 \; p^t(n_1+1)/p^t(n_1)}{\lambda_1(n_1) + \lambda_2(n_2) + \alpha(n_1,n_2)\mu_1 + \beta(n_1,n_2)\mu_2} \quad , \\
\qquad \text{if} \quad X_m^t = p^t(n_2|n_1) \text{ and } X_n^{t-1} = p^{t-1}(n_2|n_1+1) \; ; \\[4pt]
- p^t(n_1)/\left[\lambda_1(n_1) + u^{t-1}(n_1)\right], \\
\qquad \text{if} \quad X_m^t = p^t(n_1) \text{ and } X_n^{t-1} = u^{t-1}(n_1) \; ; \\[4pt]
p^t(n_1+1)/\left[\lambda_1(n_1) + u^{t-1}(n_1)\right], \\
\qquad \text{if} \quad X_m^t = p^t(n_1) \text{ and } X_n^{t-1} = u^{t-1}(n_1+1) \; ; \\[4pt]
0 \; , \quad \text{otherwise.}
\end{cases}
\tag{1.14}
$$

It doesn't seem easy to determine which one among the many possible matrix norms yields the closest bound for the Lipschitz constant of our iterative scheme. The norm $||\ ||_1$, i.e. $\max\limits_{n} s_n$, where $s_n = \sum\limits_{m} |j_{m,n}|$, appears to be convenient. We note that the last two terms in (1.14) can be made arbitrarily small, so that we obtain from (1.14), using the solution of (1.8),

$$
s_n \leq \alpha(n_1+1,n_2)\mu_1 \, \lambda_1(n_1)/\{u^{t-1}(n_1+1)\left[\lambda_1(n_1)+ \lambda_2(n_2) + \alpha(n_1,n_2)\mu_1 + \beta(n_1,n_2)\mu_2\right]\},
$$
$$
\tag{1.15}
$$
$$
n_2 = 0,\dots,N_2 \; ; \; n_1 = 0,\dots,N_1-1 \; ;
$$

and, hence, an upper bound for L :

$$
L \leq \max_{n} s_n \leq \max(\alpha \, \lambda_1, \, \lambda_1, \, \mu_1)/\min_{n_1,n_2} \left[\lambda_1(n_1) + \lambda_2(n_2) + \alpha(n_1,n_2)\mu_1 + \beta(n_1,n_2)\mu_2\right].
$$
$$
\tag{1.16}
$$

We observe that the convergence is not always guaranteed (which does not necessarily mean that our scheme doesn't always converge, since we have obtained an upper bound for $||J||$, itself already an upper bound for L). We also observe that our intuition is confirmed in that the smaller the $\lambda_1(n_1)$ and $\alpha(n_1,n_2)\mu_1$, the smaller our bound for $||J||$. It seems interesting to note that the speed of variation of $\alpha(n_1,n_2)$ with respect to n_2 is of importance. This is because of factors of the form

$$
\alpha(n_1+1,n_2)\mu_1/u^{t-1}(n_1+1)
$$

in our bound for J.

The speed of convergence, and thus, the accuracy attained after a given number of iterations are known to depend on the Lipschitz constant :

$$||x^t - x^*|| < \frac{L^t}{1 - L} ||x^1 - x^0|| \tag{1.17}$$

where x^* is the solution searched.

As for the choice of the set of initial distributions, any x^0 (provided it satisfies $u^0(n_1) \neq 0$, $n_1 = 1,...,N_1$) will do, though, of course, some x^0's will lead faster than others to a given accuracy solution.

We give in the Appendix a few examples illustrating the iterative solution of the system of Figure 1.

Let us now return briefly to the set of equations (1.6), (1.7). The latter equation implies

$$p(n_1-1)/p(n_1) = u(n_1)/\lambda_1(n_1-1) .$$

We could use this relation directly in (1.6), and thus apply the following iterative scheme :

$$-\left[\lambda_1(n_1) + \lambda_2(n_2) + \alpha(n_1,n_2)\mu_1 + \beta(n_1,n_2)\mu_2 \right] p^t(n_2|n_1)$$
$$+ \lambda_2(n_2-1)p^t(n_2-1|n_1) + \beta(n_1,n_2+1)\mu_2 \, p^t(n_2+1|n_1) \tag{1.18}$$
$$+ u^t(n_1)p^t(n_2|n_1-1) + \alpha(n_1+1,n_2)\mu_1 \, p^{t-1}(n_2|n_1+1)\lambda_1(n_1)/u^{t-1}(n_1+1) = 0.$$

The slight increase of the computational difficulty at each iteration seems justified by the often considerable speed up of the convergence.

Another point regarding equations (1.6), (1.7) is the apparent increase of the number of unknowns and of equations as compared to (1.3). In the latter we had $(N_1+1)(N_2+1)$ variables $(p(n_1,n_2))$ tied by the normalization condition $\sum_{n_1,n_2} p(n_1,n_2) = 1$. In (1.6) and (1.7) we have a total of $(N_1+1)(N_2+1)$ plus (N_1+1) variables $(p(n_2|n_1), p(n_1),$ respectively) but these variables are tied by a number of normalization conditions : $\sum_{n_2} p(n_2|n_1) = 1$, for each n_1, and $\sum_{n_1} p(n_1) = 1$. As a consequence in (1.6) only N_2 (and not (N_2+1)) equations are needed for every n_1, and N_1 equations in (1.7), i.e. a total of $(N_1+1)N_2 + N_1$, which is exactly the number of equations really needed in (1.3). This also means that the increase of storage requirements which seems implied by (1.6), (1.7) may, in principle, be avoided, since for every n_1, one of the $p(n_2|n_1)$ is known if we know the N_2 others and anologously for $p(n_1)$. In practice, whether one chooses to store all the probabilities, or not is a question of tradeoff between storage and time for a particular computation.

As a final point in this introductory section, let us note that the use of conditional probabilities, normalized separately for each value of the condition, resembles a decomposition approach, since we replace the solution of a complex system of equations by a set of solutions of much simpler equations. Intuitively, one would also expect that this should result in a robustness with respect to error propagation problems.

In the next section we shall generalize our approach to any finite number of state variables.

GENERALIZATION OF THE METHOD

Consider a vector of k integers

$$n^k = (n_1, n_2, \ldots, n_i, \ldots, n_k) , \qquad k \geq 1.$$

Let

$$a(n^k, i) = (n_1, \ldots, n_i + 1, n_{i+1}, \ldots, n_k) ,$$
$$b(n^k, i) = (n_1, \ldots, n_i - 1, n_{i+1}, \ldots, n_k) , \qquad (2.1)$$

and

$$c(n^k, i, j) = (n_1, \ldots, n_i + 1, \ldots, n_j - 1, \ldots, n_k).$$

We shall consider queueing systems which enjoy the following properties :
. their state can be described by n^k ;
. they possess a stationary probability distribution for n^k, which will be noted $p(n^k)$;
. $p(n^k)$ satisfies equations of the form

$$- \sum_{i=1}^{k} \left[\lambda_i(n^k) + \mu_i(n^k) + \sum_{j=1}^{k} u_{ij}(n^k) \right] p(n^k)$$

$$+ \sum_{i=1}^{k} \lambda_i(b(n^k, i)) p(b(n^k, i)) + \sum_{i=1}^{k} \mu_i(a(n^k, i)) p(a(n^k, i)) \qquad (2.2)$$

$$+ \sum_{i=1}^{k} \sum_{j=1}^{k} u_{ij}(c(n^k, i, j)) p(c(n^k, i, j)) = 0,$$

where

$\mu_i(n^k) = 0$, whenever $n_i = 0$, $i = 1, \ldots, k$;

$u_{ii}(n^k) = 0$, for all n^k, $i = 1, \ldots, k$;

$p(n^k) = 0$, if n^k contains an element which is negative, or exceeds its maximum value (for finite-state systems) ;

$\lambda_i(n^k) = 0$, if n_i has its maximum possible value given n^k (for finite-state systems) ;

$u_{ij}(n^k) = 0$, whenever $n_i = 0$, $i = 1, \ldots, k$; or n_j has its maximum possible value given n^k, $j = 1, \ldots k$;

$\lambda_i(n^k), \mu_i(n^k), u_{ij}(n^k) > 0$, otherwise.

It is clear that a great number of queueing problems can be formulated in this way.

Let us introduce some more notations :

$$p(n_{l+1}|n^l) = \text{Prob}\{n_{l+1}|(n_1,\ldots,n_l)\} \quad , \; l = k - 1,\ldots,\; 1 \; ;$$

$$\lambda_i^l(n^l) = \begin{cases} \lambda_i(n^k) \; , \; \text{if } l = k \; ; \\ \sum_{n_{l+1}} \lambda_i^{l+1}(n^{l+1})p(n_{l+1}|n^l) \quad , \; i = 1,\ldots,l \; ; \end{cases} \tag{2.3}$$

$$\mu_i^l(n^l) = \begin{cases} \mu_i(n^k), \; \text{if } l = k \; ; \\ \sum_{n_{l+1}} \mu_i^{l+1}(n^{l+1})p(n_{l+1}|n^l) \; , \; \text{if } l = k - 1,\ldots,l \; ; \\ \qquad\qquad\qquad\qquad i = 1,\ldots,l \; ; \end{cases} \tag{2.4}$$

$$u_{ij}^l(n^l) = \begin{cases} u_{ij}(n^k) \; , \; \text{if } l = k \; ; \\ \sum_{n_{l+1}} u_{ij}^{l+1}(n^{l+1})p(n_{l+1}|n^l) \; , \; \text{if } l = k - 1,\ldots,l \; ; \\ \qquad\qquad i = 1,\ldots,l \qquad i \neq j. \\ \qquad\qquad j = 1,\ldots,l, \end{cases} \tag{2.5}$$

The system under consideration can be shown (again either by some algebra on (2.2) or by a direct reasoning on the corresponding state vector) to be equivalent with respect to n^l, $l = k$, $k - 1,\ldots,l$ to a system described by the following equations

$$\begin{aligned} &- \sum_{i=1}^{l} \left[\lambda_i^l(n^l) + \mu_i^l(n^l) + \sum_{j=1}^{l} u_{ij}^l(n^l) \right] p(n^l) \\ &+ \sum_{i=1}^{l} \lambda_i^l(b(n^l,i))p(b(n^l,i)) + \sum_{i=1}^{l} \mu_i^l(a(n^l,i))p(a(n^l,i)) \\ &+ \sum_{i=1}^{l} \sum_{j=1}^{l} u_{ij}^l(c(n^l,i,j))p(c(n^l,i,j)) = 0, \end{aligned} \tag{2.6}$$

so that (2.2) can be replaced by the set of (2.6) for $l = k$, $k - 1,\ldots,l$.

Now, we can write for every $p(n^l)$, $l = k$, $k - 1,\ldots,2$

$$p(n^l) = p(n_1|n^{l-1})p(n^{l-1}) \; , \tag{2.7}$$

and thus

$$p(n^l) = p(n_1) \prod_{\gamma=0}^{l-2} p(n_{l-\gamma}|n^{l-\gamma-1}).$$

Using (2.7) in (2.6) we obtain

$$p(n^{1-1})\{- \sum_{i=1}^{1} \left[\lambda_i^1(n^1) + \mu_i^1(n^1) + \sum_{j=1}^{1} u_{ij}^1(n^1)\right] p(n_1|n^{1-1})$$

$$+ \lambda_1^1(b(n^1,1))p(n_1-1|n^{1-1}) + \mu_1^1(a(n^1,1))p(n_1+1|n^{1-1})\}$$

$$+ \sum_{i=1}^{1-1} p(b(n^{1-1},i)) \left[\lambda_i^1(b(n^1,i))p(n_1|b(n^{1-1},i)) + u_{1i}^1(c(n^1,1,i))p(n_1+1|b(n^{1-1},i))\right]$$

$$+ \sum_{i=1}^{1-1} p(a(n^{1-1},i)) \left[\mu_i^1(a(n^1,i))p(n_1|a(n^{1-1},i)) + u_{i1}^1(c(n^1,i,1))p(n_1-1|a(n^{1-1},i))\right]$$

$$+ \sum_{i=1}^{1-1} \sum_{j=1}^{1-1} p(c(n^{1-1},i,j)u_{ij}^1(c(n^1,i,j))p(n_1|c(n^{1-1},i,j)) = 0, \qquad (2.8)$$

$$n_1 = 0, 1,\ldots ; \qquad 1 = k, k-1,\ldots,2 ;$$

and

$$-\left[\lambda_1^1(n_1) + \mu_1^1(n_1)\right] p(n_1) + \lambda_1^1(n_1-1)p(n_1-1) + \mu_1^1(n_1+1)p(n_1+1) = 0, \qquad (2.9)$$

$$n_1 = 0, 1,\ldots,N_1.$$

Equation (2.8) enjoys the same interesting property of being close in form to a simple one-dimensional recurrence relation for the $p(n_1|n^{1-1})$ as (1.6) of our introductory example. (Given the independent normalization conditions implied in the use of conditional probabilities we may easily generalize the remark of the preceding section regarding the apparent increase of the number of unknowns). There are a number of possible iteration schemes to solve (2.8), (2.9) depending on the order in which we want to consider the equations. A straightforward generalization of the introductory example is to start by computing, at iteration $t(t = 1, 2,\ldots)$, the $p^t(n_1)$, then the $p^t(n_2|n^1)$, etc,i.e. to consider (2.8), (2.9) for increasing $1(1 = 1, 2,\ldots,k)$. This doesn't completely specify the scheme since there are many ways, for a given 1, of enumerating the n^{1-1} states. One possible ordering is to consider the n^{1-1} states in the order of increasing sums $\sum_{i=1}^{1-1} n_i$, and for a given value of this sum (say,s) , first $(0,\ldots,0,s)$ then $(0,\ldots,1,s-1)$, $(0,\ldots,2,s-2)$, etc up to $(s,\ldots,0,0)$. Using obvious notational generalizations we can express the iterative scheme as

$$-\left[\lambda_1^{t'1}(n_1) + \mu_1^{t'1}(n_1)\right]p^t(n_1) + \lambda_1^{t'1}(n_1-1)p^t(n_1-1) + \mu_1^{t'1}(n_1+1)p^{t1}(n_1+1) = 0,$$

solved for 1 = 1 ,

and

$$p^t(n^{1-1}) \{ \sum_{i=1}^{1} \left[\lambda_i^{t'1}(n^1) + \mu_i^{t'1}(n^1) + \sum_{j=1}^{1} u_{ij}^{t'1}(n^1)\right] p^t(n_1|n^{1-1})$$

$$+ \lambda_1^{t'1}(b(n^1,1))p^t(n_1-1|n^{1-1}) + \mu_1^{t'1}(a(n^1,1))p^t(n_1+1|n^{1-1})\}$$

$$+ \sum_{i=1}^{l-1} p^t(b(n^{l-1},i))\left[\lambda^{t'l}_{i}(b(n^l,i))p^t(n_1|b(n^{l-1},i))\right.$$

$$\left. + u^{t'l}_{i1}(c(n^l,1,i))p^t(n_1+1|b(n^{l-1},i))\right]$$

$$+ \sum_{i=1}^{l-1} p^t(a(n^{l-1},i))\left[\mu^{t'l}_{i}(a(n^l,i))p^{t'}(n_1|a(n^{l-1},i))\right.$$

$$\left. + u^{t'l}_{i1}(c(n^l,i,1))p^{t'}(n_1-1|a(n^{l-1},i))\right]$$

$$+ \sum_{i=1}^{l-1}\left[\sum_{j=1}^{i} u^{t'l}_{ij}(c(n^l,i,j))p^t(n_1|c(n^{l-1},i,j))\right. \tag{2.10}$$

$$\left. + \sum_{j=i+1}^{l-1} u^{t'l}_{ij}(c(n^l,i,j))p^{t'}(n_1|c(n^{l-1},i,j))\right]\cdot p^t(c(n^{l-1},i,j)) = 0,$$

(with $p^t(n^{l-1}) = p^t(n_1)p^t(n_2|n_1)\ldots p^t(n_{l-1}|n^{l-2})$)

for $l = 2, 3,\ldots, k$;

where $t' = t - 1$.

Sufficient convergence conditions for this iterative procedure can be obtained in a manner analogous to that used in the introductory example, i.e. by considering the Jacobi matrix for (2.10). Using again the matrix norm $||\ ||_1$, we obtain the following upper bound for the Lipschitz constant

$$L \leq \max_{l=2,\ldots k} (L_1(1), L_2(1), L_3(1)),$$

where

$$L_1(1) \leq \max_{n^1} \{f(n^1)u^{t'l}_{ij}(c(n^1,i,j))/u^{t'l-1}_{ij}(c(n^{l-1},i,j))\},$$

$$i=1,\ldots,l-1 ; \ j=i+1,\ldots,l-1 ;$$

$$L_2(1) \leq \max_{n^1} \{f(n^1)\mu^{t'l}_{i}(a(n^1,i))/\mu^{t'l-1}_{i}(a(n^{l-1},i))\},$$

$$i=1,\ldots,l-1 ;$$

$$L_3(1) \leq \max_{n^1} \{f(n^1)u^{t'l}_{i1}(c(n^1,i,1))/\mu^{t'l-1}_{i}(a(n^{l-1},i))\}, \tag{2.11}$$

$$i=1,\ldots,l-1,$$

with

$$f(n^1) \leq \sum_{i=1}^{1-1} \left[\lambda_i^{t'1-1}(n^{1-1}) + \mu_i^{t'1-1}(n^{1-1}) + \sum_{j=1}^{1-1} u_{ij}^{t'1-1}(n^{1-1}) \right] /$$
$$\sum_{i=1}^{1} \left[\lambda_i^{t'1}(n^1) + \mu_i^{t'1}(n^1) + \sum_{j=1}^{1} u_{ij}^{t'1}(n^1) \right].$$

We note that (2.11), quite similarly to (1.15), depends on the speed of variation of the transition rates.

As in the case of the introductory example, this bound doesn't guarantee that our iterative scheme always converges. The choice of the initial set of probability distributions $p^o(n_1)$, $p^o(n_2|n_1)$,...,$p^o(n_k|n_1,...,n_{k-1})$ is easy, since any set will do, provided it does not make equal to zero any of the denominators in (2.11). In summary, what we propose is to replace a set of equations for a single probability distribution $p(n^k)$ by k sets of equations for k probability distributions $p(n_1)$, $p(n_1|n^{1-1})$, $1 = 2,...,k$. The equations in the latter sets can be solved iteratively in such a way that a simple one-dimensional recurrence relation has to be solved at each iteration. The advantages of this method are those of a decomposition approach provided, of course, that the number of iterations needed is not too high. Since the numbering of state variables in the state vector n^k is arbitrary, it is clear from (2.10) and (2.11) that the choice of a given numbering is not, in general, immaterial with respect to the speed of convergence. The same holds for the order in which we consider the system states. The point will be illustrated in the next section.

The queueing systems considered so far were described by balance equations with one-step transitions for each state variable. The solution of these equations by our method required the use of an iterative scheme. In the next section we apply our method to an example for which no iteration is needed, and also to a system with more-than-one-step transitions.

EXAMPLES OF APPLICATION

In this section we shall illustrate the use of our method by applying it to several queueing systems which pertain to computer systems modelling.

Example 3.1.

Consider the queueing model of an iteractive computer system represented in Figure 2. The system consists of a set of terminals, a CPU, and a secondary memory device (SM). The terminals are modelled by an exponential server with service rate $n_c \lambda$, n_c being the current number of users (processes) active at their terminals. The SM is modelled by an exponential server with service rate $u_1(n_1)$; n_1 is the current number of processes at it. The CPU, finally, is modelled by two exponential service stages corresponding to user mode execution, and overhead mode for initiating SM operations, respectively.
In user mode the rate of process completions is v_o, and the rate of SM requests is v_1. The rate of service of the exponential stage representing the SM overhead is η_1. The current number of processes at the CPU is denoted by n_o, and the service stages "user mode" and "overhead" are labelled 1 and 2. All the processes are assumed to be statistically identical and independent. Their total number, N, is constant. The queueing disciplines are all assumed to be FCFS.

It is clear that the long-run behavior of this queueing network is completely described by the stationary probability distribution $p(s)$ of the state vector $s = (n_o, n_1, i)$, where i (i=1, 2) indicates the active CPU stage, i.e. the CPU mode (i=1 -user mode ; i=2 -SM overhead). Clearly, $p(s)$ satisfies a set of

balance equations of the form (2.2), so that we could apply our method to the
state vector s. Given, however, that for current values of the model parameters
λ and v_0 (the rates of process arrivals and of process completions) are (at least)
an order of magnitude smaller than v_1, η_1, and u_1 (the rates of internal system
transitions) it is more interesting to choose $s' = (n, n_0, i)$ where $n = n_0 + n_1$,
as the state vector, and to apply our method to s'.

We have

$$p(s') = p(i|n, n_0)p(n, n_0) = p(i|n, n_0)p(n_0|n)p(n), \qquad (3.1)$$

$$n = 0,\ldots,N ; \quad n_0 = 0,\ldots,n ; \quad i = 1,2 ;$$

(note that i makes no sense for $n_0 = 0$).

We choose an initial set of probability distributions

$$p^o(i|n, n_0) \quad , \quad p^o(n_0|n) \quad ,$$

and at iteration $t(t = 1, 2,\ldots)$ we solve

$$. - \left[(N-n)\lambda + u^{t-1}(n)\right]p^t(n) + (N-n+1)\lambda p^t(n-1) + u^{t-1}(n+1)p^t(n+1) = 0,$$

$$n = 0,\ldots,N-1 ; \qquad (3.2)$$

with

$$\sum_{n=0}^{N} p^t(n) = 1 , \qquad (3.3)$$

where $\quad u^{t-1}(n) = \sum_{n_0=1}^{n} \mu_o^{t-1}(n,n_0)p^{t-1}(n_0|n) \quad , \; n=1,\ldots,N ; \qquad (3.4)$

$$(\mu_o(n_1 n_0) \text{ is given by } (3.7))$$

$$. \; p^t(n) \{-\left[u_1(n-n_0) + (N-n)\lambda + \mu_o^{t-1}(n,n_0) + \mu_1^{t-1}(n,n_0)\right]p^t(n_0|n)$$

$$+ u_1(n-n_0+1)p^t(n_0-1|n) + \mu_1^{t-1}(n,n_0+1)p^t(n_0+1|n)\} \qquad (3.5)$$

$$+ (N-n+1)\lambda p^t(n-1)p^t(n_0-1|n-1) + \mu_o^{t-1}(n+1,n_0+1)p^t(n+1)p^{t-1}(n_0+1|n+1) = 0,$$

$$n_0=0,\ldots,n-1 ; \; n=1,\ldots,N ;$$

with $\quad \displaystyle\sum_{n_o=0}^{n} p^t(n_o|n) = 1, \quad n = 1,\ldots, N$; $\hspace{2cm}$ (3.6)

and $\quad \mu_o^{t-1}(n,n_o) = v_o p^{t-1}(1|n,n_o) \; ; \; \mu_1^{t-1}(n,n_o) = \eta_1 p^{t-1}(2|n,n_o),$ $\hspace{1cm}$ (3.7)

$$n_o=1,\ldots,n \; ; \; n=1,\ldots,N \; ;$$

. $p^t(n,1) \; \{-[(N-n)\lambda + \eta_1 + u_1(n-n_o)] p^t(2|n,1) + v_1 \, p^t(1|n,1)\}$

$\hspace{1cm} + (N-n+1)\lambda p^t(n-1,0) = 0$, $\hspace{4cm}$ (3.8)

$\hspace{1cm} n = 1,\ldots,N \; ;$

. $p^t(n,n_o) \; \{-[(N-n)\lambda + \eta_1 + u_1(n-n_o)] p^t(2|n,n_o) + v_1 \, p^t(1|n,1)\}$

$\hspace{0.5cm} + u_1(n-n_o+1) \; p^t(n,n_o-1)p^t(2|n,n_o-1) + (N-n+1)\lambda p^t(n-1,n_o-1)p^t(2|n-1,n_o-1) = 0$,

$\hspace{10cm}$ (3.9)

$\hspace{1cm} n_o = 2,\ldots,n \; ; \quad n = 2,\ldots,N \; ;$

with $\quad p^t(1|n,n_o) + p^t(2|n,n_o) = 1 \quad , \; n_o = 1,\ldots,n \; ;$ $\hspace{2cm}$ (3.10)

$$n = 1,\ldots,N.$$

Owing to the choice of s', the coefficients of many of the terms in $(t-1)$ are much smaller than those of terms in t, and this results in a fast convergence. This is illustrated in the Appendix for a set of values of the model's parameters. It is interesting to note that, although any initial $p^o(n_o|n)$ and $p^o(i|n,n_o)$ leads to the correct solution, given the order of magnitude difference in transition rates, the approximate solution obtained by an equivalence and decomposition approach [2] constitutes an excellent starting point. This is also illustrated in the Appendix.

Note how, owing to the independent normalization conditions, only a part of the possible balance equations are used, e.g. (3.8) suffices to compute both $p(1|n,1)$ and $p(2|n,1)$.

Note also that we might speed up the convergence by using the formal solution for $p(n)$ $(p(n) \sim \displaystyle\prod_{i=1}^{n} \lambda(N-i+1)/u(i))$ directly in (3.5) instead of the $p^t(n)$. Finally, note that, instead of (3.1), we might use the "less decomposed" scheme

$$p(s') = p(i,n_o|n)p(n),$$ $\hspace{4cm}$ (3.11)

which would not increase significantly the complexity of the computation involved at each iteration.

Example 3.2.

Consider the queueing system of Figure 3. It represents a model of a batch system.

The arrivals of jobs are assumed to form a Poisson process with parameter λ.; the current number of jobs in the system is denoted by n, n=0,1... The jobs undergo in the system a series of k treatments. The latter are modelled by k exponential stages, labelled 1 to k, with service rates $\mu_i(n)$, i=1,...,k. The state of this system is completely described by the couple (n,i), where i=1,...,k is the number of the current active service stage. The long-run behavior of the system is described by the stationary probability distribution p(n,i), assuming it exists. Applying our approach we write

$$p(n,i) = p(i|n)p(n), \tag{3.12}$$

$$i=1,\ldots,k \; ; \; n=1,\ldots$$

(for n=0, i makes no sense).

By an equivalence with respect to the variable n we obtain

$$p(n) = G \; \lambda^n / \prod_{j=1}^{n} u(j) \quad , \quad n=0,1,\ldots \tag{3.13}$$

where

$$u(n) = \mu_k(n)p(k|n), \tag{3.14}$$

and G is a normalization constant. Using (3.12), (3.13) together with (3.14) in the system balance equations we easily obtain the following equations for p(i|n) :

$$\cdot \; -\left[\lambda + \mu_i(1)\right]p(i|1) + \mu_{i-1}(1) \; p(i-1|1) = 0 \; , \qquad i=2,\ldots,k \; ;$$

$$\tag{3.15}$$

$$\cdot \; -\left[\lambda + \mu_i(n)\right]p(i|n) + \mu_{i-1}(n)p(i-1|n)$$

$$+ \; \mu_k(n)p(k|n)p(i|n-1) = 0, \qquad i=2,\ldots,k \; ; \; n=2,3,\ldots,$$

with the set of normalization conditions

$$\sum_{i=1}^{k} p(i|n) = 1 \quad , \quad \text{for } n = 1, 2,\ldots \tag{3.16}$$

Clearly, no iteration is needed ; (3.15) is a simple recurrence relation and the p(i|n) are easy to compute if we start from n = 1.

Example 3.3

Consider the queueing model of Figure 4. It consists of two queues in tandem. The arrival process is Poisson with parameter λ_1 ; the source is finite, and the maximum number of requests which may be present in the system is N. The service at server 1 is exponential by bulks of size b, b $\geq$ 1 ; its rate is μ_1. The service at server 2 is exponential with rate μ_2. This queueing network may be used to model a buffer in which fixed-length messages are assembled before an individual analysis of message characters (server 2).

For more generality, let us assume state-dependent arrival and service rates $\lambda_1(n_1,n_2)$, $\mu_1(n_1,n_2)$, $\mu_2(n_1,n_2)$. Let $n = n_1 + n_2$. In our case

$$\lambda_1(n_1,n_2) = \begin{cases} \lambda_1 & \text{, if } n < N \text{ ,} \\ 0 & \text{, otherwise ;} \end{cases}$$

$$\mu_1(n_1,n_2) = \begin{cases} \mu_1 & \text{, if } n_1 \geq b \text{ ,} \\ 0 & \text{, otherwise ;} \end{cases} \qquad (3.17)$$

$$\mu_2(n_1,n_2) = \begin{cases} \mu_2 & \text{, if } n_2 > 0 \text{ ,} \\ 0 & \text{, otherwise.} \end{cases}$$

With these notations, we have the following equations for the joint stationary probability distribution for the numbers at the servers, $p(n_1,n_2)$,

$$- \left[\lambda_1(n_1,n_2) + \mu_1(n_1,n_2) + \mu_2(n_1,n_2) \right] p(n_1,n_2) + \lambda_1(n_1-1,n_2)p(n_1-1,n_2)$$

$$(3.18)$$

$$+ \mu_2(n_1,n_2+1)p(n_1,n_2+1) + \mu_1(n_1+b,n_2-b)p(n_1+b,n_2-b) = 0,$$

$$n_1 = 0,\ldots,N ; \quad n_2 = 0,\ldots,N-n_1.$$

Although these equations are not of the form of (2.2), the "decomposition" by use of conditional probabilities can be successfully applied to their solution. One possible scheme is to consider $p(n,n_2)$ instead of $p(n_1,n_2)$ and to write

$$p(n,n_2) = p(n_2|n)p(n). \qquad (3.19)$$

With respect to n, our system is equivalent to a simple finite M/M/1 queue with arrival rate

$$\lambda(n) = \sum_{n_2=0}^{n} \lambda_1(n-n_2,n_2)p(n_2|n) \quad , n = 0,1,\ldots,N-1 ; \qquad (3.20)$$

and service rate

$$u(n) = \sum_{n_2=0}^{n} \mu_2(n-n_2,n_2)p(n_2|n) \quad , n = 1,\ldots,N. \qquad (3.21)$$

Hence, p(n) is formally known

$$p(n) \sim \prod_{i=1}^{n} \lambda(i-1)/u(i). \qquad (3.22)$$

Using (3.19), (3.22) in (3.18) we obtain as a possible iterative scheme (Scheme 1)

$$- \left[\lambda_1(n_1, n_2) + \mu_1(n_1, n_2) + \mu_2(n_1, n_2) \right] p^t(n_2 | n)$$

$$+ \mu_1(n_1+b, n_2-b) p^t(n_2-b | n) + u^{t-1}(n) \lambda_1(n_1-1, n_2) p^t(n_2 | n-1) / \lambda^t(n-1)$$

$$+ \lambda^{t-1}(n) \mu_2(n_1, n_2+1) p^{t-1}(n_2+1 | n+1) / u^{t-1}(n+1) = 0,$$

$$n = 1, \ldots, N \; ; \quad n_2 = 0, \ldots, n \quad ; \qquad (3.23)$$

$$\sum_{n_2=0}^{n} p^t(n_2 | n) = 1, \quad n = 1, \ldots, N .$$

Another possible scheme may be derived from

$$p(n_1, n_2) = p(n_2 | n_1) p(n_1). \qquad (3.24)$$

Let

$$\gamma(n_1) = \sum_{n_2=0}^{N-n_1} \lambda_1(n_1, n_2) p(n_2 | n_1), \qquad (3.25)$$

$$\mu(n_1) = \sum_{n_2=0}^{N-n_1} \mu_1(n_1, n_2) p(n_2 | n_1). \qquad (3.26)$$

We easily obtain (Scheme 2) :

$$- \left[\gamma^{t-1}(n_1) + \mu^{t-1}(n_1) \right] p^t(n_1) + \gamma^{t-1}(n_1-1) p^t(n_1-1)$$

$$+ \mu^{t-1}(n_1+b) p^t(n_1+b) = 0 , \qquad n_1 = N, N-1, \ldots, 1 ;$$

$$\sum_{n_1=0}^{N} p^t(n_1) = 1 ; \qquad (3.27)$$

and

$$p^t(n_1) \{ - \left[\lambda_1(n_1, n_2) + \mu_1(n_1, n_2) + \mu_2(n_1, n_2) \right] p^t(n_2 | n_1)$$

$$+ \mu_2(n_1, n_2+1) p^t(n_2+1 | n_1) \} + p^t(n_1-1) \lambda(n_1-1, n_2) p^t(n_2 | n_1-1)$$

$$+ p^t(n_1+b) \mu_1(n_1+b, n_2-b) p^{t-1}(n_2-b | n_1+b) = 0, \qquad (3.28)$$

$$n_2 = 0, \ldots, N-n_1-1 \; ; \; n_1 = 0, \ldots, N \; ;$$

$$\sum_{n_2=0}^{N-n_1} p^t(n_2|n_1) = 1, \qquad n_1 = 0,\ldots,N.$$

Both Scheme 1 and Scheme 2 involve simple recurrence relations at each iteration. We give in the Appendix a numerical example of their application. Sufficient convergence conditions can be obtained for these schemes in a manner similar to that used in the previous sections.

Note that our method can also be applied to other "more-than-one-step-transition" systems, e.g. it may be applied to equations obtained by an imbedded Markov chain approach.

CONCLUSION

We have presented an approach to the numerical solution of a broad class of queueing problems. In most cases, an iterative scheme is necessary. The computation involved at each iteration is simple and does not require any matrix operation. Sufficient convergence conditions have been obtained, and the practical convergence speed, as illustrated in several numerical examples, appears to be good. The convergence is particularly fast if there are significant differences in transition rates, and if the iterative scheme (essentially the order in which the system states are considered) is arranged so as to exploit them. In such cases, the equivalence and decomposition approximation may yield an excellent starting point for the iteration. The relatively fast convergence together with the simplicity of the computation at each iteration and the moderate space requirements of the method justify this presentation.

REFERENCES

[1] Heinrici, P. Elements of numerical analysis. New York : John Wiley 1964.
[2] Brandwajn, A. A model of a virtual memory system. Acta Informatica 6, 365-386 (1976).

APPENDIX

(In all examples "iteration number 0" is the starting point).

1. Numerical results for the introductory example (scheme (1.8)).

$N_1=10$; $N_2=10$; $\alpha=0.5$; $\lambda_1=\lambda_2=\mu_1=\mu_2=3.0$;

ITERATION NUMBER: 0

P(N1)

	0	1	2	3	4	5	6	7	8	9	10
	.000	.000	.000	.000	.000	.000	.000	.000	.000	.000	.000

P(N2|N1)

	0	1	2	3	4	5	6	7	8	9	10
N2: 0	.091	.091	.091	.091	.091	.091	.091	.091	.091	.091	.091
N1: 1	.000	.001	.002	.004	.008	.016	.031	.063	.125	.250	.500
N1: 2	.000	.001	.002	.004	.008	.016	.031	.063	.125	.250	.500
N1: 3	.000	.001	.002	.004	.008	.016	.031	.063	.125	.250	.500
N1: 4	.000	.001	.002	.004	.008	.016	.031	.063	.125	.250	.500
N1: 5	.000	.001	.002	.004	.008	.016	.031	.063	.125	.250	.500
N1: 6	.000	.001	.002	.004	.008	.016	.031	.063	.125	.250	.500
N1: 7	.000	.001	.002	.004	.008	.016	.031	.063	.125	.250	.500
N1: 8	.000	.001	.002	.004	.008	.016	.031	.063	.125	.250	.500
N1: 9	.000	.001	.002	.004	.008	.016	.031	.063	.125	.250	.500
N1: 10	.000	.001	.002	.004	.008	.016	.031	.063	.125	.250	.500

ITERATION NUMBER: 1

P(N1)

	0	1	2	3	4	5	6	7	8	9	10
	.000	.001	.002	.004	.008	.016	.031	.063	.125	.250	.500

P(N2|N1)

	0	1	2	3	4	5	6	7	8	9	10
N2: 0	.002	.002	.004	.007	.014	.026	.049	.091	.160	.264	.382
N1: 1	.001	.001	.003	.005	.010	.019	.037	.070	.134	.250	.471
N1: 2	.001	.001	.002	.004	.008	.017	.033	.065	.127	.250	.493
N1: 3	.001	.001	.002	.004	.008	.016	.032	.063	.126	.250	.498
N1: 4	.001	.001	.002	.004	.008	.016	.031	.063	.125	.250	.500
N1: 5	.001	.001	.002	.004	.008	.016	.031	.063	.125	.250	.500
N1: 6	.001	.001	.002	.004	.008	.016	.031	.063	.125	.250	.500
N1: 7	.001	.001	.002	.004	.008	.016	.031	.063	.125	.250	.500
N1: 8	.001	.001	.002	.004	.008	.016	.031	.063	.125	.250	.500
N1: 9	.001	.001	.002	.004	.008	.016	.031	.063	.125	.250	.500
N1: 10	.000	.001	.002	.004	.008	.016	.031	.063	.125	.250	.500

ITERATION NUMBER: 13

P(N1)

0	1	2	3	4	5	6	7	8	9	10
.000	.001	.002	.004	.008	.016	.031	.063	.125	.250	.500

P(N2|N1)

N1 \ N2	0 (.000)	1 (.001)	2 (.002)	3 (.004)	4 (.008)	5 (.016)	6 (.031)	7 (.063)	8 (.125)	9 (.250)	10 (.500)
0	.005	.005	.007	.011	.019	.033	.057	.098	.162	.252	.351
1	.002	.003	.005	.007	.013	.023	.041	.075	.135	.244	.451
2	.002	.002	.003	.006	.010	.019	.035	.067	.128	.246	.482
3	.001	.002	.003	.005	.009	.017	.033	.064	.126	.248	.493
4	.001	.002	.002	.004	.008	.016	.032	.063	.125	.249	.497
5	.001	.001	.002	.004	.008	.016	.032	.063	.125	.249	.498
6	.001	.001	.002	.004	.008	.016	.031	.063	.125	.250	.499
7	.001	.001	.002	.004	.008	.016	.031	.063	.125	.250	.500
8	.001	.001	.002	.004	.008	.016	.031	.063	.125	.250	.500
9	.000	.001	.002	.004	.008	.016	.031	.063	.125	.250	.500
10	.000	.001	.002	.004	.008	.016	.031	.063	.125	.250	.500

ITERATION NUMBER: 15

P(N1)

0	1	2	3	4	5	6	7	8	9	10
.000	.001	.002	.004	.008	.016	.031	.063	.125	.250	.500

P(N2|N1)

N1 \ N2	0 (.000)	1 (.001)	2 (.002)	3 (.004)	4 (.008)	5 (.016)	6 (.031)	7 (.063)	8 (.125)	9 (.250)	10 (.500)
0	.005	.005	.007	.011	.019	.033	.057	.098	.162	.252	.351
1	.003	.003	.005	.007	.013	.023	.041	.075	.135	.244	.451
2	.002	.002	.003	.006	.010	.019	.035	.067	.128	.246	.482
3	.001	.002	.003	.005	.009	.017	.033	.064	.126	.248	.493
4	.001	.001	.002	.004	.008	.016	.032	.063	.125	.249	.497
5	.001	.001	.002	.004	.008	.016	.032	.063	.125	.249	.498
6	.001	.001	.002	.004	.008	.016	.031	.063	.125	.250	.499
7	.001	.001	.002	.004	.008	.016	.031	.063	.125	.250	.500
8	.001	.001	.002	.004	.008	.016	.031	.063	.125	.250	.500
9	.000	.001	.002	.004	.008	.016	.031	.063	.125	.250	.500
10	.000	.001	.002	.004	.008	.016	.031	.063	.125	.250	.500

$N_1=10 \qquad N_2=10 \qquad \alpha=0.5$

$\lambda_1=3 \qquad \mu_1=4$

$\lambda_2=0.3 \qquad \mu_2=0.3$

ITERATION NUMBER: 0

P(N1)

N1	0	1	2	3	4	5	6	7	8	9	10
P(N1)	.000	.000	.000	.000	.000	.000	.000	.000	.000	.000	.000

P(N2|N1)

N2→ / N1↓	0	1	2	3	4	5	6	7	8	9	10
N1:0	.091	.091	.091	.091	.091	.091	.091	.091	.091	.091	.091
N1:1	.000	.001	.002	.004	.008	.016	.031	.063	.125	.250	.500
N1:2	.000	.001	.002	.004	.008	.016	.031	.063	.125	.250	.500
N1:3	.000	.001	.002	.004	.008	.016	.031	.063	.125	.250	.500
N1:4	.000	.001	.002	.004	.008	.016	.031	.063	.125	.250	.500
N1:5	.000	.001	.002	.004	.008	.016	.031	.063	.125	.250	.500
N1:6	.000	.001	.002	.004	.008	.016	.031	.063	.125	.250	.500
N1:7	.000	.001	.002	.004	.008	.016	.031	.063	.125	.250	.500
N1:8	.000	.001	.002	.004	.008	.016	.031	.063	.125	.250	.500
N1:9	.000	.001	.002	.004	.008	.016	.031	.063	.125	.250	.500
N1:10	.000	.001	.002	.004	.008	.016	.031	.063	.125	.250	.500

ITERATION NUMBER: 5

P(N1)

N1	0	1	2	3	4	5	6	7	8	9	10
P(N1)	.006	.009	.013	.020	.030	.044	.067	.100	.150	.225	.337

P(N2|N1)

N2→ / N1↓	0	1	2	3	4	5	6	7	8	9	10
N1:0	.003	.001	.002	.004	.009	.017	.035	.069	.136	.262	.461
N1:1	.002	.001	.002	.004	.008	.017	.033	.066	.131	.256	.481
N1:2	.001	.001	.002	.004	.008	.016	.032	.064	.128	.253	.490
N1:3	.001	.001	.002	.004	.008	.016	.032	.063	.127	.251	.495
N1:4	.001	.001	.002	.004	.008	.016	.032	.063	.126	.250	.498
N1:5	.001	.001	.002	.004	.008	.016	.031	.063	.125	.250	.499
N1:6	.001	.001	.002	.004	.008	.016	.031	.063	.125	.250	.500
N1:7	.001	.001	.002	.004	.008	.016	.031	.063	.125	.250	.500
N1:8	.001	.001	.002	.004	.008	.016	.031	.063	.125	.250	.500
N1:9	.000	.001	.002	.004	.008	.016	.031	.063	.125	.250	.500
N1:10	.000	.001	.002	.004	.008	.016	.031	.063	.125	.250	.500

ITERATION NUMBER: 24

P(N1)

0	1	2	3	4	5	6	7	8	9	10
.006	.009	.013	.020	.030	.044	.067	.100	.150	.225	.337

P(N2|N1)

N2:	0	1	2	3	4	5	6	7	8	9	10
N1: 0	.011	.004	.003	.005	.009	.018	.036	.070	.137	.259	.448
N1: 1	.006	.003	.003	.005	.009	.017	.034	.067	.132	.253	.469
N1: 2	.004	.003	.003	.004	.008	.017	.033	.065	.129	.251	.484
N1: 3	.002	.002	.002	.004	.008	.016	.032	.064	.127	.250	.491
N1: 4	.001	.001	.002	.004	.008	.016	.032	.064	.126	.250	.494
N1: 5	.001	.001	.002	.004	.008	.016	.032	.063	.126	.250	.497
N1: 6	.001	.001	.002	.004	.008	.016	.032	.063	.126	.250	.498
N1: 7	.000	.001	.002	.004	.008	.016	.032	.063	.125	.250	.499
N1: 8	.000	.001	.002	.004	.008	.016	.031	.063	.125	.250	.499
N1: 9	.000	.001	.002	.004	.008	.016	.031	.063	.125	.250	.500
N1:10	.000	.001	.002	.004	.008	.016	.031	.063	.125	.250	.500

ITERATION NUMBER: 25

P(N1)

0	1	2	3	4	5	6	7	8	9	10
.006	.009	.013	.020	.030	.044	.067	.100	.150	.225	.337

P(N2|N1)

N2:	0	1	2	3	4	5	6	7	8	9	10
N1: 0	.011	.004	.003	.005	.009	.018	.036	.070	.137	.259	.448
N1: 1	.006	.003	.003	.005	.009	.017	.034	.067	.132	.253	.469
N1: 2	.004	.003	.003	.004	.008	.017	.033	.065	.129	.251	.484
N1: 3	.002	.002	.002	.004	.008	.016	.032	.064	.127	.251	.490
N1: 4	.001	.001	.002	.004	.008	.016	.032	.064	.126	.250	.494
N1: 5	.001	.001	.002	.004	.008	.016	.032	.063	.126	.250	.497
N1: 6	.001	.001	.002	.004	.008	.016	.032	.063	.126	.250	.498
N1: 7	.000	.001	.002	.004	.008	.016	.032	.063	.125	.250	.499
N1: 8	.000	.001	.002	.004	.008	.016	.031	.063	.125	.250	.499
N1: 9	.000	.001	.002	.004	.008	.016	.031	.063	.125	.250	.500
N1:10	.000	.001	.002	.004	.008	.016	.031	.063	.125	.250	.500

$$N_1=10 \qquad N_2=10 \qquad \alpha=0.5$$
$$\lambda_1=0.03 \qquad \mu_1=0.04$$
$$\lambda_2=0.3 \qquad \mu_2=0.3$$

ITERATION NUMBER: 0

P(N1)

	0	1	2	3	4	5	6	7	8	9	10
	.000	.000	.000	.000	.000	.000	.000	.000	.000	.000	.000

P(N2|N1)

	0	1	2	3	4	5	6	7	8	9	10
N2:0	.091	.091	.091	.091	.091	.091	.091	.091	.091	.091	.091
N1:1	.000	.091	.002	.004	.008	.016	.031	.063	.125	.250	.500
N1:2	.000	.001	.002	.004	.008	.016	.031	.063	.125	.250	.500
N1:3	.000	.001	.002	.004	.008	.016	.031	.063	.125	.250	.500
N1:4	.000	.001	.002	.004	.008	.016	.031	.063	.125	.250	.500
N1:5	.000	.001	.002	.004	.008	.016	.031	.063	.125	.250	.500
N1:6	.000	.001	.002	.004	.008	.016	.031	.063	.125	.250	.500
N1:7	.000	.001	.002	.004	.008	.016	.031	.063	.125	.250	.500
N1:8	.000	.001	.002	.004	.008	.016	.031	.063	.125	.250	.500
N1:9	.000	.001	.002	.004	.008	.016	.031	.063	.125	.250	.500
N1:10	.000	.001	.002	.004	.008	.016	.031	.063	.125	.250	.500

ITERATION NUMBER: 4

P(N1)

	0	1	2	3	4	5	6	7	8	9	10
	.006	.003	.013	.025	.030	.044	.067	.100	.150	.225	.337

P(N2|N1)

	0	1	2	3	4	5	6	7	8	9	10
N2:0	.033	.035	.040	.047	.058	.073	.092	.115	.142	.171	.195
N1:1	.005	.008	.011	.016	.022	.031	.047	.074	.126	.227	.432
N1:2	.001	.002	.004	.007	.011	.020	.035	.065	.125	.244	.484
N1:3	.001	.001	.002	.005	.009	.017	.032	.063	.125	.249	.496
N1:4	.001	.001	.002	.004	.008	.016	.031	.063	.125	.250	.499
N1:5	.001	.001	.002	.004	.008	.016	.031	.063	.125	.250	.500
N1:6	.001	.001	.002	.004	.008	.016	.031	.063	.125	.250	.500
N1:7	.001	.001	.002	.004	.008	.016	.031	.063	.125	.250	.500
N1:8	.001	.001	.002	.004	.008	.016	.031	.063	.125	.250	.500
N1:9	.000	.001	.002	.004	.008	.016	.031	.063	.125	.250	.500
N1:10	.000	.001	.002	.004	.008	.016	.031	.063	.125	.250	.500

Numerical results for Example 3.1

Values of model parameters :
$1/\lambda$ = 10 sec. ; $1/v_0$ = 0.5 sec. ; $1/v_1$ = 7 msec. ; $1/u_1$ = 5 msec. ;
$1/\eta$ = 3 msec. ; N = 10.

Starting point : equiprobability

ITERATION NUMBER: 0

P(N)

N:0	N:1	N:2	N:3	N:4	N:5	N:6	N:7	N:8	N:9	N:10
.091	.091	.091	.091	.091	.091	.091	.091	.091	.091	.091

P(NOIN)

N	0	1	2	3	4	5	6	7	8	9	10
N:0	1.000										
N:1	.500	.500									
N:2	.333	.333	.333								
N:3	.250	.250	.250	.250							
N:4	.200	.200	.200	.200	.200						
N:5	.167	.167	.167	.167	.167	.167					
N:6	.143	.143	.143	.143	.143	.143	.143				
N:7	.125	.125	.125	.125	.125	.125	.125	.125			
N:8	.111	.111	.111	.111	.111	.111	.111	.111	.111		
N:9	.100	.100	.100	.100	.100	.100	.100	.100	.100	.100	
N:10	.091	.091	.091	.091	.091	.091	.091	.091	.091	.091	.091

ITERATION NUMBER: 1

P(N)

N:0	N:1	N:2	N:3	N:4	N:5	N:6	N:7	N:8	N:9	N:10
.068	.136	.184	.196	.172	.124	.072	.033	.011	.002	.000

P(NOIN)

N	0	1	2	3	4	5	6	7	8	9	10
N:0	1.000										
N:1	.455	.545									
N:2	.275	.330	.395								
N:3	.187	.224	.268	.322							
N:4	.135	.161	.193	.232	.278						
N:5	.101	.121	.145	.174	.208	.250					
N:6	.078	.093	.112	.134	.160	.192	.231				
N:7	.061	.073	.088	.105	.126	.151	.181	.217			
N:8	.048	.058	.069	.083	.100	.119	.143	.172	.207		
N:9	.039	.046	.056	.067	.080	.096	.115	.138	.166	.199	
N:10	.031	.037	.045	.054	.064	.077	.093	.111	.134	.161	.193

ITERATION NUMBER: 5

P(N)

.270	.289	.210	.126	.064	.028	.010	.003	.001	.000	.000

P(NOIN)

N											
N: 0	1.000										
N: 1	.333	.667									
N: 2	.116	.327	.557								
N: 3	.044	.123	.313	.521							
N: 4	.017	.048	.122	.306	.508						
N: 5	.007	.019	.048	.121	.303	.502					
N: 6	.003	.008	.019	.048	.121	.303	.500				
N: 7	.001	.003	.008	.019	.048	.120	.301	.500			
N: 8	.000	.001	.003	.008	.019	.048	.120	.301	.499		
N: 9	.000	.000	.001	.003	.008	.019	.048	.120	.301	.499	
N:10	.000	.000	.000	.001	.003	.008	.019	.048	.120	.301	.499

ITERATION NUMBER: 7

P(N)

.270	.289	.210	.126	.064	.028	.010	.003	.001	.000	.000

P(NOIN)

N											
N: 0	1.000										
N: 1	.333	.667									
N: 2	.116	.327	.557								
N: 3	.044	.123	.312	.521							
N: 4	.017	.048	.122	.305	.508						
N: 5	.007	.019	.048	.121	.303	.503					
N: 6	.003	.008	.019	.048	.120	.301	.501				
N: 7	.001	.003	.008	.019	.048	.120	.301	.500			
N: 8	.000	.001	.003	.008	.019	.048	.120	.301	.499		
N: 9	.000	.000	.001	.003	.008	.019	.048	.120	.301	.499	
N:10	.000	.000	.000	.001	.003	.008	.019	.048	.120	.301	.499

Starting point : decomposition

Consider the closed queueing network composed of the CPU and the SM of Figure 2, obtained by "cutting off" the links with the terminals. Let n be the total number of processes in it, and denote by $p_n(n_0, i)$ the stationary probability distribution for the number at the CPU (n_0 = 0, 1,...,n), and for the CPU mode (i = 1 - user mode ; i = 2 - overhead). This probability distribution is easy to bbtain. Let

$$P_{n,n_0}(i) = \text{Prob} \{\text{CPU mode } i | n, n_0\} ,$$
$$n = 1,...,N ; \qquad n_0 = 1,...,n ;$$

and

$$P_n(n_0) = \text{Prob} \{n_0 \text{ processes at CPU}|n\} ,$$
$$n_0 = 0, 1,...,n.$$

We have

$$P_n(n_0, i) = P_n(n_0) \cdot P_{n,n_0}(i)$$

where

$$P_n(n_0) = C \prod_{j=1}^{n_0} u(n-j+1) / [\eta_1 P_{n,j}(2)] ,$$

(C is a normalization constant) ;

and $P_{n,n_0}(2)$ can be computed from the following recurrence relation :

$$P_{n,1}(2) = v_1 / [u_1(n-1) + v_1 + \eta_1]$$

$$P_{n,n_0}(2) = v_1 / [u_1(n-n_0) + v_1 + \eta_1(1-P_{n,n_0-1}(2))] ,$$

$$n_0 = 2,...,n .$$

We have, of course, $p_{n,n_0}(1) = 1-p_{n,n_0}(2)$, $n_0 = 1,...,n$; $n = 1,...,N$.

Decomposition arguments imply

$$p(n_0, i|n) \approx P_n(n_0, i),$$

and, hence, we let

$$p^o(i|n,n_0) = P_{n,n_0}(i) , \quad \text{and} \quad p^o(n_0|n) = P_n(n_0).$$

ITERATION NUMBER: 0

.270 .289 .210 .126 .064 .028 .010 .003 .001 .000 .000 .000

P(N)

P(NOIN)

	.270	.289	.210	.126	.064	.028	.010	.003	.001	.000	.000
N: 0	.000	.667									
N: 1	.333	.327	.558	.522	.508	.503	.501	.501	.500	.500	.500
N: 2	.115	.123	.312	.305	.302	.301	.301	.300	.300	.300	
N: 3	.043	.048	.122	.121	.120	.120	.120	.120	.120		
N: 4	.017	.019	.048	.048	.048	.048	.048	.048			
N: 5	.007	.008	.019	.019	.019	.019	.019				
N: 6	.003	.003	.008	.008	.008	.008					
N: 7	.001	.001	.003	.003	.003						
N: 8	.000	.000	.001	.001							
N: 9	.000	.000	.000	.000							
N:10	.000	.000	.000								

ITERATION NUMBER: 2

.270 .289 .210 .126 .064 .028 .010 .003 .001 .000 .000 .000

P(N)

P(NOIN)

	.270	.289	.210	.126	.064	.028	.010	.003	.001	.000	.000
N: 0	.000	.667									
N: 1	.333	.327	.557	.521	.508	.503	.501	.501	.500	.500	.499
N: 2	.116	.123	.312	.305	.302	.301	.301	.301	.301	.301	.301
N: 3	.044	.048	.122	.121	.120	.120	.120	.120	.120	.120	
N: 4	.017	.019	.048	.048	.048	.048	.048	.048	.048		
N: 5	.007	.008	.019	.019	.019	.019	.019	.019			
N: 6	.003	.003	.008	.008	.008	.008	.008				
N: 7	.001	.001	.003	.003	.003	.003					
N: 8	.000	.000	.001	.001	.001						
N: 9	.000	.000	.000	.000	.000						
N:10	.000	.000	.000	.000							

Numerical results for Example 3.3

Values of model parameters :

$b = 3$; $N = 10$; $\lambda_1 = 0.1$; $\mu_1 = 0.01$; $\mu_2 = 1.0$

Scheme 1

ITERATION NUMBER: 0

P(N1,N2)

N1 \ N2	0	1	2	3	4	5	6	7	8	9	10
0	.091	.045	.030	.023	.018	.015	.013	.011	.010	.003	.008
1	.045	.030	.023	.018	.015	.013	.011	.010	.009	.008	
2	.030	.023	.018	.015	.013	.011	.010	.009	.008		
3	.023	.018	.015	.013	.011	.010	.009	.008			
4	.018	.015	.013	.011	.010	.009	.008				
5	.015	.013	.011	.010	.009	.008					
6	.013	.011	.010	.009	.008						
7	.011	.010	.009	.008							
8	.010	.009	.008								
9	.009	.008									
10	.008										

ITERATION NUMBER: 15

P(N1,N2)

N1 \ N2	0	1	2	3	4	5	6	7	8	9	10
0	.000	.000	.000	.000	.000	.000	.000	.000	.000	.000	.000
1	.001	.000	.000	.000	.000	.000	.000	.000	.000	.000	
2	.006	.001	.000	.000	.000	.000	.000	.000	.000		
3	.012	.001	.000	.000	.000	.000	.000	.000			
4	.020	.001	.000	.001	.000	.000	.000				
5	.020	.000	.001	.001	.000	.000					
6	.019	.000	.001	.001	.000						
7	.059	.005	.007	.007							
8	.067	.001	.001								
9	.068	.000									
10	.697										

ITERATION NUMBER: 29

P(N1,N2)

N2:	0	1	2	3	4	5	6	7	8	9	10
N1:0	.000	.000	.000	.000	.000	.000	.000	.000	.000	.000	.000
N1:1	.002	.000	.000	.000	.000	.000	.000	.000	.000	.000	
N1:2	.003	.000	.000	.000	.000	.000	.000	.000	.000		
N1:3	.005	.001	.001	.001	.000	.000	.000	.000			
N1:4	.010	.001	.001	.001	.000	.000	.000				
N1:5	.016	.001	.001	.001	.000	.000					
N1:6	.022	.001	.001	.001	.000						
N1:7	.072	.006	.006	.007							
N1:8	.076	.001	.001								
N1:9	.069	.000									
N1:10	.694										

ITERATION NUMBER: 30

P(N1,N2)

N2:	0	1	2	3	4	5	6	7	8	9	10
N1:0	.000	.000	.000	.000	.000	.000	.000	.000	.000	.000	.000
N1:1	.001	.000	.000	.000	.000	.000	.000	.000	.000	.000	
N1:2	.003	.000	.000	.000	.000	.000	.000	.000	.000		
N1:3	.005	.001	.001	.001	.000	.000	.000	.000			
N1:4	.011	.001	.001	.001	.000	.000	.000				
N1:5	.017	.001	.001	.001	.000	.000					
N1:6	.022	.001	.001	.001	.000						
N1:7	.072	.006	.006	.007							
N1:8	.075	.001	.001								
N1:9	.069	.000									
N1:10	.694										

ITERATION NUMBER: 0

P(N1,N2)

N2:	0	1	2	3	4	5	6	7	8	9	10
N1: 0	.008	.008	.008	.008	.008	.008	.008	.008	.008	.008	.008
N1: 1	.100	.100	.100	.100	.100	.100	.100	.100	.100	.100	
N1: 2	.010	.010	.010	.010	.010	.010	.010	.010	.010		
N1: 3	.011	.011	.011	.011	.011	.011	.011	.011			
N1: 4	.013	.013	.013	.013	.013	.013	.013				
N1: 5	.015	.015	.015	.015	.015	.015					
N1: 6	.018	.018	.018	.018	.018						
N1: 7	.023	.023	.023	.023							
N1: 8	.030	.030	.030								
N1: 9	.045	.045									
N1:10	.091										

ITERATION NUMBER: 3

P(N1,N2)

N2:	0	1	2	3	4	5	6	7	8	9	10
N1: 0	.000	.000	.000	.000	.000	.000	.000	.000	.000	.000	.000
N1: 1	.002	.000	.000	.000	.000	.000	.000	.000	.000	.000	
N1: 2	.003	.000	.000	.000	.000	.000	.000	.000	.000		
N1: 3	.005	.000	.000	.000	.000	.000	.000	.000			
N1: 4	.011	.001	.001	.001	.000	.000	.000				
N1: 5	.017	.001	.001	.001	.000	.000					
N1: 6	.022	.001	.001	.001	.000						
N1: 7	.072	.006	.006	.007							
N1: 8	.075	.001	.001								
N1: 9	.069	.000									
N1:10	.694										

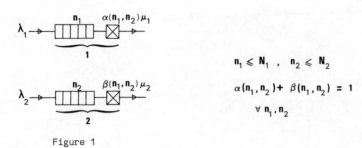

$$n_1 \leqslant N_1 \ , \quad n_2 \leqslant N_2$$

$$\alpha(n_1, n_2) + \beta(n_1, n_2) = 1$$

$$\forall \, n_1, n_2$$

Figure 1

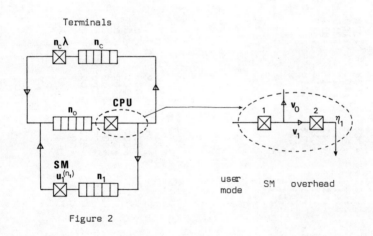

Figure 2

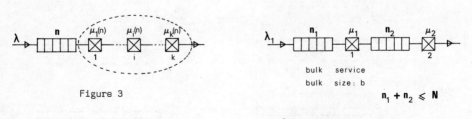

Figure 3

bulk   service
bulk   size: b

$$n_1 + n_2 \leqslant N$$

Figure 4

COMPUTER PERFORMANCE, K.M. CHANDY AND M. REISER (EDS.)
NORTH HOLLAND PUBLISHING COMPANY, 1977

THE MODELING OF SOME SCHEDULING STRATEGIES FOR AN INTERACTIVE COMPUTER SYSTEM

Y. Bard

IBM Cambridge Scientific Center
Cambridge, Massachusetts, USA

An analytic model of an interactive multiprogrammed computer
system (VM/370) decomposes the system into an inner loop,
consisting of the users receiving service, and an outer
loop, consisting of users "thinking" and waiting to receive
service. The model is solved by iteration between the two
loops. The inner loop model uses the standard closed
queueing network with multiple user classes approach. The
outer loop model relies on steady state flow equations, plus
a representation of the system's scheduling strategy, which
admits a user to service when main storage is available for
his estimated working set. Two alternative admission
policies, which are available in different versions of the
system, can be modeled: These are first-come-first-serve,
and fair-share CPU utilization, with or without priorities.
The model has been validated and used extensively in live
load situations.

I. INTRODUCTION

Many analytic models of interactive computer systems, based on queueing
networks, have appeared in the past few years [1, 2, 3, 4]. The present model,
while not radically different from most, contains some novel features. It
explicitly models the regulation of the multiprogramming level by the amount of
available storage, and it handles both FIFO and fair-share scheduling algorithms. It allows an unlimited number of user classes. The perennially difficult problem of handling the complex queueing structure of the I/O channels and
devices is handled by using an I/O system submodel, which enables one to reduce
the entire I/O subsystem to a single infinite server queue. An asymptotic
queueing model is shown to give excellent approximate solutions, which can be
used as good initial guesses for the finite model, or may in some cases be

accepted without further processing. Finally, coupled with an automatically produced characterization of an installation's workload [5], the model may be routinely used to model the effects of workload and configuration changes for a widely used complex interactive operating system, namely VM/370 [6]*.

II. TRANSACTION FLOW MODEL

The flow of transactions through a typical interactive system is depicted in Figure 1. A user seated at a terminal generates a transaction, which is classified by the system as either "trivial" or "nontrivial". In the first case, it is admitted for immediate service. In the second case, the transaction may have to wait in an "eligible set" until main storage availability permits its admission for service. Transactions receiving service are said to be in the "multiprogrammed set", while a user is said to be "dormant" from the time his transaction is completed until he has entered the next one.

Transactions, both trivial and nontrivial, may be further classified into different transaction classes. The i-th class is characterized by means of the following parameters which must be input to the model:

N_i :   No. of users entering class i transactions.

$T_{i,1}$:   Average user dormancy ("think") time.

W_i :   Average main storage required ("working set").

t_i :   Average CPU time required.

θ_i :   Average total I/O delay (see section VI for further details).

----

*   These facilities are available for use by IBM personnel only.

The workload characterization can be generated automatically for existing VM/370 workloads by means of existing measurement facilities [5].

The above description represents a simplification relative to the transaction flow in a real system. Omitted are details such as time slicing and generation of different transaction classes by the same user. Generally, a transformation can be applied to the true system representation to obtain the simplified representation given here, with no significant loss in accuracy [7].

Let $T_{i,1}$, $T_{i,2}$, and $T_{i,3}$ denote, respectively, the average time spent by a class i transaction in the dormant, eligible, and multiprogrammed sets, respectively, and let $N_{i,1}$, $N_{i,2}$, and $N_{i,3}$ be the average number of class i users in those sets at any one time. Let I_1 and I_2 denote the sets of indices corresponding to trivial and nontrivial transaction classes, respectively. The following equation is obvious:

$$(1) \quad N_{i,1} + N_{i,2} + N_{i,3} = N_i \quad (i \varepsilon I_1, I_2)$$

The Q-admission policy requires that:

$$(2) \quad S_1 + S_2 \leqslant S$$

where S is the total available main storage capacity, and S_1 and S_2 are the average amounts of main storage occupied by trivial and nontrivial users, respectively. Clearly:

$$(3) \quad S_j = \sum_{i \varepsilon I_j} N_{i,3} W_i \quad (j = 1,2)$$

According to Little's formula [8], the average number of transactions in each set is proportional to the average time spent by a transaction in that set. Thus:

$$(4) \quad N_{i,k} = \lambda_i \, T_{i,k} \quad (i \epsilon I_1, \, I_2; \, k = 1,2,3)$$

where λ_i is the class i transaction flow rate. Summing the above equations over k, we find:

$$(5) \quad N_i = \lambda_i \, (T_{i,1} + T_{i,2} + T_{i,3}) \quad (i \epsilon I_1, \, I_2)$$

Furthermore,

$$(6) \quad \frac{N_{i,k}}{N_i} = \frac{T_{i,k}}{T_{i,1} + T_{i,2} + T_{i,3}} \quad (i \epsilon I_1, \, I_2; \, k = 1,2,3)$$

By assumption, $T_{i,2} = 0$ for $i \epsilon I_1$. Hence, from (6):

$$(7) \quad N_{i,2} = \frac{T_{i,3} \, N_i}{T_{i,1} + T_{i,3}} \quad (i \epsilon I_1)$$

and,

$$(8) \quad S_1 = \sum_{i \epsilon I_1} \frac{T_{i,3} \, N_i \, W_i}{T_{i,1} + T_{i,3}}$$

Before proceeding, we must take stock of which variables are known and which must be calculated. Specifically, the following are given in the workload description:

N_i, $i\epsilon I_1$, I_2:   active users in class i

W_i, $i\epsilon I_1$, I_2:   class i working set

$T_{i,1}$, $i\epsilon I_1$, I_2:   class i think time

Furthermore, S (main storage capacity) is given in the configuration description. We shall also assume for the time being that the $T_{i,3}$ are known for all
$i\epsilon I_1$, I_2. We can now evalaute S_1, using (8). If it turns out that $S_1 \gtrsim S$, then
the system is entirely saturated with trivial transactions, and no further
analysis takes place. If $S_1 < S$, then the storage requirement for nontrivial
transactions is computed on the assumption that $T_{2,i} = 0$, $i\epsilon I_2$, i.e., that
nontrivial transactions are admitted into Q2 immediately. Analogously to (8),
this storage requirement is:

$$(9) \quad S_2^* = \sum_{i\epsilon I_2} \frac{T_{i,3} \, N_i \, W_i}{T_{i,1} + T_{i,3}}$$

Now, if $S_2^* \leqslant S-S_1$ it follows that the assumption is correct and indeed $T_{i,2} = 0$
for $i\epsilon I_2$. If $S_2^* > S-S$, storage is saturated, so that $S_2 = S-S_1$, or:

$$(10) \quad \sum_{i\epsilon I_2} \frac{T_{i,3} \, N_i \, W_i}{T_{i,1} + T_{i,2} + T_{i,3}} = S-S_1$$

The solution of this equation depends on the system scheduling discipline as
shown in the next two sections, which describe two algorithms available with
different versions of the VM/370 System [6, 9].

One could easily model constraints on resources other than main storage by
introducing appropriate inequalities analogous to (2).

III. FIFO SCHEDULER

A FIFO scheduler treats all classes equally, so that expected   admission wait time should be about the same for all. Hence we may assume

$$(11) \ T_{i,2} = Q \ (i\epsilon I_2)$$

where Q is an unknown constant. Substituting in (10) we find:

$$(12) \ \sum_{i\epsilon I_2} \frac{T_{i,1} \ N_i \ W_i}{T_{i,1} + Q + T_{i,3}} = S-S_1$$

This is a single equation in the single unknown Q, which may be solved, say by means of the Newton-Raphson method.

IV. FAIR SHARE SCHEDULER

A fair share scheduler [9] guarantees equal amounts of CPU time to all CPU-bound users. Let t_i $(i\epsilon I_2)$ be the CPU time required per transaction, which is given in the workload description.   The CPU consumption rate for each class i active user is

$$(13) \ U_i = \frac{\lambda_i t_i}{N_i}$$

Substituting for λ_i from (5), we find that $U_i = t_i/(T_{i,1} + T_{i,2} + T_{i,3})$. Equating all U_i to a common "fair share" value U, we obtain the equation:

$$(14) \ T_{i,1} + T_{i,2} + T_{i,3} = \frac{t_i}{U} \quad (i\epsilon I_2)$$

which, when substituted in (10) yields:

$$\sum_{i \epsilon I_2} \frac{T_{i,3} \, N_i \, W_i \, U}{t_i} = S - S_1$$

or,

$$(15) \quad U = \frac{S - S_1}{\sum\limits_{i \epsilon I_2} \dfrac{T_{i,3} \, N_i \, W_i}{t_i}}$$

and, from (14):

$$(16) \quad T_{i,2} = \frac{t_i}{U} - T_{i,1} - T_{i,2} \quad (i \epsilon I_2)$$

It may turn out that (16) gives negative values for some $i \epsilon I_2$. This indicates that the corresponding user classes are not CPU bound. Let J be the set of indices for which (16) is negative. We then assign

$$T_{i,2} = 0 \quad (i \epsilon J)$$

and modify (15) to compute a new value of U:

$$(17) \quad U = \frac{S - S_1 - \sum\limits_{i \epsilon J} \dfrac{T_{i,3} \, N_i \, W_i}{T_{i,1} + T_{i,3}}}{\sum\limits_{i \epsilon I_2 - J} \dfrac{T_{i,3} \, N_i \, W_i}{t_i}}$$

If resources other than the CPU are to be fair shared, only a redefinition of the t_i is required. In particular, the t_i may be defined as a weighted sum of different resources used per transaction.

The fair share scheduler permits user priorities to be specified. These priorities may be translated into relative CPU utilizations [9].

The priorities could be modeled as follows:

Let b_i be the relative CPU utilization assigned to members of user class i. Hence, instead of having $U_i = U$ for all $i \epsilon I_2$, we now have $U_i = b_i$ U, and (15) must be modified to:

$$(18) \quad U = \frac{S - S_1}{\sum_{i \epsilon I_2} \frac{T_{i,3} N_i W_i b_i}{t_i}}$$

Equation (16) becomes:

$$(19) \quad T_{i,2} = \frac{t_i}{b_i U} - T_{i,1} - T_{i,3}$$

and (17) is also modified correspondingly.

If main storage capacity is large enough to admit all transactions immediately, the Resource Management PRPQ still allocates compute-bound users equal shares of CPU time. This is achieved by assigning to users in the multiprogrammed set dispatching priorities inversely related to their CPU utilizations. Our model fails to take note of this effect. The model also fails to predict the response time degradation suffered by users who generate trivial transactions at so fast a rate that they become CPU bound.

V. OVERALL SYSTEM MODEL

Once the $T_{i,j}$ are computed, all other quantities are easily determined. In particular, we obtain:

$$(20) \quad N_{i,3} = \frac{T_{i,3} \, N_i}{T_{i,1} + T_{i,2} + T_{i,3}} \quad (i \epsilon I_1, \ I_2)$$

Recall that $N_{i,3}$ is the average number of class i users who are in the multiprogrammed set. When in that set, users receive CPU bursts, execute I/O operations, etc. These events occur frequently, on a milliseconds time scale, while Figure 1 state transitions occur relatively infrequently, on a seconds time scale. Hence, to the rest of the system, the multiprogrammed set appears to be in an equilibrium state. The system may, therefore, be decomposed [10], and the multiprogrammed set may be treated as a closed queueing network with a constant user population $N_{i,3}$ $(i \epsilon I_1, \ I_2)$. A suitable queueing network model (see Sections VI and VII) may be used to find the steady state solution for the network. This solution yields estimates for the network residence times, which are the $T_{i,3}$. We have, therefore, the makings of an iterative procedure:

(i)   Assume initial guesses for the $T_{i,2}$ and $T_{i,3}$.

(ii)   Apply the transaction flow model to compute the $N_{i,3}$.

(iii)   Apply the queueing network model to recompute the $T_{i,3}$.

(iv)   Return to step (ii).

The cycle is broken when values of $T_{i,2} + T_{i,3}$ from successive iterations do not differ significantly. Although we have no convergence proof, experience with hundreds of practical cases shows that convergence generally takes place in two to ten iterations, where as initial guesses we take $T_{i,2} = 0$ and $T_{i,3}$ to be equal to the CPU time plus the sum of all channel data transfer times for all I/O's generated by a class i transaction. To guard against the possibility of infinte looping, if convergence has not been attained after twenty iterations, the program terminates with a warning message.

VI. MULTIPROGRAMMED SET MODEL

The multiprogrammed users cycle among a set of queues: CPU queue, channel queues, and device queues. To compute the service time at each I/O channel and device, an I/O system submodel is required. This submodel takes as inputs the record lengths, placement of data sets on devices, and access rates to all data sets. It turns out that models of this type [11, 12, 13] also compute, at little additional cost, the average response time to each I/O request. Let θ_i be the sum of response times to all I/O requests generated by a class i transaction. This is the total delay suffered by this transaction due to its I/O activity. But the same delay would be suffered by the transaction if all the channel and device queues were replaced by a single infinite-server queue with service time θ_i. Thus, the original network may be replaced by a two-queue network, consisting of a single-server CPU queue and an infinite-server I/O queue.

The convolution algorithm [14] applied to this network works as follows: An L-dimensional array G is initialized as follows:

$$(21) \quad G(j_1, j_2, \ldots, j_L) = \prod_{i=1}^{L} \frac{\theta_i^{j_i}}{j_i!} \quad (j_i = 0, 1, \ldots, N_{i,3}^*)$$

where $N_{i,3}^*$ is the smallest integer containing $N_{i,3}$, and L is the number of transaction classes.

This represents the infinite-server. The array G is transformed by applying the following feed-back filter representing the CPU queue:

$$(22) \quad G\,(j_1, j_2, \ldots, j_L) \leftarrow G(j_1, j_2, \ldots, j_L) +$$

$$+ \sum_{(i\,|\,j_i>0)} t_i\, G\,(j_1, \ldots, j_i-1, \ldots, j_L)$$

where, as before, t_i is the CPU time per class i transaction. Equation (22) must be applied in order of increasing values of the indices. The expected time in the multiprogrammed set for class i transactions with a population of $N_{1,3}^*$ is now given by:

$$(23) \quad T_{i,3}^* = \frac{N_{i,3}^*\, G\,(N_{1,3}^*,\, N_{2,3}, \ldots, N_{L,3})}{G\,(N_{1,3}^*, \ldots, N_{i,3}^* -1, \ldots N_{L,3}^*)}$$

Similar equations hold for any other integral user population not exceeding $N_{i,3}^*$. To determine average responses $T_{i,3}$ at the (possibly) non-integral population $N_{i,3}$, a set of L+1 integral populations surrounding $N_{i,3}$ is selected, the corresponding responses are computed, and $T_{i,3}$ is estimated by interpolation.

VII. ASYMPTOTIC MULTIPROGRAMMED SET MODEL

The computational and storage demands of the algorithm described in the preceding section grow rapidly as the number of transaction classes and the multiprogramming level increase. It is, therefore, of interest to determine what happens as the $N_{i,3}$ increase beyond bounds, and whether such asymptotic results can provide useful approximations in practical cases.

Before proceeding, we define the following quantities:

$N = \sum_i N_{i,3}$ is the total multiprogramming level.

$a_i = N_{i,3}/N$ is the fraction of class i transactions in the multiprogrammed set.

x_j = Fraction of multiprogrammed transactions in the j-th server queue.

$\tau_{i,j}$ = Average j-th server service time for a class i transaction.

$f_j(n_j)$ = j-th server service rate (number of simultaneously busy servers) when there are n_j transactions in its queue. Clearly, on the average, $n_j = x_j N$.

Assume that N approaches infinity in such a way that the a_i remain constant (i.e., all transaction classes increase proportionately). Then, it has been shown [15] that for a network satisfying the separability criteria with processor sharing servers, the x_j approach values which can be computed using the following iterative scheme:

$$(24) \quad x_j^{(v+1)} = x_j^{(v)} \sum_i \frac{a_i \, \tau_{i,j}}{f_j(x_j^{(v)} N) \sum_k \frac{\tau_{i,k} \, x_k^{(v)}}{f_k(x_k^{(v)} N)}}$$

where the superscript v refers to the iteration number. The iterations may be started with any set of positive x_j . In our case, we have two servers:

$j=1$ is the single server CPU, with $\tau_{i,1} = t_i$ and $f_1(n_1) = 1$.

$j=2$ is the infinite server I/O subsystem, with $\tau_{i,2} = \theta_i$ and $f_2(n_2) = n_2$.

Substituting these values into (24) we find after simplification:

$$x_1^{(v+1)} = x_1^{(v)} \sum_i \frac{a_i\, t_i}{t_i\, x_1^{(v)} + \dfrac{\theta_i}{N}}$$

$$x_2^{(v+1)} = \sum_i \frac{a_i\, \theta_i}{N\,(t_i x_i^{(v)} + \dfrac{\theta_i}{N})}$$

It is clear that meaningful results can be obtained only if it is assumed that the θ_i increase in proportion with N. Hence, let $\beta_i = \theta_i/N$ be assumed constant. Then:

$$(25)\quad x_1^{(v+1)} = x_1^{(v)} \sum_i \frac{a_i\, t_i}{t_i\, x_i^{(v)} + \beta_i}$$

$$(26)\quad x_2^{(v+1)} = \sum_i \frac{a_i\, \beta_i}{t_i\, x_i^{(v)} + \beta_i}$$

It is now possible to apply the iterative scheme (25) by itself, then substitute x_1 in (26) to compute x_2 directly (or, more simply, set $x_2 = 1-x_1$). We shall show, however, that even (25) need not be used in some cases.   From (25) it is evident that:

$$x_1^{(v)} < x_1^{(0)} \left[\sum_i \frac{a_i t_i}{\beta_i}\right]^v$$

Therefore, if $\sum_i a_i\, t_i/\beta_i < 1$, then $x = \lim_{v\to\infty} x_1^{(v)} = 0$.

We shall now compute the average time $T_{i,3}$ spent by a class i transaction in the multiprogrammed set when N is large. The time spent in the I/O subsystem is θ_i, and the CPU service time is t_i. Hence

$$(27) \quad T_{i,2} \leq \theta_i + t_i$$

When $x_1 = 0$, CPU queueing time is negligible compared to $\theta_i = N\beta_i$, and (27) holds with equality sign. If $x_1 > 0$, then the CPU queue contains, on the average, Nx_1 transactions, and, for large N is almost never empty. Hence CPU utilization is 100%, and the CPU utilization per transaction in queue is $1/Nx_1$. To obtain t_i seconds of CPU time, a transaction must spend $t_i Nx_1$ seconds in the CPU queue. Therefore,

$$(28) \quad T_{i,3} = \theta_i + t_i Nx_1$$

but, because of (27), this result can be valid only for $Nx_1 \geq 1$. We may combine this remark with equation (28) into the single result:

$$(29) \quad T_{i,3} = \theta_i + \max (t_i, N_1 x_1 t_i)$$

Equation (29) gives remarkably accurate results even for fairly small values of N, as illustrated in Tables 1 and 2, and its computation is much faster than (23). In view of this, the following strategy has been adopted for the model:

(a) Apply the overall iterative scheme of Section V using equation (29) in step (iii) until convergence is obtained (no value of $T_{i,2} + T_{i,3}$ has changed by more than 5% from one iteration to the next).

(b) If storage capacity is insufficient to contain the entire G array, or if N >15, terminate. Otherwise:

(c) Continue the iterations of Section V, using equation (23) in step (iii), until once more convergence is obtained.

In small problems, this scheme is slightly slower than using equation (23) from the start, since the total number of iterations is somewhat increased. In large problems, this scheme can be several fold faster, since generally only one or two applications of equation (23) are required.

VIII. MODEL OUTPUTS

Once the model has converged, many performance measures can be computed easily from available quantities. We list some of these below:

Class i transaction average response time:

$$T_i = T_{i,2} + T_{i,3}$$

Note that this is the internal response time, i.e., the time elapsed from the system scheduler's recognition of the transaction's arrival until the CPU's completion of the transaction processing. It does not include transmission delays between the CPU and the user's terminal. To the model, such delays appear as part of the think time.

Class i transaction rate, from equation (4):

$$\lambda_i = N_{i,3}/T_{i,3}$$

Class i CPU utilization:

$$V_i = \lambda_i\, t_i$$

Total CPU utilization:

$$V = \sum_i V_i$$

I/O channel and device utilizations are obtained as by-products of the I/O system submodel. Furthermore, the total response time T_i can be easily broken up into service and queueing times for the different system resources.

IX. MODEL VALIDATION

The model is typically used in the following fashion: The VM/370 Monitor facility [8] is turned on to collect data for, say, two hours of peak load time, on a running VM/370 installation. The data are reduced to produce:

1. A summary of the system's performance during the measured period.

2. A characterization of the installation's workload.

The latter is input to the model, together with the description of the actual system configuration. The model's output is then compared to the observed system performance. If the two match to the user's satisfaction, the model is considered validated for this installation. It is now possible to vary the model's inputs to reflect changes in workload, configuration, or both, and thus to explore the system's predicted performance under a wide variety of circumstances. If the match is unsatisfactory, the model can be "tuned" by manipulating some of the more doubtful input parameters - e.g., I/O block lengths, seek patterns, and assignment of disk areas to the various user classes.

Table 3 presents the results of several such validations, which show that the model can reasonably match the observed performance of the measured systems. Of greater interest, however, is the question of how accurately the model can predict the performance of a projected system, rather than of the actually measured one. Since a true workload measured on an existing system cannot generally be reproduced after the system has been changed, this type of validation requires a controlled benchmark environment. For this purpose, a benchmark stream consisting of four user classes (see Table 4) was run repeatedly on a System/370 Model 158 with varying main storage sizes and total number of users. The data from one of these runs were used to derive the workload characterization, and the model was then invoked to predict the performance for all the runs. Comparisons of predicted and measured performance appear in Table 5. Once more, the accuracy of the predictions is quite adequate for the purposes of configuration and capacity planning.

All the above validation results were attained without any attempt to "tune" the model. The results, therefore, indicate what can be achieved by an inexperienced user in a limited amount of time.

X. CONCLUSIONS

The model described here has been programmed in APL for use by IBM personnel. A typical case requires 2-20 seconds of System/370 Model 168 time.

Improved model accuracy can probably be best attained through better modeling of:

1. The paging process - particularly better prediction of the relation between paging rate, system configuration, and workload characteristics.

2. Priority dispatching within the multiprogrammed set.

Our model ignores all delays incurred in data transmission between the CPU and remote user terminals. To predict response times actually experienced by users at remote terminals, the model would have to be coupled to a data transmission network model. The same type of iteration described in Section V could be used to alternate between the network model and the host VM/370 model.

While some of the details are specific to the VM/370 system, the model should be readily applicable to many other interactive multiprogrammed computer systems. Perhaps the most important feature of VM/370 which makes it easy to model is that the only interference between users in the multiprogrammed set is through contention for physical resources: CPU and I/O paths. Blocking through software locks to prevent simultaneous access to data items is largely absent. However, it should be possible to model software locks so the θ_i computed by the I/O subsystem model reflect these delays, leaving the logic of the rest of the model unchanged. The possibility of modeling other scheduling algorithms would have to be investigated on a case by case basis.

XI. REFERENCES

1. A. Sekino, Performance Evaluation of Multiprogrammed Time-Sharing Computer Systems, MIT Project MAC Report TR-103, Cambridge, Mass. (1972).

2. Y. Bard, An Analytic Model of CP-67 and VM/370, in Computer Architectures and Networks, E. Gelenbe and R. Mahl (eds.), North Holland Publishing Co., Amsterdam (1974), pp. 419-460.

3. J. E. Neilson, An Analytic Performance Model of a Multiprogrammed Batch-Timeshared Computer, Proceedings of the International Symposium on Computer Performance Modeling, Measurement, and Evaluation, Cambridge, Mass. (1976), pp. 59-70

4. M. Reiser, Interactive Modeling of Computer Systems, IBM Systems Journal, 309-327 (1976).

5. Y . Bard, A Characterization of VM/370 Workloads, Proceedings of the International Workshop on Modelling and Performance Evaluation of Computer Systems, Stresa, Italy (1976), pp. 35-56.

6. IBM Virtual Machine Facility/370, Introduction, Form No. GC20-1800, IBM Data Processing Division, White Plains, N.Y. (1972).

7. Y. Bard, An Analytic Model of the VM/370 System, IBM Cambridge Scientific Center Report GC320-2121, Cambridge, Mass. (1977).

8. J.D.C. Little, A Proof of the Queueing Formula L= W, Operations Research 9, 383-387 (1961).

9. VM/370 Resource Management Programming RPQ PO-9006, Programmer and System Logic Guide, Form No. LY20-1996-0, IBM Data Processing Division, White Plains, N.Y. (1976).

10. P. J. Courtois, Decomposability, Instabilities, and Saturation in Multiprogrammed Systems, Communications of the ACM 18, 371-377 (1975).

11. P. H. Seaman, R. A. Lind, and T. L. Wilson, On Teleprocessing System Design, Part IV: An Analysis of Auxiliary Storage Activity, IBM Systems J. 5, 158-170 (1966).

12. Y. Bard, Task Queueing in Auxiliary Storage Devices with Rotational Position Sensing, Technical Report G320-2070, IBM Cambridge Scientific Center, Cambridge, Mass. (1971).

13. N. C. Wilhelm, A General Model for the Performance of Disk Systems, J ACM 24, 14-31 (1977).

14. M. Reiser and H. Kobayashi, Queueing Networks with Multiple Closed Chains: Theory and Computational Algorithms, IBM J. Research and Development 19, 283-294 (1975).

15. B. Pittel and M. Reiser, Some Asymptotic Results for Closed Exponential Queueing Networks, Including Cases with Processor Sharing and with Blocking, Proceedings ORSA-TIMS National Meeting, Miami, 1976.

No. of Users in Multiprogrammed Set		Time in Multiprogrammed Set Finite model (eq. 23) Asymptotic model (eq. 29)	
$N_{1,3}$	$N_{2,3}$	$T_{1,3}$	$T_{2,3}$
1	1	4.00 3.56	2.67 2.28
2	2	7.44 7.53	4.37 4.27
3	3	11.43 11.52	6.31 6.26
4	4	15.45 15.52	8.30 8.26
5	5	19.46 19.51	10.29 10.26
10	10	39.48 39.51	20.27 20.25
4	1	9.78 9.82	5.50 5.41
8	2	19.79 19.81	10.45 10.40
16	4	39.79 39.80	20.42 20.40

Table 1

Comparison of asymptotic and finite multiprogrammed

set models, with $t_i = 2, 1$ and $\theta_i = 1, 1$.

No. of Users in Multiprogrammed Set			Time in Multiprogrammed Set Finite model (eq. 23) Asymptotic Model (eq. 29)		
$N_{1,3}$	$N_{2,3}$	$N_{3,3}$	$T_{1,3}$	$T_{2,3}$	$T_{3,3}$
1	2	3	19.19 20.87	18.51 17.43	8.71 8.14
2	4	6	53.28 54.98	34.57 34.49	14.03 13.83
4	8	12	125.31 126.12	70.02 70.06	25.77 25.69
8	16	24	269.32 269.72	141.82 141.86	49.66 49.62
3	2	1	28.46 29.17	22.47 21.59	10.00 9.53
6	4	2	63.48 64.04	39.39 39.02	15.60 15.34
12	8	4	135.05 135.39	74.84 74.69	27.36 27.23
24	16	8	278.86 279.04	146.58 146.52	51.24 51.17

Table 2

Comparison of Asymptotic and Finite Multiprogrammed

Set Models, with t_i = 6, 3, 1 and θ_i = 2, 8, 5.

CPU Model	Average Logged Users	Percent CPU Utilization		Percent Virtual CPU Time		Average Trivial Response (Seconds)		Average Nontrivial Response (Seconds)	
		Measured	Predicted	Measured	Predicted	Measured	Predicted	Measured	Predicted
135	4	17.1	17.2	5.3	5.2	0.7	1.0	19.0	24.1
145	8	84.0	84.8	42.5	42.9	0.25	0.24	3.9	3.1
145	15	96.6	97.4	40.8	41.4	0.51	0.44	26.6	19.7
155-II	20	22.2	22.2	6.7	6.6	0.05	0.06	1.2	1.1
155-II	23	36.9	35.7	10.7	10.3	0.08	0.11	2.8	3.6
158	37	59.2	55.4	31.5	28.7	0.21	0.26	21.8	18.4
158	46	70.3	69.0	37.8	36.7	0.14	0.12	2.5	1.6
158	24	68.8	71.3	52.2	55.5	0.07	0.09	6.1	5.3
168	72	36.0	35.2	14.5	14.6	0.13	0.11	7.8	6.7
168	117	96.3	99.7	56.0	57.9	0.46*	0.41	8.0	9.7
						0.48*	0.53	13.9	10.7
						0.55*	0.58	19.2	19.2
						0.83*	0.73	28.3	26.0

Table 3

Validation of Model on Real Workloads

Note: Predictions differ somewhat from those presented in 4 due to changes in the model.

* These response times refer to four separate user classes. Classification was based on ratio of trivial to nontrivial transactions.

Class Name	Description	Number of Users in Workload With Total User Number =		
		20	40	60
TRVU	Generates a trivial transaction after every 10 seconds of think time	8	16	24
MEDU	Generates a nontrivial transaction (FORTRAN compilation) after every 40 seconds of think time	8	15	23
HVYA	Generates a continuous stream of PL/1 compilations, FORTRAN compilations, and assemblies	2	4	6
HVYB	Generates a continuous stream of assemblies	2	5	7

Table 4

Description of Benchmark Workloads

Run	Main Storage Size (K Bytes)	No. of Users	Percent CPU Utilization		Percent Virtual CPU Time		Average Response* (Seconds)		
			Measured	Predicted	Measured	Predicted		Measured	Predicted
1	512	20	48.4	48.0	35.0	29.7	TRVU	0.33	0.16
							MEDU	32.0	50.5
							HVYA	36.7	46.0
							HVYB	44.0	45.8
2	1024	20	81.1	95.8	58.1	67.4		0.31	0.21
								15.0	12.2
								15.5	13.7
								16.3	12.3
3**	1024	40	84.4	91.9	58.4	59.9		0.38	0.25
								49.1	49.8
								38.8	46.0
								45.8	43.8
4	1024	60	86.7	82.2	50.7	48.4		0.41	0.26
								127.7	122.4
								75.1	83.7
								84.6	84.6
5	2048	40	96.8	100	69.3	73.4		0.25	0.31
								44.8	34.0
								32.6	38.2
								30.0	33.6
6	2048	60	98.5	100	67.5	69.1		0.34	0.44
								78.2	76.5
								61.7	60.8
								57.5	55.1

Table 5

Validation of Model on Benchmark Workload

* Response times for HVYA and HVYB are per second of virtual CPU time.
** Workload characterization derived from run No. 3

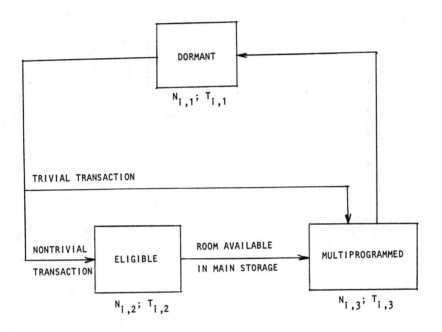

Figure 1: Transaction Flow

COMPUTER PERFORMANCE, K.M. CHANDY AND M. REISER (EDS.)
NORTH HOLLAND PUBLISHING COMPANY, 1977

AN EMPIRICAL EVALUATION OF ANALYTICAL MODELS
FOR COMPUTER SYSTEM PERFORMANCE PREDICTION

M. A. Diethelm
Honeywell Information Systems
Phoenix, Arizona, USA

The results of an evaluation of the computer system
performance prediction capability of a number of
analytical computer performance models are presented.
The evaluation is based upon a set of controlled
measurement experiments made on Honeywell 6000 series
systems. The evaluation indicates the particular
areas of weakness of each model structure as well as
provides a set of quantitative model prediction
errors. A model which includes both channels and
devices in its disc subsystem representation is
shown to provide the most consistently accurate
performance predictions. The generality of the
Honeywell system based evaluation is tested by a
limited analysis using previously published IBM
system measurement data.

1.0 INTRODUCTION

There has been in the past few years a surge of enthusiasm for the
application of analytical models to the problem of characterizing
current system performance and quantitatively predicting proposed
future system performance.

The application of analytical models based on queueing theory is
directed toward answering questions about the effects on system
performance caused by changes in the system hardware structure,
operating system software structure, and/or the workload to be processed. While several such applications have been reported to be
successful (cf. 2,10,15) some of the reported results are somewhat
unsettling. Rose (15) for example states, "It is, in actual practice, very difficult with current analytical techniques and measurement devices to accurately model and measure the I/O channel behavior
of modern computer systems". Even after a numerical model
"calibration", Rose reported 20% errors in predicted CPU utilization
and 6 to 28% errors in channel utilization for an IBM 370/155 system
(14; 108). Bhandiwad and Williams (2) reported good success in
modelling IBM 370/145 systems but admitted the fallibility of the
model structure in the I/O area, "Representation of channels ... is
not faithfully done ... but channel utilizations are low so we
proceed confident that errors introduced on their account will remain

low". Software structures have also caused wrinkles in the veneer
of general model success. Due to the IBM practice of allocating
main memory prior to allocation of peripherals, the peripheral wait
time can become a significant portion of memory residence time.
This means that an area of memory is tied up but not eligible for
processing by the active system resources. To account for this,
both Bhandiwad and Williams and Giammo (10) included a tape mount
delay stage in their model. While this technique was successful,
it is not general and is completely inappropriate for H6000/GCOS
systems. These reported experiences indicate that the potential
usefulness of an analytical model is very much dependent upon the
structural relationships between the model and the system being
modelled. A more general structural characteristic of current
systems is the presence of a disc subsystem consisting of one or
more data transfer channels and a number of moveable head data
storage devices. Representation of both the channels and device
configuration of a disc subsystem has been omitted in analytical
models to data as evidenced by the above statements of Rose and
Bhandiwad and Williams.

This paper reports the results of an evaluation of the computer
system performance prediction capability of a number of analytical
models. The evaluation is based upon a set of controlled measurement experiments made on Honeywell large scale computer systems.
The analytical models included in the evaluation were the following.

1. The deterministic (constant service time) and machine repairman
   (exponential service time) models presented by Boyse and Warn (3).

2. The "classical" central server form of queueing network model
   including I/O servers to represent either devices or channels
   (cf. 2, 4, 8, 10, 14).

3. An extension to the "classical" central server model which
   includes both channels and devices among the I/O servers (7).

4. A two class central server model which includes both disc
   channels and devices (7).

The system configuration elements which were varied in the experiments
included the following.

>   1. The number of disc channels and devices.

>   2. The quantity of main memory.

>   3. The central processor capability.

>   4. Time sharing load.

The next section briefly describes each of the models included in
the evaluation. Then the models are evaluated by comparing their
predictions to measurement results. The generality of this

Honeywell system based evaluation is then addressed by a brief
evaluation of the central server form models' results compared to
previously published (14, 15) IBM system measurement data.

2.0 ANALYTICAL MODELS

The following paragraphs briefly describe each model included in the
evaluation including the input quantities required for each.

2.1 Deterministic Model (DM)

The "constant service time" form of deterministic model can be used
to estimate computer system performance effects for either a batch
or time sharing workload (but not both). Figure 1 depicts this
model. In this model there are N jobs known to the system. Only K
jobs may be processed at a time, i.e., the multiprogramming depth is
K, therefore, N-K jobs are always waiting for a place in the set of
K actively processing jobs. The processing system is represented as
a single central processor server and K I/O servers, one for each of
the K jobs actively processing. The service times at the CPU and
the K I/O devices are constants which are input quantities. Each
I/O server has the same constant service time. The inputs required
for this model are:

N : Total number of jobs in the system,

K : Multiprogramming depth,

S : Central processor service time per job,

I : I/O device service time per job,

U : Time sharing user think time (optional).

The model produces for each set of inputs estimates of the throughput (jobs per unit time), response or turn around time (time for a
job from entry into the system until completion of processing), and
the central processor server utilization (Reference: 3).

2.2 Machine Repairman·Model (MRM)

The same model shown in Figure 1 can be analysed with the constant
service time assumption replaced with the assumption that service
times are randomly distributed according to a negative exponential
probability distribution function. The solution under this assumption
follows the form of the machine repairman queueing model where the K
I/O servers are the "machines" and the central processor server
represents the "repairman". While the solution form is much different,
the usage of this model is very similar to the deterministic model.
The input and output quantities are the same with the philosophical
difference that for this model the input service times are the mean
values for exponentially distributed service time variables. Similarly,
the output performance estimates are mean values. (Reference: 3)

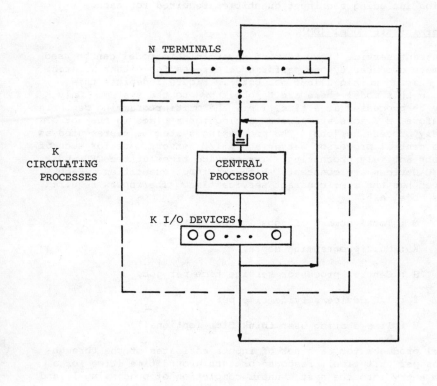

"STRAIGHTFORWARD" MODEL

FIGURE 1

2.3 Central Server Model (CSM)

Figure 2 shows the central server model. This model is a special
queueing network form and is shown as representing the computer
system by a central processor server and three peripheral servers.
Each server provides service from its own unique exponentially distributed service time distribution. Each server may have a state-
dependent service characteristic whereby the rate at which service
is provided is a function of the number of jobs at that server.
K jobs (K is the multi-programming depth) constantly circulate among
the servers in the network with routings determined randomly by the
given branching probabilities (p_i). All jobs obtain central processor
service on each trip through the network. Each then receives service
from one of the peripheral servers as randomly directed by the p_i.
Following this peripheral service the job returns to the central
processor server and begins another cycle.

The inputs required for this model are:

    K: Multiprogramming depth,

    p_i: Branching probability from the central processor
         server to the i-th peripheral server, (or N_i, the
         mean number of accesses to the i-th server per job),

    I_i: Mean service time for the i-th peripheral server,

    C: Mean central processor service time.

If any server is to be state dependent, the service time factors for
each possible number of customers at that server must also be input.
The quantities p_i and I_i may be replaced by their product, the mean
total peripheral i service time per job, if more convenient for the
analysis.

The outputs from this model, which is basically a model of batch
processing, include estimates of the mean job throughput, turnaround
time, and utilization of each of the servers. (References: 4, 5, 8)

2.4 Central Server Model With Disc Subsystem (CSMD)

Figure 3 shows a central server model enhanced by a more complete
representation of a disc storage subsystem. The single disc subsystem server of Figure 2 has been replaced by an imbedded queueing
network which has a server to represent the data channel and a
server for each of the disc storage devices. The imbedded disc subsystem branching probabilities, q_i, represent the proportionate
utilization of each of the devices in the subsystem. The channel
service time represents the data transfer time for a data record and
some, or all, of the rotational latency time dependent upon the
latency reduction capabilities of the subsystem. The mean seek time
is the device service time which may be also augmented by all or
some part of the latency time. This model requires as input data
(in place of the usual Central Server Model peripheral data) the

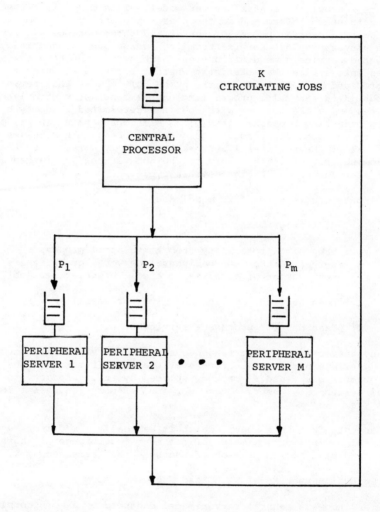

CENTRAL SERVER MODEL

FIGURE 2

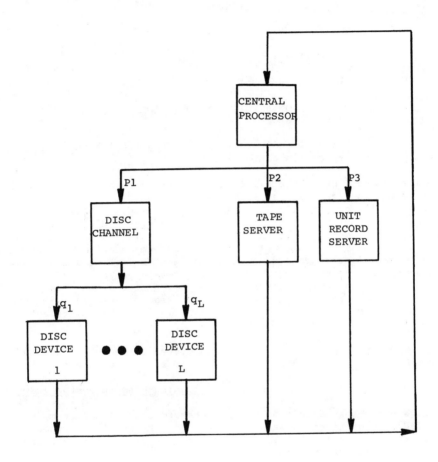

<u>CENTRAL SERVER MODEL WITH DISK SUBSYSTEM</u>

FIGURE 3

quantities necessary to describe the average job usage of the disc
subsystem:

N: The mean number of disc accesses per job,

L: The number of devices,

D: The mean data transfer time,

A: The mean latency time,

M: The mean seek time,

q_i: Proportionate utilization of the i-th disc
device, and

X: A binary indicator of the subsystem latency
reduction capability

Figures 4 and 5 shown the similarity in structure between the disc
subsystem and a central server model representation of it. For
computational convenience the disc subsystem model can be solved
independently of the total system model yielding the subsystem
throughput (accesses per unit time) as a function of the number of
access requestssimultaneously in the subsystem (multiprogramming
depth equivalent). This throughput is then the set of state dependent service rates to be used in the total system model for a
single state dependent server representation of the disc subsystem.
This is an approach similar to that proposed by Rice (13) although
the subsystem model Rice proposed has a significantly different
mathematical structure.

This model produces estimates of mean system throughput, mean turnaround time per job and server utilizations. (Reference : 7)

2.5 Two Class Central Server Model Including Disc Subsystem (CSMD2)

Figure 6 shows an extension of the enhanced central server model to
include two distinct classes of jobs. For the specific purposes of
this research these two classes were defined to be batch processing
jobs and time sharing jobs.

On Figure 6 the routing probabiliteis for the batch jobs are indicated by αi and for time sharing jobs as βi. Only the time
sharing jobs are routed to an additional server in the network which
represents the time sharing terminals. The mean service time of this
server is the average time sharing user think time (plus line transmission time) and the server is modelled as a state dependent server
such that no queueing delay is ever encountered. For the central
processor, tape, and unit record servers, unique mean server time
requirements may be specified for each type of job (b.n. service
discipline is processor-shared, not first-come-first served). For
the disc subsystem, however, the service rate quantities of mean
data transfer, latency seek times are the same for any user. The

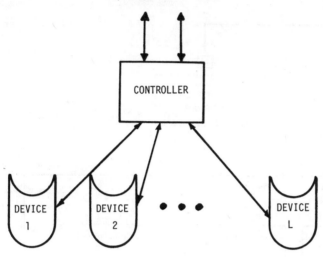

DISC STORAGE SUBSYSTEM

FIGURE 4

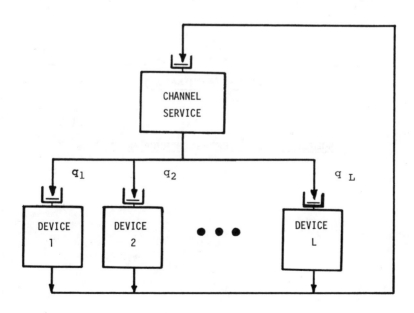

CENTRAL SERVER MODEL OF DISC SUBSYSTEM

FIGURE 5

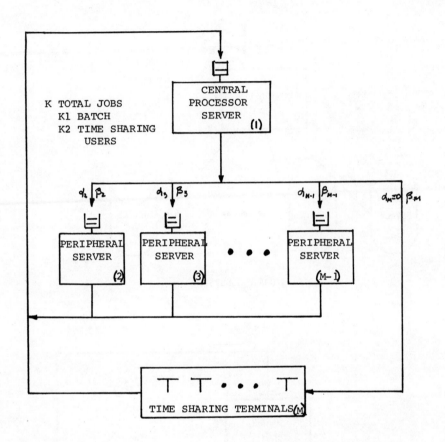

MULTIPLE CLASS CENTRAL SERVER MODEL

FIGURE   6

number of accesses (hence routing probability to the disc subsystem) may be unique for each user class however. State dependent service factors must also be input for appropriate servers.

With the additions noted above, this model requires essentially the same inputs as the previously discussed central server model with disc subsystems. The outputs produced include throughput, turn-around time and server utilization for each class of user.

This model can also be used to model two distinct classes of batch jobs (no time-sharing jobs) by eliminating the terminal server. State-dependent service rate factors may also be used if desired. The service discipline at all servers with job class unique service rates is processor shared as dictated by the mathematical solution assumptions of the model. (References: 1, 16, 7)

Another interesting multiple class model is the numerical model presented by Gaver and Humfeld (9). This model was not included in the evaluation for time and logistical reasons but is of interest because it allows multiple classes with first-come-first-served discipline.

3.0 EVALUATION OF MODELS

The results of a set of empirical evaluation experiments performed on Honeywell large computer systems were used to provide input quantities for each of the models as well as to provide the real system performance measurements. The comparison of these performance measurements to the performance predicted by each of the models is described in the following evaluation of the models. Measurements were taken by both hardware and software monitors as well as by standard accounting data recording.

3.1 Disc Subsystem Reconfiguration

The first experiment performed was directed toward prediction of system performance for changed mass storage configurations. A fixed multiprogramming depth of eight test programs was maintained during the experiment. The measurement results for a single channel and two devices were used to generate the inputs for each model. Measurements were then taken for single and dual channel configurations with two, four and eight disc devices. The configuration description inputs to the models (i.e., number of channels, and/or devices) were then varied to conform to the measured configurations. The resulting predictions of system throughput are summarized in Figures 7 and 8.

The "straightforward" models (i.e., DM and MRM) are not effective in predicting the performance changes due to mass storage subsystem changes. This is because their structure does not allow an arbitrary number of channels and devices.

The central server model with devices used as the peripheral servers representing the disc subsystem (CSM (Devices)) provides better pre-dictions than the "straightforward" models but not very accurate. It

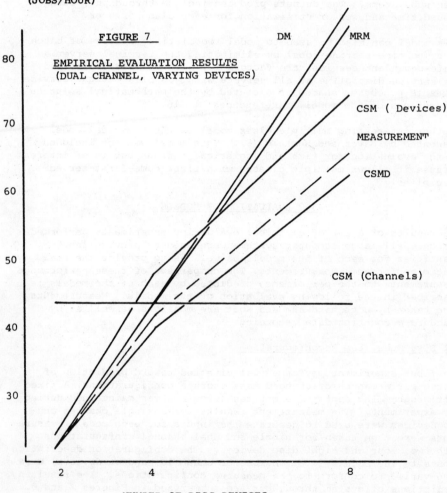

SYSTEM
THROUGHPUT
(JOBS/HOUR)

FIGURE 7

EMPIRICAL EVALUATION RESULTS
(DUAL CHANNEL, VARYING DEVICES)

DM   MRM

CSM (Devices)

MEASUREMENT

CSMD

CSM (Channels)

NUMBER OF DISC DEVICES

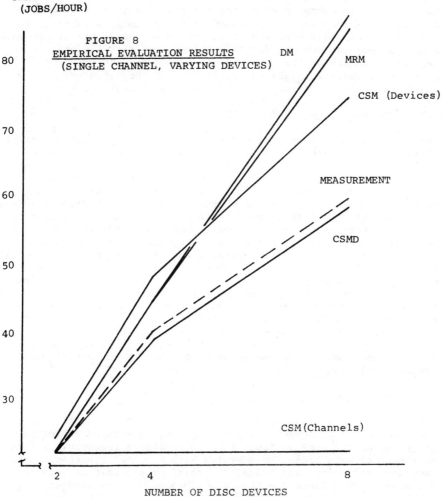

SYSTEM
THROUGHPUT
(JOBS/HOUR)

FIGURE 8
EMPIRICAL EVALUATION RESULTS
(SINGLE CHANNEL, VARYING DEVICES)

DM

MRM

CSM (Devices)

MEASUREMENT

CSMD

CSM(Channels)

NUMBER OF DISC DEVICES

also has the inability to predict the effects of single vs. dual
channels as the channels are not structurally represented in the
model.

The central server model with channels used as the peripheral servers
representing the disc subsystem (CSM (Channels)) is able to predict
the performance changes due to channel configuration changes. Its
predictions, however, are also not very accurate (in spite of being
precisely "calibrated" at the two devices, single channel point).
This model also cannot predict the effects of a changed number of
devices since they are not represented in the model structure. The
central server model with a disc subsystem included which represents
both channels and devices (CSMD) provides significantly better predictions than any of the other model structures. At the "worst"
point (dual channel, eight devices) the CSMD throughput prediction
is less than 5% different than the measured throughput.

3.2 Memory Reconfiguration

Another experiment which was performed was directed toward prediction
of system performance for changed main memory capacity. A fixed
collection of programs was run from an IMCV tape to provide a repeatable workload and measurements were taken at memory capacities of
192K, 256K and 512K words. The 192KW configuration measurements
were taken as the base and the multiprogramming depth for the models
was varied to obtain their prediction of throughput. In this case,
all models performed reasonably well. At 512K words the system was
processor bound which made the model structures diminish in
importance as long as they reasonably faithfully represented the CPU
resources. The 256K word point thus was the best test of prediction
capabilities. Figure 9 shows the model throughput prediction results
in terms of the percentage deviation from the measured system
throughput. The significant observation from Figure 9 is that again
the "straightforward" models are poor predicters. All forms of
central server model however did quite well (within 5% error). It is
believed that a "subsystem active" characteristic of the channel time
measurement accounts for the accuracy of the CSM (Channels) model
predictions.

3.3 Processor Speed Reconfiguration

The next experiment performed was directed to the prediction of
performance for changed CPU capability. Again a fixed collection of
programs was run from an input tape to provide a repeatable workload.
Measurements were taken for a system with a "slow" processor, a single
"regular" processor, and a dual "regular" processor configuration.
The measurements taken for the "slow" processor case were taken as
the base and model predictions were obtained for the two improved
CPU capability configurations. Figure 10 displays the predictions
of throughput made by the models and the measured system throughputs.

Figure 10 again indicates that the "straightforward" models are not
good performance prediction tools. All the forms of central server

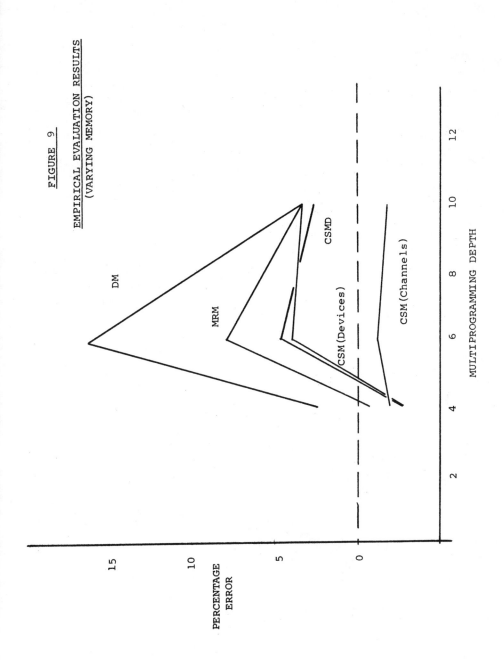

FIGURE 9

EMPIRICAL EVALUATION RESULTS
(VARYING MEMORY)

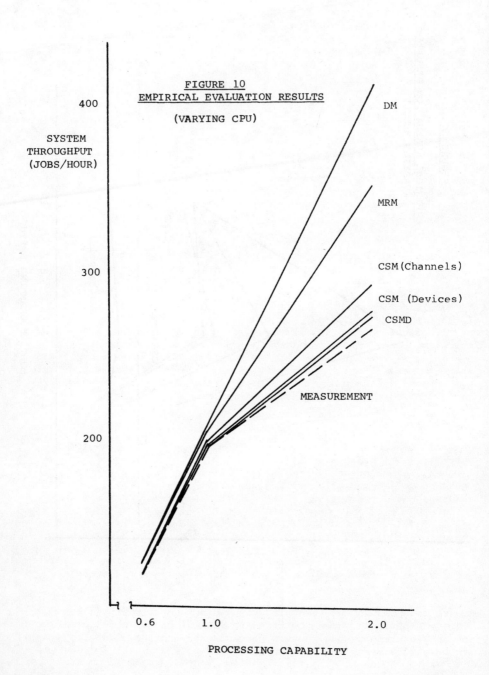

FIGURE 10
EMPIRICAL EVALUATION RESULTS
(VARYING CPU)

model, however, provided reasonably accurate predictions. The
accuracy of each form of CSM will vary in any given workload situation. For example, if the disc I/O is composed of large data
transfers it is expected that the CSM (Channels) would be better than
the CSM (Devices). If the disc I/O is composed of more seeking and
short data transfers, the opposite would be true. In either case
the CSMD, which can represent each situation uniquely, is expected
to provide <u>consistent</u> predictions with good (less than 10% error)
accuracy.

3.4 Time Sharing Load

The last experiment performed was directed to the prediction of
performance with a variable number of time sharing users along with
a batch load. The batch load was again supplied by an input program
tape. Time sharing load was provided by a terminal emulator system
proprietary to Honeywell. Measurements were taken for 30 and 60
time sharing users. The model implementation was such, however, that
the 30 and 60 line data had to be lumped into "effective" user loads
of 8 and 17 users.

Figures 11 and 12 show the batch and time sharing throughputs measured
as well as those predicted by a two class central server model which
included a disc subsystem. While the absolute errors in throughput
are not extremely bad it is significant to note that batch throughput
is consistently over predicted and time sharing throughput is consistently under predicted. It is conjectured that this is caused by
the processor shared CPU service discipline of the model which does
not provide any priority service to time sharing transactions. The
operating system software does provide such priority service to time
sharing transactions. The predicted response times were approximately
twice those measured which is also at least partially caused by the
lack of priority discipline representation.

3.5 IBM System

Rose (14) included a large amount of measurement data taken on IBM
systems (370/158 and 370/168). Due to difficulty in modelling the
I/O behavior of these systems, Rose resorted to a "calibration"
technique of arbitrarily scaling the input data to provide more
accurate model predictions. Some of this published data was used
to assess the gain in predictive accuracy provided by using central
server model which included the more complete disc subsystem
representation. Figure 13 shows a measurement point taken from Rose
(14) and predictions by the central server model including disc
channels and the central server model including both channels and
devices. The relative superiority of completely representing the
disc subsystem is clear.

Figure 14 shows another example using measurements published by Rose
(14). This figure shows the standard central server model predictions,
the "calibrated" central server predictions, and the predictions made
by the central server mode which included both channels and devices.
It is interesting to note that the latter model produced better

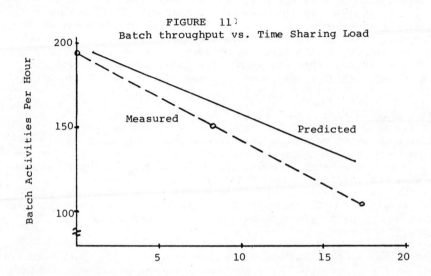

FIGURE   11
Batch throughput vs. Time Sharing Load

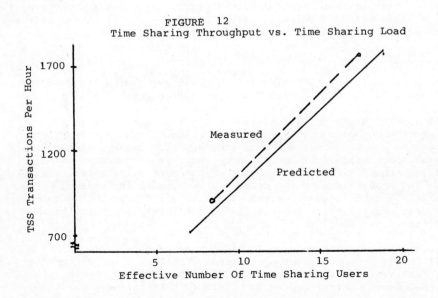

FIGURE   12
Time Sharing Throughput vs. Time Sharing Load

FIGURE 13

MODEL PREDICTIONS FOR IBM SYSTEM*

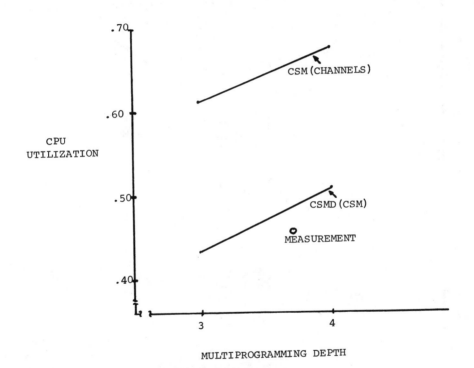

MULTIPROGRAMMING DEPTH

* MEASURED DATA FROM ROSE 75

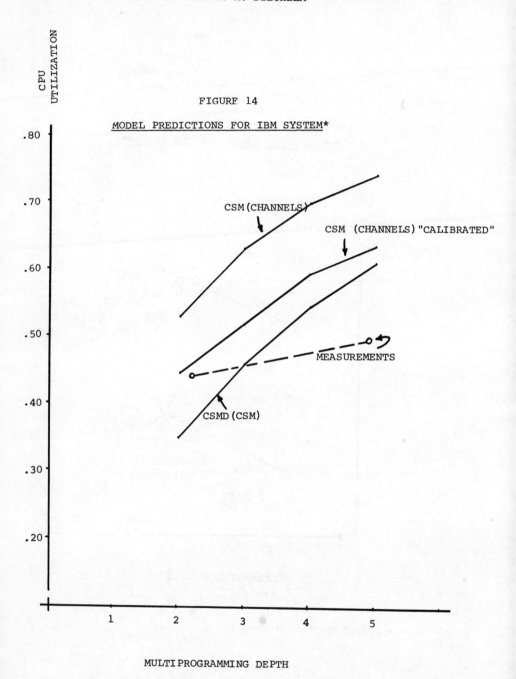

FIGURE 14

MODEL PREDICTIONS FOR IBM SYSTEM*

MULTI PROGRAMMING DEPTH

* MEASURED DATA FROM ROSE 75

predictions at a multiprogramming depth of 5 than did even the "calibrated" model.

4.0 CONCLUSIONS AND RECOMMENDATIONS

The evaluation positively indicates that network queueing models can be used to provide reasonably accurate predictions of computer system performance. The deterministic and machine repairman forms, on the other hand, did not produce predictions with useful accuracy.

The model form recommended for use is a central server model which includes a disc subsystem representation with both channels and devices. The imbedded central server form described herein has been shown to be effective. The results from use of the IBM system data indicate that an iterative calibration exercise is not necessary if a more suitably structured model, such as that recommended, is used.

The evaluation did not provide such positive results for the two class (batch and time sharing) form. While CPU utilization can be predicted reasonably accurately the decomposition of processing into batch and time sharing throughputs was not predicted accurately nor was response (or turnaround) time. This is a potentially very useful direction for future model development and evaluation. It is likely that a more complete model representation of the system communications facility and some form of priority CPU service discipline will be necessary to provide a useful model.

5.0 ACKNOWLEDGEMENTS

The support and counsel of Mr. Barry Wallack of the Defense Communications Agency (which supported in part the research reported herein under Contract DCA 100-73-6-0055 with Honeywell Information Systems), and of Dr. W. E. Lewis of Arizona State University are gratefully acknowledged.

REFERENCES

1. Baskett, F., Chandy, K., Muntz, R. and Palacios, F.   Open closed, and mixed networks of queues with different classes of customers.   J. ACM 22, 2 (April 1975), 248-260.

2. Bhandiwad, R. A. and Williams, A. C.   Queueing network models of computer systems.   Proceedings of the Third Texas Conference on Computing Systems.   (November 1974).

3. Boyse, J. W. and Warn, D. R.   A straightforward model for computer performance prediction.   ACM Computing Surveys 7, 2 (June 1975).

4. Buzen, J. P.   Queueing network models of multiprogramming. AD731575 (August 1971).

5. Buzen, J. P. Computational algorithms for closed queueing
    networks with exponential servers. C. ACM 16, 9 (September
    1973).

6. Diethelm, M. A. An evaluation of analytical models for com-
    puter system performance prediction. Presented at 1976 CPEUG
    meeting. San Diego, California.

7. Diethelm, M. A. An empirical evaluation of analytical computer
    systems performance models. Ph. D. Dissertation, Department of
    Industrial Engineering. Arizona State University (1977).

8. Gaver, D. P. The construction and fitting of some simple prob-
    abilistic computer models. NPS556v75011, Naval Postgraduate
    School, Monterey, California (January 1975).

9. Gaver, D. P. and Humfeld, G. Multitype multiprogramming
    probability models and numerical procedures. Proceedings ACM
    Computer Performance Symposium (1976), 38-43.

10. Giammo, T. P. Validation of a computer performance model of
    the exponential queueing network family. Proceedings, ACM
    Computer Performance Symposium (1976), 44-58.

11. Jackson, J. R. Jobshop-like queueing systems. Management
    Science 10, 1 (October 1963).

12. Reiser, M. and Kobayashi, H. Queueing networks with multiple
    closed chains: Theory and Computations algorithms. IBM
    Journal of Research and Development (May 1975), 283-294.

13. Rice, D. R. An analytical model for computer system perfor-
    mance analysis. Ph. D. Dissertation, University of Florida
    (1971).

14. Rose, C. S. Measurement and analysis of computer performance
    evaluation. Ph. D. Dissertation, George Washington University
    (September 1975).

15. Rose, C. S. Validation of a queueing model with classes of
    customers. Proceedings, ACM Computer Performance Symposium
    (1976), 318-326.

16. Wong, J. Queueing network models for computer systems.
    UCLA-ENG-7579 (October 1975).

COMPUTER PERFORMANCE, K.M. CHANDY AND M. REISER (EDS.)
NORTH HOLLAND PUBLISHING COMPANY, 1977

THE RESOLUTION AND RETRIEVAL OF END-USE DATA PROCESSING WORKLOADS

M. J. Marcus and A. A. Cerino
International Business Machines Corporation
Poughkeepsie, New York, USA

INTRODUCTION

To the best of our knowledge, DP workload characterizations are inadequate and/or configuration-dependent. This paper describes how a particular DP workload was characterized so that: (1) all the transactions are represented; (2) the resource demands that determine if a response time is met are included; and (3) appreciable changes can be made in the systems configuration without making it necessary to change the form in which the DP workload is expressed.

Background Considerations

The adequate characterization of any workload, whether it be manufacturing, road building, or data processing, must take place in the context of a clear notion of the purpose of the activity, in other words a definition of performance. Further, the workload description must be drawn in terms of the resource system with which it will be accomplished.

Data processing systems performance is concerned with the timely completion of the population of transactions impinging on an information system in the course of some specified operating period. The unit of performance is the transaction, a transaction being a task completed by the system across its logical periphery. To the degree that timeliness requirements are met with accurate output for the transaction set, then systems performance is adequate.

Accordingly, timeliness requirements are a key descriptor of DP workload. Two transaction populations, identical except for their contrasting response times (such as three seconds versus thirty seconds), would usually represent dramatically different workloads. This is so because timeliness differences have an impact on the rate at which the resource demands of a transaction must be met. Furthermore, the relationship in time that each transaction bears to any other, particularly when there is multiple overlapping, also determines the rate at which demands are made on system resources. It follows that the start time of a transaction as well as its due time must be included.

Most basic, DP workload is concerned with the collective requirement that the transaction population has for the services of various resources that will be configured into the information processing system. To adequately characterize workload, data is needed covering this demand on each of the resource types.

Given that timeliness and resource demand are essential characteristics of a DP workload, then the relationship between this demand and the total time used by a resource, once so dedicated, will depend on resource operating rate. The operating rate (such as MIPS, access time, megabytes per second) of a resource type (such as processor, DASD storage, channel unit) is different from one implementation to another. When configuring/reconfiguring his system, the customer chooses a particular version of a resource type.

Therefore, the demand made on a system resource (such as number of instructions to be executed, total accesses required, sum of the bytes to be transmitted) is fundamental to a description of the DP workload. In contrast, the rate at which the resource functions is basic to the particular system configuration and should be kept independent of the DP workload description.

Consolidation of Batch and Real Time

Beginning in the early 1950s, for over a decade of computer applications, batch and real time (at first mostly sensor base) workloads were implemented on separate systems. Occasionally, as we came into the 60s, two such workloads might be run on the same system but in separate periods of time. In the view of developers at both the systems and applications level, batch and real time were almost antithetical computing entities.

With the more recent appearance of successful real time human interactive applications such as APL, BASIC, and TSO along with supporting DBDC implementations such as BETACOMM, COSMOS TP, CICS, and IMS, this dualism has faded. Many of the large systems in today's DP environments handle a workload that includes a nearly continuous spectrum of contrasting jobs, from an extensive batch payroll requiring several processing hours to brief batch jobs that may spend a few minutes in the system, as well as thousands of real time human interactive inquiries with response time requirements of a few seconds. In today's computing environments, the adequate characterization of DP workload must move batch, human interactive, and sensor base processing requirements into a common conceptual framework.

The attribute that all three of these main end-use environments have in common is the transaction (Tn). We abbreviate the term transaction to Tn and use it interchangeably with job. As stated earlier, the Tn is the information processing unit of performance. Generally, batch Tn's are "longer" than interactive ones; these differences must be reflected in associated demands on system resources. However, they both have a start time when the Tn is initiated and a due time when the system output is required by an end-user. The difference between due time and start time is the response time or timeliness requirement of the Tn, whether it be a batch run or a single round in a protracted interactive inquiry.

Related to the differences among contrasting end-use environments is the distinction between real time and non-real time processing. These two can be brought into the same frame of reference by considering a typical batch Tn and converging it on a real time state.

Batch Tn's are usually initiated by a systems staging specialist who knows when the Tn output is due. The specialist has determined the start time by backing off some reasonable interval before it is due. In most systems situations, a batch Tn could actually be started earlier. And in fact it often occurs that because of increased workload and/or reduced system resource the start of that Tn is rescheduled to an earlier time. If the rescheduling goes through several such cycles, a limit will be reached when the Tn

can no longer be started because of dependence on data concerning
events yet to occur in the environment outside the system.

Stated in a more general way, when completion of a batch job depends
on retrieving data concerning events occurring close to the time the
job must be started, then we are at the border of real time processing. The consequence of this for DP workload characterization is
that the scheduling limit, or as we refer to it, prerequisite time,
of non-real time Tn's must be listed.

RESOLVING THE DP WORKLOAD

Many of today's DP systems handle more than 100,000 Tn's in
a twenty-four hour period. In our own operation a typical day
involves some 163,000, about 1200 of them batch production and
batch programming test jobs. For us it was a foregone conclusion
that we would not resolve this workload down to each Tn or to the
idiosyncratic demand that it might make on the system resources.
The sheer volume of a fully resolved workload characterization
would render it useless for our purposes.

Therefore, the questions were how to approach detailing some parts
of the workload and approximating others, and on what basis would
it be decided which segments of the load should be so treated.
Two overall considerations governed our decisions. First, the
entire workload had to be represented in some manner or form.
This is consistent with the earlier discussion of timeliness and
concurrent resource demand. Second, the projected use of the
workload characterization determined the level of detail to be
incorporated.

In common with many DP environments, our system runs characteristically different workloads from one day of the week to the next.
For the phase of the work described here, we chose to represent a
twenty-four-hour Thursday period, chosen as a "normal" weekday workload by the operations staff, rather than attempt to cover all five
working days or average them into a single twenty-four-hour period.

Batch Workload Segment

The batch segment of the workload has 1210 jobs, 600 being the key
production set. The remaining 610 jobs support the programming test
requirements of the facility. A 180-transaction subset of the production load represents the "critical job stream" of the DP operation. These jobs are large consumers of system resource and are
highly interdependent (that is, the initiation of many of these jobs
is contingent on the completion of others). While the number of
jobs in the subset represents about 15 percent of the batch workload,
their processing demand has been estimated at 75 percent of the
batch total. These are the batch jobs we decided to detail as individual events (in our terms, "particularizing" each of these 180
batch Tn's). The remaining 420 batch production jobs and the 610
test jobs were generalized into five representative Tn's. The
resource demands content for each representative Tn is typical of
the jobs it covers. A representative Tn is run in the frequency and
on the starting schedule of each of the jobs in its set.

In Figure 1, the first of the five representative batch Tn's (#181)
covers the short production jobs; the next four cover the long and
short TEST and CAPTAIN jobs. "Long" jobs are those having an
elapsed time of more than 18 minutes in the CPU or more than 5 min-

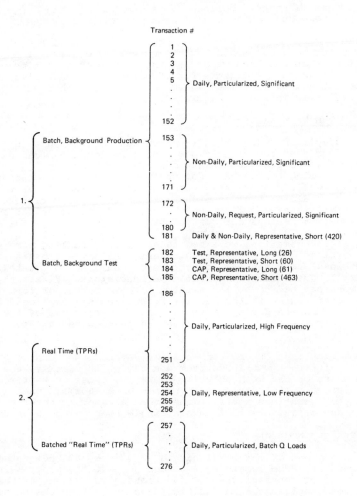

Figure 1. Listed Transaction Dimension of the DP Workload Table

utes active time. The remainder are "short" jobs.

Real Time Workload Segment

The bulk of the 162K real time segment of the workload is human interactive and is run between 7:00 a.m. and 6:00 p.m. Real time Tn's involve the use of a TPR (transaction processing routine), of which we have 200 in systems residence. Sixty-six of these TPRs are run at high frequencies, making up almost 90 percent of the daily Tn's. We have particularized these 66 TPRs (#186-251 in Figure 1) and covered the occurrence of the remaining 134 TPRs with five representative Tn's. The frequencies with which these 71 Tn's (#186-256, Figure 1) are run are ʻecorded in six-minute intervals across the working day.

The exception to the use of TPRs in human interactive mode is the
Q-loads where aggregates of these Tn's that do not require an
immediate response are queued into a batch job. We have 20 such
jobs which, taken together, cover 35,000 TPR runs. We have particularized these batch jobs in respect to their content across the
71 listed Tn's and have identified the start time of each of the 20.

Transaction Dimension

We have discussed above one of three dimensions in the workload
characterization, the Tn dimension. The argument we have traced
shows the basis on which we decided to resolve our particular
163,000-Tn load at a 276-Tn level. From one DP installation to
another, decisions on the appropriate degree of contraction in
moving from the real workload to its characterization will depend
on the composition of the load, the use to which the characterization will be placed, and the cost of performing the characterization. The basic technique, however, can remain the same: (1)
singling out the individual transactions that are the major resource
consumers and/or are highly interdependent; (2) including other
transactions that are repeated with high frequency; and (3) replacing the usually large number of remaining Tn's with a small number
of representative ones.

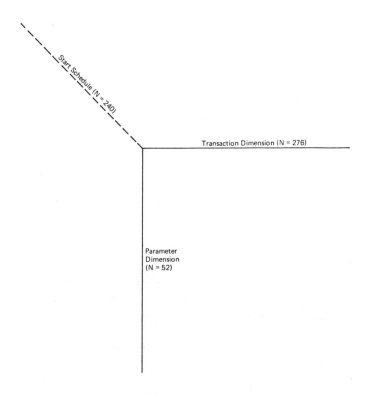

Figure 2. DP Workload Table Structure

Parameter Dimension

Figure 2 indicates how the DP workload characterization is organized
as a three-dimensional structure. The <u>workload</u> <u>table</u> carries the
listed Tn's along its first dimension. The resource demand of each
Tn is profiled in the vertical <u>parameter</u> dimension. And finally,
the <u>start schedule</u> <u>dimension</u> of the table carries 240 six-minute
slots where the starting time or start frequencies of the listed
Tn's are indicated.

The parameter dimension of the load table (Figure 3) reflects three
categories of information: (I) the services a Tn may demand of each

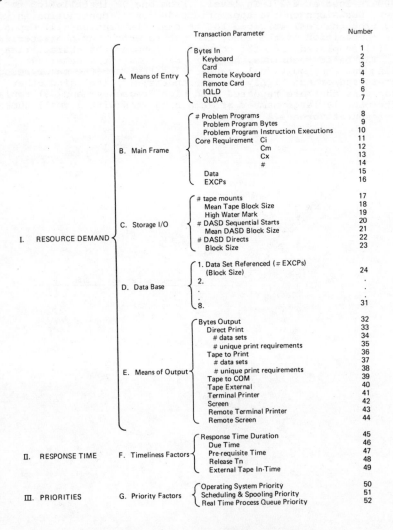

		Transaction Parameter	Number
	A. Means of Entry	Bytes In	1
		Keyboard	2
		Card	3
		Remote Keyboard	4
		Remote Card	5
		IQLD	6
		QLOA	7
	B. Main Frame	# Problem Programs	8
		Problem Program Bytes	9
		Problem Program Instruction Executions	10
		Core Requirement Ci	11
		Cm	12
		Cx	13
		#	14
		Data	15
		EXCPs	16
I. RESOURCE DEMAND	C. Storage I/O	# tape mounts	17
		Mean Tape Block Size	18
		High Water Mark	19
		# DASD Sequential Starts	20
		Mean DASD Block Size	21
		# DASD Directs	22
		Block Size	23
	D. Data Base	1. Data Set Referenced (≠ EXCPs) (Block Size)	24
		2.	.
		.	.
		.	.
		8.	31
	E. Means of Output	Bytes Output	32
		Direct Print	33
		# data sets	34
		# unique print requirements	35
		Tape to Print	36
		# data sets	37
		# unique print requirements	38
		Tape to COM	39
		Tape External	40
		Terminal Printer	41
		Screen	42
		Remote Terminal Printer	43
		Remote Screen	44
II. RESPONSE TIME	F. Timeliness Factors	Response Time Duration	45
		Due Time	46
		Pre-requisite Time	47
		Release Tn	48
		External Tape In-Time	49
III. PRIORITIES	G. Priority Factors	Operating System Priority	50
		Scheduling & Spooling Priority	51
		Real Time Process Queue Priority	52

Figure 3. Workload Table, Transaction Parameter Dimension

resource type configured into the system; (II) its timeliness factors; and (III) any priority levels associated with it. Resource
demand has been subdivided (see A through E) to an approximation of
the usual progression of a Tn through the system. Fifty-two variables listed in Figure 3 are discussed below. Since different Tn's
make use of differing resource subsets, a Tn ordinarily exercises
about half of the 52 listed parameters.

A. Bytes In (#1) is the basic parameter that starts the Tn. It is
the number of bytes of information that must be entered at some
point on the periphery of the system to initiate the Tn. The
means of entry may involve card, keyboard, or tape (#2-7); it
also provides some limited information on where the transaction is entered, whether local or remote.

B. For the batch segment of the workload, # Problem Programs (#8)
corresponds to the number of job steps required during mainframe primary processing. For most of the real time segment
there is just a single program involved, a TPR. Related
parameters are Problem Program Bytes (#9), the total number
of bytes taken up by the object code brought into core, and
Problem Program Instruction Executions (#10), the primary
processing demand the job makes on the CPU resource. The
memory or core occupancy requirement of a Tn is an important
factor in its resource demand in the mainframe phase of its
processing. Therefore, the initial core required (Ci), the
maximum core of all the steps (Cm), and the mean core required
by all the steps (Cx) are parameters (#11, 12, 13) for relevant Tn's. Σ#> (#14) applies to multistep jobs and indicates
the number of times a job step calls for more core than the
one which went before it. Σ Data (#15) is the total bytes of
data a job will bring in and out to support its overall problem
program instruction execution stream; Σ EXCPs (#16) is the sum
of EXCPs that were issued in support of the job before it
exited the CPU.

C. Storage Input/Output resource requirements are covered by parameters #17-23. We record the number of tape mounts a job
requires (#17) and the block size used once a tape is sequencing
its data to and from the CPU (#18). In jobs coming in under
scheduling and spooling software (such as ASP and JES3), a high-
water mark entry (#19) is included. This is the maximum number
of tape frames a job requires at any point in time during primary processing. In our operation this determines the number
of tapes that will be pre-mounted. DASD Sequential Starts (#20
is analogous to tape mounts, each event involving the lining up
of a data set which can then be sequenced into core in the
block size (#21) indicated. DASD Directs (#22) is the remaining form of access, where each block of data (#23) retrieved is
searched for independent of the last.

D. Parameters #24-31 provide information on the data sets
referenced by each listed Tn, naming the data set, the number
of times it is referenced, and the block size per referencing
event. These parameters make it possible to track the relationship between the job stream and contention waits within the
organization of the data base.

E. Bytes Out (#32) is the outcome or output of the Tn which signals
completion. The number of bytes of information in the Tn output bears on the demand it places on the resource(s) employed.

The means of output (#33-44) indicates which resource types
will be involved in output and whether they are local or remote.

F. Timeliness factors cover the contingencies involved in real
   time and batch Tn response time. Most of the real time Tn's in
   the workload are assigned a simple response time duration
   (#45), such as 15 seconds. Whenever one of these Tn's is
   initiated, it then has a due time that is 15 seconds later.
   Any particularized batch Tn is given a due time (#46), the time
   of the day when the completed output should be available to its
   end-user(s). The time it is initiated by the staging crew is
   listed on the start schedule dimension. Pre-requisite Time
   (#47) is the time of day when the last information needed to
   initiate the Tn becomes available in the "outside world."
   This marks the time before which the Tn cannot be initiated.
   When the workload table is used as a basis for rescheduling
   Tn's, this parameter sets the early boundary on possibilities
   to be considered.

   Many of the particularized batch Tn's are dependent upon the
   prior running of other batch Tn's; these form a "Tn net," a
   characteristic of the critical job stream which has an important bearing on whether timeliness requirements are met or
   missed. In the case of a batch job dependent on a previous one,
   Release Tn (#48) identifies this contingency. Some batch
   jobs are dependent on the availability of a prior tape output
   from another Tn run in our own system or sent from another
   system. This is covered by External Tape In-Time (#49), the
   time of day the tape is received at the station where it is
   used.

   Each of the five representative batch jobs (#181-185, Figure 1)
   is given a simple response time. At whatever time a job is
   started, its due time is determined by its assigned response
   time. While test jobs are not interdependent, the 420 short
   production jobs (#181) sometimes are. In this treatment of our
   load table, this element of accuracy was relinquished to gain
   the usability resulting from the shortening of the number of
   Tn's listed on the first dimension of the workload table.

G. There are three priority factors in our operation (#50-52),
   with most of the Tn's subject to two of the three. The operating system priority (#50) is in effect while the job is in the
   mainframe. For jobs scheduled and spooled under a control
   program, the priority listed in #51 applies during those
   phases of the processing. In the real time segment of the
   load, a Tn is assigned to a particular process queue (#52) from
   which it is moved over a channel for back end processing. The
   process queue number itself is a priority relative to other
   queues where Tn's may be waiting for back end facilities used
   in common.

START SCHEDULE DIMENSION

This dimension (see Figure 2) covers the starting schedule for each
of the Tn's listed on the first axis of the workload table. The
start schedule is set up in 240 time slots of six minutes each to
cover the twenty-four hours of the operating day. Each particularized batch Tn (#1-180, Figure 1) has an assigned start time listed
in the appropriate start cell. In contrast, Tn's #181-256 are run
multiple times and their respective starts are carried in the

appropriate six-minute start cells. For the twenty Q-loads (#257-276), the start time is handled the same way as particularized batch.

DP WORKLOAD RETRIEVAL

Data Sources

It was one matter to design the workload table but quite another to populate it with valid data. The first pass at filling in the table was time consuming and tedious. It involved working through massive system monitoring printouts and long discussions with programmers and end-users. While this effort on a one-time basis was not unreasonable, the expense of repeating even a part of it each time we wanted to update the workload table would become prohibitive. Furthermore, as in most large DP operations, the workload is frequently subject to change; the week or two it would take to characterize a workload would often leave it already out-of-date. So we began to automate the workload data retrieval process.

We use a number of monitoring and data collection facilities in running our DP system. Almost all of the data needed to populate the load table is available from the four support facilities discussed below. There were two problems, however, that had to be solved: the relatively small amount of relevant data was obscured by the sheer mass of other data collected in the same run; and the data we wanted had to be moved into the format of the load table. This required the writing of a number of bridging programs, which are described in Figures 4 and 5.

We use the SMF (System Management Facility) with the Data Set Volume option in place as a prime source for batch Tn data. Also used is our scheduling data base, designed and maintained locally, which centralizes operations information so that each functional area within the operations department works from a common set of data. The scheduling data base tracks batch Tn scheduling requirements and attainments and provides load table data on the input and output phases of batch Tn's. Also utilized in batch Tn data collections is a computer operations-maintained file of production card reader procedures, the MHV.JCLDECK. This file provides data on JCL entries, unique output from requirements, Tn priority assignments, and the dependent job control network. From the network information, it is possible to generate a flowchart-type document describing prerequisite and postrequisite Tn relationships. The real time data collection uses a logging file which tracks Tn's from entry to exit in our telecommunications front end. This file provides most of the information we need to cover real time Tn's.

In designing our load table data collection method, we have tried whenever possible to use sources already available in our system. While they do contain most of the data we require, they are not provided in a convenient end-use format. Therefore, it has been necessary to modify a series of existing programs and to design and code a number of new programs to process this raw data.

It may be noted that, with the exception of SMF, the data sources we used are unique to our installation. These sources are significant for our operation; and we expect that many large computer systems will have this data available in some form. In most instances, a similar bridging activity will have to be undertaken to achieve an end-use load table.

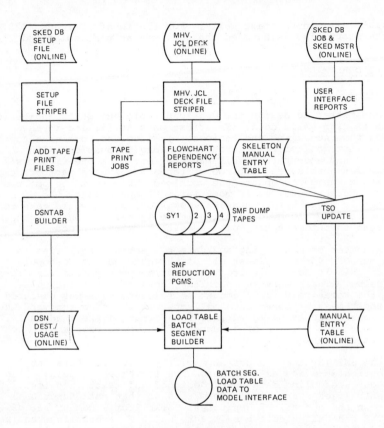

Figure 4. Retrieval Flow Diagram; Batch Segment of Workload Table

Figure 4 covers the batch segment workload data collection flow. The actual collection is driven from SMF reduction programs but dependent upon prior data collection from the scheduling data base (left and right top) and the card reader deck history. Data from the scheduling data base and the MHV.JCLDECK are grouped into two tables. The Data Set Name/Destination Usage table is collected from the scheduling data base setup file and MHV.JCLDECK. The manual entry table uses two data sources (right top down). On interrogation of the MHV.JCLDECK, a skeleton manual entry table is generated. This is used as input by a conversational/prompting program running under TSO. The TSO session updates the skeleton manual entry file with data from the scheduling data base job and scheduling user interface reports. Once these tables are built and verified, they need not be updated until significant changes occur in the DP workload.

The data collection for the real time segment of the load (see Figure 5) is rather direct. The Log File provides tracking from Tn entry to exit. System events between these two points are time stamped; those of interest to the workload table are retrieved by the real time segment builder program.

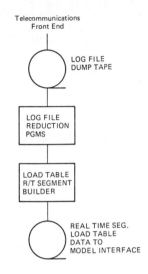

Figure 5. Retrieval Flow Diagram; Real Time Segment of Workload Table

Mechanics of Data Retrieval

In the paragraphs below, which correspond to the Tn parameter grouping in Figure 3, we outline the mechanics of obtaining the data for
the Tn parameter dimension of the workload table. Figure 6 uses the
same format to summarize the source(s) of data.

In the last column of the matrix we indicate parameters where data
retrieval has not to this date been satisfactorily solved.

    A. **Means of Entry.** Recording bytes in for batch Tn's requires
       identification of three types of records: JCL (job control
       language) cards, scheduling control cards, and end-user sub-
       mitted input on system utility control cards. The sources for
       recording bytes in for batch Tn's are SMF records and
       MHV.JCLDECK.

       A table entry is created for every job residing on MHV.JCLDECK.
       This entry contains a count of control cards. As SMF records
       are processed, a table lookup is performed to calculate the
       byte volumes. SMF records also provide the number of card
       images from DD * or DD DATA files. The byte volume of
       these files (if any) is then added to the control card byte
       volume to create the total card entry byte volume. Since a
       particular job number is associated with this byte volume, it
       is a simple matter to deduce whether this entry was made via
       normal or via remote card entry.

       For real time entry (except tape) the source of data is the
       Log File maintained as part of the telecommunication front end.
       An entry record is generated for each Tn, and flags in the
       record include device type, terminal name, and length of input

Transaction Parameter	No.	SMF	SKED DB	MHV JCL DECK	LOG FILES	MANUAL	NOT RESOLVED
A. Means of Entry							
Bytes In	1	X		X	X		
Keyboard	2				X		
Card	3	X	X		X		
Remote Keyboard	4				X		
Remote Card	5	X			X		
IQLD	6	X	X		X	X	X
QLOA	7	X	X		X	X	X
B. Main Frame							
= Problem Programs	8	X					
Problem Program Bytes	9	X					
Problem Program Instruction Executions	10						X
Core Requirement Ci	11	X					
Cm	12	X					
Cx	13	X					
#	14	X					
Data	15	X					
EXCPs	16	X					
C. Storage I/O							
= tape mounts	17	X	X				
Mean Tape Block Size	18	X					
High Water Mark	19	X	X				
= DASD Sequential Starts	20	X					
Mean DASD Block Size	21	X					
= DASD Directs	22	X	X				
Block Size	23	X					
D. Data Base							
1. Data Set Referenced (= EXCPs) (Block Size)	24	X					
2.	.	.					
.	.	.					
8.	31	X					
E. Means of Output							
Bytes Output	32	X			X		
Direct Print	33	X	X		X		
≠ data sets	34	X					
≠ unique print requirements	35	X	X	X			
Tape to Print	36	X	X	X			
≠ data sets	37	X					
≠ unique print requirements	38	X	X	X			
Tape to COM	39	X	X				
Tape External	40	X	X				
Terminal Printer	41				X		
Screen	42				X		
Remote Terminal Printer	43				X		
Remote Screen	44				X		
F. Timeliness Factors							
Response Time Duration	45	X	X		X		
Due Time	46	X					
Pre-requisite Time	47		X	X		X	
Release Tn	48		X	X		X	
External Tape In-Time	49	X				X	
G. Priority Factors							
Operating System Priority	50			X			
Scheduling & Spooling Priority	51		X	X			
Real Time Process Queue Priority	52			X			

Figure 6. Transaction Parameter Data Source Summary

string. From this entry record, the input string byte volume of each Tn can be determined. Type of entry can also be determined from the entry record flags.

In the case of IQLD and QLOA inputs (the batched real time Tn's (#257-276 in Figure 1), another mode of recording is required. These are identified by unique data set names, and SMF records provide byte volumes.

B. <u>Mainframe</u>. System Management Facility (SMF) is the primary source of data for recording mainframe usage. It covers core requirements for the life of a Tn, initial core request, and maximum core. A count of the number of times a Tn requests more core than previously requested is also made. This is of some importance in our environment as it reflects the chance of a Tn being "rolled out," that is, waiting for a larger amount

of core than had previously been allocated to it. The sum of
data transferred in and out, measured in bytes and EXCP (execute channel program) counts, is also provided by SMF data.

One problem area in our data collection is program instruction
execution counts, a level of detail not provided by SMF. The
use of a systems hardware measurement instrument cabled to a
mainframe to provide the instruction execution counts by Tn is
presently under investigation.

C. Storage I/O and Data Base. SMF and a local link in the sche-
&   duling and spooling system are used to provide data for
D. storage I/O. The scheduling data base system intercepts
    messages for use in schedule attainment reports. From these
intercepts, the tape high-water mark (HWM) pre-mount count
and subsequent operating system issued tape mount counts are
obtained. SMF with its DSV option allows data collection by
discrete data set name within Tn. Device type is determined
as well as EXCP counts and mean block sizes by device type
group.

The activity on files accessed directly either by real time or
batch Tn's has a more detailed level of collection. Since
these online files are shared by many end users and form the
basic record of the "critical job stream" detailing the
demand placed on them during the life of Tn's, we can determine file/Tn interaction and interdependency.

E. Means of Output. From the scheduling data base setup file, a
    table of data set name destinations is built. Entries created
from MHV.JCLDECK identify tape-to-print data set names and are
included in the above. This table is used to determine the
classification of batch Tn tape and disk output. For direct
card/print output, the SYSOUT class can be determined from the
SMF records by interrogating the DSN field. The type of forms
required for output can be determined using MHV.JCLDECK. Knowing the standard forms present in the printer pool, it is
possible to determine unique print requirements.

The main source of output byte volume for real time Tn's will
be the Log File. This file has flags for type of output device
as well as output byte volume by Tn.

F. Timeliness Factors. SMF will be used to track the duration of
    actual CPU runs. Scheduling data base records and the opera-
tions group provides user due time, prerequisite time, and
external tape-in time. Since these timeliness parameters may
vary considerably, their inclusion in the load table is via a
table entry. A conversational/prompting program running under
TSO is used to create or update timeliness parameters. A means
of identifying a particular Tn's prerequisite(s) and post-
requisite(s) has been developed using the network control cards
found on MHV.JCLDECK. A program is in place to create dependency records which, in turn, create a base flowchart of
installed jobs. The prerequisite(s) and postrequisite(s), if
any, are then added to the table.

G. Priority Factors. Knowing the relative priority of a Tn will
    be important in any workload characterization. The operating
system execution priority is obtained from the PRTY parameter
of the JCL job card; in its absence, the default priority

assigned by the reader interpreter is used. This priority is
in effect only during Tn life on the mainframe. Before and
after mainframe processing for many batch Tn's, a scheduling
and spooling priority is in effect. This priority is obtained
from the scheduling control card found on MHV.JCLDECK.

The real time process queue assignment in our environment is
not static. The operations group makes adjustments to balance
workload. To allow for this balancing, we make use of a table
recording process queue assignment by real time Tn. This
table resides in a TSO-created data set and is updated via a
TSO "edit" session.

USEFULNESS OF THE DP WORKLOAD TABLE

Most fundamental, the workload characterizations are a step in
solving a problem large computer installations have had too long,
the paradox of collecting huge quantities of operations data while
suffering from too little operations information. The workload
table, as complex as it may appear at first glance, is a simple,
extremely flexible structure. It culls load information from
performance information and organizes it in a form so that the
DP workload can be understood as a single entity. And it accom-
plishes this with a small fraction of the data most large systems
collect in the course of a day's operation.

In using a completed workload table, you start from an overall
view of the job the system must do; reasoning from this, it is convenient to look at selected segments of it. The segment chosen
can be examined and understood as a part of the whole workload.
Tn starts in bands of time can be tracked in the plane of the listed
transaction and start schedule dimensions (see Figure 2). The plane
formed by the listed transaction and parameter dimensions will
provide resource demands by Tn class (vertical bands) or particular
resources demands by Tn class (horizontal bands). These planes,
used in combination, can provide resource capacity demands by time
segments through the operating period of the workload table. Any
combination subset of these two planes can be inspected, provided
the resolution the user looks for does not exceed the level of
detail defined on the three axes of that particular load table.

For any given workload, the table is useful as a tuning aid, in
terms of possible resource variations and/or in scheduling
adjustments. It is under conditions of workload change or projected
change that the comparison of two tables becomes useful. In many
computer installations a workload can increase for reasons outside
the control of the DP operation. A human interactive Tn demand can
shift in time or can increase in number. Or more subtly, the Tn
demand rate and pattern can remain the same, but the resource demand
of the Tn mix can vary appreciably. Delta changes in load of this
type can be tracked through comparison of workload tables drawn at
different periods in time.

When sizing a planned prospective increment to an existing load,
its implications for systems performance can be understood in the
context of the current workload table. Later, when the change
has been run on the system, the actual increment can be recorded
and compared with earlier estimates. Both projected and retrospec-
tive load table comparisons can be used in resource capacity planning, that is, in observing which of the resource types configured
in the system are soon to be, or are being, stressed.

In addition to tuning and resource capacity planning uses of the
workload table, it can also serve as a workload simulation. Used
in this way it can be fed to modeled representations of part or all
of the installed function in a computing system. When nearly all of
a DP workload and most of the function configured in a system are
represented, then two necessary conditions have been met for
modeled predictions of systems performance.

COMPUTER PERFORMANCE, K.M. CHANDY AND M. REISER (EDS.)
NORTH HOLLAND PUBLISHING COMPANY, 1977

IBM 3850 MASS STORAGE SYSTEM, PERFORMANCE EVALUATION USING A CHANNEL MONITOR

H. Hempy

International Business Machines Corporation
Boulder, Colorado, USA

This paper presents an overview of a Channel Utilization Monitor
and Performance Analysis System, which is a hardware monitor used
on the IBM 3850 Mass Storage System (MSS), as well as the many
uses of a channel monitor for evaluating MSS performance.
Included are some examples of computer-generated reports which
are used specifically for MSS evaluation.

INTRODUCTION

The letters MSS stand for IBM's 3850 Mass Stoarge System. An MSS contains a
library of tape cartridges, several disk drives (called staging drives) to hold
active data, and various mechanisms that are used for staging: moving data from
the library to the staging drives when the data becomes active, and destaging:
moving data from the staging packs to the library when the data becomes inactive.

Tape cartridges are stored in a set of pigeonholes called the cartridge store (CS)
which is similar to a two-walled honeycomb. A cartridge acessor moves on a track
between the two walls, taking a cartridge from one location (pigeonhole) and
delivering it to another. The accessor can also deliver cartridges to any of the
data recording devices (DRD's) where data can be read from or written onto the
cartridge. There is also a data recording control (DRC) for each pair of DRD's
which controls the operation of the DRD's. There are from one to four DRC's and
two to eight DRD's, depending on the model.

The staging and destaging of data between the staging drives and the cartridge
store is controlled by microprogrammed processors called staging adaptors (SA's).
Each SA contains a staging buffer used to match speeds between the DRC's and the
faster staging drives. Additionally, SA responds to CPU requests to read and
write data just as a disk control unit does, but the SA has the additional function
of keeping up-to-date directories (SA tables) of staged data and translating the
virtual data address received from the CPU to the real address of the data on the
staging drive. This process is called virtual-to-real translation.

A mass storage controller (MSC) controls the processes for making data active and
inactive. Its functions include instructing SA's what data to stage and destage,
allocating space on the staging drives, and instructing the accessor in the cartridge store to move cartridges to and from DRD's.

The MSC is connected by a byte-multiplexor channel to one or more CPU's and the
CPU's use this interface to send commands to the MSC. I will describe two
particular CPU-to-MSC commands, MOUNT and ACQUIRE, which will be used as examples
throughout this paper.

MOUNT COMMAND

With the mount command, the CPU causes the MSC to mount a virtual 3330 volume in a
manner analogous to a human operator mounting a physical disk pack on a disk drive.

The sequence of operations by the MSC is as follows. The microcode for the mount
command is read into the control store of the MSC from the MSC table pack. This
microcode reads the Mounted Volume Table (MVT) to determine whether the virtual

volume is already mounted. Assuming it is not mounted, the MSC tables are updated
to indicate the new volume is mounted and space is allocated on one of the staging
drives to hold the volume table of contents (VTOC) of the virtual volume. The
VTOC is assumed to be on the first cylinder (cylinder zero) of the virtual volume.
The MSC presents Device End after writing a record to the Schedule Queue Table (SQT)
which will cause cylinder zero to be staged into the allocated space asynchronously.

The stage scheduler function of the MSC processes the asynchronous portion of MSC
commands. Records are read from the SQT and the work indicated is done. For the
mount command, the stage scheduler first issues an order to the cartridge accessor
to deliver the cartridge containing cylinder zero of the virtual volume to a
specified DRD. When the cartridge is moved and loaded into the DRD, the completion
is indicated by a Device End from the DRD, through an SA, to the MSC. Next, the
cartridge table of contents (CTOC) is read into the MSC's CTOC buffer via a series
of commands from the MSC to an SA to a DRC. Figure 1 shows these command
interfaces.

The CTOC is checked to see that the right cartridge is in the DRD and then a stage
order is sent to the SA. The SA stages the cylinders indicated (only cylinder zero
in this case) and returns Device End to the MSC on completion. The MSC sends an
order to each SA which can access the staging drive involved, causing the SA's to
update their tables indicating that the cylinder staged is valid and may be
referenced by the CPU. Finally, the MSC instructs an SA to send a Pack Change
Interrupt to the CPU, indicating that the mount is completed.

ACQUIRE COMMAND

The CPU will typically read the VTOC of a virtual volume to determine the location
of a particular data set and then issue an ACQUIRE command to the MSC, specifying
the cylinders of the virtual volume that may be read or written.

An option of the ACQUIRE command is whether to stage or inhibit staging of the
data. The inhibit stage option is generally used when the ACQUIRE is for an output
data set.

The processing of the ACQUIRE by the MSC is similar to a MOUNT; for example, if the
data needs to be staged, the cartridge is moved to a DRD and the data is staged to
the staging packs. In either case, the appropriate cylinders are validated in
each SA that can access the data.

CHANNEL MONITOR OVERVIEW

The channel monitor is a hardware measurement device which is attached to the IBM
channel (multiplexor, selector, or block multiplexor) interface. The monitor can
also be attached to the MSC's lower interface which uses the standard channel
command protocol. As many as three interfaces can be monitored by one channel
monitor at a time. Multiple channel monitors can be hooked up as needed.

The channel monitor collects data for each interaction between the channel and the
devices attached to it, whether the interaction is a channel command or a response
by a device to a command. The content and format of the logical reocrds collected
for each interaction is shown in Figure 2. The logical records are assembled in a
2008-byte buffer which, when full, is recorded on the magnetic tape of the channel
monitor.

Figure 3 shows a sample of output from the basic channel monitor trace report
program. Each line represents one logical channel monitor record. A description
of each field of the report follows.

XLATED DATA BYTES - This is a translation of the data bytes transferred for the
command to printable EBCDIC characters. Nonprintable characters are translated to
a period.

BYTE COUNT - This is the number of bytes transferred for the command. For example, a READ of an 80-byte record will result in a byte count of 80, a SEARCH ID EQ will result in a byte count of 5, and a device-end response to a SEEK will produce a byte count of 0.

CMD EXEC TIME - This is the amount of time in microseconds for the channel to execute the command. In particular, for disconnected operations, this is the time the channel was actually connected to the selected control unit.

CHAN IND HEX - This is a hexadecimal representation of the channel indicator bits as described in Figure 2.

STATUS - This is an 8-bit representation of the final status bits as described in Figure 2.

CMD CODE HEX - For channel-initiated commands, this is the command code in hexadecimal. For other commands this field is zero.

DATA BYTES - This is a hexadecimal representation of the data bytes transferred for the command. For commands with a byte count of zero, this field is ignored.

CHA-CU-DEV - This is the address of the device selected for the command, i.e., channel monitor interface, control unit address, device address.

ELAPSED TIME - This is the clock time at the initial selection for the command.

MSS ACTIVITY TRACE

When we began using this trace to study MSS performance, the process was slow. We spent days looking through hundreds of pages of this kind of listing, trying to understand what was happening in the MSS. For example, Figure 3 shows three instances of a particular bottleneck which we called SA command-buffer serialization, but locating them required a lot of time and patience.

To improve this time-consuming process we modified the basic channel monitor trace program, adding the MSS Activity Trace to the report. Figure 4 is a sample of the MSS Activity Trace showing the SA Command-Buffer Serialization. The report is from the same channel monitor data as shown in Figure 3. Figure 4 will be addressed in more detail in the section, 'Detecting Performance Bottlenecks.'

Each field (Ø4Ø, 21X, 23X, and 281) of the activity trace represents one component of the MSS: Ø4Ø is the MSC, 21X is the first SA, 23X is the second SA, and 281 is the cartridge accessor. The function being performed by the component is indicated by a mnemonic, starting on the line that the function was begun and continuing on each line until completion. The mnemonics used in this paper are defined in Figure 5.

For example, in Figure 4 at line 11 the MSC received an ACQUIRE from the host, processed the ACQUIRE through line 23, and at that point returned a device end to the host. In particular, at line 19, the MSC was doing an ACQUIRE for the host (AQD), the MSC was reading the data buffer in the first SA (RDB), the second SA was staging data (STG), and the cartridge accessor was idle (...).

Let's go through an example of the commands issued by the MSC to the SA's and to the cartridge accessor to stage a data set. Referring to Figure 6: In lines 1 through 11 the accessor is moving a cartridge to the DRD specified in a move-cartridge command (not seen in the example). When the accessor controller returns Device End (line 11) the cartridge has just been placed in the DRD entry chute. The cartridge slides down this chute to the DRD, where the protective cover is removed and the tape is threaded and positioned to be read. When this is completed,

the DRD sends a Device End to the MSC through an SA (line 19). At this time the
MSC knows it can read the cartridge.

The MSC reads the cartridge table of contents (CTOC) to verify that the correct
cartridge is in the DRD. The sequence of MSC-to-SA commands used is seek (SEK),
read tape to SA buffer (RDT), and read SA buffer (RDB). Lines 20 through 24 show
this sequence in the second SA (23X). The translated data bytes field on line 24
shows the first four characters in virtual volume ID to be '0119'. The last two
characters in the volume ID are not recorded by the channel monitor.

Next, the MSC issues a move data command (STG) to the SA (line 25). This command
causes the SA to stage the virtual cylinders specified onto staging drives. At
completion, the SA returns a Device End to the MSC (line 29).

Before the staged data can actually be referenced by the host CPU, the virtual-to-
real translation tables in the SA's must be modified to indicate that the staged
cylinders are now valid. To validate the cylinders, the MSC sends an SA table-
access command (VAL) to each SA which can reference the staged data (lines 30 and
31). At this point the data is staged and can be used by the host CPU.

The MSC still has to update the CTOC and put the cartridge away as shown in lines
36 through 52 of this sequence.

Line 36 is a seek to the beginning of the tape. Lines 38 through 40 read the CTOC.
Line 41 is a no-operation (no-op). Line 42 is a seek to the beginning of the tape
again. Lines 44 through 46 write the updated CTOC on the tape. The cartridge
unload (line 47) unthreads the tape, replaces the protective cover and drops the
cartridge into the DRD exit port. The cartridge move command (line 49) moves the
accessor to the exit station and returns the cartridge to its home cell (completed
on line 52).

DETECTING PERFORMANCE BOTTLENECKS

The claim was made earlier that with the addition of the MSS Activity Trace to the
basic channel monitor trace report it became easier to determine what was happening
in the MSS. With this claim in mind, let's go back to Figure 4 and see what observations can be made about MSS performance. Note that this data was collected on an
early version of the MSC microcode (February 1976) and that the bottlenecks found
here have since been eliminated.

On line 12 some virtual cylinders are validated in the first SA (21X). The MSC
cannot issue the validate to the other SA (23X) because the SA command buffer is
occupied with a stage command. Thus, the second validate is held up until the
completion of the staging (line 21), in this case about 18 seconds. Also, after
the second SA completes the stage command on line 21, the MSC cannot issue
validates for the data staged because now the first SA is staging data. In this
case (line 21 to 31) the delay is about 78 seconds.

Also, in Figure 4, on line 46 the tables in the first SA are validated but the
second SA is being used to rewind a cartridge and update the CTOC. This was done
with a single-channel program and so the second validate was delayed.

These are examples of what I called SA command buffer serialization. We asked the
microprogrammers if they could devise a way to access the SA tables without having
to wait for the command in the SA command buffer to complete. They implemented a
microcode change which used the DASD command buffer in the SA for SA-table-access
commands instead of the MSC/SA command buffer.

In the performance area we wanted to monitor the change to be sure it worked as
planned. To do this, we added two more columns to the MSS Activity Trace as shown
in Figure 7.

The old columns, 21X and 23X, have been relabeled SAØ and SA1 and still refer to the two SA's, specifically they denote the command in the MSC/SA command buffer.

The two new columns are labeled DPØ and DP1. The mnemonic DPØ means 'dasd path table update to SAØ. For example, line 10 in Figure 7 indicates that SAØ is doing a validate and the validate command itself is in the dasd command buffer. At the same time the MSC/SA command buffer in SA1 contains a stage command.

The next line (line 11) shows the validate being done in SA1, using the dasd command buffer, while the MSC/SA command buffer still contains the stage command. Figure 7 shows many uses of the dasd buffer in SA1 that previously would have had to wait until the end of the stage-and-seek operations in SA1. Thus, we verified that the implemented change worked as expected.

Using the MSS activity trace in the same way, we have identified inefficiencies and bottlenecks involving serialization on the CTOC buffer in the MSC: destaging before staging, cylinder interleaving of DRD's on a single DRC, DRD to SA path allocation problems, CPU/SA cylinder fault loop, and serialization on the diagnose command buffer in the MSC. Most of these have been either remedied or judged to be of trivial importance.

MSC TABLE I/O REPORT

This section describes the MSC table I/O report and useful applications of the report. First, an overview of the use of the MSC tables is given. Next, an example of the table activity for a mount command is presented. Lastly, actual and potential uses for the report are discussed.

The MSC uses and maintains a set of tables, called the primary MSC tables. The tables exist on a staging drive and are read from and written to by the MSC using standard DASD channel programs. A second staging drive holds a duplicate of the tables, called the secondary MSC tables. The secondary tables are not read from except in abnormal situations such as recovery. The secondary tables are written to whenever the primary tables are written to.

The tables contain MSC microcode overlay segments, MSS and virtual volume status information, processing control information, the recovery journal, and MSC trace records.

Figure 8 is an example of the MSC Table I/O Report. The table accesses are annotated on the right-had side of the listing. Microcode overlay lines begin two characters to the left of (e.g., lines 1, 6, 11, 18). Line 7 is a write to the Schedule Queue Table (SQT). Writes to the journal occupy two lines; for example, lines 34 and 35 inidicate a write to the journal of a record from the data portion of the Mounted Volume Table (MVT).

An example of the table accesses for the synchronous portion of a MOUNT command can be seen in Figure 8, beginning at line 22 of Figure 8A and ending at line 23 of Figure 8C.

This report is useful for validating the flow of control between overlay segments and the table accesses made by each segment. It has been used extensively for developing a detailed MSC simulator and for analyzing MSC processing of individual commands.

SUMMARY REPORTS

There are also two summary type reports as opposed to the trace type reports discussed previously. The first is the Command Mix Summary Report for the MSC and each MSC-to-SA interface. The second is the MSC Table Access Statistics Report.

Figure 9 shows an example of the Command Mix Summary Report. The first page of
the report (Figure 9A) is the host-to-MSC command mix. The number of commands of
each type, percentage of each type, and rate of each type is reported. The EXECUTE
command (command code 87) has several possible functions: MOUNT, DEMOUNT, ACQUIRE,
and RELINQUISH. The particular function is determined by an order code which is
contained in the first byte of data transferred to the MSC from the host as a
result of the 87-command. The number, percentage, and rate of each of these order
codes is reported on the second half of the first page of the report.

The second page of the report, Figure 9B, shows the MSC-to-SA command mix with the
number, percentage, and rate of each command type.

The second page also reports on the messages sent to the MSC from the SA in the SA
message buffer. The most common message types are cylinder fault, reserve, and
release. In this example, Figure 9B, no messages were sent.

Figure 10 shows an example of the MSC Table Access Statistics Report. The first
part of this report contains the number of reads and writes to each of the MSC
tables. In this example there were 17 reads from the staging/drive group (SDG)
table and 164 reads of microcode overlay segments (CODE). The rest of the report
provides more detail on specific tables: the distribution of accesses to individual records in the SDG table, accesses to the four sections of the mounted volume
table (MVT), accesses to the recovery journal, accesses to the MSC trace area,
and the number of reads of each microcode overlay segment.

This report has not yet been used extensively, but has potential use for optimizing
microcode packaging and MSC microcode residency, placing of tables, and reducing
the number of table accesses.

CONCLUSIONS

This paper has given examples of the use of special purpose data-reduction programs
to analyze MSS operation and evaluate MSS performance from data collected by the
channel monitor. The use of any peripheral device attaching to an IBM channel by
an IBM computer or any other driver can be studied in similar detail by specialized
computer programs using channel monitor. In a complex system, such measurement and
analysis is essential for understanding performance.

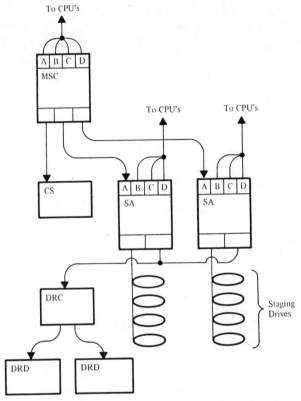

Figure 1. MSS Command Interfaces

Content	Format
Control unit address, device address	2 hex digits
Channel monitor	2 bits
Pad and length indicator	2 bits
Live register	12 bits
Channel indicator bits:	8 bits
1. Channel initiated selection	
2. Select in on channel attempted selection	
3. Command chained	
4. Stacked status	
5. Control unit busy	
6. Control unit disconnect	
7. Byte count exceeded 64K bytes	
8. Channel in polling mode	
End time of connection in microseconds	one full word*
Command code	2 hex digits
Final status bits:	8 bits
1. Attention	
2. Status modifier	
3. Control unit end	
4. Device busy	
5. Channel end	
6. Device end	
7. Unit check	
8. Unit exception	
Number of data bytes transferred	one half word
Initail selection time in microseconds	one full word*
First data bytes transferred as a result of the command	8 bytes
This field exists only if the number of data	
bytes is nonzero.	

*The full time field is 5 bytes long, consisting of one high order byte which is recorded in the monitor status bytes at the end of each physical record written, followed by the full word.

Figure 2.   Channel Monitor Content and Format

-- ADAPTED FROM 'BOULDER PRODUCT TEST LABORATORY-DCCL2' REPORT

VS2 RUN 5 - FEB 5, 1976 (TEMP64) 1 OF 2 DATE=76.048 TIME=17:04:44

	XLATED DATA BYTES	BYTE COUNT	CMND EXEC TIME	CHAN IND HEX	STATUS ASUCCDUU TMEBEECX	CMND CODE HEX	---- DATA 1 2	3 4	BYTES 5 6	--- 7 8	CCD HUE A V	ELAPSED TIME MMM:SS.SSSS
1	....	2	91	31	00001000	07	0001	0000	0000	0000	231	120:40.1833
2	....	0	48	31	00000100	00	000C	00CC	CCCC	CCC0	231	12C:40.1932
3	....	0	77	31	00001C00	33	0000	0000	0000	0000	231	120:40.1933
4	....	0	48	31	00000100	00	0C0C	000C	CC00	CCC0	231	12C:40.2114
5	VO.100.5	256	244	31	00001100	06	E5C6	00F1	F0F0	C0F5	231	12C:40.2114
6	....	16	176	31	00001000	27	0003	0042	C40C	C77F	231	120:40.2119
7	....	0	121	81	00000100	00	000C	00CC	CC0C	CCC0	281	12C:41.5844
8	....	0	11	40	C0000100	00	000C	0000	0000	0000	040	120:43.3401
9	....	0	25	40	00001100	03	0000	0000	CC0C	CCC0	040	120:43.3401
10	....	0	428	40	00100000	00	1F00	000C	CC00	CC00	040	120:43.4000
11	0098	28	657	40	00001C00	87	020C	0001	FCFC	F9F8	040	120:43.4009
12	.......F	12	138	10	00001100	37	0002	0043	0B03	02FF	210	12C:43.4070
13	....	0	54	15	CC000100	00	0000	000C	0000	0000	215	120:46.2779
14	....	0	5	15	01010C00	00	0000	0000	CCCC	CCC0	215	12C:46.5814
15	....	2	103	15	00001000	07	0001	0000	0C0C	CC00	215	120:46.5877
16	....	0	48	15	0C0C01CC	00	0000	00CC	CC0C	C000	215	120:46.5983
17	....	0	80	15	00001000	33	0000	0000	0000	0000	215	12C:46.5983
18	....	0	48	15	CC000100	00	0000	0000	CC00	0000	215	120:46.6178
19	VOL10094	256	234	15	00001100	06	E5D6	D3F1	FCF0	F9F4	215	12C:46.6178
20	... .	16	173	15	00001000	27	0003	0040	021A	C87F	215	120:46.6183
21	....	0	48	31	0C0C01CC	00	000C	000C	CC0C	C000	231	121:01.7000
22	.......F	12	138	30	00001100	37	0002	0044	0B03	02FF	230	121:01.7002
23	....	0	13	40	0C000100	00	3A00	0000	0C00	0000	040	121:07.7915
24	....	0	22	40	00001100	03	3A0C	000C	CC0C	CCCC	040	121:07.7916
25	0098	28	651	40	00001000	87	0200	2001	F0F0	F9F8	040	121:07.8388
26	....	0	13	40	0C000100	00	D01E	0A1C	CC0C	CC00	040	121:15.3459
27	....	0	24	40	00001100	03	D01E	0A10	0000	0000	040	121:15.3460
28	....	0	3488	40	0C100C00	00	0000	001A	000A	C000	040	121:15.3675
29	0094	28	643	40	00001000	87	020C	2001	FCFC	F9F4	040	121:15.3716
30	....	0	48	15	00000100	00	0000	0000	0000	0000	215	121:19.5379
31	.......F	16	174	10	00001100	37	0003	0043	CCC4	C6FF	210	121:19.5382
32	.......F	16	180	30	00001100	37	0003	0044	0C04	06FF	230	121:19.5385
33	....	0	5	11	01010000	00	0000	0000	0000	0000	211	121:19.6593
34	....	16	177	11	00001100	37	0003	0042	C40C	C77F	211	121:19.6698
35	....	16	176	31	00001100	37	0003	0042	0400	077F	231	121:19.6701
36	.......F	8	99	10	00001100	37	0C01	C044	CA04	C3FF	210	121:20.0561
37	.......F	8	101	30	00001100	37	0001	0045	0A04	03FF	230	121:20.0564
38	....	8	100	10	00001100	37	0001	0044	0E03	011F	210	121:20.0568
39	....	8	100	30	00001100	37	0C01	0045	CE03	C11F	230	121:20.0571
40	.......F	8	105	10	00001100	37	0001	0044	0A04	03FF	210	121:20.0576
41	.......F	8	98	30	00001100	37	0CC1	0045	CAC4	03FF	230	121:20.0579
42	....	8	101	10	00001100	37	0001	0044	0E03	011F	210	121:20.0583
43	....	8	97	30	00001100	37	0001	0045	0E03	011F	230	121:20.0585
44	....	2	93	31	00001000	07	0001	000C	CCCC	CCC0	231	121:20.4387
45	....	0	5	15	01010000	00	0000	0000	0000	0000	215	121:20.5853
46	... .	16	176	15	00001100	37	0003	004C	C21A	C87F	215	121:20.5863
47	....	0	48	31	00000100	00	0000	0000	0C00	C000	231	121:22.4795
48	....	0	77	31	00001C00	33	0000	00C0	CC00	0000	231	121:22.4796
49	....	0	48	31	00000100	00	000C	000C	CC0C	CCC0	231	121:22.4976
50	VO.100.5	256	246	31	00001100	06	E5D6	00F1	F0F0	00F5	231	121:22.4977
51	.......J	28	88	31	00001100	A4	0131	000C	A40C	00D1	231	121:22.4980
52	....	2	95	31	00001C00	07	0001	0000	0C00	CC00	231	121:22.4982
53	....	0	48	31	00000100	00	0000	0000	CC00	0000	231	121:22.5016

Figure 3. Basic Channel Monitor

-- ADAPTED FROM 'BCULDER PRODUCT TEST LABORATORY-DCCL2' REPCRT

VS2 RUN 5 - FEB 5, 1976 (TEMP64) 1 OF 2 CATE=76.048 TIME=17:04:44 STATLS 00CC2CCCCCC04000

XLATED DATA BYTES	BYTE CCUNT	CMND EXEC TIME	CHAN IND HEX	STATLS A SUCC DUU TMEBEECX	CMND CODE HEX	---- DATA BYTES --- 1 2	3 4	5 6	7 8	CCD HUE A V	ELAPSEC TIME MMM:SS.SSSS	ACTIVITY TRACE 040	21X	23X	281	HOSTCHAN D T
1.........	2	91	31	00001000	07	0001	0000	0000	0000	231	120:40.1833	AQS	...	SEK	MV	***...
2.........	0	48	31	00000100	00	00CC	00CC	CCCC	CCCC	231	12C:40.1932	ACS	...	SEK	MV	.+....
3.........	0	77	31	00001C00	33	000C	0000	0000	0000	231	120:40.1933	AQS	...	RCT	MV	.+....
4.........	0	48	31	00000100	00	CCCC	000C	CC00	CCC0	231	12C:40.2114	AQS	...	RCT	MV	......
5VO.100.5	256	244	31	00001100	06	E5C6	00F1	F0F0	C0F5	231	12C:40.2114	AQS	...	RCB	MV	......
6.........	16	176	31	00001C00	27	0003	0042	C40C	C77F	231	120:40.2119	ACS	...	STG	MV	......
7.........	0	121	81	00000100	00	000C	0CCC	CC0C	CCC0	281	12C:41.5844	ACS	...	STG	MV	***...
8.........	0	11	40	C0000100	00	000C	0000	0000	0000	040	120:43.3401	AQS	...	STG	...	***...
9.........	0	25	40	00001100	03	000C	0000	CC0C	CCC0	040	120:43.3401	...	...	STG	...	......
10.........	0	428	40	00100000	00	1F00	000C	CC00	CC00	040	120:43.4000	...	...	STG	...	**....
11....0098	28	657	40	00001C00	87	020C	0001	FCFC	F9F8	040	120:43.4009	ACD	...	STG	...	+.....
12........F	12	138	10	00001100	37	0002	0043	0B03	02FF	210	12C:43.4070	AQD	VAL	STG	...	+.....
13.........	0	54	15	CC000100	00	000C	0000	C000	0000	215	120:46.2779	ACD	.E.	STG	...	***...
14.........	0	5	15	01010C00	00	0000	0000	CCCC	CCC0	215	12C:46.5814	ACD	...	STG	...	**....
15.........	2	103	15	00001000	07	0001	0000	0C0C	CC00	215	120:46.5877	ACD	SEK	STG	...	......
16.........	0	48	15	0C0CC1CC	00	0000	00CC	CCCC	C000	215	120:46.5983	ACD	SEK	STG	...	......
17.........	0	80	15	00001000	33	0000	0000	0000	0000	215	12C:46.5983	AQD	RCT	STG	...	......
18.........	0	48	15	CC000100	00	0000	0000	CC00	0000	215	120:46.6178	ACD	RCT	STG	...	......
19VOL10094	256	234	15	00001100	06	E5D6	D3F1	FCF0	F9F4	215	12C:46.6178	AQD	RCB	STG	...	......
20...	16	173	15	00001000	27	0003	0040	021A	C87F	215	120:46.6183	AQD	STG	STG	...	......
21.........	0	48	31	0C000C1CC	00	000C	000C	CC0C	C000	231	121:01.7000	ACD	STG	STG	...	***...
22........F	12	138	30	00001100	37	0002	0044	0B03	02FF	230	121:01.7002	AQD	STG	VAL	...	......
23.........	0	13	40	0C000100	00	3A00	0000	CC00	C000	040	121:07.7915	AQD	STG	...	...	***...
24.........	0	22	40	00001100	03	3A0C	000C	CC0C	CCCC	040	121:07.7916	...	STG	...	...	......
25....0098	28	651	40	00001000	87	0200	2001	F0F0	F9F8	040	121:07.8388	AQS	STG	...	...	*.....
26.........	0	13	40	0C000100	00	D01E	0A1C	CCCC	CC00	040	121:15.3459	ACS	STG	...	...	**....
27.........	0	24	40	00001100	03	D01E	0A10	0000	0000	040	121:15.3460	...	STG	...	...	......
28.........	0	3488	40	0C100000	00	0000	001A	C00A	C000	040	121:15.3675	...	STG	...	...	......
29....0094	28	643	40	00001000	87	020C	2001	FCFC	F9F4	040	121:15.3716	ACS	STG	...	...	......
30.........	0	48	15	00000100	00	0000	0000	0000	0000	215	121:19.5379	AQS	STG	...	...	***...
31........F	16	174	10	00001100	37	0003	0043	CCC4	C6FF	210	121:19.5382	ACS	VAL	...	...	......
32........F	16	180	30	00001100	37	0003	0044	0C04	06FF	230	121:19.5385	AQS	...	VAL	...	......
33.........	0	5	11	01010000	00	0000	0000	0000	C000	211	121:19.6593	AQS	...	...	...	*.....
34.........	16	177	11	00001100	37	0003	0042	C40C	C77F	211	121:19.6698	AQS	VAL	...	...	......
35.........	16	176	31	00001100	37	0003	0042	0400	077F	231	121:19.6701	AQS	...	VAL	...	......
36........F	8	99	10	00001100	37	0C01	0044	CA04	C3FF	210	121:20.0561	ACS	VAL	...	...	*.....
37........F	8	101	30	00001100	37	0001	0045	0A04	03FF	230	121:20.0564	AQS	...	VAL	...	......
38.........	8	100	10	00001100	37	0001	0044	0E03	011F	210	121:20.0568	AQS	VAL	...	...	......
39.........	8	100	30	00001100	37	0C01	0045	CE03	C11F	230	121:20.0571	ACS	...	VAL	...	......
40........F	8	105	10	00001100	37	0001	0044	0A04	03FF	210	121:20.0576	AQS	VAL	...	...	......
41........F	8	98	30	00001100	37	0CC1	0045	CAC4	C3FF	230	121:20.0579	ACS	...	VAL	...	......
42.........	8	101	10	00001100	37	0001	0044	0E03	011F	210	121:2C.0583	AQS	VAL	...	...	......
43.........	8	97	30	00001100	37	0001	0045	CE03	011F	230	121:20.0585	AQS	...	VAL	...	......
44.........	2	93	31	00001000	07	0001	000C	CCCC	CCC0	231	121:20.4387	ACS	...	SEK	...	**....
45.........	0	5	15	01010000	00	0000	000C	0000	0000	215	121:20.5853	AQS	...	SEK	...	*.....
46...	16	176	15	00001100	37	0003	004C	C21A	C87F	215	121:20.5863	ACS	VAL	SEK	...	+.....
47.........	0	48	31	00000100	00	0000	0000	0C00	C000	231	121:22.4795	AQS	...	SEK	...	++....
48.........	0	77	31	00001C00	33	0000	00C0	CC00	0000	231	121:22.4796	ACS	...	RDT	...	++....
49.........	0	48	31	00000100	00	000C	000C	CC0C	CCC0	231	121:22.4976	ACS	...	RCT	...	+.....
50VD.100.5	256	246	31	00001100	06	E5D6	00F1	F0F0	00F5	231	121:22.4977	AQS	...	RCB	...	+.....
51........J	28	88	31	00001100	A4	0131	000C	A40C	00D1	231	121:22.4980	ACS	...	A4	...	+.....
52.........	2	95	31	00001C00	07	0001	0000	0000	C000	231	121:22.4582	AQS	...	SEK	...	+.....
53.........	0	48	31	00000100	00	0000	0000	CC00	C000	231	121:22.5016	AQS	...	SEK	...	+.....

Figure 4. MSS Activity Trace

AQD	Acquire data (host to MSC)
AQS	Acquire inhibit stage (host to MSC)
DIA	Diagnose
DMT	Demount virtual volume (host to MSC)
DST	Move data—destage (MSC to SA)
.E. or .+.	Device end – cartridge load complete (DRD to MSC)
INV	Invalidate SA tables (MSC to SA)
MT	Mount virtual volume (host to MSC)
MV, MOV	Move cartridge (MSC to accessor)
RDB	Read data from SA buffer (MSC to SA)
RDC	Read SA command buffer (MSC to SA)
RDT	REad cartridge to SA buffer (reads CTOC) (MSC to SA)
SDE	Send suppressible device end to host (MSC to SA)
SEK	Seek to a position on a cartridge (MSC to SA)
STG	Move data—stage from cartridge to staging drive (MSC to SA)
UDE	Send unsuppressible device end to host (MSC to SA)
UNL	Unload cartridge (MSC to SA)
VAL	Validate SA tables (MSC to SA)
WRB	Write data to SA buffer (MSC to SA)
WRT	Write SA buffer to cartridge (writes CTOC) (MSC to SA)
...	Device idle

Figure 5. MSS Activity Trace Mnemonics

BOULDER PRODUCT TEST LABORATORY-DOOL2   * * * * * D 2 C L P E R F . A N D M E A S .* * * *

| SUBSYSTEM 'A' TEST | TRACE | DATE=75.324 | TIME=14:09:48 | STATUS 01E1E00000004000 | PAC |

COMMAND EXECUTION TIME. USEC	CCD HUE A V	LRG	CHAN IND ISCSCCBP SICSBDCL	HC EM XD	STATUS ASUCCOUU TMEBEECX	BYTE COUNT	01	02	03	04	05	06	07	08	XLATED DATA BYTES	ELAPSED TIME HH:MM:SS.MMMUUU	ACTIVITY TRACE 040 21X 23X 281
1 9835	040	000	10100000	42	00001100	512	C0	26	C0	25	00	1D	00	39	*......*	01 29 14 444062	DIA ... ... MOV
2 20	040	000	10000000	03	00001100	0										01 29 14 453906	... ... MOV
3 75	281	000	00100000	00	00000000	0	00	00	00	00	00	00	00	00	*........*	01 29 14 647997	... ... MOV
4 470	281	000	10000000	71	00001000	4	4A	EE	5B	F2	00	C0	C0	00	*....2....*	01 29 14 648105	... ... MOV
5 107	040	000	10100000	26	00001100	0										01 29 14 741367	RD ... ... MOV
6 11	040	000	00100000	00	00000100	0	E0	1B	C5	01	00	00	00	00	*........*	01 29 14 809966	RD ... ... MOV
7 4695	040	000	10100000	06	00001100	248	0C	94	40	00	F1	F1	F1	F0	*...:1110*	01 29 14 809986	RMB ... ... MOV
8 23	040	000	10000000	03	00001100	0										01 29 14 814677	... ... MOV
9 89	281	000	00100000	00	00000000	0	00	00	00	00	00	00	00	00	*........*	01 29 17 110145	... ... MOV
10 468	281	000	10000000	71	00001000	4	7A	F1	5B	D6	00	00	00	00	*.1.0....*	01 29 17 110274	... ... MOV
11 110	281	000	00000000	00	00000100	0	00	00	00	00	00	C0	00	00	*........*	01 29 19 571316	... ... MOV
12 53	230	000	00000000	00	00000100	0	00	00	00	00	00	00	00	00	*........*	01 29 21 490116	... .+. ...
13 94	210	000	10100000	00	00001100	2	00	01	CC	00	00	C0	00	00	*........*	01 29 21 775206	... SEK ... ...
14 46	210	000	00100000	00	00000100	0	00	00	00	00	00	00	00	00	*........*	01 29 21 777392	... SEK ... ...
15 76	210	000	10100000	33	00001100	0	00	00	00	00	00	00	00	00	*........*	01 29 21 777450	... RDT ... ...
16 46	210	000	00100000	00	00000100	0	00	00	00	00	00	00	00	00	*........*	01 29 21 795502	... RDT ... ...
17 231	210	000	10000000	06	00001100	256	E5	C6	C3	F1	F1	F1	F5	F6	*VOL11156*	01 29 21 795560	... RDB ... ...
18 161	210	000	10100000	27	00001000	8	80	C1	C0	4E	09	C7	0B	F8	*......8*	01 29 21 795970	... DST ... ...
19 53	232	000	00000000	00	00000100	0	00	00	00	00	00	00	00	00	*........*	01 29 23 962255	... DST .+. ...
20 90	234	000	10100000	07	00001100	2	C0	01	00	00	00	00	00	00	*........*	01 29 23 972619	... DST SEK ...
21 46	234	000	00100000	00	00000100	0	00	00	00	00	00	00	00	00	*........*	01 29 23 973370	... DST SEK ...
22 79	234	000	10100000	33	00001100	0	00	00	00	00	00	C0	00	00	*........*	01 29 23 973427	... DST RDT ...
23 47	234	000	00100000	00	00000100	0	C0	C0	CC	00	00	00	00	00	*........*	01 29 23 991495	... DST RDT ...
24 245	234	000	10000000	06	00001100	256	E5	C6	C3	F1	F0	F1	F1	F9	*VOL10119*	01 29 23 991553	... DST RDB ...
25 212	234	000	10100000	27	00001100	44	C0	CA	00	00	0F	00	01	7F	*........*	01 29 24 036002	... DST STG ...
26 46	210	000	00000000	00	00000100	0	00	00	00	00	00	C0	00	00	*........*	01 29 29 980801	... DST STG ...
27 82	210	000	10000000	37	00001100	8	80	01	00	4E	09	07	0B	F8	*......8*	01 29 30 007788	... INV STG ...
28 58	210	000	10000000	37	00001100	4	C8	C0	2C	30	00	C0	00	00	*H......*	01 30 29 771882	... 37 STG ...
29 46	234	000	00000000	00	00000100	0	00	00	00	00	00	00	00	00	*........*	01 30 41 328067	... ... VAL ...
30 663	214	000	10000000	37	00001100	44	C0	0A	00	4A	0F	00	01	7F	*........*	01 30 41 338129	... ... VAL ...
31 664	234	000	10000000	37	00001100	44	00	CA	00	00	0F	00	01	7F	*........*	01 30 41 338901	... ... VAL ...
32 85	230	000	10000000	37	00001100	8	80	01	00	00	C9	07	0B	F8	*......8*	01 30 41 403711	... ... INV ...
33 101	210	000	10000000	37	00001100	8	C0	C1	C0	4A	0F	00	01	FF	*......F*	01 30 41 440162	... ... VAL ...
34 106	230	000	10000000	37	00001100	8	00	01	00	00	0F	00	01	FF	*......F*	01 30 41 440438	... ... VAL ...
35 68	210	000	10000000	37	00001100	4	20	C0	75	4A	C0	C0	00	00	*........*	01 30 41 440833	... ... UDE ...
36 92	234	000	10100000	07	00001000	2	00	01	C0	00	C0	00	00	00	*........*	01 30 41 551554	... ... SEK ...
37 46	234	000	00100000	00	00000100	0	00	00	00	00	00	00	00	00	*........*	01 30 47 150118	... ... SEK ...
38 78	234	000	10100000	33	00001100	0	00	00	00	00	00	00	00	00	*........*	01 30 47 150175	... ... RDT ...
39 48	234	000	00100000	00	00000100	0	00	00	00	00	00	00	00	00	*........*	01 30 47 168242	... ... RDT ...
40 245	234	000	10100000	06	00001100	256	E5	D6	D3	F1	F0	F1	F1	F9	*VOL10119*	01 30 47 168300	... ... RDB ...
41 87	234	000	10000000	A4	00001100	28	01	31	00	00	A4	00	34	01	*......J*	01 30 47 168552	... ... A4 ...
42 91	234	000	10100000	07	00001100	2	00	01	00	00	00	00	00	00	*........*	01 30 47 168846	... ... SEK ...
43 46	234	000	00100000	00	00000100	0	00	00	00	00	00	00	00	00	*........*	01 30 47 172212	... ... SEK ...
44 928	234	000	10100000	05	00001100	256	E5	C6	C3	F1	F0	F1	F1	F9	*VOL10119*	01 30 47 172269	... ... WRB ...
45 77	234	000	10100000	3F	00001100	0	CC	C0	C0	00	00	C0	00	00	*........*	01 30 47 173204	... ... WRT ...
46 43	234	000	00100000	00	00000100	0	00	00	00	00	00	00	00	00	*........*	01 30 47 150457	... ... WRT ...
47 102	234	000	10100000	17	00000100	0	C0	C0	00	00	00	00	00	00	*........*	01 30 47 190516	... ... UNL ...
48 48	234	000	00000000	00	00000100	0	00	00	00	00	00	00	00	00	*........*	01 30 52 344052	... ... UNL ...
49 470	281	000	10000000	71	00001000	4	93	C6	3A	F1	00	00	00	00	*.0.1....*	01 30 52 344308	... ... MOV
50 4	210	000	10000100	00	01010000	0	00	C0	00	00	00	C0	00	00	*........*	01 30 52 619582	... ... MOV
51 92	210	000	10100000	07	00001000	2	00	01	00	00	00	C0	00	00	*........*	01 30 52 619764	... SEK ... MOV
52 108	281	000	00000000	00	00000100	0	C0	00	00	00	00	00	00	00	*........*	01 30 54 999193	... SEK ... MOV
53 46	210	000	00100000	00	00000100	0	00	00	00	00	00	00	00	00	*........*	01 30 56 960556	... SEK ... ...

Figure 6. MSS Activity Trace Example-Staging a Data Set

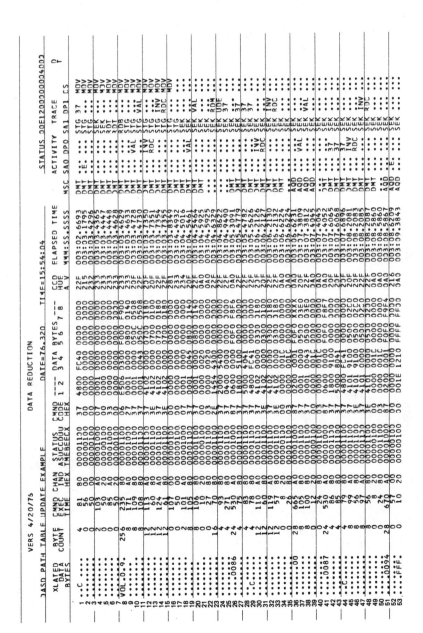

Figure 7. Verification of DASD Path Table Update Implementation

VERS 4/20/76 DATA REDUCTION

1 INIT MERGE HOST ON CHAN 2 -- 76.231-1 DATE=76.231 TIME=12:23:59 STATUS 00E120000000004000 PAGE 260

	XLATED DATA BYTES	BYTE COUNT	CMND EXEC TIME	CHAN IND HEX	STATUS ASUCCDUU TMEBEFCX	CMND CODE HEX	---- DATA BYTES --- 1 2	3 4	5 6	7 8	CCD HUF A V	ELAPSED TIME MMM:SS.SSSS	ACTIVITY TRACE MSC	SAO	DPO	SA1	DP1	CS	D T
1	....	264	390	A0	00001100	06	D01E	1111	0000	0000	200	008:06.6218	MT	...	...	...	...	...	SPC CNV/QCB SCAN/QCB FIFO
2	....	5	534	A0	01001100	31	001B	000B	0D00	0000	200	008:06.6526	MT	...	...	...	...	...	JOURNAL:
3	....	264	385	80	00001100	05	C01C	0005	0002	0445	200	008:06.6531	MT	...	...	...	...	...	SQT
4	....	5	569	A0	01001100	31	001B	000B	0D00	0000	224	008:06.6718	MT	...	...	...	...	...	JOURNAL:
5	....	264	384	80	00001100	05	C01C	0005	0002	0445	224	008:06.6724	MT	...	...	...	...	...	SQT
6	....	264	389	A0	00001100	06	D01E	0C01	0000	0000	200	008:06.6972	MT	...	...	...	...	...	SPACE ALLOC/DELAYED RESP
7	....	264	385	80	00001100	05	C01C	0005	0002	0445	200	008:06.7158	MT	...	...	...	...	...	WR SQT
8	....	264	386	80	00001100	05	C01C	0005	0002	0445	224	008:06.7350	MT	...	...	...	...	...	WR SQT
9	....	264	385	80	00001100	05	2009	0B15	0002	0445	200	008:06.7569	MT	...	...	...	...	...	WR MVT DATA
10	....	264	388	80	C0001100	05	2009	0B15	0002	0445	224	008:06.7761	MT	...	...	...	...	...	WR MVT DATA
11	....	264	387	A0	C0001100	06	D01F	0201	0000	0000	200	008:06.7970	MT	...	...	...	...	...	MOUNT OVLY 1
12	....	5	178	A0	01001100	31	001B	000B	0100	0000	200	C08:06.8301	MT	...	...	...	...	...	JOURNAL:
13	....	264	388	80	00001100	06	701A	0A05	0002	0445	200	008:06.8303	MT	...	...	...	...	...	READ BEFORE NULL
14	....	5	176	A0	01001100	31	001B	000B	0100	0000	200	008:06.8468	MT	...	...	...	...	...	JOURNAL:
15	....	264	386	80	00001100	05	0000	0000	0002	0445	200	008:06.8470	MT	...	...	...	...	...	NULL
16	....	5	179	A0	01001100	31	001B	000B	0100	0000	224	008:06.8659	MT	...	...	...	...	...	JOURNAL:
17	....	264	386	80	00001100	05	0000	0000	0002	0445	224	008:06.8661	MT	...	...	...	...	...	NULL
18	....	264	390	A0	00001100	06	D01E	1201	C000	0000	200	C08:06.8803	MT	...	...	...	...	...	CONF DATA UPDATE
19	....FFF.	0	7	20	00000100	00	D01E	1210	FFFF	FF00	0A0	008:06.8886	MT	...	...	...	...	...	
20	....FFF.	0	25	80	00001100	03	D01E	1210	FFFF	FF00	0A0	008:06.8886	...	...	...	...	...	...	
21	0097	17	331	A0	00001000	87	0800	0000	F0F0	F9F7	0A0	008:06.8995	MT	...	...	...	...	...	
22	....	264	390	A0	00001100	06	D01E	0B01	0000	0000	200	008:06.9135	MT	...	...	...	...	...	MNT/INDEX SRCH
23	....	264	388	80	00001100	06	701A	0A01	0000	0000	200	008:06.9468	MT	...	...	...	...	...	RD CONFIG INDX/ID CONV
24	....	5	175	A0	01001100	31	001B	000B	0100	0000	200	008:06.9633	MT	...	...	...	...	...	JOURNAL:
25	....	264	387	80	00001100	05	701A	0A06	0002	0446	200	008:06.9635	MT	...	...	...	...	...	CONFIG SA 1, IFACE B
26	....	5	176	A0	01001100	31	001B	C00B	0100	0000	224	008:06.9657	MT	...	...	...	...	...	JOURNAL:
27	....	264	384	80	00001100	05	701A	0A06	0002	0446	224	008:06.9659	MT	...	...	...	...	...	CONFIG SA 1, IFACE B
28	....	264	391	80	C0001100	06	2008	1005	0002	0257	200	008:06.9821	MT	...	...	...	...	...	RD MVT INDX
29	....	5	569	A0	01001100	31	001B	000B	0200	0000	200	008:06.9967	MT	...	...	...	...	...	JOURNAL:
30	....	264	387	80	00001100	05	2008	1005	0002	0446	200	008:06.9973	MT	...	...	...	...	...	MVT INDX
31	....	5	613	A0	01001100	31	001B	000B	0200	0000	224	008:06.9991	MT	...	...	...	...	...	JOURNAL:
32	....	264	389	80	00001100	05	2008	1005	0002	0446	224	008:06.9997	MT	...	...	...	...	...	MVT INDX
33	....	264	388	80	00001100	05	2009	0B16	0002	043F	200	008:07.0237	MT	...	...	...	...	...	RD MVT DATA
34	....	5	526	A0	01001100	31	001B	000B	0300	0000	200	008:07.0471	MT	...	...	...	...	...	JOURNAL:
35	....	264	387	80	00001100	05	2009	0B16	0002	0446	200	008:07.0477	MT	...	...	...	...	...	MVT DATA
36	....	5	555	A0	01001100	31	001B	000B	0300	0000	224	008:07.0495	MT	...	...	...	...	...	JOURNAL:
37	....	264	384	80	00001100	05	2009	0B16	0002	0446	224	008:07.0501	MT	...	...	...	...	...	MVT DATA
38	....	264	391	A0	00001100	06	D01E	0E01	0000	0000	200	008:07.0633	MT	...	...	...	...	...	**********
39	....	264	389	80	00001100	06	1008	000A	0002	0445	200	008:07.1011	MT	...	...	...	...	...	RD SDG 000 DVB
40	....	5	517	A0	01001100	31	001B	000B	0400	0000	200	008:07.1142	MT	...	...	...	...	...	JOURNAL:
41	....	264	384	80	00001100	05	1008	000A	0002	0446	200	008:07.1148	MT	...	...	...	...	...	SDG 000 DVB
42	....	5	537	A0	01001100	31	001B	000B	0400	0000	224	008:07.1166	MT	...	...	...	...	...	JOURNAL:
43	....	264	388	80	00001100	05	1008	000A	0002	0446	224	008:07.1171	MT	...	...	...	...	...	SDG 000 DVB
44	....	264	389	A0	00001100	06	D01E	0B01	0000	0000	200	008:07.1299	MT	...	...	...	...	...	MNT/INDEX SRCH
45	....	264	387	80	00C01100	05	1008	000A	0002	0446	200	008:07.1510	MT	...	...	...	...	...	WR SDG 000 DVB
46	....	264	386	80	00001100	05	1008	000A	0002	0446	224	008:07.1700	MT	...	...	...	...	...	WR SDG 000 DVB
47	....	264	388	80	00001100	06	1008	000B	0002	0445	200	008:07.1848	MT	...	...	...	...	...	RD SDG 000 LPB
48	....	5	616	A0	01001100	31	001B	000B	0500	0000	200	008:07.1978	MT	...	...	...	...	...	JOURNAL:
49	....	264	387	80	00001100	05	1008	000B	0002	0446	200	008:07.1985	MT	...	...	...	...	...	SDG 000 LPB
50	....	5	629	A0	01001100	31	001B	000B	0500	0000	224	008:07.2168	MT	...	...	...	...	...	JOURNAL:
51	....	264	384	80	00001100	05	1008	000B	0002	0446	224	008:07.2174	MT	...	...	...	...	...	SDG 000 LPB
52	....	264	386	80	00001100	05	1008	000B	0002	0446	200	008:07.2347	MT	...	...	...	...	...	WR SDG 000 LPB
53	....	264	384	80	00001100	05	1008	000B	0002	0446	224	008:07.2536	MT	...	...	...	...	...	WR SDG 000 LPB

Figure 8A. MSC Table I/O Report Example

VERS 4/20/76   DATA REDUCTION

1 INIT MERGE HOST ON CHAN 2 -- 76.231-1   DATE=76.231   TIME=12:23:59   STATUS 00E1200000004000   PAGE 261

	XLATED DATA BYTES	BYTE COUNT	CMND EXEC TIME	CHAN STATUS HEX	CHAN ASHC CHU TME	STATUS CODE HEX	CMND CODE 1 2	DATA BYTES 3 4 5 6 7 8	CCD HUE AV	ELAPSED TIME MMM:SS.SSSS	MSC	ACTIVITY SAO DPO SA1 DPI CS	TRAFF D
1	....	264	391	A2	00001100	06	001F	3201 0000 0000	200	008:07.2797	MT	......	MOUNT OVLY 1
2	....	264	386	80	01001100	05	701A	3406 0002 0446	224	008:07.3187	MT	......	WR CONFIG SA 1, IFACE B
3	....	264	388	80	01001100	05	A01A	3201 0002 0445	200	008:07.3297	MT	......	WR CONFIG SA 1, IFACE B
4	....	264	623	80	01001100	31	A01B	0008 0600 0000	200	008:07.3315	MT	......	RD VVA-TBL
5	....			A0	00001100	06	001B	0000 0600 0000	200	008:07.3321	MT	......	JOURNAL:
6	....	265	609	A0	01001100	31	001B	0608 0002 0446	224	008:07.3504	MT	......	VVA-TBL
7	....	264	386	90	01001100	05	A01B	3201 0002 0446	224	008:07.3509	MT	......	JOURNAL:
8	....	264	386	90	00001100	05	A01B	3201 0002 0446	224	008:07.3561	MT	......	WR VVA TBL
9	....	264	387	A0	01001100	06	001A	0804 0002 0445	200	008:07.3811	MT	......	WR VVA TBL
10	....	264	389	90	00001100	05	001B	0804 0002 0445	200	008:07.3901	MT	......	RD VVA-VOL SA 1
11	....	264	545	A0	01001100	31	001B	0700 0002 0446	224	008:07.3986	MT	......	JOURNAL:
12	....	264	387	80	00001100	05	001A	3804 0002 0446	224	008:07.3992	MT	......	VVA-VOL SA 1
13	....	264	388	90	01001100	05	001A	3804 0002 0446	224	008:07.4008	MT	......	JOURNAL:
14	....	264	386	80	00001100	05	001A	0804 0002 0445	200	008:07.4114	MT	......	WR VVA-VOL SA 1
15	....	264	389	80	00001100	05	001A	0804 0002 0445	200	008:07.4312	MT	......	WR VVA-VOL SA 1
16	....			A0	00001100	05	001A	0804 0002 0446	224	008:07.4322	MT	......	WR VVA-VOL SA 1
17	.FFF..	265	380	A0	01001100	05	001F	EEEE 0002 0446	200	008:07.4496	MT	......	JOURNAL:
18	.FFF..	264	537	A0	01001100	31	001A	0008 0002 0446	224	008:07.4478	MT	......	SA BACK OUT
19		264	386	80	00001100	05	001F	EEEE 0002 0446	224	008:07.4684	MT	...RDC..	SA BACK OUT
20	......			A2	00001100	06	001F	5642 0000 0000	200	008:07.4491	MT	......	JOURNAL:
21	......	265	350	A0	01001100	36	001A	0008 0000 0000	200	008:07.4495	MT	......	SPACE ALLOC
22	......	265	508	A2	00001100	31	001A	0000 0002 0444	200	008:07.4995	MT	......	JOURNAL:
23	......			A0	00001100	06	001B	0009 0002 0446	224	008:07.5017	MT	......	SDG 000 PAB
24	......	264	473	A0	01001100	31	001A	0009 0002 0446	224	008:07.5021	MT	......	JOURNAL:
25	......	264	386	A0	00001100	05	001E	0E01 0002 0000	200	008:07.5127	MT	......	SDG 000 PAB
26	......	265	393	A0	00001100	06	001A	0009 0002 0446	224	008:07.5344	MT	......	**********
27	......			90	00001100	05	001B	0009 0002 0000	200	008:07.5509	MT	......	JOURNAL: 000 LPB
28	......	265	389	A0	01001100	05	001B	0400 0002 0446	224	008:07.5520	MT	......	JOURNAL: 000 LPB
29	......	264	524	A0	01001100	31	001A	0008 0002 0446	224	008:07.5627	MT	......	SDG 000 LPB
30	......			A0	00001100	06	001E	0001 0002 0446	200	008:07.5442	MT	......	SPACE ALLOC
31	......	264	390	80	00001100	05	1C08	0009 0002 0446	224	008:07.6029	MT	......	WR SDG 000 LPB
32	......	264	387	80	00001100	05	001A	0008 0002 0446	224	008:07.6186	MT	......	WR SDG 000 LPB
33	......	264	388	80	00001100	05	001B	0008 0002 0430	200	008:07.6186	MT	......	RD SDG 000 PAB
34	....	265	429	A0	00001100	06	001B	0006 0002 0446	224	008:07.6317	MT	......	WR SDG 000 PRM 5
35	8			A0	00001100	05	001A	0008 0002 0446	224	008:07.6504	MT	......	JOURNAL:
36	......	264	432	A0	00001100	31	001B	0008 0002 0446	224	008:07.6508	MT	......	JOURNAL: 000 PRM 5
37	......	264	386	A0	01001100	05	001A	0008 0002 0446	224	008:07.6690	MT	......	WR SDG 000 PRM 5
38	......	264	390	A0	00001100	06	001F	1111 0003 0000	200	008:07.6695	MT	......	SDG 000 PRM 5
39	......	264	388	80	00001100	05	001C	0009 0002 0446	224	008:07.6683	MT	......	SPACE ALLOC/DELAYED RESP
40	......			A0	00001100	05	001C	0009 0002 0446	224	008:07.7458	MT	......	SPC ENV/QCB SCAN/QCB FIFO
41	......			A0	00001100	05	001E	02E8 0000 0000	200	008:07.7703	MT	......	PD SQT
42	......			A0	00001100	05	001C	0009 0002 0000	200	008:07.7996	MT	......	JOURNAL:
43	......	264	386	80	00001100	05	001A	0002 0002 0446	200	008:07.8178	MT	......	SQT
44	......	264	431	80	01001100	05	001B	0009 0002 0000	200	008:07.8359	MT	......	JOURNAL:
45	......	264	387	80	00001100	05	001C	0009 0002 0446	224	008:07.8363	MT	......	SQT

Figure 8B. MSC Table I/O Report Example

VERS 4/20/76

DATA REDUCTION

1 INIT MERGE HOST ON CHAN 2 -- 76.231-1   DATE=76.231   TIME=12:23:59   STATUS 00E1200000004000   PAGE 262

The right-hand column (ACTIVITY TRACE) lists entries including:

- SPACE ALLOC/DELAYED RESP
- WR SQT
- SPC CNV/QCB SCAN/QCB FIFO
- JOURNAL:
- SQT
- SPACE ALLOC/DELAYED RESP
- WR SQT
- WR MVT DATA
- WR MVT DATA
- MOUNT ONLY 1
- JOURNAL: BEFORE NULL
- NULL
- JOURNAL:
- NULL
- WR SQT
- CONE DATA UPDATE
- WR SQT
- WR SQT
- WR SQT
- RD SQT
- WR SQT
- WR SQT
- WR SQT
- WR SQT
- WR SQT
- WR SQT
- WR SQT

Figure 8C. MSC Table I/O Report Example

```
         VERSION 1.0 -- 7/15/76
       EXAMPLE                              DATE=76.320    TIME=15:04:58
DEVICE = 21X = SA0      TIME INTERVAL = 00:00:00 TO 00:01:00
```

SATBL (COMMAND MIX)

COMMAND CODE	NUMBER OF COMMANDS	PERCENTAGE OF TOTAL COMMANDS	RATE/HOUR
00 - TIO	28	*******	1680
05 - WRD	3	5.4	180
06 - RDD	6	10.9	360
07 - SEK	9	16.3	540
17 - UNL	3	5.4	180
27 - MVD	3	5.4	180
33 - RTB	6	10.9	360
37 - TBS	14	25.4	840
3E - RCB	5	9.0	300
3F - WBT	3	5.4	180
A4 - RBL	3	5.4	180
TOTAL	83	100	4980

*CODES 00 AND 03 NOT INCLUDED IN PERCENTAGE

RMBTBL (MESSAGE TYPE MIX)

MESSAGE TYPE	NUMBER OF MESSAGES	PERCENTAGE OF RMB MESSAGES	RATE/HOUR
TOTAL	--------	100	--------

Figure 9A. MSC Command Mix Report Example

```
-- VERSION 1.0 -- 7/15/76
EXAMPLE                                          DATE=76.320    TIME=16:04:58          STATUS 00E1200000004000
DEVICE = OAO = MSC     TIME INTERVAL = 00:00:00 TO 00:01:00

NUMBER OF CHANNEL PROGRAMS FROM HOST TO MSC =        26
MSCTBL  (COMMAND MIX)
 COMMAND CODE      NUMBER OF COMMANDS                   PERCENTAGE OF TOTAL COMMANDS          RATE/HOUR
    00 - TIO               26                                   *******                          1560
    03 - NOP               26                                   *******                          1560
    27 - MVD               13                                      32.5                           780
    42 - DIR               13                                      32.5                           780
    99******                2                                       5.0                           120
    87 - EX                12                                      30.0                           720
    TOTAL---         -------92                                  ----100                      -----5520

*CODES 00 AND 03 NOT INCLUDED IN PERCENTAGE

MSCTBL(COMMAND MIX) FOR CODE 87 COMMANDS
 COMMAND TYPE      NUMBER OF COMMANDS                   PERCENTAGE OF COD87 COMMANDS          RATE/HOUR
       MT                   8                                      66.6                           480
       AQD                  4                                      33.3                           240
    TOTAL---         -------12                                  ----100                      -----720
```

Figure 9B. MSS Command Mix Report Example

TABLE I/O STATISTICS - VERSION 0.1 - 4/27/76

	VERIFIC SDG	MVT	SCR CART VOL	INV	TRAN VOL	VVA-VOL	CONFIG	TABLE NAME PST	IMG	CELL MAP	VVA TBL	***ERROR	RQT CODE	MSG BUFF*****ERR
RD	17	53		11		11	11	24			11	19	164	
WR	60	72		11		22	22	22			22	106		

SDG ACCESSES (READS)

SDG NUM	RPM 0	RPM 1	RPM 2	RPM 3	RPM 4	PRM 5	RPM 6	RPM 7	PAB	DVB	LPB
0											
1	1		1	3		6		4	1	1	
2											
3											
4											
5											
6											
7											
8											
9											
A											

SDG ACCESSES (WRITES)

SDG NUM	RPM 0	RPM 1	RPM 2	RPM 3	RPM 4	PRM 5	RPM 6	RPM 7	PAB	DVB	LPB
0											
1	2		2	6		12		8	28	2	
2											
3											
4											
5											
6											
7											
8											
9											
A											

Figure 10A. MSC Table Access Statistics Report

MVT ACCESSES

	CNTL	INDX	OVFL	DATA
RD	11	38		4
WR	22	22		28

RECOVERY JOURNAL ACCESSES

NULLS: BEFORE NULLS: 52
READ BACK OUT: READS: 26   22 WRITES:
SA BACK OUT:

OTHER JOURNAL ACCESSES:

	VERIFIC	SDG	MVT	SCR	CARTVOL	INV	TRAN	VCL	VVA-VCL	TABLE NAME CONFIG	PST	IMG	CELL	MAPVVA	TBL	***ERRORSQT	CODE	MSG BUFF*****ERR
RD	60	106						22	22	22	22				22			
WR																52		

MSC TRACE ACCESSES

READS: 12 ; WRITES:

Figure 10B. MSC Table Access Statistics Report

COMPUTER PERFORMANCE, K.M. CHANDY AND M. REISER (EDS.)
NORTH HOLLAND PUBLISHING COMPANY, 1977

THE STATISTICAL ESTIMATION OF TURNAROUND FUNCTIONS FOR FIRST-IN, FIRST-OUT SCHEDULED BATCH JOBS

*P. L. Chouinard**
Northwestern University
Evanston, Illinois, USA

Execution turnaround is modeled using statistically estimated
execution residency functions. A separate function is found
for each batch job class in a mixed timesharing and batch
multiprogrammed environment. A simple model for expected
execution residency is presented. Model parameter estimates
are calculated using the preliminary test estimator. Use of
these functions to predict execution turnaround, for first-in
first-out scheduled batch jobs, is shown.

1. INTRODUCTION

Individual users at large installations, for example at university research sites,
are interested in having a reasonable estimate of when their job will be out once
it has been submitted. Computer center managers are concerned with turnaround to
the extent that they are aware of user discontent over poor or poorly predicted
turnaround. This paper focuses on the problem of predicting turnaround for batch
jobs in a mixed batch and timesharing environment through the use of statistically
estimated batch job execution residency functions. A separate function is found
for each batch job class under the assumptions that each incoming batch job is
assigned a job class designation based upon an estimate of computer resources it
will require, and that jobs within each jobclass are scheduled on a first-in
first-out basis.

The portion of total turnaround considered here is <u>execution turnaround</u>, the
elapsed wall clock time between when a batch job is read into the system and when
it finishes execution. Execution turnaround consists of the time waiting to go
into execution, the <u>execution queue time</u>, plus the wall clock time that a job is
part of the executing job mix, the <u>execution residency time</u>. Execution queue time
depends upon the execution residency times of all jobs ahead of it in its own job
class and the number of multiprogramming levels servicing that job class. Peripheral time, that portion of total turnaround between execution termination and the
termination of all peripheral activity, such as printing, punching, and plotting,
was not modeled because the necessary data would have been too difficult to
collect for the system at hand. The effort to collect such data would not have
been rewarded by any new methodological insights.

---

*This work was done as part of the author's Ph.D. dissertation and was partially
supported by the Computing Services Office, University of Illinois at Urbana-
Champaign.

2. THE TURNAROUND MODEL

Whereas turnaround is the amount of time required per unit of work, throughput is the amount of work done per unit of time. These two performance measures are inversely related representations of the same phenomenon taken from two different points of view. The throughput measure is taken from the point of view of the system, and the turnaround measure is taken from the point of view of the collection of individual jobs. In a mixed batch and timesharing system, and under the assumption that timesharing work executes at a higher priority than batch, the batch throughput rate is not constant but rather it varies inversely with the amount of timesharing activity. In this situation, changes in the batch throughput rate is an important determinant of execution residency, and hence batch turnaround.

It was noted that for systems in which total CPU utilization approached 100% if no one jobclass tended to be more CPU bound than other jobclasses, then for some multiprogramming level, L, the jobs running in each multiprogramming partition would get, on average, 1/L of the available throughput rate. For example, if L = 5 and the batch throughput rate were 60% of wall clock time, then a randomly chosen job which required 36 seconds of CPU time would be expected, on average, to have an execution residency time of 5 minutes. This expected value relationship is expressed as

(1a) $$\frac{\text{execution residency}}{\text{CPU time}} = \frac{\text{multiprogramming level}}{\text{throughput rate}}$$

or equivalently

(1b) $$\text{execution residency} = A \frac{L \ (\text{CPU time})}{\text{throughput rate}}$$

where L is the multiprogramming level and A is a multiplicative constant that is one for jobclasses which get their "fair share" of the CPU. Job classes which get more than their fair share would have shorter residency times and A would be less than one, whereas for job classes which were dominated, A would be greater than one.

In formulating this job execution residency model, it was implicitly assumed that the average long term effects of job to job variations in any other variables were nil. The argument is that a job which must wait for core because it is large, for example, will later hold up other jobs once it gets core, thereby balancing out the effect of previously having to wait. This working assumption was tested.

The approach taken was first to estimate an ordinary least squares model of the form

(2) $$Y = XB + u$$

where Y is an $N \times 1$ vector of observed residency times, N the number of observations; X is an $N \times K$ full rank matrix of K independent variables, $K < N$; B is a $K \times 1$ vector of unobservable population parameters to be estimated; and u is an $N \times 1$ vector of identically and independently distributed normal random variables with expected value and covariance given by

(3a) $E(u) = 0$
(3b) $E(uu') = qI$

where q is the variance of each of the u variables, and I is an identity matrix of order N. Note that the scalar A in (1b) is one of the elements in the vector B.

Under these assumptions, ordinary least squares estimates for the vector B ,

(4) $b = (X'X)^{-1}X'Y = CX'Y$

are linear, unbiased, maximum likelihood, and have minimum variance within the class of all linear unbiased estimators. Furthermore, the ordinary least squares estimator is minimax, that is, within the class of linear unbiased estimators it minimizes the Mean Square Error. An unbiased estimate, s , of the variance, q , is

(5) $s = \dfrac{(Y-Xb)'(Y-Xb)}{(N-K)} = \dfrac{e'e}{(N-K)}$.

The covariance matrix for b is

(6a) $qC = q(X'X)^{-1}$

and an unbiased estimate is given by

(6b) $sC = s(X'X)^{-1}$.

The multiprogramming level times job CPU time divided by throughput rate was an independent variable with additional independent variables measuring the levels of I/O activity, the number of steps in the job, and the amount of core memory used by the job.

Next it was hypothesized that the coefficients of all independent variables were zero except for the coefficient of the CPU variable weighted by the ratio of the multiprogramming level to the throughput rate. These hypotheses were expressed in the form

(7) $RB = r$

where R was a JxK restriction matrix of rank J , $J < K$, J the number of restrictions to be imposed, and r was a Jx1 vector, which in this case was the zero vector. The estimator for the exact restricted model (2), (3a), (3b), and (7) is

(8a) $b* = b - CR'(RCR')^{-1}(Rb-r)$

and an unbiased estimate of the variance is

(8b) $s* = \dfrac{(Y-Xb*)'(Y-Xb*)}{(N-K+J)} = \dfrac{e*'e*}{(N-K+J)}$.

In the case that the R matrix makes no linear restrictions other than restricting specific B elements to zero, the $b*$ solution given is computationally equivalent to performing an ordinary least squares solution on the remaining unrestricted independent variables and setting the restricted coefficients, as hypothesized, to zero. Under the assumption that the hypothesized prior information (7) is correct, $b*$ is minimum variance, linear, unbiased, and maximum likelihood. The covariance matrix for $b*$,

(9) $E(b*-B)(b*-B)' = qC* = q(C - CR'(RCR')^{-1}RC)$,

has zero variance and covariances for all restricted coefficients, and the variances and covariances for unrestricted coefficients are identical to the corresponding variances and covariances which result from an OLS solution on the unrestricted variables alone. Note that $qC*$ is necessarily singular.

The hypotheses were tested using

(10) $$F = \frac{(e*'e* - e'e)}{J} \frac{(N-K)}{(e'e)}$$

as a test statistic. This statistic, under the assumption that the prior information is true, has an F distribution with J and $N-K$ degrees of freedom. Use of (10) as a test statistic for determining the acceptance or rejection of the prior information (7) resulted in the preliminary test estimator

(11) $$\tilde{b} = I(0,c)b* + I(c,\infty)b$$

where c is the critical value which determines the acceptance, $F < c$, or the rejection, $c < F$, of (7), and in general the indicator function $I(a,b) = 1$ if $a < F < b$ and $= 0$ otherwise. The preliminary test estimator was discussed in Bock, Yancy, and Judge (1973).

This model gives expressions for the expected residency of a job given its class and amount of computer resources that it uses during execution. Note, however, that while a job's job class is determined at the time it is read into the system, its use of CPU time and other resources are not known until it actually executes. This requires a solution of a resource prediction problem if one is interested in predicting execution residency on the basis of resource usage. Unfortunately, in a research environment, as contrasted with a business environment, user supplied estimates (guesses) of the maximum amount of CPU time and I/O activity that his job will require are poor predictors of the job's actual resource use. In applying this model, one would estimate the use of each resource by jobs in each job class with sample means or moving averages. An estimate of a job's expected residency time, therefore, would be the predicted execution residency of an "average" job in its class as determined by substituting mean resource usage into the estimated residency equation for its class. The expected execution turnaround of a particular job would be the sum of its expected execution residency time and the expected execution residency times of all jobs ahead of it in its own job class divided by the number of multiprogramming levels servicing that class.

This estimate for turnaround takes into explicit account both the number of jobs in each class queue and the multiprogramming level servicing each class. Changes in these turnaround parameters are ignored when average turnaround is used as an estimate of a job's expected turnaround. Generalization of this approach to non-FIFO scheduling algorithms would require the estimation of job characteristics for jobs which have yet to be submitted.

3. THE SYSTEM

The particular machine considered was the IBM 360/75 system at the Computing Services Office, University of Illinois at Urbana-Champaign. The system included one million bytes of IBM fast core memory and two million bytes of Ampex slow core memory; four selector channels, one of which was dedicated to a high speed drum with the remaining three selector channels being connected to 2314-type Ampex disk drives; and one multiplexor channel for magnetic tape drives, local unit record equipment, a remote job entry controller, and two minicomputers for front end processing of timesharing users. This system ran under the multiprogramming system OS/MVT and Hasp.

Jobs were read into the system under control of Hasp. Each job which did not have Hasp ID card errors, errors which would have caused immediate flushing of the job, was spooled for later execution and was assigned to one of the job classes A, B, C, D, E, F, G, or X. A job was scheduled as a class X job if SYSTEM=EXPRESS was specified by the user as an ID card parameter. Class X jobs were immediately scheduled for a higher priority, Express dedicated, OS/MVT partition. Hasp assigned

one of the job classes A through G to a non-Express job on the basis of user
specified ID card resource limits according to the formula

(12)   "magic number" = 3*CPU + .05*IO + .01*K*K

where CPU was the number of central processor seconds requested for the job; IO
was the number of Execute Channel Program supervisor calls (i.e. input/output
requests) exclusive of calls for cards read, lines printed, cards punched, or
plotting requested for the job; and K was the amount of primary memory kilobytes
requested for the job. A job's class, A through G, was chosen on the basis of
where its "magic number" fell in relation to the jobclass boundaries given in
Table 1. Within each jobclass, jobs were selected by Hasp modules, known as
initiators, for execution according to a first-in first-out, or FIFO, discipline.
Once a job had been selected for execution it was placed in the OS/MVT Job Queue.
The Hasp system was capable of holding a maximum of six hundred jobs. This limit
was never approached during the time data was collected for this study.

Table 1
Job Class Boundaries

Class	"magic number" - MN
A	0 < MN <= 450
B	450 < MN <= 850
C	850 < MN <= 1600
D	1600 < MN <= 2800
E	2800 < MN <= 4500
F	4500 < MN <= 7000
G	7000 < MN <= 32767

Each Hasp initiator could select only one job at a time for execution so that the
number of active Hasp initiators was the number of Hasp jobs in the OS/MVT job
queue. The number of active Hasp initiators, that is the multiprogramming level,
and the jobclass queues from which each initiator chose jobs was under experimental
control. Once a Hasp initiator had selected a job for the OS/MVT job queue, its
previous Hasp jobclass was irrelevant since OS/MVT had no knowledge of what the
Hasp designation had been for the job. After a job had terminated execution, Hasp
scheduled it for peripheral activity.

Job priorities were used by the OS/MVT supervisor to select the task to be resumed
upon completion of any interrupt processing. Hasp jobs ran at priority 6, Hasp
itself ran at priority 13, the timesharing system Plorts ran at priority 12, and
Express ran at priority 11. Two additional monitors, Civil and UOI, ran at
priorities 10 and 13 respectively. With full job queues for each initiator, CPU
time available for batch work, and hence batch throughput rate during any particular
sampling period, was largely a function of the amount of Plorts, Express, and
system work which had to execute first.

4. THE DATA

Data for batch job turnaround consisted of records from two data bases, SMF and
ARDS. SMF is a data gathering facility for IBM operating systems and is described
in IBM manual number GC28-6712-7 (1973). ARDS was the Accounting Record Data Set
used by the Computing Services Office for all account billings. ARDS did not
contain accurate times of when jobs went into or finished execution, but ARDS did
have the execution residency time for each job, and SMF job termination records
did have the time of day that the job terminated execution. From this information
it was trivial to calculate when Hasp placed each job into the OS/MVT jobqueue.
The procedure followed was to read the SMF job termination records for jobnames,
the time when each job ended execution, and the number of steps in each job. Each
jobname was then looked up in a table of available ARDS records jobnames. A
correspondence table then pointed to job information in a random access organized

copy of the ARDS data base. If the jobname was unique in ARDS, then that job was
included in the sample, otherwise it was not. The total number of jobs excluded
because of duplicate jobnames was 202. No effort was made to retrieve SMF step
termination records by jobname. Data on 763 class A jobs, 203 class B jobs, 94
class C jobs, and 5 class D jobs were collected. The class D jobs were discarded
because the sample of jobs was too small.

The ARDS records provided execution residency time, billed CPU time, the amount of
fast and slow core memory, and the number of I/O requests used by the job exclusive
of requests for peripheral activity. Also in ARDS was the amount of peripheral
activity, that is, the number of cards read, cards punched, lines printed and
seconds of plotter time generated by the job.

Since the throughput rate was an essential piece of information in the execution
residency model, some suitable measure of this rate was necessary. The throughput
rate for batch jobs was defined to be the amount of SMF accountable CPU seconds
for Hasp batch (i.e. non-Express, non-timesharing, non-system) jobs accumulated
during a fifteen minute sampling period. Since an additional experiment was being
carried on at the same time, namely the estimation of batch throughput functions,
data were collected over nominal fifteen minute intervals which then had to be
prorated to a precise fifteen minute interval. Data from SMF step termination
records were used to calculate this throughput rate. The CPU time for jobsteps
which were in execution at the beginning or ending of any sampling period was
proportionally distributed across the period boundary. For example, if 40% of the
wall clock time that a jobstep was in execution residency occurred during a
particular sampling period, then that sampling period's throughput was credited
with 40% of that jobstep's CPU time. Although this implicitly assumed that the
CPU time for a jobstep was uniformly distributed over its step residency time, it
was felt that the few jobsteps this affected, 2*(number of initiators), was
relatively small, and that any other assumption was equally likely.

Data from a total of 111 fifteen minute sampling periods, of which 89 were finally
used, were collected during the time from September 19 through October 4, 1974.
Of the 89 periods, six of them were collected while running with four Hasp
initiators, forty-one were collected with five initiators, twenty-seven were
collected with six initiators, and fifteen were collected with seven initiators.

Afternoon hours were used exclusively since the diurnal nature of mankind and a
deliberate choice of management scheduling policy caused the character of the workload to shift radically by time of day. Afternoon hours were characterized by lots
of small and medium sized jobs being run. Nighttime saw the large and huge jobs
being run while morning hours were relatively lightly loaded so that the initiators
would sometimes become inactive.

Morning hours could not be used since it was necessary that all non-drained
initiators be active. If there had been, say, five non-drained initiators but one
or more of them had been sometimes active and sometimes not, a question would have
arisen as to whether the data from such an observation period were indicative of
how the system handled five or a fewer number of initiators. In order to avoid
such measurement error, only observations which were taken when there was a
backlog for all non-drained initiators were considered. Indeed, the 111-89=22
sampling periods which were unused were thrown out because initiators had emptied
their assigned queues even though it was afternoon and supposedly a busy time of
day.

Measurement error of another type was the reason that nighttime hours could not be
used. Due to the fact that knowledge of how much CPU time any jobstep took (i.e.
the amount of throughput the job generated) was available only at its step
termination when an SMF record was written, some throughput measurement error was
present during each of the 89 sampling periods. For each jobstep which started
and ended within a single sampling period, no measurement error was generated.

However, each jobstep which was in execution over a sampling period boundary
necessarily generated some measurement error because of the decision to prorate
such a jobstep's CPU time uniformly over its residency time. As a result, night
hours could not be used because of the substantial measurement error which would
have resulted from applying this decision rule to jobsteps which were in execution
for several hours.

To summarize, data were collected during afternoon hours when there were no
initiators with empty queues and when individual jobsteps were not running for
excessively long residency periods. In particular, no class E through class G
jobs were run during sampling periods. The afternoon hours were relatively high
usage hours for Express and timesharing work with sufficient variability so that
data were also being collected over fluctuating levels of the batch throughput rate.

5. EXECUTION RESIDENCY ESTIMATION

To model expected execution residency times, job execution residency functions were
estimated for each of the jobclasses A, B, and C. The independent variables, and
the names by which they are referred, are:

1. CONSTANT – column of ones
2. L*CPU/TH – Hasp multiprogramming level times job CPU seconds divided by
                the system throughput rate
3. IOREQ   – number of job IO requests exclusive of requests for reading
                cards, punching cards, printing lines, and plotting
4. RGN0   – hundred kilobytes of high speed core memory
5. RGN1   – hundred kilobytes of slow speed core memory
6. STEP   – number of jobsteps in the job
7. JOBREAD   – number of cards read by the job
8. JOBPUNCH – number of cards punched by the job
9. JOBPRINT – number of lines printed by the job
10. JOBPLOT   – seconds of plotter time generated by the job

The dependent variable is identified by the name RESIDE. Table 2 gives the sample
means and standard deviations for the residency variables in each of the jobclasses
considered. The variables L*CPU/TH and RESIDE are measured in seconds. Ordinary
least squares estimates, and their corresponding t-ratios, are given in Table 3.

Table 2
Means and Standard Deviations of Execution Residency Data by Class

VARIABLE	CLASS A MEAN	CLASS A ST. DEV.	CLASS B MEAN	CLASS B ST. DEV.	CLASS C MEAN	CLASS C ST. DEV.
L*CPU/TH	130.8455	188.9304	253.2274	398.1240	700.3682	1066.2295
IOREQ	297.1835	475.8803	304.8916	399.0410	1257.5851	2580.4859
RGN0	1.1811	.3150	1.7825	.3905	2.1365	.7916
RGN1	.0005	.0102	.0896	.2108	.1483	.2803
STEP	1.7785	.9227	1.6552	.8762	2.1170	1.2704
JOBREAD	342.4836	614.2224	309.8177	436.7106	463.9681	599.4597
JOBPUNCH	54.4626	300.6418	3.6502	41.6804	11.2021	52.6471
JOBPRINT	621.5033	2531.3724	652.4877	812.1435	1395.6915	1966.6624
JOBPLOT	8.3971	38.6619	13.4138	65.8754	20.7766	140.0837
RESIDE	165.5609	187.2538	315.7192	343.6127	679.2660	698.0862

Table 3
Job Execution Residency Model Parameter Estimates and T-Ratios
Ordinary Least Squares

VARIABLE	CLASS A COEFF.	CLASS A T-RATIO	CLASS B COEFF.	CLASS B T-RATIO	CLASS C COEFF.	CLASS C T-RATIO
CONSTANT	-27.5966	-1.140	-75.4277	-0.744	-28.5122	-0.153
L*CPU/TH	0.5291	15.960	0.6026	12.032	0.4193	7.830
IOREQ	0.0590	4.614	0.0478	0.877	0.0607	2.877
RGN0	86.6472	5.042	106.4253	2.244	147.3806	2.212
RGN1	-221.7544	-0.423	-4.9220	-0.053	-183.4167	-0.973
STEP	6.0071	0.980	37.4996	1.467	21.5536	0.478
JOBREAD	-0.0107	-1.096	-0.0402	-0.846	-0.0440	-0.491
JOBPUNCH	-0.0002	-0.010	-0.2902	-0.669	0.1670	0.173
JOBPRINT	-0.0020	-0.905	-0.0179	-0.731	0.0155	0.546
JOBPLOT	-0.1916	-1.371	-0.1599	-0.572	0.0704	0.204

On the basis of the t-ratios in Table 3, the coefficients for L*CPU/TH and RGN0
were significantly different from zero in all three classes, and the coefficient
for IOREQ was significantly different from zero in classes A and C. The coefficients for L*CPU/TH and IOREQ remained fairly stable across job classes while the
coefficient for RGN0 increases by 20 seconds per hundred kilobytes from class A to
class B and by 41 seconds per hundred kilobytes from class B to class C. The
coefficients for CONSTANT, RGN1, STEP, JOBREAD, JOBPUNCH, JOBPRINT, and JOBPLOT
were consistently not significantly different from zero. The sum of squared error,
estimate of variance, and coefficient of multiple correlation for each of the
models are given in Table 4.

Table 4
Ordinary Least Squares Job Residency Models by Job Class
Summary Statistics

	Sum of Squared Error	Variance	Multiple Corr.
CLASS A	.164462E 08	.218409E 05	.621
CLASS B	.120226E 08	.622933E 05	.706
CLASS C	.177090E 08	.210821E 06	.783

Next, exact linear restrictions (hypotheses) were imposed on the regression
parameters in each of the three models. These linear hypotheses, made prior to
having looked at the ordinary least squares results given in Tables 3 and 4, were
each of a form restricting nine of the parameters to zero. The only coefficient
in each model which was not restricted to zero was the coefficient for the variable
L*CPU/TH. The results of these restrictions, given in Table 5, may be compared
against Table 3. In each jobclass, the coefficient for L*CPU/TH is larger in
Table 5 than in Table 3, but in no instance is this coefficient equal to, or
greater than one.

Table 5
Job Execution Residency Model Parameter Estimates and T-Ratios
Restricted Least Squares

VARIABLE	CLASS A COEFF.	CLASS A T-RATIO	CLASS B COEFF.	CLASS B T-RATIO	CLASS C COEFF.	CLASS C T-RATIO
L*CPU/TH	0.8019	30.126	0.7779	18.105	0.6286	13.985

For each of the exact restricted job residency models, the sum of squared error,
the estimate of variance, and the coefficient of multiple correlation are given in
Table 6. These results may be compared with the results in Table 4.

Table 6
Exact Restricted Least Squares Job Residency Models by Job Class
Summary Statistics

	Sum of Squared Error	Variance	Multiple Corr.
CLASS A	.217560E 08	.285512E 05	.432
CLASS B	.168536E 08	.834336E 05	.545
CLASS C	.287409E 08	.309042E 06	.610

Table 7
Job Residency Model Hypothesis Test Results

	F-Ratio	Prob.	Degrees of Freedom
CLASS A	27.01	.000	9 , 753
CLASS B	8.62	.000	9 , 193
CLASS C	5.81	.000	9 , 84

F tests were performed to test the hypotheses that the sample and hypothesized prior information were compatible. As shown by Table 7, the hypotheses were rejected in all three models.

The fact that the hypothesized prior information was rejected in each model raised the question of whether or not the variable L*CPU/TH was a "better" predictor of execution residency than, say, unweighted CPU time. This question was informally considered by calculating ordinary least squares estimates using the full set of ten independent variables as were used in the regressions of Tables 3 and 4, except that CPU was substituted for L*CPU/TH. A comparison of the coefficients of multiple correlation, given in Table 8, suggested that L*CPU/TH was "better" than unweighted CPU for predicting execution residency. The first column of Table 8 is the same as the Multiple Corr. column in Table 4.

Table 8
Execution Residency Models
Ordinary Least Squares Multiple Correlation Coefficients

	using L*CPU/TH	using CPU
CLASS A	.621	.535
CLASS B	.706	.599
CLASS C	.783	.727

6. CONCLUDING REMARKS

Although the hypotheses were rejected, it was felt that the variable L*CPU/TH was a useful construct and that the hypotheses were rejected simply because IOREQ and RGNO did have a measurable effect on job residency. The usefulness of L*CPU/TH underlines the fact that two of the primary performance measures of Calingaert (1967), turnaround and throughput, are not independent measures but are inversely related measures of the same phenomenon. If this model were to be estimated from new data, it is recommended that only the coefficients for RGN1, STEP, JOBREAD, JOBPUNCH, JOBPRINT, and JOBPLOT be hypothesized to be zero. It would be unfair to make such a test using the current set of data since we already have a clear indication, from the t-ratios in Table 3, that such a hypothesis would not be rejected.

The coefficient of L*CPU/TH was consistently less than one. It had been anticipated that those job classes which got less than their "fair share" of CPU time,
on average, would have L*CPU/TH coefficients greater than one. Since this never
happened, apparently no such effect is present along class lines. Rather in all
classes, jobs which were CPU prone had shorter residency times, and each 16 to 20
I/O requests which a job required caused an increase in the job's execution
residency of approximately one second.

Whereas the coefficients for L*CPU/TH and IOREQ were relatively stable across job
classes, the coefficient for RGN0, the only other significant coefficient,
increased sharply across job classes. It is felt that the reason for this is that
the time spent waiting for region allocation is probably not a linear function of
the amount of region requested, coupled with the fact that as one proceeds from
class A to class B to class C jobs, the mean region requested increases.

As an example of the estimation of execution turnaround for a job, suppose that a
class A job is submitted and becomes the fortieth job in the class A queue.
Further assume that five Hasp initiators are active, two of which are processing
class A jobs, that Hasp throughput is 35% of wall clock time, and that these
conditions are expected to prevail at least until our test job finishes execution.
Suppose that the expected value of resources to be used by each of the forty jobs
is given in Table 9.

The expected value of the L*CPU/TH variable would therefore be 5*8/.36 = 114.3 .
Using the parameter estimates in Table 3, the expected execution residency for any
one class A job is 155.11 seconds. For the entire forty jobs, the expected
residency is 40*155.11 = 6204.4 seconds, and since there are two class A initiators,
our test job can be expected to finish execution in approximately half that time,
or 3102.2 seconds after it was read in. Notice that this estimate of remaining
queue time improves for jobs further back in the queue due to the law of large
numbers. Another way of looking at this result is that the system is disgorging a
class A job approximately every 155.11/2 = 77.55 seconds. For simplicity we have
ignored the two class A jobs which were in execution when our test job was read in.
If the throughput rate suddenly shifted to 55% of wall clock time, and all other
quantities remained constant, the system would complete execution of class A jobs
on the average of one every 66.56 seconds.

The above calculations were not dependent upon the existence of either Plorts or
Express but only upon the rate of batch job throughput per unit of wall clock time,
the initiator settings, and the expected resource usage characteristics of class A
jobs. Also, this model takes into account changing queue position. This model
can be used dynamically to explicitly take into account for changes in the total
number of initiators, the number of initiators servicing particular job classes,
changes in the throughput rate, and changes in the resources which jobs may be
expected to use.

Table 9
Turnaround Example
Assumed Class A Expected Job Characteristics

CPU	8.00	seconds of CPU time
IOREQ	300.00	I/O requests
RGN0	1.16	hundred kilobytes of fast core
RGN1	0.00	hundred kilobytes of slow core
STEP	1.77	job steps
JOBREAD	350.00	cards read
JOBPUNCH	50.00	cards punched
JOBPRINT	620.00	lines printed
JOBPLOT	8.40	seconds of plotter time

The difficulty with using linear models in performance measurement is in finding the appropriate transformation of variables such that the techniques of linear model estimation can be applied. In the model at hand, it is perfectly reasonable to assume that execution residency is linear in some function of region size. The problem is in finding what the form of that function is. When the dependent variable is measured in time units, which are typically treated as being linear, linear models can be an effective tool for computer performance measurement.

REFERENCES

Bard, Y., "Performance Criteria and Measurement for a Time-Sharing System," IBM Systems Journal, 10 (1971), 193-216.

Bard, Y. and Suryanarayana, K.V., "On the Structure of CP-67 Overhead," in Walter Freiberger, ed., Statistical Computer Performance Evaluation, New York: Academic Press, 1972, 329-346.

Bock, M.E., Yancy, T.A., and Judge, G.G., "The Statistical Consequences of Preliminary Test Estimators in Regression," Journal of the American Statistical Association, 68 (March, 1973), 109-116.

Boehm, B.W. and Bell, T.E., "Issues in Computer Performance Evaluation: Some Consensus, Some Divergence," Performance Evaluation Review, 4 (July, 1975), 4-39.

Calingaert, P., "System Performance Evaluation: Survey and Appraisal," Communications of the ACM, 10 (January, 1967), 12-18.

Chouinard, P.L., The Statistical Estimation of Throughput and Turnaround Functions for a University Computer System, Report No. UIUCDCS-R-76-799, Department of Computer Science, University of Illinois at Urbana-Champaign, May, 1976.

Drummond, M.E., Jr., "A Perspective on System Performance Evaluation," IBM Systems Journal, 8 (1971), 252-263.

Goldberger, A.S., Econometric Theory, New York: John Wiley & Sons, Inc., 1964.

Grenander, U. and Tsao, R.F., "Quantitative Methods for Evaluating Computer Performance: A Review and Proposals," in Walter Freiberger, ed., Statistical Computer Performance Evaluation, Academic Press, New York, 1972, 3-24.

IBM Corporation, MVT Guide, Order Number GC28-6720-4, March, 1972.

IBM Corporation, MVT Supervisor, Order Number GY28-6659-5, January, 1971.

IBM Corporation, OS SMF, Order Number GC286712-7, April, 1973.

Kimbleton, S.R., "The Role of Computer System Models in Performance Evaluation," Communications of the ACM, 15 (July, 1972), 586-590.

Kimbleton, S.R., "Performance Evaluation - A Structured Approach," AFIPS Conference Proceedings, 40 (Spring Joint Computer Conference), Montvale, New Jersey: AFIPS Press, 1972, 411-416.

Mamrak, S.A., Simulation Analysis of a Pay-For-Priority Scheme for the IBM 360/75, Report No. UIUCDCS-R-73-605, Department of Computer Science, University of Illinois at Urbana-Champaign, August, 1973.

Schatzoff, M. and Bryant, P., "Regression Methods in Performance Evaluation: Some Comments on the State of the Art," Proceedings of Computer Science and Statistics: Seventh Annual Symposium on the Interface, Ames, Iowa: Iowa State University, 1973, 8-57.

Theil, Henri, Principles of Econometrics, New York: John Wiley & Sons, Inc., 1971.

COMPUTER PERFORMANCE, K.M. CHANDY AND M. REISER (EDS.)
NORTH HOLLAND PUBLISHING COMPANY, 1977

A HYBRID SIMULATION/REGRESSION MODELING APPROACH
FOR EVALUATING MULTIPROGRAMMING COMPUTER SYSTEMS

H. Gomaa
Department of Computing and Control
Imperial College of Science and Technology
London, England

This paper describes how two different modelling techniques,
regression and simulation modelling, have been combined
within a hybrid simulation/regression model of a computer
system. In the model, a simulation framework is created
which models task arrival and termination. Within this
framework, a regression submodel predicts each task's
elapsed time in the absence of competition from other
tasks. This approach has been applied to modelling a
non-virtual storage system, namely a CDC 6000 computer
system, and is currently being applied to modelling a
virtual storage system, namely an IBM VM/370 system. In
both models, the memory management subsystem is modelled
in considerable detail, whereas the rest of the system is
modelled in much less detail.

1. Introduction

For a computer system performance model to be of most value to computer installation managers, it should be capable of modelling the system's performance
in a fraction of the real world time. In such conditions, it is more economical
to experiment with the model than the system itself.

There are a number of ways of building computer system performance models. One
method is to use simulation techniques. A simulation model may model a computer
system at almost any required level of detail. However, there is a tendency for
many simulation models to model systems in considerable detail. In these cases,
the greatest drawback to simulation modelling is probably its relatively high
cost (19).

A more promising alternative is to combine simulation with different modelling techniques to produce hybrid models of computer system performance. Kimbleton has described an analytically driven computer system simulator (17, 18) which combines simulation and queuing modelling techniques. The method described in this paper combines regression techniques with simulation techniques.

A regression model (16) is a fast statistical model of computer system perform- ance which relies on workload and performance data collected from the system being evaluated. However, it has the disadvantage of not being capable of modelling logical and structural relationships in the system. A simulation model does not suffer from this limitation. However, a simulation model which produced results similar to a regression model would probably need to model the system in considerably more detail, and consequently be more expensive to implement.

By combining simulation and regression techniques within a hybrid model, the advantages of both techniques may be exploited. Simulation modelling techniques are used to model those aspects of the system of particular interest in consider- able detail. Regression modelling techniques are used to model the rest of the system in much less detail.

This paper describes how hybrid simulation/regression models of both non-virtual storage and virtual storage systems may be constructed. It describes how the Memory Management Model of a CDC 6000 (Cyber) system was developed. It also describes how a hybrid model of the IBM Virtual Machine 370 system is being developed.

2. Hybrid Simulation/Regression Modelling of a Non-Virtual Storage System

2.1 Introduction

In the hybrid simulation/regression model of a non-virtual storage system, a simulation framework is created which allows each task's progress through the system to be modelled dynamically. Within this framework, two submodels (22) are used. A regression submodel predicts each task's elapsed time in the absence of competition from other tasks. A numerical submodel predicts the time delay experienced by a task due to the competition from other tasks, for each period when the number of tasks executing is constant. The time spent by a task waiting to be admitted into the multiprogramming set is explicitly simulated.

2.2 Task Elapsed Time

A task's elapsed time t_e, that is the time from when a task starts executing to the time it terminates, may be considered as consisting of two terms:

$$t_e = t_j + t_w \qquad\qquad (1)$$

t_j is the elapsed time a task would experience if no other task were competing
with it for resources, i.e. if it were executing in a monoprogramming environment.
It is referred to as the task execution time from now on.

t_w is the delay a task experiences due to competing with other tasks for system
resources, e.g. CPU, I/O and main store. Hence t_w is equal to zero if the task
experiences no competition from other tasks. It is convenient to split t_w into
two terms. These are the time when the task is waiting for main store t_s and the
time when the task is in main store but is waiting (i.e. queuing) for the CPU or
I/O. This latter time is called the task delay time t_d.

It is assumed that a task displays the properties of a sequential process, hence
its CPU and I/O operations are not overlapped. A typical process state transition
diagram is shown in Figure 1. It may thus be assumed that the task's progress
through the system is a linear function of its resource demands, providing it
experiences no competition for resources. Consequently, the task execution time
t_j may be predicted by a linear regression submodel:

$$t_j = f\ (r_1,\ r_2\ \ldots\ r_n) \qquad\qquad (2)$$

where $(r_1,\ r_2\ \ldots\ r_n)$ are the task's resource requirements, e.g. CPU time and
I/O requirements.

As the model is trace driven, a task's arrival time and resource requirements are
obtained from an input trace. At the simulated time of task arrival, the task's
execution time is predicted using equation (2).

2.3 Time Intervals

A time interval is defined as a period of time during which the number of tasks
in the multiprogramming set is constant. In an interval t_i, each executing task
experiences some useful execution t_{ji}, i.e. time being serviced by the system,
and some delay t_{di} due to competition from other tasks for system resources.

Thus:

$$t_i = t_{ji} + t_{di} \qquad\qquad (3)$$

It is further assumed that in any given time interval, each task is subjected to

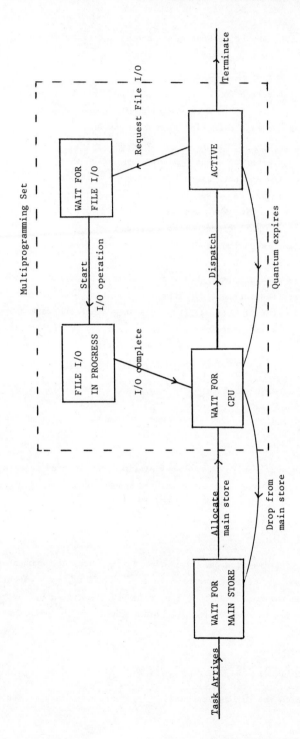

Figure 1: State Transition Diagram in Non-Virtual Storage System.

the same delay t_{di}. Hence it is assumed that each task experiences the same execution time t_{ji}. However, how this execution time is divided up into CPU time and I/O time is dependent on the characteristics of the task. Thus a compute bound task will use more CPU time than an I/O bound task in t_i.

2.4 Modelling Delay Time

As described in 2.2, a task's elapsed time t_e may be expressed as:

$$t_e = t_j + t_d + t_s$$

$$= t_j + \sum_{i=1}^{k} t_{di} + t_s$$

where k is the number of time intervals a task passes through while being executed in main store.

The delay time t_{di} is estimated for each time interval. It is assumed that the delay experienced by each task in a time interval is a function of the number of tasks, N, competing for resources with it, i.e.

$$t_{di} = t_i \, g(N)$$

It is to be expected that the delay is a non-linear function of N. Assume it is a polynomial in N in which only the first two terms in N are significant. Then:

$$t_{di} = (a_o + a_1 N + a_2 N^2) \, t_i$$

Furthermore, as t_{di} is defined to be equal to zero if only 1 task is executing (i.e. N = 0), then for any time interval t_i in which there are N + 1 tasks executing:

$$t_{di} = (a_1 N + a_2 N^2) \, t_i \qquad\qquad (4)$$

From (3), substituting for t_{di}:

$$t_{ji} = (1 - a_1 N - a_2 N^2) \, t_i \qquad\qquad (5)$$

2.5 Estimating Time Interval Length

A time interval is terminated either by a new task arriving or a task terminating. On some systems, another possible event is a task dropping from the multiprogramming set due to it having exceeded some time allowance (slice). This happens if the cumulative CPU time used by the task exceeds a system parameter, the CPU time

slice T_s. If a task has a total CPU requirement which exceeds T_s, then the execution time t_{js} it uses before being dropped may be estimated, assuming uniform
resource utilization.

$$t_{js} = t_j \ \frac{T_s}{T} \tag{6}$$

At the start of each time interval, each task in the multiprogramming set has a
remaining execution time t_{jr}, which is the real time a task would use before
terminating execution or being dropped if no other tasks were competing for resources. As it is assumed that each task experiences the same execution time in
a given time interval, then it follows that the task with the minimum t_{jr} (given
by t_{jrm}) is the one that will terminate/drop first. The time interval t_{im}
necessary to complete execution of the task with execution time t_{jrm} is computed
using equation (5).

$$t_{im} = \frac{t_{jrm}}{1 - a_1 N - a_2 N^2}$$

t_{im} is then compared with the time of the next task arrival t_a to determine
whether the next event is a task arrival or a task termination/drop. Hence the
length of the next time interval t_i is given by:

$$t_i = \min (t_{im}, t_a)$$

Given t_i, the execution time t_{ji} and delay time t_{di} for this interval may be
computed using equations (5) and (4) respectively. t_i is added to the value of
the elapsed time so far for each task in the system. t_{ji} is subtracted from the
value of the execution time remaining (t_{jr}) for each task in the multiprogramming
set. This procedure continues until t_{jr} is reduced to zero for a particular task.
This represents the time at which the model predicts the task will terminate or
drop. The accumulated elapsed time at the simulated time of task termination is
the predicted elapsed time for that task.

3. Applying the Hybrid Model of a Non-Virtual Storage System

3.1 The System Modelled

A hybrid model of the Imperial College CDC Cyber 73 (6400) system, called the Memory
Management Model (MMM), has been developed. The system has one central processor
(CPU), ten peripheral processors and 64K 60-bit Central Memory (CM). The oper-
ating system used is Kronos. It supports a multiprogramming system with dynamic

storage allocation including rollin/rollout (12).

At the time the system was modelled, it supported a 'cafeteria' service for short batch jobs, a local batch service and a remote batch service. Batch jobs may fall into one of five job categories. In this paper, jobs in the smallest category are referred to as short jobs, while jobs in the other four categories are referred to as long jobs. Short jobs may use up to 16 seconds CPU time, 25K Central Memory and no magnetic tapes.

3.2   Simulating the Memory Management Subsystem

3.2.1 Applying the Hybrid Model

Referring to the state transition diagram in Figure 1, the time spent by a task (in this case a job) being serviced by the system, e.g. using the CPU or doing I/O, is predicted by the regression submodel (equation 2 in 2.2). The time spent by a job waiting for the CPU or user I/O is predicted by the delay time submodel (equation 4 in 2.4). The time spent by a job waiting for Central Memory is explicitly simulated. Events simulated in the model are job arrival, job starts execution, job rollout and rollin, time slice expiry and job termination.

3.2.2 Job Commencement

In Kronos, when a job first enters the system, it is placed in the Input Queue. A job rolled out of CM is placed in the Rollout Queue. For the purpose of memory allocation, the Job Scheduler (which handles memory as well as job scheduling) treats the Input and Rollout queues as one queue. On the IC Kronos system, short jobs have priority over long jobs in the allocation of main store.

In the Memory Management Model, at the simulated time of job arrival, the job's execution time is predicted by the regression submodel. The model then determines whether sufficient memory is available for the job. If sufficient memory is available, an entry is set up for the job and is linked onto the end of the Execution List. This list contains an entry for each simulated job executing in CM (see Figure 2).

If insufficient memory is available, then for long jobs the entry is linked onto the end of a combined Input/Rollout Queue for long jobs. For short jobs, the model checks if there is enough 'eligible' memory, in addition to free memory, to allow the job to start execution. Eligible memory is that used by executing jobs which are eligible for rollout. This includes all long jobs and those short jobs which have exceeded their time slice (see 3.2.3). If there is now sufficient

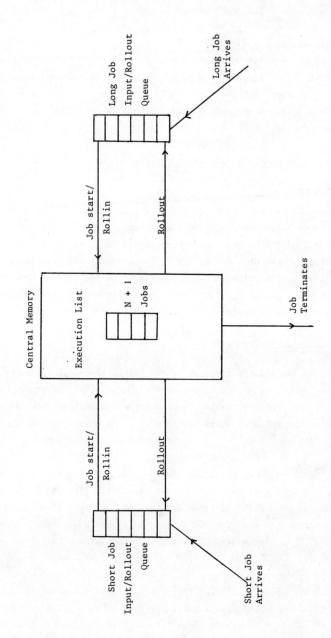

Figure 2: Memory Management Model.

memory, as many 'eligible' jobs as necessary are rolled out, and the new job is linked onto the Execution List. If insufficient memory is available, the job is linked onto the end of the short job Input/Rollout Queue.

3.2.3 Job Rollout and Rollin

In Kronos, each job resident in CM is given two time slices, a CPU time slice (see 2.5) and a CM time slice. The CM time slice is the real time a job is allowed to be resident in CM before becoming eligible for rollout. If a job exceeds its CPU or CM time slice, its state is set to 'eligible for rollout'.

At each event occurence, the model checks if sufficient memory is available for one or more jobs in first the short job and then the long job Input/Rollout queues. If so, the job is brought into CM and placed onto the end of the Execution List.

3.3   Implementation of the Model

The data used for the evaluation was derived entirely from the CDC Dayfile. The Dayfile is a system file which collects workload and performance data and is used primarily for accounting purposes (12). The Kronos Dayfile provides sufficient data to allow the batch workload to be modelled at the job level.

The contents of the Kronos Dayfile need to be reduced into a more convenient form for input to the Memory Management Model. The Dayfile for a particular session is input to a suite of Dayfile Processing programs collectively called the Preprocessor. The Preprocessor prepares a workload trace, representing a given session, for input to the model. The trace consists of a set of short jobs ordered by job arrival time. Each job is represented by a vector of its resource requirements which is input to the model at the simulated time of job arrival.

The model outputs the predicted elapsed time, execution time and delay time for each job. A Postprocessor analyzes the file generated by a run of the Memory Management Model and carries out a statistical analysis of the results.

3.4   Regression Modelling

3.4.1 The Workload Model

There are a number of examples of the application of regression modelling techniques to the evaluation of computer system performance (1, 2, 11, 16). The

regression submodel used in the Memory Management Model was based on a regression
model of the IC Kronos system called the Workload Model. The model is described
in detail in reference (13). A brief description of it follows.

The Workload Model was constructed after a detailed analysis of system performance
and of the characteristics of the workload. It is a regression model (i.e.
equation) which models the performance of a subset of the batch workload, namely
the short job workload, on the IC Kronos system. The dependent (output) variable
is job elapsed time. The independent (input) variables are of two types: measures
of each job's resource demands and measures of the system load experienced by the
job.

The Workload Model is represented by:

$$t_e = 3.25 + 2.25T + 1.08K + 5.32N \qquad\qquad (7)$$

where t_e is the job elapsed time, T is the CPU time required, K is the number of
job steps, and N is the average number of short jobs in competition with this job
over its lifetime. Given the values of T, K and N for a particular batch job, the
model will predict the job's elapsed time.

3.4.2 The Regression Submodel

The equation

$$t_j = b_o + b_1T + b_2K \qquad\qquad (8)$$

was found to be a suitable model for the subset of the short job workload which
did not experience any competition from other short jobs (i.e. N = 0). Consequently, this is the regression submodel used in the MMM for predicting short job
execution time. This submodel is also used for predicting the execution time of
long jobs. Considerable difficulty was experienced modelling the long job workload (13) and so a separate regression submodel for this workload was not available. Hence, the objective of modelling the long job workload is to estimate the
competition experienced by short jobs.

The subset of the short job workload used in constructing equation 8 was not
representative. Hence, the values of the parameters b_o, b_1 and b_2 (known as
regression coefficients) of the model are not appropriate for the regression submodel. Normally in a regression model, these parameters are estimated by means
of least squares fitting techniques (9). However, in this case, the values of
the job execution time t_j, i.e. the elapsed time in a monoprogrammed environment,

are not generally known. Hence, the parameters of the model have to be estimated
by a different method which is described next.

3.5   Calibration and Validation

Calibration is an iterative procedure whose objective is to reduce the difference
in behaviour between the model and the real system by adjusting the parameters of
the model (5). Two sets of parameters were adjusted during the calibration of the
Memory Management Model:

(a) The parameters b_o, b_1 and b_2 of the regression submodel for the job execution
    time (equation 8).
(b) The parameters a_1 and a_2 of the delay time submodel (equation 4).

The calibration was carried out by applying a given workload trace to the model
and adjusting the parameters by means of an iterative tuning procedure. The mean
absolute value of the residuals (for each job the residual is the actual elapsed
time minus the predicted elapsed time) was used as a 'figure of merit'. The
regression Workload Model was used as a standard against which the MMM predictions
were compared. The approach was based on that used in the calibration of a simulation model of OS/360 under LASP (6) and is described in detail in reference (15).

After the calibration process, the model was validated. Validation of the LAM
aims at determining the domain of situations for which the model performs with a
given accuracy, for an established calibration (5). Hence, the objective of the
validation process is to find a set of parameter values, determined during calibration, with which the model predictions are not significantly different for
other traces (15).

Three workload traces were used in developing the model, representing three
different sessions. The model was calibrated using the 30/1/75 trace and validated using the 27/1/75 and 30/4/75 traces (14). The results are summarized in
Table 1.

3.6   Discussion of Results

The Memory Management Model was written in Fortran. It required 4.6 seconds CPU
time to model a $3\frac{1}{2}$-hour session consisting of 354 short jobs and 61 long jobs.
Thus the model is very economical.

Table 1, however, shows that the mean absolute value of the residuals as a percentage of mean actual elapsed time is between 24 and 27%. The main reason for

H. GOMAA

Table 1: The Memory Management Model

Parameter Settings

$$b_o = 4.7 \qquad b_1 = 1.9 \qquad b_2 = 0.7$$

$$a_1 = 0.07 \qquad a_2 = 0.01$$

Model Predictions

Session Modelled	Actual $\overline{t}_e$ (secs)	Predicted $\overline{t}_e$ (secs)	$|\overline{r}_r|$	$|\overline{r}_s|$	P	$\dfrac{|\overline{r}_r|}{\overline{t}_e}$ (%)	$\dfrac{|\overline{r}_s|}{\overline{t}_e}$ (%)
27/1/75	17.4	15.4	5.08	4.51	0.037	29.2	25.9
30/1/75	16.8	15.2	4.42	3.99	0.046	26.4	23.8
30/4/75	17.0	15.7	4.72	4.58	0.133	27.8	26.9

Key: $\overline{t}_e$: mean job elapsed time

$|\overline{r}_r|$: mean of absolute residuals of regression Workload Model (WM)

$|\overline{r}_s|$: mean of absolute residuals of hybrid Memory Management Model

P : probability that there is no difference between Workload Model and Memory Management Model – Wilcoxon Test (15).

the comparatively large residuals in the model is due to the limitations of the available data, derived entirely from the Kronos Dayfile. The main limitations are:

(a) In Kronos, memory is usually allocated to a job at the job step level. However, the only information on memory allocation available from the Dayfile is the average memory used by a job during its execution. Consequently, the model assumes that a job uses its average memory requirement throughout its execution. It would be a simple extension to the model to handle memory allocation at the job step level, if the data was available.

(b) The time a job is rolled out of CM is not recorded. This data could be used for developing a more accurate regression model and to assist in the calibration of the Memory Management Model.

(c) No good measures of each job's I/O requirement are available. Better measures such as the job's non-overlapped I/O time and count of I/O requests made would probably result in an I/O term appearing in the regression submodel.

With additional data, it is believed that the accuracy of the model could be substantially improved.

4.   Hybrid Simulation/Regression Modelling of a Virtual Storage System

4.1   Introduction

In this section, the hybrid simulation/regression modelling approach is extended to modelling demand paged virtual storage systems.

It should be noted that reference in this section to simulating the memory management subsystem means simulating that part of the system concerned with deciding which tasks should be admitted into the multiprogramming set (as in the Memory Management Model). It does not imply a detailed simulation of the paging subsystem.

4.2   Task Elapsed Time

Consider a task executing alone in a virtual storage system with unlimited main store available to it, so that there is no paging overhead. Let t_m be the task's monoprogrammed elapsed time in this case. It is again assumed that the task displays the properties of a sequential process, so that its progress through the system is a linear function of its resource demands. As before, the monoprogrammed elapsed time may be predicted by means of a regression submodel, which it is assumed is of the form:

$$t_m = b_o + b_1 T + b_2 F \qquad\qquad (9)$$

where T is the task's CPU time and F is the number of file I/O requests.

If the task is executing in an environment where the physical store available to it is less than its virtual storage requirements, there will be a paging overhead. The task's elapsed time in this monoprogrammed environment t_j will depend on the number of paging operations performed. Thus, again assuming the sequential properties of a task:

$$t_j = b_o + b_1 T + b_2 F + b_3 P \qquad\qquad (10)$$

where P is the number of page faults for this task.

Let $\qquad\qquad t_p = b_3 P \qquad\qquad (11)$

where t_p is the estimated real time spent doing page I/O.

Then $\qquad\qquad t_j = t_m + t_p \qquad\qquad (12)$

where t_j is termed the task execution time.

Now, if the task is executing in a multiprogramming environment, then it will experience a delay t_d due to competing for resources with other tasks, i.e. time spent waiting for the CPU, waiting (i.e. queuing) to do file I/O and page I/O. Furthermore, it may spend some time t_s waiting to be admitted into the multiprogramming set. The complete state transition diagram for the task is shown in Figure 3. Hence, the task's elapsed time may be expressed as:

$$t_e = t_j + t_d + t_s$$

4.3   Time Intervals

It is again assumed that in each time interval each task in the multiprogramming set experiences the same delay t_{di} and hence the same execution time t_{ji}. However, how that execution time is divided up into CPU time T_i, file I/O F_i, and page I/O P_i is dependent on the characteristics of each task. For example, since

$$t_{ji} = t_{mi} + t_{pi} \qquad\qquad (13)$$

then if a task pages at a high rate, t_{pi} will be high and consequently t_{mi} will be low.

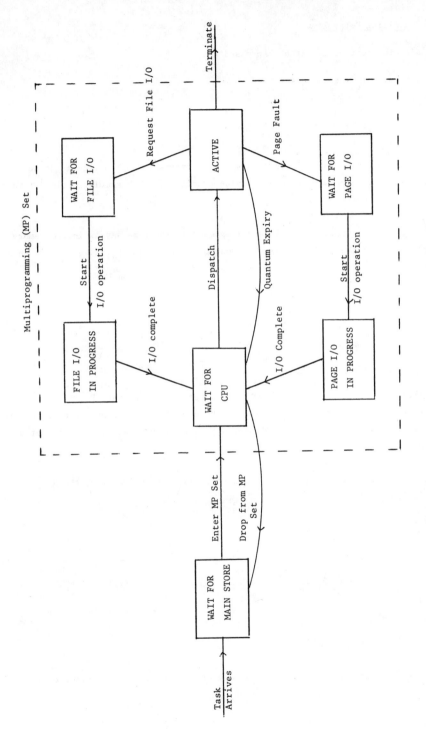

Figure 3: State Transition Diagram in Virtual Storage System.

4.4   Modelling Delay Time

A task's elapsed time t_e may be expressed as:

$$t_e = t_j + t_d + t_s$$

$$= t_m + \sum_{i=1}^{k} t_{pi} + \sum_{i=1}^{k} t_{di} + t_s$$

where k is the number of time intervals a task passes through while in the multi-programming set. For each task, t_m may be predicted at the simulated time of task arrival using equation (9).

t_{di} is estimated for each time interval in exactly the same way as in the Memory Management Model (see 2.4). Thus the equations for t_{di} and t_{ji} also hold in this environment.

$$t_{di} = (a_1 N + a_2 N^2) t_i \qquad\qquad (4)$$

$$t_{ji} = (1 - a_1 N - a_2 N^2) t_i \qquad\qquad (5)$$

4.5   Paging Characteristics

Each task has a parachor curve (7) which relates its paging rate R_p, i.e. the number of page faults/second CPU time, to the number of page frames p available to it (see Figure 4). Thus, a task allocated p pages of main store will page at a rate of R_p pages/CPU sec.

During an interval t_i, in which the task consumes T_i secs CPU time, the number of page faults P_i will be:

$$P_i = R_p T_i$$

From (11) $\qquad t_{pi} = b_3 P_i$

$$= b_3 R_p T_i \qquad\qquad (14)$$

Since $\qquad t_{ji} = t_{mi} + t_{pi} \qquad\qquad$ from (13)

then $\qquad t_{ji} = t_{mi} + b_3 R_p T_i \qquad\qquad (15)$

If we assume that a task uses its resources uniformly during execution, then

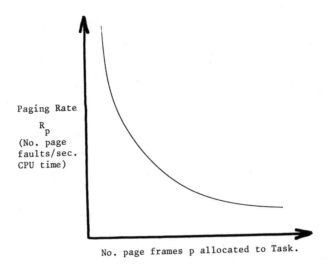

Figure 4: <u>Typical Parachor Curve</u>

$$t_{mi} = \frac{T_i}{T} \; t_m$$

Substituting for t_{mi} in (15)

$$t_{ji} = \frac{T_i}{T} \; t_m + b_3 \; R_p \; T_i$$

$$= T_i \; (\frac{t_m}{T} + b_3 \; R_p) \tag{16}$$

This equation relates the task execution time in an interval t_i to its CPU time T_i. All the other variables in the equation are constant for a given task during the interval: t_m is the monoprogrammed elapsed time which is predicted at the simulated time of task arrival. T is the task's total CPU requirement. R_p is the task's paging rate which is assumed constant for this interval.

4.6   Estimating Time Interval Length

At the start of a time interval, each task will have a certain amount of mono-programmed elapsed time remaining t_{mr} before it terminates or drops from the multiprogramming set due to exceeding its time slice. t_{mr} is a function of the CPU time remaining for this task T_r and the file I/O remaining F_r. Each task will also have p pages allocated to it and page at a rate R_p. Hence the execution time remaining for this task t_{jr} is given by equation (16):

$$t_{jr} = T_r \; (\frac{t_m}{T} + b_3 \; R_p)$$

Thus t_{jr} may be computed for each task. It is assumed, as before, that the task that will terminate or drop first is the task with the minimum execution time remaining t_{jrm}. The time interval t_{im} necessary to complete execution of the task with execution time t_{jrm} is computed using equation (5).

$$t_{im} = \frac{t_{jrm}}{1 - a_1 N - a_2 N^2}$$

t_{im} is then compared with t_a (the time to the next task arrival) to determine whether the next event is a task arrival or a task termination/drop. Hence, the length of the next time interval t_i is computed and is added to the value of the elapsed time so far for each task in the system.

Given t_i, the execution time t_{ji} for this interval may be computed using equation (5). T_i may then be computed for each task using equation (16):

$$T_i = \frac{t_{ji}}{\dfrac{t_m}{T} + b_3 R_p}$$

Given T_i, the time spent by this task doing page I/O in this interval, t_{pi}, may be computed using equation (14):

$$t_{pi} = b_3 R_p T_i$$

The monoprogrammed elapsed time used in the interval, t_{mi}, may then be computed from equation (13) by subtracting t_{pi} from t_{ji}. t_{mi} is then subtracted from t_{mr}, for all tasks in the multiprogramming set, to obtain the updated value of mono-programmed elapsed time remaining. This procedure continues until t_{mr} is reduced to zero for a particular task. This represents the time at which the model predicts the task will terminate or drop. The accumulated elapsed time at the simulated time of task termination is the predicted elapsed time for that task.

5.   Applying the Hybrid Model of a Virtual Storage System

5.1   The System Modelled

The hybrid simulation/regression model of a virtual storage system is being applied to modelling the Virtual Machine (VM) Operating System on an IBM/370 system (21). The Virtual Machine Monitor on this system is called the Control Program (CP). It supports a number of virtual machines executing concurrently. The system being modelled is an IBM 370/135 at Imperial College (IC) which supports batch and terminal users. Each terminal user has a dedicated virtual machine in which the Conversational Monitor System (CMS) is executed. Batch jobs are executed sequentially by a CMS Batch Virtual Machine.

5.2 Applying the Hybrid Model

In the model, a task refers to an interactive transaction for terminal users, e.g. the execution of a command. For batch users, a task refers to a job.

Referring to the state transition diagram in Figure 3, the time spent by a task being serviced by the system, i.e. using the CPU, doing user I/O, doing page I/O, is predicted by the regression submodel (equation 10 in 4.2). The time spent by a task waiting for the CPU, for user I/O and for paging I/O is predicted by the delay time submodel (equation 4 in 4.4). The memory management policies in VM, and hence the time spent by a task waiting to be admitted into the multiprogramming set are explicitly simulated.

5.3 Simulating the Memory Management Subsystem

The aspects of memory management which are explicitly simulated are shown in
Figure 5. There are two eligible lists maintained by VM for tasks waiting to be
admitted into the multiprogramming set, one for interactive tasks and one for
non-interactive tasks. Interactive tasks have priority over non-interactive tasks
in the competition for main store. There are also two lists maintained for tasks
in the multiprogramming set, namely the interactive queue (Q_1) and the non-
interactive queue (Q_2).

At the simulated time of task arrival, the task's monoprogrammed elapsed time t_m
is predicted by the regression submodel (equation 9). An entry is then set up
for the task on the Q_1 eligible list in a position determined by the memory
scheduling algorithm (4). Next, the highest priority task on the eligible lists
is checked to determine whether there is sufficient main store available to
accommodate the task's estimated working set (10). If there is, the task is
brought into the multiprogramming set and the next task on the eligible lists is
checked. If there is insufficient space available (and providing certain special
cases do not hold), the search is stopped.

A task in the multiprogramming set may eventually either terminate or be in-
voluntarily dropped from the set if it exceeds its time slice, which is a cumulative CPU time allowance. This happens if the task's CPU requirement T is greater
than the time slice T_s of the queue it is currently in. It is estimated that this
occurs after a monoprogrammed elapsed time of $t_m \dfrac{T_s}{T}$, assuming uniform resource
utilization.

A task that drops due to exceeding its time slice is rescheduled onto the Q_2
eligible list in a position determined by its memory scheduling priority. After
a task termination or drop, the eligible lists are checked to see if one or more
tasks may be brought into the multiprogramming set.

5.4 Input Data to the Model

For each task, the following trace data is required, and is input to the model at
the simulated time of task arrival:

a) The task's CPU requirement T.
b) The number of file I/O requests F made by the task.
c) The average working set size of the task w.

Also required are the task's elapsed time t_e and the time spent in the multi-

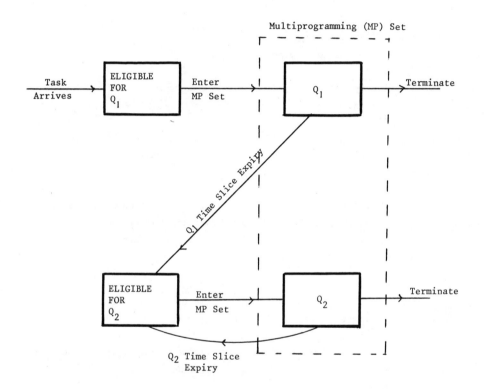

Figure 5: Hybrid Model of VM/370.

programming set t_q. These performance variables are used in the calibration of
the model.

This trace data is collected by the VM Monitor software monitor available on
VM/370 systems (8). In particular, the Schedule class of data is used. This
generates a trace record every time the following events occur (see Figure 5):

(i)   A task enters the eligible list.
(ii) A task enters the multiprogramming set.
(iii) A task leaves the multiprogramming set.

Each task processed by the system generates at least three Schedule records and
can generate considerably more if it cycles through the queues a number of times.

The Schedule trace is input to a program which outputs one record for each task.
This contains the cumulative resource utilization of the task from the time it
first arrived in the system to the time it left the system.

Parachor Curves (see 4.5) may also be derived from the VM Schedule trace data
using the method described in (3). Parachor Curves are currently being developed
for the major classes of workload on the IC VM/370 system. Initially, this is
being limited to the following classes as suggested in (4):

(i)   Trivial interactive tasks that terminate within the Q_1 time slice.
(ii) Non-trivial interactive tasks that exceed the Q_1 time slice.
(iii) Large non-interactive tasks such as compilations and batch jobs.

Eventually, when they have been developed, the parachor curves will also be input
to the model.

5.5   Aspects of Developing the Model

The first version of the model has been implemented and is currently being
calibrated. In this version, some simplifications have been made to the model
from that described in section 4. As the parachor curves are not yet ready, one
simplifying assumption being made is that a task in the multiprogramming set has
a constant number of pages available to it equal to the task's average working
set size. It is also assumed that a task pages at a constant rate throughout.
In addition, each task's paging rate is assumed known and is input to the model.
This follows the approach described in (20) where performance data is initially
used as input to the model. Later, as confidence in the model increases, each
task's paging rate will be predicted by the model, with the aid of the parachor

curves. Furthermore, a task's predicted paging rate will be allowed to vary, but will be assumed constant during each interval.

The CPU time T referred to in section 4 is a task's virtual CPU time, i.e. CPU time required by the task. In addition to this, there is also the system (Control Program) overhead to be considered. Important system parameters such as the CPU time slice take into account total CPU time used, which includes system overhead time.

Currently, the system overhead time experienced by a task is input to the model. Later, it is planned to predict each task's system overhead by means of a regression submodel as described by Bard (1, 2). A regression model of the IC VM/370 system has been developed in which system overhead time is the dependent variable. The independent variables are the number of page faults, file I/Os and spool I/Os experienced by a task. This model gives a very good fit, accounting for over 90% of the variation in the data.

5.6 Calibration of the Model

The calibration of the model is being carried out in two stages. One stage involves finding appropriate values for the parameters of the regression submodel:

$$t_j = b_o + b_1 T + b_2 F + b_3 P \qquad (10)$$

and the delay time submodel:

$$t_{di} = (a_1 N + a_2 N^2) \qquad (4)$$

These parameters are being estimated by means of the same iterative tuning procedure used in the calibration of the Memory Management Model (see section 3.5). In this case, however, the figure of merit is the mean absolute value of the residuals of the time spent by a task in the multiprogramming set (i.e. either in Q_1 or Q_2 in Figure 5).

Another stage in the calibration is to correct structural inadequacies in that part of the model which simulates the memory management subsystem. In this case, the figure of merit is the mean absolute value of the residuals of the time spent by a task in the eligible lists.

Regression models of the system are also being developed to provide:

(i)   a guide to the appropriate parameter settings of the regression submodel.

(ii) A standard against which the hybrid model can be compared.

The regression models relate the time spent by a task in the multiprogramming set t_q to its resource requirements:

$$t_q = b_o + b_1 T + b_2 F + b_3 P$$

and a task's elapsed time t_e to its resource requirements:

$$t_e = b_o + b_1 T + b_2 F + b_3 P$$

Models with very good fits have been constructed, accounting for over 80% of the variation in the data.

5.7 Status of the Hybrid Model of VM/370

The hybrid model of VM/370 is written in Fortran. The current version requires 8.5 seconds CPU time on a CDC 6400 to model a half-hour session consisting of 459 tasks and 1260 intervals. Thus the model is fast although it is slower than the Memory Management Model (see 3.6) because of its greater level of detail.

The first version of the model is in its initial stages of calibration. Initial results from a slightly tuned model show that the mean absolute value of the residuals as a percentage of mean time in the multiprogramming set is 24%. The figure for elapsed time is higher because of a structural inaccuracy in the model which is being corrected.

Work on this version of the model is continuing. The second version, incorporating the features described in section 5.5, is due to be started shortly. It is hoped to report on these in a future paper.

6. Conclusions

This paper has described how hybrid simulation/regression models of both non-virtual storage and virtual storage systems may be constructed. By this means the advantages of both simulation and regression techniques are exploited. Regression analysis provides a fast statistical method of modelling a system or subsystem at a gross level. Simulation provides a method of modelling the system in more detail by representing logical and structural relationships in the system.

The hybrid modelling approach has been applied to modelling a non-virtual storage system, namely a CDC 6000 computer system, and is currently being applied to modelling a virtual storage system, namely an IBM VM/370 system. In both models, the memory management subsystem is modelled in considerable detail, whereas the rest of the system is modelled in much less detail.

The Memory Management Model of the CDC system is economical, although the error in the model is comparatively large. This is mainly due to the limitations of the data used in developing the model.

The first version of the hybrid model of VM/370 has been developed and is currently being calibrated. When the model has been calibrated and validated, it is planned to use it for experimenting with different memory scheduling algorithms and different system parameter settings.

7. Acknowledgments

I am indebted to Professors D.J. Howarth and M.M. Lehman and to Dr. H. Beilner for their invaluable advice and assistance.

8. References

1) Y. Bard, 'Performance Criteria and Measurement for a Time Sharing System', IBM Systems Journal, Vol. 10, No. 3, 1971.

2) Y. Bard and K.R. Suryanarayana, 'On the Structure of CP Overhead', in Statistical Computer Performance Evaluation, W. Freiberger (ed.), Academic Press, 1972.

3) Y. Bard, 'Characterization of Program Paging in a Time Sharing Environment', IBM Journal of Research and Development, Vol. 17, 387-393, 1973.

4) Y. Bard, 'A Characterization of VM/370 Workloads', Proc. International Workshop on Modelling and Performance Evaluation of Computer Systems, Stresa (Italy), October 1976.

5) H. Beilner, 'Problems in Calibrating and Validating Simulation Models', Proceedings of 2nd Seminar on Experimental Simulation, Liblice (CSSR), 1973.

6) H. Beilner and G. Waldbaum, 'Statistical Methodology for Calibrating a Trace-Driven Simulator of a Batch Computer System', in Statistical Computer Performance Evaluation, W. Freiberger (ed.), Academic Press, 1972.

7) L.A. Belady and C.J. Kuehner, 'Dynamic Space Sharing in Computer Systems', Communications ACM, Vol. 12, No. 5, 1969.

8) P.H. Callaway, 'Performance Measurement Tools for VM/370', IBM Systems Journal, Vol. 14, No. 2, 1975.

9) C. Daniel and F. Wood, 'Fitting Equations to Data', Wiley, 1971.

10) P.J. Denning, 'The Working Set Model for Program Behaviour', Communications ACM, Vol. 11, No. 5, 1969.

11) H.P. Friedman and G. Waldbaum, 'Evaluating System Changes Under Uncontrolled Workloads: A Case Study', IBM Systems Journal, Vol. 14, No. 4, 1975.

12) H. Gomaa and M.M. Lehman, 'Performance Analysis of an Interactive Computing System in a Controlled Environment', Proc. Online Conference on Computer System Evaluation, September 1973.

13) H. Gomaa, 'Regression Models for the Evaluation of Computer System Performance', Proc. Eurocomp conference on Computer Performance Evaluation, London, September 1976.

14) H. Gomaa, 'A Modelling Approach to the Evaluation of Computer System Performance', Proc. International Workshop on Modelling and Performance Evaluation of Computer Systems, Stresa (Italy), October 1976.

15) H. Gomaa, 'The Calibration and Validation of a Hybrid Simulation/Regression Model of a Batch Computer System', Submitted for publication.

16) U. Grenander and R. Tsao, 'Quantitative Methods for Evaluating Computer System Performance: A Review and Proposals', in Statistical Computer Performance Evaluation, W. Freiberger (ed.), Academic Press, 1972.

17) S.R. Kimbleton, 'A Fast Approach to Computer System Performance Prediction', in Computer Architectures and Networks - Modelling and Evaluation, E. Gelenbe and R. Mahl (eds.), North-Holland, 1974.

18) S.R. Kimbleton, 'A Heuristic Approach to Computer Systems Performance Prediction', Proc. AFIPS National Computer Conference, 1975.

19) H.C. Lucas, 'Performance Evaluation and Monitoring', ACM Computing Surveys, Vol. 3, No. 3, 1971.

20) J.D. Noe and G.J. Nutt, 'Validation of a Trace-Driven CDC 6400 Simulation', Proc. AFIPS Spring Joint Computer Conference, 1972.

21) R.P. Parmelee, T.I. Peterson, C.C. Sullivan, D.S. Hatfield, 'Virtual Storage and Virtual Machine Concepts', IBM Systems Journal, Vol. 11, No. 2, 1972.

22) G. Waldbaum and H. Beilner, 'Submodel Simulation', Proc. Summer Simulation Conference, 1973.

COMPUTER PERFORMANCE, K.M. CHANDY AND M. REISER (EDS.)
NORTH HOLLAND PUBLISHING COMPANY, 1977

A CASE STUDY OF PERFORMANCE MODELING
A LARGE COMPUTER SYSTEM

A. Guillon

G.I.X.I. ingenierie informatique s.a.

Orsay, France

We present a performance analysis of the CDC 7600 machine
using measurements and an experimentally validated mathematical model. The queueing network used is solved by a decomposition method. An application is presented to the analysis
of system bottlenecks and to the prediction of the effect
of the modification of the computer's configuration.

We show that mathematical modelling is for our purposes the
most cost-effective performance analysis tool.

1 - INTRODUCTION

CISI, affiliate of C. E. A. (COMMISSARIAT A L'ENERGIE ATOMIQUE), gathering all
the civilian part of the computing resources, has a large number of machines,
among which : IBM 360/91, IBM 370/168, CDC 7600, CDC 6600, etc...

For the last ten years, our permanent concern has been to improve performance.
In this view many years have been spent making numerous experiments regarding
both software and hardware. These experiments clearly pointed out the limitations of measurements techniques for making extrapolations concerning performance under system modifications.

Therefore, to answer such concern for predictions, simulation experiments were
first attempted, mainly in GPSS. The results were quite disappointing, because
of the lack of precision*, and because of the cost.

This is the reason why it was then decided to explore new methods using mathematical modelling. A model has been created for each computer, 360/91, 370/168
and CDC 7600. Then after many trial and errors, each model managed to reproduce
numerical values of CPU utilisation rate. These values almost never depart by
more than 1 % from the values measured in real experiments.

These results appeared quite surprising to us, since we had dared to make rather
important approximations both as regards model conception and their mathematical
use.

We now use these tools as privileged means for making predictions of the behaviour of our systems.

---

* It appeared difficult to obtain better than a 95 % confidence interval with a
range of ± 5 % of the CPU rate. This excludes all possible serious predictions
on non-obvious effects of modifications.

2 - THE CDC 7600 SYSTEM

The general system architecture (see fig. 1) can be briefly described as follows :

All the card readers, line printers, transmission lines are located on a service computer (6400 or CYBER or any computer of 6000 class), linked to the 7600 by a rather slow hardware half-duplex link (the maximum rate is about 0,5 MØ sec.).

The 7600 is surrounded by peripheral computers in charge of the control of transfers on :

- the 7600's own disks
- the link with the 6000

On its own disks are to be found the active files and the inactive files most frequently used. Among the active files are, of course, those which are being transferred on the link.

The jobs initialized in the 7600 are located on three different memory types :

a) Disk : they are the support of all jobs for which a file is trans-ferred on the link. They are then said to be in staging. They also contain other jobs which could not be loaded in LCM.

b) LCM (Large Core Memory) : Besides I/O buffers and various tables, jobs ready for processing or awaiting end of I/O disk are stored here.

c) SCM (Short Core Memory) : Besides channel buffers,the whole code needed for immediate processing is stored here ; consequently, besides the various parts of the system, it also stores the jobs which are being processed.

Therefore, a job to be processed must be in SCM. As soon as such a job requests an I/O, for which it must wait[*], it is immediately swapped out, and a resident job in LCM, if there is one ready for processing, is also swapped in SCM.

d) PPU (Peripheral Processing Unit) : In 7600 system, the PPU are only used as very sophisticated channels both for disk transfer and link transfer. Therefore they will not be considered apart from the channels.

---

[*] These I/O called "recall I/O".

3 - MODELLING

It is impossible to find a mathematical model which describes accurately all
the main phenomena which are to be taken into account. Especially, the number
of jobs in LCM and SCM limited - by LCM size, of course - There are also several
I/O anomalies such as service time dependence on the request rate,...

Therefore, using a systematic method, we shall divide the problem in several
levels, through a top-down approach. Each leval can be solved through iteratively. We shall first present the problem breakdown, under this first heading :
design of the model. A second section will contain the formalisms used and a
third will summarize the iterative process.

3.1 - Design of the model

3.1.1 - Global level

Considered at the most global level, a job is seen as a customer requiring either
the 7600 system - called s - or a file on the 6000. Three types of files can be
delivered simultaneously, and will therefore constitute three parallel stations.
These are : 7-track tapes (t7), 9-track tapes (t9), disk files (D).

Moreover, a preliminary service must be delivered on the tape corresponding to
the time for mounting the unit (MT).

The above considerations immediately lead to the following network :

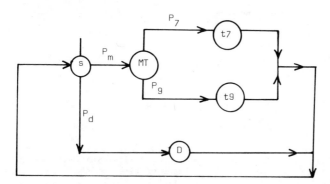

fig. 2

3.1.2 - 7600 internal flow

Job flow between LCM and SCM is ignored for the following reasons : in case of
swapping - in or out - it leads to CPU service monopolisation, which can then
be considered as an extra utilisation, associated to the corresponding I/O. To
make the problem easier it was decided to add to the CPU time used by I/O, the
value of this additional utilisation, weighted by swapping probability - that
is the probability that CPU queue is not empty -

It is then possible to consider only that the jobs effectively loaded in LCM endlessly flow between CPU and I/O requests. Therefore, with n disks the resulting network will be :

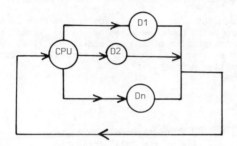

fig. 3

3.1.3 - 7600 disks

It is now time for a closer look at the disk stations. Three main elements should be analyzed : channel conflicts, optimisation of system requests and the disturbance due to staging and other I/O.

3.1.3.1 - Channel conflicts

There are two channels for data transfer to - and from - LCM. The transfer time is about 5 % of the total I/O time.

(Transfer is generally of 20 KC and channel speed is 6,5 Mc/sec ; on the other hand, average disk request is about 80 ms, mainly because of long arm seek time).

The largest configuration studied included four volumes. That way, a case with all disks completely saturated corresponds to only a 20 % channel utilisation. The resulting conflict on channel must remain much smaller than what would be determined by M/M/1 ($\rho/1-\rho$) that is 1/4 of transfer time, which in the end makes only 1 % of the hardware time disk. But, disk having been supposed satured, the conflict for getting volume is at least on the same time than hardware time disk itself. Finelly it results that channel conflict will remain at most on the order of 0,5 % of volume conflict + volume time, and is therefore set neglectable.

3.1.3.2 - Optimisation of requests

The system optimizes the disk requests with respect to both rotational delay and seek time. The former will be disregarded, since its influence is apparently of no significance. On the other hand, we decided to take into account the latter, using Denning's approximation whenever the mean queue length exceeded 1.

Besides, it should be pointed out that the maximum considered time of arm movement is estimated as the maximum physical length times the volume filling rate.

3.1.3.3 - Other I/O disturbances

Within job flow between CPU and disks, we only considered the I/O leading to
effective job delay, that is the recall type I/O. Several other I/O are generated without recall, especially during the processing of sequential files.
Even more, all I/O caused by staging must be taken into account, as all transfers with the station pass through the same disks. The first I/O set must not
modify the CPU queue length and, so, cannot be integrated in the network. For
the same reason, the second set cannot be integrated ; if we did, we would be
forced to limit the number of jobs because of LCM size.

It is to be noted that all these additional I/O account, at the most, for 30 %
of all the I/O in the CPU disk network. This is why we decided to treat them
as disturbances. The only effect is to lengthen the mean time of the I/O
effectively accounted for in the network.

3.2 - Formalism

The above networks (see figures 2 and 3) are of course supposed to fulfil
conditions of Jackson [1] networks in order to obtain an analytic solution. We
still have to establish the connection between both and the insertion of pro-
sesses particular to 7600 disks.

3.2.1 - Global network

Let us consider the following notations :
μ_7 station service rate : 7-track tape file
μ_9 station service rate : 9-track tape file
μ_d station service rate : disk file
μ_m station service rate : tape mounting

These parameters refer to job patterns and to configuration. In a similar way
we shall call e , ê , e_m , e_d the visit rates of jobs to each of the stations
[3].

For each CPU time unit consumed by an average job, are respectively issued
α_7, α_9, $\alpha_m = \alpha_7 + \alpha_9$ requests to these stations. (These values represent job
pattern parameters).

Therefore we obtain :

$$e = \frac{\alpha_7}{\alpha_7 + \alpha_9 + \alpha_d} \qquad\qquad ê = \frac{\alpha_9}{\alpha_7 + \alpha_9 + \alpha_d}$$

$$e_m = \frac{\alpha_m}{\alpha_m + \alpha_d} \qquad\qquad e_d = \frac{\alpha_d}{\alpha_m + \alpha_d}$$

The only remaining unknown parameter is the service rate of station s. Now,
for each CPU time unit $\alpha_m + \alpha_d$ staging request are issued. Therefore, should
we know the real time d necessary for an average CPU unit processing, we would
obtain one staging request issued every :

$$\frac{d}{\alpha_m + \alpha_d}$$

and consequently μ_s, the service rate of station s, would be :

$$\mu_s = \frac{\alpha_m + \alpha_d}{d}$$

d, being, of course, the inverse of CPU service rate - considering that the s system is not empty - is therefore calculated in the following network. As our main interest inside this global network is the CPU loading rate, we are mainly interested in the probabilities P_0, P_1, ... P_n of finding 0, 1, 2 ... n jobs in station s   n being the maximum number of jobs which can be simultaneously stored in LCM.

Calling $\bar{k}$ the state vector of the other stations besides s :

$$\bar{k} = < k_7, k_g, k_m, k_d >, \text{ with } k = k_7 + k_g + k_m + k_d$$

and p_i ($\bar{k}$) the probability that i jobs be in s and the k others distributed according to $\bar{k}$ we obtain [3] :

$$p_i(\bar{k}) = K (\frac{1}{\mu_s})^i (\frac{e}{\mu_7})^{k_7} (\frac{\hat{e}}{\mu_g})^{k_g} (\frac{e_m}{\mu_m})^{k_m} (\frac{e_d}{\mu_d})^{k_d}$$

where K is a normalisation constant obtained by writing that the sum of all probabilities equals 1. This give us, if N is the number of the initialized jobs :

$$p_i = \sum_{k=N-i} p_i(\bar{k})$$

Numerical values are obtained either using Buzen's algorithm [5] or by direct factorisations.

3.2.2 - CPU network

3.2.2.1 - CPU rate with i jobs

Similary calling :

μ_0 = CPU service rate

μ_j = service rate of jth disk volume, $i \leq j \leq n$,

and e_j the visit rate of the jth volume we shall compute rate ρ_i of the CPU knowing that i jobs are loaded in LCM :

$$\rho_i = \sum (\frac{1}{\mu})^{l_0} \prod_1^n (\frac{e_j}{\mu_j})^{l_j}$$

$$l_j \geq 0$$
$$l_0 \geq 1$$
$$l_0 + l_1 + ... + l_n = i$$

μ_0 is the i verse of average CPU process for each I/O and is therefore a job parameter ; the e_j are also job parameters. The μ_j are the I/O times and are determined in the next section.

3.2.2.2 - Global_CPU_rate

The p_i' probability there should be i jobs in LCM is determined in section 3.2.1

$$p_i' = p_i \text{ if } i < M$$
$$= \sum_M^N p_j \quad f \ i \geq M$$

where M is the maximum number of jobs to be stored in LCM and N is the total number of initialized jobs.

The real processing time, d, corresponding to one CPU time unit represents the inverse of the CPU activity rate, knowing that system s is active.

Consequently :

$$d = \cfrac{1}{\cfrac{\sum_1^M \rho_i\, p_i'}{1 - \rho_0}} = \frac{1 - p_0}{\sum_1^M \rho_i\, p_i'}$$

And ρ the global CPU activity rate equals :

$$\rho = \sum_1^M \rho_i\, p_i'$$

3.2.3 - Disk stations

To obtain the mean time of the disk stations service, the disk service time d_{io} must be increased by a factor representing the extra I/O. These are perfectly determined once the staging request rates and size of corresponding files are known, as well as the rate of I/O without recall and I/O of jobs rolling in or out. All these parameters can be measured and therefore this request rate α is assumed to be a job parameter. This implies :

$$\mu_d = \frac{1}{(1+\alpha)\, d_{io}}$$

Disk service time, d_{io}, is obtained adding arm movement, rotational delay and transfer, that is respectively : d_b, d_r, t

$$d_{io} = d_b + d_r + t$$

On CDC transfer size is constant for each type of file. Therefore this size is known if request rate for each type has been measured. d_r is systematically supposed equal to half a rotation.

There remains the problem of arm movement. We shall now deal with it as follows. First, a probability p_b is determined, then an average arm movement d_{bm}, which implies :

$$d_b = d_{bm} p_b$$

The probability of arm movement is taken equal to 1 for the following I/O :

- non-sequential files

- roll in - roll out : an empty cylinder is nessary here

- staging as link rate generates a maximum of 5 I/O per second. Henceforward, under normal operation, if a job active in s, as it generates much more I/O, it will have a better chance to "steal" the arm. If there is no active jobs, this implies they are all staging and that, therefore, several files are yielded simultaneously.

For the I/O generated by jobs on sequential files, the probability of arm movement is calculated as follows : let v be the number of volumes, and i the number of jobs in LCM. The allocations are supposed uniformly distributed in the v volumes. Henceforth the I/O on one file will be without arm movement if no other file is allocated in the same volume. Knowing the number f of simultaneous sequential files for each job, there are (if) active sequential files. Let a file be in a given volume, the probability that none of the (if-1) others should be in the same volume is :

$$(1 - \frac{1}{v})^{if-1}$$

Therefore, if β is the proportion of job I/O on sequential files,

$$P_b = 1-\beta + \beta \ (1-\frac{1}{v})^{if-1}$$

To estimate an average arm movement, on one hand a maximum arm movement will be determined weighted by the volume allocation rate γ. On the other hand, Denning approximation will be either used or not whether average length of file or disk n_d exceeds 1 or not. Therefore :

$$d_m = d_{min} + \gamma \ (d_{max} - d_{min}) \ \frac{1 + \frac{1}{n_d + 2}}{2 \ (n_d + 1)} \quad \text{if } n_d > 1$$

$$d_m = d_{min} + \gamma \ (\frac{d_{max} - d_{min}}{3}) \ \text{if } n_d < 1$$

Note : The working out of n_d obviously implies marginal probabilities at disk station, as in 3.2.4 but this can often be dispensed with. For instance if i_0 is the average number of jobs at the CPU, if i jobs are in LCM and if disk stations are supposed more or less balanced :

$$n_d \approx \frac{i - i_0}{v}$$

3.3 - Iterative computations

The global computation is worked out as follows. From the pattern parameters, CPU model is solved for i = 1, 2, ..., min (N,m). Let us remark that in certain cases an iterative computation is necessary when an explicit value of $n_d > 1$ must be calculated. This determines the ρ_i.

Taking an arbitrary value for d, the global model is solved, thus supplying all the p_i which with the help of all the ρ_i will enable to work out a new value of d̄. If this value is different from the preceding one, it will be necessary to iterate with an intermediate value.

3.4 - Validation

Without a rigourous basis to tackle the problem, we shall be content with an
intuitive type of validation which provides an estimate of the range of error
on a few cases. In this prospect, we shall only compare carefully measured cases
with the vehaviour predicted by the model. Each comparison relates to a set
of measurements with the essential particularity that all the values of the
parameters it includes are sumultaneously defined on the same processing period.
These parameters include on one hand all the necessary date needed for the
model, and, on the other hand, the one or various essential values concerned
with this computation, as we are interested in the comparison beetween their
measured value and their calculated one :

the small variation ε observed on several rather different sets, will be
called reasonable validation and will warrant - with a rather large probability -
that the model can be used within a reasonable range in order to assure a useful
prediction for any modification : with widely larger effects than this variation
ε.

The following table gives measured and computed values for 2 differents sets
of measurements on the initial 7600 configuration (2 volumes).

	SET N°1	SET N°2
Measured CPU utilisation	33,2 %	56 %
Calculated CPU utilisation	34 %	57 %

The absolute difference is of about 1 %. We are not yet quite able to explain
the reasons for such a small variation. Yet, with the help of our experience
supported by other models, we are convinced that, as regards CPU utilisation,
a difference well above 1 % is always the sign of bad modelling : bad representation of a physical phenomenon or, more often non-detection of a physical
important phenomenon.

4 - MODEL USE

Placed again at the level of the computation center operation manager, we see
that his concern is mainly for the best possible operation for his hardware at
the smallest possible cost. He has at his disposal a model providing accurate
predictions, that is a high-grade tool to help answering many questions.
Among these, the main ones are those referring to an appreciation of the various
bottlenecks which influence global operation. The secondary ones are those
which will assist him in making the most efficient decisions, both as regards
configuration evolution and load modifications.

4.1 - Classification of the main bottlenecks

The 7600 turned out to be seldom able to rise above 50 % CPU utilisation. Thus,
though it easily managed with the load, this type of observation soon became
the main concern of the operation teams, and, of course, they gave their opinion on the question. They particularly complained about LCM size - which could
not hold more than 4 medium jobs - and also about the link rate.

Yet, the model enables to make out a very different classification. First, the problem of the link is immediately discarded : once it is ascertained that its rate allows for a faster delivery of files than it is necessary for a saturated central unit, there only remains to initialize enough jobs so that the probability to have less than four of them in station becomes small.

Consequently, the model shows that when LCM is well loaded, especially for i = 4 jobs, the I/O service is very close to saturation. On the other hand this point is easily seen before model solving, in checking the utilisation of CPU and I.O, that must remain proportionnal to a same constant :

$$\frac{u_i}{e_i \mu_i} \quad (u_i \text{ being utilization of service i})$$

In fact a typical job parameter is 30 to 40 I/O executed for one CPU second ; at 80 ms per I/O and two volumes, this would make 100 % volume utilization at 62,5 % to 83 % CPU utilization. Then, increasing LCM in order to store more jobs inside it, though it leads to no I/O reduction, does not really open up any hope of a better operation. This observation is actually strengthened by the fact - contrary to all expectations - that the load of the 2 volumes in the initial configuration was far from being balanced.

For instance in case study when CPU run at 56 %, first volume was working at 82 % and the other one at 59 %.

Therefore, quite naturally, the next sequence of necessary modifications will follow - classified by decreasing importance :

- software problem : better volume balancing

- problem of the reduction of I/O overloading : increasing number of volumes

- if really necessary, increasing of LCM

4.2 - Configuration extrapolation

Our previous analysis has brought out the necessity to reduce sooner or later I/O overloading. This only implies increasing the number of volumes. Various assumptions have been made in order to test their efficiency, namely :

- adding 1 type 844 volume

- adding 2 type 844 volumes

- adding 2 type 819 volumes (faster)

The following table illustrates the results obtained for different profiles. It also points out the improvements added by volume balancing and the eventual result an extension of LCM would have led to (50 % memory increase).

This leaves time to check that the last solution (several time more expensive than the addition of 2 volumes) still leads to a very poor efficiency compared to disk volume extension.

		CPU RATE	
		PROFILE N° 1	PROFILE N° 2
Measured CPU utilisation		56 %	
Calculated CPU utilisation for initial configuration		57 %	52 %
Volume balancing		63 %	57 %
Disk volume extension	adding 1 x 844	68 %	62 %
	adding 2 x 844	73 %	66 %
	adding 2 x 819	84 %	78 %
LCM extension (+ 50 %)		64 %	58 %

4.3 - Extrapolation of profiles

Even though we may know that a given configuration will be able to reach a
satisfactory CPU utilisation - about 80 % - for a given profile, all the
concerns of the operation manager are not yet solved. There is no proof, in
fact, that this profile will not change. At least two phenomena can determine
such an evolution, namely accounting and the activity of commercial departments.

4.3.1 - Accouting

Any sensible customer will try to act upon available parameters in order to
reduce job cost, if he is acquainted with the formulas used for job accouting.
This naturally leads to a modification of job profile. Therefore it is particularly important for the operation manager, to avoid that these manipulations
lead to a gradual loss of global receipt. This implies that the coefficients
of main facturable services (I/O, CPU, memory size...) should be adapted so
that, on the average, the user will tend to strive for an optimum operation.
For instance, a memory size, priced too low will urge the user towards extension, thus leading to an excessive reduction of multiprogramming rate ; on the
contrary, when priced too high, the programs size will excessively decrease
but will, on the other hand, generate too many I/O, thus leading to a new
overloading of the service.

4.3.2 - Commercial previsions

On the side of the computer, it is obvious, for similar reasons, that it is
not possible to assume equivalent all the eventual applications. Therefore, it
is now necessary there should be a two-way interaction between operation and
commercial management. The operation manager should convey the specifications
of the "interesting" jobs for the machine : the commercial division must
inform sufficiently behorehand of interesting productions jobs - though normally outside the specifications - so that the corresponding impact should be
figured out and that eventually the decision of a configuration adaptation
should be taken.

5 - CONCLUSIONS AND PROSPECTS

We are perfectly aware that we only used classical techniques for mathematical modelling. Indeed, many problems remain unsolved, especially as regards precision. Yet, the efficiency of the above methods in industrial use is already demonstrated by elementary economic considerations.

5.1 - Open problems

Among the problem which are still open, some are general and others are specific to our study.

5.1.1 - Specific problems

Most certainly, not everything is solved by this modelling and some points remain unclear. The most interesting one refers to an apparently systematic shift between computation and reality where machine behaviour is more closely observed. The illustration on page   , shows the results of the model compared to a whole day's observations, classified by the value of N - number of jobs simultaneously initialized. For small values of N, the model is not too optimistic, but it is so for large values of N (N > 10) and moreover a palpable deterioration seems to occur in the real system.

Of course, the lack of precision of the model (especially its lack of real stability) can be suspected. Yet, we do not know if this is enough or if other physical elements have an importance. A few elements can be pointed out by decreasing intuitive importance, namely :

- N, when increasing, determines an increasing size of allocated disk space, hence an increase of the arm movements. Then as the model makes out the computations on a global average, it will issue unfavourable results for N small and favourable ones for N large.

- Since free-space on disk decreases as N increases, the number of semi-permanent files -reserved on 7600 disks after end of job, with the hope that they will soon be used again - decreases, and consequently staging request rate increases.

- A particularity of a scheduler settled on the site is that it initializes jobs for N > 10, only when it considers that too many jobs are in staging.

5.1.2 - Accuracy

While doing various simplifications and approximations on one hand, we get rather accurate results on the other. We are becoming aware that we are unable to understand these facts.

The best, for us, should be to possess,as a traditional physicist, techniques for error estimation, in order to determine a priori the error made by our approximations. For certain cases, we managed to represent reality with two models, so that the results of each one could define an imprecision interval, small enough for our needs. But this is seldom the case.

That is to say we feel deeply the need for a whole set of tools that would enable us to estimate a priori the range of error.

5.2 - Economic interest of modelling

Our experience pointed out that the total cost of a modelling like the one described here, can be estimated to 2 specialist man-months, the cost of measurements not included. This cost makes the total cost twice as large. On the
other hand, for this particular case, a non-efficient decision would have been
taken without this study,   that is LCM would have been   increased would
have cost much more than what comes out of the final decision ; and this to
such an extent, that the difference would have been several times larger than
the 4 man-months necessary for the whole study.

Another striking example refers to 360/91 modelling which, unlike 7600, was
entirely saturated. Modelling enabled here to take non-obvious decisions on
the configuration modifications, resulting in increasing the observed throughput. This increase paid, within less than a month, for all the modelling
operation and for the measurements.

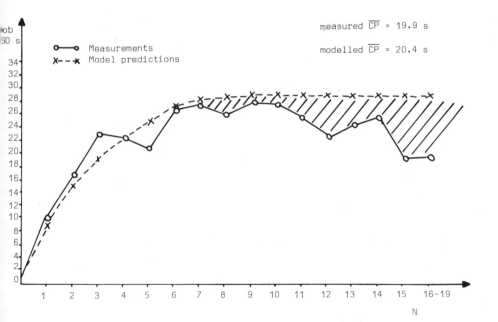

REFERENCES

[1] J.R. JACKSON, "Job-shop like queueing systems", Management Science Vol. 10, 131-142 (1963).

[2] P.J. DENNING, "Effects of scheduling on file memory operations", Proc. AFIPS Conf. Vol. 30, 9 - 21 (1967).

[3] E. GELENBE, R. muntz, "Probabilistic models of computer systems - Part I (Exact results)", Acta Information Vol. 7, 35 - 60 (1976).

[4] E. GELENBE, "On approximative computer system models", Journal ACM Vol. 22, 261 - 263 (1975).

[5] J. BUZEN, "Computational algorithms for closed queuing networks with exponential servers", Comm. ACM Vol. 16, 527 - 531 (1973).

COMPUTER PERFORMANCE, K.M. CHANDY AND M. REISER (EDS.)
NORTH HOLLAND PUBLISHING COMPANY, 1977

PERFORMANCE OF AN ESC-BASED TIME-SHARING SUBSYSTEM

V. A. Abell and S. Rosen*
Purdue University
West Lafayette, Indiana USA

This paper describes a performance study of a time-sharing
system that is based on the use of Control Data Extended Core
Storage (ECS) as swapping storage. The system differs from
most other time-sharing systems in that a task is swapped out
when a disk I-0 command occurs, and the disk I-0 is performed
between the disk file and the swapped out task in ECS.

In analyzing the system, we have found it convenient to introduce a three phase model of a user interaction in place of the
more usual two phase (think time-system time) model.

A software probe provides a detailed event trace of the running
production system. Data collected during short intervals,
(about 10 minutes each), in which more than 100 users were active
provide a great deal of useful and interesting information about
the performance of the system.

INTRODUCTION

Performance measurement and evaluation techniques have played an important part
in the design and development of the MESA-IODP time-sharing system. MESA-IODP
runs as a subsystem of the Purdue Dual-MACE operating system which uses two interconnected Control Data (CDC) 6500 computers as its main computing units and three
MODCOMP II Communications Processors as front end computers.

The most important tool for obtaining performance data in the MACE system is a
software event probe that collects event records produced by the central processor executive routine for each function that it performs. The event records provide input to data reduction routines that produce summary information at many
levels of detail for use by systems programmers and performance analysts.

The first event probe in the Purdue MACE system was installed by Joel Ewing in
1971, and was described in an internal report, Ewing (1975). Later developments
and uses of the event probe in connection with MACE and in connection with early
versions of the MESA time-sharing subsystem have been described in Schwetman
(1975) and Rosen (1976).

The MESA-IODP time-sharing subsystem differs from earlier versions of MESA and
from most other time-sharing systems in that a user's task is swapped out of central memory when a disk I-0 command occurs in a user's program. The actual input-
output transfers are then done by a system program, IODP, that causes data to be
transferred between disk files and the swapped out user space. When the I-0 command has been completed the user's task becomes eligible to be swapped back into
central memory.

*
This work was supported in part by the National Science Foundation under grant
GJ41289.

This strategy makes sense only if swapping storage is very fast relative to disk storage. The swapping storage used in the MESA system is CDC Extended Core Storage (ECS). ECS is magnetic core memory with an access time of 3.2 µsec. Only one access time is needed for a block of data, after which data can stream into or out of central memory at a maximum instantaneous transfer rate of 10,000,000 words (100,000,000 characters) per second. ECS is expensive storage, far too expensive to use in place of disks. Because of its cost, the ECS in use by the Dual MACE system has a capacity of only 504,000 words of which 437,000 are available to MESA as swapping storage. MESA programs, such as editors, macro processors, file management systems and incremental compilers, are all designed to use a maximum of 15000_8 words of storage. Code overlays are swapped in from ECS to main memory at very high speed, and since they are read-only code they do not form part of the swapped out user space. The average amount of read/write space swapped in and out for a user is about 2000 words. The average time to swap a user out and to then swap in and start up a new user's program is about 4 ms. There is usually space in ECS to swap about 140 users. When the system starts to run out of swapping space it moves the user space for relatively inactive users to disk storage, and stages them back to ECS when they need processor time.

Performance data for the earlier MESA systems which used the more conventional approach of keeping a user task in central memory while disk I-O was in progress showed that user programs could make use of central processors for only a very small fraction of the time during which they occupied central memory. The principal goal of the IODP version of MESA was to cut down on the time in central memory per user interaction (the in-core time) in order to permit more interactions to be processed per unit of time. An alternative would have been to allocate sufficient additional central memory to the time-sharing system to increase its level of multiprogramming. That alternative, if used, would have resulted in severe limitation on the number and size of the jobs that could be handled by the batch processing system. The ability of the batch processing system to turn around jobs created or called up by the time-sharing subsystem is an important factor in the total system performance, and there was therefore a very strong motivation to keep the amount of central memory used by the time-sharing subsystem as small as possible.

Most current predictions about the next generation of computers suggest that they will have a level of intermediate storage, intermediate in speed and capacity between central memory and disk file storage. In addition to their inherent interest, ECS based systems may offer some insight into how such storage levels might be used and the effect they might have on system performance.

MODEL OF A USER INTERACTION

In his classic study of the CTSS system at MIT, Scherr (1967) introduced a "user interaction model" that has been widely used in the study of time-sharing systems. In Scherr's model the time taken by an interaction starts when the user's program requires input. The interaction time consists of Think time (also called input wait time or user time) which ends when the user has finished typing an input line, and Working time (also called response time) which ends when the program again requires input. (Figure 1.)

In Scherr's study the importance of other events, in particular output events, was relatively small since output was directed only to 15 character per second typewriter terminals.

In our studies of MESA we have found it useful to introduce a slightly more complicated three phase model of an interaction. (Figure 2.) One reason is the use of a number of very much faster output devices than were available on the original CTSS system. Another is the use of communications processors as buffer machines between the central computing system and the user terminals.

In our model an interaction starts with the Think time which is defined very much
as in Scherr's model. It starts when the user's program requires input, and ends
when the user's input is finished. Think time is followed by IN-OUT time which
starts when the user's input is finished and ends when the user's program starts
providing output for the user. IN-OUT time is followed by OUT-IN time which ends
when the user's program again requires input.

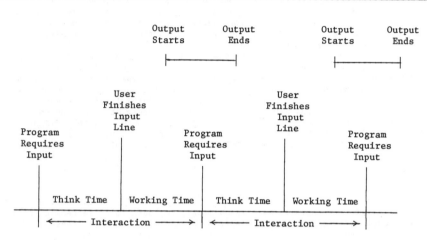

Figure 1.   Scherr Model of a User Interaction

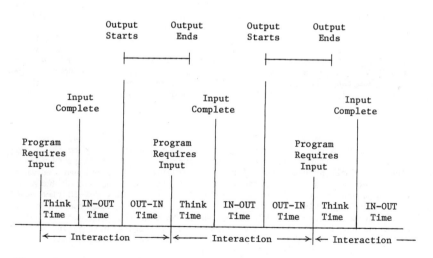

Figure 2.   Three Phase Model of a User Interaction

Because of the existence of buffer machines the user's input is not necessarily a single line. When the user is creating a file, for example, the buffer machine may collect a number of lines into a buffer area before it issues a buffer ready signal that is interpreted as an input completed signal by the central computer.

Scherr's response time represents the time it takes to complete the system's response to the user's input. This is a reasonable measure of response time if only a single number is to be used. In our model the IN-OUT time is the time it takes the system to make an _initial_ response to the user, and the OUT-IN time is the time it then takes to complete the response. In many cases the time it takes to start a response, i.e., the IN-OUT time, corresponds more closely to an intuitive notion of response time than does the time to make the entire response. Thus if a user asks the system to list a file, he might reasonably consider the response time to be the time between his request and the beginning of the listing operation. The time until the response is completed may be quite long, especially if the terminal is a 10 or 15 character per second typewriter, but that is a reflection on the speed of the output device, not on the speed of the computing system. On the other hand there are cases in which the initial response may be almost spurious. Some systems may even try to mask instances of poor response by using reassuring messages such as, "wait for output" or "there will be a slight delay." The initial response in such a case may be very fast, but it is in fact no response at all. In these cases the OUT-IN time is definitely part of the system response time. IN-OUT time may also be interpreted as the time it takes the system to make a simple response to a user who makes a small demand on the system.

The interactions for which data are obtained do not correspond exactly to the conceptual model of an interaction. As already mentioned, data is collected in the form of an event trace produced on the central computer. The data is thus all obtained and interpreted from the point of view of the central processor. Consider an interaction in which the user types in a command followed by a carriage return. That carriage return is the end of Think time from the point of view of the user, but the central processor cannot record that event until it becomes aware of it. What actually happens is that the front-end computer records the carriage return in a status array. The array is read periodically from the front-end computer's memory by an input routine in a peripheral processor of the central computer. The input routine then stimulates another peripheral processor routine to set the bit corresponding to that terminal in the central memory attention array. Only then is the end of Think time recorded for the interaction. The difference between the length of Think time from the point of view of the computer and that of the user is usually less than 100 ms., but in unusual cases it can be as high as 300 ms. These values may be insignificant relative to the total length of Think time, but they are much more significant relative to the length of the initial response time, i.e. the IN-OUT time, which may in some cases be 100-300 ms. shorter from the point of view of the central computer than it is from the point of view of the user.

All three phases do not necessarily have to be present in every interaction. OUT-IN time begins when the user's program starts to transmit output to the front-end machine, and it ends when the program indicates that it is ready for the next input. If all of the output for the interaction can be transmitted in a single burst, there will be no measured time between the start of output and the request for input, and there will be no OUT-IN time. A non-zero OUT-IN time occurs when it is not possible to transmit all of the output for the transaction in a single burst, either because of buffering constraints in the front-end computer, or because the output is not all in central memory, e.g. additional output will have to be fetched from a disk file. The OUT-IN time then lasts until all of the output data has been transmitted to the front-end computer.

In the case of an interrupt that occurs during OUT-IN time there is an immediate transition to IN-OUT status, and hence an interaction with no Think time. A

message broadcast to a terminal might appear as part of an interaction with no
IN-OUT time. These latter cases are relatively rare, and one finds, as in the
data in Table 1, that the number of IN-OUT times and THINK times are fairly close
to each other, but there are considerably fewer non-zero OUT-IN times than IN-OUT
times.

Table 1. User interaction data. IN-OUT, OUT-IN and
          Think times. All times are in seconds.

	IN-OUT Times		OUT-IN Times		Think Times	
	Nov. 1	Nov. 22	Nov. 1	Nov. 22	Nov. 1	Nov. 22
Count	1961	2319	1207	1480	1812	2213
Mean	.509	1.055	15.551	16.630	17.815	16.392
Standard Dev.	2.835	5.491	64.118	68.928	36.838	36.249
Median	.027	.026	1.317	1.462	7.220	6.410
Maximum	76.2	134.1	540.1	600.0	527.6	511.0
Total no. of users	118	125				
Total sample time	540	600				
Equivalent active users	96.2	105.5				

PERFORMANCE DATA

A user may sit at a terminal and form a subjective evaluation of the responsiveness of the time-sharing system. A major goal of measurement and evaluation is
to find a set of parameters that can be measured or calculated that will give an
objective evaluation of performance that is consistent with the subjective evaluation that would be made by most users.

The techniques used in the performance analysis of the MESA system involve gathering data while it is in normal production use by a large number of users; while
it is doing all of the things that it is designed to do. An alternative technique, that of measuring performance under a simulated or benchmark load, can
also be very useful. Studies using that alternative approach may be attempted in
the future, but the large variety of users of the MESA system, and the effects of
interaction with the host MACE system, makes it very difficult to design and to
validate such studies.

There are a number of problems and disadvantages to the use of software event
probe techniques to measure a fully loaded system. The collection of data uses
system resources, and to some extent perturbs the performance of the system. The
effect on performance can be measured and can either be ignored as inconsequen-
tial or can be factored out. The fact that the measurement uses significant resources makes it necessary to limit the measurement to short intervals of time.
The very large volume of data that is produced is another factor that makes it
desirable to limit the amount of time during which data is collected.

The data discussed here was gathered in two intervals, one nine minutes long and
one ten minutes long, on November 1 and November 22, 1976 respectively. This is,
of course, a very small sampling of data for a system that runs almost all of the
time. In using such data to describe the performance of the system there is an
implicit assumption that system performance in the intervals during which data
was collected was in some sense typical of the performance of the system for very
much larger periods of time. Actually, there are no typical intervals. A detailed analysis of any real data sample almost always reveals special events that

occurred during the time the data was collected that make that data sample somewhat atypical. The best that can be done is to select data collection times carefully to avoid obtaining or using data for intervals during which serious known
atypical conditions prevail.

The data samples from November 1 and November 22, 1976 are representative of two
different subjective levels of system performance. November 22 was a day of unusually heavy total system activity. It was the first time the MACE system ran
over 15,000 jobs in a single day, and the very heavy system load was reflected in
the relatively poor response times seen by users of the time-sharing subsystem.
It is not clear what combination of circumstances made November 1 a day on which
response was unusually good, but that seemed to be the consensus of a number of
users of the system on that day.

We shall discuss some of the performance parameters of the system as they appear
in performance analysis reports for samples of data collected on those two days.
A performance analysis report is a statistical summary derived from the analysis
of an event trace tape. An event trace tape for a nine to ten minute period of
reasonably heavy activity contains about 750,000 event records. The report contains roughly one hundred pages of tables and summary data for the MESA system as
a whole and for the various programs that run under MESA. Only very brief ex-
tracts from the two performance reports will be presented here.

INTERACTIONS

The number of IN-OUT states is used as a measure of the number of interactions.
Table 1 shows that there were 2319 interactions with an average IN-OUT time of
1.055 seconds in the ten minute measurement interval on November 22. The average
OUT-IN time for the 1480 OUT-IN times recorded was 16.630, but if a zero OUT-IN
time is assigned to those interactions for which no OUT-IN time is recorded, then
the average OUT-IN time per interaction (1480 x 16.630) ÷ 2319 is 10.61. If a
zero Think time is similarly assigned to those interactions for which no Think
time is recorded then the average Think time per interaction is 15.64 seconds.
Fig. 3 shows the average interaction times calculated in this way based on the
data for November 1 and for November 22.

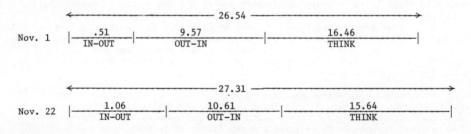

Figure 3. Average Interaction Times in Seconds
           (not drawn to scale)

The average length of an interaction on November 1 was 26.54 seconds. The average length on November 22 was 27.31 seconds. As mentioned earlier, the IN-OUT
time may be interpreted as an initial response time. This initial response time
is much shorter on November 1, but even on November 22 when system response was
considered to be relatively poor it was just about one second. This agrees with
the experience noted by users that response to trivial requests remains relatively good even when the total responsiveness of the system seems poor.

There were 125 users active during the ten minute sampling period on November 22. The number 125 represents the total number of terminals for which any activity was recorded in the interval. Continuous activity of 125 terminals for the full 600.187 seconds during which data was recorded would account for 125 x 600.187 = 75,023 seconds of interaction time. The total interaction time actually recorded, i.e. the total of all of the time in IN-OUT, OUT-IN and THINK states was 63,337 seconds. While some of this deficiency may be caused by inevitable losses of information during the data gathering process, most of it can be attributed to the fact that not all of the users for whom some activity was recorded were active throughout the entire period. The number of "equivalent active terminals" is defined as the total amount of recorded interaction time divided by the length of the sampling interval. For the November 22 sample it was 63337 ÷ 600.187 = 105.5 equivalent active terminals. In the 541.006 second sampling interval on November 1, data was recorded for 118 different users, whose total activity corresponded to that of 96.2 equivalent active terminals. These data suggest that any estimate that we make of the number of active terminals that the system can support will underestimate the number of logged on terminals that can be supported.

IN-CORE TIME

Because of the fact that disk I-O is performed for the user's program when it is swapped out of central memory, a typical interaction may have a fairly large number of relatively short intervals during which the task occupies central memory. We call such an interval an in-core time. In-core time data for the data samples on November 1 and November 22 are given in Table 2.

Table 2.   In-core time in seconds.

	All In-core		IN-OUT In-core		OUT-IN In-core	
	Nov. 1	Nov. 22	Nov. 1	Nov. 22	Nov. 1	Nov. 22
Count	13171	14516	6252	6938	6919	7578
Mean	.050	.060	.042	.055	.057	.064
Standard Dev.	.082	.113	.081	.114	.083	.111
Median	.027	.029	.023	.027	.033	.033
Maximum	1.721	2.721	1.721	2.381	1.449	2.721
In-core per IN-OUT	.339	.377				

The system attempts to enforce an in-core time maximum of 250 ms., but it is not always successful in enforcing this maximum since peripheral processor programs cannot be interrupted. Thus the maximum in-core time indicated in Table 2 is 2.721 seconds. This probably reflects the existence of a few special situations in which disk I-O for a user task must be done while the task is in core (e.g. loading a disk resident code module), and the possibility that there may occasionally be long I-O waits because of queueing for channel access and for disk unit access. An in-core time frequency distribution (Table 3) suggests that between 2 and 4% of the total number of in-core times exceed the 250 ms. maximum. The number and size of unusually large in-core times is the type of performance data that needs to be monitored with some regularity.

The average in-core time, 50 ms. on November 1 and 60 ms. on November 22, includes a total swap-out and swap-in time of about 4 msec. (Swap time can be deduced from other data included in the full report.) The difference in average in-core time on the two days can be partially explained as a result of a difference in the distribution of the types of programs that were being executed for MESA users. It is also at least in part caused by the fact that the whole MACE system was more heavily loaded on November 22.

Table 3.   In-core time frequency distribution.

Time in ms.	November 1		November 22	
	Count	Cum %	Count	Cum %
0- 31	7540	57.24	7694	53.00
32- 63	2938	79.55	3385	76.32
64- 95	1088	87.81	1396	85.93
96- 127	495	91.57	600	90.07
128- 191	449	94.98	527	93.70
192- 319	480	98.62	476	96.98*
319-1727	181	100.00	438	100.00*

*
On November 22 the last two intervals were 192-288 ms. and 288-2751 ms.

IN-CORE TIME PER INTERACTION

The amount of in-core time used per interaction is one of the critical performance parameters of the time-sharing subsystem. It was 339 ms. in the November 1 data sample and 377 ms. in that of November 22. The number of MESA tasks that can be in central memory, i.e. the degree of subsystem multiprogramming, is a MACE system parameter that is set at 2. The total in-core time that is available in an interval is thus equal to twice the length of the interval. The in-core time used was 60.9% and 72.5% of the total in-core time available in the samples of November 1 and November 22 respectively. If in-core time is the only factor considered, and if a fixed interaction length is assumed, then a rough estimate of the number of users that can be supported is the total amount of in-core time available during an interaction divided by the in-core time per interaction. The amount of in-core time available during an interaction is equal to the degree of multiprogramming multiplied by the length of an interaction. Taking the degree of multiprogramming as 2, the interaction lengths as given in Figure 3 and the in-core time per interaction as above, this rough estimate is 156.6 for November 1 and 144.9 for November 22. One might interpret these as estimates of the numbers of active users that could have been supported on those two days with roughly the same kind of response as that observed.

There are many other factors that contribute to the responsiveness of the system, but these estimates are useful as an indication that the amount of available in-core time is probably not a limiting factor in response time at the level of usage represented in these samples. From these and similar data obtained at other times it seems reasonable to conclude that the MESA subsystem multiprogramming level will not be a limiting factor in performance until the number of equivalent active users goes above the 125-130 level. If the number of users is expanded beyond that level it may be necessary to increase the level of multiprogramming to 3. At that level of utilization other factors may be more important than available in-core time in limiting the number of users that can be supported.

BIT-STATUS QUEUE

User tasks that are ready to execute are placed on a ready queue by setting a corresponding status bit in a "bit-status" array. In most cases the task becomes ready to execute because IODP has completed an input-output transfer, or because terminal input is complete, but there can be other reasons, e.g. an interrupted program requests more in-core time, or a program pause comes to an end.

The scheduler selects the next user on the ready queue to be swapped into core according to an algorithm that is described in detail in Abell (1975). The bit status array is one of the major system queues. The length of the queue, (i.e. the

number of bits set), and the time it takes for a task to be swapped in after its
status bit is set, (the queueing delay), are important indicators of the responsiveness of the system. Table 4 shows the behavior of the bit-status array queue
for the two data samples under discussion. For each queue length, the table gives
the percent of the total sampling time for which the queue had that length. It is
surprising to find that the queue length was 0 for a much larger part of the time
in the November 22 sample, but the cumulative percents, and the average values for
queue length and queueing delay, show that there was considerably more queueing in
the November 22 sample.

Table 4. Bit-status array and IODP queues.

| Queue Length | Bit-status array | | | | IODP | | | |
| | Nov. 1 | | Nov. 22 | | Nov. 1 | | Nov. 22 | |
	%	Cum. %	%	Cum. %	%	Cum. %	%	Cum. %
0	26.17	26.17	37.14	37.14	35.11	35.11	14.68	14.68
1	33.84	60.01	11.81	48.95	10.85	45.96	6.01	20.69
2	12.00	72.01	7.12	56.07	8.13	54.09	5.89	26.58
3	7.52	79.53	6.17	62.24	6.59	60.68	6.36	32.94
4	5.79	85.32	4.61	66.85	7.03	67.71	6.13	39.07
5	4.13	89.45	3.78	70.63	6.90	74.61	6.36	45.43
6	2.84	92.29	3.06	73.69	5.96	80.57	6.23	51.66
7	1.83	94.12	2.78	76.47	5.46	86.03	6.23	57.89
8	1.26	95.38	2.46	78.93	4.36	90.39	5.25	63.14
9	1.21	96.59	2.28	81.21	3.38	93.77	5.47	68.61
10	.96	97.55	1.80	83.01	2.50	96.27	4.20	72.81
11–15	1.98	99.53	8.48	91.49	3.57	99.84	17.59	90.40
16–20	.37	99.90	5.19	96.68	.06	99.90	7.61	98.01
21–31	----	-----	3.15	99.83	----	-----	1.83	99.84
Average Length	2.167		4.571		3.188		7.140	
Average Delay	.068 sec.		.190 sec.		.201 sec.		.463 sec.	

IODP

When a user program attempts to issue an I-O command, the command is almost always
intercepted by the executive routine and is converted into a directive for the
Input-Output Directive Program (IODP). The user task is then swapped out. IODP
is a separate resident program that can supervise the execution of a number of I-O
commands simultaneously. That number is a system parameter that is currently set
at 3. Data moves between disk storage units and user space in ECS through buffers
in IODP's central memory space. Conflicts for access to channels and to disk
units may occur between directives belonging to different MESA tasks, and also
between IODP and the batch programs running either on the same central computer or
on the other 6500 of the Dual MACE system. One of the functions of IODP is to attempt to lessen the impact of such conflicts on the MESA subsystem by transferring
the queueing delays to IODP. Data that is collected in connection with IODP includes the number of IODP directives executed, and the amount of time it takes
IODP to execute directives. Table 5 shows such data for the November 1 and November 22 data samples. Since up to three directives can be in process simultaneously, the total available directive processing time is taken as three times the
total sample time, and it is on this basis that IODP utilization is 81.06% on
November 1 and 90.79% on November 22. Table 4 shows the extent of IODP queueing
for the two samples. These data can be a bit misleading since the time it takes
to process a directive includes channel access time and disk access and transfer
time. What might be interpreted as an IODP capacity problem is actually a disk

system capacity problem. Data on disk channel activity reveals that the channel most critical to the performance of the MESA-IODP system was in use 70.43% of the time in the November 1 sampling period and 79.65% of the time on that of November 22. A number of new disk controllers and disk units that are scheduled to be installed in 1977 will almost certainly relieve much of the observed IODP congestion.

Table 5. IODP activity.

	Nov. 1	Nov. 22
IODP Directives	8574	9270
Ave. IODP time/dir.	.244	.238
% IODP utilization	81.06	90.79

DISK ACCESS CYCLE

The time for a complete disk access cycle consists of in-core time followed by IODP queueing delay, then IODP execution time, and finally the bit-status queue delay that precedes the next in-core time. Figure 4 shows the time taken for an average disk access cycle during the two sampling periods. Note that the average in-core time used is not that given in Table 2. It comes from a more detailed listing in the performance report which gives the average in-core time broken down by the reason for which the user was swapped out. The average in-core time prior to issuing an I-O command is considerably shorter than the average of all in-core times. It was approximately 31 ms. and 33 ms. in the November 1 and November 22 samples respectively.

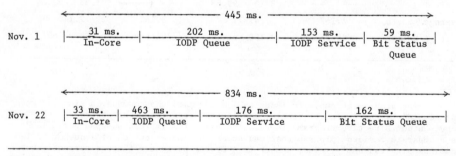

Figure 4. Disk Access Cycle
           (not drawn to scale)

The much longer disk access cycle on November 22 is a direct measure of the difference in performance level. The queueing delays in the disk access cycle occur because of the system design that forces tasks to be swapped out for I-O. In the case of a very lightly loaded system this may actually result in some degradation of performance. Data samples taken before and after the introduction of the IODP version of MESA, however, indicate a very considerable improvement in performance on a heavily loaded system. While individual I-O requests may be subject to delays that may seem unnecessary, the general approach that causes these delays results in more I-O commands and more interactions to be completed per unit time. Some data for the pre-IODP MESA system is given in Rosen(1976). That data is 3+ years old, and it would be misleading to make item by item comparisons between data collected on the system running in 1973 and that running at the end of 1976.

Subjective evaluations by long time users indicate that response time was significantly better in 1976, even though the average number of simultaneous users had
increased by about 50%. It is not possible to tell to what extent such long term
system improvement can be attributed to the handling of I-O through IODP. A number of other significant hardware and software changes were made in the interim.

TERMINAL SERVICE PROGRAMS

MESA interactions involve the execution by MESA of a large variety of terminal
service programs. These include PIRATE, a macro command system used mostly for
conversational remote batch job creation, submission, and retrieval, QED, a line-
oriented context editor, PFILES, a permanent file storage and retrieval system,
ALFIE, a BASIC language incremental compiler, and XBATCH, a program that supports
high speed card readers and printers as remote batch terminals. In all, there are
more than thirty different terminal support programs. There is a great deal of
variety in the characteristics of the interactions that use these different terminal service programs.

All of the data that have been discussed so far are average and summary data based
on all of the interactions that occurred during the two sampling periods. These
average performance data make up only a very small part of the performance analysis report. Most of the report consists of information about interactions that
used the individual terminal support programs. These classes of interactions make
very different kinds of demands on system resources as shown in Table 6 which
gives data for three terminal support programs, PIRATE, QED, and XBATCH. By almost any way of measuring response it can be seen that QED interactions use minimal system resources and provide excellent response to users. PIRATE makes large
demands on the input-output system, while XBATCH uses a great deal of in-core time
per interaction. Data of this kind is useful in indicating areas in which subsystem performance can be improved. The large amount of disk I-O represented by
PIRATE interactions points to PIRATE usage as an area in which there would be a
significant payoff if disk usage economies could be achieved. The introduction of
the line editor QED was strongly influenced by performance analysis studies that
suggested that the earlier line editor which had been a subprogram of PIRATE would
use fewer disk accesses if were made into a separate terminal support program.
This type of information also makes it possible to estimate the effect of introducing new users of various types into the system.

Table 6.   Interactions that used terminal service
           programs: PIRATE, QED, XBATCH.

	PIRATE		QED		XBATCH	
	Nov. 1	Nov. 22	Nov. 1	Nov. 22	Nov. 1	Nov. 22
Number of interactions	522	679	676	808	306	373
% of total number	26.6	29.3	34.5	34.8	15.6	16.1
Average interaction time	31.42	29.95	20.14	21.26	27.54	23.93
In-core time per int.	.457	.492	.108	.127	.527	.547
% of total in-core time	36.1	38.4	11.1	11.2	24.3	23.5
IODP calls per int.	10.12	7.77	0.95	1.08	2.05	1.67
% of total IODP calls	61.9	57.0	7.6	9.5	7.4	6.7

SYSTEM RESOURCES

The two central processors and ten peripheral processors in one of the CDC 6500
computers are the main computing resources that are shared between the MESA-IODP
subsystem and the other programs that run under the MACE operating system.

Table 7 contains data for central processor (CPU) utilization during the two sampling periods. On both days MESA along with IODP accounted for about half of the
CPU time used. CPU time is allocated in short (20 ms.) quanta by a dispatcher
that gives MESA programs priority over other user programs. The two MESA programs
that can be running simultaneously are very well served by the two central processors, and CPU availability does not seem to be a limiting factor in MESA performance. Note that the statistics gathering program uses a significant amount of CPU
time. However, from the point of view of the MESA subsystem the resources used by
the statistics program are similar in nature to those used by other batch jobs
running under MACE. On both sampling days only about 60% of the total available
CPU time was used. The nature of the workload and of the peripheral subsystems is
such that it is very unusual to find more than 60% of the available CPU time used
over an extended period. The expected value is closer to 50%.

Table 7. Central processor utilization. All times in seconds.

	Nov. 1	Nov. 22
Total CPU time available	1082	1200.4
CPU time used	637.3	746.6
% used	58.9	62.2
MESA CPU time	234.0	273.5
% of CPU time used	36.7	36.6
IODP CPU time	73.8	80.2
% of CPU time used	11.6	10.7
Probe CPU time	85.8	79.8
% of CPU time used	13.5	10.7
MESA in-core time used	658.6	870.4
MESA CPU time as % of in-core time used	35.5	31.4
MESA in-core time as % of in-core time available	60.9	72.5

Three of the ten peripheral processors (PPU's) are permanently assigned to system
tasks. The other seven peripheral processors are available for assignment to the
user programs, mostly for the handling of input-output requests. IODP, which is
given some priority over other programs in the assignment of PPU's, may use up to
three of them simultaneously if it is processing I-O commands directed to three
different channels. Table 8 shows the proportion of time during which N or more
PPU's were in use for N = 3 to 10. The fact that all ten PPU's were in use more
than 35% of the time in the November 22 sample means that during more than 35% of
the time the system had to reject and queue any requests for peripheral processors.
The number of such requests that had to be queued is the number of PPU shortages
given in Table 8. The PPU saturation problem is to a large extent a reflection of
speed and capacity problems in the disk storage system. Our experience with these
and other data samples suggests that PPU shortage statistics provide one of the
useful measures of MESA subsystem performance.

CONCLUSION

It would have been difficult and perhaps impossible to develop MESA-IODP without
the kind of performance data that was provided by the software event probe. The

performance of the time-sharing subsystem depends critically on a number of parameters of the subsystem itself and of the host MACE operating system. We are convinced that no single measure of response time is adequate to describe the performance of a time-sharing system of this type. The three-phase model of the user
interaction appears to be a useful concept to guide the presentation and analysis
of the data that is collected during production runs on a heavily loaded system.
That data plus queueing and utilization data for certain essential resources provide evaluations of performance that seem to agree with subjective evaluations.

Table 8. Peripheral processor utilization.

	% Time in Use	
Number of PPU's	Nov. 1	Nov. 22
3	100.0	99.99
4	99.99	99.98
5	99.87	99.78
6	98.57	97.89
7	92.88	90.81
8	77.49	75.73
9	54.26	56.32
10	29.93	35.42
PPU Shortages	2426	3461

REFERENCES

Abell, V. A. (1976). The MESA System. Purdue University Computing Center Document LO-MESA.

Ewing, J. (1975). CPUMTR Software Event Probe. Purdue University Computing Center
Document LO-EVNTPBE.

Rosen, S. (1976). Lectures on the Measurement and Evaluation of the Performance
of Computing Systems. A monograph in the Regional Conference Series in Applied
Mathematics. SIAM. Philadelphia, PA.

Scherr, A. L. (1967). An Analysis of Time-Shared Computer Systems. MIT Press,
Cambridge, MA.

Schwetman, H. (1975). Gathering and Analyzing Data from a Computer System: A
Case Study. Proceedings ACM National Conference, pp. 112-117.

COMPUTER PERFORMANCE, K.M. CHANDY AND M. REISER (EDS.)
NORTH HOLLAND PUBLISHING COMPANY, 1977

SINGLE SERVER QUEUES WITH CORRELATED INPUTS

B. Gopinath and J. A. Morrison
Bell Telephone Laboratories
Murray Hill, New Jersey, USA

A wide variety of queueing systems with a single server can be modeled
by the equation $b_{n+1} = (b_n-1)^+ + z_n$, where b_n denotes queue length and
z_n the input. The usual assumption about the sequence $\{z_n\}$ is that it
be a sequence of independent identically distributed (i.i.d.) random
variables. However, in many applications, this is not really the case,
$\{z_n\}$ is a sequence of correlated random variables. In this paper we
allow z_n to be of the form $\sum_{i=1}^{\ell} \sum_{j=0}^{k} \alpha_j^i x_{n-j}^i$ where $\{(x_n^1, x_n^2, \ldots, x_n^\ell)\}$ is a
nonnegative integer valued sequence of i.i.d. vector random variables,
and, for each i, α_j^i's are nonnegative integers with $\alpha_0^i > 0$. In this
case b_n is no longer a Markov process. However we show that, with the
help of a transformation, a $(k+1)$-dimensional Markov process that
suffices to describe the queueing system may be found. The first component of this Markov process is just b_n. We obtain an equation for
the steady state generating function corresponding to the joint distribution of this vector process. This equation involves a multinomial which corresponds to zero queue length. A finite system of linear
equations can be obtained to solve uniquely for the coefficients of
this multinomial. We find that a simple set of equations can be
obtained for the marginal distributions. In particular, the steady
state distribution of b_n, the queue length, can be obtained without
solving for the joint distribution.

INTRODUCTION

Several computer systems and networks involve queueing models with single server
queues. We consider a discrete time queueing system, with service time normalized to unity, modeled by the equation

$$b_{n+1} = b_n - 1 + z_n \quad \text{if} \quad b_n \geq 1$$
$$= z_n \quad \text{if} \quad b_n = 0$$

or equivalently

$$b_{n+1} = (b_n-1)^+ + z_n. \tag{1}$$

Here b_n denotes queue length and the nonnegative integer valued sequence z_n is

B. GOPINATH AND J. A. MORRISON

the input.

A vast majority of literature in queueing theory deals with the case when $\{z_n\}$ is a sequence of independent identically distributed random variables. In this situation, when the average value $Ez_n < 1, b = \lim*_{n\uparrow\infty} b_n$ is a well defined random variable, and various authors have analyzed the distribution of b, see Ghosal (1970).

The literature dealing with models where $\{z_n\}$ are not necessarily independent is relatively scant. Recently Ali Khan (1970) and Herbert (1975) have analyzed the case when z_n is the state of a denumerable Markov chain. In this case (b_n, z_n) forms a Markov process, thus relaxing somewhat the condition that $\{z_n\}$ are independent identically distributed (i.i.d.) random variables.

The queueing process that motivated the work presented in this paper arose in a data communications system. Messages are temporarily stored in a buffer before they are sent across the communications network. It is assumed that the buffer transmits one packet, the basic unit of data, in a unit time interval, provided that it is not empty. In this context, then, z_n is the number of packets that arrive at the buffer in the time interval $(n, n+1]$. It is assumed that the inputs are correlated and z_n is taken to be a sum of moving averages.

In order to illustrate the techniques, the particular example $z_n = x_n^1 + x_{n-2}^1 + x_n^2$ is first analyzed. This corresponds to the arrival of two kinds of messages. The first kind of message consists of two packets which are spread apart in time, the second packet being transmitted two units of time after the first packet. The number of such messages generated in the $(n+1)^{st}$ time unit is denoted by x_n^1. The second kind of message consists of just one packet, and the number of such messages generated in the $(n+1)^{st}$ time unit is denoted by x_n^2. It is assumed that (x_n^1, x_n^2), $n = 0,1,2,\ldots$, are independent identically distributed vector random variables. However, for each n, x_n^1 and x_n^2 may be dependent. In particular, if

$$E\begin{bmatrix} x_n^1 & x_n^2 \\ t_1 & t_2 \end{bmatrix} = \Phi[(1-\rho)t_1 + \rho t_2], \tag{2}$$

with $0 \leq \rho \leq 1$ fixed, then the probability that a message is of the first kind is $1-\rho$, and the probability that it is of the second kind is ρ.

There are several other examples where such a model for the input process z_n is more appropriate than the usual one. We give two examples. Consider a queueing system where each request for service may consist

---

*We mean here limit in distribution: for each j, $\lim_{n\uparrow\infty} \Pr\{b_n \leq j\} = \Pr\{b \leq j\}$.

of a sequence of tasks to be completed by the same server. However, these tasks may not be available for completion in the same time interval, instead they are spread out in time. Hence the random variables corresponding to the number of tasks arriving at the server may be correlated as in the above example. This model may apply to a scheduler in a computer processing system. Another example is that of a dam fed by rivers that originate at geographically distant points, which motivated the model considered by Herbert (1972). When rainfall occurs, that affects the flow in all of the rivers, the increase in flow to the dam is spread out in time since the origins of the rivers are at different distances from the dam. A discrete time model of the dam process, similar to the one in the packet network example above, can be solved by the method presented in this paper.

In general we assume that

$$z_n = \sum_{i=1}^{\ell} \sum_{j=0}^{k} \alpha_j^i x_{n-j}^i \tag{3}$$

where the sequence of vector nonnegative integer valued random variables $\{(x_n^1, x_n^2, \ldots, x_n^\ell)\}$ are independent and identically distributed, and α_j^i are nonnegative integers with $\alpha_0^i > 0$ for each i. For each n the random variables $x_n^1, x_n^2, \ldots, x_n^\ell$ may be dependent on each other. Notice that z_n by itself is not necessarily a Markov process. As far as we know there is only one work dealing with a special case of (3) which is related to ours. Herbert (1972) considers the case when

$$z_n = \sum_{j=0}^{k} \alpha_j x_{n-j} \tag{4}$$

where $\{x_n\}$ are i.i.d. random variables and α_j are positive integers. In this case whenever $x_n \neq 0$, $b_{n+i} \neq 0$, $i = 1, \ldots, k+1$, hence b_{n+r} is linearly related to b_{n+1}, $r = 2, \ldots, k+2$ from (1). Using this property formulas can be derived for the equilibrium distribution for b_n given $x_{n-1}, x_{n-2}, \ldots, x_{n-k}$. However, even in this special case our approach gives formulas for $b = \lim_{n \uparrow \infty} b_n$ itself more simply than the method of Herbert (1972).

In the general case b_n is not a Markov process, but it is shown that, with the help of a transformation, a (k+1)-dimensional Markov process that suffices to describe the queueing system may be found. The first component of this Markov process is just b_n. An equation is derived for the steady state generating function corresponding to the joint distributions. This equation involves a multinomial, which corresponds to zero queue length. It is shown that a finite system of linear equations can be obtained to solve for the coefficients in this multinomial. A simple set of equations for the marginal distributions is then derived, leading to the calculation of the steady state generating function of the queue length.

A pair of limiting cases of time-scaled versions of the input process is considered. For $m = 0,1,2,\ldots,$ let d_{jm} be a nondecreasing sequence of nonnegative integers such that $d_{j0} = 0$, $d_{j1} = j$, $j = 0,1,\ldots,k$ and $d_{jm} - d_{j-1,m} \uparrow \infty$ as $m \uparrow \infty$, $j = 1,\ldots,k$. The corresponding sequence of input processes is

$$z_n^m = \sum_{i=1}^{\ell} \sum_{j=0}^{k} \alpha_j^i x_{n-d_{jm}}^i ,$$

so that $z_n^1 = z_n$, and z_n^0 is the "fastest" version of z_n, in the sense that all the packets triggered by x_n^1 are bunched together and arrive in the same time interval. As m increases the different delayed contributions of x_n^1 are spread farther and farther apart in time. The limiting case $m \uparrow \infty$ can then be interpreted as the "slowest." Let η_n be independent identically distributed random variables such that for each n the distribution of η_n is the same as that of $z_n = z_n^1$. Then the finite dimensional distributions of the processes $\{z_n^m\}$, $m = 0,1,2,\ldots,$ converge to the corresponding distributions of $\{\eta_n\}$ as $m \uparrow \infty$. The steady state generating functions of the queue lengths are derived for the input processes z_n^0 and η_n. In the special case $\ell = 1$, and (omitting the superscript) $\alpha_j = 0$ or 1 for each j, a relationship between the generating functions for these two limiting cases is derived. In the last section we present an example of the numerical results obtained using the formulas presented here.

We must emphasize here that, for lack of space, we omit all proofs, which will be given elsewhere, the authors (1977). The terminology of Markov-chains used in this paper is consistent with that of Karlin (1966).

AN EXAMPLE

We first consider the example described in the previous section, in which there are two kinds of messages. The number of packets arriving at the buffer in the $(n+1)^{st}$ time unit is

$$z_n = x_n^1 + x_{n-2}^1 + x_n^2 . \tag{5}$$

It is assumed that (x_n^1, x_n^2), $n = 0,1,2,\ldots,$ are independent identically distributed vector random variables. The number of packets in the buffer at the end of the $(n+1)^{st}$ time unit is given as in (1) by

$$b_{n+1} = (b_n - 1)^+ + x_n^1 + x_{n-2}^1 + x_n^2 . \tag{6}$$

It is clear b_n is not a Markov process. However $(b_n, x_{n-1}^1, x_{n-2}^1, x_{n-1}^2, x_{n-2}^2)$ is a five dimensional Markov process. We will derive another Markov process from (6) that is only 3 dimensional that suffices to describe the queueing process. Define

QUEUES WITH CORRELATED INPUTS

$$y_{0n} = b_n$$
$$y_{1n} = y_{0n} + x^1_{n-2}$$
$$y_{2n} = y_{1n} + x^1_{n-1}. \tag{7}$$

Then from (6) we have

$$y_{0,n+1} = [(y_{0n}-1)^+ - y_{0n}] + y_{1n} + x^1_n + x^2_n$$
$$y_{1,n+1} = [(y_{0n}-1)^+ - y_{0n}] + y_{2n} + x^1_n + x^2_n$$
$$y_{2,n+1} = [(y_{0n}-1)^+ - y_{0n}] + y_{2n} + 2x^1_n + x^2_n. \tag{8}$$

Let $v_{0n} = v_{1n} = x^1_n + x^2_n$ and $v_{2n} = 2x^1_n + x^2_n$. Then (v_{0n}, v_{1n}, v_{2n}) is independent of (y_{0j}, y_{1j}, y_{2j}) for $j \leq n$ by assumptions about x^1_n, x^2_n. Hence (y_{0n}, y_{1n}, y_{2n}) is a 3 dimensional Markov process. The state space of the corresponding Markov-chain S can naturally be indexed by a triple of nonnegative integers. Let

$$P^n_{i_0, i_1, i_2} = \Pr\{y_{0n} = i_0, y_{1n} = i_1, y_{2n} = i_2\}. \tag{9}$$

Then

$$P^{n+1}_{i_0, i_1, i_2} = \sum_{j_0, j_1, j_2} \Pr\{y_{0,n+1} = i_0, y_{1,n+1} = i_1, y_{2,n+1} = i_2 |$$
$$y_{0n} = j_0, y_{1n} = j_1, y_{2n} = j_2\} P^n_{j_0, j_1, j_2}. \tag{10}$$

These form the equations for transition probabilities. Notice that not all states (i_0, i_1, i_2) communicate with $(0,0,0)$. For example, we can show that when $i_0 = 0$, the only states that communicate with $(0,0,0)$ are $(0,0,0)$ and $(0,1,1)$. Suppose $y_{0,n+1} = 0$, $y_{1,n+1} = i_1$ and $y_{2,n+1} = i_2$. Then $b_{n+1} = 0$. Hence, from (6), $b_n \leq 1$, $x^1_n = 0$. But $x^1_n = 0$ implies $y_{2,n+1} = y_{1,n+1}$. Also, $b_n \leq 1$ implies $x^1_{n-1} \leq 1$. Further $y_{0,n+1} = 0$ and $x^1_{n-1} \leq 1$ imply $y_{1,n+1} \leq 1$. However it can be shown that states that do not communicate with $(0,0,0)$ are transient. So we will restrict the state space to consist only of those states, denoted by A, that communicate with zero. We will continue to denote by S the Markov-chain on the restricted state space A. Then it may be shown that S is irreducible and aperiodic. Notice that for every state at time n

$$y_{0n} \leq y_{1n} \leq y_{2n}. \tag{11}$$

It may be shown that S is positive recurrent when $Ez_n < 1$. Interpreting the sums over j_0, j_1, j_2 to extend only over A we have from (8) and (10), and the definitions of v_{0n}, v_{1n}, v_{2n},

$$P^{n+1}_{i_0,i_1,i_2} = \sideset{}{'}\sum_{j_1-i_0=j_2-i_1} Pr\{v_{0n} = i_0-j_1, v_{2n} = i_2-j_2\} \, P^n_{0,j_1,j_2}$$

$$+ \sideset{}{'}\sum_{j_0>0, j_1-i_0=j_2-i_1} Pr\{v_{0n} = 1+i_0-j_1, v_{2n} = 1+i_2-j_2\} \, P^n_{j_0,j_1,j_2}. \quad (12)$$

The equilibrium distribution of S: $\lim\limits_{n\uparrow\infty} P^n_{i_0,i_1,i_2} = P_{i_0,i_1,i_2}$ has the property

that if $P^n_{i_0,i_1,i_2} = P_{i_0,i_1,i_2}$ for $(i_0,i_1,i_2) \in A$, so does $P^{n+1}_{i_0,i_1,i_2}$. So

P_{i_0,i_1,i_2} satisfies:

$$P_{i_0,i_1,i_2} = \sideset{}{'}\sum_{j_1-i_0=j_2-i_1} Pr\{v_{0n} = i_0-j_1, v_{2n} = i_2-j_2\} \, P_{0,j_1,j_2}$$

$$+ \sideset{}{'}\sum_{j_0>0, j_1-i_0=j_2-i_1} Pr\{v_{0n} = 1+i_0-j_1, v_{2n} = 1+i_2-j_2\} \, P_{j_0,j_1,j_2}$$

$$\sum_{(i_0,i_1,i_2)\in A} P_{i_0,i_1,i_2} = 1. \quad (13)$$

P_{i_0,i_1,i_2} is the unique nonnegative solution of (13), see Karlin (1966). In
principle solving the infinite system of linear equations (13) determines
P_{i_0,i_1,i_2}, hence the equilibrium distribution of (y_{0n}, y_{1n}, y_{2n}). However, we will
see a much simpler way to find equilibrium distributions of the components y_{0n},
y_{1n}, y_{2n}, without computing P_{i_0,i_1,i_2}. Denote $Es^{y_{in}}$ by $\phi_{ni}(s)$ and $Es^{v_{in}}$ by
$\phi_{iv}(s)$. Then from (8) we can derive the following equations:

$$\phi_{n+1,0}(s) = [s^{-1}\phi_{n1}(s)+(1-s^{-1})c_{1n}(s)]\phi_{0v}(s)$$
$$\phi_{n+1,1}(s) = [s^{-1}\phi_{n2}(s)+(1-s^{-1})c_{2n}(s)]\phi_{1v}(s)$$
$$\phi_{n+1,2}(s) = [s^{-1}\phi_{n2}(s)+(1-s^{-1})c_{2n}(s)]\phi_{2v}(s). \quad (14)$$

Here

$$c_{in}(s) = \sum_{j\geq 0} Pr\{y_{0n} = 0, y_{in} = j\} \, s^j, \ i = 1,2. \quad (15)$$

For any n the only admissable states in A that have $y_{0n} = 0$ are $(0,0,0)$ and
$(0,1,1)$. So $c_{in}(s)$, $i = 1,2$ are polynomials of degree 1, and $c_{1n}(s) = c_{2n}(s)$.
Let $\phi_i(s)$ denote the generating function of $y_i = \lim\limits_{n\uparrow\infty} y_{in}$ and $c_i(s) = \lim\limits_{n\uparrow\infty} c_{in}(s)$
for $i = 1,2$. Then

$$\phi_0(s) = [s^{-1}\phi_1(s)+(1-s^{-1})c_1(s)]\phi_{0v}(s)$$
$$\phi_1(s) = [s^{-1}\phi_2(s)+(1-s^{-1})c_1(s)]\phi_{1v}(s)$$

$$\phi_2(s) = [s^{-1}\phi_2(s)+(1-s^{-1})c_1(s)]\phi_{2v}(s).$$ (16)

From (16)

$$\phi_2(s) = \frac{(1-s^{-1})c_1(s)\phi_{2v}(s)}{1-s^{-1}\phi_{2v}(s)}.$$ (17)

Since $\phi_{0v},\phi_{1v},\phi_{2v}$ are known directly from the distribution of x_n^1, x_n^2, (16) gives ϕ_0,ϕ_1 in terms of $c_1(s)$ the only unknown. Let $c_1(s) = k_0+k_1 s$. Then

$$c_1(1) = Pr\{y_0 = 0, y_1 = 0\} + Pr\{y_0 = 0, y_1 = 1\}$$

$$= Pr\{y_0 = 0\} = k_0 + k_1.$$ (18)

If we take expectations of both sides of (6), and take the limit as $n\uparrow\infty$, then we obtain

$$k_0 + k_1 = 1 - E(x_n^1 + x_{n-2}^1 + x_n^2)$$

$$= 1 - Ez_n.$$ (19)

In order to derive another equation for k_0, k_1 we go back to the original equations for $P_{i_0 i_1 i_2}$, (13). From (13) we can derive the following: for $i_0 = i_1 = i_2 = 0$, since v_{in} are nonnegative, $P_{000} = Pr\{v_{0n} = 0, v_{2n} = 0\}$ $P_{000} + Pr\{v_{0n} = 0, v_{2n} = 0\}$ P_{111}. However, $v_{2n} = 2x_n^1 + x_n^2 = 0$ implies $x_n^1 = x_n^2 = 0$, so $v_{0n} = 0$. Therefore

$$k_0 = P_{000} = Pr\{v_{0n} = 0\} (P_{000}+P_{111}).$$ (20)

Similarly

$$k_1 = P_{011} = Pr\{v_{0n} = 0\} P_{112}$$

$$P_{112} = Pr\{v_{0n} = 1, v_{2n} = 2\} P_{111}$$

$$+ Pr\{v_{0n} = 1, v_{2n} = 2\} P_{000}.$$

Hence

$$k_1 = Pr\{v_{0n} = 0\} Pr\{v_{0n} = 1, v_{2n} = 2\} (P_{000}+P_{111}).$$ (21)

Notice that the various probabilities occurring on the right hand sides of (20), (21) can be calculated from the distribution of (x_n^1, x_n^2). For example:

$$Pr\{v_{0n} = 1, v_{2n} = 2\} = Pr\{x_n^1 = 1, x_n^2 = 0\}.$$

Therefore using (19) we can determine k_0, k_1, hence $c_1(s)$. From (16) therefore it is easy to derive the formula for $\phi_0(s)$, namely

$$\phi_0(s) = (1-s^{-1})c_1(s)\phi_{0v}(s) \left[1 + \frac{s^{-1}\phi_{1v}(s)}{1-s^{-1}\phi_{2v}(s)}\right].$$ (22)

To solve for the equilibrium distribution of b_n, i.e., distribution of y_0, we do not have to invert $\phi_0(s)$. It turns out that (16) can be translated to linear recursions for marginal distributions for y_0, y_1, y_2. We will not go into computational details here. They are described by Fraser, et al.

QUEUEING PROCESSES WITH MOVING AVERAGE INPUTS

The most general input process that we will consider in this paper is a finite sum of moving averages i.e.,

$$z_n = \sum_{i=1}^{\ell} \sum_{j=0}^{k} \alpha_j^i x_{n-j}^i . \tag{23}$$

Equation (1) in this setting is

$$b_{n+1} = (b_n - 1)^+ + \sum_{i=1}^{\ell} \sum_{j=0}^{k} \alpha_j^i x_{n-j}^i. \tag{24}$$

The integer k is referred to as memory of the input process z_n. The α_j^i are assumed to be nonnegative integers and, for each i, $\alpha_0^i > 0$. We will assume that the vector, nonnegative integer valued random variables $(x_n^1, x_n^2, \ldots, x_n^\ell)$ are independent and identically distributed, though for each n, $x_n^1, x_n^2, \ldots, x_n^\ell$ will be allowed to be dependent on each other. The $(k\ell+1)$ dimensional vector process $(b_n, x_{n-1}^1, x_{n-2}^1, \ldots, x_{n-k}^1, x_{n-1}^2, \ldots, x_{n-k}^2, \ldots, x_{n-1}^\ell, \ldots, x_{n-k}^\ell)$ is Markov as in the example of the previous section.

However by a transformation we will find a (k+1) dimensional Markov process that suffices to describe the queueing system.

Define:

$$y_{0n} = b_n$$

and, for $r = 0, 1, \ldots, k-1$

$$y_{r+1,n} = y_{rn} + \sum_{i=1}^{\ell} \sum_{j=r+1}^{k} \alpha_j^i x_{n-j+r}^i. \tag{25}$$

Let $\sum_{j=0}^{r} \alpha_j^i = \mu_r^i$ and $\sum_{i=1}^{\ell} \mu_r^i x_n^i = v_{rn}$ for $r = 0, 1, \ldots, k$. Then using (24) we can verify:

$$y_{r,n+1} = [(y_{0n}-1)^+ - y_{0n}] + y_{r+1,n} + v_{rn}, r = 0, 1, \ldots, k-1 \tag{26}$$

$$y_{k,n+1} = [(y_{0n}-1)^+ - y_{0n}] + y_{kn} + v_{kn}. \tag{27}$$

From the assumptions about x_n^i, $(v_{0n}, v_{1n}, \ldots, v_{kn})^t \equiv \underline{v}_n$ is independent of $\underline{y}_j \equiv (y_{0j}, y_{1j}, \ldots, y_{kj})^t$ for $j \le n$. Hence $\underline{y}_n$ is a (k+1) dimensional Markov process. We will assume hereafter that $Pr\{\underline{v}_n = 0\} > 0$ and $Pr\{v_{rn} > 1\} > 0$ for some r.

The state space corresponding to this Markov process is indexed naturally by a (k+1)-triple of nonnegative integers. Furthermore by definition of y_{in}, $i = 0,1,\ldots,k$, $n = 0,1,2,\ldots$,

$$y_{0n} \leq y_{1n} \leq y_{2n} \leq \cdots \leq y_{kn}. \tag{28}$$

Hence we can assume that if $(i_0,i_1,\ldots,i_k)$ denotes a state then

$$i_0 \leq i_1 \leq i_2 \leq \cdots \leq i_k. \tag{29}$$

Let A' denote the set of vectors satisfying (29) and S' the Markov-chain with state space A'. Of the states in A' let A denote the set of states that communicate with the state $\underline{0} = (0,0,\ldots,0)^t$. It may be shown that starting in a state belonging to A', S' will transition into a state belonging to A in at most k steps. Hence we may restrict our attention to only those states that are in A, and to the irreducible Markov-chain S, with state space A, derived from S'. It may be shown that S is aperiodic. Moreover, for each nonnegative integer j, there is a finite number of states in A with $y_{0n} = j$. This result is used in proving that S is positive recurrent when $Ez_n < 1$, i.e. when

$$E \sum_{i=1}^{\ell} \mu_k^i \, x_n^i < 1.$$

The transition probabilities for S can be derived from (26) and (27). Let $P_{\underline{i}}^n = \Pr\{y_{0n} = i_0, y_{1n} = i_1, \ldots, y_{kn} = i_k\}$.

Then

$$P_{\underline{i}}^{n+1} = \sum_{\underline{j} \varepsilon A} \Pr\{\underline{y}_{n+1} = \underline{i} | \underline{y}_n = \underline{j}\} \, P_{\underline{j}}^n \tag{30}$$

$$P_{\underline{i}}^{n+1} = \sum_{\substack{j_0=0 \\ \underline{j} \varepsilon A}} \Pr\{v_{0n} = i_0 - j_1, \ldots, v_{k-1,n} = i_{k-1} - j_k, v_{kn} = i_k - j_k\} \, P_{\underline{j}}^n$$

$$+ \sum_{\substack{j_0 > 0 \\ \underline{j} \varepsilon A}} \Pr\{v_{0n} = i_0 - j_1 + 1, \ldots, v_{k-1,n} = i_{k-1} - j_k + 1, v_{kn} = i_k - j_k + 1\} \, P_{\underline{j}}^n. \tag{31}$$

If the equilibrium probabilities $P_{\underline{i}} = \lim_{n \uparrow \infty} P_{\underline{i}}^n$ exist then $P_{\underline{i}}^n = P_{\underline{i}}$ for every $\underline{i} \, \varepsilon \, A$ implies $P_{\underline{i}}^{n+1} = P_{\underline{i}}, \underline{i} \, \varepsilon \, A$. Furthermore $P_{\underline{i}}$ is the unique nonnegative solution of

$$\sum_{\underline{i} \varepsilon A} P_{\underline{i}} = 1$$

$$P_{\underline{i}} = \sum_{j_0=0, \underline{j} \varepsilon A} P_{i_0 - j_1, i_1 - j_2, \ldots, i_k - j_k} P_{\underline{j}}$$

$$+ \sum_{j_0 > 0, \underline{j} \varepsilon A} P_{i_0 - j_1 + 1, i_1 - j_2 + 1, \ldots, i_k - j_k + 1} P_{\underline{j}}. \tag{32}$$

Here $p_{i_0,i_1,\ldots,i_k} = \Pr\{v_{0n} = i_0,\ldots,v_{kn} = i_k\}$.

GENERATING FUNCTIONS FOR JOINT DISTRIBUTIONS

We will now derive expressions for joint distributions of $(y_0,y_1,\ldots,y_k)$ assuming $E z_n < 1$, so S is positive recurrent. Let

$$E\left(\prod_{r=0}^{k} s_r^{y_{rn}}\right) = \phi_n(s_0,s_1,\ldots,s_k) \tag{33}$$

and

$$E\left(\prod_{r=0}^{k} s_r^{v_{rn}}\right) = \phi_v(s_0,s_1,\ldots,s_k), |s_i| \leq 1. \tag{34}$$

From (26) and (27) we have, using independence of $\underline{v}_n$ and $\underline{y}_n$,

$$\phi_{n+1}(s_0,s_1,\ldots,s_k) = E\left(\left(\prod_{r=0}^{k} s_r\right)^{(y_{0n}-1)^+-y_{0n}} \prod_{r=0}^{k-1} s_r^{y_{r+1,n}} s_k^{y_{kn}}\right)$$

$$\phi_v(s_0,s_1,\ldots,s_k). \tag{35}$$

It follows that

$$\phi_{n+1}(s_0,s_1,\ldots,s_k) = \left[\phi_n(1,s_0,s_1,\ldots,s_{k-2},s_{k-1}s_k)\prod_{i=0}^{k} s_i^{-1}\right.$$

$$\left. + \left(1 - \prod_{i=0}^{k} s_i^{-1}\right)\phi_n(0,s_0,s_1,\ldots,s_{k-1}s_k)\right]$$

$$\phi_v(s_0,s_1,\ldots,s_k). \tag{36}$$

When ϕ_n is the generating function of the equilibrium distribution i.e., when

$$\phi_n(s_0,s_1,\ldots,s_k) = \phi(s_0,s_1,\ldots,s_k) = E\prod_{i=0}^{k} s_i^{y_i}, \tag{37}$$

then $\phi_{n+1} = \phi$. Therefore ϕ satisfies

$$\phi(s_0,s_1,\ldots,s_k) = \left[\phi(1,s_0,s_1,\ldots,s_{k-2},s_{k-1}s_k)\prod_{i=0}^{k} s_i^{-1}\right.$$

$$\left. + \left(1 - \prod_{i=0}^{k} s_i^{-1}\right)\phi(0,s_0,s_1,\ldots,s_{k-2},s_{k-1}s_k)\right]$$

$$\phi_v(s_0,s_1,\ldots,s_k). \tag{38}$$

We note that $\phi(0,t_1,\ldots,t_k)$ is a polynomial of finite degree since the set of states $(0,i_1,\ldots,i_k)$ is finite. Knowledge of $\phi(0,t_1,\ldots,t_k)$ determines $\phi(s_0,s_1,\ldots,s_k)$ as follows. If we set $s_0 = s_1 = \cdots = s_{k-1} = 1$ then (38) becomes

$$\phi(1,1,\ldots,1,s_k) = [s_k^{-1} \phi(1,1,\ldots,1,s_k) + (1-s_k^{-1}) \phi(0,1,1,\ldots,1,s_k)]$$

$$\phi_v(1,1,\ldots,1,s_k). \tag{39}$$

This determines $\phi(1,1,\ldots,1,s_k)$ in terms of $\phi(0,1,1,\ldots,1,s_k)$:

$$\phi(1,1,\ldots,1,s_k) = \frac{(1-s_k^{-1})\phi(0,1,1,\ldots,1,s_k)\phi_v(1,1,\ldots,1,s_k)}{1-s_k^{-1}\phi_v(1,1,\ldots,1,s_k)}. \tag{40}$$

For $r = 0,1,\ldots,k$, set

$$\phi^r(s_r,\ldots,s_k) = \phi(1,1,\ldots,1,s_r,s_{r+1},\ldots,s_k). \tag{41}$$

Then (40) determines ϕ^k in terms of $\phi(0,1,\ldots,1,s_k)$. Using (38) yields:

$$\phi^r(s_r,\ldots,s_k) = \left[\prod_{i=r}^{k} s_i^{-1} \phi^{r+1}(s_r,\ldots,s_{k-2},s_{k-1}s_k) \right.$$

$$\left. + \left(1 - \prod_{i=r}^{k} s_i^{-1}\right) \phi(0,1,\ldots,s_r,\ldots,s_{k-1}s_k) \right]$$

$$\phi_v(1,1,\ldots,1,s_r,\ldots,s_k). \tag{42}$$

So starting with ϕ^k, k applications of (42) yields $\phi^0(s_0,\ldots,s_k) = \phi(s_0,\ldots,s_k)$ in terms of $\phi(0,s_1,\ldots,s_k)$. Let

$$\phi(0,s_1,s_2,\ldots,s_k) = \mu \sum_{\underline{j}}{}' c_{\underline{j}} s_1^{j_1} s_2^{j_2} \cdots s_k^{j_k}, \tag{43}$$

where $\mu = \text{Pr}\{y_0 = 0\} = 1 - Ez_n$, and the finite sum on the right hand side extends over all indices $j_1, j_2, \ldots, j_k$ such that $(0,j_1,j_2,\ldots,j_k)$ is in A. As described above $\phi(s_0,s_1,\ldots,s_k)$ can be represented in terms of $\phi(0,s_1,s_2,\ldots,s_k)$ and known functions of $s_0,s_1,\ldots,s_k$. We can show that substitution of (43) into this representation for $\phi(s_0,s_1,\ldots,s_k)$, and equating coefficients of like powers, leads to a finite system of linear equations for the coefficients $c_{\underline{j}}$. Moreover, we can prove that these equations, together with the condition $\phi(0,1,1,\ldots,1) = \mu$, uniquely determine the constants $c_{\underline{j}}$, and hence the function $\phi(0,s_1,\ldots,s_k)$.

In the case $\ell = 1$, an alternate generating function was considered by the authors (1976). The corresponding generating function here is obtained by setting $u_j = \prod_{i=j}^{k} s_i$, $j = 0,\ldots,k$, and defining

$$\phi(s_0,s_1,\ldots,s_k) = \Phi(u_0,u_1,\ldots,u_k)$$

$$= \lim_{n \to \infty} E\left(u_0^{y_{0n}} \prod_{r=1}^{k} u_r^{y_{rn}-y_{r-1,n}} \right). \tag{44}$$

In this alternate formulation, the determination of the finite system of linear equations for the coefficients in the multinomial $\Phi(0,u_1,\ldots,u_k)$ is somewhat simplified.

GENERATING FUNCTIONS FOR MARGINALS

The joint distributions of $(y_0,y_1,\ldots,y_k)$ have $(k+1)$ arguments. We will see that we can reduce the problem to "$k+1$ one-dimensional problems" when we are only interested in the marginal distributions of $y_0,y_1,\ldots,y_k$. Let us denote the generating functions of y_i by $\phi_i(s)$ and those of v_{rn} by $\phi_{rv}(s)$. Then

$$
\begin{aligned}
\phi_i(s) &= \phi(1,1,\ldots,\overset{i}{s},1,\ldots,1) \\
&= \phi(\overbrace{s,\ldots,s}^{i+1},\ \overbrace{1,\ldots,1}^{k-i}),\ i = 0,\ldots,k.
\end{aligned}
\tag{45}
$$

From (38) we then obtain for $r = 0,\ldots,k-1$

$$
\phi_r(s) = [s^{-1}\phi_{r+1}(s)+(1-s^{-1})\phi(0,1,\ldots,\overset{r+1}{s},\ldots,1)]\phi_{rv}(s)
$$

and

$$
\phi_k(s) = [s^{-1}\phi_k(s)+(1-s^{-1})\phi(0,1,\ldots,1,s)]\phi_{kv}(s).
\tag{46}
$$

Note that

$$
\phi(0,1,\ldots,\overset{r}{s},\ldots,1) = \phi(0,\overbrace{s,\ldots,s}^{r},\ \overbrace{1,\ldots,1}^{k-r}),\ r = 1,\ldots,k.
$$

Therefore once the c_i have been determined from the method presented above, equation (46) gives the marginal distributions. Once again we can translate (46) into linear equations for the distributions themselves. The marginals are finitely solvable in the sense that a finite number of components of the marginal distributions can be solved for from a finite number of linear equations.

A LIMITING CASE

For each m let d_{jm} be a nondecreasing sequence of nonnegative integers such that

$$
\begin{aligned}
&1)\quad d_{j0} = 0,\ d_{j1} = j;\ j = 0,1,\ldots,k, \\
&2)\quad \lim_{m\uparrow\infty} d_{jm} - d_{j-1,m} = \infty,\ j = 1,\ldots,k.
\end{aligned}
\tag{47}
$$

We define a sequence of processes $\{z_n^m\}$ which will be time-scaled versions of z_n.

Let $z_n^m = \sum_{i=1}^{\ell}\sum_{j=0}^{k}\alpha_j^i x_{n-d_{jm}}^i$. We observe that z_n^1 is the same as z_n, and z_n^0 is the "fastest" version of z_n, in the sense that all the packets triggered by x_n^i are bunched together and arrive at the same time. As m increases the different delayed contributions of x_n^i are spread farther and farther apart in time. The limiting case can then be interpreted as the "slowest," see Fraser, et al. Let

$\{\eta_n\}$, $n = 0,1,2,\ldots$ be a sequence of independent identically distributed random variables such that for each n the distribution of η_n is the same as that of z_n. Then it may be shown that η_n corresponds to the slowest case: the finite dimensional distributions of the processes $\{z_n^m\}$, $m = 0,1,\ldots$ converge to the corresponding distributions of $\{\eta_n\}$ as $m\uparrow\infty$.

We now define a sequence of processes b_n^m, b_n^∞ corresponding to z_n^m, η_n respectively. Formally let

$$b_{n+1}^m = (b_n^m - 1)^+ + z_n^m$$

$$b_{n+1}^\infty = (b_n^\infty - 1)^+ + \eta_n. \tag{48}$$

If $Ez_n < 1$, then it may be shown that, for each j,

$$\lim_{m\uparrow\infty} Pr\{b^m \le j\} = Pr\{b^\infty \le j\}. \tag{49}$$

Therefore b^∞ is the steady state queue size corresponding to the "slowest" version of z_n. Let $\phi_x(s_1,\ldots,s_\ell) = E\left(\prod_{i=1}^{\ell} s_i^{x_i}\right)$. Then it is easy to verify that $Es^{z_n^0}$ and Es^{η_n} are given by

$$\phi_x^0 = \phi_x\left(s^{\mu_k^1}, s^{\mu_k^2}, \ldots, s^{\mu_k^\ell}\right) \quad \text{and} \quad \phi_x^\infty = \prod_{i=0}^{k} \phi_x\left(s^{\alpha_i^1}, s^{\alpha_i^2}, \ldots, s^{\alpha_i^\ell}\right)$$

respectively.

If $\phi^0 = Es^{b^0}$ and $\phi^\infty = Es^{b^\infty}$ then

$$\phi^0 = \frac{(1-s^{-1})\phi_x^0(s)\mu}{1-s^{-1}\phi_x^0(s)}$$

$$\phi^\infty = \frac{(1-s^{-1})\phi_x^\infty(s)\mu}{1-s^{-1}\phi_x^\infty(s)}. \tag{50}$$

In the special case when $\ell = 1$, and (omitting the superscript) $\alpha_j = 0$ or 1 for each j, we have an interesting special relationship between ϕ^0 and ϕ^∞. Let $f_n^0 = Pr\{b^0 \le n\}$, $f_n^\infty = Pr\{b^\infty \le n\}$ and $F^0 = \Sigma f_n^0 s^n$, $F^\infty = \Sigma f_n^\infty s^n$. Then F^0 and F^∞ are $\frac{1}{1-s}\phi^0$ and $\frac{1}{1-s}\phi^\infty$ respectively for $|s| < 1$. We will show that

$$f_n^\infty = f_{n\mu_k}^0 \tag{51}$$

equivalently

$$\Pr\{b^\infty \le n\} = \Pr\{b^0 \le n\mu_k\} \ . \tag{52}$$

Let ω be a primitive μ_k^{th} root of unity. Then for $|s| < 1$

$$\frac{1}{\mu_k} \sum_{i=0}^{\mu_k-1} F^0(\omega^i s) = \frac{\phi_x(s^{\mu_k})}{\mu_k} \sum_{i=0}^{\mu_k-1} \frac{\mu}{\phi_x(s^{\mu_k}) - \omega^i s}$$

$$= \frac{\mu[\phi_x(s^{\mu_k})]^{\mu_k}}{[\phi_x(s^{\mu_k})]^{\mu_k} - s^{\mu_k}} = F^\infty(s^{\mu_k}). \tag{53}$$

Therefore

$$\sum_{n=0}^\infty f_n^\infty s^{n\mu_k} = \frac{1}{\mu_k} \sum_{i=0}^{\mu_k-1} \sum_{m=0}^\infty f_m^0 (\omega^i s)^m$$

$$= \sum_{n=0}^\infty f_{n\mu_k}^0 s^{n\mu_k} \ . \tag{54}$$

Since f_n^0 and f_n^∞ are both increasing and bounded by 1, (54) shows that (51) holds.

A NUMERICAL EXAMPLE

In this section we present the numerical results corresponding to the model

$$b_{n+1} = (b_n - 1)^+ + x_n + x_{n-k}. \tag{55}$$

The i.i.d. random variables x_n are assumed to be distributed according to the Poisson law, and k is set equal to 5. In the figure below

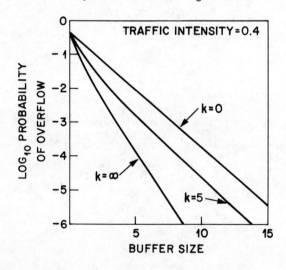

QUEUES WITH CORRELATED INPUTS

we show the logarithm of the probability that the queue size exceeds the level shown on the abscissa. The average of x_n is set equal to 0.2. The curves corresponding to k = 0 and k = ∞ are shown for comparison. From the formulas (46) it can be seen that the tail of the queue size distribution is geometric. Furthermore, the common ratio corresponding to the asymptotic geometric distribution is the same for all finite values of k. Therefore, we see that the slope of the curve corresponding to k = 5 approaches that of the curve corresponding to k = 0, for large values of the abscissa.

ACKNOWLEDGMENTS

The authors are indebted to J. McKenna for a careful reading of the manuscript, and for many helpful suggestions for improving the presentation. They are also grateful to A. G. Fraser for bringing the data communications problem to their attention.

REFERENCES

Ali Khan, M. S. (1970). J. Appl. Prob. 7, 291-303.
Fraser, G., Gopinath, B., and Morrison, J. A. (to be submittted for publication).
Ghosal, A. (1970). Some Aspects of Queueing and Storage Systems. (Springer-Verlag, Berlin).
Gopinath, B., and Morrison, J. A. (1976). Séminaires IRIA, Analyse et Contrôle de Systèmes, 201-210. (IRIA, Rocquencourt).
Gopinath, B. and Morrison, J. A. (1977). The Bell System Technical Journal (to be published).
Herbert, H. G. (1972). J. Appl. Prob. 9, 404-413.
Herbert, H. G. (1975). SIAM J. Appl. Math. 28, 657-661.
Karlin, S. (1966). A First Course in Stochastic Processes. (Academic Press, New York).

COMPUTER PERFORMANCE, K.M. CHANDY AND M. REISER (EDS.)
NORTH HOLLAND PUBLISHING COMPANY, 1977

A NEW APPROACH TO THE NUMERICAL ANALYSIS
OF MARKOVIAN MODELS

W. A. Stewart
I.R.I.S.A. Laboratoire d'informatique
University of Rennes
Rennes, France

Introduction.

It has long been known that numerical techniques may be used to obtain an exact solution for practically any class of queueing network. In this
sense it is unique, for all other methods (including simulation) are either restricted to a very narrow class of application, or else yield only approximate
results which must be validated by an independent process. The difficulty with the
numerical approach is that when the network considered has a large state space, it
often requires a prohibitively long time to obtain the solution. This is largely
due to the fact that available numerical iterative techniques usually require a
large number of iterations to converge. It is to be expected that with the advent
of high speed array and vector computers, interest in the numerical solution to
queueing networks will grow rapidly. These computers are particularly well suited
to the numerical iterative techniques employed in the analysis of Markovian models,
and will therefore permit large networks to be studied. In addition the development of more advanced techniques will reduce the amount of computation to be performed. It is with this last aspect that the present paper is concerned. More
precisely, a technique is presented for substantially reducing the number of
iterations required by numerical iterative techniques without increasing the
amount of computation involved in, and hence the time required by, a single

iteration cycle. This saving results from considering the transition rate matrix
from a different point of view and is consequently not restricted to a particular
method. It will be shown that merely by altering the manner in which the iterative techniques treat the problem, a new and efficient approach is obtained.

        In the following section, the transition probability matrix is deri-
ved, and iterative methods of solution discussed. In particular, the rates of
convergence of these methods will be analysed. In section 3, the new approach is
developed and the relations on which it is based are established. Finally, in
section 4, two areas in which the new approach will be particularly useful are
considered. Numerical examples and comparisons are included.

2. Basic Considerations.

Consider a system which is modelled by a continuous-time, homogeneous Markov chain with discrete state space. Let $P_i(t)$ be the probability that the system is in state i at time t, then we have the Chapmann-Kolmorgoroff equation :

$$P_i(t+\delta t) = P_i(t) \{1 - \sum_{j \neq i}^{n} s_{ij} \delta t\} + \{\sum_{k \neq i}^{n} s_{ki} P_k(t) \delta t + 0(\delta t)$$

in which s_{ki} is the rate of transition from state k to state i and n is the total number of states.

Let $s_{ii} = - \sum_{j \neq i}^{n} s_{ij}$, then $P_i(t+\delta t) = P_i(t) + \{\sum_{k=1}^{n} s_{ki} P_k(t) \} \delta t + 0(\delta t)$

$$\lim_{\delta t \to 0} \frac{P_i(t+\delta t) - P_i(t)}{\delta t} = \dot{P}_i(t) = \sum_{k=1}^{n} s_{ki} P_k(t)$$

In matrix notation $\dot{\underset{\sim}{P}}(t) = \underset{\sim}{S}^T \underset{\sim}{P}(t)$.

At steady state, the rate of change of $\underset{\sim}{P}(t)$ is zero, and therefore

$$\underset{\sim}{S}^T \underset{\sim}{P} = 0 \qquad\qquad (1)$$

where $\underset{\sim}{P}(t)$ is now written as $\underset{\sim}{P}$.

From equation (1), $\underset{\sim}{S}^T \Delta t \underset{\sim}{P} + \underset{\sim}{P} = \underset{\sim}{P}$ where Δt is arbitrary :

$$(\underset{\sim}{S}^T \Delta t + \underset{\sim}{I}) \underset{\sim}{P} = \underset{\sim}{P} \qquad \text{i.e.} \quad \underset{\sim}{W}^T \underset{\sim}{P} = \underset{\sim}{P}. \qquad (2)$$

where $W^T = \underset{\sim}{S}^T \Delta t + \underset{\sim}{I}$.

If Δt is chosen such that $\Delta t \leqslant (\max_i |s_{ii}|)^{-1}$, then the matrix $\underset{\sim}{W}$ is a stochastic matrix and may be regarded as the transition probability matrix for a discrete time Markov system in which transitions take place at intervals of Δt, Δt being sufficiently small to ensure that the possibility of two changes of state within this interval is negligible. From the method of construction of this matrix, it may be shown that there always exists a unit eigenvalue and that no other eigenvalue exceeds this in modulus. The required vector $\underset{\sim}{P}$ is therefore the left eigenvector corresponding to the dominant eigenvalue of the stochastic matrix $\underset{\sim}{W}$.

We now consider how the stationary probability vector $\underset{\sim}{P}$ may be determined from the transition probability matrix. Numerical iterative methods are normally recommended since the stochastic matrices involved are usually large and very sparse, and consequently compact storage schemes may be conveniently implemented and used, resulting therefore in a considerable saving in core store. Iterative methods may also result in a saving of time since highly accurate answers are not generally required and consequently, the iterative process may be halted after a certain specified tolerance has been achieved. The use of good initial approximations to the solution vector has the same desirable time-saving effect. In addition, build-up of rounding error is, to all intents and purposes, non-existant in iterative methods of the type discussed in this paper.

When the dominant eigenvalue and corresponding eigenvector of a matrix are required, as is the case here, the power method [4] is the usual iterative technique employed. This method involves successively premultiplying an arbitrary trial vector until the results obtained from consecutive iterations become proportional to one another. The vector thus obtained is the dominant right eigenvector and the constant of proportionality, the dominant eigenvalue. If we let $\underset{\sim}{A}$ be a square matrix of order n with eigensolution $\underset{\sim}{A}\underset{\sim}{x_i} = \lambda_i \underset{\sim}{x_i}$, i = 1, 2,....,n and if we suppose that $|\lambda_1| > |\lambda_2| \geqslant \ldots \ldots \geqslant |\lambda_n|$ then the power method is described by the iterative procedure : $\underset{\sim}{y_k} = \underset{\sim}{A}\underset{\sim}{y_{k-1}}$ with $\underset{\sim}{y_0}$ arbitrary, and its rate of convergence may be determined from the relationship.

$$\underset{\sim}{y_k} = \underset{\sim}{A}^k \underset{\sim}{y_0} = \sum_{i=1}^{n} \alpha_i \lambda_i^k \underset{\sim}{x_i} = \lambda_1^k \{\alpha_1 \underset{\sim}{x_1} + \sum_{i=2}^{n} (\lambda_i/\lambda_1)^k \underset{\sim}{x_i} \tag{3}$$

It may be observed that the process converges onto the dominant eigenvector $\underset{\sim}{x_1}$, and that the rate of convergence depends on the ratios $|\lambda_i|/|\lambda_1|$ for i = 2, 3,..,n, since the smaller these rations are, the quicker the summation on the right-hand side of equation (3) goes to zero. It is, in particular, the magnitude of the principal subdominant eignevalue, λ_2, which determines the convergence rate, so that the power method will not perform satisfactorily when $|\lambda_2| \simeq |\lambda_1|$. This situation, unfortunately, arises relatively frequently in stochastic matrices of large dimension.

This problem can be overcome to a certain extent by using simultaneous iteration methods. Such methods are extensions of the power method in which iteration is carried out with m trial vectors, which converge onto the eigenvectors corresponding to the m dominant eigenvalues. Within each iteration cycle,

these methods usually include a premultiplication and a reorientation, followed
by normalization and a tolerance test. Of these, the normalization and tolerance
test are trivial as far as the amount of computation is concerned. The purpose of
the premultiplication phase is to wash out the components of the lower eigenvectors in the approximations to the dominant eigenvectors, in much the same way as
occurs in the power method. However, if this was the only operation involved,
then all m trial vectors would converge onto the dominant eigenvector. It is the
purpose of the reorientation to prevent this happening by eliminating the components of the dominant eigenvectors from those subdominant to them in the set of m
trial vectors. This is sometimes called the interaction analysis since it eliminates the mutual "interactions" among approximations to the dominant eigenvectors.

Although simultaneous iteration methods have been most highly developed
for the real symmetric eigenvalue problem, there now exists several algorithms for
the real unsymmetric case. $[3, 5, 9]$. Among these latter, the lop-sided method
developed by Jennings and Stewart is particularly advantageous since only one set
of dominant eigenvectors (either the left or right eigenvector set) is obtained.
This is in contrast with other simultaneous iteration techniques in which both
left and right sets of vectors are simultaneously derived. The iteration cycle for
the lop-sided method is therefore greatly simplified and since the rate of convergence of the eigenvectors is not affected the stationary probability vector may be
determined in approximately half the time required by other simultaneous iteration
methods. In addition, the lop-sided method requires only half the core of other
methods.

The speed of convergence of simultaneous iteration is governed primarily by the rate at which the lower eigenvector components are washed out from
approximations to the dominant eigenvectors. Since we are interested in the convergence of the eigenvector corresponding to the unit eigenvalue, the convergence
rate therefore depends on the ratio $|\lambda_{m+1}|/|\lambda_1|$, i.e. $|\lambda_{m+1}|$, and since
$|\lambda_{m+1}| \leqslant |\lambda_2|$ this implies that simultaneous iteration will converge quicker than
the power method. However, since simultaneous iteration requires, on the average,
slightly more than m times the computation per iteration as the power method, it
is important that the difference between $|\lambda_{m+1}|$ and $|\lambda_2|$ be sufficiently large to
yield the result in less than 1/m times the number of iterations required by the
power method. It is therefore important that m be chosen to take advantage of
"gaps" in the eigenvalue distribution. If, for example, all eigenvalues are distributed at equal intervals apart, no benefit will be obtained from using simultaneous iteration. This problem will be raised again in section 4.

3. A New Approach.

In the preceding section it was shown that either the power method or lop-sided iteration may be used to determine the stationary probability vector P from equation (2). It is natural to ask if an alternative approach would be to obtain P from the homogeneous system of linear equations $S^T P = 0$. The standard and well known iterative methods for the solution of linear systems are the methods of Jacobi, of Gauss-Seidel and of successive overrelaxation (SOR), discussion of which may be found in any elementary text on numerical linear algebra. (See, for example Jennings, $|4|$). These methods derive from a general system of linear equations $Ax = b$, an iterative formula of the form $x_{r+1} = Bx_r + c$, i.e. the (r+1)-th approximation to the solution vector is obtained by multiplying the r-th approximation by B, which is called the iteration matrix, and adding a vector c. If x is the true solution and x_r the approximation obtained after r applications of the iterative process, then the value $e_r = x_r - x$ is a measure of the error after r iterations, and it may be shown that $e_r = B^r e_0$. For convergence, it is required that $e_r \to 0$ as $r \to \infty$, i.e. that $B^r \to 0$ as $r \to \infty$. This will only be true if all of the eigenvalues of B are strictly less than unity in modulus. However, when the three methods quoted above are employed to obtain the solution of the set of linear homogeneous equations (1), it may be shown (see below) that their iteration matrices possess a unit eigenvalue, and thus convergence cannot be guaranteed. Although this unit eigenvalue effectively rules out the possibility of using these methods, it is the key to the improved approach.

Consider the equation $S^T P = 0$.

Let $(L + D + U) = S^T$, where D is a diagonal matrix and L and U are respectively strictly lower and upper triangular matrices.

It follows from $(L + D + U) P = 0$

that $-(L + U) P = D P$

and assuming D to be non-singular, this yields the eigenvalue equation

$$-D^{-1} (L + U) P = P$$

in which P is the right eigenvector corresponding to a unit eigenvalue of the matrix $-D^{-1}(L + U)$. This matrix will immediately be recognized as the iteration matrix for the method of Jacobi. In the suite, it is denoted B_J. The stationary probability vector may therefore be determined by finding the eigenvector corresponding to a unit eigenvalue of this matrix. Since, in the transition rate matrix S,

$$s_{ii} = - \sum_{\substack{i \neq j}}^{n} s_{ij} \text{ and } s_{ij} > 0 \ \forall \ i \neq j,$$ it follows directly from the theorem of

Gersgorin, $[4]$ that no eigenvalue of B_J can have modulus greater than unity. P is therefore the eigenvector corresponding to the dominant eigenvalue of B_J and hence may be determined by the methods described in section 2.

Similar results may be derived for the Gauss-Seidel iteration matrix.
Writing $\quad (L + D + U) \, P = 0$
in the form $-U \, P = (L + D) \, P$
and assuming $(L + D)$ to be non-singular, yields the eigenvalue equation

$$- (L + D)^{-1} U \, P = P.$$

The matrix $-(L + D)^{-1} U \,(\equiv B_{GS})$ is the iteration matrix for the method of Gauss-Seidel, and the stationary probability vector is the eigenvector corresponding to its unit eigenvalue. As a consequence of the Stein-Rosenberg theorem (Varga, [10] p 70) and the fact that the Jacobi matrix possesses a dominant unit eigenvalue, it follows that the unit eigenvalue of the matrix B_{GS} is the dominant eigenvalue, and once again the iterative methods of section 2 may be employed.

Finally it may be shown that the stationary probability **vector** is also the eigenvector corresponding to the unit eigenvalue of the successive overrelaxation iteration matrix, but unfortunately, it is not necessarily true that this eigenvalue is the dominant eigenvalue. Beginning with $\omega(L + D + U) \, P = 0$, in which ω is the relaxation factor, it is possible to obtain an eigenvalue equation involving B_{SOR}, the iteration matrix for the successive overrelaxation method, as follows

$$
\begin{aligned}
(\omega U + \omega D) &= -\omega L \, P \\
= \quad (\omega U + \omega D) \, P - D \, P &= \ -\omega L \, P - D \, P \\
= \quad \left[\omega U + (\omega - 1)D\right] P &= \ - (\omega L + D) \, P \\
= \quad -(\omega L + D)^{-1}\left[\omega U + (\omega - 1)D\right] P &= P
\end{aligned}
$$

$$\text{i.e.} \quad B_{SOR} \, P = P$$

Thus P is the eigenvector corresponding to the unit eigenvalue of the matrix B_{SOR}. This eigenvalue may, or may not, be the dominant eigenvalue. Note that when $\omega = 1$, $B_{SOR} = B_{GS}$.

The same iterative methods, those of section 2, are used to obtain P from one of the four matrices W^T, B_J, B_{GS}, and B_{SOR}. The eigenvalues will not be the same from one matrix to the next (with the exception of the unit eigenvalue), so that a considerable difference in the number of iterations required to obtain convergence may be observed. It is therefore desirable to apply the iterative methods to that matrix which yields convergence in the smallest number of iterations, i.e. the matrix whose subdominant eigenvalues are, in modulus, furthest from unity.

Unfortunately there are very few theoretical results available on which to compare the relative distribution of the eigenvalues of a given matrix and those of its iteration matrices. Nevertheless, the corresponding equation solving methods have been in use for a considerable period of time and certain intuitive conclusions may be drawn about the eigenvalues of their iteration matrices. The eigenvalues of the Jacobi matrix, for example, are often grouped in pairs. This is largely due to the fact that all the diagonal elements of $\underset{\sim}{B}_J$ are zero and the matrix consequently has a tendency to be cyclic. Application of the power method to $\underset{\sim}{B}_J$ cannot therefore be recommended. In general the principal subdominant eigenvalues of the successive overrelaxation matrices with optimum parameter ω_b will be further from unity than those of $\underset{\sim}{B}_{GS}$, and in turn, the eigenvalues of Gauss-Seidel iteration matrices should be further from unity than either the eigenvalues of $\underset{\sim}{B}_J$ or of $\underset{\sim}{W}^T$. It is normally to be recommended then, that the power method and lop-sided iteration be applied to the matrix $\underset{\sim}{B}_{GS}$ unless a reasonably accurate estimate of ω_b is available. If a series of related tests is to be performed, then it is worthwhile conducting some initial experiments to determine this optimum value. When simultaneous iteration is being employed, an alternative scheme is to alter the value of ω after each p iterations until a value near the optimum is obtained. For example, an initial value of $\omega = 1$ may be chosen and p iteration cycles performed. The value of the principal subdominant eigenvalue, λ_2 is then recorded and the value of ω augmented to $\omega = 1.1$. After a further p iteration cycles a comparison is made between the current value of λ_2 and the value recorded at the beginning. If the current value is less than the previous value, then ω may be increased to $\omega = 1.2$ and the process repeated. If at any instant, the current value exceeds the previous value, the value of ω should be decreased. It is of course possible to envisage variations on this basic theme.

Finally, it should be pointed out that there is no hidden overhead in using either the Gauss-Seidel or SOR iteration matrices even though these appear to be more complicated. No extra storage arrays are needed, and the number of operations required in each iteration cycle is the same for all four different matrices. In particular, it is not necessary to construct explicitly the inverses $(\underset{\sim}{L} + \underset{\sim}{D})^{-1}$ and $(\omega\underset{\sim}{L} + \underset{\sim}{D})^{-1}$. We will now consider two examples to demonstrate the power of the new approach.

4. Numerical Examples.

The first example is related to a hybrid "iterative-numerical" method recently developed by Marie and Stewart, [7], for the approximate analysis of networks in which some, or all, of the stations contain several non-exponential

servers. Networks with stations of this nature were not previously amenable to solution by iterative techniques. A distinction should here be drawn between the numerical iterative techniques presented in section 2, and the general class of
iterative techniques developed by Chandy, Herzog and Woo, [2], and extended by
Marie, [6]. In this section, the first kind will be prefixed with the word numerical. The latter techniques obtain an approximate solution for a queueing network
by attempting to determine the behaviour of each individual station in the network.
For each such station, the only unknown is the sequence of arrival rates, and if
this can be determined exactly, then a numerical analysis of the station will yield
its exact stationary probability distribution. The purpose of the iterative method
is therefore to determine a sequence of arrival rates so that the computed behaviour
of the station approximates its exact behaviour in the network. Consequently, during each iteration, each station is supplied with a sequence of arrival rates and
a numerical iterative technique employed to obtain its stationary probability vector. This information is then used to obtain a "better" sequence of arrival rates
for the next iteration. This process is continued unitl some global criteria have
been satisfied. A numerical solution is therefore required for each station in
each iteration of the enclosing iterative method. It is therefore essential that
the time spent in obtaining this solution for a single station be kept to a minimum.

        Figure 1 shows the basic configeration for a general service station
in which the servers are considered to have Coxian service time distributions and
are represented accordingly .   To compare the convergence rates obtained by
the numerical iterative methods, it is necessary to know the eigenvalue distribution for the four different matrices W^T, R_J, B_{GS}, B_{SOR} and this can only be accurately obtained in a reasonable period of time if the model has a small state space.
Consequently, in the particular instance of the model analysed, the number of servers, r, was chosen to be 3, and the parameter which denotes the number of fictit-
ous stages in the representation of a server, k, was chosen to be 2. The number
of customers was taken as 6. For each of the servers, the value of the parameter
K^2 (=mean^2/variance) was chosen to be 10, and the mean service time 1.0. Figure 2
shows the number of iterations ℓ, required to obtain four decimal places of accuracy when the numerical iterative methods are applied to the four different matri-
ces. These values were calculated by means of the formula, $(|\lambda_{m+1}|)^\ell = 0.0001$ for
m = 1, 2,....., 9. Recall that m = 1 corresponds to the power method .

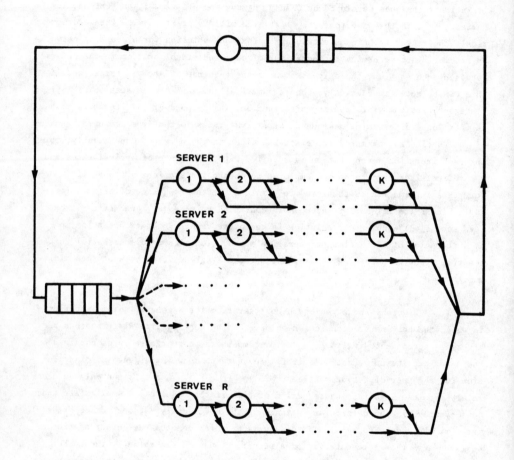

FIGURE 1.

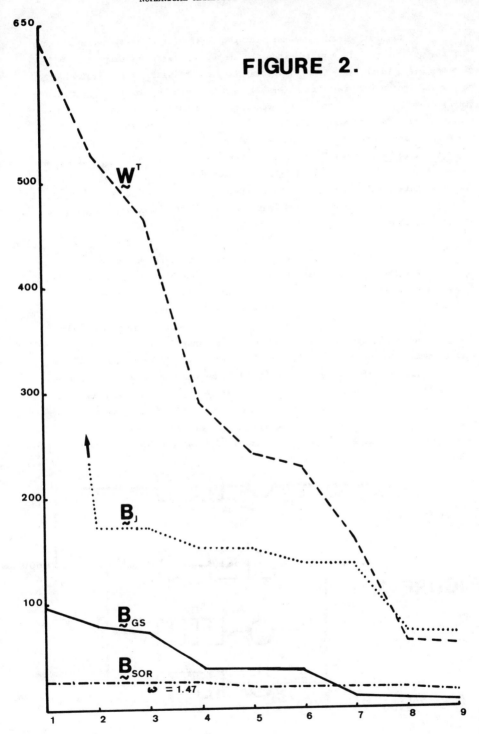

FIGURE 2.

Figure 2 clearly demonstrates the desirability of the new approach.
When the power method is applied, then the number of iterations drops from 631
with the standard matrix $\underset{\sim}{W}^T$, to 97 when applied to the Gauss-Seidel iteration
matrix. If the optimum value of ω (=1.47) is used with the matrix $\underset{\sim SOR}{B}$, then the
number of iterations required drops even further to only 26. It may also be obser-
ved that lop-sided iteration will only bring about an improvement if applied to
the $\underset{\sim GS}{B}$ iteration matrix and the value of m chosen to be 7. In particular, lop-
sided iteration should not be recommended for use with the matrix $\underset{\sim SOR}{B}$ since the
rate of convergence is practically the same, no matter what number of vectors
are used. Note finally that the curve representing the number of iterations
required when the matrix $\underset{\sim J}{B}$ is used exhibits the effect of pairs of eigenvalues
of equal modulus.

The second type of application in which the new approach will be
extremely valuable, is the analysis of nearly-decomposable networks. Such networks characteristically have a large number of eigenvalues very close to the
dominant unit eigenvalue, and therefore a very large number of iterations are required before convergence is achieved. Consider the model presented in figure 3.
This represents the system architecture of a time-shared multiprogrammed paged
virtual memory computer. It consists of a set of terminals from which users generate commands, a central processing unit (CPU), a secondary momory device (SM),
and a filing device (FD). Due to the large difference in the rates at which the
users enter commands, and the rate at which the CPU, SM and FD operate, the system
may be considered to be nearly decomposable. This system has been analysed by
several authors (e.g. Brandwajn, [1], Stewart [8]) and for further details,
readers should consult the references.

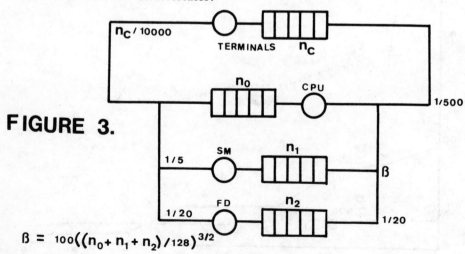

FIGURE 3.

$$\beta = 100((n_0 + n_1 + n_2)/128)^{3/2}$$

In figure 4, the logarithm of the number of iterations required to achieve a single place of accuracy is presented.

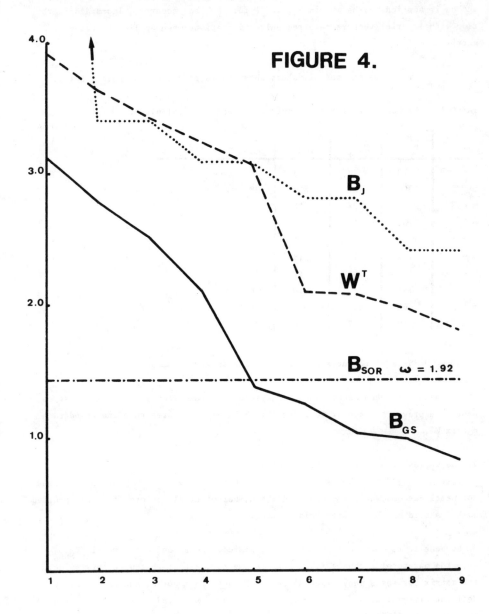

FIGURE 4.

It was necessary to plot the logarithm of ℓ against the number of different trial vectors m because of the large range of values obtained. For example, it requires 8078 iterations to obtain a single place of accuracy when the power method is applied to the matrix $\underset{\sim}{W}^T$, while for the same accuracy, lop-sided iteration with 10 trial vectors requires only 6 iterations when applied to the $\underset{\sim}{B}_{GS}$ matrix.

The complete set of values obtained is presented in table 1 below.

TABLE 1.   Number of iterations required for each decimal place.

	$\underset{\sim}{W}^T$	$\underset{\sim}{B}_J$	$\underset{\sim}{B}_{GS}$	$\underset{\sim}{B}_{SOR}$ ($\omega = 1.92$)
m = 1	8078	∞	1313	28
m = 2	4360	2627	622	28
m = 3	2658	2627	320	28
m = 4	1706	1243	129	28
m = 5	1150	1243	24	28
m = 6	131	641	18	28
m = 7	123	641	11	28
m = 8	96	259	10	28
m = 9	68	259	7	28
m = 10	59	47	6	28

Several features of these results deserve comment :

1. Iterating with the Jacobi matrix $\underset{\sim}{B}_J$ yields the same step-like characteristics as in the previous example. In general it behaves even worse than the standard matrix $\underset{\sim}{W}^T$.

2. The curves of both the Gauss-Seidel matrix $\underset{\sim}{B}_{GS}$ and the standard matrix $\underset{\sim}{W}^T$ exhibit a sharp drop, the first for m = 4, and the second for m = 5. This is usual for nearly-decomposable systems, and the number of trial vectors for the lop-sided method should be chosen with this in mind.

3. No benefit is derived from applying lop-sided iteration to the matrix $\underset{\sim}{B}_{SOR}$, when the parameter ω equals 1.92. This is due to the fact that with this value, the matrix possesses many eigenvalues which equal in modulus, the principal subdominant eigenvalue. Note, however, that the value $\omega = 1.92$ is the value which maximizes the difference between $|\lambda_1|$ and $|\lambda_2|$ and is not the optimum parameter

when more than one trial vector is used. For example, if m = 5 trial vectors are used, then the optimum value for ω is ω = 1.5 which yields one decimal place of accuracy each 3 iterations, while for m = 10, the optimum value is ω = 1.3, and yields one decimal place of accuracy in 2 iterations only.

4. Finally, it is perhaps worthwhile stressing the fact that the Gauss-Seidel iteration matrix yields very considerable savings, especially when five or more trial vectors are used.

5. Conclusions.

A new approach for the numerical analysis of queueing networks has been presented. It has been shown that simply by altering the manner in which the usual numerical iterative methods obtain the solution vector, three different possibilities arise. One of these, (the method involving the Jacobi iteration matrix), should be abandoned since it will only yield marginally better results with lop-sided iteration, and will fail completely with the power method. The remaining two permit numerical solutions to be obtained very rapidly and should therefore be used whenever possible. Normally, the method involving the Gauss-Seidel iteration matrix will be recommended, except when a series of related experiments is being conducted, in which case it is desirable to obtain an estimation of the optimum parameter for the method based on the SOR iteration matrix.

REFERENCES

1. BRANDWAJN, A.   *A Model of a Time-Sharing Virtual Memory System Solved
                          using Equivalence and Decomposition Methods.*
                          Acta Informatica, vol. 4, n° 1, 1974.

2. CHANDY, K.M.   *Approximate Analysis of General Queueing Networks.*
   HERZOG, U. and WOO, L. IBM J. Res. Develop. Jan. 1975, pp 43-49.

3. CLINT, M. and   *A Simultaneous Iteration Method for the Unsymmetric
   JENNINGS, A.   Eigenvalue Problem.*
                          J. Inst. Maths. Applics. vol. 18, 1971, pp 111-121.

4. JENNINGS, A.   *Matrix Computation for Engineers and Scientists.*
                          John Wiley and Son. 1977.

5. JENNINGS, A. and   *Simultaneous Iteration for Partial Eigensolution of
   STEWART, W.J.   Real Matrices.*
                          J. Inst. Maths. Applics. vol. 15, 1975, pp 351-361.

6. MARIE, R.   *Méthodes Itératives de Résolution de Modèles Mathéma-
                          tiques pour Systèmes Informatique.*
                          Séminaire IRIA. Nov. 1976 IRIA, 78150 FRANCE.

7. MARIE, R. and   *A Hybrid 'Iterative-Numerical' Approach to the Solu-
   STEWART, W.J.   tion of a General Queueing Network.*
                          To be presented at Third International Symposium on
                          Modelling and Performance Evaluation of Computer Sys-
                          tems. October 3-5 1977. BONN, GERMANY.

8. STEWART, W.J.   *A comparison of Numerical Techniques in Markov Model-
                          ling.*
                          Accepted for publication Comm. ACM.

9.   STEWART, W.J. and   *LOPSI : A Lop-sided Simultaneous Iteration Algorithm.*
      JENNINGS, A.   IRISA Research Report, Université de RENNES
                             35031 FRANCE.

10.   VARGA, R.S.   *Matrix Iterative Analysis.*
                             Prentice Hall, New York 1963.

COMPUTER PERFORMANCE, K.M. CHANDY AND M. REISER (EDS.)
NORTH HOLLAND PUBLISHING COMPANY, 1977

THE EFFECT OF SERVICE TIME REGULARITY
ON SYSTEM PERFORMANCE

R. W. Wolff

Department of Industrial Engineering
and Operations Research
University of California
Berkeley, California, USA

Conventional wisdom holds that the more regular the arrival
process and/or service times are, the better system performance
will be. Examples of contrary behavior are presented in three
cases: loss systems, processor sharing, and multi-channel
queues without losses. In each case, it is shown that making
service times more regular can make system performance worse.

INTRODUCTION

In undersaturated queues, queueing occurs primarily because of the stochastic
variation of the arrival process and/or service times. Thus, it is generally
believed that the more regular (in some appropriate sense) each of these processes
is, the better any of the usual performance measures will be.

This "conventional wisdom" is very useful when true. For example, we may be able
to improve system performance when the arrival and/or service processes are under
some control. Alternatively, performance measures for systems which are difficult
to analyze can be bounded by corresponding measures for easier ones. If we are
lucky, these bounds may even be good approximations.

In this paper, we briefly review published results in support of conventional
wisdom and cite one published result which is contrary. Then, in a series of
examples, we exhibit other results which are contrary to conventional wisdom. All
of our examples compare performance measures for different service distributions
under specified, sufficiently irregular arrival processes. In some cases, not only
does a performance measure move in the "wrong" direction, but also the magnitude
of the change is large. In the process, our understanding of the nature of these
effects should improve.

RESULTS IN SUPPORT OF CONVENTION WISDOM

Kingman's upper bound [7] for the expected delay in a GI/G/1 queue is in terms of
the sum of the variance of the inter-arrival and service distributions. Marshall
[13] obtained lower bounds on expected delay for this queue when the inter-arrival
distribution is more regular than the exponential (under either bounded mean
residual life or increasing failure rate). The closeness of the upper and lower
bounds shows that, in certain cases, the upper bound is a good approximation.

For heavy traffic[*], Kingman [8], [10] showed that the distribution of delay in

---

[*]Definitions of heavy traffic vary, but for most purposes, we mean heavily loaded
systems where server utilization is less than but near 1.

RONALD W. WOLFF

queue is approximately an exponential distribution with mean equal to his upper bound in [7]. Köllerström [12] extended Kingman's result to the GI/G/c queue: In heavy traffic, the delay distribution is approximately an exponential distribution with mean equal to Kingman's GI/G/1 upper bound with the variance of service, $V(S)$, replaced by $V(S/c)$. That is, in heavy traffic, a multi-server queue behaves like a "fast" single server queue. Thus, the lower bound obtained by Brumelle [1] for the expected delay in a GI/G/c queue is a good approximation in heavy traffic. Similarly, the heavy traffic approximations of Iglehart and Whitt [5] for the number of customers in a GI/G/c queue are consistent with conventional wisdom.

Bounds on the delay distribution for the GI/G/1 queue [9], [16] are also consistent with conventional wisdom.

In several papers, with the main results summarized in [15], it is shown that for the GI/G/1 queue under various definitions of regularity, the stationary delay distribution becomes more regular as the interarrival and/or service distributions become more regular. For two of these definitions, the mean delay decreases.

Finally, in a classic paper by Kiefer and Wolfowitz [6], it is shown that for a stable GI/G/c queue with positive arrival rate, the rth moment of the stationary delay distribution is finite if and only if the $(r + 1)^{st}$ moment of the service time distribution is finite.

A CONTRARY RESULT FOR THE INFINITE SERVER QUEUE

The evidence in favor of conventional wisdom is impressive. However, it should be noted that most of these results pertain to the GI/G/1 queue without losses (all customers are served). With the exception of [6], all results pertaining to the GI/G/c queue are heavy traffic approximations.

In an unpublished paper by Haji and Newell [4], summarized in Newell ([14], p. 32), an infinite server queue is analyzed for the mean and variance of N, the stationary number of busy servers.

For arrival rate λ and service time S with $E(S) = 1/\mu$ and $P(S \leq t) = G(t)$, $E(N)$ obviously depends only on these rates:

$$(1) \qquad\qquad E(N) = \lambda/\mu \ .$$

For the variance to mean ratio, $V(N)/E(N)$, Haji and Newell obtain the approximation:

$$(2) \qquad\qquad V(N)/E(N) \simeq 1 + (I - 1)v \ ,$$

where I is (roughly) the ratio of the variance to the mean number of arrivals in an interval and

$$(3) \qquad\qquad v = \int_0^\infty [1 - G(t)]^2 dt/E(S) \ .$$

THE EFFECT OF SERVICE TIME REGULARITY ON SYSTEM PERFORMANCE

Now v is a measure of service time regularity (increasing v means
greater regularity). In fact, v is maximized (v = 1) uniquely in the case
of constant service, where $(1 - G)^2 = 1 - G$ for all t .

The effect of server regularity on (2) depends on the sign of I - 1 . For a
Poisson process, I = 1 and v has no effect. For less regular arrival
processes, e.g., batch Poisson arrivals, I > 1 , and making the service more
regular in the sense of (3) *increases* V(N) .

While contrary to conventional wisdom (and, at first, quite a shock) this
observation has an intuitive explanation: For arrivals which occur in batches
and constant service, either an entire batch is present or none of it is at any
time t . Irregular service spreads out the departure times, permitting the
observance of "partial" batches, i.e., the number present from any batch is
somewhere in-between "all" and "none." Thus, we expect larger deviations from
the fixed E(N) , and hence a larger variance, when service is regular.

LOSS SYSTEMS

By a loss system, we mean a system with c servers in parallel (c channels)
such that an arrival finding all servers busy departs immediately without
receiving service (the arrival is lost). An important performance measure for
these systems is the fraction of arrivals lost.

A classic result, with a long history in the literature, is called *Erlang's Loss
Formula*, e.g., [18]: For Poisson arrivals and general independent service
(the M/G/c loss system), the stationary distribution of the number of busy
servers $\{p_n , n = 0,1, ..., c\}$ is the unique solution to:

(4) $$\lambda p_{n-1} = n\mu p_n , \quad n = 1,2, ..., c \quad \text{and} \quad \sum_{n=0}^{c} p_n = 1 ,$$

where λ and μ are the arrival and service rates.

Of course, we could exhibit the solution to (4) explicitly. It is written in
the form above to emphasize that (a) the solution depends *only* on the arrival
and service rates and (b) knowing this, (4) can be written down immediately by
assuming that G is exponential. The fraction of arrivals lost in this case
is also the fraction of time there are c busy servers, p_c .

Loss systems when the arrival process is not Poisson occur naturally in
telephone systems, in particular, when the arrival process in a loss system is
itself the overflow process of lost calls at some other loss system. The
equivalent random method, described in [2], is an approximation technique
developed to estimate the fraction of calls lost when the arrival process is a
composite of overflow processes and service is exponential.

One might expect loss systems and infinite server systems to be closely related.
The equivalent random method is based on this notion. More general
approximation methods are presently under investigation [3] which attempt to do
this explicitly for general arrival processes and service time distributions in
terms of the ratio V(N)/E(N) in (2). This ratio is called *peakedness*.

While evaluating the accuracy of various approximation methods is of
considerable interest, that is not our purpose here. Instead, we will show that
loss systems can also exhibit contrary behavior.

Our example will be for a loss system with c channels, batch Poisson arrivals
(denoted by BM) with batch arrival rate λ and constant batch size b , and

RONALD W. WOLFF

three different service distributions at rate μ : constant (D) , exponential (M) , and a special case of hyperexponential (H) ,

$$H = (1 - \alpha)U_o + \alpha \exp(\alpha\mu) ,$$

i.e., H is a mixture of an exponential with mean $1/\alpha\mu$ and a unit step at the origin.

The exponential and hyperexponential cases can be solved from balance equations. If we choose b and c so that c/b is an integer, then the constant service case can be solved using Erlang's loss formula because groups of b servers are busy and idle together. Thus, the constant service case behaves "like" an M/D/(c/b) loss system.

For b = c = 2 , the percent of calls lost for constant service is easily shown to be identical with that for exponential service. That is, it does not exhibit contrary behavior. However, this case is very special. The irregular arrivals (2 at a time) match perfectly the number of channels.

Example 1:

We now exhibit contrary behavior for the case: batch size b = 2 and ${}_*$c = 4 channels. In this case, we did not explicitly compute results for H .* In the limit $(\alpha \to 0)$ it can be shown that the hyperexponential case behaves like an M/M/4 loss system with the same offered load: $2\lambda E(S)$. In Table 1, the percent of calls lost is presented for a batch Poisson, 4 server loss system under constant (D), exponential (M), and the limiting case of hyperexponential service (the M/M/4 loss system), as a function of offered load.

TABLE 1

	BM/D/4	BM/M/4	M/M/4
$2\lambda E(S)$	% lost	% lost	% lost
.5	2.4	2.0	0.16
1	7.7	6.6	1.5
2	20.0	18.4	9.5
3	31.0	29.5	20.6
4	40.0	38.7	31.1
6	52.9	52.1	47.0
8	61.5	61.0	57.5

Notice that the direction of the effect of service regularity is independent of the offered load. The effect, at least in this case, appears to be greater to the right (less regular) side of the exponential, and can be substantial.

While this example is consistent with infinite server results, the b = c = 2 case shows that peakedness alone may be an inadequate measure, particularly if the number of servers is small.

---

* Explicit results for the hyperexponential case will be presented later in example 2.

THE EFFECT OF SERVICE TIME REGULARITY ON SYSTEM PERFORMANCE

PROCESSOR SHARING

Priority rules for processing jobs at a computer system central processor often permit interrupting jobs. An idealized version of such a rule is called *Round Robin*: jobs (customers) join the end of a single queue at a single server (the CPU). On entering service, each job is allocated an amount of CPU time, $\delta > 0$. The job either completes service during δ or, if not, is interrupted after receiving δ and joins the end of the same queue. This is repeated until each job completes service and departs.

The limiting version of the round robin rule as $\delta \to 0$ is called *Processor Sharing*. Under a work-conservation assumption, it was first shown in [17] that the M/G/1 Processor Shared (PS) queue possesses a remarkable property analogous to Erlang's loss formula: the stationary distribution of the number of customers in systems, $\{p_n\}$ is

(5) $$p_n = (1 - \rho)\rho^n , \quad n = 0,1, \ldots, \text{ and}$$

(6) $$L = \sum np_n = \frac{\rho}{1 - \rho} ,$$

where $\rho = \lambda E(S)$, *independent* of the form of the service distribution.

For non-Poisson arrivals, can the PS rule exhibit contrary behavior? By now, it should be clear how to proceed.

Example 2:

Consider a batch Poisson arrival process with batch rate λ and random batch size ν .

(a) For exponential service, L is independent of the rule, e.g., L under PS is the same as L under the usual first-in-first-out (FIFO) rule:

(7) $$L_{PS} = L_{FIFO} = \frac{\rho}{1 - \rho} \cdot \frac{E\{(\nu)(\nu + 1)\}}{2E(\nu)} .$$

(b) For hyperexponential service with $H = (1 - \alpha)U_0 + \alpha \exp (\alpha\mu)$, the customers with zero service time go through immediately under a PS rule. This leaves customers with exponential service. Thus, this system is equivalent to a BM/M/1 FIFO queue composed only of "long" service time customers. Therefore,

(8) $$L_{PS} = \frac{\rho}{1 - \rho} \cdot \frac{E\{(\nu_\ell)(\nu_\ell + 1)\}}{2E(\nu_\ell)} ,$$

where ν_ℓ is the number of "longs" in a batch of size ν . It is easily shown that

(9) $$\frac{E\{(\nu_\ell)(\nu_\ell + 1)\}}{2E(\nu_\ell)} = \frac{2E(\nu) + \alpha[E(\nu^2) - E(\nu)]}{2E(\nu)} ,$$

and

(10)
$$\lim_{\alpha \to 0} L_{PS} = \frac{\rho}{1 - \rho} \ .$$

(c) For constant service, restrict the batch size to be a constant $\nu = b$. Sharing customers is equivalent to sharing batches, where the expected number of batches in system is given by (6). Since each batch in system contains exactly b customers,

(11)
$$L_{PS} = \frac{\rho b}{1 - \rho} \ .$$

In this example, the effect of service regularity can be large. If b is large, (11) is nearly double (7). For fixed ρ , we can make (7) as large as we want by making batches large and/or irregular. The effect of hyperexponential service is to remove the batch effect, i.e., for fixed ν and sufficiently small α , ν_ℓ is likely to be 0 or 1 .

We also remark that quite apart from the arrival process, Processor Sharing is a terrible rule when service is sufficiently regular. For constant service, *every* customer departs later under PS than under FIFO (strictly later, except for those jobs that end busy periods).

When interruptions are permitted, one needs to interpret conservation laws with care, e.g., for the conservation law on pg. 199 of [11], it is not true that reducing the delays of some jobs can only be achieved by increasing the delays of others.

MULTI-CHANNEL FIFO QUEUES WITHOUT LOSSES

We previously observed that in heavy traffic, multi-channel queues behave like fast single channel queues. Contrary behavior of the usual first moment measures of performance is possible only for sufficiently "light" traffic.

In fact, one might expect that for a sufficiently irregular arrival process, there will be a "crossover" point of server utilization such that irregular service is preferred below that point and regular service is preferred above. (The crossover point would presumably depend on the distributions being compared.) The following example exhibits this behavior.

Example 3:

Consider a batch poisson arrival process at batch rate λ with constant batch size $b = 4$ and $c = 2$ channels, with server utilization $\rho = 2\lambda/\mu$.

(a) For the BM/M/2 queue, the generating function of the state probabilities $P(z) = \sum_n p_n z^n$ was found and differentiated, yielding

(12)
$$L = \frac{\rho}{4 + \rho} + \frac{5\rho}{2(1 - \rho)} \ .$$

THE EFFECT OF SERVICE TIME REGULARITY ON SYSTEM PERFORMANCE

(b) The BM/D/2 queue may be analyzed as two BM/D/1 queues with batch arrival
     size b = 2 at each. Finding L is now easy:

$$(13) \qquad\qquad L = 2\rho + \frac{\rho(\rho + 1)}{(1 - \rho)} .$$

There is a crossover point at $\rho = \rho_o \approx .35$, with exponential service preferred
for $\rho < \rho_o$ and constant service preferred for $\rho > \rho_o$.

For the case c = b = 2 , no crossover points exists. Constant service is
preferred to exponential service for all ρ .

CONCLUSIONS AND SUGGESTIONS FOR FURTHER RESEARCH

The results of this paper are provacative rather than definitive.

In all three examples, we compared service distributions for specified sufficiently
irregular arrival processes. Exhibiting contrary behavior in the converse
situation appears to be much more difficult. It is this author's judgment that
contrary behavior for arrival processes will occur only when there are very
special structural relationships between the arrival process and service facility.
For example, batches of size three might perform better than batches of size two
for a loss system with three servers.

The Poisson process appears to be a boundary between irregular arrival processes
which can exhibit contrary behavior and regular arrival processes which cannot.
Contrary behavior also depends on structure, e.g., it occurs in processor sharing
under circumstances in which it does not occur in loss systems.

The competing effects which account for the crossover in the multichannel case
(Example 3) tend to diminish the effect of service time regularity on system
performance. Thus, the mathematically convenient assumption of exponential service may result in surprisingly good approximations for system performance in
moderately loaded multi-channel queues with irregular arrivals.

For arrival processes which are more regular than Poisson in some appropriate
sense (including the Poisson itself) it is conjectured that contrary behavior
cannot occur. In particular, this author would expect results similar to those
in [15] to be true.

REFERENCES

[1] Brumelle, S. L., (1971),   "Some Inequalities for Parallel-Server Queues,"
     Operations Research 19, 402-413.
[2] Cooper, R. B., (1972), Introduction to Queueing Theory, Macmillan, New York.
[3] Eckberg, A. E., and A. A. Fredericks (1976) personal communication, Bell
     Telephone Laboratories, Holmdel, NJ 07733.
[4] Haji, R., and G. F. Newell, (1971), "Variance of the Number of Customers in
     an Infinite Channel Server," University of California, unpublished.
[5] Iglehart, D. L. and W. Whitt, (1970), "Multiple Channel Queues in Heavy
     Traffic I," Adv. Appl. Prob., 2, 150-177.
[6] Kiefer, J., and J. Wolfowitz (1956), "On Characteristics of the General
     Queueing Process with Applications to Random Walk," Ann. Math. Stat., 27,
     147-161.
[7] Kingman, J. F. C., (1962(a)), "Some Inequalities for the GI/G/1 Queue,"
     Biometrika, 49, 315-324.
[8] Kingman, J. F. C., (1962(b)), "On Queues in Heavy Traffic," J. Roy. Stat. Soc.,
     B24, 383-392.
[9] Kingman, J. F. C., (1964), "A Martingale Inequality in the Theory of Queues,"
     Proc. Camb. Phil. Soc., 59, 359-361.

RONALD W. WOLFF

[10] Kingman, J. F. C., (1965), "The Heavy Traffic Approximation in the Theory of Queues," Ch. 6 in Proceedings of the Symposium on Congestion Theory, W. L. Smith and W. E. Wilkinson (eds) University of North Carolina Monograph Series in Probability and Statistics.

[11] Kleinrock, L., (1976), Queueing Systems Vol. II: Computer Applications, John Wiley and Sons, New York.

[12] Köllerström, J., (1974), "Heavy Traffic Theory for Queues with Several Servers. I," J. Appl. Prob., 11, 544-552.

[13] Marshall, K. T., (1968) , "Some Inequalities in Queuing," Operations Research 16, No. 3, 651-665.

[14] Newell, G. F., (1973), Approximate Stochastic Behavior of n-Server Service Systems with Large n, Springer-Verlag, New York.

[15] Rolski, T. and D. Stoyan, (1976), "On the Comparison of Waiting Times in GI/G/1 Queues," Operations Research 24, 197-200.

[16] Ross, S. M., (1974), "Bounds on the Delay Distribution in GI/G/1 Queues," J. Appl. Prob., 11, 417-421.

[17] Sakata, M., S. Noguchi and J. Oizumi (1969), "Analysis of a Processor-Shared Queueing Model for Time-Sharing Systems," Proc. Second Hawaii International Conference on System Sciences, University of Hawaii, Honolulu, Hawaii 625-628.

[18] Takács, L., (1969), "On Erlang's Loss Formula," Ann. Math. Statist., 40, 71-78.

ACKNOWLEDGMENTS

Partially supported by the Air Force Office of Scientific Research, AFSC, USAF, under Grant AFOSR-77-3213.

A Portion of this research was completed while the author was a visiting consultant to the Operations Research Projects Department, Bell Telephone Laboratories, Holmdel, N. J. 07733.

PROCESSOR PRIORITY MODEL WITH DIFFERENT USER TASKS AND OPERATION SYSTEM PHASES

W. Kraemer
Institute of Swtiching and Data Techniques
University of Stuttgart
Stuttgart, Germany

ABSTRACT

A processor model is considered with different types of user tasks
as well as different operating system phases. The processing of
user code (in problem state) and the processing of operating system
code (in supervisor state) are scheduled by interrupt schemes and
by dispatching rules. The operating system phases may consist of
interrupt handling, scheduling, channel program construction,
paging overhead functions... There are m different types of user
tasks with different dispatching priorities. The operating system
phases initiated by the user tasks are running with higher priority
than the associated user tasks. This results in a single server
queueing model with feedbacks into higher (and lower) priority
classes. Such a model is analyzed under the assumptions of

- a Poisson input process of arriving I/O-interrupt requests and
- general distribution functions for the processing times of
  user and system tasks.

Main results are the waiting times in the different queues of the
operating system as well as response times for the different user
tasks.
Numerical results are shown and compared with those obtained by
simpler models.

1 INTRODUCTION

Queueing models for multiprogrammed computer systems have achieved
great importance for the determination of global performance values
of systems with several programs in main storage. For a fixed degree

of multiprogramming these models are so-called closed or cyclic
models, but also so-called open models are considered for a variable
degree of multiprogramming. They are used to calculate the different
utilizations of the servers (I/O devices, processor(s)) as well as
the associated queue lengths or waiting times.

The central part of such queueing networks is represented by a
central processing unit CPU (central server model"/4/). The utilization of the CPU is a most important measure for system throughput,
which - often together with response time constraints - normally is
tried to be maximized. This can be done e.g. by different scheduling
disciplines for the CPU, denoted in the following as "processor".

The most simple discipline is FIFO (first-in, first-out) between
all user tasks, which leads to a standard single server FIFO model
for the processor.

In case of time-slicing, it is often more suited to apply processor
models with the so-called processor sharing discipline (see also /2/).
This discipline automatically favours jobs with short CPU times at
the cost of longer ones. Fortunately, this processor discipline is
included in queueing networks with "local balance" or "product
solution" /3,15/, for which a universal queueing analysis software
tool QNET 4 has been implemented /16/.

To increase system throughput, very often fixed priorities are
assigned to different user tasks, i.e. the different user tasks
reside e.g. in different partitions with different priorities.
Normally highest throughput is achieved when high CPU dispatching
priority is given to jobs or user tasks with high I/O activity.

To calculate the times these different jobs are in the system, it
is necessary to determine the different flow or response times of the
central processing unit. For this purpose, ordinary priority models
(e.g. preemptive resume) cannot be used generally, since for the
scheduling of the operating system queues the priority of the
associated user task often is not considered. This, naturally, is
useful since operating system phases are used by all user programs
concurrently.

The consideration of system overhead can be done e.g.

- by defining global processor occupations including overhead
  (e.g. /13/), thus preserving a single queue model or
- by explicit consideration of operating system phases with
  associated queues and priorities, thus leading to single
  server queueing models with multiple queues, priorities
  and feedbacks.

The subject of this paper is a separate processor model with several
operating system phases of different priorities and with several types
of user tasks having different dispatching priorities.

The aim of the queueing analysis of this model is

- to determine the influence of system overheads on the response
  times of user tasks
- to calculate waiting times within internal operating system
  queues
- to investigate the influence of the grade of interruptibility
  of operating system phases (i.e. of the proportion of supervisor code running enabled)
- to compare the results for the response times of the different
  jobs with response time results of simpler models

It is possible to consider and use this model as a CPU module within
an (open) network of a total computer system, also representing the
I/O subsystem (disks, drums, channels...), since I/O scheduling often
is done without regarding user priorities.

2   PROCESSOR MODEL

2.1 Definition of User Task Phases

The total flow of a batch job or also transaction through a multiprogrammed computer system can be described essentially by a
sequence of alternating occupations of the central processor and
the I/O devices. Each time a program has to perform an access to
an I/O device, a switch into the operating system is necessary to
construct e.g. appropriate channel programs and to perform queue
scheduling for the I/O system as well as to reschedule the processor
itself. Such I/O accesses may be accesses to user files in case of
user specified I/O (READ/WRITE) or may be accesses to the page data
set in case of a page fault in virtual storage systems.

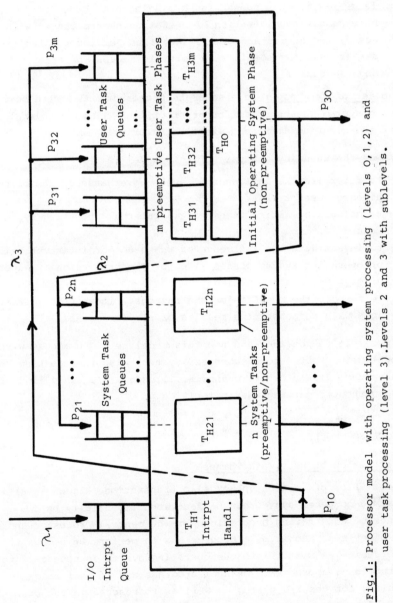

<u>Fig.1:</u> Processor model with operating system processing (levels 0,1,2) and user task processing (level 3).Levels 2 and 3 with sublevels. (λ_i=arrival rates,T_{Hi}=service times,p_{ij}=branching probabilities)

The phases of a user task between such two subsequent switches into
supervisor state for performing I/O here are called "user task phases".
The mean pathlength of such a user task phase can be obtained by
dividing the total number of user instructions performed during
processing a job in problem state by the total number of its physical
I/O accesses.

2.2 Structure of the Processor Model

Figure 1 shows the structure of the processor model with its
different queues,   priority levels and feedbacks.
The service boxes within the processor represent the processing of
user or operating system (supervisor) code. They are labeled for a
level i with their service or holding times T_{Hi}, resulting from
associated pathlengths and processor speeds (MIPS values).
The model contains queues at different levels

- the I/O-interrupt queue at level 1

- n system task queues for n($\geq$ O) system tasks at level 2

- m user task queues for m($\geq$ 1) types of user tasks with
   different dispatching priorities within level 3.

Furthermore, a priority level indexed with i=0 is contained, which
always is non-preemptive and for which no request must wait, since
the user task phases on level 3 throughout are running enabled with
respect to I/O-interrupt requests (i.e. they always can be interrupted).
So, levels 0,1 and 2 represent the processing of operating system
code in supervisor state, whereas level 3 is the level for the
processing of user task phases in problem state.

In the following, the operating system parts are described.

The processor model is considered on the level of user task phases
defined above and is driven by external I/O-interrupt requests,
arriving with rate λ_1 from the I/O subsystem. These requests
represent messages from the channels and devices which have to be
investigated and handled by processing appropriate I/O-interrupt
handling routines.

In most cases, the I/O interrupt is signalizing the end of a data
transfer between main and secondary storage (channel end, device
end). The consequence of such a message is first an attempt to

issue the next START-I/O, i.e. to reschedule the same device or
channel. After this has been done, the associated user task of
the I/O interrupt is dispatchable again, i.e. is selectable for the
beginning of its next user task phase. This is represented by the
branch from level 1 into the associated queue of level 3.

There might be further reasons for I/O interrupts e.g. 'SEEK-end'
of a disk, which does not result in making the associated user task
dispatchable again. This is represented by a branch leaving the
processor after level 1. In the model this path is selected by an
arbitrary fraction p_{10} of I/O-interrupt requests. This fraction
e.g. is 0 if for each physical I/O request   only 1 interrupt is
needed. Consider e.g. disks with RPS (rotational position sensing,
see also e.g. /5/), where normally no separate I/O interrupt for
a seek end is necessary since the I/O can be performed with one
channel program.
Thus the total pathlengh of level 1 service may be interpreted to
include

  - a part for the analysis of the type of interrupt (a general
    entry routine)

  - the proper interrupt handling routine

  - the channel device scheduling

  - the dispatcher performing a task switch.

Level 3 of the model consists of $m (\geqslant 1)$ different queues for m
different types of user tasks with different user priorities. This
means, if a user task phase of a user task of the last priority m
has been interrupted by an I/O interrupt making a class 1 user task
dispatchable, this class 1 user task is dispatched before resuming
the interrupted user task phase of a class m user task. When the
end of a user task phase is reached, an immediate switch into
supervisor state is performed (e.g. by a supervisor call SVC) to
prepare the I/O access. This   includes an entry routine, the
construction of appropriate channel programs , queue entries, channel
scheduling and the dispatching of the next task. There are further
activities necessary, depending on the type of I/O. This may be in
case of user -I/O the translation of the channel program (CCW Translation) or in case of a page fault the execution of the page replacement algorithm.

In the model all these activities are represented by a general non-preemptive operating system part at level 0 and by n different system tasks at level 2.

"System tasks" here are considered to be internal tasks of an operating system combining a certain amount of work for a special purpose.This may be e.g. a page manager which is responsible for the paging,or may be a task for the fetching of transient parts of the operating system.

If in case of an I/O access such a system task is needed, then during the non-preemptive operating system phase with index 0 the queue entry for a system task is prepared, performed and analyzed by the dispatcher. If no system task is included, requests leave the processor in the branch labeled with the associated fraction p_{30}.

As can be seen, in the terminology used, operating system phases correspond to levels 0, 1 and 2, whereas only in level 2 system tasks are processed.

2.3 Processor Scheduling

To completely define the functioning of the model, it is necessary to describe the interrupt scheme (i.e. which service may be interrupted by I/O interrupt requests) and the procedure for the scheduling of waiting requests (dispatching rule).

INTERRUPT SCHEME:

The only requests arriving from outside of the processor (i.e. being asynchronous) are the I/O-interrupt requests with index 1. Table 1 shows, whether a class i service may be interrupted by an arriving I/O-interrupt request.

level	0	1	2	3
status	n	n	p if $c_{12}=0$ n if $c_{12}=1$	p

Table 1: Interrupt Scheme (p=preemptive resume,n=non-preemptive, c_{12}= control variable)

Note that class 0 service cannot be interrupted at all, i.e. class 0
service is running disabled for all I/O-interrupt requests. Also, I/O-
interrupt requests do not interrupt themselves. For ease of notation
a control variable c_{12} has been introduced, indicating purely
preemptive system tasks ($c_{12}=0$) or purely non-preemptive system
tasks ($c_{12}=1$). These two bordering cases for level 2 have been
included, since often operating system phases are a sequence of
preemptive and non-preemptive parts of code, implemented e.g. by
ENABLE and DISABLE commands. Also interruptions might be allowed only
at certain predetermined points.

Naturally all user code (running in problem state) is preemptive.

DISPATCHING RULE:

This rule determines which request of the waiting requests will get
the control on the processor (will be dispatched) if a service has
reached a normal end.

If there are requests waiting for processor service, a request with
momentary highest dispatching priority (lowest priority index) is
chosen for service. Note that level 3 might be considered to consist
of m separate interrupt levels (i.e. class 3_1 always is dispatched
before an interrupted class 3_2 request).
Within each single queue the queue discipline FIFO is adopted.

2.4 Definitions and Assumptions

The model consists of levels 0,1,2 and 3. In addition, level 2 is
composed of $n(\geqslant 0)$ sublevels where n is the number of system tasks.
Also level 3 is formed by $m(\geqslant 1)$ sublevels with m as the number of
different types of user tasks. Let these levels and sublevels be
denoted by i ($i=0,1,2,3,2_1...2_n,3_1...3_m$).

Now, the total flow or response time for a request from its
arrival at the I/O-interrupt queue and the time being completely
served by the processor (i.e. the time instant leaving the
processor) is the sum of the flow times in the different levels
involved. The flow time T_{Fi} for a priority level i is

$$T_{Fi} = T_{Wi} + T_{WSi} + T_{Hi} \qquad (1)$$

T_{wi} is the initial waiting time for a level i, i.e. the waiting time from the arrival up to the first period of service. If level i is interruptible, the service time T_{Hi} may not be given continuously due to interrupts. These interrupts induce a total subsequent waiting time T_{WSi}. The sum of service time and subsequent waiting time often is called residence time /7/.

Let each level or sublevel i be characterized by

λ_i = arrival rate of requests

$h_i = E(T_{Hi})$ mean service time

$A_i = \lambda_i \cdot h_i$ offered traffic (utilization) for level i   (2)

The distribution functions of all service times may be arbitrary with

c_{Hi} = coefficient of variation (standard deviation/mean value).

It is assumed throughout that the arrival process of class 1 is a Poisson process and that the service times are independent of each other.

Furthermore, probabilistic branching is assumed. The associated branching probabilities be p_{ij}. The probability of leaving the processor after the class 1 service is p_{10}, whereas with probability p_{30} no system task is involved.

Naturally,

$$\sum_{j=1}^{n} p_{2j} = 1 \quad \text{and} \quad \sum_{j=1}^{m} p_{3j} = 1 \ .$$

It is very simple to calculate all arrival rates λ_i and all utilizations A_i for the model.

For ease of notation, let

$$A_2 = \sum_{j=1}^{n} A_{2j} \quad , \quad A_3 = \sum_{j=1}^{m} A_{3j} \tag{3a,b}$$

$$z_i = \frac{1+c_{Hi}^2}{2} \cdot h_i \cdot A_i = \frac{\lambda_i}{2} \cdot E(T_{Hi}^2) \tag{4}$$

$$h_0' = h_0 + (1-p_{30}) \cdot \sum_{j=1}^{n} p_{2j} \cdot h_{2j} \tag{5}$$

$$A'_{3j} = \lambda_{3j} \cdot (h_{3j}+h'_0) = \lambda_1 \cdot (1-p_{10}) \cdot p_{3j} \cdot (h_{3j}+h'_0) \qquad (6)$$
$$j=1...m$$

2.5 Related Models

Priority systems with feedbacks have been investigated e.g. by ENNS /8/.
Also the well-known time-sharing models belong to this type of queueing systems /11/.

A processor model with explicit operating system phases has been considered by LEWIS,SHEDLER /14/ as part of a cyclic queueing system.
That closed queueing model has been treated by Imbedded Markov Chain
analysis,assuming a finite number of identical jobs with same priority.

Recently,HERZOG /10/ investigated flexible priority models for
communication processors serving different classes of jobs or requests
and taking into account system overhead especially for interrupt
handling.That processor model with so-called preemption-distance
priorities (cf.e.g. /9/) is for the special case of pure preemptive
priorities identical with a simplified version of the model treated
here,having $p_{10}=0,p_{30}=1,h_0=0$ and no system tasks (n=0).

3 QUEUEING ANALYSIS

3.1 Method of Analysis

For the investigation of priority systems with feedbacks,several
methods can be and have been used,which are sometimes more or less
related.These methods include in many cases the consideration of
certain requests,often called test-requests,during their flow through
the system.From this,the moments of the random variables involved
(waiting time,response time) are calculated.

This basic principle was used e.g. by HERZOG /9,10/ and applied to
systems with preemption-distance priorities in order to calculate the
first moment of the waiting or response times.

Furthermore,when considering test-requests it is tried to define partially equivalent M/G/1 systems /7,8,11/ in order to directly apply
known results for this single server system without priorities,also
for higher moments.

The method of analysis used for the special processor model treated
in this paper,can be considered to be a congenial extension and
application of COBHAM's calculation method /6/,which has been developed and applied to priority systems with non-preemptive priorities.
As will be explained,this method mainly consists of two parts

- the calculation of total initial amounts of work
- the application of results of generalized busy periods for
  M/G/1 systems

When calculating different initial amounts of work,it was in part
necessary to consider test-requests during part of their flow
through the system as it was demonstrated by HERZOG.

As will be also shown in the following,special attention had to be
given to the mechanism of interruptions.This means that at an arbitrary instant also interrupted requests are present,only requiring
part of a service time to be completed.

3.1.1 Initial Waiting Times

The calculation of the mean initial waiting times $E(T_{Wi})$ of a
request in queue i is performed in two steps:

- First, a so-called initial amount of work T_{Oi} is calculated.
  This is a certain backlog of processor work at that instant,
  the considered request of class i arrives at queue i.It is
  composed only by that services,which - according to the
  interrupt and dispatching disciplines - have to be done before
  the considered request might be dispatched for class i service.

This initial amount of work may be enlarged by external requests
arriving later on.
  - Therefore,secondly,the extension of the waiting time is calcu-
    lated being induced by arriving external requests.
Since the external arrivals form a Poisson process,it can be easily
shown that

$$E(T_{Wi}) = \frac{E(T_{Oi})}{1 - A_i^*} \qquad (7),$$

where A_i^* is a partial effective server utilization induced by external arrivals.This result,already applied by COBHAM /6/,can also be
obtained by considering generalized busy periods in M/G/1 systems
(cf. e.g./1,7,11/).

Due to the FIFO discipline within all queues,requests arriving
later on in class 1 do not influence the initial waiting time of a
considered class 1 request,and therefore

$$A_1^* = O \qquad\qquad (8)$$

All class 1 requests arriving during the initial waiting time of
a request in any class 2 queue will be dispatched previously,but
only for receiving service in class 1.So

$$A_{2j}^* = A_1 \qquad\qquad j = 1...n \qquad (9)$$

Regarding a request waiting in queue 3_i, it must be taken into
account that all class 1 requests are dispatched previously and
that some of them are continued in a higher priority class of
level 3 and then possibly in class 2:

$$A_{3i}^* = A_1 + \sum_{j=1}^{i-1} A_{3j}' \qquad\qquad (10)$$

The appropriate initial amounts of work will be calculated separately in chapters 3.2 ff.

3.1.2 Subsequent Waiting Times

The calculation of the subsequent waiting times for interruptible
services analogously result in

$$E(T_{WSi}) + E(T_{Hi}) = \frac{E(T_{Hi})}{1 - A_i^{**}} \qquad\qquad (11a)$$

or

$$E(T_{WSi}) = \frac{A_i^{**}}{1 - A_i^{**}} \cdot E(T_{Hi}) \qquad\qquad (11b)$$

with A_i^{**} as another effective server utilization.
In this model

$$A_i^{**} = \begin{cases} O \text{ for non-interruptible service} \\ A_i^* \text{ else} \end{cases} \qquad (12)$$

Using the well-known Little's theorem,for each waiting time also
corresponding queue lengths can be obtained.

3.2 Class 1 Waiting Time

The (initial) waiting time of class 1 requests in the I/O-interrupt queue is identical with the initial amount of work T_{O1} for this queue.This backlog of work is composed of requests of different classes,each request needing a certain time or residual time to be served.Table 2 shows the mean or expected number of requests together with their service demand.

Mean number	A_O	A_1	$\lambda_1 \cdot E(T_{W1})$	$c_{12} \cdot A_{2\gamma}$ ($\gamma=1\ldots n$)
Mean (residual) time	$\dfrac{1+c_{HO}^2}{2} \cdot h_O$	$\dfrac{1+c_{H1}^2}{2} \cdot h_1$	h_1	$\dfrac{1+c_{H2\gamma}^2}{2} \cdot h_{2\gamma}$

Table 2: Components of the mean initial amount of work
        for class 1

If at an arbitrary instant a request of class 1 arrives,with probability A_i a class i service is in progress,having an expected residual service time of

$$\frac{1+ c_{Hi}^2}{2} \cdot h_i \qquad (i = 0,1).$$

This is a well-known result from renewal theory.

The mean number of waiting class 1 requests is $\lambda_1 \cdot E(T_{W1})$,each requiring a full class 1 service.If class 2 service cannot be interrupted ($c_{12}=1$),a further part has to be added.
So the mean waiting time in the I/O-interrupt queue turns out to be

$$E(T_{W1}) = \frac{z_0 + z_1 + c_{12} \cdot \sum_{\gamma=1}^{n} z_{2\gamma}}{1 - A_1} \qquad (13)$$

3.3 Class 2 Waiting Times

To calculate the initial waiting time of a request in a queue 2_i, consideration of a test request may start when it begins service at level 0.Then no other requests are present in the queues of levels 1 or 2,since user task phases are always interruptible.

So the initial waiting time of a class 2_i request is identical with the sum of all class 1 service times of all requests arrived during the non-preemptive phase O,possibly enlarged by further arriving class 1 requests.At the end of the service time T_{HO} of the considered request in the mean $\lambda_1 \cdot h_O$ class 1 requests have arrived, each claiming for a mean service time h_1.Therefore the initial amount of work is

$$E(T_{O2i}) = A_1 \cdot h_O$$

So

$$E(T_{W2i}) = \frac{A_1}{1 - A_1} \cdot h_O \qquad i=1...n \qquad (14)$$

The subsequent waiting time is

$$E(T_{WS2i}) = (1 - c_{12}) \cdot \frac{A_1}{1 - A_1} \cdot h_{2i} \qquad (15)$$
$$i=1...n$$

3.4 Class 3 Waiting Times

To calculate the initial waiting time of a class 3_i request,it is necessary to pursue such a request (cf. fig.2).

Let such a class 3_i request arrive at time t at queue 1 and after waiting and service time it arrives at time t' at queue 3_i.

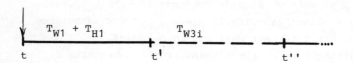

Fig 2: Time diagram for considered test request of class 3_i

The initial amount of work for this test request at time t' is composed of

        - requests already present in the system at time t

and   - requests arrived during t and t'

Table 3 is a survey on these different components of the initial amount of work $E(T_{O3i})$.

	Mean Number	Residual Mean Time
1)	$\lambda_1 \cdot E(T_{W1}) + A_1$	$\sum_{\gamma=1}^{i} (1-p_{10}) \cdot p_{3\gamma} \cdot (h_{3\gamma} + h_0')$
2)	$\lambda_{2\gamma} \cdot E(T_{W2\gamma})$	$h_{2\gamma}$
3)	$\lambda_{2\gamma} \cdot E(T_{WS2\gamma})$	$\dfrac{1+c_{H2\gamma}^2}{2} \cdot h_{2\gamma}$
4)	$A_{2\gamma}$	$(1-c_{12})\dfrac{1+c_{H2\gamma}^2}{2} \cdot h_{2\gamma}$
5)	A_0	$(1-p_{30}) \cdot \sum_{\gamma=1}^{n} p_{2\gamma} \cdot h_{2\gamma}$
6)	$\lambda_{3\gamma} \cdot E(T_{W3\gamma})$	$h_{3\gamma} + h_0'$
7)	$\lambda_{3\gamma} \cdot E(T_{WS3\gamma})$	
8)	$\lambda_{3\gamma} h_{3\gamma}$	$\dfrac{1+c_{H3\gamma}^2}{2} h_{3\gamma} + h_0'$
9)	$\lambda_1 \cdot (E(T_{W1}) + h_1)$	$h_1 + \sum_{\gamma=1}^{i-1} (1-p_{10}) \cdot p_{3\gamma} \cdot (h_{3\gamma} + h_0')$

(Rows 2–5: $\gamma = 1 \ldots n$; Rows 6–8: $\gamma = 1 \ldots i$)

Table 3: Components of the mean initial amount of work $E(T_{O3i})$ for class 3_i

Lines 1 to 8 refer to requests being already at time t in the system, having different residual mean times.

Line 9 refers to requests arriving during t and t'. They all will receive class 1 service, whereas only classes 3_1 up to 3_{i-1} of them are receiving total service before the considered class 3_i request.

With

$$E(T_{W3i}) = \frac{E(T_{O3i})}{1 - A_{3i}^{\ast}}$$

after standard manipulations it is obtained

$$E(T_{W3i}) = \frac{1}{1-A_1-\sum_{\gamma=1}^{i} A'_{3\gamma}} \cdot \left[\sum_{\gamma=1}^{i-1} A'_{3\gamma} \cdot E(T_{W3\gamma}) + \ldots \right.$$

$$\ldots + \left[E(T_{W1}) + h_1 \right] \cdot \left\{ A_1 + A'_{3i} + 2\sum_{\gamma=1}^{i-1} A'_{3\gamma} \right\} + \ldots \qquad (16)$$

$$\left. + \frac{1}{1-A_1} \cdot \left[A_1 A_2 h_0 + (1-c_{12})\sum_{\gamma=1}^{n} z_{2\gamma} \right] + \sum_{\gamma=1}^{i} \frac{z_{3\gamma} + A_{3\gamma} h'_0}{1-A_1-\sum_{j=1}^{\gamma-1} A'_{3j}} \right]$$

From this recursive formula for the mean initial waiting time in a queue 3_i $(i=1\ldots m)$, with the help of a homogeneous and a particular solution of the resulting inhomogeneous difference equation it is possible to derive an explicit solution

$$E(T_{W3i}) = \frac{(1-A_1)\cdot E(T_{F1}) + A_1 A_2 h_0 + (1-c_{12})\sum_{\gamma=1}^{n} z_{2\gamma} + \sum_{j=1}^{i} z_{3j} + h'_0 \cdot \sum_{j=1}^{i} A_{3j}}{\left[1-A_1-\sum_{j=1}^{i-1} A'_{3j} \right] \cdot \left[1-A_1-\sum_{j=1}^{i} A'_{3j} \right]} - E(T_{F1})$$

$$i=1\ldots m \quad (17)$$

where

$$E(T_{F1}) = E(T_{W1}) + h_1 \qquad (18)$$

is the expected flow time of class 1 requests.
It has been already indicated that the subsequent waiting time of a class 3_i request (cf.(10),(11),(12)) is

$$E(T_{WS3i}) = \frac{A_1 + \sum_{j=1}^{i-1} A'_{3j}}{1 - A_1 - \sum_{j=1}^{i-1} A'_{3j}} \cdot h_{3i} \qquad (19)$$

3.5 Response Times

The response time for a request belonging to a user task of class i i.e. of user priority i $(i=1\ldots m)$ is the time from the arrival of the associated I/O interrupt up to the final release of the processor:

$$E(T_{Ri}) = E(T_{F1}) + E(T_{W3i}) + E(T_{WS3i}) + h_{3i} + h_0 + \ldots \qquad (20)$$

$$\ldots + (1-p_{30}) \cdot \sum_{j=1}^{n} p_{2j} \cdot \left[E(T_{W2j}) + E(T_{WS2j}) + h_{2j} \right]$$

The mean total time   a job of user priority i is in the total
computer system would be obtained by adding the mean time in the
channel device subsystem per I/O access and by multiplication with
the mean number of physical I/O accesses.

4 NUMERICAL RESULTS

4.1 Influence of System Overhead

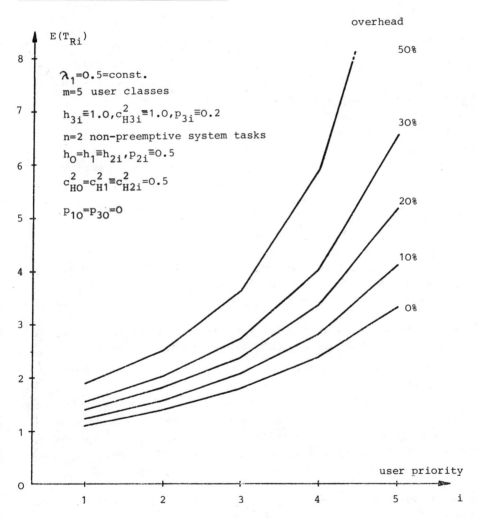

Fig 3: Influence of system overhead on the mean response times
       of different user classes

Fig.3 shows the influence of the operating system phases on the
mean response times of m=5 different user priority classes.
The processor utilization for user task processing has been taken
fixed

$$A_3 = \sum_{i=1}^{m} A_{3i} = 0.5$$

whereas the additional system overhead $A_0 + A_1 + A_2$ has been varied
up to 0.25.

4.2 Waiting Times within Internal Operating System Queues

It has been confirmed by several calculations that the waiting
times within internal operating system queues often can be neglected
compared with the waiting times in a user task queue.
To give some figures,for the highest user priority the fraction of
waiting in internal operating system queues (levels 1,2) was up to
10% for a system with 50% overhead and up to 20% for the same
number of user and operating system instructions (100% overhead).

4.3 Comparison of Total Response Times

For many purposes it is sufficient to consider the processor as a
black box and to describe its behaviour by the different response
times for different user priorities.Of special interest here is
the question,how large is the influence of the operating system
phases on the discrimination of the different user priority classes.

Fig.4 shows the response times for a processor model with 3 user
priorities as a function of the total processor utilization.

Compared with the calculation results are results for corresponding
models without feedbacks.
If system overhead is considered to globally enlarge user task
phases,a comparison model with 3 queues is obtained,each with a
mean service time of h =1.4 and a squared coefficient of variation
of 0.612.This model has been calculated for the two bordering cases
of pure preemptive and pure non-preemptive services.

There is another possibility to calculate approximately the response
times by assuming for each of the 6 queues in the example a Poisson
input process.The resulting model with a mixture of preemptive and

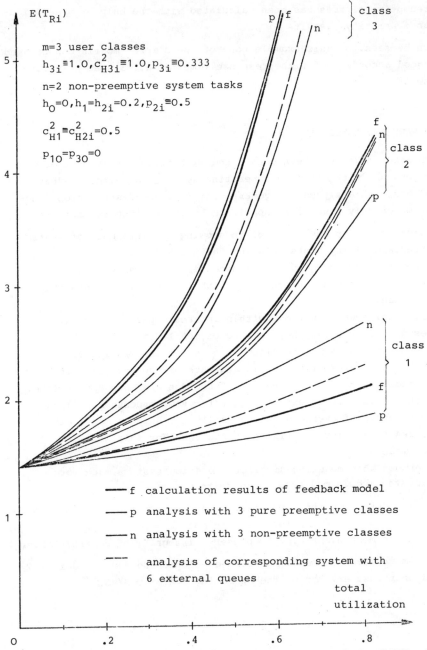

$E(T_{Ri})$

m=3 user classes
$h_{3i} \equiv 1.0, c_{H3i}^2 \equiv 1.0, p_{3i} \equiv 0.333$
n=2 non-preemptive system tasks
$h_0 = 0, h_1 = h_{2i} = 0.2, p_{2i} \equiv 0.5$
$c_{H1}^2 \equiv c_{H2i}^2 = 0.5$
$p_{10} = p_{30} = 0$

——f calculation results of feedback model

——p analysis with 3 pure preemptive classes

——n analysis with 3 non-preemptive classes

– – – analysis of corresponding system with
        6 external queues

total
utilization

<u>Fig. 4</u>: Comparison of total response time results of the feedback
        model and of models without feedbacks

nonpreemptive classes has been calculated with the help of preemption-distance priority results /10/.

As can be seen,for this example none of the simpler models can be used with good accordance for the response times of all 3 user priority classes.

5 SUMMARY AND CONCLUSION

A processor model has been considered with different priorities of user jobs and with different operating system phases.The feedback model has been analyzed for general service time distribution functions,which only have to be specified by their first two moments.

Numerical examples have been given showing the influence of system overhead,and giving hints relating the necessity of modeling internal operating system queues.This necessity,as expected,heavily depends on the amount of overhead which can be selected properly in the model.
In any case,if waiting times within internal operating system queues are of interest,they have to be modeled.
The assumption of a Poisson input process of the I/O interrupts could be considered as a certain drawback of the analysis,since often models with a finite number of sources are more appropriate. Nevertheless,it can be expected that for same processor utilization and percentage of overhead the necessity for using a model with feedbacks is smaller for finite source than for this infinite source model.
Furthermore,when modeling distinct operating systems,much more complicated models may result,e.g. with

- feedbacks from the I/O-interrupt queue to system task queues
- I/O-compute overlap for the same job
- gating mechanisms e.g. to preserve integrity of control tables

Such a more detailed model has been developed and described in /12/ based on the supervisor of the operating system DOS/VS.

REFERENCES

/1/ ADIRI,I.   Introduction to queueing theory with applications
                 to computer systems
                 Computer Science Department Monograph Series,RA 42,
                 IBM Research Division,Yorktown Heights,1972

/2/ ANDERSON,H. Approximating pre-emptive priority dispatching in
        A.Jr.   a multiprogramming model
                 IBM Journal of Res.Dev. 17(1973)4,533-539

/3/ BASKETT,F.   Open,closed,and mixed networks of queues with
    CHANDY,K.M.   different classes of customers
    MUNTZ,R.R.   JACM 22(1975)2,248-260
    PALACIOS,F.G.

/4/ BUZEN,J.P.   Queueing network models of multiprogramming
                  Thesis,Harvard Univ. Camb. Mass.,1971

/5/ BUZEN,J.P.   I/O subsystem architecture
                  Proc. IEEE 63(1975)6,871-879

/6/ COBHAM,A.   Priority assignment in waiting line problems
                  Operations Research 2(1954),70-76

/7/ CONWAY,R.W.   Theory of Scheduling

    MAXWELL,W.L. Addison-Wesley Publishing Company,1967

    MILLER,L.W.

/8/ ENNS,E.G.   Some waiting-time distributions for queues with
                  multiple feedback and priorities
                  Operations Research 17(1969)3,519-525

/9/ HERZOG,U.   Optimal Scheduling Strategies for Real-Time Computers

                  IBM J.Res.Dev. 19(1975)5,494-504

/10/ HERZOG,U.   Priority models for communication processors
                  including system overhead
                  8th International Teletraffic Congress (ITC),
                  Melbourne,November 1976,Paper 623

/11/ KLEINROCK,L. Queueing systems,Vol I,II
                  John Wiley,1975/76

/12/ KRAEMER,W.   Performance investigations with a DOS/VS based
                  operating system model
                  Submitted to an IBM Journal

/13/ KUEHN,P.   Zur optimalen Steuerung des Multiprogramminggrades
                  in Rechnersystemen mit virtuellem Speicher und Paging
                  Lecture Notes in Computer Science,Vol 34,Springer,
                  Berlin/NY 1975,567-580
/14/ LEWIS,P.A.W. A cyclic-queue model of system overhead in multi-
     SHEDLER,G.S. programmed computer systems
                  JACM 18(1971)2,199-220

/15/ REISER,M.   Queueing networks with several closed subchains:
     KOBAYASHI,M. theory and computational algorithms
                  IBM Research Rpt RC 4919,July 1974

/16/ REISER,M.   Interactive modeling of computer systems
                  IBM Systems Journal 15(1976)4,309-327

COMPUTER PERFORMANCE, K.M. CHANDY AND M. REISER (EDS.)
NORTH HOLLAND PUBLISHING COMPANY, 1977

BIN-PACKING PROBLEMS AND THEIR APPLICATIONS
IN STORAGE AND PROCESSOR ALLOCATION

E. G. Coffmann, Jr.
Columbia University
New York, New York, USA

J. Y-T. Leung
Virginia Polytechnic Institute
and State University
Blacksburg, Virginia, USA

D. Ting
Bell Telephone Laboratories
Holmdel, New Jersey, USA

I.   INTRODUCTION

There are a number of important sequencing (scheduling) and storage
allocation problems connected with the efficient use of parallel
devices in computer systems which are superficially different but
in fact subject to the same mathematical model. We consider three
such problems, noting that each is a particular one-dimensional
bin-packing problem[1]. Approximation algorithms for these problems
will be presented and their performance studied.

We now provide informal but abstract definitions of bin-packing
problems, after which the specific applications in computer systems
will be outlined. For each of the problems we consider, a collection of bins $B_1, B_2, \ldots, B_m$ is assumed where each bin has the same
capacity c. For each problem we are given a collection $p_1, \ldots, p_n$
of pieces which are to be packed into the bins as so that no bin
capacity is exceeded and some measure of the packing (or bins) is
optimized. We shall let p_i also denote the size of p_i (this
ambiguity will always be easily resolved by context), and for all
i we assume $p_i \leq c$. The three problems to be studied are:

P1.   For c fixed the minimum number, m, is to be found
      such that the entire set of pieces can be packed in m
      bins of capacity c.

P2.   For a fixed m the minimum number, c, is to be found
      such that the entire set of pieces can be packed in m
      bins of capacity c.

P3.   For fixed m and c the maximum number $n' \leq n$ is to be
      found such that n' of the n pieces can be packed in
      m bins of capacity c.

Problem P1 is the classical bin-packing problem [2,3] having numerous applications in industry, e.g. coil-slitting and cable-length
optimization, where a set of pieces has to be obtained from some
resource provided in standard lengths. Clearly, each of these

applications can also be considered mutatis mutandis for the other problems. In computer design storage allocation problems of essentially equivalent structure occur in table-formatting, paginating variable-size records, and assigning variable-size records to autonomous storage units such as disk cylinders. Note that in P1 the unit design is fixed and the number of units used is to be minimized; in P2 the number of units is fixed while a minimum capacity is to be designed; and in P3 the entire system is fixed and maximum usage of it is to be obtained.

In scheduling multiprocessors P1 is the problem of minimizing the number of processors necessary for completing all tasks by a given deadline; P2 is simply the schedule length (makespan) minimization problem. In general, a correspondence between storage allocation and scheduling applications can be made by the term associations: storage unit-processor, capacity-deadline, allocate-schedule, record-task.

It is readily verified that each of P1,P2 and P3 is NP-complete. Therefore, the approach that has been taken towards solving these problems is to design and analyze very fast, structurally simple approximation algorithms. (See [1] for approaches concerned with more complex and time-consuming enumeration and high-accuracy techniques.) Despite their simplicity, analyses of these algorithms entail very difficult combinatorial problems. For this reason past studies, as well as the present one, focus on the evaluation of worst-case performance. Although worst-case performance bounds are often not very informative measures of "goodness", we shall see that this is not the case with efficient bin-packing rules, which provide near-optimum performance even in the worst-case.

We shall consider for each of P1,P2, and P3 the basic bin-packing rules whereby a given list L of the pieces is scanned from left-to-right with successive pieces being packed in the first bin in which they fit (the bins are also scanned from left-to-right, i.e. in the sequence $B_1, B_2, \ldots$). The more effective rules which are our main concern perform an initial ordering of the pieces. For P1 and P2, L is initially placed in non-increasing order of piece size which gives us the so-called first-fit-decreasing (FFD) rule. Although the FFD rule can also be used in P3 we shall focus on the first-fit-increasing (FFI) rule which places L in non-decreasing order of piece size.

     As an illustration consider c=1 and the piece sizes*
{ 2/9x6, 5/18x6, 4/9x4, 5/9x4} packed in bins under the circumstances of P1. Below we indicate successive bin contents by columns of piece sizes headed by a number u_i giving the unused capacity of B_i. In sequence are shown the optimum, FFD, and an "arbitrary" packing.

---

*pxk denotes k pieces of size p.

u_i:	0	0	0	0	0	0	0
					2/9	2/9	2/9
					2/9	2/9	2/9
	4/9	4/9	4/9	4/9	5/18	5/18	5/18
	5/9	5/9	5/9	5/9	5/18	5/18	5/18

L = (5/9x4, 4/9x4, 5/18x2, 2/9x2, 5/18x2, 2/9x2, 5/18x2, 2/9x2)

Optimum - m=7

u_i:	0	0	0	0	1/6	1/6	1/9	5/9
							2/9	
					5/18	5/18	2/9	
	4/9	4/9	4/9	4/9	5/18	5/18	2/9	2/9
	5/9	5/9	5/9	5/9	5/18	5/18	2/9	2/9

L = (5/9x4, 4/9x4, 5/18x6, 2/9x6)

FFD - m=8

u_i:	1/9	1/9	0	0	0	4/9	4/9	4/9	4/9
			2/9	2/9	5/18				
			2/9	2/9	5/18				
	4/9	4/9	5/18	5/18	2/9				
	4/9	4/9	5/18	5/18	2/9	5/9	5/9	5/9	5/9

L = (4/9x4, 5/18x2, 2/9x2, 5/18x2, 2/9x4, 5/18x2, 5/9x4)

m=9

Another bin-packing rule of interest is the best-fit-decreasing (BFD) rule in which successively smaller pieces are placed in the left-most bin for which the resulting unused capacity is least, i.e. in the bins in which they best fit. The performance bound for the BFD rule is the same as for the FFD rule when applied to P1, although the BFD performance can be better over certain classes of lists. The BFD rule has not been applied to P2 or P3 and it appears rather more difficult to analyze. For this reason we shall have little more to say about this rule.

In the next section we shall present the results known for the performance of bin-packing rules applied to P1-P3. In section III we shall provide proof of the main result for the most recently studied problem, P3.

II. RESULTS

We shall consider P1-P3 in sequence. P1 is the best studied of the three problems and the one for which most is known. Let $m_D(L)$ denote the number of bins required by the FFD rule to pack L in bins whose common capacity is understood. Let $m_0(L)$ denote the corresponding number of bins required by an optimization rule. We have

<u>Theorem 1</u> [2] For all lists L

$$m_D(L) \leq \frac{11}{9} m_0(L) + 2$$

As we shall see below the coefficient 11/9 is smallest possible. However, let us first introduce the parameter $\alpha(L) \varepsilon [0,c]$, denoting the largest piece size in L. Also, to eliminate consideration of the additive constants that appear in results like Theorem 1 we define the following limit. Consider the supremum of the ratio $m_D(L)/m_0(L)$ over all lists for which $m_0(L)=m$ and $\alpha(L)=\alpha$. Let $R_D(\alpha)$ denote the limit of this supremum as $m \to \infty$. Then we have

<u>Theorem 2</u> [2] For all lists L and $\alpha=\alpha(L)$

$$R_D(\alpha) = \begin{cases} 11/9 & \alpha \varepsilon (\frac{1}{2},1] \\ 71/60 & \alpha \varepsilon (\frac{8}{29},\frac{1}{2}] \\ 7/6 & \alpha \varepsilon (\frac{1}{4},\frac{8}{29}] \\ 23/20 & \alpha \varepsilon (\frac{1}{5},\frac{1}{4}] \end{cases}$$

and each of these bounds is smallest possible.

Note that the parameter α allows one to assess improvements in worst-case performance as capacity is increased. It is conjectured that the complete form of Theorem 2 is obtained by replacing the last bound by

$$R_D(\alpha) = 1 + \frac{k-2}{k(k-1)} \quad \text{for} \quad \alpha \leq \frac{1}{4}, \quad k = \lfloor \alpha^{-1} \rfloor$$

For an idea of the importance of ordering L, it has been shown that $R_F(1)=17/10$, where $R_F(1)$ is the analog of $R_D(1)=11/9$ when L is allowed to be in an arbitrary order [2].

To verify that the 11/9 bound in Theorem 2 is best possible consider the example below for c=1. Note that Xk beneath a column denotes k bins with the pieces shown, that $\varepsilon > 0$ is to be chosen suitably small, and that r is any positive integer.

u_i:	0	0
		$\frac{1}{4} - 2\varepsilon$
	$\frac{1}{4} - 2\varepsilon$	$\frac{1}{4} - 2\varepsilon$
	$\frac{1}{4} + \varepsilon$	$\frac{1}{4} + 2\varepsilon$
	$\frac{1}{2} + \varepsilon$	$\frac{1}{4} + 2\varepsilon$
	(X6r)	(X3r)

Optimum: $m_0 = 9r$

u_i:	$\frac{1}{4} - 3\varepsilon$	$\frac{1}{4} - 3\varepsilon$	8ε
			$\frac{1}{4} - 2\varepsilon$
		$\frac{1}{4} + \varepsilon$	$\frac{1}{4} - 2\varepsilon$
	$\frac{1}{4} + 2\varepsilon$	$\frac{1}{4} + \varepsilon$	$\frac{1}{4} - 2\varepsilon$
	$\frac{1}{2} + \varepsilon$	$\frac{1}{4} + \varepsilon$	$\frac{1}{4} - 2\varepsilon$
	(X6r)	(X2r)	(X3r)

FFD: $m_D = 11r$

Similar examples can be found for the remaining bounds in Theorem 2 [2]. It has been shown that Theorem 2 also applies to the BFD rule. Although these are the major results of interest to us here, a number of similar results for certain extensions of the model can be found summarized in [1,2,3]. As a final note it is readily verified that the worst-case time complexity of the FFD rule is $O(n \log_2 n)$, where use is made of the fact that with a binary search technique the FFD assignment can be done in at most $O(n \log_2 m)$ time.

Problem P2 has only recently been studied [4], with the original motivation being the makespan minimization problem in scheduling theory. The main result bounds the capacity required by the FFD rule in order to guarantee being able to pack a set of pieces in m bins. For a set L of pieces let $c_D(L)$ denote the minimum capacity needed by the FFD rule for packing L into m bins, where m is understood; and let $c_0(L)$ denote the minimum capacity needed by an optimization rule.

Theorem 3 [4]   For all   L

$$\frac{c_D(L)}{c_0(L)} \leq \begin{cases} 8/7 & m=2 \\ 15/13 & m=3 \\ 20/17 & 4 \leq m \leq 7 \end{cases}$$

and for all   m   and   L

$$\frac{c_D(L)}{c_0(L)} \leq \frac{61}{50}$$

Moreover, the bounds for $m \leq 7$ are smallest possible.

Although 20/17 is conjectured to be a best bound for all $m > 4$, the arguments for $4 \leq m \leq 7$ have not been extendable to the general case. The proof of the 61/50 result extends the weighting function approach used in Theorems 1 and 2. The structure of the proof, which can be applied with certain modifications to P3, is as follows.

Proceeding by contradiction a list   L   is assumed which violates the bound. It is then shown without much difficulty that such a list must produce an FFD packing with at least 2 and at most 5 pieces per bin, and an optimum packing having at least 3 and at most 5 pieces per bin. For this reduced problem a weighting function of piece size is defined. Finally, it is shown that the total weight of pieces in an FFD packing with   m   bins of capacity 61/50 $c_0(L)$ is at least that of an optimum packing with   m   bins of capacity $c_0(L)$. This part of the proof, which provides the final contradiction, is basically an exhaustive examination of all possible bin configurations in both FFD and optimum packings (under the above bin cardinality constraints), computing weight bounds for each.

The examples below show that the 8/7, 15/13, and 20/17 bounds are smallest possible. The 20/17 example is easily extended to arbitrary   m   simply by introducing   m-4   pieces of size $c_0(L)$. Note that the FFD packings shown are those produced in   m   bins when it is assumed that the bin capacity for the FFD rule is chosen to be strictly less than $c_D(L)$.

```
u_i:         0         0        c-6  c-6

             2         2             2     6≤ α ≤8
             2         2        3    2     ‾‾‾m=2
             3         3        3    2     n=6
          Optimum              FFD (p_n=2 does not fit)


u_i:    0    0    0             c-12  c-12  c-12

                  3                          3
        3    4    3                   4      3     12≤ α ≤15
        3    4    3             5      4      3     ‾‾‾m=3
        7    5    4             7      4      3     n=10
          Optimum              FFD (p_n=3 does not fit)


u_i:   0    0    0    0         c-16  c-16  c-16  c-16

                 4    4                      4     4
       4    4    4    4                5      4     4    16≤ α ≤20
       4    6    4    4         7      5      4     4    ‾‾‾m=4
       9    7    5    5         9      6      4     4    n=14
          Optimum              FFD (p_n=4 does not fit)
```

Clearly, since $c_0(L)$ can not be efficiently computed, neither can $61/50 \; c_0(L)$. Thus, in order to make use of this result some search mechanism must be designed. An efficient such algorithm can be constructed using binary search over a range bounded by

$$\max \{ \max_i p_i, \; \sum_{i=1}^{n} p_i/m \} \leq c \leq 2 \max \{ \max_i p_i, \; \sum_{i=1}^{n} p_i/m \}$$

These bounds on $c_0(L)$ and $c_D(L)$ are easily proved.

The algorithm iteratively uses capacities selected by binary search over the above range, applying the FFD rule in each case. It is easily verified that this algorithm will converge to a value for the capacity satisfying Theorem 3. One can show [4] in general that after the kth iteration a capacity of $[r_m+1/2^k]c_0(L)$ will always suffice, where r_m denotes the bounds in Theorem 3. In practice, the algorithm performs much better, and it has been found that after about 7 iterations no further improvement is obtained by the algorithm. For k iterations the worst-case time complexity of the algorithm is $O(n \log_2 n+k \; n \log_2 m)$ and provides an attractive alternative to largest-processing-time-first (LPT) scheduling [1].

The latest bin-packing results concern problem P3. First, observe that in considering algorithms for this problem we may restrict ourselves to those which pack a prefix of the list L arranged in nondecreasing order. That is, we do not need to consider packings in which there is a piece whose size exceeds that of some unpacked piece. Algorithms packing pieces drawn from a list in non-decreasing order of size will be called prefix algorithms.

Let $n_A(L)$ denote the cardinality of the subset of pieces packed by algorithm A from list L in m bins, where m is understood. As before $n_0(L)$ denotes the number packed by an optimization rule. In a packing produced by a prefix algorithm all of the unpacked pieces have a size exceeding u_i for all $i (1 < i < m)$. Thus, for any prefix algorithm $n_0(L) - n_A(L) < m-1$. Since $n_A(L) \geq m$ must hold if $n_A(L) < n_0(L)$ we have

Theorem 4   For any prefix algorithm A and all L and $m \geq 1$

$$n_0(L) - n_A(L) \leq m-1$$

and

$$\frac{n_0(L)}{n_A(L)} \leq 2 - 1/m$$

The above bound can be achieved by an algorithm that packs successively larger pieces into bins currently having lowest level (sum of the sizes of the pieces contained in a bin). The example shown below for $m=4$ is easily generalized for arbitrary m.

u_i:	0	0	0	0	3/4	3/4	3/4	3/4
	1/4							
	1/4							
	1/4							
	1/4	1	1	1	1/4	1/4	1/4	1/4
	$n_0(L) = 7$					$n_A(L) = 4$		

$$m=4, \quad c=1, \quad L=(\tfrac{1}{4},\tfrac{1}{4},\tfrac{1}{4},\tfrac{1}{4},1,1,1)$$

A more promising algorithm is the FFI algorithm according to which the bins are filled one by one, smallest piece first. An example is shown below. Note that once a piece is encountered which will

u_i:	0	0	0	0	0	1/6	0	1/3	0	1/4
	1/3	1/6	1/6			1/4				
	1/3	1/3	1/3	1/4	1/4	1/4	1/3			
	1/3	1/2	1/2	3/4	3/4	1/6	1/3	1/3	1/2	
						1/6	1/3	1/3	1/2	3/4
	$n_0(L) = 13$						$n_I(L) = 12$			

$$m=5, \quad c=1, \quad L=(\tfrac{1}{6} \times 2, \ \tfrac{1}{4} \times 2, \ \tfrac{1}{3} \times 5, \ \tfrac{1}{2} \times 2, \ \tfrac{3}{4} \times 2)$$

not fit into a bin B, no as yet unpacked pieces will fit either, so that B may be removed from further consideration in the packing sequence. Note also that the numbers of pieces in individual bins form a non-increasing sequence. Clearly, this simple rule has an execution time dominated by the time required to sort L (i.e. $O(n \log_2 n)$).

The following result shows the improvement provided by FFI sequencing; it is proved in the next section.

Theorem 5   For all   L   and $m \geq 1$

$$\frac{n_0(L)}{n_I(L)} \leq 4/3$$

and this bound is achievable for all even m.

To verify that 4/3 is achievable consider the following example for m=6. (The example is easily generalized to arbitrary even m.)

u_i:	0	0	0	0	0	0
	3/8	3/8	3/8	3/8	3/8	3/8
	5/8	5/8	5/8	5/8	5/8	5/8

$$n_0(L) = 12$$

u_i:	1/4	1/4	1/4	3/8	3/8	3/8
	3/8	3/8	3/8			
	3/8	3/8	3/8	5/8	5/8	5/8

$$n_I(L) = 9$$

$$m=6, \quad c=1, \quad L=(\tfrac{3}{8} \times 6, \tfrac{5}{8} \times 6)$$

An interesting result in which piece size is effectively a parameter has also been derived [5]. Let $k=|B_m|$ denote the smallest number of pieces packed in any bin of an FFI packing. Let $N_I(k)$ be the limit as $n \to \infty$ of the supremum of $n_I(L)/n_0(L)$ over all lists for which $n_I(L)=n$ and $|B_m|=k$. Then one can show

Theorem 6   For each $k \geq 1$

$$N_I(k) = \frac{(k+1)^2}{k^2+k+1}$$

and is achievable for all m a multiple of k+1.

The example of $L=((\frac{1}{k+1} - k\varepsilon) \times \frac{m}{k+1}), \ (\frac{1}{k+1} + \varepsilon) \times \frac{km}{k+1})$ with $\varepsilon > 0$ suitably small, shows that the ratio is achievable for all k.

With the objective of a more effective algorithm, the FFD rule has also been applied to P3. In order to keep with prefix algorithms it is necessary to consider an iterative rule, since the size of the largest piece packed is unknown at the outset. Let $(p_1,...,p_n)$ be the list L in non-decreasing order of piece size, and let s be the largest index such that $\sum_{i=1}^{s} p_i \leq m$. The iterated FFD (called)

the FFD*) rule first attempts to pack $p_s,...,p_1$ in m bins using the FFD rule. If it succeeds, the algorithm terminates; otherwise, the largest piece is removed and the FFD rule is applied to $p_{s-1},...,p_1$. Largest pieces are successively discarded until a fit of the remaining pieces in m bins is finally found. It is not difficult to show that at most m iterations are necessary, and hence we have an $O(n \log_2 n + m \ n \ log_2 m)$ worst-case time complexity for the FFD* rule. Let $N_{D*}(k)$ be defined for the FFD* rule as $N_I(k)$ was defined for the FFI rule, and let $N_{D*} = \max_k N_{D*}(k)$.

Theorem 7

$$8/7 \leq N_{D*} \leq 7/6$$

Other related results as well as the rather arduous proof of Theorem 7 will be the subject of a future paper.

III. PROOF OF THE 4/3 BOUND

In this section we provide a proof of the bound in Theorem 5: $n_I(L)/n_0(L) \leq 4/3$. Recall that the example following Theorem 5 verifies that 4/3 is achievable. For convenience we assume c=1.

It will be convenient to introduce the following notation. We let P_I denote an FFI packing, and n_I the number of pieces in P_I; the list of pieces being packed will be clear in context. Similarly, P_0 and n_0 are defined for an optimum packing. We let k_i and v_i denote, respectively, the number of pieces in B_i and the level of B_i, $1 \leq i \leq m$. B_i and k_i will always refer to an FFI packing P_I; B_i^0 and k_i^0 will refer to a corresponding optimum packing P_0. We define the index r as the largest integer such that $k_r > k_m = \min\{k_i\}$ in P_I. Also, we let $d = n_0 - n_I$. Because of space constraints some of the routine details of the proof are omitted. The proof is based on the following four claims. The first follows from simple capacity arguments.

<u>Claim 1</u> For any list packed into m bins we must have $d \leq r k_m$.

By definition of the FFI packing the smallest piece in B_{i+1} must be larger than the unused capacity in B_i. This simple property is instrumental in the proof of

<u>Claim 2</u> In an FFI packing let $x_j = \sum_{i=1}^{j} v_i$. If for some k>1 we have $|B_{i+1}| = k$ and $v_i \leq k/(k+1)$, then $v_j > k/(k+1)$,

$1 \leq j < i$, $v_i + v_{i+1} > 2k/(k+1)$ and $x_{i+1} > (i+1)k/(k+1)$.

Using Claim 2 we may next prove

Claim 3 For a given list L packed into m bins suppose d>0, and let x_j' be the following sum of largest piece-sizes in an optimum packing P_o: $x_j' = \sum_{i=j}^{m} v_i + \Sigma_{p \varepsilon P_o - P_F}\, p$.   Then for all s=r, r+1,...,m we have $x_j' > (m-s+1)k_m/(k_m+1) + d/(k_m+1)$.

Note that $x_i + x_{i+1}' \le m$ must hold, since the cumulative size of the pieces in P^i can not exceed the capacity, m, of m bins. A key result for this and the following theorem is given next.

Claim 4 Suppose list L is packed into m bins such that $n_0/n_I > f(k_m) \equiv (k_m+1)^2/(k_m^2+k_m+1)$. Suppose further that there is no shorter list $L' \subset L$ for which a packing into $m' \le m$ bins is such that $n_0'/n_I' > f(k_{m'})$. Then we must have $k_i^o > k_m$, $1 \le i \le m$, and either $n_0 \ge (k_m+2)m-k_m$, or $r \ge m-k_m+1$ (and hence $n_I \ge mk_m+r \ge (k_m+1)m-(k_m-1)$).

Proof In P_o suppose $k_i^o \le k_m$ and let S be the set of k_i^o largest pieces in P_o. It is easily seen that the packings P_o' and P_I' of the list L'=L-S into m'=m-1 bins provide a smaller example for which $n_0'/n_I' > f(k_{m'})$ - a contradiction.

For the second part, suppose both $n_0 < (k_m+2)m-k_m$ and $r < m-k_m+1$. Note that these inequalities and $k_i^o > k_m$, $1 \le i \le m$, imply that P_o has at least k_m+1 bins with exactly k_m+1 pieces, and P_I has at least k_m bins with exactly k_m pieces. It is not difficult to verify that the packings P_o' and P_I' of the list $L'=L-B_r$ into $m'=m-(k_m+1)$ bins again provide us with a smaller example for which $n_0'/n_I' > f(k_{m'})$.

We may now proceed with a proof of the theorem. We distinguish three principal cases.

Case 1 ($k_m \ge 3$) Since $n_I \ge 3m$ we have immediately from Theorem 4: $d \le m-1$, and $n_0/n_I = 1+d/n_I \le 1+(m-1)/3m < 4/3$, $m \ge 1$.

Case 2 ($k_m = 2$) Suppose L is such that $n_0/n_I > 4/3 > (k_m+1)^2/(k_m^2+k_m+1) = 9/7$. If $n_0 < 4m-2$ and $r < m-1$ then from the arguments in Claim 4 there must be a shorter list, L', violating 4/3 in $m' < m$ bins. Moreover, we can not, according to Case 1, assume that the packing of L' is such that $k_m' \ge 3$. Thus, if we assume, as we may, that L is the shortest list for which $k_m=2$, then we require that either $n_0 \ge 4m-2$ or $r \ge m-1$ and hence $n_I \ge 3m-1$. But if $n_0 \ge 4m-2$ then for all $m \ge 1$, $n_0/n_I = n_0/(n_0-d) \le (4m-2)-(m-1) < 4/3$, and if $n_I \ge 3m-1$ then for all $m \ge 1$,

$n_0/n_I = 1 + d/n_I \le 1 + (m-1)/(3m-1) < 4/3$. We obtain a contradiction in either case.

Case 3 $(k_m = 1)$ Suppose we have a shortest list L such that $k_m = 1$ and $n_0/n_I > 4/3$. We consider two sub-cases based on the level of B_r.

Case 3a $(v_r > 2/3 = (k_m + 1)/(k_m + 2))$ Since the cumulative size of the pieces in P_0 must not exceed the total capacity m, we must have $m \ge x_r + x'_{r+1}$ (see Claims 2 and 3). From $v_r > 2/3$ and Claims 2 and 3 we get $x_r > 2r/3$ and $x'_{r+1} > (m-r)/2 + d/2$. Hence, $m > 2r/3 + (m-r+d)/2$. On using $d < rk_m = r$ from Claim 1, we obtain $d < 3m/4$ or $d \le (3m-1)/4$.

Omitting the details, one can now verify from Claim 4 that $n_0 \ge 3m-1$ for the present case. Using this result along with $d < (3m-1)/4$ we have $n_0/n_I = n_0/(n_0 - d) \le (3m-1)/((3m-1) - (3m-1)/4) = 4/3$, the desired contradiction.

Case 3b $(v_r \le 2/3)$ In this case every piece in $B_1, \ldots, B_{r-1}$ has a size no greater than $1/3$. Hence, $k_i \ge 3$, $1 \le i \le r-1$, and a count of the pieces in P_I must give $n_I \ge 3(r-1) + 2 + (m-r) = m + 2r - 1$. On applying Claim 1 we obtain $n_0/n_I = 1 + d/n_I \le 1 + r/(m+2r-1) \le 1 + (m-1)/(3m-3) = 4/3$. This contradiction completes the proof of the bound 4/3.

IV. OPEN PROBLEMS

Clearly, a tightening of the bounds in Theorems 3 and 7 would be highly desirable; however, this would appear to be rather difficult. More interesting perhaps is the extension of the bin-packing results to systems containing more than one bin capacity. See [2] for further discussion.

The generalization to two-dimensional bin-packing is indeed intriguing. Unfortunately, one is faced with an initial, serious obstacle in that very fast algorithms of the type considered here are very difficult to find with a worst-case performance moderately close to optimum. The nature of the problem apparently suggests the study of more elaborate efficient enumeration and approximation techniques such as limited backtrack branch-and-bound.

REFERENCES

1. Coffman, E.G., Jr., Computer and Job-Shop Scheduling Theory, Wiley and Sons, 1975.
    Chapter 5 - R.L. Graham, "Bounds on the Performance of Scheduling Algorithms".

    Chapter 6 - W.H. Kohler and K. Steiglitz "Enumerative and Iterative Computational Approaches".
2. Johnson, D.S., A. Demers, J.D. Ullman, M.R. Garey, and R.L. Graham, "Worst-Case Performance Bounds for Simple One-Dimensional Packing Algorithms", SIAM Journal on Computing, 3 (1974), 299-326.

3. Johnson, D.S., "Fast Algorithms for Bin Packing", <u>Journal of
    Computer and System Sciences</u>, <u>8</u> (1974), 272-314.
4. Coffman, E.G., D.S. Johnson, and M.R. Garey, "An Application of
    Bin-Packing to Multiprocessor Scheduling", <u>SIAM Journal on Com-
    puting</u> (to appear).
5. Coffman, E.G., Jr., J. Y-T. Leung, and D. Ting, "Bin-Packing:
    Maximizing the Number of Pieces Packed", <u>Acta Informatica</u> (to
    appear).

COMPUTER PERFORMANCE, K.M. CHANDY AND M. REISER (EDS.)
NORTH HOLLAND PUBLISHING COMPANY, 1977

PERFORMANCE ANALYSIS OF THE CHAINING METHOD
FOR RANDOM-ACCESS ADDRESSING

H. Mendelson and U. Yechiali
Tel Aviv University
Tel Aviv, Israel

Consider a random-access file with N storage locations.
Records are added to the file from time to time. A record
with key $\omega \in \Omega$ is hashed to storage location $F(\omega)$.
A collision is resolved by the following chaining method:
All records hashed to the same location are chained to each
other to form a list structure. The first record of a list
is stored either at location $F(\omega)$ or at an alternative
start if location $F(\omega)$ is occupied. For this process the
multi-dimensional time-dependent generating function is
derived and the expected values of various state-variables
are calculated. These values are used to obtain formulae
for the expected number of I/O operations needed for
retrieval, updating or addition of a record.

Two measures of retrieval performance are calculated:

(i)   the expected number of additional probes needed to
      find a record in the file. This measure is uniformly
      bounded by 2/3.

(ii) the expected number of additional probes required to
      discover that a record is not in the file. This
      performance measure is always smaller than the first
      and is uniformly bounded by 1/2.

Addition of a record consists of two steps: (i) finding
an empty location, and (ii) writing the record and
updating all the pointers involved. The number of I/O
operations needed for the first step depends on the
amount of information available on the occupancy of the
file. For various information levels the relevant
performance measures are calculated and compared. As
for the updating of chains, the possibility of maintaining

341

an additional pointer directly to the end of each list
is considered. It is found that the additional pointer
does not improve the performance of the updating
procedure.

INTRODUCTION

Consider a random-access file with N (equivalent) storage locations $1,2,\ldots,N$.
Fixed-length records are added to the file from time to time. Each record is
identified by a key ω belonging to a key-set Ω. Let ω_k $(k = 1,2,3,\ldots)$
denote the key of the k-th record added to the file. A record with key $\omega \in \Omega$
is hashed to storage location $F(\omega)$, where the hashing function F is given
(see [2], [3]).

Let $F_i = F(\omega_i)$ be the storage location to which the i-th record is mapped. We
assume that $F_1, F_2, F_3, \ldots$ is a sequence of i.i.d. random variables uniformly
distributed over the set of integers $A = \{1,2,\ldots,N\}$. A collision occurs when
two distinct records are hashed to the same location - i.e., when $F(\omega_i) = F(\omega_j)$
for $\omega_i \neq \omega_j$.

Several methods for collision resolution are known ([2], [4], [5], [6]). In this
work we analyze in detail the so-called chaining method. According to this method,
all records mapped to the same location are chained to each other to form a list
structure. The first record of a list is stored either at location $F(\omega)$ or,
if location $F(\omega)$ is occupied, at a randomly selected empty location which is
termed alternative start.

Our aim is to calculate various measures of performance for the chaining method.
Retrieval performance is evaluated via two measures: (i) the expected number of
probes needed to find a record in the file, and (ii) the expected number of probes
required to discover that a record is not in the file.

Measures of performance for addition of a record are also derived. Record addition
is composed of two steps: (i) finding an empty location, and (ii) writing the
record and updating all the pointers involved. The number of I/O operations
needed for the first step depends on the amount of information available on the
occupancy of the file. For various information levels the relevant performance
measures are calculated and compared.

Updating an existing record consists of two stages: reading the record and
rewriting it. Since the location of the record remains the same, no pointers
have to be changed. Thus, the expected number of I/O operations needed is equal

to the expected number of probes needed to find the record in the file plus one.

A special case of our general problem has been studied by Johnson [1], who treated the problem of addressing on secondary keys. He derives an approximate formula for the expected number of probes for retrieval of a record in the file. An exact formula which is easily derived from our general results shows that Johnson's approximation is a good one.

The paper is composed of the following sections. Section 2 describes the chaining method and defines the underlying stochastic process. In section 3 we derive the multi-dimensional time-dependent generating function of the process and calculate the moments of various state-variables. These formulae are used in section 4 to calculate the retrieval performance measures. In section 5 the process of record addition is analyzed. We consider the possibility of maintaining an additional pointer directly to the end of each list, and find that the additional pointer does not improve the performance of the addition process.

THE CHAINING METHOD

Consider a random-access file with N storage locations. Let $F: \Omega \to A$ be the hashing function. We assume that F is a random variable uniformly distributed over the set $A = \{1,2,\dots,N\}$. Records are added to the file from time to time. Suppose that a record with key $\omega \in \Omega$ is to be added to the file. The record is hashed to storage location $F(\omega)$. If this location is empty, the record is stored there. If the storage location is occupied, the record has to be assigned to some empty location which is randomly selected from the set of empty locations. From symmetry considerations the actual method of assignment is irrelevant to the future development of the process, since the empty locations are interchangeable.

For retrieval purposes it is necessary to keep track of the actual addresses of the records. All records hashed to the same location are chained to each other to form a list structure. Retrieval of a record requires a search along the list generated by all records mapped by F to the same location. Once the beginning of the list is found, the required key is searched along the list. However, it might require additional effort to determine the beginning of the list, since the first record in the chain might have found an occupied location and may have had to be assigned to an alternative address.

We start the process at time $\tau_o = 0$ with an empty file.

Let $0 < \tau_1 < \tau_2 < \dots < \tau_k < \dots$ be the sequence of arrival instants of records. τ_k is the instant of arrival of the k-th record with key ω_k.

We assume that the inter-arrival times $\tau_k - \tau_{k-1}$ (k = 1,2,...) are indepedent

random variables and imbed the process at instants $\{\tau_k+0\}_{k=0}^{\infty}$. We say that the
system is in stage (step) k when there are k records in the file. Storage
locations are gradually numbered (for the analysis) along with the development
of the process: the location occupied by the k-th record is denoted as the k-th
storage location. That is, at the k-th step k   storage locations are occupied
and numbered by the numbers 1,2,...,k. Once a number is assigned to a location,
it does not change. Addition of records to the file generates lists. We say that
a record with key $\omega \in \Omega$ belongs to list $\hat{F}(\omega)$, where $\hat{F}(\omega)$ is the number given
by our numbering procedure to the location to which the record is hashed. The
records of the same list are chained to each other by <u>pointers</u> according to the
order of arrival.

List $\hat{F}(\omega)$ = i starts either at location i or at some alternative location j
(j ≠ i). It starts at location i if the first record in the list, which
arrives at instant τ_i, is hashed to an empty location. Otherwise, if it is
hashed to an occupied location, it is assigned to an <u>alternative start</u>, j. It
follows that two pointers are required for each occupied location:

(a)   a <u>link</u> to the next record in the list, if any, or an indication, ϕ, that the
      record is the last (so far) in the list.

(b)   an address of the alternative start, if any, or ϕ, if none exists.

Let $X_i^{(k)}$ be the number of records in the file belonging to list i at the k-th
step, and let $Y_i^{(k)}$ be defined as follows:

$$Y_i^{(k)} = \begin{cases} 1, & \text{if location i is occupied by a foreign record at the k-th step} \\ 0, & \text{otherwise} \end{cases}$$

where a foreign record is one with a key ω such that $\hat{F}(\omega) \neq i$.

It follows that whenever $Y_i^{(k)}$ = 1 and $X_i^{(k)}$ > 0 list i has an alternative
start. Also, $Y_i^{(i)}$ = 1 implies $Y_i^{(k)}$ = 1 for k > i. The chaining method
is best illustrated graphically. A storage location is represented by a
rectangle shown in figure 1.

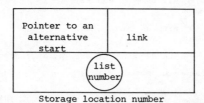

Figure 1: Graphic representation of a storage location

In figure 2 we demonstrate a list (list i, say) with no alternative start in
stage k:

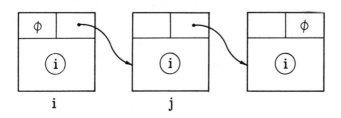

Figure 2:   List with no alternative start.

In this case, $X_i^{(k)} = 3$, $Y_i^{(k)} = 0$.

Now consider list j of figure 2.   If no record has been mapped to list j   up to
this step (the k-th), then $X_j^{(k)} = 0$, yet $Y_j^{(k)} = 1$.   Suppose $X_j^{(k)} = 2$;   then we
get the configuration shown in figure 3, for which $X_i^{(k)} = 3$, $Y_i^{(k)} = 0$, $X_j^{(k)} = 2$,
$Y_j^{(k)} = 1$.

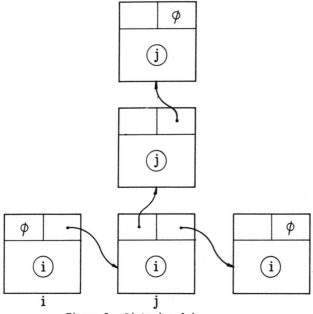

Figure 3: Lists i and j.

THE MULTI-DIMENSIONAL TIME-DEPENDENT GENERATING FUNCTION

Consider the 2N-dimensional stochastic process $\{(\underline{X}^{(k)}, \underline{Y}^{(k)}), \ k = 0,1,2,\ldots\}$ where $(\underline{X}^{(k)}, \underline{Y}^{(k)}) = (X_1^{(k)}, X_2^{(k)}, \ldots, X_N^{(k)}, Y_1^{(k)}, Y_2^{(k)}, \ldots Y_N^{(k)})$. The process $\{(\underline{X}^{(k)}, \underline{Y}^{(k)}), \ k = 0,1,2,\ldots\}$ is Markovian, but its transition probabilities are non-stationary. For each k, we define the 2N-dimensional generating function

$$G^{(k)}(\underline{z},\underline{v}) = E(\underline{z}^{\underline{X}^{(k)}} \cdot \underline{v}^{\underline{Y}^{(k)}}) \tag{1}$$

where, $\underline{z}, \underline{v} \in R^N$, $\underline{z}, \underline{v} \geq \underline{0}$ and, for non-negative $\underline{a}, \underline{b} \in R^N$, we define $\underline{a}^{\underline{b}} \equiv \prod_{i=1}^{N} a_i^{b_i}$. We derive a recursive equation for $G^{(k)}(\underline{z},\underline{v})$.

Theorem 1: $G^{(k)}(\underline{z},\underline{v})$ satisfies the following recursive equation:

$$G^{(k+1)}(\underline{z},\underline{v}) = (1/N)\underline{v}_{k+1}(\sum_{i=1}^{k} z_i)G^{(k)}(\underline{z},\underline{v}) + (1-k/N)z_{k+1}G^{(k)}(\underline{z},\underline{v}) \tag{2}$$

$$(k = 0,1,2,\ldots)$$

where $G^{(0)}(\underline{z},\underline{v}) = 1$.

Proof: $\hat{F}(\omega_{k+1}) = i$ ($i = 1,2,\ldots,k$) with probability $1/N$. On the other hand, ω_{k+1} belongs to a non-occupied location - which will be numbered as the (k+1)st storage location - with probability $1-k/N$. That is,

$$\hat{F}(\omega_{k+1}) = \begin{cases} i & \text{w.p.} \quad 1/N \quad (i = 1,2,\ldots,k) \\ \\ k+1 & \text{w.p.} \quad 1-k/N \end{cases}$$

If $\hat{F}(\omega_{k+1}) = i$ ($i = 1,2,\ldots,k$), the (k+1)st record becomes a foreign record in location k+1, so $Y_{k+1}^{(k+1)} = 1$. This record belongs to the i-th list. Hence, $X_i^{(k+1)} = X_i^{(k)} + 1$. On the other hand, if $\hat{F}(\omega_{k+1}) = k+1$, $Y_{k+1}^{(k+1)} = 0$ and $X_{k+1}^{(k+1)} = 1$ since a new list - list k+1 - starts at location k+1. We have

$$G^{(k+1)}(\underline{z},\underline{v}) = \sum_{i=1}^{k} E(\underline{z}^{\underline{X}^{(k+1)}} \cdot \underline{v}^{\underline{Y}^{(k+1)}} \mid \hat{F}(\omega_{k+1}) = i) \cdot P(\hat{F}(\omega_{k+1}) = i)$$

$$+ E(\underline{z}^{\underline{X}^{(k+1)}} \cdot \underline{v}^{\underline{Y}^{(k+1)}} \mid \hat{F}(\omega_{k+1}) = k+1) \cdot P(\hat{F}(\omega_{k+1}) = k+1)$$

$$= \sum_{i=1}^{k} E(\underline{z}^{\underline{X}^{(k)} + \underline{e}_i} \cdot \underline{v}^{\underline{Y}^{(k)} + \underline{e}_{k+1}}) \cdot 1/N + E(\underline{z}^{\underline{X}^{(k)} + \underline{e}_{k+1}} \cdot \underline{v}^{\underline{Y}^{(k)}})(1-k/N)$$

where $\underline{e}_j$ is the unit vector with 1 in the j-th place. Since $\underline{a}^{\underline{e}_j} = a_j$, equation (2) readily follows,   Q.E.D.

It is interesting to write specifically the generating functions $G^{(k)}(\underline{z},\underline{v})$ for $k = 0,1,2$ and interpret them. $G^{(0)}(\underline{z},\underline{v}) = 1$, since in step 0 the file is empty. $G^{(1)}(\underline{z},\underline{v}) = z_1$. Indeed, the first record is assigned - by our numbering method - to location 1. $G^{(2)}(\underline{z},\underline{v}) = (1/N)z_1^2 v_2 + (1-1/N)z_1 z_2$, for the second record is hashed to storage location 1 with probability $1/N$ and to an empty storage location with probability $1-1/N$.

Theorem 2: $G^{(k)}(\underline{z},\underline{v})$ is a polynomial in $\{z_i\}_{i=1}^k$ and $\{v_i\}_{i=1}^k$. The maximal power of z_i is $k-i+1$ $(i = 1,2,\ldots,k)$, and of v_i is 1.

Proof: By induction on k.

Remark: Theorem 2 represents the following facts:

(i) $X_i^{(k)} = Y_i^{(k)} = 0$ for $i = k+1,k+2,\ldots,N$.

(ii) $Y_i^{(k)} = 0,1$ for all i,k.

(iii) $X_i^{(k)} \leq k-i+1$ for $k = 1,2,\ldots,N$; $i = 1,2,\ldots,k$ since list i may be augmented by records only at instants τ_j for $j \geq i$.

Given the recursive equation (2) various moments - which will be needed in the sequel - may be calculated. We summarize the results in corollary 1.

Corollary 1: For every $k = 1,2,\ldots,N$; $i = 1,2,\ldots,k$

$$E(Y_i^{(k)}) = (i-1)/N \tag{3}$$

$$E(X_i^{(k)}) = 1+(k-2i+1)/N \tag{4}$$

$$E((X_i^{(k)})^2) = (k-i)(3N-3i+k+1)/N^2+1-(i-1)/N \tag{5}$$

$$E(X_i^{(k)}Y_i^{(k)}) = (k-i)(i-1)/N^2 \tag{6}$$

Proof: Differentiating equation (2) with respect to v_i and putting $\underline{z} = \underline{v} = \underline{1}$, we get $E(Y_i^{(k+1)}) = E(Y_i^{(k)})$. (The interpretation is obvious: $Y_i^{(k)}$ is determined at step $k = i$ and does not change thereafter). Also, using the fact that

$\frac{\partial}{\partial v_{k+1}} G^{(k)} (\underline{z}, \underline{v}) = 0$, we have $E(Y_{k+1}^{(k+1)}) = \frac{\partial}{\partial v_{k+1}} G^{(k+1)} (\underline{z}, \underline{v})\big|_{\underline{z}=\underline{v}=\underline{1}} = k/N$, which

implies equation 3. In a similar method we derive $E(X_{k+1}^{(k+1)}) = 1-k/N$. Now,

$$E(X_i^{(k+1)}) = \frac{\partial}{\partial z_i} G^{(k+1)} (\underline{1}, \underline{1}) = 1/N + E(X_i^{(k)}).$$

Thus,

$$E(X_i^{(k)}) = \sum_{j=i}^{k-1} 1/N + E(X_i^{(i)}) = (k-i)/N + 1-(i-1)/N$$

$$= 1 + (k-2i+1)/N.$$

To get (5) we write

$$\frac{\partial}{\partial z_i^2} G^{(k)} (\underline{1}, \underline{1}) = \sum_{j=i}^{k-1} (2/N) E(X_i^{(j)}).$$

Substituting equation (4) in the above yields (5).

Finally,

$$E(X_i^{(k+1)} Y_i^{(k+1)}) = \frac{\partial}{\partial z_i} \frac{\partial}{\partial v_i} G^{(k+1)} (\underline{1}, \underline{1}) =$$

$$= E(X_i^{(k)} Y_i^{(k)}) + (1/N) E(Y_i^{(k)}).$$

Using (3) and the fact that $X_i^{(i)} Y_i^{(i)} = 0$ we get

$$E(X_i^{(k)} Y_i^{(k)}) = \sum_{j=i}^{k-1} (i-1)/N^2 = (k-i)(i-1)/N^2 \qquad Q.E.D.$$

We note that equations (3), (4), (5) and (6) may also be derived by using direct probabilistic arguments.

RETRIEVAL PERFORMANCE MEASURES

In the previous section, we analyzed the Markov process $\{(\underline{x}^{(k)}, \underline{y}^{(k)}), k = 0,1,2,...\}$. The results obtained there will now be used to derive various performance measures. We restrict the analysis to input-output (I/O) considerations, which are frequently dominant in management information systems. In this section we deal with the costs associated with the retrieval of records where we measure costs by the number of probes needed for retrieval

of a single record. In the next section, we calculate the costs incurred by the
addition of records to the file.

Consider a retrieval request for a record with key $\omega \in \Omega$, where k records are
in the file. The retrieval procedure may be described by the flow-chart in
figure 4. We use the following notation:

a = address of current storage location read,

key(a) = key of record in storage location a,

link(a) = address of next record in the list to which a belongs.

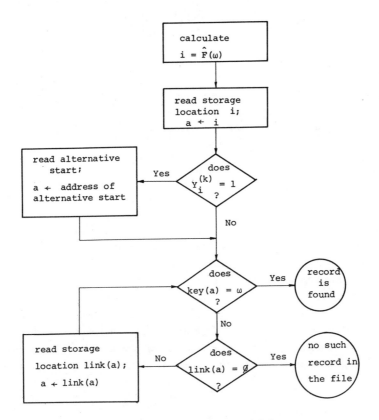

Figure 4: Flow chart for retrieval of a record with key ω.

Let C(k) be the expected number of probes needed for retrieval of one of the
k records currently stored in the file. We assume that each of the k records is
equally likely to be requested. A record in the file belongs to list i with
probability $x_i^{(k)}/k$. The search for a record in list i consists of (a) finding
the beginning of the list, which requires $Y_i^{(k)}$ probes, and (b) moving along
the list until the record is found. Since each record in the list has the same
probability of being requested, the average number of moves is $(X_i^{(k)}+1)/2$.
Hence ,

$$C(k) = \sum_{i=1}^{k} E[\frac{x_i^{(k)}}{k} (Y_i^{(k)} + \frac{x_i^{(k)}+1}{2})] \tag{7}$$

Note that when we sum in (7) from 1 to k we allow for the possibility
of empty lists with $x_i^{(k)} = 0$. Since $\sum_{i=1}^{k} X_i^{(k)} = k$, we have

$$C(k) = \frac{1}{2} + \frac{1}{k} \sum_{i=1}^{k} [E(X_i^{(k)} Y_i^{(k)}) + \frac{1}{2}E(X_i^{(k)})^2]$$

Substituting from equations (6) and (5) yields

$$C(k) = 1 - \frac{1}{2NK} \sum_{i=1}^{k} (i-1) + \frac{1}{2N^2 k} \sum_{i=1}^{k} (k-i)^2 + \frac{3N-1}{2N^2 k} \sum_{i=1}^{k} (k-i)$$

By algebraic manipulation we finally obtain

<u>Theorem 3:</u> $C(k) = 1 + (k-1)(3N+k-2)/(6N^2)$ $(k = 1,2,...,N)$ \qquad (8)

It is seen that C(k) is a monotone increasing convex function of k and, for
fixed k, it is a monotone decreasing convex function of N.

Suppose a record with key ω, which is <u>not</u> in the file, is requested at the k-th
step.   Let D(k) be the expected number of probes needed to discover that the
required key is not there. The key is hashed to an empty location with probability
1-k/N. In such an event the number of probes is one. For each i = 1,2,...,k
$\hat{F}(\omega) = i$ with probability 1/N. In that case the number of probes required is
$X_i^{(k)} + Y_i^{(k)}$. The expected number of probes, given that $\hat{F}(\omega) = i$ is, by (3)
and (4),

$$E(X_i^{(k)} + Y_i^{(k)}) = 1+(k-i)/N. \tag{9}$$

Note that equation (9) may be obtained directly as follows: The search is done
along all records sent to location i. At time τ_i a record was stored in

location i. This could have been the first record in list i or a foreign record.
In the following k-i steps a record is hashed to location i with probability 1/N.
Thus, equation (9) readily follows. We have

Theorem 4: $D(k) = (1-k/N) \cdot 1 + \sum\limits_{i=1}^{k} (1/N)[1 + (k-i)/N] = 1 + k(k-1)/(2N^2)$ (10)

$D(k)$ has the same qualitative properties as $C(k)$.

In figure 5 we illustrate the behavior of $C(k)$ and $D(k)$ for a file with
$N = 1,000$ storage locations.

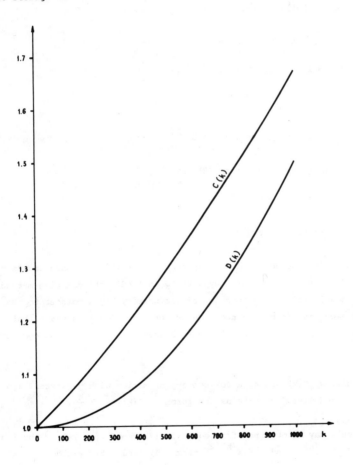

Figure 5: Behavior of $C(k)$ and $D(k)$

From figure 5 it is evident that $C(k)$ and $D(k)$ possess the following properties:

Corollary 2:   (i) $C(k) \geqslant D(k)$ $k = 1,2,\ldots,N$

(ii) $C(k) < 5/3$ $k = 1,2,\ldots,N$

(iii) $D(k) < 1.5$ $k = 1,2,\ldots,N$

(iv) For $k \ll N$, $C(k) \sim 1 + (1/2N) \cdot k$

Proof: (i) follows from equations (8) and (10) since

$$C(k) - D(k) = (k-1)(3N-2k-2)/(6N^2) \geqslant 0.$$

(ii) From (8) we have

$$C(k) \leqslant C(N) = 1 + (N-1)(4N-2)/(6N^2) < 5/3.$$

(iii) From (10),

$$D(k) \leqslant D(N) = 1 + N(N-1)/(2N^2) < 1.5.$$

(iv) Rewrite equation (8) as

$$C(k) = 1 + \frac{k-1}{N}(\frac{1}{2} + \frac{1}{6}\frac{k}{N} - \frac{1}{3N}) \ .$$

For $k \ll N$, the result follows.

The above results may be compared with Johnson's work [1]. Johnson treats the problem of addressing on secondary keys, using an 'indirect' chaining method. Since a record's location is a function of the primary key a pointer to the beginning of each list is maintained. In our presentation this means that $Y_i^{(k)} = 1$ for all $i \leqslant k$. Obviously, this reduces the dimension and complexity of the problem.

Johnson calculates $C(k)$ using a Poisson approximation with parameter k/N for the length of each list. He obtains the formula $C(k) = 2 + \frac{k}{2N}$.

The exact result may be obtained from equation (7) when $Y_i^{(k)} = 1$. Substituting the values of $E(X_i^{(k)})$ and $E((X_i^{(k)})^2)$ from (4) and (5) yields,

$$C(k) = 2 + \frac{k-1}{2N} \tag{11}$$

Comparing equations (11) and (8), it is clear that Johnson's method requires more I/O operations. For $k = 1$, the difference is one probe; when k approaches N, the difference approaches 5/6.

ADDITION OF RECORDS

Consider the (k+1)st record arriving at instant τ_{k+1} where there are already k records in the file. The addition of the record is composed of two stages: (1) searching for an empty location, and (2) storing the record there and updating the relevant pointers. Each of the two stages may be analyzed separately.

First consider the searching procedure. The record is mapped to location $\hat{F}(\omega_{k+1})$. An input operation is always required to read the content of location $\hat{F}(\omega_{k+1})$. If $\hat{F}(\omega_{k+1})$ is empty, the search is completed. Otherwise, an alternative location has to be found.

The amount of effort needed to select the alternative location depends on the level of information available on the occupancy of the file. Three different levels of information will be analyzed:

(i) No information.   In this case a location is selected randomly among all N locations in the file. If the location so selected is empty, the record will be stored there. Otherwise, another similar independent trial is repeated until an empty location is found. Since no information is gathered during this process it might happen that an occupied location will be selected more than once.
We indicate this information level with the subscript n.

(ii) Partial information · Here we keep track of the locations which have been tried in this search and found occupied. These locations are no longer candidates for storing the (k+1)st record.
This information level will be indicated by the subscript p.

(iii) Full information.   With this level of information the addresses of all
                               k occupied locations are known. (Such information
                               may compactly be maintained in a bit-map). The
                               subscript f will indicate this level of information.

Let $S(k)$ be the number of input operations starting from reading $\hat{F}(\omega_{k+1})$
until an empty location is found for the $(k+1)$st record. For each of the
above levels of information, denote the expected value of $S(k)$ by
$L_n(k)$, $L_p(k)$ or $L_f(k)$ respectively. We have,

Theorem 5: For $k = 0,1,2,\ldots,N-1$

$\quad$ (i) $\quad L_n(k) = \dfrac{1}{1-k/N}$ $\hspace{10cm}$ (12)

$\quad$ (ii) $\quad L_p(k) = \dfrac{1}{1-k/(N+1)}$ $\hspace{8cm}$ (13)

$\quad$ (iii) $L_f(k) = 1+k/N$ $\hspace{9cm}$ (14)

Proof: (i) It is readily seen that $S(k)$ has a geometric distribution with
a probability of success (= finding an empty location) $1-k/N$. Hence,
$L_n(k) = 1/(1-k/N)$.

$\quad$ (ii) To indicate the dependence of $L_p(k)$ on N we write $L_p(k,N)$
instead of $L_p(k)$. $L_p(k,N)$ satisfies the recursive equation

$\quad L_p(k,N) = (1-k/N)\cdot 1 + (k/N)[1 + L_p(k-1,N-1)]$

or

$\quad L_p(k) = 1 + (k/N)L_p(k-1,N-1)$ $\hspace{7cm}$ (15)

Equation (13) now follows by induction on N for each $k = 0,1,2,\ldots,N-1$ and
from the uniqueness of the solution for equation (15).

$\quad$ (iii) Location $\hat{F}(\omega_{k+1})$ is occupied with probability k/N. Hence,
$L_f(k) = (1-k/N)\cdot 1 + (k/N)\cdot 2 = 1+k/N$.

Note that in deriving $L_f(k)$ we assume that the content of a storage location
has to be read before it is updated.

<u>Corollary 3</u>: $L_f(k) \leq L_p(k) \leq L_n(k)$

<u>Proof</u>: Rewriting the expressions for $L(k)$ in equations (12) and (13) we have

$$L_f(k) = 1 + \frac{k}{N} \leq L_p(k) = 1 + \frac{k}{N+1-k} \leq L_n(k) = 1 + \frac{k}{N-k} \quad .$$

As was expected the number of I/O operations increases as the level of
information decreases. The improvement obtained by partial information relative
to no information is negligible when k is not close to N.   This fact may
be understood by considering the process of finding an empty location as
sampling from an urn containing N balls, of which k are red and N-k are
white, until a white ball is drawn. The case of no information is equivalent
to sampling with replacement, while the case of partial information is equivalent
to sampling without replacement. The difference between $L_n(k)$ and $L_p(k)$
is due to the different sampling methods.

When k approaches N, both $L_n(k)$ and $L_p(k)$ increase rapidly while $L_f(k)$
increases only linearly. These facts are seen in figure 6 for the case of
N = 1,000.

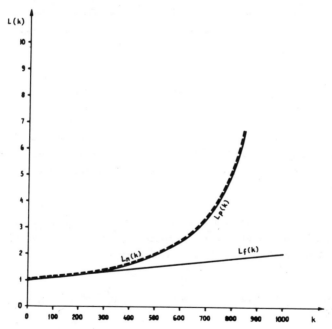

Figure 6: $L_n(k)$, $L_p(k)$ and $L_f(k)$.

We now calculate the number of I/O operations required for the second stage of record addition - i.e., for storing the record and updating the pointers. We assume here that the cost of writing a record is the same as its reading cost. (Our results may easily be generalized when assuming that the above costs are not equal). Besides writing the record it has to be chained to its list, which requires passing along the list up to its last record. Suppose $\hat{F}(\omega_{k+1}) = i$. The number of I/O operations needed in this stage depends on the values of $X_i^{(k)}$ and $Y_i^{(k)}$ as given in table 1.

Case	$X_i^{(k)}$	$Y_i^{(k)}$	number of I/O operations needed for		
			Scanning the list to find the last record	pointer updating	storing the record
(a)	0	0	0	0	1
(b)	0	1	0	1	1
(c)	≥ 1	0	$X_i^{(k)} - 1$	1	1
(d)	≥ 1	1	$X_i^{(k)}$	1	1

Table 1: number of I/O operations needed for various (sub)steps in the second stage of record addition.

Table 1 is constructed as a consequence of the following considerations.

Case (a): Location $\hat{F}(\omega_{k+1})$ has already been read in the first stage; all
          that remains is to write the record there.

Case (b): In this case location i is occupied by a foreign record and the (k+1)st
          record starts list i. Therefore, a pointer to the alternative start
          is registered in $\hat{F}(\omega_{k+1})$ and the record is stored at the (k+1)st
          location.

Case (c): List i starts at location $\hat{F}(\omega_{k+1}) = i$, which has already been read.
          Scanning the rest of the list requires $X_i^{(k)} - 1$ operations. Storing
          the record and updating the last link requires two additional
          operations.

Case (d): Since $\hat{F}(\omega_{k+1})$ does not belong to list i, $X_i^{(k)} + 2$ operations are
          needed.

Let V(k) be the number of I/O operations required for the second stage of
adding the (k+1)st record.

Case (a) occurs when location $\hat{F}(\omega_{k+1})$ is empty. This happens with probability
1-k/N and requires V(k) = 1 operations.

In cases (b), (c) and (d), $V(k) = X_i^{(k)} + Y_i^{(k)} + 1$, hence,

$$E[V(k)] = (1-k/N) \cdot 1 + \sum_{i=1}^{k} (1/N) E[X_i^{(k)} + Y_i^{(k)} + 1] =$$

$$= 1 + (1/N) \sum_{i=1}^{k} E[X_i^{(k)} + Y_i^{(k)}]$$

Substituting result (9) yields

$$E[V(k)] = 1 + k/N + k(k-1)/(2N^2) \tag{16}$$

which is a convex increasing function of k.

We now consider a variant of the addition procedure in which an additional
pointer directly to the end of each list is maintained. The additional pointer
nullifies the need to scan a list in order to find its last record. Location i
will now contain three pointers as sketched in figure 7.

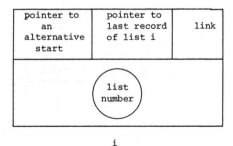

Figure 7: Location i with 3 pointers.

A typical list (list i, say) without an alternative start is shown in figure 8.

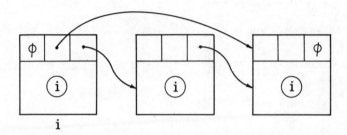

Figure 8: List with no alternative start using an
additional pointer.

A list with an alternative start is shown in figure 9. Observe that the
pointer to the end of list i is recorded in storage location i and not in the
alternative start.

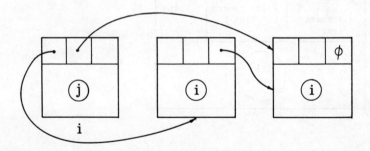

Figure 9: List with an alternative start using an
additional pointer.

We now calculate $E[U(k)]$, the expected number of I/O operations for the
second stage of addition of the (k+1)st record when we use an additional pointer.

If location $\hat{F}(\omega_{k+1}) = i$ is empty, then $U(k) = 1$. If location i is occupied, then some or all of the following four operations may be needed.

(i) Finding and reading the last record in list i. This requires a single input operation, since the last record is directly pointed to.

(ii) Updating the link in the last record. The link will now point to location k+1.

(iii) Updating the pointer to the last record in list i. This requires a single writing operation in location $\hat{F}(\omega_{k+1})$.

(iv) Storing the (k+1)st record.

All four operations are needed except for the following two cases: (a) When $X_i^{(k)} = 0$ and $Y_i^{(k)} = 1$, the first two operations are not needed. The pointers to the end of the list and to the alternative start are both updated in storage location i in a single output operation. Together with storing the new record, a total of two I/O operations is needed.

(b) If $X_i^{(k)} = 1$ and $Y_i^{(k)} = 0$, the last record in list i is obviously stored in location $\hat{F}(\omega_{k+1}) = i$. Thus, a total of two output operations will suffice.

Therefore,

$$E[U(k)] = (1-k/N)\cdot 1 + (1/N) \sum_{i=1}^{k} [4 - 2P(X_i^{(k)} = 0, Y_i^{(k)} = 1)$$

$$- 2P(X_i^{(k)} = 1, Y_i^{(k)} = 0)] \qquad (17)$$

Since $P(X_i^{(k)} = 0, Y_i^{(k)} = 1) = \dfrac{\partial}{\partial v_i} G^{(k)}(\underline{z},\underline{v})\Big|_{\substack{z_i = v_i = 0 \\ z_j = v_j = 1}}$ for $j \neq i$

We have by differentiating equation (2) with respect to v_{k+1} and v_i, respectively, that

$$P(X_{k+1}^{(k+1)} = 0, Y_{k+1}^{(k+1)} = 1) = k/N \quad \text{and}$$

$$P(X_i^{(k+1)} = 0, Y_i^{(k+1)} = 1) = (1-1/N)P(X_i^{(k)} = 0, Y_i^{(k)} = 1) \quad \text{for} \quad i = 1,2,\ldots,k$$

Hence, by induction, for $i = 1,2,\ldots,k$,

$$P(X_i^{(k)} = 0, \; Y_i^{(k)} = 1) = \frac{i-1}{N}(1-\frac{1}{N})^{k-i} \tag{18}$$

The expression for $P(X_i^{(k)} = 1, \; Y_i^{(k)} = 0)$ is derived similarly from equation (2) by taking derivatives with respect to z_{k+1} and z_i. We have

$$P(X_i^{(k)} = 1, \; Y_i^{(k)} = 0) = (1 - \frac{i-1}{N})(1 - \frac{1}{N})^{k-i} \tag{19}$$

Finally, by substituting equations (18) and (19) in (17), we get

$$E[U(k)] = 1 + \frac{3k}{N} - \frac{2}{N} \sum_{i=1}^{k} (1 - \frac{1}{N})^{k-i} \tag{20}$$

Note that $P(X_i^{(k)} = 0, \; Y_i^{(k)} = 1) + P(X_i^{(k)} = 1, \; Y_i^{(k)} = 0) = P(X_i^{(k)} + Y_i^{(k)} = 1)$

$= P\binom{\text{records } i+1, \; i+2,\dots,k}{\text{do not belong to list } i} = (1 - \frac{1}{N})^{k-i}$. So, equation (20) could have been derived directly.

Now, $\sum_{i=1}^{k} (1 - \frac{1}{N})^{k-i} = \dfrac{1-(1 - \frac{1}{N})^k}{1/N}$. Hence,

$$E[U(k)] = -1 + \frac{3k}{N} + 2(1 - 1/N)^k \tag{21}$$

It is readily seen that $E[U(k)]$ is a monotone increasing convex function of k.

It is of interest to compare the performance of the two addition procedures. The result is that the addition of a pointer to the last record in the list does not improve the performance - i.e.:

Theorem 6: $E[U(k)] \geqslant E[V(k)]$ for every $k = 1,2,\dots,N$.

Proof: For $k = 1,2,\dots$ $(1 - \frac{1}{N})^k$ may be expanded to

$(1 - \frac{1}{N})^k = 1-k/N + \frac{k(k-1)}{2} (\frac{1}{N})^2 - \frac{k(k-1)(k-2)}{6} t^3$

where $0 < t < 1/N$. Hence

$$E[U(k)] = 1 + \frac{k}{N} + \frac{k(k-1)}{N^2} - \frac{k(k-1)(k-2)}{3} t^3$$

$$= E[V(k)] + \frac{1}{2} \frac{k(k-1)}{N^2} - \frac{k(k-1)(k-2)}{3} t^3$$

$$\geqslant E[V(k)] + \frac{k(k-1)}{N^2}[\frac{1}{2} - \frac{k-2}{3N}] \geqslant E[V(k)]$$

where equality holds only when k = 1.

Theorem 6 somewhat contradicts one's intuition. To understand this phenomenon,
we constructed table 2 in which the number of I/O operations in both methods is
compared.

$X_i^{(k)} + Y_i^{(k)}$	Number of I/O operations	
	without additional pointer	with additional pointer
0	1	1
1	2	2
2	3	4
3	4	4
4	5	4
5	6	4
.	.	.
.	.	.
.	.	.

Table 2: number of I/O
operations with and
without an additional
pointer

It is evident that the additional pointer decreases the number of I/O operations
only when $X_i^{(k)} + Y_i^{(k)} \geq 4$. However, the probability of $X_i^{(k)} + Y_i^{(k)} \geq 4$ (i.e.,
the probability of relatively long lists) is small, and therefore the expected
value of the number of I/O operations is smaller without the additional pointer.

REFERENCES

[1]   Johnson, L.R., "An Indirect Chaining Method for Addressing on Secondary
      Keys", CACM 4 (1961) 218-222.
[2]   Knuth, D.E., The Art of Computer Programming, Vol. 3, Section 6.4
      pp. 506-518, Addison Wesley, 1973.
[3]   Lum, V.Y., Yuen, P.S.T. and Dodd, M., "Key to Address Transform Techniques:
      A Fundamental Performance Study on Large Existing Formatted Files," CACM 14
      (1971), 228-239.
[4]   Morris, R., "Scatter Storage Techniques", CACM 11 (1968), 38-44.
[5]   Peterson, W.W.,"Addressing for Random-Access Storage", IBM J. of Research
      and Development 1 (1957), 130-146.
[6]   Van Der Pool, J.A., "Optimum Storage Allocation for Initial Loading of a
      File", IBM J. of Research and Development 16 (1972), 579-586.

COMPUTER PERFORMANCE, K.M. CHANDY AND M. REISER (EDS.)
NORTH HOLLAND PUBLISHING COMPANY, 1977

A PROGRAM BEHAVIOR MODEL FOR PAGING SYSTEMS

We-Min Chow and W. W. Chiu
Thomas J. Watson Research Center
Yorktown Heights, New York, USA

A program behavior model in a periodic aging environment is
analyzed. Properties of this model are derived based upon
the assumption that successive references made to the
contents of the same page form a renewal process. Using
this model we obtained the mean number of page exceptions
during an interval for the working set and LRU page
replacement algorithms. Finally, measurements from an
actual system are compared to the model results.

I. INTRODUCTION

An important component in contemporary virtual storage operating
systems is the management of real storage. These systems, in an
attempt to utilize system resources efficiently, keep only those
recently used program pages in storage. Since programs are known to
exhibit locality of storage references, algorithms such as LRU
(least-recently used) and working-set, have been proposed. However,
actual implementations, due to overhead reasons, can only approximate
such algorithms. In particular, IBM's OS/VS1, OS/VS2 systems employ
a periodic aging mechanism to identify those longest unreferenced
program pages for replacement [1,2]. In this paper, we analyze a
paging model, with periodic aging characteristics, to study the
performance of LRU and working-set algorithms. Particularly the mean
number of page exceptions during an interval are derived and
compared. The model uses the renewal program behavior assumption
introduced by Opderbeck and Chu [3]. We also compare data measured
from an MVS system to the model results.

II. THE MODEL

The paging model is motivated by the page aging mechanism in IBM's
MVS [2] operating system. The mechanism has supported both LRU and
working-set algorithms in the various releases of MVS. It works in
the following way. Associated with each page in real storage are a
page ID, a reference bit (RB) and an unreferenced interval counter
(UIC). RB is turned on by hardware when a reference is made to the
contents of the page. At periodic intervals, say h time units, the
status of RB is examined by software. If RB = 1 (on), both RB and
UIC are reset to zero. If RB = 0 (off), then UIC is incremented by
one. Figure 1(a) shows the status of pages before the end of an
h-interval. After having examined RB's, the values of UIC's are
updated as shown in Figure 1(b). In the case of LRU strategy only
pages with the largest UIC are replaced in response to page requests.
(Note that this is not strictly LRU since pages with the same UIC are
treated identically). For working-set strategy, pages with UIC
exceeding some criterion number are considered outside the
working-set and are removed. In this case, the UIC's of a
working-set are updated based on elapsed virtual processing time,
e.g. h is in CPU time units.

In essence, these two storage management strategies are implemented by looking at ages of pages (i.e. UIC numbers), instead of the order of page references. We next introduce a stochastic model to study the paging behavior under these two different strategies. In particular, we are interested in the mean number of page exceptions during an h-interval.

For convenience the model consists of infinitely many stages as shown in Figure 2, where stage numbers are one to one correspondent to UIC values. Let n_i be the number of pages in state i, i.e. n_i pages have their UIC's equal to i. A page in stage i is called an i-page. For each h-interval, all RB's are examined and each of the n_i pages has UIC changed from i to either $i+1$, if not referenced, or 0 otherwise. Referring to the model, it is clear that a total of n_i pages leave stage i after an h-interval. Let r_i be the return probability or the probability that an i-page is referenced in the next h-interval. The branching probability that a page leaves stage i for stage j is given by

$$P_{ij} = \begin{cases} r_i , & j=0 , \\ 1-r_i , & j=i+1 , \\ 0 , & \text{otherwise} , \quad i=0,1,\dots . \end{cases} \qquad (1)$$

One would expect that r_i is decreasing in i due to the well-known locality property that it is more likely to use the most recently referenced page than any others.

To complete our model construction, the following postulates are used:

   (i)   The total number of pages N in the logical memory is fixed such that

$$N = \sum_{i=0}^{\infty} n_i.$$

   All pages are treated independently and identically.

  (ii)   There is no distinction between CPU time and elapsed time. (This will be discussed in the last section).

 (iii)   The sequence of references made to the same page forms a renewal process with an inter-reference time T and a continuous distribution $F(.)$ such that $F(\infty) = 1$ and $E[T] < \infty$. Therefore, once a page is referenced, it simply takes another finite random time T to be re-referenced.
         (This assumption is first introduced in [3], where different pages may however have different F distributions).

The event that a page is in stage i implies that this page has not been referenced for at least ih time units. Consequently, the return probability at stage i is

$$r_i = P[\, ih < T \leq (i+1)h \mid T > ih \,]$$

$$= \frac{F_{i+1} - F_i}{1 - F_i} > 0 , \text{ if } h > 0 . \qquad (2)$$

where $F_i = F(ih) = P[T \leq ih]$, $i=0,1,\ldots$

In general one would expect that F is a DFR (decreasing failure rate) function, i.e. for $f(t) = F'(t)$

$$r(t) = \frac{f(t)}{1-F(t)} \qquad (3)$$

is non-increasing in t. Such a class of distributions implies that $P[T < t] < 1$, for any finite t and $r_i \geq r_j$, if $i < j$. There are several well-known distributions that fall into this class, such as hyperexponential.

Note that equation (2) does not present a precise measure of $\{r_i\}$. Because the age of a page is expressed as the number of h-intervals, the actual age of an i-page is between $(i+1)h$ and $(i+2)h$. However, the result is still considered to be accurate if h is small and is exact if F is exponential.

III. MODEL SOLUTION

Since a page's UIC value can only be changed at each h-interval, the status of each page can be characterized by a Markov Chain, imbedded at the beginning of each h-interval, with a transition matrix $P = ||P_{ij}||$. Since F is assumed to be an honest distribution with a finite mean and $r_i > 0$ for all i, it is easy to show that such a chain comprises of an irreducible aperiodic positive recurrent class and hence the steady-state distribution exists. After an h-interval the status of each page can be considered as the outcome of an independent trial either returns to stage zero or moves to the next stage. Let

$$\lim_{k \to \infty} P_{ij}^{(k)} = P_j \text{, for all i and j,}$$

Since pages are treated independently and identically, the age distribution of each individual page is $\{P_j\}$ and the number of j-pages has a binomial distribution with parameters N and P_j.

Note that $||P_{ij}||$ is the transition matrix for a single page, and $\{P_i\}$ can be obtained by solving

$$\sum_{i=0}^{\infty} P_{ij} P_i = P_j \text{ , for all j} \qquad (4)$$

$$\sum_{i=0}^{\infty} P_i = 1 .$$

According to (1), the transition matrix P is given by

$$P = \begin{bmatrix} r_0 & 1-r_0 & 0 & 0 & \\ r_1 & 0 & 1-r_1 & 0 & \\ r_2 & 0 & 0 & 1-r_2 & \\ \cdot & \cdot & \cdot & \cdot & \\ \cdot & \cdot & \cdot & & \cdot \\ \cdot & \cdot & \cdot & & & \cdot \end{bmatrix}$$

Equations (4) can then be rewritten as

$$P_0 = \sum_{i=0}^{\infty} r_i P_i$$

$$P_j = (1-r_{j-1}) P_{j-1} , \ j = 1,2,..$$

which, together with (2) imply

$$P_j = P_0 \prod_{i=0}^{j-1} (1-r_i)$$

$$= P_0 \prod_{i=0}^{j-1} \frac{1-F_{i+1}}{1-F_i} \qquad (5)$$

$$= \overline{F}_j \ P_0$$

where $\overline{F}_j = 1-F_j = P[T > jh]$.

Hence, $P_0 = (\sum_{j=0}^{\infty} \overline{F}_j)^{-1}$. $\qquad (6)$

We next derive the mean number of page exceptions during an h-interval under two replacement algorithms:

(i) Working-set strategy

Let N_i = number of i-pages under an equilibrium situation,
    X_i = number of i-pages being referenced during an h-interval
and k = window size.

A page belongs to the working-set if its UIC is less than or equal to k. A page exception occurs if a reference is made to a page which is not a member of the working-set. Therefore, the number of page exceptions is a function of k and given by

$$Z_W(k) = \sum_{i=k+1}^{\infty} X_i \qquad (7)$$

Note that given N_i, the conditional probability distribution of X_i is subject to a binomial form with N_i trials and a probability of success r_i. Thus

$$E[X_i] = E[E[X_i| N_i]]$$

$$= E[N_i] r_i$$

$$= N P_i r_i$$

$$= N (\overline{F}_i - \overline{F}_{i+1}) / S ,$$

where $S = \sum_{j=0}^{\infty} \overline{F}_j$

The expected number of page exception is

$$E[Z_W(k)] = \sum_{i=k+1}^{\infty} N(\overline{F}_i - \overline{F}_{i+1}) / S$$

$$= N\overline{F}_{k+1} / S \tag{8}$$

(ii)   LRU Strategy

Under LRU storage management strategy, the expectations of the number of page exceptions can be evaluated by means of order statistics [4]. As mentioned earlier, the status (UIC value) of pages can be interpreted as the outcome of   N independent identical experiments. Let $Y_1 \leq Y_2 \ldots \leq Y_N$ be the order statistics observed from these N experiments subject to the same distribution, $\{P_i\}$.

Thus, Y_j is the age of the jth most recently referenced page.   Let

   M = the real storage capacity in terms of pages

$$I_j = \begin{cases} 1, & \text{if the } Y_j\text{-page (i.e. the page of age } Y_j) \text{ is referenced during h} \\ 0, & \text{otherwise} \end{cases}$$

A page exception occurs if a page outside real storage is referenced, then the number of page exceptions during h is

$$Z_L(M) = \sum_{j=M+1}^{N} I_j \tag{9}$$

By definition of order statistics,

$$P[Y_i \leq k] = P[\text{ at least } i \text{ outcomes} \leq k]$$

$$= \sum_{v=i}^{N} \binom{N}{v} H_k^v (1-H_k)^{N-v}$$

$$\text{where } H_k = \sum_{j=0}^{k} P_j = \sum_{j=0}^{k} \overline{F}_j / S.$$

Consequently, the mean value is given by

$$E[Z_L(M)] = \sum_{j=M+1}^{N} P[I_j = 1]$$

$$= \sum_{j=M+1}^{N} \sum_{k=0}^{\infty} r_k \, P[Y_i = k] \tag{10}$$

$$= \sum_{i=M+1}^{N} \sum_{k=0}^{\infty} \sum_{v=i}^{N} \left(1 - \frac{\overline{F}_{k-1}}{\overline{F}_k}\right) \binom{N}{v} [H_k^v \overline{H}_k^{N-v} - H_{k-1}^v \overline{H}_{k-1}^{N-v}]$$

where $\overline{H}_k = 1 - H_k = \sum\limits_{j=k+1}^{\infty} \overline{F}_j \, / \, S$.

PAGE EXCEPTION RATE

We next compute page exception rate R which is defined by

$$R = \lim_{h \to 0} \frac{E\,[Z(h+t) - Z(t)]}{h} \text{ , for all } t \geq 0, \tag{11}$$

where $Z(t)$ is the number of page exceptions occurred during $(0,t)$.

The page exception rate under a working-set strategy, with a window size $v = ih$, becomes

$$R_W(v) = N \frac{\overline{F}(v)}{E[T]} \tag{12}$$

Note that $N/E[T]$ is the reference rate. The probability that a page does not belong to the working-set is $\overline{F}(v)$. The page exception rate is the rate of references made to the contents of the pages outside the working-set.

The page exception rate under LRU strategy can be written as

$$R_L(M) = \frac{N}{E[T]} \int_0^\infty \sum_{i=M}^{N-1} B\,(i \mid N-1, G(t))\, f(t)\, dt, \tag{13}$$

where $B\,(i \mid N,p) = \binom{N}{i} p^i \,(1-p)^{n-i}$, for $i = 0,1,\dots,N$, and $0 < p < 1$.

and $G(t) =$ Probability that a page has age less than t. Note that

$$\sum_{i=M}^{N-1} B(i \mid N-1, G(t))$$

is the probability that at least M out of $(N-1)$ pages have ages less than t. Consequently, the integration in (13) gives us the probability that a page is not in the LRU stack. For computational purposes, these binomial terms can be evaluated by normal approximations [5].

IV. MODEL RESULTS

In this section we compare measurement data from an MVS system with the model results. The measurement tool used is a software monitor called RESMON [9]. RESMON both samples periodically and traces system and workload information. Measurements are obtained during

the execution of a benchmark job stream of 10 jobs in uni-programming
mode (i.e. one batch initiator). The sample interval output includes
status information on each batch program page. Since the working-set
window parameter chosen for this experiment is set to be very large
no explicit page stealing occurs and the sampling frequency is always
higher than the UIC update frequency. Program page status includes
RB and UIC. Figure 3 is the age (or UIC) histogram from these
samples. The histogram is fitted with a theoretic function which
then becomes the input to the model. To minimize the distortion on
the experiment we chose not to measure the required page
inter-reference distribution since instruction tracing introduces too
much overhead. The histogram is fitted with a k-phase
hyper-exponential,

$$g(t) \quad = \quad \sum_{j=1}^{k} \beta_j \, \alpha_j \, e^{-\alpha_j t} \;, t > o$$

The parameters are obtained from **Min-Chi-Square** estimators [8]. The
cases with k=2,3 and 4 are investigated and the results are given in
Table I. Since the improvement is not significant when k is
increased from 3 to 4, it is assumed that k = 3 and then $(\alpha_1, \alpha_2, \alpha_3)$ =
(3.91, 0.49, 0.13) and $(\beta_1, \beta_2, \beta_3)$ = (0.62, 0.17, 0.21). The observed
histogram and the theoretical plot are shown in Figure 3. From the
age distribution, g(t), we obtain the inter-reference time
distribution. According to renewal theory this distribution function
is given as follows

$$F(t) \quad = \quad 1 - g(t) \, E[T]$$

$$= \quad 1 - \sum_{j=1}^{k} \lambda_j \, e^{-\alpha_j t}$$

where $\lambda_j \quad = \quad \beta_j \, \alpha_j \, / \, \sum_{i=1}^{k} (\beta_j \, \alpha_i) \, , j = 1,..,k$.

then

$$\overline{\lambda} \quad = \quad (0.957, 0.032, 0.011)$$

Figure 4 shows the density function, f(t), the tail distribution,
$\overline{F}(t)$, and the failure rate function, r(t) = f(t)/$\overline{F}(t)$. The mean and
the variance of inter-reference time are respectively 0.395 and
0.847. Since a total of 26747 UIC's are read in 828 samples we let
$N \simeq 26747/828 \simeq 32$.

The page exception rates per page are computed. The case of LRU is
given in Figure 5 and working-set case in Figure 6. When the window
size is 0.6, the page exception rate per page is about 0.325 and an
average working-set size equal to 20. From Figure 5 under an LRU
strategy with M = 20, the rate is approximately the same (i.e.
0.325). This very result holds for the entire computed range.

Finally, we compare our theoretical results with measurements. Let
x_i be the total count that an i-page is changed into a 0-page.
Thus, if the window size is set to be k·h (i.e. the working-set
includes those pages with UIC numbers less than or equal to k-1), the

average number of page exceptions per page during the h-interval is given by

$$\sum_{j=0}^{k-1} x_i \bigg/ \sum_{i=0}^{\infty} x_i .$$

We compare in figure 7 this observed number and the expected number computed by using equation (8). For small k (e.g. k = 1,2,3) the relative difference is about 10 - 30%. The curve shows a good match in the range of k = 4 to 15. For k > 15, the worst case may produce 50% relative error. But this region is very unstable because the observed number of page exceptions are very few. The detailed computational results are given in Table II.

V. DISCUSSION AND CONCLUSION

We have presented a paging model to compute the mean number of page exceptions during a given time interval under LRU and working-set strategies. It can be shown by using equations (12) and (13) that

(1) Page exception rates are the same for the LRU and working-set replacement algorithms under the exponential inter-reference time assumption when the average working-set size is equal to the LRU stack length.

(2) These rates are linear functions of the average number of allocated pages for identical exponential inter-reference times, and are decreasing convex functions if inter-reference time distribution is hyperexponential.

Numerical results indicate that the expected number of page exceptions during a fixed interval is not sensitive to replacement algorithms. (see also [6], [7]).

The assumption of identical pages in our model can be relaxed as in [3]. Assuming that pages have different inter-reference times, however, will introduce two difficulties:

   (1) More computational effort is required, this is particularly the case if N is large.

   (2) Some pages may be referenced very infrequently, and that it is not easy to obtain a good theoretical distribution for small sample size.

In spite of its simple structure our model compares reasonably well with empirical observations for the case of working-set replacement. We are not able to obtain an LRU stack list (the measured system does not implement LRU method). However, one would expect that theoretical and observed results are close to those under working-set strategy. Another attractive feature is that it is much easier to measure age distribution than inter-reference time distribution. The renewal assumption allows us to have a rather simple relation between these two distributions. Consequently, UIC values can be used as input to our model.

When the computer system is running under multiprogramming environment, the UIC's of all pages are updated based upon either CPU time (for working-set strategy or LRU with a set of fixed individual stack lengths) or elasped time (for global LRU). In the latter case, if a program received less CPU time due to a lower dispatching priority and/or longer I/O delays its allocated pages (pages in the global LRU stack) may be reduced and thus, the program would experience a higher page exception rate. Consequently, postulate (ii) in Section (II) is no longer acceptable. This case should be the subject of future work.

VI. <u>REFERENCES</u>

[1] Wheeler, T.F. (1974). "OS/VS1 Concepts and Philosophies," IBM System Journal, Vol. 13, No. 3.
[2] "OS/VS2 Scheduler and Supervisor Logic," Vol 1. Form SY28-0624-0, IBM Data Processing Division, White Plains, N.Y.
[3] Opderbeck, H. and Chu, W.W. (1975). "The Renewal Model for Program Behavior," SIAM J. Computer, Vol. 4, No. 3.
[4] David, H.A. (1970). "Order Statistics," John Wiley.
[5] Raff, M.S. (1956). "On approximating the point Binomial," J. Am. Stat. Ass., Vol. 51.
[6] Denning, P.J. and Schwartz, S.C. (1972). "Properties of the Working-Set Model," CACM, Vol. 15, No. 3.
[7] Fagin, R. (1975). "Asymptotic Miss Ration over Independent References," IBM Research RC report 5415.
[8] Kendall, M.G. (1951). "The Advanced Theory of Statistics," Hafner, N.Y.
[9] Chiu, W. and Galati, G. "RESMON: A Software Monitor for MVS." (in preparation).

TABLE I   MIN CHI-SQUARE FIT

UIC i	OBSERVED FREQ.	THEORETICAL FREQ.		
		K=2	K=3	K=4
0	18651	18540	18563	18638
1	2009	2051	1999	2007
2	1198	922	1202	1203
3	892	799	880	886
4	699	673	668	674
5	440	569	522	526
6	485	482	419	420
7	354	407	344	343
8	280	344	287	286
9	232	291	243	241
10	188	246	207	206
11	150	208	179	178
12	153	176	155	155
13	142	149	134	135
14	144	126	117	118
15	119	107	102	104
16	91	90	89	91
17	67	76	78	80
18	71	65	69	70
19	70	55	60	62
20	46	46	53	54
21	40	39	46	48
22	43	33	41	42
23	32	28	36	37
24	26	24	31	32
25	28	20	27	28
26	29	17	24	24
27	21	14	21	21
28	17	12	19	18
29	17	10	16	15
30	13	9	14	13
TOTAL	26747	26747	26747	26747
CHI-SQUARE VALUE		188	49.8	48.7
DEG. OF FREEEDOM		27	25	23

TABLE II   PAGE EXCEPTION RATE PER PAGE

i	EXPECTED	OBSERVED
1	0.04214	0.03250
2	.01816	.02183
3	.01289	.01492
4	.00961	.01103
5	.00740	.00770
6	.00586	.00621
7	.00475	.00497
8	.00393	.00400
9	.00331	.00325
10	.00282	.00269
11	.00242	.00239
12	.00209	.00209
13	.00181	.00179
14	.00158	.00142
15	.00138	.00116
16	.00121	.00082
17	.00106	.00064
18	.00093	.00056
19	.00081	.00034
20	.00071	.00026
21	.00063	.00022
22	.00055	.00022
23	.00048	.00022
24	.00042	.00022
25	.00037	.00022
26	.00033	.00015
27	.00029	.00015
28	.00025	.00011
29	.00022	.00011
30	.00019	.00011

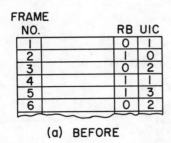
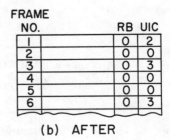

(a) BEFORE   (b) AFTER

FIG. 1   STATUS OF PAGES BEFORE AND AFTER THE END
         OF AN H-INTERVAL

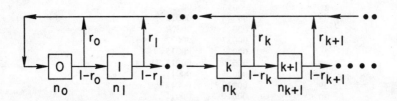

FIG. 2   TRANSITION DIAGRAM OF PAGE UIC's

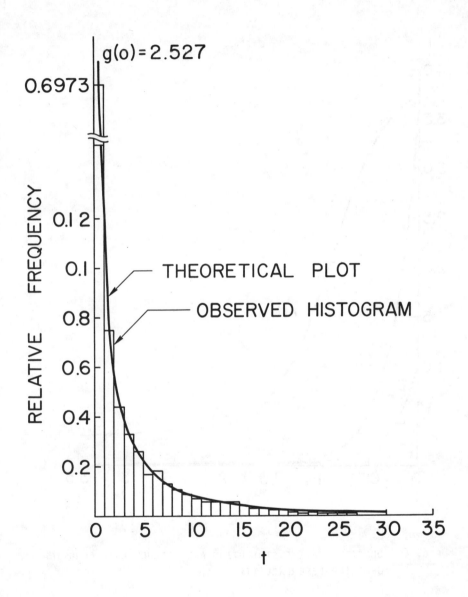

FIG. 3. OBSERVED UIC HISTOGRAM AND THEORETICAL AGE DENSITY

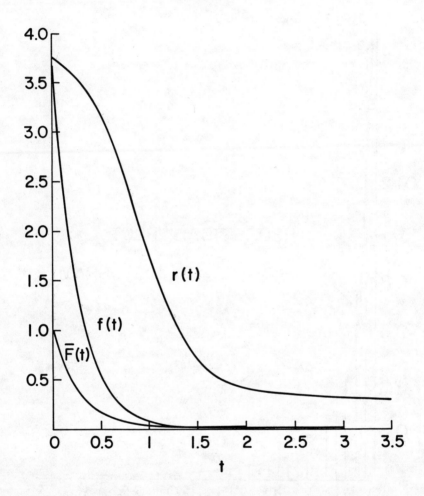

FIG. 4   DENSITY, TAIL DISTRIBUTION AND FAILURE RATE FUNCTION
         OF INTER-REFERENCE TIME

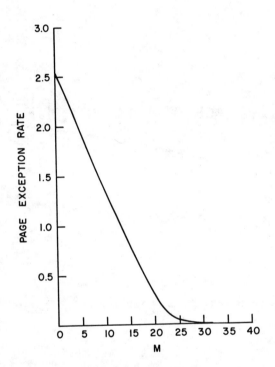

FIG. 5   PAGE EXCEPTION RATE UNDER LRU STRATEGY

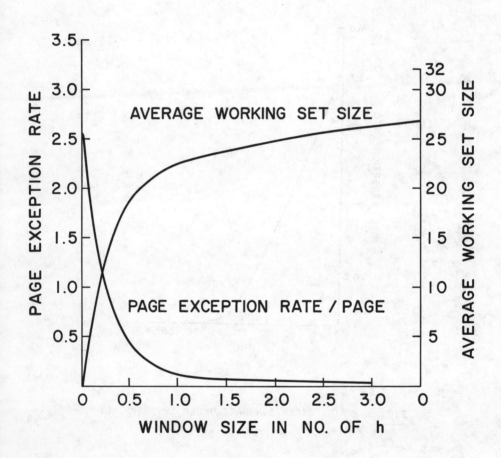

FIG. 6   PAGE EXCEPTION RATE AND AVERAGE WORKING SET SIZE

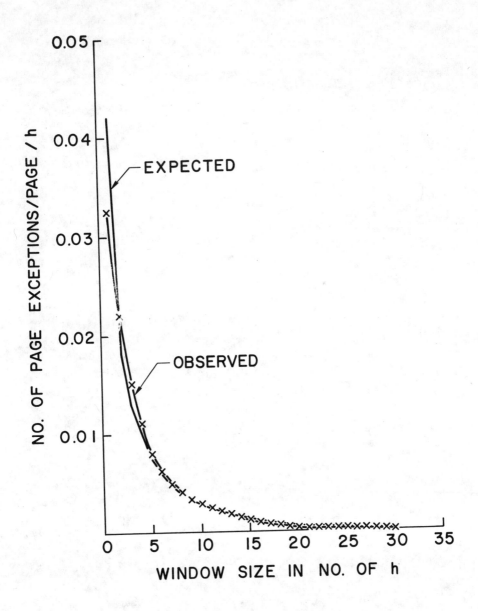

FIG. 7   NUMBER OF PAGE EXCEPTION PER PAGE PER H-INTERVAL

COMPUTER PERFORMANCE, K.M. CHANDY AND M. REISER (EDS.)
NORTH HOLLAND PUBLISHING COMPANY, 1977

A STATISTICAL APPROACH TO THE STUDY OF PROGRAM BEHAVIOR VIA REFERENCE STRING ANALYSIS

A. Schroeder
I.R.I.A. Laboria
Le Chesnay, France

Reference strings are widely used to describe the dynamic
behaviour of programs. According to the level of detail of
the description, these strings may be sequences of virtual
memory addresses, of page references, of symbolic instructions, etc...

We propose a statistical approach based on data analytic
methods to analyse such strings. We show how multivariate
statistical methods such as Correspondence Analysis and
clustering techniques may be advantageously used for this
purpose. A statistical notion of "locality" can then be derived, which is consistent with the various empirical definitions of "locality" given in the literature.

This approach may be used for the description of reference
strings at any level of detail. As an example we present
experiments on observed page reference strings.

1. INTRODUCTION

The study of program behaviour is a capital step in the development of most research
on operating systems. It is particularly essential when such techniques as analytical modelling and simulation are used for performance evaluation and prediction.
The utilization of these tools requires that the system workloads are clearly
characterized and quantified. This characterization may be done at various levels
of detail : global statistics on the number and requirements of the users of a
computer centre, classification of different kinds of jobs, or models for the sequence of addresses referenced by a job.

In this paper, we shall focus our attention on using this last type of information
to find "localities" of references. The presence of localities is a most interesting feature in the behaviour of a program. It means that the execution time may be
divided into distinct steps during which the program references mainly belong to
some favoured set of addresses. The concept of locality of memory references is of
great importance for the design of virtual memory systems, and it has been used
explicitly in various memory management policies implemented in such systems. It
has already been described by probabilistic models [ShT 72, FrG 75]. A quantitative
characterization of localities may be deduced from such models, like in [FrG 75].

381

Other characterizations which does not rely on a stochastic model have also been
introduced : the notion of "working-set" [Den 68] and, more recently, the "activity
sets" and "bounded locality intervals" (BLI) [MaB 76]. The working set model gives
a simple and operational mean to exhibit local memory requirements of a program.
The activity sets and BLI describe its behaviour at various levels of detail via
hierarchies of nested localities ; though quite appealing this last approach seems
too heavy for an on-line use.

Statistical analyses of reference strings have already been carried on but not
directly in the purpose of locality detection. In [GaL 74, LeS 73] for instance,
the aim was first to suggest a point process model for a process associated with
the reference string (the sequence of page exceptions), and then to estimate and
validate it. From an other point of view [Bry 75, BuL 76, Rod 73] give descriptive
statistical results on the working-sets behaviour. In [Bry 75] the results are used
to build a predictive model for the working-set sizes.

Our own approach is based on the idea that the phenomenon of locality is an objective property of each program which must be directly observed on its reference
strings. We thus propose a characterization of localities which is deduced from
descriptive analyses of reference strings. The statistical tools used are descriptive multivariate methods : Correspondence Analysis and a clustering algorithm.

In the next section of this paper, we shall present the reference strings which
we analyze and we shall illustrate experimentally the notion of locality. Then a
formal definition of locality will be given in the 3rd section while the statistical tools we use to exhibit such localities will be presented in section 4.
Finally, applications on real page references strings will be discussed in section
5.

2. MEASUREMENTS OF PROGRAMS BEHAVIOUR

2.1 - Reference strings

The dynamic behaviour of a program may be described by different strings :
       - the string of addresses which is the sequence of all the virtual ad-
dresses referenced by the program during its execution. This string only depends
on the program itself and its input data. It depends neither on the structure of
the physical memory nor on the memory allocation strategy.
       - the page string, easily deduced from the string of addresses as soon as
the page size is given, is the sequence of page references.
       - more generally, strings of blocks may be considered where "blocks" is
used as a general name for any subset of addresses (modules, segments,...).
       - the symbolic reference string describes the execution at the source
language level [Bat 76].

In the following, we shall use the word "reference" in the most general meaning
(address, page number, source language instruction, etc...).

2.2 - Notion of locality

Let R be the space of references and N its size. Then $R = \{r_1, r_2,...,r_N\}$. The
available observed information on R is a reference string $S = \{s_1,...,s_t,...,s_T\}$
where s_t is the tth reference and T is the number of observed references. In the
following, the mean time between two successive references will be taken as the
time unit. Hence, the indices $\{1,...,T\}$ represent a time scale.

Figure 1 illustrates the page reference string of a LISP
interpreter executing one program and Figure 2 that of a
FORTRAN compiler compiling two different modules (for
further details on the collection and representation of
such strings, see BuL 76). On the horizontal axis is
plotted the page set R, the vertical axis is a time axis
in the following sense : Each line represents a working-
set of window-size equal to 5000 references, by the mean
of a "I" for pages in the working-set and a blank for
the others. The time is running from top to bottom. The
sampling of these workings-sets is detailed in §3.1.

These graphs obviously show phases in the execution of
the programs, which are associated with different localities. Moreover a more careful observation reveals that
there is not one definite locality structure. It would be
better to talk of different levels of localities. For
instance, in Figure 1, four main phases appear (the 2nd
and the 4th one corresponding to the same locality), but,
when going into further details several other subphases
can be noticed.

These indications are the kind of observation we shall try
to obtain automatically. For this purpose, we shall define
on R as well as on $\{1, 2,...,T\}$ two structures describing
those kinds of phases : determined subsets of references
which the program addresses during determined time intervals.

3. A TIME x REFERENCE REPRESENTATION OF LOCALITIES

3.1 - The data

The basic information we shall use from now on to describe
localities will consists in occurrence tables between the
set R of references and the set of instants $[1,...,T]$.
Since the execution of any program may consist in several
millions references, it is essential to sample them in
order to extract a manageable information. A point sampling
would not be appropriate since we are interested in analysing a neighbourhood behaviour. We shall therefore have to
sample intervals. We chose here the simplest interval sampling procedure, though
more sophisticated procedures could also be adapted. The observed periods are intervals of equal size s (or "windows") sampled every t_0 units of time ; they will
be denoted by :

$$I_1 = [t_0, t_0 + s], \quad I_2 = [2t_0, 2t_0 + s], \quad I_M = [Mt_0, Mt_0 + s]$$

where $M = \max\{m \in \mathbb{N} \mid mt_0 + s \leq T\}$.

It is easy to note that this sampling process consists in sampling working-sets of
window size s every t_0 references. This is important from a practical standpoint
in order to get indications on the parameters t_0 and s (see §5.1). Moreover, the
practical use that has already been made of working-sets legitimates the sampling
strategy.

Let I be the set $\{I_1, I_2,...,I_M\}$. In the sequel of the paper, the analysis will be
conducted on the contingency table C between R and I. C is defined by :

Figure 1

$$C(I_i, r_j) = a_{ij} = \begin{cases} 1 \text{ if } r_j \text{ has been referenced during } I_i \\ \\ 0 \text{ otherwise} \end{cases}$$

So, the ith row of C is nothing else than the characteristic function of the ith "working-set" WS_i of window size s :

$$\forall i \in \{1, 2,...,M\} \qquad WS_i = \{r_j / 1 \le j \le N \text{ and } a_{ij} = 1\}$$

Let us use the following notation :

$$\forall i \in \{1, 2,...,M\} \qquad a_{i*} = \sum_{j=1,N} a_{ij}$$

$$\forall j \in \{1, 2,...,M\} \qquad a_{*j} = \sum_{i=1,M} a_{ij}$$

and
$$a_{**} = \sum_{i=1,M} \sum_{j=1,N} a_{ij}$$

$$C = \begin{bmatrix} a_{11} & \cdots & a_{1j} & \cdots & a_{1N} \\ \vdots & & \vdots & & \vdots \\ a_{i1} & \cdots & a_{ij} & \cdots & a_{iN} \\ \vdots & & \vdots & & \vdots \\ a_{M1} & \cdots & a_{Mj} & \cdots & a_{MN} \end{bmatrix} \longrightarrow a_{i*}$$

$$\downarrow \qquad\qquad\qquad\qquad \downarrow$$

$$a_{*j} \longrightarrow a_{**}$$

Thus a_{i*} is the ith working-set size, a_{*j} the number of working-sets which contain r_j and $a_{**} = M.\overline{WS}$, where $\overline{WS}$ is the mean working-set size.

3.2 - The multidimensional approach

Once the data on the relationships between the set R of references and the set I have been collected, we propose to analyse them by using multidimensional statistical techniques. In these techniques the two sets R and I are considered as finite sets of vectors in spaces of respective dimensions M and N. For instance, the page r_j is identified with the vector $(a_{1j}, a_{2j},...,a_{Mj})$ which is the jth column of the table C and thus completely describes how r_j is used throughout the sampled time intervals. Symmetrically, each sample window is represented by the corresponding line of C which is the characteristic function of its working-set. Multidimensional techniques attempt by different means to provide a clear description of such sets of objects placed in multidimensional spaces. In order to do that, these spaces are assigned a measure of distance and the problem of description can then be stated in geometrical teams.

For our purpose of locality detection, we shall use two of those techniques : Correspondence Analysis and a clustering procedure. They provide different forms of description of the data which prove to be complementary. They will be described more precisely in the following section 4. For both techniques, given distances d_1 and d_2 have to be taken for the two sets I and R. Correspondence analysis also requires weights to be assigned to the sets. We shall now see more precisely which are those distances and weights.

i) Weights and distance on the set I :

Each sampled time interval or "window" I_i is weighted by the number of distinct references that have been accessed during its duration, i.e. by its working-set size a_{i*}.

The distance between the kth and the ℓth windows is given by :

$$d_1^2(I_k, I_\ell) = M \overline{WS} \sum_{j=1,M} \frac{1}{a_{*j}} \left[\frac{a_{kj}}{a_{k*}} - \frac{a_{\ell j}}{a_{\ell *}} \right]^2$$

Let us recall that :

$$\frac{a_{ij}}{a_{i*}} = \begin{cases} 1/a_{i*} & \text{if } r_j \text{ belongs to the } i^{th} \text{ working set} \\ 0 & \text{Otherwise} \end{cases}$$

It is easy to see that two time intervals are represented by a unique point in I if and only if they have identical working sets :

$$d_1^2(I_k, I_\ell) = 0 \iff \{j/a_{kj} \neq 0\} = \{j/a_{\ell j} \neq 0\}$$

Moreover, when the working-sets are different, I_k and I_ℓ are considered the closer their non common references are more frequently referenced. This is due to the terms $1/a_{*j}$ appearing in the sum defining this distance which is imposed by the use of Correspondence Analysis.

ii) Weights and distance on R :

Each reference r_j is weighted by the number a_{*j} of sampled working-sets which contain it. The distance between two references r_k and r_ℓ is given by :

$$d_2^2(r_k, r_\ell) = M \overline{WS} \sum_{i=1,N} \frac{1}{a_{i*}} \left[\frac{a_{ik}}{a_{*k}} - \frac{a_{i\ell}}{a_{*\ell}} \right]^2$$

As seen above in the case of the time intervals, we have :

$$\forall i, \quad 1 \leq i \leq M$$
$$\frac{a_{ij}}{a_{*j}} = \begin{cases} 1/a_{*j} & \text{if } r_j \text{ belongs to the } i^{th} \text{ working set} \\ 0 & \text{Otherwise} \end{cases}$$
$$\forall j, \quad 1 \leq j \leq N$$

Two references are considered as identical when they occur in the same working-sets. They are closer or further away from each other according to whether the working-sets in which only one of them occurs are larger or smaller.

Finally, we see that the notions of "Importance" and of "Closeness" for references and for time intervals that will are introduced by the statistical techniques reflect well enough the empirical definition of "localities" of references.

4. THE STATISTICAL TOOLS

4.1 - Correspondence Analysis

Due to J.P. Benzecri [Ben 69, Ben 73], this multivariate statistical method is derived from Fisher's Canonical Analysis of contingency tables and is closely related to other multivariate statistical techniques, such as Principal Components and
Canonical Analysis [And 58, Hil 74, Sch 76].

As seen in the previous paragraph the two sets I and R to analyse may be considered
as sets of vectors in a N-dimension and in a M-dimension spaces. The aim of Correspondence Analysis is to give the best possible representation of such a multidimensional set in a space of low dimension (in a plane, for instance, in order to get
the structure of the set directly legible). The problem of finding that subspace
on which the data set can be projected with a minimal loss of information is
solved by using mechanical arguments : it is the principal inertia subspace of the
data set. The quality of the representation obtained is measured by the ratio :

$$\frac{\text{dispersion of the projected set}}{\text{total dispersion of the data set}}$$

This ratio indicates the part of information which is preserved after the projec-
tion. The dispersions involved in the ratio are dispersions in the sense of the
distance chosen for the analysed set (here d_1 for I and d_2 for R).

Thus, Correspondence Analysis provides a low-dimension representation for the two
sets I and R and a measure of the quality of these representations. Moreover, the
theoretical properties of the method ensure that the two representations of I and
R can be interpreted simultaneously with the help of each other. The use and the
interpretation of the graphical representations provided by such an analysis will
appear more clearly in section 5 in which applications are presented.

Let us note that the choice of the particular distances d_1 and d_2 is characteristic
of Correspondence Analysis and that it is this choice which allows the simultaneous
interpretation of the two representations. With any others distances, good representations of each set could be obtained by a Principal Components Analysis, but
there would not be any results allowing to compare the two representations. These
distances also have a property, called by J.P. Benzecri, "distributional equivalence" which will be illustrated in §5.1.

4.2 - A clustering procedure

Given a finite set of vectors on which a distance measure is chosen, clustering
techniques find out a partition of this set which is optimum for some quality
criterion. Those techniques differ from one to another by their criterion and the
algorithm they use to get an optimum (or, most generally, a local optimum) of the
criterion.

The method we use here is due to G. Govaert [Gov 76]. It is a particular case of
the large family of clustering techniques known as Dynamic Clusters type methods
[DiS 74]. It requires that the number k of classes required in the partition is
given and considers the weights and distances introduced in 3.2. The two sets I
and R are analysed separately by this method. Since they play symmetrical parts,
we shall only detail the analysis of I. The analysis of I provides a partition
$(I_1, I_2,...,I_k)$ of I.

Notation :

$$\left.\begin{array}{l} \forall \ell = 1, k \\ \\ \forall j = 1, N \end{array}\right\} \qquad b_{\ell j} = \sum_{\{i/I_i \in I_\ell\}} a_{ij}$$

and

$$b_{\ell *} = \sum_{\{i/I_i \in I_\ell\}} a_{i *}$$

So $C' = [b_{\ell j}]_{\ell=1, k}^{j=1, N}$ is the contingency table deduced from C by partitioning I into $(I_1, \ldots, I_k)$ and $b_{\ell *}$ is the total weight of the class I_ℓ.

The partition obtained maximizes the following criterion :

$$K^2 = \sum_{\ell=1,k} b_{\ell *} \sum_{j=1,N} \frac{1}{a_{*j}} \left[\frac{b_{\ell j}}{b_{\ell *}} - a_{*j} \right]^2$$

This criterion expresses the strength of the correlation between the set I divided into the k classes $(I_1, \ldots, I_\ell)$ and the set R. (Under classical hypotheses, this quantity is proved to be distributed as a χ^2 variable and is commonly used as a test of homogeneity in contingency tables).

5. APPLICATIONS

The statistical methods have been applied to various examples.

The data were collected at the University of Rennes (France) by interpreting the execution of programs running on a CII 10070 Computer. The traces obtained are the address strings of the observed programs, i.e. the sequence of all addresses referenced during the execution. These references may be identified as instruction or data references. Further detail on these reference strings may be found in ⌈BuL 76⌉.

5.1 - Analysis of the FORTRAN compiler

The first string we have chosen to analyse because of its typical local behaviour, is that of a FORTRAN compiler of 30K words compiling two different modules and containing 3 207 168 references ($\cong$ 3 seconds). It has first been converted in two page reference strings assuming respectively the page size to be 512 or 256 words. Thus, in the sequel, the set R of references will be either R_1 (page size = 512 words) or R_2 (page size = 256 words). The corresponding traces are presented in Figures 2 and 3.

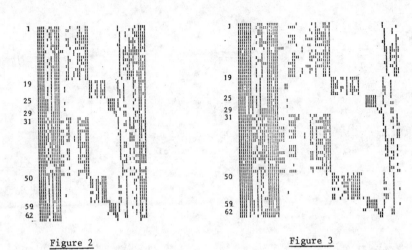

Figure 2   Figure 3

From R_1 we have also deduced two other page reference strings : R_{1i} and R_{1d} by making a distinction between instruction references (R_{1i}) and data references (R_{1d}). This will permit to compare the specific behaviour of data and instructions references with the global one.

The next step is to sample time intervals. This sampling, as seen in 3.1 depends on two parameters : the size s of the intervals (window size) and the sampling period t_0. Guided by the experience of authors who have analysed working-set properties [BuL 76] or implemented working-set memory management [Rod 73], we made experiments with the following values for those parameters.

> s = 2 000, 5 000 or 10 000 references
> t_0 = 10 000 or 50 000 references.

The value s = 5 000 and t_0 = 50 000 have been finally kept since they give the best results with the fewest number of references to deal with. However, it should be noted that the choice of these values may depend on the program to analyse and a first investigation of the data must be made to get an idea of the "size" of possible localities.

i) Correspondence Analysis

Four analyses have been performed : analyses of the Table C between I and the sets R_1, R_2, R_{1i} and R_{1d}.

We shall first present the detailed results of the analysis of C between I and R_1 which appeared to be the most informative of the four performed analyses. Then, the other ones will be more briefly described and compared to this one and to one another.

- Analysis of $I \times R_1$:

This analysis provides plane representations for I and R_1 which bring 36 % of the global information contained in the Table C. The representation of I is shown in Figure 4.

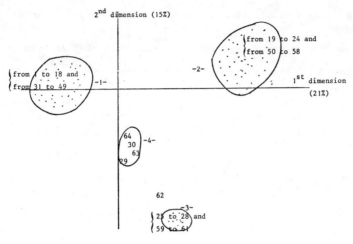

Figure 4

Four clusters appear, indicated by numbers 1, 2, 3 and 4 in Figure. Group 1 contains two phases in the execution of the program (from the 1st to the 18th sampled windows and from the 31st to the 49th). In the same way, the three other obvious phases of the execution seen in Figure 2 are represented here in the groups 2, 3 and 4.

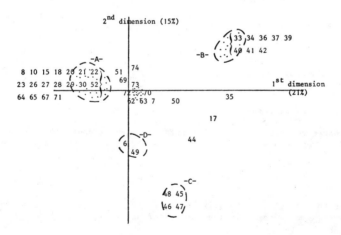

Figure 5

Simultaneously, we can see on the representation of R_1 (Figure 5) which pages characterize those phases. Around the centre of gravity are clustered the most frequently referenced pages : they are accessed during all the execution and cannot characterize a particular phase. The others are clustered according to a pattern similar to the one displayed in that of the time interval of Figure 4 (groups A, B, C and D on Figure 5).

The 1st and 5th phases in the execution time are both characterized by references
to the pages represented in Group A on Figure 5, and so on for the other groups.
Several isolated points represent pages which are shared by different phases.

By taking one more dimension into account, we can add 10 % of information. This
gain is not important compared with the 36 % of information brought by the two
first dimensions. We shall however examine it to see whether it contains relevant
information or not. The plane representation of I on the 1st and 3rd axes is shown
on Figure 6. One can note that if the groups 2, 3 and 4 of Figure 4 are still the
same, the group 1 is split into subgroups. One of the two subgroups is very close
to group 4. By observing the representation of R_1 on these same axes (not reproduced here), we can see that the two subgroups of group 1 are characterized by the
use they make of pages 18, 19, 21, 22, 64, 65, 67, 69 on one hand and of pages 8,
15, 27, 28, 71 on the other.

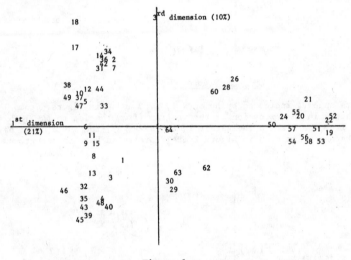

Figure 6

– Analyses of $I \times R_{1i}$ and $I \times R_{1d}$:

There are 54 pages containing data references and only 14 containing instructions
references. Both representations of I and R_{1d} are very close to the representations
issued from $I \times R_1$. This is certainly due to the fact that pages references are
most often data references as noted just above. The interesting point is that the
similarity is still true in the results of $I \times R_{1i}$. This observation may indicate
that the detected phases are phases in the instructions sequence of the program
which, of course, imply phases in the data references.

– Analyses of $I \times R_2$:

The sampling process is still the same as above, but the page size is 256 words
i.e. half of that for R_1. The representation of I is almost the same as in the
analysis of $I \times R_1$. This means that the phases are the same when observing the
behaviour of the program at these two different levels of detail. This conclusion
is confirmed by observing the traces in Figures 2 and 3. This illustrates the stability of the results of the analyses when aggregating (or disaggregating) classes

of elements that are close to one another. It is due to the property of "distributional equivalence" that we have mentioned in §4.1. (This property is the
following : if two elements in one of the two sets we analyse, let us say r_{j_1} and
r_{j_2} in R, are at a null distance from each other, they can be replaced by a unique
point, weighted by the sum of their weights : $a_{*j_1} + a_{*j_2}$, without changing anything to the distances d_1 between the elements of I).

ii) Clustering

The clustering procedure has been applied to the set I of the working-sets corresponding to R_1. Since the results obtained coincide exactly with those of Correspondence Analysis it has not been necessary to cluster the set of references : the
characteristic references of the observed phases have already been obtained.

Three experiments have been made asking respectively for three, four or five
classes in the partition.

Partition obtained with three classes :

$$I_1 = \{I_1 \text{ to } I_{18} \quad \text{and} \quad I_{29} \text{ to } I_{65}\} : \text{groups 1 and 4 of Figure 4}$$

$$I_2 = \{I_{19} \text{ to } I_{24} \quad \text{and} \quad I_{50} \text{ to } I_{58}\} : \text{group 2 of Figure 4}$$

$$I_3 = \{I_{25} \text{ to } I_{28} \quad \text{and} \quad I_{59} \text{ to } I_{62}\} : \text{group 3 of Figure 3}$$

In the partition obtained with four classes, I_2 and I_3 remain the same and I_1 is
split into the two subclasses which have been found in the 2nd plane given by
Correspondence Analysis (Figure 6). When asking for five classes, it is the small
group 4 of Correspondence Analysis which is separated from the subclass of group 1
to which it was so close.

NB : The quality criterion of the partitions obtained is of course increasing with
the number of classes required : it has to be maximum when there are as many classes as elements in the set. When making several experiments with different number
of classes, it is important to examine whether asking for one more class significantly improves the criterion or not. If it does not it means that the lowest
number of classes is a "good" one, in the sense that clustering cannot be improved
by adding a new class.

In this particular application, the criterion increases noticeably and regularly
when passing from three classes to four, and from four to five. So, all successive
partitions bring worthwhile information.

The clustering method and the Correspondence Analysis exhibit the same locality
structure for the FORTRAN compiler under study. Since the structure was a very
pronounced feature, it could have been unambiguously deduced from Correspondence
Analysis graphs. However, these graphs are not always so easy to interpret because
of poor representation in a low dimension space or of overlapping classes. In these
cases, clustering is the method which is able to display relevant classes. Moreover,
results provided by Correspondence Analysis have a more attractive form than those
of any clustering algorithms, but from a computational standpoint a Correspondence
Analysis is more expensive than the clustering method used here.

5.2 - Analysis of the LISP interpreter

The LISP interpreter requires 14K words of core and interprets a whole user LISP
program. Its reference string contains 3 663 872 references ($\cong$ 3.7 seconds). We

analysed its page reference string (Figure 1) with a page size of 512 words. Let R be the set of these pages. The values of the sampling parameters (see 3.1) are : $s = 5\ 000$ and $t_0 = 20\ 000$. They have been selected after some experiments as in 5.1.

i) Correspondence Analysis

A first analysis has been performed on $I \times R$. It has not been of great interest since the only feature it could point out is the fact that the two first sampled working-sets are completely apart from all the others : on the representations, all the other working-sets are gathered on a single point. When looking at the trace (Figure 1), it appears that these two working-sets I_1 and I_2 belong to an initialization phase in which the program will never return.

We then analysed $(I - \{I_1,\ I_2\})$. The parts of information brought by the successive dimensions are :

        1st dimension : 33 %
        2nd   "   : 17 %
        3rd   "   : 10 %
        4th   "   : 7 %, etc...

On the plane of the two first dimension (global information : 50 %) the working-sets are represented on Figure 7 and the pages on Figure 8. The 1st dimension (horizontal axis) separates the working-sets I_{67} to I_{126} and I_{146} ti I_{180} (except I_{86}, I_{97}, I_{115}, I_{177}) from all the others. We can see on Figure 1 that those working-sets obviously constitue one locality which is held during two long phases (the 4 exceptions appear like outliers). The 2nd dimension (vertical axis) puts apart the phase containing I_{127} to I_{144} though a subphase I_{138} to I_{144} can be distinguished. These phase and subphase are also noticeable on Figure 1. Eventually, on this first plane, remains the first phase of the execution (I_3 to I_{65} with some exceptions).

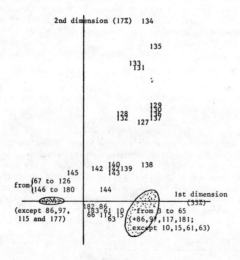

Figure 7

The characteristic references of these classes of working-sets are easy to read on Figure 8.

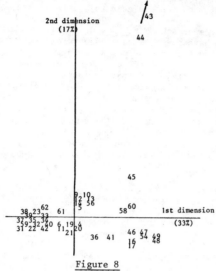

Figure 8

When observing the third dimension (not represented here) the only new feature is a partition of the 1st phase into two classes : I_{25} to I_{29} and I_{52} to I_{60} on one hand, the rest on the other. Once more these subphase may be seen on Figure 1.

Using three dimensions, which represent 60 % of the information, it has been possibe to detect the major phases in the execution of the program, while all the incertain points on the resulting graphs are the small localities which are seen as isolated working-sets on Figure 1. (I_{10}, I_{15}, I_{30}, etc...).

      ii) Clustering

Five experiments have been made asking respectively for three, four, five, six and seven classes. The criteria obtained at the four last experiments were almost equal to the value obtained with three classes. This means (see §5.1.ii)) that there is a robust structure of three classes in the set $I - \{I_1, I_2\}$ to analyse and that the gain obtained by partitioning it into more classes is negligible.

We found two different partitions into three classes which have equal quality criteria. Both of them exhibit the three main phases : I_3 to I_{65}, I_{127} to I_{137} and (I_{66} to I_{126} + I_{145} to I_{182}), with the same outliers as those noticed in Correspondence Analysis. The only difference is in the assignment of the subphase I_{138} to I_{144} which is classified either with $I_3 - I_{65}$ or with $I_{127} - I_{137}$. This intermediate position was already noticed on Figure 7.

6. CONCLUDING REMARKS

We have presented in this paper an attempt to characterize localities by a descriptive analysis of the reference string of a program. The major benefit of this approach is its objectivity, since no underlying model for the locality structure has to be assumed. It must also be noticed that the description obtained is a detailed one. It is able to display different levels of nested localities, and this description is derived by only observing a limited subset of the string (from 10 to 20 percent of the total number of references).

A first application of our approach is to provide convenient tools for on-line detection of localities. We have seen how sampled working-sets of a program may be considered as N-vectors, how they can be compared to one another by using the distance defined in §3.2, and how a locality may be defined as a cluster of those vectors. Thus, a new sampled working-set may be identified as belonging to one of the detected localities by measuring its distance to the different clusters representing those localities and being assigned to the locality the closest to which it is. The only hypotheses needed to make such a prediction valid is that the phases of a program are the same from one execution to another ; no assumption has to be made concerning the lengths and orders of the phases. Such on-line methods which identify in which locality a program is running may be used to design adaptive memory management policies using predictive loading techniques such as those presented in [BaS 76].

The description of localities of references we have presented can also be applied to program restructuring : the known restructuring techniques [Fer 75, MaS 74, AcB 76] are clustering methods applied to connection tables between logical blocks of the program. Our method could either improve those blocks definition or suggest restructuring procedures directly built on our obtained pages clusters.

It should also be noted that the approach we have presented here can be extended to the characterization of localities at other levels of the program behaviour, such as file access sequences or transaction initiations in a data base system. From a technical point of view, sampling and analysis tools have still to be studied and refined.

ACKNOWLEDGEMENTS

Special thanks are due to Dominique POTIER, Domenico FERRARI and one of the referees for their helpful criticisms and comments.

REFERENCES

[AcB 76] M.S. Achard, J.Y. Babonneau, G. Morisset - "Adaptation automatique des programmes au milieu paginé" - Research Report n° 196, IRIA-LABORIA - Octobre 1976 - (an English version of this paper will be presented at the 6th ACM Symposium on Operating Systems principles to be held at Purdue University - November 1977 - with the following title : "Automatic and general solution to the adaptation in the paging environment").

[And 58] T.W. Anderson - "Introduction to multivariate statistical analysis" - John Wiley - 1958.

[BaS 76] J.L. Baer, G.R. Sager - "Dynamic improvement of locality in virtual memory systems" - IEEE Trans. on Software Engineering - Vol. SE-2 - n° 1 - pp. 54-62 - March 1976.

[Bat 76] A. Batson - "Program behavior at the symbolic level" - Computer - Vol. 9 - n° 11 - pp. 21-28 - November 1976.

[Ben 69] J.P. Benzecri - "Statistical analysis as a tool to make patterns merge from data" - in Methodologies of Pattern Recognition (S. Watanabe, ed.)- pp. 35-60 - Academie Press N.Y. - 1969.

[Ben 73] J.P. Benzecri et Coll. - "L'analyse des données T.1 : La taxinomie, T.2 : L'analyse des Correspondances" - Dunod - Paris - 1973.

[BuL 76] P. Burgevin, J. Leroudier - "Characteristics and models of program behavior" - National Conference ACM 76 - Houston - Texas - October 1976.

[Den 68] P. Denning - "The working-set model for program behavior" - Communications of the ACM - Vol. 11 - pp. 323-333 - May 1968.

[DiS 74] E. Diday, A. Schroeder, Y. Ok - "The dynamic clusters method in pattern recognition" - Information Processing 74 - IFIP - Stockholm - North-Holland Publishing C. - pp. 691-697 - 1974.

[Fer 75] D. Ferrari - "Tailoring programs to models of program behavior" - IBM J. Res. Develop. - pp. 244-251 - May 1975.

[FrG 75] W.F. Freiberger, U. Grenander, P.D. Sampson - "Pattern in program references" - IBM J. Res. Develop. - pp. 230-243 - May 1975.

[GaL 74] D.P. Gaver, P.A.W. Lewis, G.S. Shedler - "Analysis of exception data in a staging hierarchies" - IBM J. Res. Develop. - Vol. 18, n° 5 - pp. 423-434 - September 1974.

[Gov 77] G. Govaert - "Algorithme de classification d'un tableau de contingence" - Journées Analyse des Données et Informatique - IRIA - Rocquencourt - France - Septembre 1977.

[Hil 74] M.O. Hill - "Correspondence analysis : a neglected multivariate method" - Appl. Statist. - 23 - n° 3 - pp. 340-354 - 1974.

[LeS 73] P.A.W. Lewis, G.S. Shedler - "Empirically derived micro models for sequences of page exceptions" - IBM J. Res. Develop. - pp. 86-100 - March 1973.

[MaB 76] A.W. Madison, A.P. Batson - "Characteristics of program localities" - Communications of the ACM - Vol. 19 - n° 5 - pp. 285-294 - May 1974.

[MaS 74]   T. Masuda, J. Shiota, K. Noguhi, T. Ohki - "Optimization of program or-
           ganization by cluster analysis" - IFIP 1974 - Stockholm - North-Holland
           Publishing C. - 1974.

[Rod 73]   J. Rodriguez-Rosell - "Empirical working-set behavior" - Communications
           of the ACM - Vol. 16 - n° 9 - pp. 556-560 - September 1973.

[Sch 76]   A. Schroeder - "Descriptive methods in multidimensional data analysis" -
           IFIP Workshop on Decision Making and Medical Care (Dombal and Grémy,
           eds) - North-Holland Publishing C. - 1976.

[ShT 72]   G.S. Shedler, C. Tung - "Locality in page reference strings" - SIAM J.
           Comp. - Vol. 1 - n° 3 - pp. 218-241 - September 1972.

COMPUTER PERFORMANCE, K.M. CHANDY AND M. REISER (EDS.)
NORTH HOLLAND PUBLISHING COMPANY, 1977

CONGESTION IN MULTILEVEL PAGING HIERARCHIES

J. A. Hamilton
Digital Equipment Corporation
Maynard, Massachusetts, USA

Several current large scale operating systems contain multilevel paging hierarchies. These systems all use a migration algorithm to move little used pages to successively lower levels in the hierarchy. Such hierarchies may exhibit a form of congestion due to the lack of free pages at intermediate levels. This paper presents several analytical models for the determination of occupancy distributions in these hierarchies. First, a Markov chain determines the probability mass function for the occupancy of individual levels, based on arrival and departure rates of pages at those levels. Then a set of simple models relates the parameters of the occupancy distribution model to the total system load and to the system configuration. It is then possible to determine the load at which a given configuration will become congested, or conversely, the configuration required to support a given load without congestion. This work also contains what is probably the first treatment of the program dependent processes by which pages are created and deleted. All of the results presented are supported by detailed measurements from the Michigan Terminal System (MTS).

INTRODUCTION

The concept of a storage hierarchy is now quite well known. A collection of storage devices are assigned to levels, numbered 1 through N, such that if C_i is the capacity and T_i the access time of devices at level i, then

$$C_1 < \ldots < C_i < \ldots < C_N$$

and

$$T_1 < \ldots < T_i < \ldots < T_N$$

A paging hierarchy is just a storage hierarchy in which the storage elements are pages, which have a fixed size. The interface presented to a user program is that of a large virtual store in which all pages appear to be directly addressable at a single level.

Several important performance evaluation and optimization problems have been formulated and studied in the area of storage hierarchies. These can be summarized (with some representative references) as follows:

1. Given some technology cost function, determine the optimal (i.e. minimal cost) number of levels, and the capacity and access time to be used at each level [1,2,3].

397

2. Given a particular hierarchy, and a knowledge of hardware, operating system, and application constraints, choose an appropriate hierarchy management strategy. This strategy will specify the paths by which pages can move from one level to another [4].

3. Given a hierarchy management strategy, specify algorithms to choose which pages to move (this is the so-called replacement algorithm), and when (and possibly where) to move them [5].

4. Given all of the above, plus a knowledge of program behavior, determine the distribution of references (hit ratios) to each level of the hierarchy [6].

5. Given 1 and 4 above, determine the resulting total system performance, e.g. response time and throughput [7].

These areas are all interrelated of course, and a thorough treatment would address all of them simultaneously. In spite of this, significant theoretical advances have been made on several of these problems independently.

After a brief discussion of items 2 and 3, this paper examines a particular phenomenon, which we will call congestion, that can significantly degrade system performance by indirectly affecting access time.

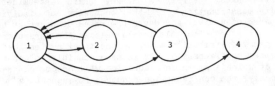

The Direct Placement Strategy

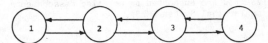

The Staging Strategy

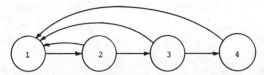

The Migration Strategy

Figure 1: Alternative Hierarchy Management Strategies

HIERARCHY MANAGEMENT

Of the many possible methods of interconnecting the levels of a paging hierarchy, there are three that have been studied and used extensively. These are illustrated in figure 1. The direct placement strategy is most appropriate for special purpose systems for which the page reference distribution can be determined in advance. The staging strategy seems appropriate for hardware implementation, where storage devices communicate with one another directly rather than via the main store of a central procesor. Examples include many high speed cache implementations, and mass storage facilities such as the IBM 3850 [8]. The migration strategy is most appropriate to software implementation in virtual memory operating systems, and at least four general purpose systems (MTS [9], MULTICS [10], TSS [11], and EMAS [12]) which include multilevel hierarchies use this approach. The migration strategy is the one we shall explore in the remainder of the paper, although some of the results are applicable to the staging strategy as well. It should be pointed out that a software implementation of the migration strategy will normally require downward movements to be physically implemented by a read into a main storage buffer followed by a write to the next lower level.

Regardless of the interconnection structure, two decisions must be made before a page can be moved from one level to another: which page to move, and when to move it. Pages move upward in the hierarchy either on demand or because their imminent use is anticipated. In either case this can be viewed as a program dependent sequence of requests for immediate transfers, and the stochastic properties of this sequence can be measured. For pages moving downward in the hierarchy, the algorithm which selects pages to move is generally called a replacement algorithm, although the actual replacement will not normally occur until sometime after the transfer is complete, when the storage is actually needed. Replacement algorithms have been, and continue to be studied extensively. Fortunately, the results of this paper do not depend on any particular replacement algorithm, although in some instances their accuracy will be improved if a "stack" algorithm [6] is used.

The simplest algorithm for deciding when to migrate pages downward is the occupancy threshold algorithm, which migrates a page out of level i whenever the occupancy of level i exceeds some fixed threshold. Although it is easy to devise more complex algorithms, which would probably reduce page traffic in some situations, we shall see that no algorithm can prevent congestion. The occupancy threshold algorithm is used, with minor variations, in all of the operating systems mentioned above, and its performance is the subject of the remainder of this paper.

The objective of the occupancy threshold algorithm is to prevent any level from becoming so full that the allocation of new pages at that level must be delayed. This is the phenomenon we call congestion. It is particularly important to avoid congestion on devices which require rotational latency or access motion, like drums and disks, because a shortage of available pages will increase the delays due to these factors. Even in main storage, congestion is more severe than it might seem, because measurements show that the majority of activity in virtual memory operating systems involves short lifetime pages which never leave main storage. See [13] for details. This activity is enormously degraded if delays are encountered in the allocation of such pages. When congestion occurs at an intermediate level it impedes the flow of pages into that level from the next higher level, and this may cause that level to become congested as well. This phenomenon may propogate all the way to main storage, thus causing the entire system to run at the rate of the highest non-congested level.

It is worth distinguishing congestion from the unrelated phenomenon called "thrashing", which is the interaction of processor scheduling with a replacement algorithm in such a way that pages may be removed from main storage before they are used.

In the next section a Markov chain model will be developed which predicts the occupancy distribution for individual levels of a hierarchy. It will be seen that certain parameter values in this model correspond to the onset of congestion. In the following section these parameter values are related to system load, and to the capacities of the levels, thus determining the maximum load which a given configuration can support, and conversely, the configuration required to support a given load without congestion.

THE OCCUPANCY DISTRIBUTION MODEL

At any point in time the state of a hierarchy can be defined as the N-tuple $(n_1,\ldots,n_N)$ where n_i is the number of occupied page frames at level i. Transitions from one state to another can occur in the following ways:

1. A new page arrives at level one, either because it is brought in from level i or because it is created there for the first time. In the former case the copy remains at level i. In either case n_i is incremented.

2. A page is removed from level i, either because it has been selected for migration and a copy exists at level i+1, or because it is deleted from the system by the program using it. In either case n_i is decremented.

3. A page is migrated from level i to level i+1. In this case n_i is decremented and n_{i+1} is incremented. This occurs only when $n_i > t_i$ where t_i is the occupancy threshold for level i.

If one assumes that these three processes are Markovian, which they almost surely are not, then this forms a rather complex, multidimensional Markov chain.

Unfortunately there is no known general solution to this type of Markov chain, primarily due to the finite capacities of the levels. Therefore although it is known to be incorrect, we will examine a much simpler model for a single level. This model is shown in figure 2. The subscript i will be omitted for the remainder of this section. The state is simply the integer n. There is an arrival process, with rate λ, which is either the arrival process at level 1, described above, or the migration process from level i-1. This latter process is known to be non-Markovian, and that is the source of the error in approximating the more complex model described above. However, this assumption seems no worse than the assumption that any of the other processes involved are Markovian. There is also a departure process, with rate μ of pages deleted from level i, and a migration process, which moves pages to level i+1 with rate η, whenever $n \geq t$.

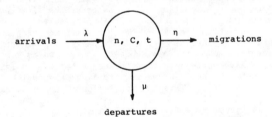

Figure 2: The Single Level Model

Measurements of the interarrival time distributions for these three processes, taken from the Michigan Terminal System (MTS) [9], show that the arrival and departure processes tend to be hyperexponential in nature, with the departure process having the greatest variance; the migration process tends to be Erlangian in shape, since it involves a transfer time. The model can be solved for processes with these distributions, and the solutions are given in [13]. The results do not differ significantly in form from those obtained using exponential distributions for all three interarrival times.

We now give a brief description of the all exponential solution. The state diagram is shown in figure 3. Note that for n<t the states are split because a migration, once begun when $n \geq t$, may not finish until several departures have

occurred, leaving n<t. There are three separate regions in this diagram, and a general solution, containing two indeterminate coefficients, can be obtained for each by solving the balance equations in the usual way. See Kleinrock [14] for a description of the method. The coefficients can be determined by solving the special balance equations at the boundaries, plus the requirement that the probabilities sum to one.

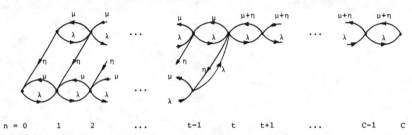

Figure 3: State Transition Diagram for Exponential Transition Processes

Several sample solutions are presented graphically in figure 4. It should be evident that a critical point of the solution will occur whenever the input rate equals the maximum output rate, namely when $\lambda = \mu + \eta$. The results in figure 4 are obtained by fixing μ and η, and choosing four values of λ, one well below the critical point, a second just below the critical point, a third just at the critical point, and the fourth just above it. The striking conclusion from figure 4 is that a very small change in parameters, only a few percent, takes the system from an acceptable mode of operation into fairly severe congestion. Thus for many purposes, this is effectively a two state system, operating acceptably, when $\lambda < \mu + \eta$, and congested, when $\lambda > \mu + \eta$. In the next section we show how these parameters are related to system load, and to system configuration.

Figures 5 and 6 compare the results of the occupancy distribution model to measurements made in MTS, which has a three level hierarchy consisting of main store, drum, and disk. Figure 5 shows the occupancy distribution for the drum, and although the variance in the measurements is considerably greater than that in the model, the general form of the distribution is quite accurate. Figure 6 shows the distribution for main storage. The agreement is not as good as for the drum, mainly because the migration algorithm from main storage to drum moves several pages at a time, rather than one at a time as the model assumes.

Figure 7 illustrates the effect of changing the threshold t, of a congested level. Changing the threshold clearly cannot prevent congestion. In fact it should be clear that as long as $\lambda > \mu + \eta$, no algorithm for the "when to migrate" decision can prevent congestion. A better replacement algorithm may prevent it, however, by effectively changing the parameters.

When a level is not congested, however, the threshold is relevant, and the occupancy distribution model can be combined with a model for rotating storage devices to determine the appropriate threshold. In addition the combined models can predict the amount of degradation that results when a level becomes congested. See [13] for details.

Although most of these results do not depend on the specific details of the Markov model, and in fact would hold under much less stringent conditions, the model is still useful as a simple demonstration of their validity, and might also be useful in other applications involving occupancy thresholds and migration.

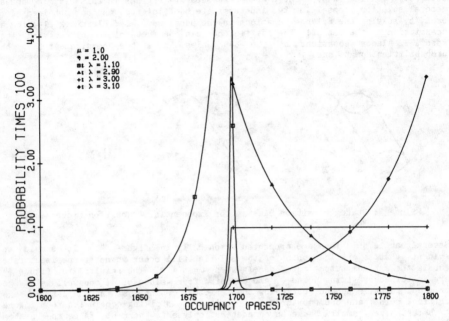

Figure 4: The All Exponential Solution

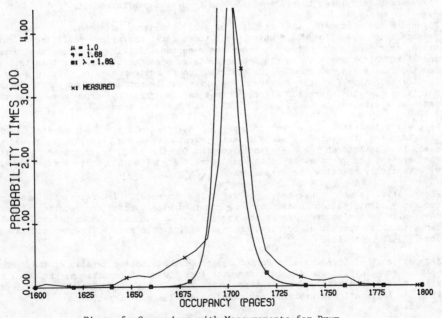

Figure 5: Comparison with Measurements for Drum

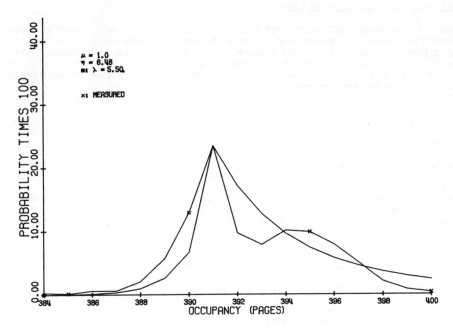

Figure 6: Comparison with Measurements for Main Storage

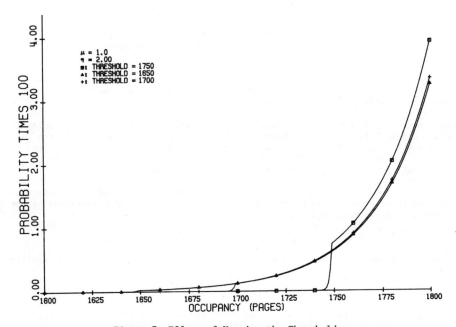

Figure 7: Effect of Varying the Threshold

RELATING PAGE FLOW RATES TO LOAD

One of the most difficult problems in performance evaluation is the characterization of system load, because it depends so critically on the mixture of different types of jobs being executed. For our purposes we sidestep this issue by assuming that the job mix remains relatively constant but that it grows and shrinks in magnitude, as measured by the total number of active virtual pages in use. By "active" we mean part of the address space of some existing process. The distinction is relevant for systems like MULTICS in which every file is potentially part of some address space. For systems with many users in a largely unchanging environment, such as university computing centers, this assumption appears to be reasonably accurate. Numerical results from one such system cannot be expected to be valid for another, however.

Although it is not really accurate, let us assume that the migration rates n_i depend only on the characteristics of the storage devices and the operating system software that controls them, and not on system load. This is not really true because system load effects page fault rates, and the read operations which satisfy page faults use the same data paths as the write operations for the migrations. There does not appear to be any simple way to account for this interaction, however.

It remains, then, to determine how the arrival rates, λ_i, and the departure rates, μ_i, vary with v, the number of virtual pages in the system. First some definitions are required. λ_1, the arrival rate at level one, is just the total page-fault rate, plus np, the rate at which new pages are created in the system. Define $\lambda_{1,i}$ to be the rate of page faults to pages stored at levels greater than i. $\lambda_{1,1}$ would be the total page-fault rate, for example. Also define C_i^* to be the sum of the capacities of levels 1 through i,

$$C_i^* = \sum_{j=1}^{i} C_j$$

Now $\lambda_{1,i}$ is just the page-fault rate for a buffer of size C_i^*. This quantity has been studied extensively and we will see shortly how to adapt these results to produce the functional relationship between $\lambda_{1,i}$ and v.

Analogous to $\lambda_{1,i}$ define ω_i to be the rate at which pages are deleted from levels greater than i (but which do not have copies at level i or lower). Exactly the same techniques will be applicable to ω_i as are applicable to $\lambda_{1,i}$.

Using these definitions, it is possible to derive an equation for the critical point for each level. If the hierarchy is in steady state, the rate of flow into a level will equal the rate of flow out of that level. The rate of flow into a level is just λ_i. The outward flow is the sum of the page-deletion rate μ_i and the actual migration rate (as opposed to the maximum rate n_i) out of level i. Pages which are migrated from level i must eventually either be deleted from some level greater than i, or be paged in from some level greater than i. Otherwise the number of pages at levels greater than i is increasing, and the system is not in steady state. Thus we have the relation

$$\lambda_i = \lambda_{1,i} + \omega_i + \mu_i.$$

Substituting this into the critical point equation from the previous section yields

$$\lambda_{1,i} + \omega_i = n_i \tag{1}$$

It remains to express $\lambda_{1,i}$ and ω_i as functions of v and C_i^*, which will yield an equation relating system load, v, to configuration parameters C_i^* and n_i.

The relation between page-fault rate and buffer capacity is given by the headway function, h(C), which yields mean time between page faults as a function of capacity C. It is implicit in the definition of h that the number of pages in the system, v, is constant. In a multiprogramming environment changes in v are largely due to changes in the number of users. Two users executing the same program, for example, might incur the same page-fault rate as one such program executing in a buffer of half the capacity. Thus, although it is highly challengable, we make the assumption that variations in v are equivalent to inverse variations in C. If the headway function is measured for some particular load, call it v_m, then for load v, it would be $h(Cv_m/v)$.

It is also implicit in the definition of h that the rate of references to memory is constant. Assuming a constant instruction mix, this is the same as saying that the CPU utilization is constant. In a multiprogramming system a variety of bottlenecks both related and unrelated to paging may cause variations in CPU utilization as a function of v. Define U(v) to be the CPU utilization as a function of v. The page-fault rate varies in direct proportion to the memory reference rate (i.e. CPU utilization). Noting that the buffer capacity relevant to $\lambda_{1,i}$ is just C_i^*, these several factors can be combined to yield the desired result for page-fault rates:

$$\lambda_{1,i} = \frac{U(v)}{U(v_m)h(C_i^* v_m/v)}$$

It is straightforward to measure the function U(v), and Mattson et. al. [6] have shown how a single pass over a page reference trace is sufficient to measure h(C), if the replacement algorithm is a "stack" algorithm. Greenberg [15] applied this method to the measurement of the headway function for MULTICS. Figure 8 is the result of a similar measurement for MTS, and shows that over a wide range the headway function is clearly exponential. The shape of the curve at the high end is inaccurate due to the finite duration of the trace data. It is interesting to compare this result to Saltzer's measurements [16] indicating a linear headway function. The replacement algorithm used in MTS is approximately a global (as opposed to per process) LRU algorithm. Using these measurements we can check the accuracy of the above formula for $\lambda_{1,i}$ by comparing it against corresponding measurements of that quantity. The results are shown in figures 9 and 10, for $\lambda_{1,1}$ and $\lambda_{1,2}$, respectively. The accuracy is acceptable for total page-fault rate, and quite good for disk page-fault rate.

In an exactly analogous way, we can define a function f(C) which yields the mean time between page deletions for pages which are not in a buffer of capacity C. This yields an identical formula for ω_i, with h replaced by f. Measurements show that in MTS f is approximately exponential in C^2. Figure 11 compares the results of the formula for ω_i with measurements. (The measurements are actually of $\omega_{i-1} - \omega_i$.)

We are now in a position to calculate the main storage and drum critical points for MTS. First, the expressions for $\lambda_{1,i}$ and ω_i are substituted into the critical point equation (1). Then f and h are measured for some particular load v_m, and U is measured. C_i^* and η_i are parameters of the system configuration. The resulting equation is transcendental in v, but can easily be solved iteratively, and for MTS results in a value of 5974 pages for main storage congestion, and 6744 pages for drum congestion. In order to test these results, mean occupancies of main storage and drum were measured and plotted as a function of v. According to the occupancy distribution model, the mean occupancy at the critical point should be halfway between the threshold and the total capacity of the level. Therefore the value of v at which the mean occupancy passed through this halfway point was taken to be the measured critical point. The results were approximately 6100 pages for

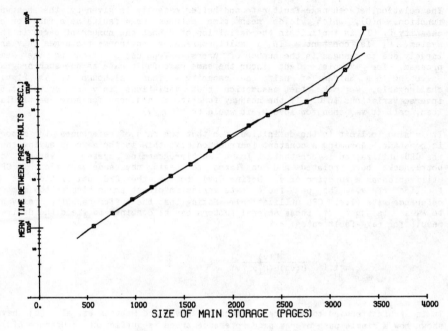

Figure 8: Mean Headway Function, h

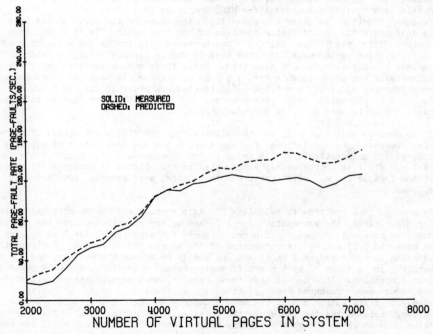

Figure 9: Variation of Total Page-fault Rate with System Load

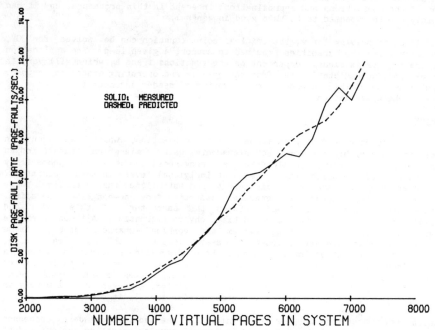

Figure 10: Variation of Disk Page-fault Rates with System Load

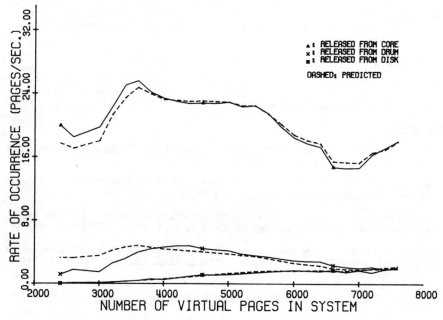

Figure 11: Variation of Released-page Rates with System Load

main storage, and 6700 pages for drum. This agreement is surprisingly accurate in light of the assumptions and approximations inherent in this procedure, and it can probably not be expected to be this good in general.

In addition to solving for v, the critical point equation can be solved for C_i^*, thus determining the capacities required to support a given load. The application of these results is clearly dependent on the functions f and h, which will vary in complex and unpredictable ways from one job mix and operating system to another. The elimination of this dependence must await much needed advances in the area of workload characterization.

SUMMARY

This paper has described a phenomenon called congestion, which can occur in multilevel paging hierarchies. For hierarchies using a migration strategy and an occupancy threshold migration algorithm, a Markov model predicts the probability distribution of occupied page frames at individual levels in such a hierarchy. This model shows how congestion comes about, and establishes that a critical point in its parameters separates congested operation from non-congested operation. Relationships were then developed between the parameters of this model and variables representing system load and hierarchy configuration. Although they are heavily dependent on operating system and workload characteristics, these relationships allow the prediction of the system load at which congestion sets in, for a given configuration, or conversely, the configuration required to support a given load without congestion. It does not guarantee acceptable system performance in terms of response time or throughput. Other models exist (e.g. [7]) which can help to predict these quantities. Congestion is merely an additional factor which can severely degrade performance if it occurs.

A unique feature of this work is its treatment of the program dependent processes by which pages are created and deleted in general purpose operating systems. Most research simply ignores these rather significant factors, and this sometimes makes practical applications more difficult. Since measurements in MTS have shown that these processes play a significant role in system performance, it would appear that further research in their characterization and their performance implications would be useful.

ACKNOWLEDGEMENT

I would like to give credit to Professor Ralph Disney of the University of Michigan Department of Industrial Engineering for his help in formulating and solving the occupancy distrubution model.

REFERENCES

1. Chow, C.K., "On Optimization of Storage Hierarchies", IBM Journal of Research and Development, 18, (July, 1974), pp. 316-327.

2. Gecsei, J., and Lukes, J.A., "A Model for the Evaluation of Storage Hierarchies", IBM Systems Journal 13,2 (1974), pp. 163-178.

3. Ramamoorthy, C.V., and Chandy, K.M., "Optimization of Memory Hierarchies in Multiprogrammed Systems", Journal of the ACM, 17,3 (July, 1970), pp. 426-445.

4. Morenoff, Edward, and McLean, J.B., "Application of Level Changing to a Multilevel Storage Organization", Communications of the ACM, 10,2 (March, 1967), pp. 149-154.

5. Denning, P.J., "Virtual Memory", Computing Surveys, 2,3 (Sept. 1970), pp. 153-190.

6. Mattson, R.L., Gecsei, J., Slutz, D.R., and Traiger, I.L., "Evaluation Techniques for Storage Hierarchies", IBM Systems Journal, 2,1 (1970), p.   78.

7. Arora, S.R., and Gallo, A., "The Optimal Organization of Multiprogrammed Multilevel Memory", Proceedings of the ACM Workshop on System Performance Evaluation, Harvard University, 1971, pp.   104-141.

8. IBM Corp., The 3850 Mass Storage Facility, Form No.   G520-2932, New York: IBM Corporation, 1975.

9. Alexander, Michael T., "Organization and Features of the Michigan Terminal System", AFIPS Conference Proceedings. 1972 Fall Joint Computer Conference, 40, pp.   585-591.

10. Organick, E.I., The MULTICS System: An Examination of Its Structure, Cambridge: MIT Press, 1972.

11. IBM Corp., System/360 Time Sharing System: Resident Supervisor, Form No. GY28-2012, New York: IBM Corporation, 1971.

12. Shelness, N.H., Stephens, P.D. and Whitfield, H., "The Edinburgh Multi-Access System: Scheduling and Allocation Procedures in the Resident Supervisor", Proceedings of the IRIA International Symposium on Operating Systems Theory and Practice, Paris, 1974.

13. Hamilton, J.A., Performance Analysis of Multilevel Paging Hierarchies, Ph.D. Dissertation, University of Michigan, Dept.   of Computer and Communication Sciences, 1976.

14. Kleinrock, Leonard, Queueing Systems. Volume I: Theory, New York: Wiley, 1975.

15. Greenberg, Bernard S., An Experimental Analysis of Program Reference Patterns in the MULTICS Virtual Memory, Project MAC report MAC TR-127, Jan.   1974.

16. Saltzer, Jerome, "A Simple Linear Model of Demand Paging Performance", Communications of the ACM, 17,4 (April, 1974), pp.   181-186.

COMPUTER PERFORMANCE, K.M. CHANDY AND M. REISER (EDS.)
NORTH HOLLAND PUBLISHING COMPANY, 1977

ON THE RELATIVE CONTROLLABILITY OF MEMORY POLICIES

G. S. Graham
Computer Systems Research Group
University of Toronto
Toronto, Canada

P. J. Denning
Computer Sciences Department
Purdue University
West Lafayette, Indiana, USA

Abstract

We investigate the ability of memory management policies
to act as load controllers in a multiprogrammed, virtual
memory computer system. We consider in detail the knee
criterion (operate a program so that its resident set size
is constrained to average near the knee of its lifetime
function). The Working Set (WS), Page Fault Frequency
(PFF), and Least Recently Used memory policies are used as
representative policies and are compared as to their knee
criterion performance. The issue of dynamic adjustment of
memory policy parameter values is also discussed. We
conclude that WS has several performance advantages over
PFF.

*Authors' addresses: G. Scott Graham, Computer Systems
Research Group, University of Toronto, Toronto, Ontario,
Canada, M5S 1A4. Peter J. Denning, Computer Sciences
Department, Purdue University, W. Lafayette, Indiana, U.S.A.
47907.

This work was supported in part by the Connaught Fund at the
University of Toronto, National Research Council Grant
A9274, and National Science Foundation Grant GJ-41289.

411

Introduction

One of the earliest problems encountered in multiprogrammed, virtual memory computer systems was that of thrashing - the collapse of performance due to an overcommitment of main memory caused by operating at too high a load (degree of multiprogramming) [2]. This is illustrated in Figure 1, where system throughput (job transactions completed per unit time) is the performance measure. Operating at an average load greater than n2 produces thrashing.

The objective of a load controller is to regulate both the load and memory policy so that system performance remains near optimal. (We choose system throughput as our performance measure of interest because it is closely related to mean response time and processor utilization [4].) Figure 1 shows that we can conveniently define a plateau (n1,n2) on the throughput curve T(n) so that throughput is within some specified tolerance (e.g., 5%) of the optimal T(n0).

Perhaps the simplest load controller is one that simply searches by varying the load n and observing T(n) for an optimal throughput. This method has several limitations: the search may find a local maximum, or it may be in error because conditions in the system may not be accurately reflected by observing jobs departing from the system.

Denning et al. [4] have investigated a variety of adaptive load control mechanisms. They observed that a practical controller must avoid the high overhead of searching for the maximum of a control function. Instead, it should use supplemental measures whose values indicate the most desirable direction for an adjustment of load or memory policy parameter. Further, the most useful supplemental measures are related to program behaviour because load changes are strongly correlated with changes in the main memory allocation available to each program.

They investigated three supplemental measures in the context of a simple queueing network model and found that these measures were effective in locating optimal loads. The supplemental measures considered were:

the knee criterion: operate each program so that its mean resident set size averages near the knee of its lifetime function,

the L=S criterion: operate the system so that the system lifetime L(n) is approximately equal to S, where S is the page swap time,

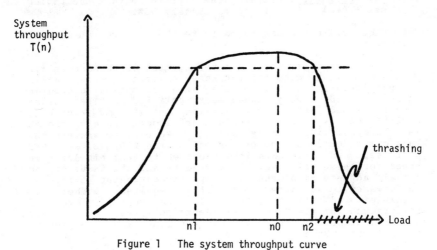

Figure 1   The system throughput curve

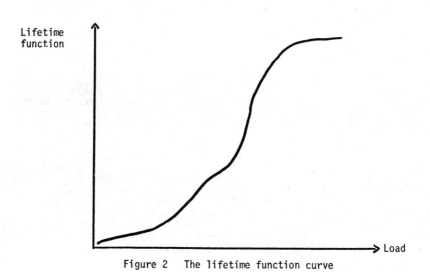

Figure 2   The lifetime function curve

the 50% criterion: operate the system so that the paging
device utilization is approximately 50%.

The knee criterion was found to be the most robust control
policy.

This paper continues the investigation of Denning et al.
One purpose is to consider the knee criterion more fully.
In particular, we relate the knee criterion to program
behaviour and memory management policies. The Least
Recently Used (LRU) [3], Working Set (WS) [2], and Page
Fault Frequency (PFF) [1] replacement algorithms are chosen
as representative memory policies. We examine whether the
knee criterion is a good criterion for the LRU, WS, and PFF
policies, and how hard it is to operate near the lifetime
knees for these policies. We also consider the issue of the
dynamic adjustment of the memory policy parameter to improve
performance. We investigate the required number of
parameter adjustments to achieve a certain level of
performance for the WS and PFF memory policies. This gives
an indication of the overhead present in the respective
controllers. We also describe certain pitfalls connected
specifically with adjustment of the PFF parameter.

The context of our study is also a simple queueing
network model, with extensive use of address reference
strings from actual virtual memory programs to generate
parameter values for the model. Our results corroborate
those of Denning et al. and also provide interesting
empirical data on WS and PFF performance. We begin with a
review of background material.

Background

We first consider performance measures. The lifetime
function $L(x)$ of a program under a given memory policy is
the mean virtual time between page faults (mean interfault
interval) when the program's resident set averages x pages.
Empirical lifetime functions usually have an approximately
convex region for small x followed by an approximately
concave region, with local variations, as shown in Figure 2.
The lifetime function is the reciprocal of the familiar page
fault rate function $F(x)$. The memory space-time product
$ST(x)$ of a program under a given memory policy is the
product of the amount of memory occupied by the program and
the real time spent occupying it, when the program's
resident set averages x pages in virtual time. $ST(x)$ can
conveniently be expressed as the sum of a virtual time
component and a real time component (in units of page-
seconds, for example)

$$ST(x) = K \cdot x + \sum_{i=1}^{P} D \cdot x(i)$$

where K is the reference string length, D is the mean real time delay to service a page fault, P is the number of page faults, and $x(i)$ is the memory size during the ith page fault.

We turn now to memory policies. The LRU policy is a fixed partition policy with memory size as its parameter. At any time, the resident set under LRU with memory size m consists of those m pages most recently referenced. The WS policy is a variable partition policy with window size as its parameter. At time t, the resident set under WS, $W(t,T)$, is the set of those pages contained in a backward-looking window of size T, including the reference at time t, $r(t)$, i.e., $W(t,T) = \{r(t-T+1),\ldots,r(t)\}$. The PFF policy is also a variable partition policy with window size as its parameter. At page fault time t, the resident set under PFF is determined by observing the time t' of the previous page fault and comparing the interfault interval with a standard parameter value THRESH. The resident set $x(t)$ for parameter THRESH is specified as

$$x(t) = \begin{cases} x(t') + r(t) & t-t' < \text{THRESH} \\ W(t,t-t') & \text{otherwise} \end{cases}$$

Intuitively, PFF attempts to decrease the memory allocation at page fault time if the most recent interfault interval is "too long".

Finally, we consider load control methods, both program and load-driven. It is useful to classify these methods based on the variable that is directly controlled. A program-driven method specifies a resident set of guaranteed content for each program and requires that the load be determined as the number of resident sets that can exist together in main memory. Its free variable is the memory policy parameter, such as window size, and the load is a dependent variable. In contrast, a load-driven method specifies a load, requiring that the memory policy determine a memory partition that accommodates the given load. Its free parameter is the load and the memory partition is a dependent variable.

Additional background material can be found in [4,7]. Before considering the knee criterion in more detail, we briefly discuss our experimental methodology.

Experimental Methodology

Six virtual memory programs were traced and produced eight output trace tapes. Two criteria were used to select programs for tracing. First, the programs represented a range of program behaviours. Second, the programs were

heavily-used and were a substantial load on the system.
Care was taken to ensure that the reference string length
used in the experiments was sufficient to exhibit consistent
experimental results. Lifetime functions and space-time
products were measured for several fixed partition and
variable partition policies. Further details can be found
in [7].

The Knee Criterion

A knee of a lifetime function curve is the operating
point beyond which the curve tends to flatten out. The
primary knee is defined geometrically as the point of
tangency between the curve and the ray of maximum slope,
from the origin, which is tangential to the curve. Knees of
higher order can be defined similarly in terms of rays of
smaller slopes. As a load control rule, the knee criterion
constrains the mean resident set size of a program to
average near the primary knee of the program's lifetime
function. The knee criterion is suited for a program-driven
control method because it uses detailed information about
the dynamic behaviour of individual programs.

The knee criterion is an intuitively appealing rule,
because the primary knee represents the "point of
diminishing returns" on the lifetime function. However,
there is much more to it than intuitive appeal. The primary
knee maximizes the ratio $L(x)/x$. Suppose one page fault
incurs a mean execution delay of D (corresponding to page
swap time and time spent queueing). P page faults in a
program will span a real time interval whose expected length
is $P \cdot L(x) + P \cdot D$. The memory space-time product per
reference is then

$$\frac{x \cdot (P \cdot L(x) + P \cdot D)}{P \cdot L(x)} = x + D \cdot \frac{x}{L(x)}$$

Thus, operating at the primary knee minimizes the component
of memory space-time due to paging $((D \cdot x)/L(x))$. Because
I/O device speeds and request rates are independent of x,
total memory space-time per job tends to be minimized [4].

Consider now a complementary argument. Observe a system
with load n for V time units. The total system space-time
product in the system is $M \cdot V$ (for main memory capacity M),
and the total number of job completions is $V \cdot T(n)$. The
system space-time per job is then $(M \cdot V)/(T(n) \cdot V)$, or $M/T(n)$.
Because Smith has observed that memory space-time calculated
in a uniprogramming mode is related to system space-time
measured in a multiprogramming load [10], minimizing system
space-time (and hence memory space-time) is equivalent to
maximizing throughput.

We now have the chain of arguments: the primary knee
tends to minimize memory space-time per job, and memory
space-time per job is minimized exactly when throughput is
maximized. The implication therefore is that the knee
criterion seems to define a load at which throughput is
optimal. The foregoing is not a proof; rather, it is a
plausibility argument supporting the knee criterion.
Denning et al. found the knee criterion to be the most
robust of the three control methods investigated [4]. It
consistently produced near optimal throughputs under a
variety of operating conditions. The purpose here is to
draw conclusions about the interaction between the knee
criterion and the memory policies producing the lifetime
functions.

The Experiments

We first tested the correspondence between the lifetime
knees and the space-time minima for the WS, PFF, and LRU
policies. The correspondence was in terms of the relative
percentage difference between the lifetime knee memory
space-time value and the minimum memory space-time value. A
summary of the data for the eight trace tapes is displayed
in Table 1. WS had both the lowest mean and lowest maximum
relative percentage difference between the space-time values
of the lifetime knee operating points and the minima of the
space-time product. PFF ranked next, LRU last. The table
shows that the correspondence between knees and local space-
time minima is extremely strong for the WS policy and is
also present, though not as strongly, for the PFF and LRU
policies. It is important to note that PFF did produce
errors exceeding 10% in the correspondence for two knees on
one reference string; we observed no such erratic behaviour
for WS. LRU showed the weakest correspondence. LRU also
has the troublesome feature that an adaptive control method
cannot systematically locate the LRU space-time minimum in a
simple way because the LRU space-time curve typically has a
sharp minimum [1,7]. We show later that WS and PFF appear
to be more controllable in that the knees and minima can be
found by indirect methods.

To investigate further the plausibility argument, we
tested the correspondence between lifetime knee and optimal
throughput in a simple queueing network model [3,7]. The
correspondence here was in terms of the relative percentage
difference between the lifetime knee throughput and the
optimal throughput. Two values of mean page swap time D and
two plateaux of good performance - within 5% and 10% of
optimal throughput - were used. Denning et al. had observed
that their results depended upon whether D exceeded the knee
lifetime by a significant amount [4]. We also observed this
dependence. A summary of the data for the eight trace tapes
is presented in Table 2. The correspondence between the

	WS	PFF	LRU
Number of knees-primary, secondary, tertiary	8, 6, 2	8, 5, 1	8, 0, 0
Mean relative percentage difference between lifetime knee ST value and ST minimum	.35, .37, .95	1.96, 3.48, .90	3.40, -, -
Maximum relative percentage difference	1.64, .97, 1.45	11.46, 10.28, .90	11.70, -, -

Table 1   Summary of lifetime knee - minimum
space-time correspondence data

	D=5			D=10		
	mean relative percentage difference between knee T(n) and max T(n)	number of programs within specified control		mean relative percentage difference between knee T(n) and max T(n)	number of programs within specified control	
		5%	10%		5%	10%
WS	5.7	6	6	14.9	3	4
PFF	4.9	5	6	12.5	5	5
LRU	12.3	4	6	25.6	1	2

Table 2   Summary of knee criterion data

lifetime knee and optimal throughput operating points (i.e.,
the knee criterion) for the small D value was very good for
all policies; at the large D value, where the knee criterion
was failing, PFF showed a better correspondence than WS,
with LRU showing poor correspondence.

The table shows that for each memory policy the knee
criterion began to break down when the value of D became
much larger than the knee lifetime. The reason is that D
represents the system delay in responding to a change of
locality sets.   If LT is the lifetime at the primary knee
and D >> LT, then D is long compared to the periods of
constant memory demand by the program and the load control
policy can no longer adapt to changes in locality in a
timely manner [7].   PFF does better than WS in this case
because its tendency to allocate more memory during locality
changes gives it a larger resident set and isolates it from
this problem.

In this experiment, the related question of the width of
the load range for the 5% and 10% plateaux allowed by WS and
PFF was also investigated. The load range is determined by
the smallest and largest loads which cause the model to
operate on a plateau. For two values of D, four
combinations of conditions were possible. As shown in Table
3, WS allowed a wider load range in three of four cases.
PFF was marginally better for D=10 on the 5% plateau.   Two
results follow from this.   WS is more robust than PFF
because it operates at near optimal over a wider range of
operating conditions.   Also, PFF performs better than WS
when the mean page swap time is significantly larger than
the knee lifetime, as it did for the lifetime knee - system
throughput correspondence test. This latter case, however,
does not represent a desirable situation for system
operation.

To summarize the results of this part of the
investigation: the WS knee criterion worked well, as
expected.   The PFF and LRU knee criteria also showed good
correspondence. The PFF policy, however, exhibited erratic
behaviour on one reference string when its lifetime knees
produced space-time values differing by more than 10% from
the space-time minima values.   In the queueing network
experiments, WS allowed a wider load range for two plateaux
on the throughput curve than PFF.   The WS and PFF knee
criteria were comparable when the average relative
difference between lifetime knee throughput and optimal
throughput was considered. The value of the mean page swap
time D affected all the results. Increasing the value of D
well beyond the knee lifetime ruined the knee criterion.
Further comparisons of memory policies are given in the next
section.

	D=5		D=10	
	5%	10%	5%	10%
WS	4.9	5.8	2.5	4.8
PFF	3.8	5.0	2.6	3.9

Table 3   Load ranges for WS and PFF on the throughput
plateaux

Dynamic Adjustment of Memory Policy Parameters

Program-driven load controllers specify a program's
resident set size and content by tracking its reference
string. In doing so, they detect changes in locality sets
and specify a memory allocation that at all times is an
estimate of the current locality set. The variable
partition policies WS and PFF use a memory parameter of
constant size to detect locality set changes - the window
size T for WS and the threshold window size THRESH for PFF.
It is appealing to consider changing parameter values, based
on trends in page referencing, to produce better estimates
of locality sets. When the locality set is small, for
example, the WS window size T can be made smaller to
estimate a smaller resident set size.

Several studies have pursued this approach. Smith
proposed to reduce the window size at locality set changes,
thereby removing unreferenced pages of the old locality set
and damping increases in working set size [10]. Prieve
assigned a different, fixed window size to each page of a
program in his Page Partition replacement policy and showed
that it improved page fault rate at the same mean memory
size over WS [8]. The difficulty with these two methods is
that the improvements in general were not significant enough
to justify the cost of implementation. T-modifying
proposals are based on assumptions that controlling the
window size during program execution is beneficial and
improves performance. However, it is not clear whether
dynamic window control is of any use. Chu and Opderbeck
observed a wide plateau in their WS and PFF space-time
curves, indicating that the choice of the window parameter
value was not critical [1]. According to their data, it
sufficed for each program to be assigned its own fixed
parameter setting.

Dynamic parameter adjustment is useful only if its cost
is less than its reward [9]. To resolve the different
approaches mentioned above, we investigated controller
criteria more fully. We considered two plateaux for the
space-time product and determined the width of the window
size intervals associated with the WS and PFF load ranges.
If the space-time curve exhibited narrow plateaux, then so
would the throughput curve.

A note of caution: our results may depend on the set of
programs present in our study. If we discovered that a
window of a specific size gave (say) a 10% level of control
for WS, we would not necessarily expect that window size
value to be correct for a different set of programs. We are
not making general conclusions about good choices of window
sizes; instead, we are presenting a methodology for
assessing the overhead of memory policy controllers.

Our interest was in the interval(s) of window size necessary to force each of the eight reference strings to operate within some specified level of the memory policy's minimum space-time cost. (As a result of the previous section, this is equivalent to the question: how hard is it to find the knee?) We studied a 5% and a 10% plateau as illustrated in Figures 3 and 4. The horizontal lines in these figures represent the range of window sizes causing the program to operate on a given plateau. In Figure 3, the vertical line A shows setting T=73,000 would cause each of the reference strings to operate on its own 10% WS space-time plateau (although several would operate on their extremes - P2,P4,P7). Thus, one value of T would be sufficient to establish a 10% level of control. Were a 5% level of control required for WS, at least two values of T, shown by the vertical lines B1(T=50,000) and B2 (T=118,000) would be needed. It would not be necessary to change constantly between these two values during program execution; only an initial selection between them would be needed. The results for PFF were different. PFF would need at least three threshold window sizes to give a 10% level of control for these reference strings. At the 5% level, PFF would need at least four threshold window sizes.

These results suggest that PFF is inherently more difficult to control than WS because it requires more distinct parameter values to achieve a comparable level of performance over a set of reference strings. A well-designed PFF controller therefore would likely generate more overhead than a well-designed WS controller. This, in turn, would offset the benefits of PFF's simpler implementation [1].

There are also stability problems present in a PFF controller. We have observed both anomalous and gap behaviours in PFF reference strings [7]. Anomalous behaviour is present when changes in parameter values do not produce the desired performance improvements. For example, increasing the PFF threshold window size may unexpectedly lead to a smaller mean memory allocation or a higher page fault rate, or both (see Figure 5 and [6]). No such behaviour is possible for the WS window size [5]. Gap behaviour is present when a small increase in threshold window value produces a small increase in lifetime value, but a large jump in mean resident set size (see Figure 6). In other words, a small upward adjustment in parameter value may cause some programs to place a sudden heavy demand on the memory subsystem. No such behaviour was observed for WS.

To summarize the results of this part of our investigation: a WS load controller contains less overhead than a PFF controller; it consistently requires fewer parameter settings for the set of programs to achieve both

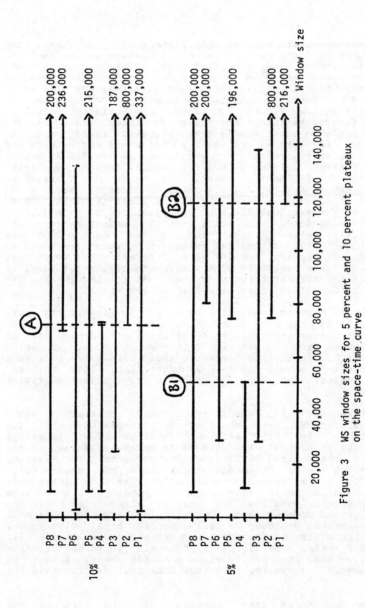

Figure 3   WS window sizes for 5 percent and 10 percent plateaux
on the space-time curve

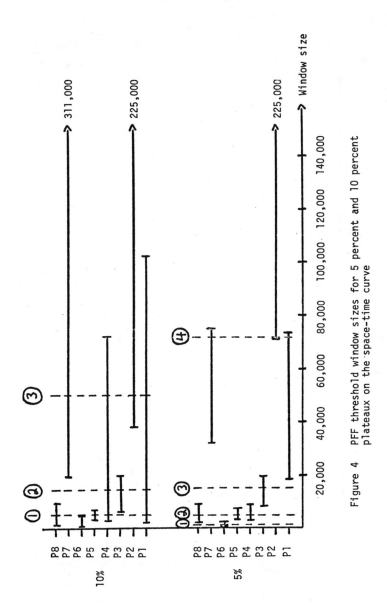

Figure 4   PFF threshold window sizes for 5 percent and 10 percent
plateaux on the space-time curve

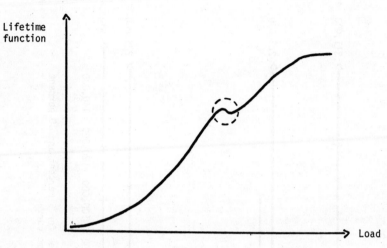

Figure 5   An anomalous lifetime function

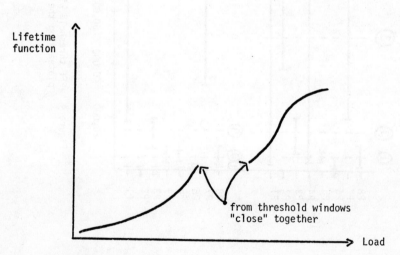

Figure 6   A lifetime function exhibiting gap behaviour

5% and 10% plateaux in the space-time curves. Moreover, a WS controller is more stable than a PFF controller because it is not subject to anomalous or gap behaviours.

Conclusions

Gap and anomalous behaviours are certainly vexing problems for a practical PFF load controller. We have observed both in practice. However, it is probable that over large increases in PFF threshold window size there is little practical likelihood of observing control problems relating to the lifetime function during computer system operation.

What is more troublesome is the observation that, for the set of eight trace tapes, there did not exist a single PFF threshold window size which would give a 10% level of control, as there was for WS. A PFF controller must classify a program and select its proper parameter setting, involving overhead not present for a WS controller at the 10% level. Given the knee criterion and dynamic parameter adjustment results, we conclude that the apparent ease of PFF implementation should be balanced against the performance benefits of WS when considering the design or modification of a memory policy.

Acknowledgements

The authors thank W.D. Elliott and A.I. Levy for their valuable comments.

References

1. Chu, W.W. and Opderbeck, H. The page fault frequency algorithm. Proc. FJCC (1972) 597-609.

2. Denning, P.J. The working set model for program behavior. Comm. ACM 11,5 (May 1968) 323-333.

3. Denning, P.J. and Graham, G.S. Multiprogrammed memory management. Proc. IEEE Vol. 63,6 (June 1975) 924-939.

4. Denning, P.J., Kahn, K.C., Leroudier, J., Potier, D., and Suri, R. Optimal multiprogramming. Acta Informatica 7 (1976) 197-216.

5. Denning, P.J. and Schwartz, S.C. Properties of the working set model. Comm. ACM 15,3 (March 1972) 191-198.

6. Franklin, M.A., Graham, G.S., and Gupta, R.K. Anomalies
    with variable partition paging algorithms. Accepted for
    publication in Comm. ACM.

7. Graham, G.S. A study of program and memory policy
    behaviour. Ph.D. thesis, Comp. Sci. Dept., Purdue
    University (December 1976).

8. Prieve, B.G. Page partition replacement algorithm.
    Ph.D. thesis, Dept. of Elec. Eng. and Comp. Sci.,
    University of California, Berkeley (December 1973).

9. Saltzer, J.H. On the modeling of paging algorithms.
    ACM Forum, Comm. ACM 19,5 (May 1976) 307-308.

10. Smith, A.J. A modified working set algorithm. IEEE
    Trans. E.C. (September 1976) 909-914.

COMPUTER PERFORMANCE, K.M. CHANDY AND M. REISER (EDS.)
NORTH HOLLAND PUBLISHING COMPANY, 1977

AN APPROACH TO USE EVALUATION NETS FOR THE PERFORMANCE EVALUATION OF TRANSACTION-ORIENTED BUSINESS COMPUTER SYSTEMS

J. Schwandt

Philips Research Laboratory
Hamburg, Germany

The use of Evaluation nets for modelling transac-
tion-oriented business computer systems and networks composed of such computers in order to evaluate their expected performance by simulation, as a
support to product planning and configuration planning is presented. System models consist of segre-
gated modules, interconnected via predefined interfaces, representing the instruction sequences of
application programs, the operating system functions and the hardware components of the system.
This approach permits the modules to be created
independently and to be exchanged against alternatives for the simulation. An own-developed discrete-event simulation program package SAMO (ALGOL-
based) complemented by an E-net implementation
program SAMEN is used for the simulation. The models available have been calibrated and validated.
Some stand-alone as well as network configurations
have been modelled and simulated.

1 INTRODUCTION

The project "Optimization of Computer Networks with Intelligent Terminals" had the objective to develop concepts for application-ori-
ented computer networks composed of small business or "office" computers or using them as intelligent terminals. These system designs
had to be evaluated and optimized under the constraints of the selected applications. For the performance evaluation modelling and
simulation should be used. Appropriate modelling techniques and simulation programs had to be provided. As a result a reservoir of system component models and application models available for further
investigations, a methodology for terminal-oriented system conception, and a proven performance evaluation tool have been accomplished.

2 METHOD OF SYSTEM CONCEPTION

A system design method has to start with the consideration of application functions and the sequences and interdependencies of tasks

The described work was supported by the German Federal Ministry for
Research and Technology (BMFT) under no. 081 2008 72. Only the author
is responsible for the contents of this publication.

within an organization. This information allows to identify the system components and their performance parameters under given constraints of execution time and data volume. Alternative system configurations may then be evaluated on a model basis by simulation.
This approach may be equally applied to assess the performance specification of <u>new</u> system components or systems or to support configuration planning for given applications, using available system components.

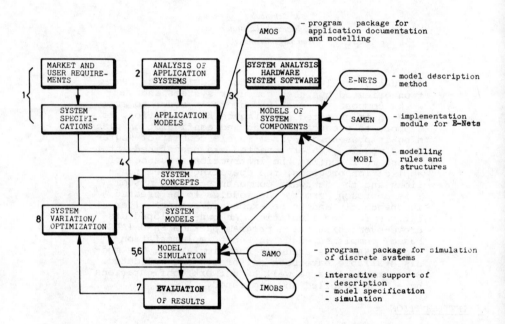

FIGURE 1: Steps of system design with modelling and simulation

Fig. 1 illustrates the major steps in simulation-based system design
and indicates in the right part the software tools available:

- 1 Based on user requirements the application has to be described
    and the performance be defined.
- 2 The application description identifies the essential system
    functions (input, output, processing, storage, retrieval) and
    information flows in hardware-independent form. It is the basis
    for conceiving alternative system designs for which the essen-
    tial system components are identified.
- 3 Models of the identified system components (hardware, system
    software) are generated or called from a library.
- 4 For each configuration the connection of the required component
    and subsystem models is specified. The respective application
    models are generated and precompiled with AMOS to serve as simu-
    lation load of the system model.
- 5 Experiments are formulated by activating measuring points in the
    models, initializing parameter values and specifying application
    process sequences.
- 6 Simulation is started, measured values are edited.

- 7 The simulation output is evaluated and related to the parameters
  of the real system to be considered for performance evaluation.
- 8 Performance evaluation shall lead to acceptance or modification
  of the conceived system which in turn may be evaluated.

3 MODELLING CONCEPT

To offer the user of this evaluation method the flexibility of easily
exchanging parts of models during simulation experiments, a modular
approach was followed which preserves roughly the structure of the
real system in its model. Mainly a three-partite concept is used so
that the application description, called the application software
model (ASM), the system software model (SSM), and the system hardware model (SHM) are kept apart from each other and are composed to
a simulation model via predefined interfaces (Fig. 2). This approach

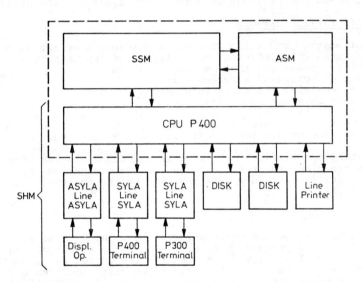

FIGURE 2: Three-partite model of a computer network

not only offers easy exchangeability of ASM, SSM, and SHM against
alternatives of each of them, but also allows the preparation of
ASM, SSM, and SHM by different teams of experts. The three parts are
representing the functional and time determining aspects of the respective parts of the real system. They control each other via
interfaces for statements or pointers. A statement transfers all information needed for its interpretation while the use of a pointer
which references a global list may reduce the information flow via
the interface.

The next step is the choice of appropriate methods for the description of the components. These methods are closely related to the
tasks of the components and to the fact, that modelling and simulation are performed to get answers to questions which are asked to
the SHM and the SSM. In our examples these questions concern primarily the execution time of programs under the constraints of concurrent operation of several programs and several subsystems. Therefore the models have to contain these time aspects.

- The application software model (ASM) represents the workload of
  the system and is described by lists. The control list contains
  the control information and the instruction list the process information of the job.
- The system software model (SSM) is described by representing the
  structure of its modules which process system software instructions
  for the purpose of allocating system resources to the application
  processes. The SSM modules are described by their functional structure and the time elapsing for running through alternative branches. This time may be either generated in the SSM itself, or the
  execution of SSM processes is also treated as workload of the SHM.
- The system hardware model (SHM) represents the functional structure of the hardware and has to deliver all time information with
  respect to the execution of instruction sequences on behalf of the
  application programs and the system software functions as well as
  for the execution of input or output operations via the devices.

4 MODEL DESCRIPTION METHODS

To accomplish this modelling concept, a suitable description method
had to be found which offered capabilities of representing
- parallel processes and their synchronization
- the logic structure of a system part
- transient entities and their information content
- propagation delay or execution time.
In addition to that a graphical representation of the model structure for better comprehension and a suitability of the model description to easy implementation for simulation are required.

From existing description methods we investigated program flow
charts, state diagrams, Petri nets and Nutt's evaluation nets. We
found that our requirements were best met by the evaluation nets
(E-nets) [1,2].

4.1 Evaluation Nets

Evaluation nets allow the description of parallel processes, control
and data flow, and processing time, they offer a graphical representation and a complementary formal description suited as simulation
input. They allow hierarchical levels of description in that a given
portion of a system may be expanded or compressed in detail compared
to the rest of the model.

Transitions, locations, and tokens are the elements of an E-net.
Tokens may be regarded as information carriers. A token may represent a job, a message, a command, or status information moving
through the system. Tokens reside in locations, one at a time, and
control their motion mutually at transitions. Transitions may represent time-less actions (events) or time-consuming actions (activities). Fig. 3 shows the five basic transition types. A transition
"fires" if the activities represented by that transition are executed. This means that after elapse of the transition time tokens
are moved from their input locations to the output locations and
that their attributes, representing the information carried, are
possibly changed according to the transition procedure. Every transition is described by its schema, by a transition procedure which
affects the attributes, by a time procedure if the transition time
is not zero, and in the case of the X- and Y-transition by a resolution procedure which allows the control of token advance according
to the status of the net or the actual values of token attributes.

Macro transitions [3] allow the use of more than two input or output locations per transition.

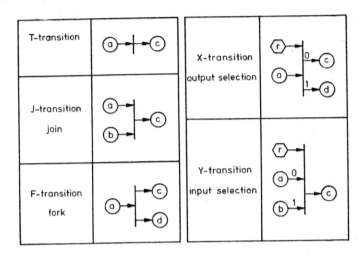

FIGURE 3: Basic transition types of E-nets

When working with evaluation nets we had to define an additional type of transition in order to describe the interruption of the transition time already started. This concept was required for modelling the interrupt behaviour of a system [4]. The TI-transition allows to signal an interrupt to an active transition and to terminate the lapse of transition time. Such a transition is used in Fig. 4 to generate the instruction execution time of the central processor.

4.2 Aspects of model representation

Modelling with evaluation nets offers flexibility in model representation. Parts of the system structure may be represented by the net graph or by transition procedures. A model with a well structured net graph is clear and easy to survey, but its simulation may take a considerable amount of computer time. With growing experience, the model builder tends to represent the system structure by structured transition procedures mainly, but a certain net structure level should be kept.

The expenses for shifting the evaluation procedure from the real object to an abstract level depend also on the degree of abstraction or detail of the model which affects model preparation time, simulation time and storage demand. Therefore one is forced to find a trade-off between detail of the model expressed in preparation time and simulation costs, and the benefits of the information we except from simulation results.

5   TOOLS

5.1 Application modelling system AMOS

Applications are described in terms of tasks and data flow. Tasks contain the functional sequences of operations to be performed, the

data flow contains the data elements connecting two tasks or serving
as input or output data [5]. For the documentation of application
description and for the generation of an application load for the
simulated computer system, an application modelling system AMOS was
conceived. It consists of four modules:

The module UPDOC is used for the storage of task and data element
descriptions and their structural relations. The module CONNEX allows the definition of input-output relationship within tasks. The
module ALIGEN generates a model of the specified application consisting of model commands like e.g.
    BOOLOOP [<Taskname>|<Filename>]↕ <No of repetitions>
    OPEN <Filename><No of groups or elements>
    JUMPOFF <condition>
    ARITHM[=|+|-|*|/]↕
The ALIGEN commands are converted by the program AMOC according to
the actual configuration and special parameters of the modelled system. The results serve as input data for the application software
model at simulation run time.

5.2 Simulation program package SAMO

The simulation and modelling program package SAMO supports event controlled simulation of time discrete systems [6]. The object to be
simulated is represented as a system of black boxes and interconnec-
tions transmitting information only at discrete times. The entire
model is generated in two steps. In the first step the black box
structure of the model is defined by describing the connection net
using the connection model description format COMOL. In the second
step the functional behaviour of each black box type has to be defined. For this purpose a black box input format BOMOL is used.
BOMOL is based on ALGOL 60 supplementing it by some simple rules
for the description of delay times and time-parallel operations. The
black boxes and the connection net are converted to an ALGOL program
by the SAMO translator. SAMO then takes care of the generation of
the model time, event scheduling and administration of the entities:
black box types, connection nets, data, procedures. Extensions enable interactive parameter variation during run time and step-by-
step simulation for the segmentation of long simulation runs.

5.3 E-net Implementor SAMEN

A simple approach for the implementation of E-nets appears if its
formal description is compared with an ALGOL program. It contains a
declaration part which defines the locations, tokens with their attributes, and other variables. The description of a single transition
is similar to a procedure call. The specifications of resolution and
transition procedures are similar to procedure declarations in ALGOL.
Following this approach a very simple pattern for the description of
E-nets was defined in the SAMEN (simulation and modelling with evaluation nets) implementation module, according to the formal description of E-nets and to the black box input format BOMOL of the SAMO
simulation program package [7,8].

The usage of SAMEN and SAMO allows the network to be decomposed into
several subnets, independently described. Each subnet is implemented
as one black box. Each black box contains its own local simulation
routine which controls the token flow in the box. The transitions
are represented by transition type procedures which imitate their
logical behaviour. Special interfaces connecting the peripheral
locations of the subnets and the SAMO connections organize the token

flow between the boxes by a handshaking mechanism. The information flow via the box connections as well as the model time are controlled by the SAMO package.

The modification of the graphic representation of E-nets on a screen and the subsequent code generation have been realized by means of a program GIPSIE [9]. A dialogue for the parametrization of models and the initialization of simulation runs may be generated and executed with the dialogue implementation program DIMPLE. The dialogue programs have the collective name IMOBS (for interactive modelling and simulation).

6 EXAMPLES OF MODELS

In the following we describe two examples of computer system design where we applied the evaluation net as model description method and performed simulation with the program packages SAMEN and SAMO.

6.1 Model of a Stand-Alone Office Computer

The first example concerns a stand-alone office computer system equipped with several input/output devices which is used for the execution of invoicing in a wholesale company. In this case the interaction of the hardware with the system software and the concurrent operation of the peripherals were considered. Also the effects of processing up to four application programs in parallel using the multiprogramming mode could be studied and the execution time for each program partition could be obtained from simulation. For this example the modelling concept was extended:
- Data transfers between subsystems do not take place. Instead of that, a start signal SIOS starts the time procedure of the subsystem model which generates the data transfer time and the command execution time as a function of the amount of data to be transferred; elapse of this time generates a signal ISP indicating completion of the data transfer.
- Errors and error handling routines are not modelled since the frequency of errors is considered to be several orders of magnitude smaller than the frequency of error-free operations.

Fig. 4 gives an impression of the functions represented in the model of the central processor. The model generates in transition a2 the time required for the execution of system software instructions and application program instructions by looking up the respective times in lists after receiving pointers from the SSM or the ASM. Each sequence of instructions in process may be interrupted by completion signals ISP from IO devices thus taking into account the time elapsed for IO operations during the time running down for the execution of instructions. All other transitions have no delay time, a1 and a9 serve as selectors for incoming requests for actions to be taken by the central processor forwarding them according to priority rules laid down in the decision procedures r1 and r9. The remaining transitions forward IO commands to devices (a10) or synchronize the operations of the SHM with the SSM and the ASM (a4 to a7). Transition a3 represents the interpretation of classes of statements to be executed.

To the central processor the IO devices keyboard, control printer, magnetic ledger card unit and disk are connected, representing the peripheral equipment typical for a so-called office computer or visual record computer. Their models consist mainly of a transition which represents the operation time depending on type of devices,

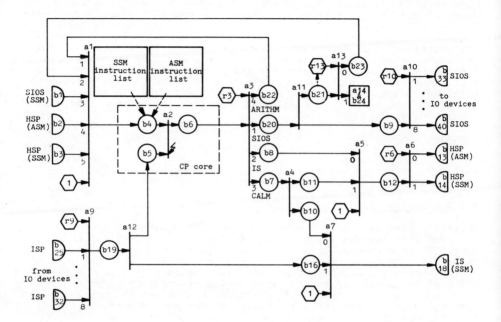

FIGURE 4: Central processor model of an office computer

command and amount of information to be processed. Also some control
functions may be modelled.

The system software model (SSM) consists of E-nets representing the
logic structure of the disk-oriented operating system DOS 400 it is
based upon. One subnet each describes the modules
- interrupt handler which steers interrupts to the respective system
  routines of the SSM and after their completed execution starts the
  scheduler;
- multifunc which processes interrupts and starts input/output
  operations;
- scheduler which monitors process priorities and starts the process
  of highest priority;
- step manager which interprets job control statements and initiates
  allocation of resources to jobs;
- section load which initiates loading of not memory-resident system
  software modules by request.

The SSM routines are considered as being executed on the SHM which
is the only time-consuming model. Therefore the SHM works at the instruction list of the SSM after being started by a pointer at b3
(see Fig. 4) and signals completion via b14 back to the SSM.

The complete model (ASM, SHM, SSM) needed about 250 K Bytes of memory. IO devices covered 4 K Bytes, the CPU and the SSM each about
60 K Bytes.

The execution of an invoicing transaction of 90 seconds office computer time was simulated repeatedly and delivered information on CPU

and IO device utilization which could be used to validate the CPU and device models. On the host computer, a Philips P1400 (comparable to an IBM 370/138) 90 minutes simulation time were needed. Abandoning the hierarchical structure of SSM and CPU by using constant execution times for the SSM transitions instead of transferring the execution to the SHM, simulation time went down to 7.5 minutes without changing the simulation results. As a variation of the model, the multiprogramming feature was activated for additional application programs. The simulation results for the invoicing program remained unchanged.

The models were calibrated and validated in the following manner: For the CPU model, which represented a CPU still under development, instruction execution times were determined on the basis of a real CPU with similar instruction set and structure. Their execution times were measured and multiplied by a constant factor which could be validated when the modeled CPU was available for measurements. Execution times were determined per type of instruction and for different operand lengths.

Execution times for system software instruction sequences were determined taking into account the number and distribution of instructions per sequence and the CPU times.

For the IO device models, the operational behaviour was analyzed on the basis of development specifications, and the operation times were expressed as functions of command types, amount of data, and device-dependent parameters. These algorithms became part of the time procedures of the IO device models. They could be validated by hardware measurements compared to the simulation results.

6.2 Model of a Terminal System

In Fig. 2 a terminal system for materials management in a factory was represented. In this terminal system, the behaviour of the control station during the peak hour of data communication with three tributary stations provides most information regarding the performance of the complete system. Therefore, the model of the control station, the central P400, contains all functions needed to assess its performance while the tributary station models have been abstracted to time procedures which represent the process sequences required to load the control station model. According to the three-partite model concept, the control station P400 has been modeled in three black boxes which represent the ASM, the SHM, and the SSM. The IO devices disk 1 and disk 2, line printer, and data communication units (ASYLA and SYLA) are separate boxes connected to the central processor box. Also, the coarse models of the tributary stations are separate boxes.

6.2.1 The Central Processor Model

The model of the central processor P400 (Fig. 5) has been derived from that of the stand-alone office computer (Fig. 4). Since it does not process system software instructions, no system software instruction list has been included. On the other hand a mechanism had to be provided which blocks the central processor while the SSM is active and vice versa. If a system software process is started, the forwarding of interrupt signals from active IO devices via transition a5 is blocked. After the completion of the system software process is signalled via transitions a2 and a1, this masking of the central processor is raised.

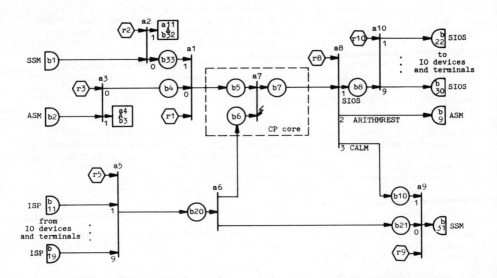

FIGURE 5: Central processor model of the terminal network

The main task of the central processor model is to determine the execution time of application software instructions. These enter via
location b2. Each sequence of application instructions up to the
next Call Monitor CALM is compressed and provides information for
the determination of the needed processing time which is generated
in the TI-transition a7.

This processing time may be interrupted by a signal from an IO device entering via transition a5 and delivering an interrupt token
into location b6 of the TI-transition a7. In this case the remaining processing time for the respective application instruction sequence is determined, and the process is steered back to the ASM. A
system software process taking care of the interrupt is started via
transition a9.

An input/output operation is started by the SSM if it sends a start
input/output statement SIOS via location b1 to the central processor. The respective device is then activated via transition a8. Requests for service (interrupts) from the devices enter via locations b11 to b19 and are forwarded according to the device priorities controlled by transition a5.

6.2.2 The Device Models

The device models consist mainly of time procedures which generate
the operation time of the respective device according to the type of
command received and the number of characters to be processed. E.g.
the disk drive model determines the time required for the seek and
read/write operation, taking into account the position of the access
mechanism after the proceeding access. After elapse of this operation time, a completion signal is sent back to the central processor
and causes an interrupt.

In the printer model the acknowledgement is signalled to the central processor immediately after the receipt of the command which contains information on the number of characters to be printed. However, the execution of further print commands which might have been received by the printer, is delayed until the time required for the first printing operation has elapsed. Thus the central processor may work concurrently with the printer, and the printer is not delayed by SSM operations.

6.2.3 The Terminal Models

The terminal models consist mainly of an X-transition the time procedure of which determines the time required for the operation initiated by the respective data communication command received. After completion of this operation an acknowledgement is sent back to the control station or is absorbed in cases where no further action is to be initiated. Since it is assumed that all processes executed in the intelligent terminals P300 and P400 run under the control of the control station, autonomous program execution in the remote stations which would present unsolicited service requests to the central station is not considered.

Differences exist in the time procedures of each tributary station. The office computers P300 and P400 have different instruction execution times. The P300 is assumed to have a magnetic tape cassette attached on which the data transmitted are stored before the execution of the terminal process is started. This operation requires an additional time. Both P300 and P400 terminal models are equipped with buffers for queuing subsequent data communication commands. These queues are modelled by chaining several T-transitions. The display terminal cannot buffer commands. Its time procedure includes the reaction time of the terminal operator. The times used in these models have been measured on test arrangements.

6.2.4 The System Software Model

The SSM contains the modules of the DOS 400 operating system (see 6.1) and in addition to that a DC scheduler which generates data communication-dependent start input/output statements to be processed by the tributary stations. Another addition is the General SIO module required for the control of the input/output and data management operations.

All time-consuming transitions now contain time procedures. Thus the execution of system software routines is simulated in the SSM itself and is not transferred to the SHM so that the simulation-time-intensive token transfers between SHM and SSM are reduced. Each module of the SSM consists of an evaluation net which describes the logical structure of that module so that for each distinguishable sequence of system software operations the execution time can be determined, and the appropriate control information can be sent to the ASM and the SHM.

6.2.5 The Application Software Model

The application being modelled comprises four programs of a materials management system executed in multiprogramming mode in four partitions of the central computer P400.

In partition 1 the articles master file of an inventory control program is updated by transactions entered via the display terminal in

the store. In partition 2 inventory is calculated, and inventory information is transmitted record by record to the P300 terminal
located in the store administration where it is stored on magnetic
tape cassette. In partition 3 an articles movement list is processed
by accessing records in the articles master file and listing it on
the line printer of the central P400. In partition 4 a program is
executed which processes in background out-of-stock information and
transmits it to the P400 terminal located in the purchase department
where it is stored on a disk for order processing.

The application software model contains the sequences of language
elements describing these functions. These are chains of arithmetic
and move instructions interspersed with Call Monitor (CALM) instructions requiring action of the system software, mainly to initiate
input or output operations. These instruction sequences are transferred to the SHM for execution if initiated by the SSM via a RUN
statement.

Another part of the ASM consists of file descriptions and job control information. File descriptions are treated as initialization
data referring to the data volumes stored on the storage modules,
and influence the dynamic performance of these devices. The control
information determines the dynamic execution of each job, e.g. how
often a loop has to be processed. This takes care of conditions
which - in the real system - are affected by the data to be processed.

6.2.6 Measuring Data Collection and Evaluation

During each simulation run measuring data have to be collected which
- after evaluation - provide information on the system performance
and eventually indicate variations of the system concept. This was
accomplished by adding procedure calls to every relevant transition
in the evaluation net of a model which may be initialized arbitrarily
before a simulation run is started. These procedures if activated
collect e.g. the attribute values specified at a certain transition
every time this transition fires. These values are stored together
with an identification of the box and transition and of the model
time of each event. This allows later evaluation according to any
appropriate algorithm in order to produce e.g. bar graphs or curves.
These evaluation algorithms may be programmed in a dialogue at the
display terminal using an instruction set similar to that of a
scientific pocket calculator.

6.2.7 Results

The complete model of the computer network covered 350 K Bytes of
storage. About 80 seconds of object time were simulated which needed
about 150 minutes of computer time on the host computer, P1400. Compared to the model of the stand-alone office computer, the relation
of simulation time to object time was considerably higher due to the
higher number of events to be processed per model time intervall,
which is caused by the concurrent operation of several system parts
and of the rather detailed modelling of the system software.

In a number of simulation runs, the following performance indicators
were determined for varied combinations of system component parameters:
- job execution time
- system response time appearing to the display and terminal oper-
  ators

- average intervall between application instruction execution interrupts
- average disk access time under the constraints of file layout and
access method specified
- load and concurrent operation of CPU and IO devices.

These results were plotted in bar graphs and curves. It was learned
from these graphs that e.g. the terminal response times showed a nonlinear dependency of data transmission line speed, and that a shortening of file access time by a new storage concept would not improve
throughput since in the applications under consideration, file accesses were fully overlapped by other operations and did not at all
influence the system performance. Also a 3 times faster CPU did not
improve the performance very much.

REFERENCES

[1] Nutt, G.J. (1972). The formulation and application of evaluation
    nets. Ph. D. Dissertation, University of Washington. Computer
    Science.
[2] Nutt, G.J. (1972). Evaluation nets for computer system perform-
    ance analysis. Fall Joint Comp. Conf. 1972, AFIPS Conf. Proc.,
    41, p. 279 - 286.
[3] Noe, J.D., Nutt, G.J. (1973). Macro-E-Nets for representation of
    parallel systems. IEEE Tr. on Comp., C-22 No. 8, p. 718 - 727.
[4] Stewen, L. (1975). Auswertungsnetze als Hilfsmittel zur Modell-
    bildung - Probleme und deren Lösungen (Evaluation nets as aid to
    modelling - problems and their solutions.) GI - 5th annual con-
    ference 1975, Oct. 8 - 10. Lecture Notes in Computer Science
    Vol. 34, p. 462 - 474.
[5] Seidel, H.A., Von Studnitz, P. (1977). A methodology for de-
    terministic model building and simulation of computer systems.
    Simulation '77, Montreux, June 22 - 24. Conference Proceedings.
[6] Lagemann, K. (1974). Das Simulationsprogrammpaket "SAMO". (The
    simulation program package "SAMO".) Angewandte Informatik, 16,
    11, p. 488 - 492.
[7] Behr, J.-P., Isernhagen, R., Pernards, P., Stewen, L. (1975).
    Modellbeschreibung mit Auswertungsnetzen. (Model description
    with evaluation nets.) Angewandte Informatik 17, 9, p. 375 - 382.
[8] Behr, J.-P., Isernhagen, R., Pernards, P., Stewen, L. (1975).
    Erfahrungen mit Auswertungsnetzen - Implementierung, Alternati-
    ven. (Experiences with evaluation nets - implementation, alter-
    natives.) Angewandte Informatik 17, 10, p. 427 - 432.
[9] Behr, J.-P. (1976). Graphical interactive modelling for simula-
    tion with evaluation nets. GI 6th annual conference 1976, Stutt-
    gart, Sept. 29 - Oct. 1. Short communications, p. 65.

COMPUTER PERFORMANCE, K.M. CHANDY AND M. REISER (EDS.)
NORTH HOLLAND PUBLISHING COMPANY, 1977

GRAPHICAL MODELS AND THE LAM HARDWARE DISCRETE EVENT SIMULATOR

M. Parent
I.R.I.A. Laboria
Le Chesnay, France

F. Prunet, J. M. Dumas and Y. Moreau
Laboratoire d'Automatique de Montpellier
Universite des Sciences et Techniques du Languedoc
Montpellier-Cedex, France

This paper presents a hardware and software tool used to
simulate descrete event systems. This new technique is based
on a graphical description of the system to be simulated but
does not lead to a standard simulation program to be run on
a general purpuse sequential computer. Instead, each node of
the graphical description is simulated by a simple hardware
component and the different components are connected by
plugged-in wires as specified by the graph. A mini-computer
monitors the hardware to handle complex events and to perform
data collection and processing.

1. INTRODUCTION

In the past few years, the need for performance evaluation at the design stage of large scale systems, such as computer systems for example, has led
to the development of several modeling methodologies. Discrete-event simulation is
one of th eapproaches that has lately received considerable attention /1/. This
technique consists in representing the state of the system of interest by elements
of a finite-state machine (e.g., a digital computer) and observing (or measuring)
the state changes which are specified by a number of fixed rules (e.g., a computer
program). This state changes are usually referenced with respect to time which is
represented either by some fraction of real (or execution) time or by one particular variable of the finite-state machine. This time which is used to reference the
occurence time of state changes (or events) is called "simulation time".

As distinguished from continuous-system simulation which has been developped on a wide variety of physical devices (e.g. electrical, mechanical and flui-
dic analog simulators), descrete-event simulation has been developped almost exclusively on general-pupose electronic digital computers. This derives from the fact
that the technology of digital computers is the only one largely available to represent a finite state machine. On the other hand, the concept of a stored program,
which is basically sequential, is quite inappropriate to perform state changes as
the simulation time advances. This is clearly illustrated by the variety of simulation languages and by the difficulty of programming any large-scale simulator.
Indeed, all simulation languages attempt, in a more or less successful way, to provide facilities to express the intrinsic parallelism of activities in a simulation.

443

Due to the intrinsic nature of digital computers, all simulation programs remain sequential both in the description and in the execution of any simulation. This is why another approach, based on a graphical description, has been investiga- ted to improve the description part of the system to be simulated (i.e. the state changes and their sequencing need not be explicitly specified). This approach was first used in the development of GPSS, a widely used simulation language based on a graphical description. The simulator is simply described by a graph built from 36 different types of blocks each representing the evolution of entities through time (generation, delays, branching, queueing, ...). A similar approach was deve- lopped in the LOGOS project /2/, to describe more specifically computer systems with Control Graph Models /9/. Although they may be used in other applications, these models which use only eight different types of nodes are not as flexible as GPSS models but they are well suited to study the problems of resource sharing. Unfor- tunately, the Control Graph Models have not been implemented as a simulation tool and they remain a description facility for the moment.

A similar approach has been developped at the same time and has recently produced an operational simulation tool. This tool uses a graphical description ba- sed on an extension of Petri networks called E-nets or Pro-nets. The graphical des- criptions are used as the entries of a classical simulation program through a gra- phical editor /4, 5/.

The LAM simulator we will present in this paper is also based on a gra- phical description, but this time the execution of the simulation is not controlled by a program on a general-purpose computer. Instead, each node of the graphical description is simulated by an electronic circuit and the nodes are physically con- nected by means of electric wires. Conditions expressing the routing of entities through the network are also expressed physically by boolean values issued from electronic circuits or from a computer and also carried by electric wires. The ope- ration of this type of simulator is thus very similar to the operation of an analog simulator except that the circuits carry binary information, thus enabling us to perform discrete-event simulation.

Figures 2-5 show the graphical representation based on GPSS, a Control Graph, an E-net, and a LAM Simulation Graph of the queueing network of figure 1 respectively. This network of three servers is a simple model based on a central server (the CPU), of a virtual-memory time-shared computer /3/. For each represen- tation, only the graph has been represented on the picture : more information must be given to specify the operation of each node. It should be mentioned that each representation can take into account various service-time distributions and the overheads at the end of each CPU service. In figs. 4 and 5, a macro node has been used to represent the graph of a queue. Such a graph has been represented explici- tely with a LAM Simulation Graph in Fig. 6 and the boolean expressions on each arc have been expressed. Such a macro node could easily be implemented in one hardware module and used as a single node in the LAM Simulator.

We will now look in more detail into the LAM hardware simulator, since it provides a new technique for discrete event simulation. We will then compare it with other graphical simulation models. Finally, we will present some evaluation of the performance of this hardware simulator.

2. THE LAM SIMULATION GRAPH MODEL

As with the other models, the system to be studied and simulated must be described by a graph consisting of nodes and arcs and by entities which flow through the graph. The graph and the rules which generate and process the entities in time constitute the model of the system. Let us now look in detail at how these rules are specified in the context of the LAM Simulation Graph Models.

A LAM Simulation Graph Model consists first of all of a set of nodes, identical in nature, and a set of directed arcs connecting the nodes :

set of nodes : N = (Ni, i = 1, 2, ..., n)
set of arcs : A = (Aij = (Ni, Nj) Ni $\in$ N, Nj $\in$ N)

Now, at any time t, there exists a (possibly variable) number of entities
called processes which are located in various nodes called the active nodes (an
active node may contain several processes) :

set or processes at time t : X(t) = (Xj, j = 1, ..., m(t))
location of Xj at time t   : Lt(Xj) = Ni   Ni $\in$ N

Each process may have a fixed or variable number of attibutes which may
be modified in time :

attributes of Xj at time t : At(Xj) = (xj1, xj2, ...)

Finally, there exists a number of variables called the entries which represent the environment of the system :

entries of the system at time t : E(t) = (e1(t), e2(t), ...)

The state of the system is defined by the position of all the processes
in the graph and the values of their attributes. As in any discrete event simulation / 1 ·   ./, this state is defined only at the occurence of an event which is in
our case the instant where a process changes position in the graph. These events
are caused by the evolution of time (end of a delay) or by a modification (in time)
of an entry variable. Therefore, it is necessary to be able to describe the evolution of all the attributes in term of these events and their occurence time.

One boolean expression F(Aij) whose value may depend on the state of the
system, on the time and on the values of the entry variables, is attached on each
arc Aij. When such an expression is true, the corresponding arc is said to be validated if and only if the issuing node is active. Each time an arc is validated, one
of the processes of the issuing node is taken by a selection procedure (e.g. FIFO)
to be sent to the next node and its attibutes may be changed according to an event
procedure attached to the arc. Therefore, to each validation of an arc corresponds
the occurence of an event and vice-versa. If several arcs are validated at the same
time, the event is a composite event which is executed in parallel at least concep-
tually. This does not cause any problem if the validation and the event procedures
consider the system as it was just before the event and not as it may be during the
execution of the composite event /9/. If validation is not done this way, one could
obtain ill-defined state changes which would depend on the execution of the composite event. The example below shows this clearly :

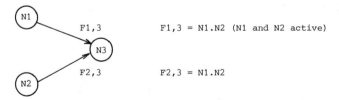

F1,3 = N1.N2 (N1 and N2 active)

F2,3 = N1.N2

A state change can occur with one process in N1 and one process in N2. A correct
sequencing lead to two processes in N3 and none in N1, N2. Incorrect sequencing in
the evaluation of the boolean functions (evaluation of F1, 3 or F2, 3 after a process move) would lead to one process in N3 and one in N2 or one process in N3 and
one in N1.

If several arcs issued from a same active node become validated at the
same time, the selected process is duplicated with its attributes in all the

corresponding successors (this is equivalent to an F-transition in an E-net or to an AND node in a Control Graph, but in this last case, the parent-infant structure of the processes is implicitly kept).

Now, if the displacement of one process causes the validation of a new arc (or maintains the validation of an arc holding several processes), this leads to a new event and validation must go on until there is no validated arc remaining. This is a stepwise process and in order to isolate clarly each event, the simulation time is increased by an amount "dt" which may be arbitrarily small between two events.

A new process is generated each time a process is removed from a node with no predecessor. These nodes-which must be initialised with at least one process- act as the IN nodes of the Control Graph models and the delays between the generations are controlled by the boolean functions of the outgoing arcs.

Similarly, processes which arrive at nodes with no successors are removed from the graph just as with the OUT nodes of the Control Graphs.

In conclusion, it can be said that a LAM Simulation Graph Model G is defined as :

$$G = (N, A, E, X (0), B, R)$$

where

    N = set of nodes
    A = set of directed arcs between the nodes
    E = set of entry variables (the environment)
    X(0) = set of processes at time 0 with their location and their attributes
    B = set of boolean functions defined on the system state, the entry variable and the time
    R = set of rules defining the selection procedure and the attribute modification at each validation.

A simpler model, called Organiphase /6, 7/, has been developped previously to describe and test the operation of automatisms. The Organiphase can be seen as a LAM Simulation Graph Model where the processes have no attributes (and therefore lose their identity) and where the environment variables are all boolean. Furthermore, each node may hold at most one process. This means that if a process arrives at an active node, it disappears (the node remains active). In fact, in the Organiphase, one does not speak of processes but of active and idle nodes.

Graphical representation of the simulation model

The graphical representation of the LAM Simulation Models is particularly simple since there is only one type of node. The representation is also very close to the hardware implementation (see the next section) which allows very convenient programming. The graphical model is drawn as a set of circles representing the nodes, linked by arrows representing the arcs. The processes may be represented by dots or numbers in the corresponding circles to specify a particular state (such as the initial state).

The boolean functions expressing the conditions on the arcs may be indicated explicitly on each arc or by way of dotted arcs issued from the variables used in the boolean function. In particular, these dotted arcs may be issued from another node (the arc carries a true value if the node is active) or from another arc (true value = arc validated) and can carry a delayed truth value. This last function which is particularly important in simulation is represented by a squared box on the arc (an incoming true value initializes the delay). Of course different variables may be combined graphically by way of the standard AND and OR nodes to express complex boolean functions.

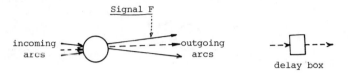

Graphical representation of the nodes and signals

3. HARDWARE IMPLEMENTATION OF THE LAM SIMULATION MODEL

We will initially describe the hardware implementation of the Organiphase which led to the hybrid implementation of the simulation graph models.

The state of the organiphase is defined at each instant by the state of each node (active/idle) and the value of each boolean entry. The state of a node changes according to the following rules depending on the validation of incoming or outgoing arcs (recall that the validation of an arc is defined by a true value on the arc function and an issuing node being active) :

R1 - If at a given instant at least one incoming arc of a node is validated, the node is active at the following instant.

R2 - If at a given instant, no incoming arc of an active node is validated and at least one outgoing arc is validated, the node is idle at the following instant.

R3 - The state of all other nodes remains unchanged.

These simple rules have been implemented in hardware by using a J-K flip-flop to represent the state of a node (Fig. 6) and a synchronous mechanism to define the notion of "next instant". Time is therefore made discrete by a clock signal, and transitions can occur only during the rising edge of this signal. When the two conditions (node active and boolean arc function true) are met, the wire representing the arc carries a digital impulse (one) which activates the next node (Rule R1). At the same time, if an active node has no incoming validated arc, the node becomes idle (Rule 2). The memory property of the flip-flop keeps all other nodes unchanged (Rule 3). This solution leads to a very simple, repetitive, and secure system and allows one to control the evolution speed of the simulation. Its only drawback is that two changes of an entry variable must be separated by at least one clock tick to be taken into account.

The arc functions are expresses simply by means of a hardware combination of various digital signals. These signals can be boolean input variables, state of nodes, or validation signals issued from other arcs, or they can be issued from two hardware boxes expressing delay conditions or branching conditions.

The delay module is a hardware device (Fig. 7) which sends a signal a given number of occurences of a particular event after it has been initialized. This number of occurences can be specified by the user (fixed delay) or issued from a random number generator (random delay). The event selected for counting can be an arbitrary event expressed by a combination of boolean signals, or it can be each clock tick in which case the delay is simply a time delay.

The two-way branching module is another hardware device (Fig. 8) which at each request sets a signal to one with a given probability assigned by the user. Using this signal and its complement as the validation function of two arcs issued from a same node, one obtains a probabilistic branching similar to the OR node in

M. PARENT, F. PRUNET, J.M. DUMAS, Y. MOREAU

Control Graph Models :

If Prob (F = 1) = p, this is equivalent to the OR function of the Control Graphs :

The probability p is set manually on the module itself by increments of 1/16.

Using a certain number of these modules plus random number generators and simple gates to connect several signals, it is possible to "program" various simulation problems. Figure 9 shows for example how a queueing system with finite waiting room G/G/1/n can be expressed by an organiphase model. The queue itself (nodes N1 to Nn) could easily be implemented as an extensible hardware module to be used in queueing network simulation. To simulate this system, one must simply be able to generate using hardware, the desired random numbers expressing the input process and the service process. This is done by generating signals "a" and "s" with delay modules periodically with time intervals corresponding to the interarrival time or to the service time. Various time distributions can be generated directly by hardware methods /8/.

Results from a simulation run can be obtained first of all by observing the state of the nodes at various simulation speeds (a light indicates whether the node is active or not). This "qualitative" method is very usefull for debugging the system and for observing transient or erratic behavior which is difficult to characterize quantitatively. Quantitative evaluation can be done by using hardware signal counters which can measure a number of events, time between events, or activation time of nodes. By using this last possibility in our example on each node N0 through Nn, one can obtain directly by a division with the total simulation time, the server utilization ratio and the queue length distribution.

Extension of the Organiphase Hardware

The existing modules of the organiphase simulator previously described are not sufficient to program complex simulations. In particular, it is not possible to attach attibutes to the processes which travel through the graph, arbitrary random variables cannot be generated, and complex measurements such as a correlation between variables are difficult if not impossible to perform.

To solve these problems, an approach similar to the one used with analog simulators was taken by considering a hybrid system. The organiphase simulator models the activity of nodes and keeps track of the time between events, but complex events and measurement procedures are performed using a digital computer. In particular, the computer can keep track of and modify the attributes of entities and can also generate arbitrary random variables to be used by the hardware modules.

Although a solution involving several micro-processors attached to various nodes (or to various events) and possibly sharing a common memory could have been proposed, a simpler approach using a single mini-computer (a Telemecanique T 1600 in our case) was selected. The hardware simulator is then considered as an input/output device which is connected to the computer through a special interface.

The computer initializes the simulator by placing processes in specific nodes and possibly by initializing the delays and the branching modules with the appropriate random numbers. The hardware simulator is then started with its clock. At the occurence of any specific event which has been programmed, the clock is stopped and the computer takes the control. Depending on the event, a specific routine is executed. This routine can read and modify the state of the hardware before the simulator is allowed to run again. Before or after the simulator is re-started, the computer can perform several measurements on the last event which caused the interruption.

4. EXECUTION OF A SIMULATION

Once a system has been described by a LAM graphical model, the procedure for executing one or several simulation runs is extremely simple. It is a relatively simple matter to connect the modules representing the different nodes of the graph, since each arc of the graph corresponds to one wire. Then, the conditions on the arcs must be wired. For this, extra modules performing the logic functions, the delays, and the branching must be used. These in turn may use one or several hardware random number generators.

If no special event needs the intervention of the computer, the simulation can be run either wih or without the control computer. Measurements can be performed with hardware event counters. If the system is run under the control of the computer, a simple language allows one to verify the execution of the simulation step-by-step, but this can also be done directly with the hardware.

On the other hand, if the computer is needed in the execution of the simulation, each event which requires the computer has to be wrired into the interface, and a program has to be written to treat this event. Special software tools give convenient access to the state of the hardware and allows one to modify it or to initialize delays. This may appear similar to classical discrete-event simulation programming, but one has to remember that the complex task of event scheduling is now performed in parallel by the hardware. Furthermore, the state of the system is held partly by the hardware, and many state changes can be handled in parallel without the execution of any instructions on the computer.

Since the clock can be tuned to any speed up to 1 MHz or pulsed manually step-by-step, it is very convenient for checking the execution of the simulation. Furthermore, any event which calls the computer can halt the simulation if this is preprogrammed. During these interruption, the operator can examine the state of the system (hardware and software) and modify it as desired.

At its maximum speed, simulated events can take place every micro-second if computer intervention is not required. However, since this is basically a time-driven simulation, many clock ticks can separate two events : it is therefore the responsability of the user to select an appropriate unit of time in order to achieve both good accuracy and acceptable performance (a similar problem is found with analog simulators).

The first experiments performed with this system demonstrated that execution times of a queueing system, where the computer generates the random variables, are comparable to the execution times of a simulation of the same system performed with GPSS on an IBM 360-65. However, the software on our mini-computer used a time consuming routine to compute the needed random variables (700 instructions on the average to generate a Poisson variable), and a factor of ten could easily be gained in the execution speed of this specific simulation.

5. CONCLUSION

The simulation tool presented in this paper is still under active development and the software aids on the mini-computer especially need to be further

expanded. However, even in its current form, this tool has proved to be very useful, since it allows the user to "program" complex or simple simulation models in
a very convenient way. Furthermore, the speed and the low cost of this system make
it now feasible to perform the very long simulation runs needed to obtain statistically meaningful reasults.

REFERENCES

/1/ Jacques Leroudier, Michel Parent, "Discrete event simulation modelling of
     computer systems for performance evaluation", Rapport de recherche n° 177,
     IRIA/LABORIA, June 1976.

/2/ Charles W. Rose, "LOGOS and the software engineer", Proceedings of the FJCC,
     Vol. 41, 1972.

/3/ Marc Badel, Erol Gelenbe, Jacques Leroudier, Dominique Potier, "Adaptive
     optimization of a time-sharing system's performance", IEEE Proceedings on
     Interactive Computer Systems, June 1975.

/4/ Jerre D. Noe, Gary J. Nutt, "Macro E-Nets for representation of parallel sys-
     tems", IEEE Transactions on Computers, Vol. C-22, n° 8, August 1973, 718-727.

/5/ C. P. Crowley, J. D. Noe, "Interactive graphical simulation using modified
     Petri nets", SIGSIM/NBS Symposium of the Simulation of Computer Systems, NBS,
     Boulder, Col., August 1975, 1-20.

/6/ Jean-Michel Dumas, François Prunet, "A method for local and reduced studies in
     parallel process models", Digital Process, Vol. 2, n° 2, Summer 1976, 99-118.

/7/ Jean-Michel Dumas, "L'organiphase : un modèle facilitant l'analyse et la syn-
     thèse des automates logiques", Thèse de 3e cycle, Université des Sciences et
     Techniques du Languedoc, Avril 1974 (French).

/8/ Yves Moreau, Philippe Coiffet, François Prunet, "Génération digitale de varia-
     bles statistiques", Rapport du Lam, Université des Sciences et Techniques du
     Languedoc, 1976, (French).

/9/ Michel R. Parent, "The control graph models : a unified approach to performan-
     ce evaluation", Ph. D. Thesis, Case Western Reserve University, March 1976.

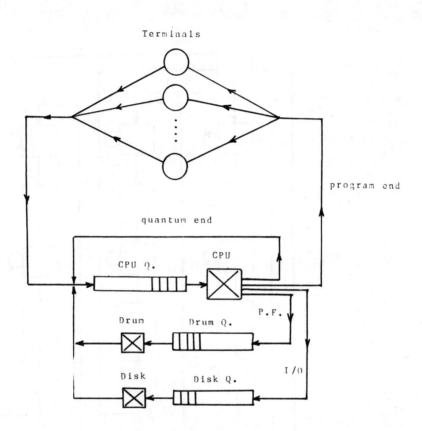

<u>Figure 1</u> : Queueing model

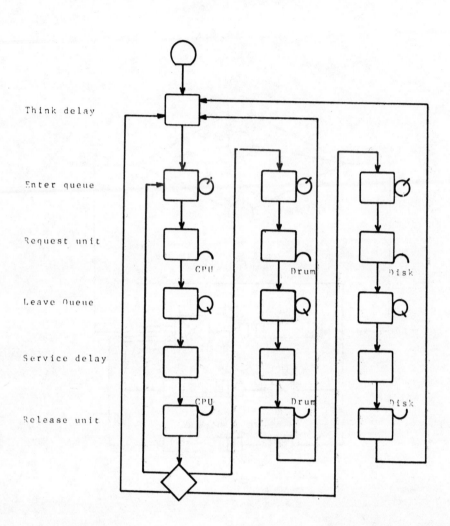

Think delay

Enter queue

Request unit

Leave Queue

Service delay

Release unit

Figure 2 : GPSS Model

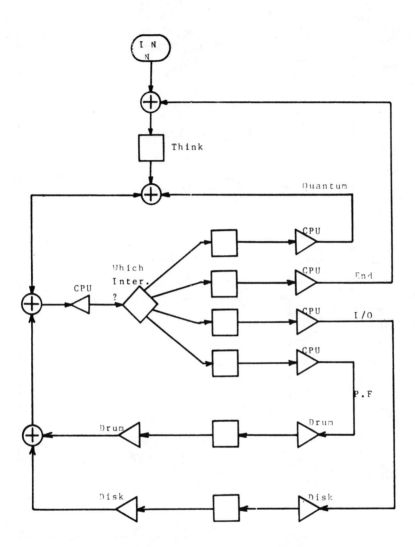

Figure 3 : Control Graph Model

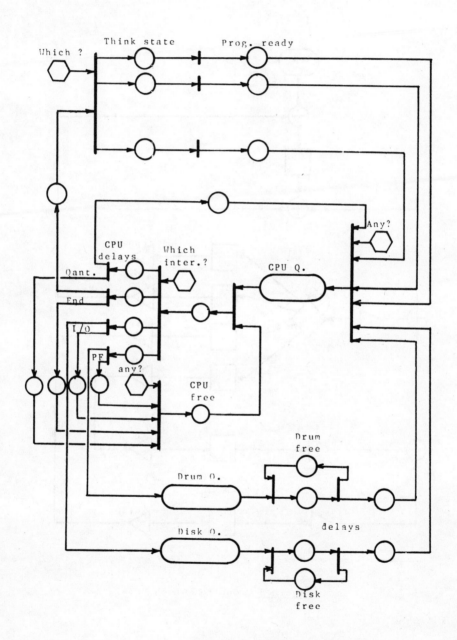

Figure 4 : E-Net model

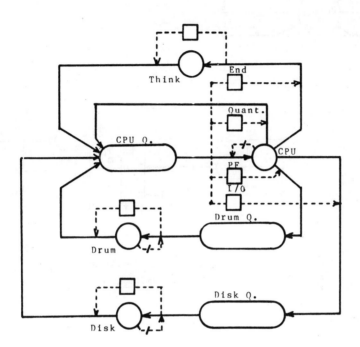

Figure 5 : LAM Simulation Model

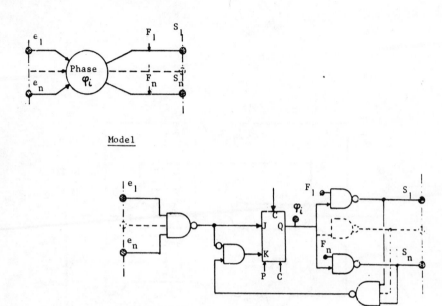

Model

Figure 6   Implementation

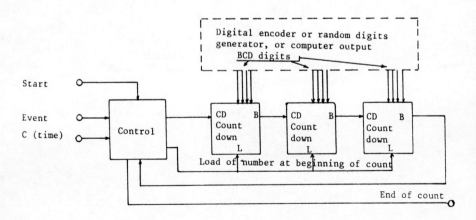

Figure 7 : Delays

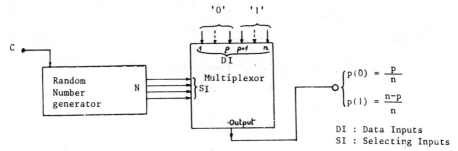

The number of '0' and '1' input values of D-Inputs is
selected by switches, or given by a computer output.

Figure 8

s = end of service signal

a = arrival signal

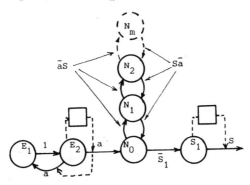

Figure 9 : Organiphase model of a
G/G/1/n queueing model

Annex : Implementation and actual results on the
        exemple of figure 5

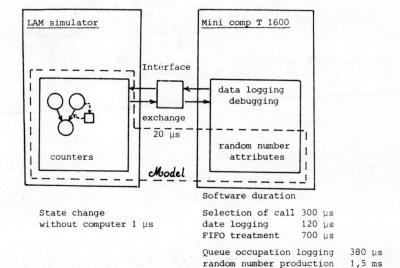

Software duration

State change   Selection of call 300 µs
without computer 1 µs   date logging   120 µs
                            FIFO treatment   700 µs

                            Queue occupation logging   380 µs
                            random number production   1,5 ms

Global result :

- 500 process with attribute through the system
- 138000 time units . 10000 calls
- 35 seconds of simulation

CONTROL VARIABLES APPLIED TO THE SIMULATION
OF QUEUEING MODELS OF COMPUTER SYSTEMS

S. S. Lavenberg, T. L. Moeller and P. D. Welch
Thomas J. Watson Research Center
Yorktown Heights, New York, USA

We develop control variables which can be applied to increase the
efficiency of simulations of a broad class of closed queueing networks.
These networks are extensions of current analytically tractable queueing networks and incorporate such features of computer systems as
scheduling based on priorities, blocking due to capacity constraints and
non-exponential service times. The control variables are estimators of
the steady state work done at specified points per network service
completion. We also report on experiments conducted to evaluate
these control variables.

1. INTRODUCTION

Queueing networks are commonly used to model the contention for resources which occurs in
interactive multiprogrammed computer systems (see, e.g., [14]). Such steady state response characteristics of these networks as mean waiting times and server utilizations correspond to performance
measures of interest for the system being modeled. In recent years the class of queueing networks
whose steady state behavior can be obtained analytically has been expanded considerably (see, e.g.,
[3]). However, networks which explicitly represent such features of real systems as scheduling based
on priorities, blocking due to capacity constraints and non-exponential service times are not, in
general, analytically tractable. Two approaches which have been used to study networks which have
some of these features are numerical techniques for computing steady state probabilities for Markov
processes (see, e.g., [15]) and approximate analytic techniques (see, e.g., [2, 5, 6, 10]). However, the
state space is often so large that it is not practical to apply numerical techniques, and the accuracy of
approximate techniques has not been established in general. Thus, it is often necessary to resort to
simulation. Furthermore, simulation can be used to assess the accuracy of analytic approximations.

Such simulations are generally substantial consumers of computing time and, hence, costly. It is
therefore important to carry them out as efficiently as possible. Toward this end we are currently
concerned with the application of variance reduction techniques, particularly control variables, to the
simulation of a broad class of queueing networks. In these networks priorities, blocking and general
service times are allowed. Control variables are random variables whose expectation is known and
which are correlated with an estimator of interest. They can be combined with the estimator to reduce
its variance while not changing its expectation. They have a long history of application in statistics
and have been applied by a number of authors to the simulation of queueing systems (see, e.g., [4, 7,
8, 9, 11, 12]).

2. THE CLASS OF CLOSED NETWORKS UNDER CONSIDERATION

The networks consist of a finite number S of interconnected *service centers*. A service center is a
single server or multiple server queue. The networks are *closed* in that customers can neither enter nor

leave. There are N customers and they circulate indefinitely among the service centers in a manner to be described shortly. Each service center has a finite set of entry points and the entry points for different service centers are given distinct labels. A customer arrives at a service center at one of its entry points. The entry point determines the probability distribution function of the customer's service time and determines the probability distribution of the customer's next entry point. We let I denote the number of entry points. We make the following assumptions:

(a)   The sequence of service times at entry point i (sequenced by the order of arrival of customers at entry point i) is a sequence of independent and identically distributed non-negative random variables, each distributed as the random variable T_i which has finite mean and variance. (Zero service times are allowed.)

(b)   The sequence of entry points for each customer is an irreducible Markov chain with state space $\{1, 2, ..., I\}$ and transition matrix $P = (p_{ij})$.

(c)   The service time sequences (there is one for each entry point) and the entry point sequences (there is one for each customer) are mutually independent random sequences.

Although the sequence of entry points for a customer is a Markov chain, this does not imply that the sequence of service centers visited by a customer, called the *route*, is a Markov chain. Entry points play a similar role to that played by customer classes in [3]. In particular, entry points can be used to represent routes which are not Markov chains. Note that the Markov chains for all customers are assumed to be probabilistically identical. The more general case, where different customers can follow different Markov chains, is treated in [13]. The class of networks just defined is rather general. We made no assumptions about the queueing disciplines or about the capacity of a service center or group of service centers.

3. REVIEW OF CONTROL VARIABLES

Let μ be an unknown deterministic quantity to be estimated and let Y be an unbiased estimator of μ, i.e., $E[Y] = \mu$. A random variable C is a control variable if its expectation μ_C is known and it is correlated with Y. We use C to construct an unbiased estimator of μ which has smaller variance than Y.

For any constant a,

$$Y(a) = Y - a(C-\mu_C), \qquad (3.1)$$

is also an unbiased estimator of μ. Now

$$\text{Var}[Y(a)] = \text{Var}[Y] - 2a\,\text{Cov}[Y,C] + a^2\,\text{Var}[C]. \qquad (3.2)$$

Hence, if

$$2a\,\text{Cov}[Y,C] > a^2\,\text{Var}[C] \qquad (3.3)$$

Y(a) has a smaller variance than Y. The value of a which minimizes Var [Y(a)] is easily shown to be

$$a^* = \text{Cov}[Y,C]/\text{Var}[C] \qquad (3.4)$$

and the resulting minimum variance is

$$\text{Var}[Y(a^*)] = \text{Var}[Y](1-R_{YC}^2), \qquad (3.5)$$

where

$$R_{YC} = \text{Cov}[Y,C]/(\text{Var}[Y]\text{Var}[C])^{1/2}$$

is the correlation coefficient between Y and C. In general, Cov[Y,C], Var [Y] and Var[C] are not known so that a* is not known.

The above development can be extended to the case of more than one control variable. Let $C = (C_1,...,C_Q)$ be a vector of control variables, let $\mu_C = (\mu_1,...,\mu_Q)$, where $\mu_q = E[C_q]$, let $a = (a_1,...,a_Q)$, and let X' denote the transpose of a row vector X. Then,

$$Y(a) = Y - a(C' - \mu_C') \qquad (3.6)$$

is an unbiased estimator of μ and the value of a which minimizes Var[Y(a)] is (see, e.g. [1])

$$a^* = \sigma_{YC}\, \Sigma_C^{-1}, \qquad (3.7)$$

where Σ_C is the covariance matrix of C and is assumed to be non-singular, and σ_{YC} is a Q-dimensional row vector whose components are the covariances between Y and the C_q's. The resulting minimum variance is

$$\text{Var}[Y(a^*)] = \text{Var }[Y](1 - R_{YC}^2), \tag{3.8}$$

where

$$R_{YC}^2 = \sigma_{YC} \Sigma_C^{-1} \sigma_{YC}' / \text{Var}[Y] \tag{3.9}$$

is the square of the multiple correlation coefficient between Y and C. We call $1-R_{YC}^2$ the *minimum variance ratio*.

To successfully apply control variables one has to: (a) find good control variables, i.e., control variables for which R_{YC}^2 is large (greater than .5 say, so that the minimum variance ratio is less than .5), and (ii) construct valid confidence intervals using these control variables which reflect the reduced variance of (3.8). We next address these tasks.

4. CONTROL VARIABLES FOR CLOSED NETWORKS

We consider only the case where customers are of the same type, i.e., they follow the same Markov chain. (The case of more than one type of customer is treated in [13].) Let π denote the unique stationary probability vector for the Markov chain over the set of entry points. Then π is the unique solution to the equations

$$\pi P = \pi ,$$
$$\sum_{i=1}^{I} \pi_i = 1. \tag{4.1}$$

We assume that π has been computed. The probability π_i is equal to the long-run frequency of occurence of entry point i in the customer's entry point sequence.

We define an *event* in the simulation of a queueing network to be the departure of a customer from any service center. We define a type i event to be the departure of a customer whose arrival was at entry point i. With these definitions, let

$$e_i (K) = \text{number of type i events which occur}$$
$$\text{in the first K events,} \tag{4.2}$$

and

$$W_i(K) = \text{sum of the service times associated}$$
$$\text{with the above } e_i(K) \text{ events.} \tag{4.3}$$

Then, $e_i(K)/K$ is the fraction of events associated with entry point i and $W_i(K)/e_i(K)$ is the sample mean service time associated with entry point i. Their product $W_i(K)/K$ is the amount of completed work associated with entry point i per event in the network. We call $e_i(K)/K$ a *flow variable*, $W_i(K)/e_i(K)$ a *service time variable* and $W_i(K)/K$ a *work variable*. In [13] we show that the asymptotic expectations of these random variables are known and that

$$\lim_{K \to \infty} E[e_i(K)/K] = \pi_i, \tag{4.4}$$

$$\lim_{K \to \infty} E[W_i(K)/e_i(K)] = E[T_i], \tag{4.5}$$

$$\lim_{K \to \infty} E[W_i(K)/K] = \pi_i E[T_i]. \tag{4.6}$$

Hence, we assume that for large K the expectations of the flow, service time and work variables are known and given by (4.4)-(4.6).

We expect the flow, service time and work variables associated with each entry point to be correlated with estimators of response characteristics for the network. Hence, any or all of these random variables could serve as control variables. Since the work variables reflect both flow and service time effects, they appear to be a particularly attractive set of control variables. We next explore this possibility.

5. SOME EXPERIMENTAL RESULTS

5.1 *Introduction*

In Section 4 we defined service time, flow and work control variables for each entry point in the network. We saw there that the work control variables reflect both service time and flow effects and, hence, appear attractive, apriori, as a set of control variables. However, the comparison of work variables with other control variables and the assessment of the overall value of control variables in this context are empirical questions which can only be settled through simulation experience. Toward this end we are conducting a sequence of experiments designed to provide information on the potential of control variables (particularly work variables) in this context and the extent to which this potential can be achieved in valid confidence intervals. In this section we give a brief report on the beginning phases of these experiments.

5.2 *The Networks Studied*

We will describe the results of experiments on a set of networks of the form depicted in Figure 1.

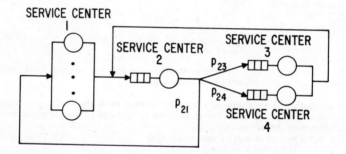

Figure 1.   Type of Network Studied

This is a model of a primitive terminal driven system with a single processor and two auxiliary storage devices. Service center 1 represents the terminals. The number of customers N is the same as the number of servers (terminals) at service center 1. Service center 2 represents the processor and service centers 3 and 4, the storage devices. There is a single entry point for each service center. All the service times are exponentially distributed and the customers are served in order of arrival.

Seven such networks were studied. For each network

$$E[T_1] = 100, E[T_2] = 1$$
$$p_{21} = .2, p_{23} = .72, p_{24} = .08. \qquad (5.1)$$

Let U_i denote the utilization for service center i. The seven networks differed in the value of N and/or the relative values of U_2, U_3, and U_4.
These are given in Table 1.

Network	1	N=15	$U_2 = U_3 = U_4$
	2	N=25	$U_2 = U_3 = U_4$
	3	N=15	$U_2 = 2U_3 = 2U_4$
	4	N=25	$U_2 = 2U_3 = 2U_4$
	5	N=15	$2U_2 = U_3 = U_4$
	6	N=15	$2U_2 = U_3 = 2U_4$
	7	N=15	$2U_2 = 2U_3 = U_4$

Table 1.
Description of Networks Studied

The response characteristics considered were the following:

a) wt_i, i=2, 3,4, the steady state expected waiting times at service centers 2,3, and 4;

b) λ, the steady state overall service completion rate for the network (all the service center utilizations can be derived from λ),

c) rt, the steady state expected terminal response time, i.e., the expected elapsed time between the departure of a customer from service center 1 and its subsequent arrival at service center 1.

The networks studied are analytically tractable and these five quantities can be calculated exactly. Such networks were selected for the initial experiments so that we could validate the simulation program and so that the validity of confidence intervals could be accurately estimated. Experiments are planned on more complex networks for which these response characteristics cannot be analytically determined.

5.3 *Comparison of Control Variables and Estimation of the Minimum Variance Ratio*

In Section 3 we defined the minimum variance ratio, $1-R_{YC}^2$, where R_{YC} is the multiple correlation coefficient between a vector C of control variables and an estimator Y. The minimum variance achievable is the product of this ratio and the variance of Y.

For each network studied, 1000 statistically independent repetitions of a simulation of 4000 events were made. These repetitions started from the same fixed initial conditions. On each repetition data from the period of the first 1000 events were discarded. Estimators and control variables were obtained from the remaining sequence of 3000 events. Hence, K = 3000 in the notation of Section 4.

The estimators for the expected waiting times wt_i, i = 2,3,4, we designate as $\hat{wt}_i$, i = 2,3,4. They were the averages of the waiting times at the respective service centers over the period described above. We let

$$T= \text{time required for the last 3000 events.} \qquad (5.2)$$

The overall service completion rate λ was estimated by

$$\hat{\lambda} = 3000/T. \qquad (5.3)$$

Finally, the expected terminal response time rt was estimated by

$$\hat{rt} = [\hat{wt}_2 + E[T_2] + p_{23}(\hat{wt}_3+E[T_3]) + p_{24}(\hat{wt}_4 + E[T_4])]/p_{21}. \qquad (5.4)$$

(Equation (5.4) can be obtained by applying Little's formula to the problem of estimating the steady state expected sojourn time in any subnetwork of a closed queueing netowrk. For a general discussion and proof see [13]).

From the 1000 repetitions we estimated the minimum variance ratios for the estimators $\hat{wt}_i$, i = 2,3,4, $\hat{\lambda}$ and $\hat{rt}$ and various subsets of the flow, service time and work control variables. The results of these experiments on the seven networks can be summarized as follows.

1) Work variables gave roughly the same variance reduction as service time and flow variables combined.

2) The entire set of four work variables gave substantially more variance reduction than any work variable taken alone.

3) The minimum variance ratios varied, roughly, from .15 to .7. This is the potential factor by which the variance could be reduced while keeping the simulation length constant.

4) In the balanced networks (networks 1 and 2 of Table 1) the variance reductions for the mean waiting time estimators were approximately equal. In the unbalanced networks the largest variance reduction for the mean waiting time estimators occured at the service center with the highest utilization.

As an example, in Table 2 we give some estimated minimum variance ratios for network 4 of Table 1.

Control Variables

		All Service Time Variables	All Flow Variables	All Service Time and Flow Variables	All Work Variables
	$\hat{wt}_2$	.48	.74	.20	.21
	$\hat{wt}_3$	.67	.82	.50	.51
Estimators	$\hat{wt}_4$	.67	.88	.54	.55
	$\hat{\lambda}$	.52	.68	.18	.20
	$\hat{rt}$	.53	.67	.19	.21

Table 2
Estimated Minimum Variance Ratios

5.4 *Comparison of Confidence Intervals With and Without Control Variables*

For the networks studied in Section 5.3 we saw that the minimum variance ratios indicated substantial benefits from the application of work control variables. However, the minimum variance ratio assumes that the optimum coefficient vector, a^*, is known and in practice this must be estimated from the data. More generally, estimates of a^* must be incorporated in a procedure which generates valid confidence intervals. In fact, in order to get a meaningful assessment of the value of control variables one must have methods of obtaining valid confidence intervals with and without control variables. Then the reduction in average confidence interval width for the same length of simulation is the correct measure of the gain.

There are a number of methods of obtaining confidence intervals for the response characteristics of a simulated model. For these initial experiments we chose the simplest, most direct and most general of these, the method of repeated trials. In this method one generates independent repetitions of the simulation and, hence, independent realizations of the estimators and the control variables. Confidence intervals for the case with no control variables are obtained by using standard methods based on the t distribution.

In forming confidence intervals using control variables and the method of repeated trials we investigated two alternative methods. The first is based on the assumption that the estimator and the control varaibles have a joint normal distribution. It results in an application of classical regression techniques. We call it "Method 1". The second is more robust and is obtained by jackknifing the regression estimate. We call it "Method 2". Both methods are discussed in detail in [13].

An experiment in this context consisted of 20 repetitions of the basic simulation described in Section 5.3. Each repetition yielded, for our purposes, a run of 3000 events. From the 20 repetitions, 90% confidence intervals were generated with no control variables and with the four work control variables. Both Method 1 and Method 2 were applied.

Now, in order to estimate the reduction in the average confidence interval width and the probability that the confidence interval covers the true value it is necessary to, in turn, repeat the above experiment. A meta-experiment, consisting of 50 independent repetitions of the above experiment, was conducted for each of the seven networks.

In these seven meta-experiments (each consisting of $50 \times 20 = 1000$ independent simulation runs) the following general results were observed.

1) Valid confidence intervals, i.e. intervals with approximately 90% coverage, were generated from both methods of applying control variables.

2) Method 1 yielded significantly narrower confidence intervals than Method 2.

3) There was some increase (about 15% in the case of Method 1) in the average width of the confidence intervals over that which would occur if the optimum coefficient vector, a^*, were known. However, the reductions in average width were still substantial.

As a typical example we again consider network 4 of Table 1 whose minimum variance ratios were summarized in Table 2. For this network the coverage of the confidence intervals and the reduction in their average width relative to intervals generated with no control variables are summarized in Table 3. The reduction in the confidence interval width if a^* were known is simply $(1-R^2)^{1/2}$, where $1-R^2$ is the estimated minimum variance ratio.

	$(1-R^2)^{1/2}$	Coverage No Controls	Width Reduction Method 1	Coverage Method 1	Width Reduction Method 2	Coverage Method 2
$\hat{wt}_2$	.46	.86	.52	.86	.57	.90
$\hat{wt}_3$	.71	.88	.84	.86	.99	.94
$\hat{wt}_4$	.74	.86	.83	.98	.96	.98
$\hat{\lambda}$	.45	.90	.53	.88	.61	.90
$\hat{rt}$	.46	.90	.53	.92	.61	.90

Table 3
Actual Confidence Interval
Width Reduction and Coverage

To graphically display the reduction in confidence interval width and maintenance of proper coverage we have plotted in Figure 2 the 50 confidence intervals both with and without control variables for wt_2 of this example. The horizontal line is drawn at the height of the true value. The confidence intervals with control variables were obtained using Method 1.

6. SUMMARY

We have developed a class of work control variables which appear to have promise for achieving substantial reductions in the simulation time required for the study of an important class of computer queueing models.

This paper is an initial report on work which is continuing along the following lines:

1) evaluation of more complex networks involving priorities, blocking and multiple types of customers following separate Markov chains,

2) application of other confidence interval generation techniques such as batch means and the regenerative method,

3) extensions to open networks and to mixed (open and closed) networks,

4) evaluation of other work type control variables involving higher moments of the service times,

5) selection of subsets of the set of work variables when the networks being simulated are very large.

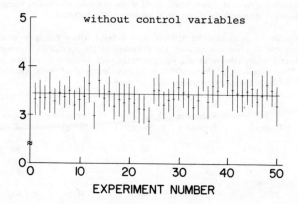

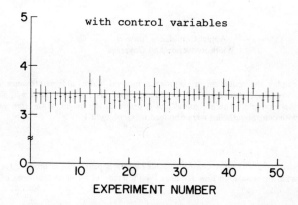

Figure 2.   Confidence Intervals for wt_2 with
             and without work control variables

REFERENCES

1.   T.W. Anderson, *An Introduction to Multivariate Statistical Analysis*, John Wiley and Sons, Inc., New York, 1958.

2.   B. Avi-Itzhak and D.P. Heyman, "Approximate Queueing Models for Multiprogramming Computer Systems," *Oper. Res.* 21, 1212-1230 (1973).

3.   F. Baskett, K.M. Chandy, R.R. Muntz and F.G. Palacios, "Open, Closed and Mixed Networks of Queues with Different Classes of Customers," *J. Assoc. Comp. Mach.* 22, 248-260 (1975).

4.   A. Beja, "Multiple Control Variates in Monte Carlo Simulation (with Application to Queueing Systems with Priorities)", *Advances in Operations Research*, Vol. I, (Ed. B. Avi-Itzhak) 1969.

5.   K.M. Chandy, U. Herzog and L. Woo, "Approximate Analysis of General Queueing Networks," *IBM J. Res. Develop.* 19, 43-49 (1975).

6.   P.J. Courtois, *Decomposability: Queueing and Computer System Applications*, Academic Press, New York, 1977.

7.   D.P. Gaver and G.S. Shedler, "Control Variable Methods in the Simulation of a Model of a Multiprogrammed Computer System," *Naval Res. Logist. Quart.* 18, 435-450 (1971).

8.   D.P. Gaver and G.L. Thompson, *Programming and Probability Models in Operations Research*, Brooks/Cole Publishing Co., Monterey, California, 1973.

9.   J.P.C. Kleijnen, *Statistical Techniques in Simulation Part I*, Marcel Dekker, Inc., New York, 1974.

10.   H. Kobayashi, "Application of the Diffusion Approximation to Queueing Networks: Part I–Equilibrium Queue Distributions," *J. Assoc. Comp. Mach.* 21, 316-328 (1974).

11.   S.S. Lavenberg, "Efficient Estimation Via Simulation of Work-Rates in Closed Queueing Networks," *Proceedings in Computational Statistics*, Physica Verlag, Vienna, 353-362, 1974.

12.   S.S. Lavenberg, T.L. Moeller and C.H. Sauer, "Concomitant Control Variables Applied to the Regenerative Simulation of Queueing Systems," IBM Research Report RC 6413, Yorktown Heights, New York, 1977.

13.   S.S. Lavenberg, T.L. Moeller and P.D. Welch, "Control Variables Applied to the Simulation of Closed Queueing Networks," to appear as an IBM Research Report, 1977.

14.   R.R. Muntz, "Analytic Modeling of Interactive Systems," *Proc. IEEE* 63, 946-953 (1975).

15.   V.L. Wallace and R.S. Rosenberg, "Markovian Models and Numerical Analysis of Computer System Behavior," *Proceedings Spring Joint Computer Conference*, 1966.

COMPUTER PERFORMANCE, K.M. CHANDY AND M. REISER (EDS.)
NORTH HOLLAND PUBLISHING COMPANY, 1977

ANALYSIS OF INEQUITY OF SERVICE FOR A PARTICULAR FEP POLLING AND PACKET REMOVAL SCHEME

A. E. Eckberg, Jr.

Bell Telephone Laboratories

Holmdel, New Jersey, USA

We consider a switching node in a packet switched data network and focus attention on a particular processor P_0 in this node.

Three assumptions concerning P_0 are:

    i) P_0 receives its inputs (in the form of packets) from K front end processors (FEP).

    ii) P_0 performs its own input functions, periodically interrupting its activities every T time units to enter an input phase and accept packets from the FEPs.

    iii)   As a form of overload control, P_0 accepts a maximum of L packets during each input phase.

Since in general there may be more than L packets waiting in the FEP buffers at the start of the input phase, P_0 must decide which packets must wait for a future input phase.

In this paper we analyze the performance of one possible scheme for making this decision. Although this scheme may be described as being "robustly optimal" with respect to minimizing the maximum FEP buffer requirements, the analysis quantifies an "inequity of service" that results whenever there is an imbalance among the arrival rates to the FEP buffers, with packets in lightly loaded FEPs experiencing much longer delays than are seen by packets in heavily loaded FEPs. The results suggest that other schemes would benefit from an analysis focused on possible inequities of service.

1. INTRODUCTION

In a packet switched data network, a switching node will generally consist of several processors between which data, usually in the form of packets, is expected to flow in an orderly manner. We shall focus attention on a particular processor P_0, and make the following assumptions:

    i) P_0 receives its inputs (packets) from K front end processors (FEP).

    ii) P_0 performs its own input functions, periodically interrupting its activities every T time units to enter an input phase and accept packets from the FEPs.

iii) The maximum total number of packets accepted during any input phase
        is L.

The condition iii) can be thought of as a form of overload control, which prevents
P_0 from spending the majority of its real time performing input tasks while packets accumulate within P_0's buffers and incur large processing delays. Since in
general there may be more than L packets waiting in the FEP buffers at the start
of the input phase, P_0 must decide which packets to accept and which must wait
for a future input phase.

It may be noted that if the overall mean delay of packets in the FEPs'
buffers were to be used as a performance measure, then all schemes for making
the above decision would perform equally well, since by the theorem of Little
(1961) the overall mean delay is invariant from scheme to scheme. However, the
performance of a particular scheme can also be judged by other criteria, such as
the distributions of queue size and delay in the individual FEP buffers. For
example, an overall FIFO scheme will provide equal delay distributions for all the
FEPs; but an imbalance in the loads to the FEPs will result in a corresponding
imbalance in the queue size distributions, thereby necessitating fairly conserva-
tive engineering of the sizes of all the FEP buffers.

In this paper we analyze the performance of one possible scheme for
deciding which of the waiting packets are to be accepted. This scheme can be
characterized as being "robustly optimal" with respect to minimizing the
maximum FEP buffer requirements, in that it tends to realize this objective
without knowledge of the rates at which packets enter the various FEP buffers.
Briefly, the scheme attempts to leave behind, at the end of an input phase, an
equal number of packets in each of the FEP buffers. During any input phase,
this is accomplished by establishing a threshold level and removing packets from
each FEP buffer (FIFO, for each buffer) down to this threshold. A more precise
description follows in Section 2.

While this scheme tends to minimize the maximum FEP buffer requirements
by approximately equalizing the queue sizes in all the buffers, it does so at
the expense of increasing the delays of packets in lightly loaded FEPs, thus
introducing an "inequity of service." To quantify both this inequity of
service and the above mentioned reduction in maximum FEP buffer requirements,
a simple stochastic model is constructed in Section 3; in this model the arrival
processes at the FEP buffers are taken as independent and Poisson.

In Sections 4 and 5, bounds are derived for the distributions of delay
and queue size in a given FEP buffer; these bounds can then be used to quantify
the inequity of service. For comparison purposes, the exact distributions of
delay and queue size resulting from an overall FIFO discipline are derived in
Section 6. Numerical results are presented in Section 7. From their derivations,

one can argue that certain of the bounds of Sections 4 and 5 should actually
be good approximations; this is confirmed by comparison with simulation results
in Section 7.

The general conclusion of this paper is that probably many service
disciplines would benefit from an analysis focused on possible "inequities of
service."

2. THE SCHEME TO BE CONSIDERED

Consider the system depicted in Figure 1 consisting of the processor P_0
and K FEPs. The arrival rate of packets to FEP_k is λ_k, and this is also the rate
at which packets enter the buffer of FEP_k, there to await their acceptance into
P_0. We assume that P_0 has a clocked schedule, interrupting every T time units to
enter its input phase, and that a fixed limit L is placed on the total number of
packets accepted by P_0 during any input phase. Clearly, to guarantee stability
of the entire system it is necessary that

$$\lambda \triangleq \sum_{k=1}^{K} \lambda_k < L/T. \tag{1}$$

The scheme that dictates which packets P_0 will accept during an input
phase is illustrated in Figure 2. N_k denotes the number of packets waiting in
the buffer of FEP_k at the start of the input phase,* and U_k denotes the number
of packets to be accepted from FEP_k, determined as follows. If $N_1+\ldots+N_K \leq L$,
then $U_k = N_k$, $1 \leq k \leq K$. Otherwise, the unique integer n is determined
satisfying

$$\sum_{k=1}^{K} (N_k-n)^+ \leq L \quad \text{and} \quad \sum_{k=1}^{K} (N_k-n+1)^+ > L,$$

and then U_k is determined as

$$U_k = (N_k-n)^+ + u_k, \quad 1 \leq k \leq K,$$

where the u_k are chosen in some arbitrary manner subject only to the conditions

$$u_k = 0 \text{ or } 1 \tag{2a}$$

---

* We shall allow only those packets present at the start of the input phase
to be eligible for removal during that phase.

$$u_k = 0, \quad \text{if} \quad N_k < n \tag{2b}$$

$$\sum_{k=1}^{K} u_k = L - \sum_{k=1}^{K} (N_k - n)^+. \tag{2c}$$

In the above, $x^+ = \max(x,0)$. After the determination of U_k, this number of packets will be removed from the buffer of FEP_k according to a FIFO discipline.

The determination of the U_k is illustrated in Figure 2, where n is seen to be a threshold above which packets are removed from every FEP and below which possibly one packet is removed from some of the FEPs. Thus no more than n of the original packets will remain in any FEP buffer.

3. THE STOCHASTIC MODEL

An analysis of the system in Figures 1 and 2 requires a stochastic model, specifically to describe the arrival processes of packets into the FEPs' buffers. For the purposes of this paper, we shall model these processes as independent, stationary Poisson processes. Thus, the packet process entering the buffer of FEP_k is specified solely by its rate, λ_k.

This model has been chosen merely to provide a simplified analysis for illustrating the point we are trying to make - a possible inequity of service. The actual processes of packets entering the FEP buffers may look either smoother or more variable than Poisson, depending on the relative throughputs of P_0 and the various FEPs, as well as the smoothness of data traffic entering the switching node.

An important quantity in the subsequent analysis is the random variable X, defined as

X = total number of packets in all the FEP buffers at the end of an input
    phase, at equilibrium.

Letting V denote a random variable, independent of X, and equal to the total number of packets entering all FEP buffers during the interval separating two successive input phases, it can be seen that

$$X \stackrel{d}{=} [X+V-L]^+ \tag{3}$$

where "$\stackrel{d}{=}$" means "is distributed as."

The distribution of X is easily determined via probability generating functions (pgf). A sketch follows; details may be found in e.g., Boudreau et al (1962). Defining $\phi(z) \stackrel{\Delta}{=} E[z^X]$ and noting that, since V is a Poisson variable,

$$\psi(z) \triangleq E[z^V] = e^{\lambda T(z-1)}, \qquad (4)$$

it follows easily from (3) that

$$\phi(z) = z^{-L}\phi(z)\psi(z) + \sum_{\ell=0}^{L-1} (1-z^{\ell-L})a_\ell \qquad (5)$$

where $\{a_\ell\}$ is the distribution of $X + V$, i.e.,

$$\sum_{\ell=0}^{\infty} z^\ell a_\ell = \phi(z)\psi(z).$$

From (5) we conclude that

$$\phi(z) = (z^L-\psi(z))^{-1} \sum_{\ell=0}^{L-1} (z^L-z^\ell)a_\ell \qquad (6)$$

where the a_ℓ, $0 \leq \ell \leq L - 1$, are yet to be determined.

Since $\phi(z)$ is the pgf for a nonnegative random variable, it is analytic in the closed unit disc. It can be seen from Rouché's theorem and the condition (1) that the function $z^L - \psi(z)$ has exactly L zeroes in this region (one being at $z = 1$); thus we conclude that the polynomial $P(z) = \sum (z^L-z^\ell)a_\ell$ has its L zeroes at precisely these locations. Since $P(z)$ automatically has a zero at $z = 1$, these requirements provide $L - 1$ equations for the unknowns a_ℓ. An additional equation follows from the requirement that $\phi(1) = 1$:

$$\sum_{\ell=0}^{L-1} (L-\ell)a_\ell = \dot{P}(1) = L - \lambda T.$$

4. THE DELAY IN AN FEP BUFFER

We define the random variable W_k as the waiting time of a "test" packet in the buffer of FEP_k, i.e., the amount of time from its insertion into the buffer until its removal by P_0. The complementary distribution function of W_k will be denoted by F_k:

$$F_k(x) = P[W_k > x], \quad x \geq 0.$$

As the exact determination of F_k is quite difficult, we shall derive upper and lower bounds on F_k:

$$F_k^{(\ell)}(x) \le F_k(x) \le F_k^{(u)}(x), \qquad x \ge 0. \tag{7}$$

It will be seen that, in the high load region of interest (i.e., $\lambda T \cong L$), $F_k^{(\ell)}$ is a good approximation to F_k when $\lambda_k \ll \lambda$, and a fair approximation to $F_k =$ when $\lambda_k \cong \lambda$.

The derivation of the bounds in (7) follows a simple argument. We first note that the waiting time of the test packet can be decomposed as

$$W_k = T - \tau + M_k T \tag{8}$$

where τ denotes the time from the most recent input phase until the arrival of the test packet in the buffer, and M_k equals the number of input phases for which the packet is denied removal by P_0. Because the processes are Poisson, τ is uniformly distributed over $(0,T]$; also, note that M_k depends statistically on τ. The bounds will be developed by determining upper and lower stochastic bounds on M_k, conditioned on τ.

We note by V_τ the total number of packets placed in the FEPs' buffers during the τ-interval from the most recent input phase until the arrival of the test packet in the buffer of FEP$_k$. Thus, just after the packet arrives there will be a total of $X + V_\tau + 1$ packets in all the buffers, where X has been determined in Section 3. Subsequent to the arrival of the test packet, and before the next input phase, more packets arrive in the K buffers; denote these quantities of packets by $V_i^{(0)}$, $1 \le i \le K$. We note that X, V_τ, and the $V_i^{(0)}$ are independent (conditioned on τ) with pgf's given by (6) and

$$E\left[z^{V_\tau}\right] = e^{\lambda\tau(z-1)}$$

$$\tag{9}$$

$$E\left[z^{V_i(0)} \,\middle|\, \tau\right] = e^{\lambda_i(T-\tau)(z-1)}, \quad 1 \le i \le K.$$

Finally, in the following interinput intervals more packets will arrive at the buffers. We denote by $V_i^{(j)}$ the number of packets arriving at the buffer of FEP$_i$ during the jth such interinput interval, and note that

$$E\left[z^{V_i^{(j)}} \,\middle|\, \tau\right] = e^{\lambda_i T(z-1)}, \quad 1 \le i \le K \text{ and } j \ge 1.$$

We now note that, under the scheme described in Section 2, if the packet is still present at a given input phase, its removal during that input phase depends on its present position relative to the positions of other packets in the FEPs' buffers. In particular, it can be seen from Figure 2 that if the total number of packets present at the start of an input phase equals N, and if the test packet occupies position s, measured from the input end of the buffer of FEP_k, then the following statements can be made:

S1: the test packet will be removed only if $N - Ks < L$

S2: the test packet will be removed if $N - s < L$.

Statement S1 follows from the fact that Ks is an upper bound on the number of packets that occupy positions which are not better than that of the test packet; thus at least $N - Ks$ packets occupy better positions. Similarly S2 uses the fact that no more than $N - s$ packets can occupy positions better than that of the test packet. Some reflection reveals that S1 is an "approximate if and only if statement" when $\lambda_k << \min_{i \neq k} \lambda_i$.[*]

Based on S1 and S2, and the fact that exactly L packets are removed for each input phase during which the test packet is denied removal, we now see that M_k can be stochastically bounded as follows:

$$P\left[M_k^{(\ell)} > m \,\middle|\, \tau\right] \leq P[M_k > m \,|\, \tau] \leq P\left[M_k^{(u)} > m \,\middle|\, \tau\right]$$

where

$$M_k^{(\ell)} = \inf\left\{ m \geq 0 \,\middle|\, X + V_\tau + \sum_{i \neq k} \sum_{j=0}^{m} V_i^{(j)} - (K-1)\left(1 + \sum_{j=0}^{m} V_k^{(j)}\right)\right.$$

$$\left. - (m+1)L < 0 \right\} \tag{10}$$

---

[*]Strictly speaking, this assumes that packets in the buffer of FEP_k receive preferred treatment in the sense that (using the terminology of (2)) $u_k = 1$ whenever this is consistent with (2).

$$M_k^{(u)} = \inf \left\{ m \geq 0 \,\Big|\, X + V_\tau + \sum_{i \neq k} \sum_{j=0}^{m} V_i^{(j)} - (m+1)L < 0 \right\} \qquad (11)$$

Since the random variables X, V_τ, and $V_i^{(j)}$ are mutually independent (conditioned on τ), both $M_k^{(\ell)}$ and $M_k^{(u)}$ have the interpretations of boundary cross-ing epochs associated with random walks; it follows that the conditional distri-butions of $M_k^{(\ell)}$ and $M_k^{(u)}$ can be easily obtained numerically, e.g., by using fast Fourier transform techniques as outlined in Cooley et al (1967). Finally, using (8), the bounds in (7) can be computed as

$$F_k^{(\ell)}(x) = \frac{1}{T} \int_0^T P\left[M_k^{(\ell)} > \frac{x-T-t}{T} \,\Big|\, \tau = t \right] dt \qquad (12)$$

$$F_k^{(u)}(x) = \frac{1}{T} \int_0^T P\left[M_k^{(u)} > \frac{x-T-t}{T} \,\Big|\, \tau = t \right] dt \qquad (13)$$

5.   THE QUEUE SIZE IN AN FEP BUFFER

Because the scheme described in Section 2 is intended to reduce the FEP buffer requirements, it is also of interest to obtain the distribution of queue size in the buffer of FEP_k just before an input phase commences, i.e., the distri-bution of the random variable N_k defined in Section 2. Of most interest is the distribution of N_{k*}, where k* is the index of the most heavily loaded FEP:

$$\lambda_{k*} = \max_k \lambda_k.$$

Denote by G_k the complementary distribution function of N_k:

$$G_k(n) = P[N_k > n], \quad n = 0,1,\ldots$$

The exact determination of G_k is quite difficult, and will not be attempted here. Rather, a simple lower bound on G_k will be derived, thereby providing a stochastic lower bound on N_k.   It will be seen that the lower bound on G_{k*} is actually also a good approximation to G_{k*} in the case where

$$\lambda_{k*} \tilde{=} \lambda,$$

i.e., the case where the traffic loads on the FEPs are grossly nonuniform.

Also derived is a simple "approximate lower bound" on G_{k*}, which will be seen to be a good approximation to G_{k*} in the case of near-uniform FEP loading, i.e., when

$$\lambda_{k*} \tilde{=} \lambda/K.$$

Denote by X_k the number of packets left behind in the buffer of FEP_k at the end of an input phase, and let V_k denote the number of packets that arrive at FEP_k during the subsequent interinput interval (V_k is independent of X_k). Then clearly,

$$N_k \stackrel{d}{=} X_k + V_k,$$

but the distribution of X_k is not easily determined.

What we do know about X_k is that it satisfies

$$X_k \stackrel{d}{=} \left[X_k + V_k - f_k \left(X_1 + V_1 ; \ldots ; X_k + V_k \right) \right]^+$$

where f_k is the (possibly random) mapping which dictates the maximum number of packets that can be removed from the buffer of FEP_k, via the scheme of Section 2. Although the mappings f_k are quite complicated, it is clear that

$$f_k \leq L,$$

and thus the following stochastic inequality results:

$$X_k \geq [X_k + V_k - L]^+.$$

Some reflection reveals that if $\hat{X}_k$ is a random variable, independent of V_k and satisfying

$$\hat{X}_k \stackrel{d}{=} \left[\hat{X}_k + V_k - L \right],$$

then

$$G_k(n) \geq P\left[\hat{X}_k + V_k > n\right], \quad n = 0,1,\dots . \tag{14}$$

Note that the distribution of $\hat{X}_k$ is easily obtained via the method of Section 3.

For the case where there is a high imbalance amongst the FEP loads, i.e., when $\lambda_{k*} \gg \max_{i \neq k*} \lambda_i$, the following is an "approximate stochastic equality":

$$f_{k*} \overset{\sim}{=} L.$$

Thus, in this situation, we expect the bound (14) to be a good approximation.

Unfortunately, (14) cannot be expected to yield a good approximation to G_{k*} when the loads on the FEPs are approximately uniform. However, in this case, i.e., when $\lambda_{k*} \overset{\sim}{=} \lambda/K$, we can observe that

$$X_{k*} \overset{\sim}{>} [X/K]$$

where $[y]$ denotes the largest integer less than or equal to y, and

$$X = \sum_{k=1}^{K} X_k.$$

Thus, an approximate bound on G_{k*} for this case is given by

$$G_{k*}(n) \overset{\sim}{>} P[[X/K] + V_{k*} > n] \tag{15}$$

where   the distribution of X has been determined in Section 3.

Combining (14) and (15) results in the following "approximate stochastic lower bound" on N_{k*}:

$$P[N_{k*} > n] \overset{\sim}{>} \max\left\{ P\left[\hat{X}_{k*} + V_{k*} > n\right],\ P\left[[X/K] + V_{k*} > n\right] \right\}. \tag{16}$$

Finally, it may be observed that the random variable $\hat{N}_{k*}$ which would result from a FIFO discipline, rather than the discipline of Section 2, is very nearly a stochastic upper bound on N_{k*}; the distribution of $\hat{N}_{k*}$ is derived exactly in Section 6.

6. DELAY AND QUEUE SIZE FOR FIFO DISCIPLINE

For comparison with the results of Sections 4 and 5 we now consider an overall FIFO discipline for removing packets from the FEPs' buffers. That is, each packet arrival time is recorded and, at each input phase, the L packets which have been waiting longest are removed. This is clearly the most equitable discipline in regards to waiting times in the various FEP buffers, but it may necessitate larger buffer capacities. Exact analyses are easily performed for the distributions of waiting times of packets in the buffer of FEP_k, and for the queue size in the buffer of FEP_k just before an input phase.

For the waiting time, it is easily seen that (8) is still a valid representation for W_k, but now (using the random variable definitions of Section 4)

$$M_k = [(X+V_\tau)/L].$$

The distribution of M_k is easily obtained via (6) and (9), and then the distribution of W_k can be computed as in (12).

For the distribution of N_k, i.e., the number of packets in the buffer of FEP_k just before an input phase, we note that the total number of packets in all buffers is just $X + V$ (as defined in Section 3). Since the K arrival processes are Poisson and independent, at any given input phase N_k has the same distribution as $\hat{N}_k$ where

$$\hat{N}_k = \sum_{i=1}^{X+V} \eta_i$$

and where the η_i are i.i.d. random variables, independent of $X + V$, and $P\{\eta_i = 1\}$ $= 1 - P[\eta_i = 0] = \lambda_k/\lambda$. It follows that the probability generating function of N_k is

$$E[z^{N_k}] = \psi\left(1 + \frac{\lambda_k}{\lambda}(z-1)\right)\phi\left(1 + \frac{\lambda_k}{\lambda}(z-1)\right)$$

where ψ and ϕ are given by (4) and (6).

7. QUALTITY OF BOUNDS AND INEQUITY OF DELAY PERFORMANCE

In this section we investigate the usefulness of the bounds in (7) and (16) as good approximations to the distribution of delay and queue size. The quality of approximation will be judged by comparison with results obtained via simulation. Then the bounds and simulation results will be used to quantify the inequity of service resulting from the scheme of Section 2, and to compare the performance of this scheme with a FIFO scheme.

For all the results, the value of the limit L was taken to be $L = 10$. The length of each simulation run corresponded to 100,000 interinput intervals (i.e., 100,000 T), which was deemed sufficient to provide fairly accurate results.

7.1 The Quality of the Bounds as Approximations

The lower bound $F_k^{(\ell)}$ in (7) was found to be an excellent approximation to F_k in the range $\lambda_k \ll \lambda$, and still a good approximation for the larger values of λ_k. Figures 3 and 4 illustrate the quality of approximation in this latter range. Plotted in these figures are the bounds $F_k^{(\ell)}$ and $F_k^{(u)}$, and estimates of F_k obtained via simulation. (Deviations of this latter curve below $F_k^{(\ell)}$ are results of simulation inaccuracies.)

The lower bound (16) for the queue size distribution of the most highly loaded FEP was also found to be a fairly good approximation. The quality of this approximation is illustrated in Figures 5 and 6.

7.2 The Inequity of Delay Performance

Figures 7 and 8 illustrate, for a variety of parameter values, the increase in delay, as seen by lightly loaded FEPs, over that resulting from a FIFO discipline. The solid curves in these figures are the lower-bounding functions $F_1^{(\ell)}$; however, as has been previously noted, for the range of values of λ_1 in Figures 7 and 8, $F_1^{(\ell)}$ is a good approximation to F_1. These figures dramatically demonstrate the increased delays to packets in lightly loaded FEP buffers which can result from the use of the scheme of Section 2.

To define a measure of the inequity of service, we assume that FEP_1 receives the lightest load, and consider the ratio

$$R = \frac{E[W_1]}{\min\limits_{2 \le k \le K} E[W_k]}.$$

Using either the result of Little (1961) or that of Kleinrock (1965) it can be seen that $\overline{W}_{FIFO}$, the mean waiting time using an overall FIFO scheme, has the representation

$$\overline{W}_{FIFO} = \frac{1}{\lambda} \sum_{k=1}^{K} \lambda_k E[W_k],$$

whence it is seen that

$$\min\limits_{2 \le k \le K} E[W_k] \le \frac{1}{\lambda - \lambda_1} (\lambda \overline{W}_{FIFO} - \lambda_1 E[W_1]).$$

Therefore, R is bounded from below as

$$R \geq \frac{(\lambda - \lambda_1)E[W_1]}{\lambda \bar{w}_{FIFO} - \lambda_1 E[W_1]} \; .$$

Figures 9 and 10 depict this lower bound on R for various parameter values.

7.3 Comparison with the FIFO Scheme

Figure 5 serves to illustrate the advantage, in terms of buffer requirements, of using the scheme of Section 2. In this example, the FEP buffer requirements are reduced about 30 percent below the requirements when an overall FIFO scheme is employed. However, Figure 6 indicates that both schemes are comparable when the loads are balanced, perhaps with a slight advantage given to FIFO.

In terms of waiting times, however, Figures 7 and 8 illustrate the drastic increases in delays to packets in lightly loaded FEPs, when the scheme of Section 2 is used. Of course, to compensate for these increases in delays, the scheme of Section 2 produces reduced delays for heavily loaded FEPs. This is illustrated in Figure 11.

8. CONCLUSION

Bounds and approximations have been developed to evaluate the performance of a particular algorithm for removing packets from FEP buffers. It has been demonstrated that, while this algorithm tends to reduce buffer requirements of heavily loaded FEPs, the delays to packets in lightly loaded FEPs are considerably increased. This can result in a gross inequity of service.

The implications of providing very poor delay performance to a small fraction of packets are not known. However, since in this case the poor service is localized to all packets in a lightly loaded FEP, this situation would probably be considered unacceptable. The results of this paper also suggest that other algorithms for removing packets from FEPs for processing should be carefully analyzed with a possible "inequity of service" in mind.

Finally, note that there are several heuristic ways of doctoring the scheme of Section 2 to remove this inequity of service. For example, for the case $K \leq L$ one could add the requirement that at least one packet should be removed from each nonempty FEP buffer. The analyses of the resulting schemes have not been undertaken, but could be the subject of future work.

REFERENCES

Boudreau, P. E., Griffin, J. S. and Kac, M. (1962), "An Elementary Queueing Problem," Amer. Math. Monthly, 69, pp. 713-24.
Cooley, J. W., Lewis, P.A.W., and Welch, P. D. (1967), "Application of the Fast Fourier Transform to Computation of Fourier Integrals, Fourier Series, and Convolution Integrals," IEEE Trans. Audio Electro., AV-15, pp. 79-84.
Kleinrock, L. (1965), "A Conservation Law for a Wide Class of Queueing Disciplines," Naval Res. Log. Quant., 12, pp. 181-92.

Little, J. D. C., (1961), "A Proof for the Queueing Formula: L = λW," Op. Res.,
9, pp. 383-87.

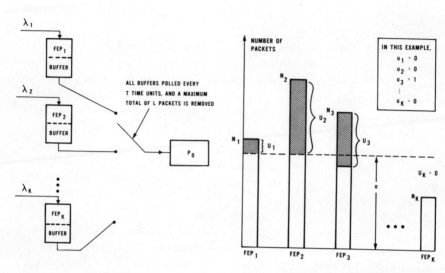

FIGURE 1 - PACKET FLOW BETWEEN THE K FEPs AND P₀

FIGURE 2 - DETERMINATION OF THE NUMBERS OF PACKETS
(THE Uᵢ) TO BE REMOVED FROM THE FEP BUFFERS

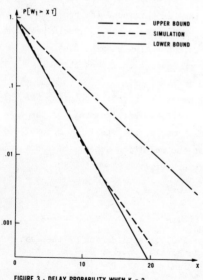

FIGURE 3 - DELAY PROBABILITY WHEN K = 2,
λ = 9.5, λ_1 = 2.0

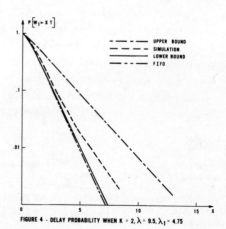

FIGURE 4 - DELAY PROBABILITY WHEN K = 2, λ = 9.5, λ_1 = 4.75

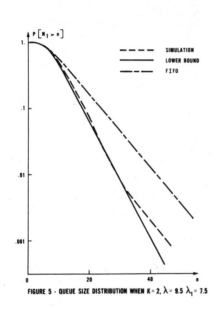

FIGURE 5 - QUEUE SIZE DISTRIBUTION WHEN K = 2, λ = 9.5 λ_1 = 7.5

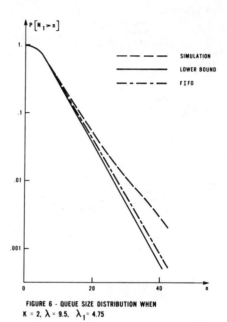

FIGURE 6 - QUEUE SIZE DISTRIBUTION WHEN
K = 2, λ = 9.5, λ_1 = 4.75

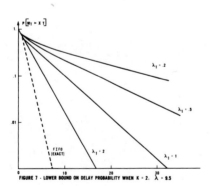

FIGURE 7 - LOWER BOUND ON DELAY PROBABILITY WHEN K = 2, λ = 9.5

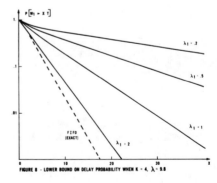

FIGURE 8 - LOWER BOUND ON DELAY PROBABILITY WHEN K = 4, λ = 9.8

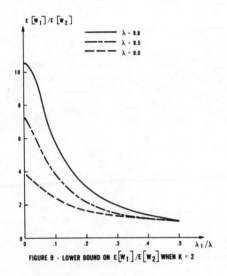

FIGURE 9 - LOWER BOUND ON $E[W_1]/E[W_2]$ WHEN K = 2

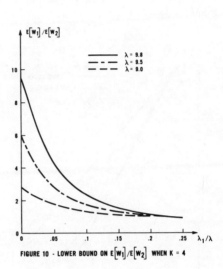

FIGURE 10 - LOWER BOUND ON $E[W_1]/E[W_2]$ WHEN K = 4

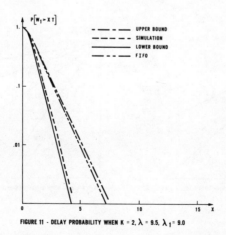

FIGURE 11 - DELAY PROBABILITY WHEN K = 2, λ = 9.5, λ_1 = 9.0

COMPUTER PERFORMANCE, K.M. CHANDY AND M. REISER (EDS.)
NORTH HOLLAND PUBLISHING COMPANY, 1977

A HIERARCHICAL ROUTING AND FLOW CONTROL POLICY (HRFC)
FOR PACKET SWITCHED NETWORKS

W. W. Chu and M. Y. Shen
Computer Science Department
University of California
Los Angeles, California, USA

A new policy that can effectively handle message routing and
flow control simultaneously in a packet switched computer
network is presented. In such a policy, the network is partitioned into regions and logically organized into a hierarchical structure (supervisor node and local node). A supervisor is assigned to monitor the channel traffic loads
in each region. The supervisors communicate with each other
and thus have complete traffic status of the entire network.
A traffic threshold level is assigned for each channel in
the network. If all the channels along the preassigned
primary route from a source to its destination do not exceed
the predetermined traffic threshold level, then the primary
route is used. Otherwise, alternative route(s) are used.
When all the alternative routes from a source to a destination become unavailable, then the input traffic from that
source to that destination is temporarily rejected. Hardware
counters may be used to measure the traffic intensities of
all the channels in the network. Under normal conditions,
that is, when the traffic intensity is below the predetermined
threshold level, the primary route is used, which does not
require overhead for signaling and route selection. Simulation results of the behavior and performance of such a routing
and control policy are presented. The implementation of the
policy is also discussed. The paper concludes that this new
policy is simpler to implement and yields better performance
than that of the distributed routing policy which is currently
being used in many packet switched networks.

INTRODUCTION

Management of traffic flow in a computer network can be generally divided into two
main tasks: message routing and flow control. To manage the traffic flow in a
network such that it provides a prespecified performance specification is an important and difficult problem. Because of the complex nature of the problem, routing
and flow control have been studied separately in the past. Message delay or cost
is a commonly used parameter to design routing policy [1-5] and buffer size is the
often-used parameter for flow control algorithms [6-11]. However, both routing
and flow control are intimately related to each other and influence the network
performance. Therefore, it is desirable to study them jointly. From queuing
theory, it is well known that the traffic intensity is closely related to delay

*This research was supported by the U.S. Office of Naval Research, Contract No.
Noool4-75-C-0650.

and queue length. This motivates us to use the channel traffic intensity as a
common parameter to jointly optimize the routing and flow control in a packet (a
unit of partitioned message) switched network.

Message routing algorithms used in many currently operating networks, e.g., ARPA-
NET, are based on distributed routing policy [1]. The next link in a path for
transmitting a packet from a source node to a destination node is selected at the
current node according to traffic information reported periodically from all its
nearest neighbors. Such a technique requires a large amount of overhead for handling and transmitting of routing update packets, which can cost the total line
utilization as high as twenty percent or more [12-13]. Further, such a routing
policy provides only a local optimization. Therefore, this motivates us to investigate a new traffic flow management policy that requires low overhead to implement
and yet provides global optimization.

In this paper we shall first describe a new hierarchical routing and flow control
policy (HRFC) which can effectively handle message routing and flow control simultaneously. To reduce the overhead, to imrpove the speed in traffic status reporting among all the nodes in the networks, and to manage the traffic flow in a more
organized way, the network is partitioned into regions and logically organized
into a hierarchical structure. Next, we present the implementation of this new
policy. Finally, we use simulation to study the behavior and performance of this
new policy and compare with that of the distributed routing policy.

A HIERARCHICAL ROUTING AND FLOW CONTROL POLICY

Since traffic intensity plays a major role in influencing the network throughput
and delay, we are motivated to use channel traffic intensity as a parameter to manage the traffic flow (routing and flow control) in a computer network. Based on
the traffic pattern and the desired performance, such as response delay and throughput, we preassign each channel in the network a traffic threshold level and a primary route from all the source and destination pairs in the network. When the
traffic intensities of all the channels along the preassigned primary route from a
source to its destination are below the specified channel threshold level, the
primary route is used to send a packet from the source to its destination. The
main motivation for using the primary route under this condition is because at low
traffic load, the system works well in most cases. Further, the primary route is
fixed and is simple to implement. Whenever the traffic intensity of one or more
channels along a primary route exceeds the given threshold level, alternative
route(s) are used to share the traffic load in order to reduce the traffic load in
the congested channel(s). If no suitable alternative route is available at that
time, input traffic (but not the through traffic) from that source node to its
destination is temporarily rejected in order not to congest the network and degrade
performance. When the traffic load of the congested channel(s) decreases to the
prescribed traffic threshold level, that source node will resume accepting input
traffic to its destination.

When a packet is enroute from a source to its destination, if congestion develops
in all the routes from the current node to its destination, this packet should follow
the predetermined primary route to its destination to avoid looping problems in
routing. On the other hand, should a malfunction develop in one of the channels or
nodes along the route, the current node according to the traffic status, selectes
the best alternative route to send the packet to its destination.

Clearly, monitoring facilities are required to determine whether each channel is
operating below or above the prespecified traffic level. Each node in the network
is assigned to measure the traffic intensity of all its connecting channels, for
example, all its output (or input) channels. The channel traffic intensity is
measured and averaged over a predetermined period. Whenever the traffic intensity
of a channel changes its state from below to exceeding the prescribed threshold
level (averaged over a measurement period), or vice versa, this information is

reported to its regional supervisor; otherwise no traffic reporting is necessary, which does not require overhead. To speed up the traffic updating in response to variation of traffic load and to reduce the overhead for handling these traffic status reports, we partition the network into regions (the partition may be based on geographical clusters) and logically organize them into a hierarchical structure. We assign one of the nodes in a region as a supervisor node* which monitors the traffic status of all the channels in its region.   The supervisor summarizes the channel traffic status of its region and broadcasts this information to other supervisors in the network. Thus, each supervisor has complete traffic status of the entire network. Further, each supervisor reports relevant channel traffic information to all local nodes in its region. With such a hierarchical structure for traffic information handling and by assigning traffic reporting packets a higher priority than data and acknowledgement packets, the response to channel status changes can be rapidly forwarded to all the nodes in the network.

Hierarchical traffic reporting structures provide all the supervisors with global traffic information. The alternative route(s) generated based on such information provide better performance than the distributed routing algorithm (currently being used by many packet switched networks) that based on local traffic information.

IMPLEMENTATION

Let us now discuss the implementation of the Hierarchical Routing and Flow Control Policy. We shall first discuss the implementation of the traffic monitoring facilities. The traffic intensity of all the channels in the network are monitored. We assign each node to monitor the traffic intensity of all its output channels and average it over a predetermined period of time. The traffic intensity may be measured in packets/sec or bits/sec. Because packets may be of variable size, it is more accurate to measure the traffic load in terms of bits/sec. A simple hardware counter may be used for such purposes. The measurement counter is reset after each measurement period. For example, for a 50 k bit/sec channel, with a threshold level = 0.7 and a measurement period of 0.5 sec, the measurement counter threshold is $0.7 \times 0.5 \times 50 = 17.5$ k bits. The monitor sends the traffic reports to its supervisor only when there is a change in its channel traffic status from below to above the prescribed threshold level or vice versa. The supervisor summarizes the traffic status of its region and broadcasts to the rest of the supervisors in the network. Therefore, each supervisor has the updated traffic status of the entire network. Each supervisor selects the relevant traffic information and sends it to corresponding local nodes in its region to update the Routing Information Table.

There is a Routing Information Table as shown in Table 1 residing at each node. The first column of the table lists all the destination addresses in the network. The second column is the congestion indicator vector of the primary route from the current node j to the desired destination node k. The third column designates the output link for the next node of the predetermined primary route for sending packets from the current node to the destination. The fourth column is the congestion indicator for the alternative route. The fifth column designates the output link for next node of the predetermined alternate route for sending packets from the current node j to the destination node k. There may be more than one alternate route for a source to send a message to its destination. In this case, a congestion indicator is assigned for each alternate route to indicate its congestion status. The last column of the table is the traffic splitting probability among the primary route and the alternative route(s) whenever the channel traffic load exceeds the threshold level.

*For reliability purposes, each region may assign a node as a back-up supervisor and capable of switching over when the supervisor node fails. In this case, communication links among the back-up supervisors must be provided. Another approach, probably more desirable, is to have a back-up communication processor at each supervisor node capable of switching over whenever a malfunction develops in the supervisor communication processor.

DESTIN- ATION NODE ADDRESS K	CONGESTION INDICATOR FOR PRIMARY ROUTE CI (A_0; j, k)	LOGICAL OUTPUT CHANNEL NUMBER FOR PRIMARY ROUTE	CONGESTION INDICATOR FOR FIRST ALTER- NATIVE ROUTE CI (A_1; j, k)	LOGICAL OUTPUT CHANNEL NUMBER FOR FIRST ALTER- NATIVE ROUTE	...	TRAFFIC SPLITTING PROBABILITY P(A_0, A_1 ..., A_m)
1						
. . .						
. . .						
j – 1						
j + 1						
. . .						
n						

n: NUMBER OF NODES   m: NUMBER OF ALTERNATIVE ROUTES

A_0: PRIMARY ROUTE A_i: i^{th} ALTERNATIVE ROUTE

Table 1   Routing Information Table for the jth Node

The congestion indicator $CI(x;j,k)$ of a route x indicates whether the traffic intensities of one or more channels in that route from the current node j to the destination node k has exceeded the prescribed threshold level. When the traffic
intensity of one or more channels of a route has exceeded the prescribed threshold
level, its corresponding congestion indicator changes from zero to one. The regional supervisor computes the congestion indicator for each route for itself and
all the local nodes in its region. The decision to use the predetermined primary
route or to use an alternative route for sending a message to its destination is
based on the Routing Information Table. When the congestion indicators of all the
routes from a source node to a destination become congested, then input traffic
generated from that source node to that destination node is temporarily rejected.

The policy to select an optimal route has been studied previously [2,4]. The commonly used policy is to select the route that minimizes the channel utilization
and to balance the traffic load among all the channels in the network. Therefore,
the path that carries the least amount of traffic and the least number of hops
from a source to its destination should be selected. Such a route does not necessarily imply the shortest distance path. A heuristic and simple method is to select the alternative route that requires approximately the lease number of hops and
also least utilized channels from a source to its destination.

The primary as well as the alternative routes are predetermined by the supervisor
based on the assumed or prior traffic statistics. These routes are selected by
the regional supervisor (which has the traffic status of the entire network), and

may be revised by the supervisor whenever there is a significant change in traffic pattern. This change can be detected by a degradation of network throughput and user response time.

When a node wishes to communicate with another node in the network, the source node, based on the Routing Information Table (which in part is generated and updated by its regional supervisor) decides whether a primary or alternate route should be used. Under normal operation (i.e., all the channel traffic loads are lower than the prescribed threshold level), a packet is routed according to its predetermined primary route from a given source to its destination. This does not require overhead in signaling, traffic reporting and route selection. When the traffic level of one or more channels along the primary route exceeds its prescribed threshold level, an alternative route is used to share the traffic load. The traffic load is split between the primary route and the alternative route(s) according to the traffic splitting probability in the Routing Information Table. The reason for load splitting is to provide a more even traffic load among the channels in the primary and alternative route during heavy traffic loads. The traffic splitting probability at each node can be determined locally based on the prescribed channel threshold, the measured traffic intensity and the channel congestion indications of the alternative routes. For example, the amount of traffic that exceeds the threshold level of the primary route may be detoured to the first available alternative route or distributed evenly among the uncongested alternative routes to that destination. In the latter case, the traffic splitting probability from node j to destination k = $[C(A_o;i,k)-C\cdot T\cdot\theta]/ C(A_o;i,k)\cdot[m-\sum_{i=1}^{m}CI(A_i;j,k)]$ where $C(A_o;i,k)$ is the measured traffic count of the primary route from node i to destination k after a measurement peroid T, C is the channel capacity, θ is the preassigned traffic threshold level, therefore $C\cdot T\cdot\theta$ is the measurement counter threshold value, and m is the total number of alternative routes from node j to node k.

The size of the Routing Information Table is fairly small. For example, for each route it requires 1 bit for channel congestion indication, 3 bits for output channel logical numbers (which is lower than the ARPANET distributed routing table that requires 16 bits to represent the delay for each connecting output channel). Further, usually the number of routes (primary and alternative) are smaller in number than the connecting channels of a node; the Routing Information Table of the HRFC Policy should require less table space than that of the distributed routing policy. Also, the distributed routing policy is required to perform many more tasks, such as periodically computing, updating, and transmitting minimum message delay from each node to all its nearest neighboring nodes.

From the above discussion, we conclude that the implementation of the HRFC policy should be simpler and lower in cost than the distributed routing policy.

A SIMULATION STUDY OF THE HRFC POLICY

Because of the many interdependent parameters in the flow control and routing policy for a computer network, it is difficult to obtain analytical solutions to estimate the behavior and performance of these policies without making grossly simplified assumptions. Therefore, we shall use simulation to study the behavior of the proposed new policy and compare with that of a distributed routing policy.

For our study, a ten-node computer network with three regions as shown in Fig. 1 is used in our simulation. Nodes 3, 7, and 10 are the three regional supervisor nodes. The rest of the nodes are local nodes. There are two types of packets in the network: data packets and control packets. The data packet is for sending data, while the control packet is for sending acknowledgments, routing information, traffic reporting, etc. and usually has a shorter length than the data packet. We assume that the data packets generated at each node are Poisson distributed. The data packet length has a minimum of 64 bits and a maximum of 1024 bits and is assumed to be truncated geometrically distributed with an average of 256 bits as shown in Fig. 2. Further, all the data are in single packets. The channels are

WESLEY W. CHU and MICHAEL Y. SHEN

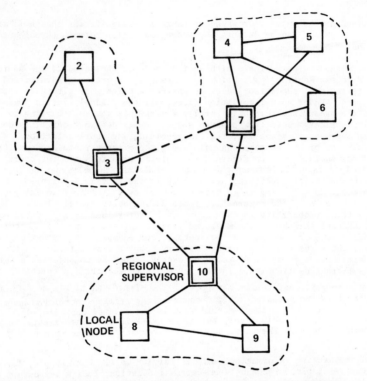

Figure 1   The Topology for the Simulated Communication Network

assumed to be so reliable that errors causing packet retransmission have negligible
effects on the performance of the network. Thus, we ignore such errors in the
simulation. Whenever a data packet is received at a node, a control packet is
sent to the sender to positively acknowledge correct receipt of the data packet.
The buffer size at each node is 61.4 Kbits or 60 packets. For the distributed
routing policy and fixed routing policy ($\theta=1.0$), the buffer flow control policy
used is that whenever the buffer occupancy exceeds 50% of its capacity, no new
input traffic (not the through traffic) is admitted into the network from that
node. For the HRFC Policy, the flow control is based on the parameter θ value.
When buffer overflows, the sender is notified to retransmit that packet without
time delay. The average control packet length is assumed to be 112 bits. In the
simulation model, we assumed that from every node to each destination in the network there is a primary route and an alternative route. The traffic threshold
levels for all the channels in the network are set at an identical value. The
traffic intensity of all the channels in the entire network is measured and
averaged over a period of 0.5 seconds. We have assumed uniform traffic between
each node pair; that is, data packets generated at any node have equal probability
of sending to each of the nodes in the network, and the input rate is the same for
each node. Further, all the channels in the network are assumed to be identical
and have a capacity of 50 Kbits/sec. The flow chart of the simulation is shown
in Fig. 3. The simulation program is written in GPSS (General Purpose Simulation
System) language. The clock time used in the simulation is 20 microseconds which
is equal to the time to transmit a bit of data in a 50Kbits/sec channel. The
simulation time required for each experiment (corresponding to a point on the
performance curve) depends on the traffic threshold level and the amount of network

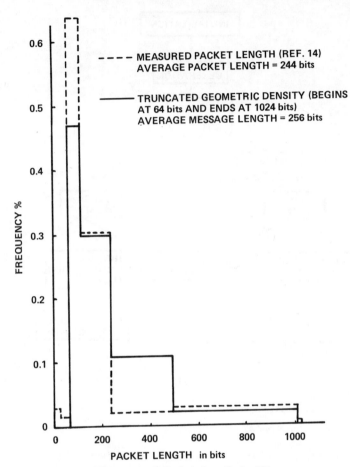

Figure 2 Histogram of Packet Length in Bits

input traffic needing to be generated. Higher input traffic and higher traffic threshold levels require more processing time than the lower input traffic and lower threshold level cases. Snapshots of performance values are generated at fixed intervals to test if the system reaches its steady state. A typical experiment takes about 10 to 15 seconds of real time network operation to reach its stability and requires about 2 to 30 minutes of IBM 360/91 processing time.

DISCUSSION OF RESULTS

Before we discuss the simulation results, let us define a few performance measures: the network input traffic is defined as the total amount of traffic in bits/sec that input to the communication network. The throughput of the network is defined as the total number of single packets that are successfully delivered from source nodes to destination nodes per second. The input rejection rate is defined as the percentage of the total rejected packets over the total generated input traffic.

Figure 4 portrays the network throughput for various network input traffic at selected traffic threshold levels θ. We notice that the network throughput increases as the network input traffic increases. After reaching a certain maximum

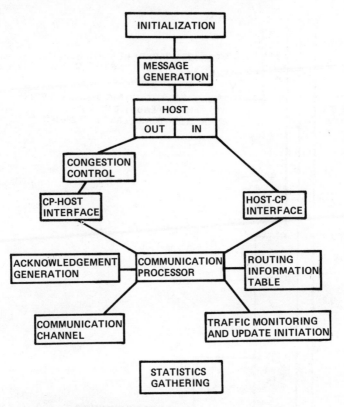

HOST: HOST PROCESSOR

CP: COMMUNICATION PROCESSOR

Figure 3 Functional Diagram for Computer Network Simulation

network throughput value, the throughput reaches its saturation. For $\theta < 1$, the
maximum network throughput increases are θ increases. However, for a given network
input traffic, the input rejection rate decreases as θ increases as shown in Fig. 5.
This is mainly because the flow control (input rejection) of the proposed policy
is based on the θ value. As a result of input rejection, the average packet delay
increases as θ increases as shown in Fig. 6. In general, for a given network
input load, a lower threshold level yields lower response delay and lower network
throughput, but more input rejection; a higher threshold level yields a higher
response delay, higher throughput, but less input rejection. Therefore, the parameter
θ plays an important role in influencing the network throughput and packet response
delay. The optimal threshold traffic level should be determined by the amount of
network input traffic, the user desired response delay, and the desired network
throughput.

When $\theta = 1$, then the proposed policy becomes a fixed routing policy. In this case,
the network throughput decreases when the network input traffic reaches 300 Kbits/
sec as shown in Fig. 4. This is because at high network input traffic, the amount
of the retransmission of the rejected packets (due to buffer overflow) increases
and eventually uses up a large portion of the network capacity. Therefore, using
input rejection as flow control greatly increases the network throughput and
reduces the response delay of those packets that are admitted into the network.

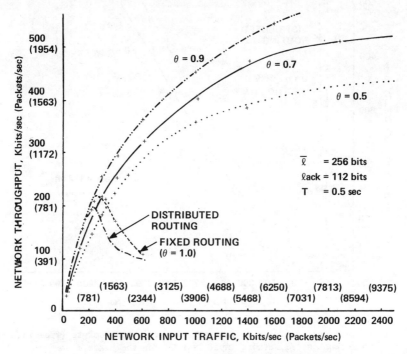

Figure 4   Throughput VS Network Input Traffic for the Network Example

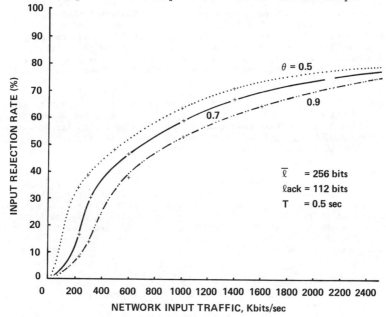

Figure 5   Input Rejection Rate VS Network Input Traffic for the Network Example

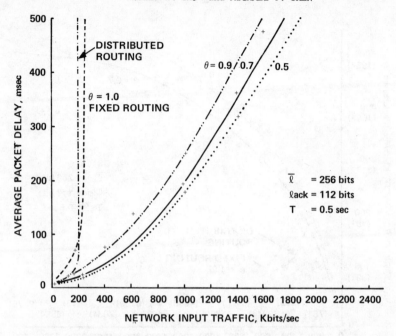

Figure 6   Average Message Delay of successfully Delivered Packets (from initiation
to reception) VS Network Input Traffic for the Example

We also notice that the HRFC policy yields a higher throughput than that of the
distributed routing policy.[*] This is mainly because the distributed routing policy
uses only local traffic information in its route selection, while the proposed
hierarchical routing and flow control policy is based on the global traffic information in selecting its route. Thus, in general, it takes fewer hops to transmit
a packet from the source to its destination than the distributed routing policy
as shown in Figure 7.

We also notice that as the network input traffic increases, the input rejection
increases, and the average number of hops for delivering a packet decreases. This
is because those messages that require more hops (from source to its destination)
have more chance of being rejected at the source than those messages that require
fewer hops from the source to their destinations.

Figure 8a portrays the packet delay distribution of the distributed routing policy
while Figure 8b portrays the packet delay distribution of the HRFC policy. We
notice that the HRFC has a higher concentration in low delay regions than that of
the distributed routing policy, and HRFC has a lower concentration in high delay
regions than that of the distributed routing policy. As mentioned earlier, this
is mainly due to the fact that the average number of hops required to successfully
deliver a packet from a source to its destination for the distributed routing
policy is higher than that of the HRFC policy.

---

*The simulation program used for evaluating the network throughput of the distrib-
ted routing policy is based on the program used in Reference [1].

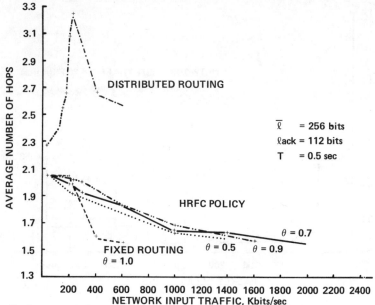

Figure 7 Average Number of Hops for the Successfully Delivered Packets VS Network
Input Traffic for the Network Example

Figure 9 displays the dynamic behavior of the HRFC policy for sending traffic from
node 4 to node 10 by presenting the probability of using an alternate route as a
function of time. We notice that due to congestion occurring on the primary route,
part of the traffic is switched from a primary route to an alternate route. Due
to input rejection and sharing of traffic load by the alternate route, the traffic
is switched back from the alternate route to the primary route. Furthermore, a
higher threshold level provides less load sharing by the alternate route(s) than
that of a lower threshold level. Thus, the HRFC policy is less sensitive in performance to sudden changes of network input traffic, and provides the capability
of self recovery from network congestion.

CONCLUSIONS

A hierarchical routing and flow control policy for packet switched networks is
proposed in this paper. Such a policy is capable of providing routing and flow
control simultaneously via the prescribed channel threshold level. Using such a
policy, each supervisor has complete traffic information of the network and thus
is able to provide a global optimal rather than local optimal route. Further, a
network with flow control (selective input rejection) provides much better performance (throughput and delay) than the ones without it. The simulation result
supports our intuition that the proposed new policy provides better performance
than that of the distributed (adaptive) routing policy that is based on local
traffic information.

Because there are relatively few supervisors and because in most cases, the primary
route is used for sending packets in the network, no traffic reporting is necessary.
The operating overhead of the proposed policy is fairly low. Further, because a
network can be easily organized logically into a hierarchical structure which
provides more efficient communication among the supervisors and because the monitoring of channel traffic intensity is rather simple, the HRFC policy is also rather
easy to implement. We conclude that since HRFC is easy to implement, requires
fairly low overhead in its operations, and yields better performance than the
distributed routing policy, it should have high potential to be used in future
packet switched computer networks.

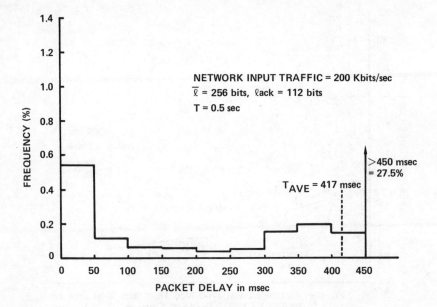

a) DISTRIBUTED ROUTING POLICY

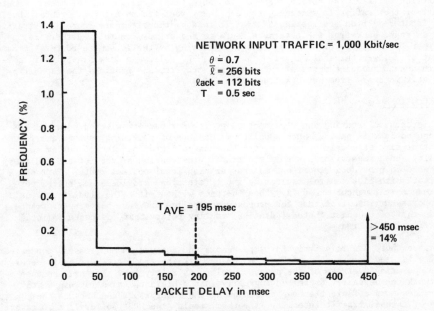

b) HRFC POLICY

Figure 8 Delay Distribution of Successfully Delivered Packets
from Initiation to Reception for the example.

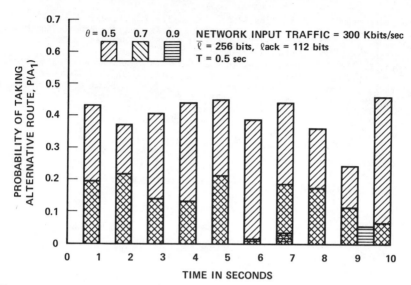

Figure 9 Probability of using primary route and alternative route for sending messages from node 4 to node 10 for the Example. Primary route is use when $P(A_1) = 0$

ACKNOWLEDGMENT

The authors wish to thank M. Gerla and W. Naylor for their critical reading of a draft of this manuscript.

REFERENCES

[1] Fultz, G.L., and Kleinrock, L. (1971). Adaptive Routing Techniques for Store Store-and-Forward Computer-Communication Networks, Proc. 1971 Int. Conf. Communications, Montreal, P.Q., Canada, pp. 39/1-8.

[2] Chou, W., and Frank, H. (1972). Routing Strategies for Computer Network Design, Proc. Symp. Computer Communications Networks and Tele-Traffic, PIB, New York, pp. 301-309.

[3] Gerla, M., Chou, W., and Frank, H. (1973). Computational Considerations and Routing Problems for Large Computer Communications Network, Proc. of Natl. Telecommunication Conference, pp. 2B/1-5.

[4] Cantor, D., and Gerla, M. (1974). Optimal Routing and a Packet-Switched Computer Network, IEEE Trans. on Computers, C-23, No, 10. pp.1062-1068

[5] Rudin, H. (1976). On Routing and Delta Routing: A Taxonomy and Performance Comparison Techniques for Packet Switching Networks, IEEE Trans. on Communications, COM-24, pp. 43-59.

[6] Chu, W.W. (1972). Demultiplexing Considerations for Statistical Multiplexors, IEEE Trans. on Communications, COM-20, pp. 603-609.

[7] Chu, W.W. (1973). Dynamic Buffer Management for Computer Communications, Proc. of Third Data Communications Symposium, Tampa, Florida, pp. 68-72.

[8] Gimpelson, L.A. (1974). Network Management: Design and Control of Communications Networks, Electrical Communication, 49, No. 1, pp. 4-22

[9] Cerf, V.G., and Kahn, R.E. (1974). A Protocol for Packet Network Intercommunication, IEEE Trans. on Communications, COM-22, pp. 637-648.

[10] Price, W.L. (1974). Simulation Studies of an Isarithmetically Controlled Store-and-Forward Data Communication Network, IFIP Congress Proc., Stockholm, Sweden, pp. 151-154. Also in Chu, W.W.(ed) (1976). Advances in Computer Communications, (Artech House), (2nd ed.).

[11] Porizin, L. (1976). Flow Control in Data Networks - Methods and Tools, Proc. of Third Intl. Conference on Computer Communications, pp. 467-474.

[12] Kleinrock, L., Naylor, W., and Opderbeck, H. (1976). A Study of Line Overhead in the ARPANET, CACM, 19, pp. 3-13.

[13] Rinde, J. (1976). TYMNET I: An Alternative to Packet Technology, Proc. of Third Intl. Conference on Computer Communication, pp. 268-293.

[14] Kleinrock, L., and Naylor W. (1972). On Measured Behavior of the ARPA Network, AFIPS Proc., SJCC, 40, pp. 255-270.

COMPUTER PERFORMANCE, K.M. CHANDY AND M. REISER (EDS.)
NORTH HOLLAND PUBLISHING COMPANY, 1977

ON HEAVY TRAFFIC DIFFUSION ANALYSIS AND DYNAMIC ROUTING IN PACKET SWITCHED NETWORKS

G. J. Foschini
Bell Telephone Laboratories
Holmdel, New Jersey, USA

For a node in a packet network we develop an idealized model for the queueing of packets for transmission over outgoing trunks. Each packet is typed in accordance with the subset of trunk facilities the controller can use for relaying the packet. The model provides a setting for analytical exploration of an important routing issue pertaining to any confluence of packet types occurring at a node at which there are K outgoing trunks capable of handling μ_1, μ_2,...μ_K packets per second respectively.

The focus here is on the question: What do dynamic (i.e., state sensitive) routing policies have to offer over static policies in terms of enhancing the resistance to delay performance degradation in a crisis situation when the node nears overload? We are interested in dynamic control related to the policy of dispatching packets to the feasible outgoing trunk that offers the least expected delay. Static controllers are represented as dispatching packets in accordance with the outcomes of throws of (optimally biased) dice whose faces are in correspondence with the permissible routing options.

In a recent document [3] a heavy traffic diffusion analysis was used to answer, under the assumptions of the model, the aforementioned question for a basic situation involving queues for two trunks of equal speed. From our general vantage point we see that there are two more basic effects that need to be explored. The first involves arrival streams with distinct but overlapping sets of alternatives. The second has to do with differing trunk speeds. Using diffusion we analyze these features in the situations of minimum dimensionality in which they arise. The results we obtain along with the results in [3] lead us to conjecture* that

$$ a = \left(\sum_1^K \sqrt{\mu_k} \right)^2 \bigg/ \sum_1^K \mu_k $$

expresses the average delay advantage under very general conditions.

---

* This conjecture was recently established by B. Gopinath and the author and will be reported in a forthcoming paper.

1. INTRODUCTION

We present a framework for comparing dynamic and static routing at a node in a computer network. The framework accommodates the routing problem solved in [3] plus the formulation of a variety of new questions of interest. We shall explore two of the most fundamental problems in detail. These solutions along with the solutions in [3] hint at a general expression for the advantage of dynamic over static control.

2. THE MATHEMATICAL FRAMEWORK

2.1 The General Model and the Standard Approach

In Figure 1 we present an idealized representation of a node in a computer network where a confluence of differing packet types occur and future disposition of these packets is to be decided. Packet arrivals are assumed to be Poisson and packet size is assumed to be exponentially distributed.

There are K servers and the term μ_k^{-1} denotes the mean exponential service time for the k-th server. If for example the server is an outgoing trunk, the μ parameters combine the effect of exponential packet size and trunk speed. So if M is the mean packet size (bits) and S is the trunk speed (bits per second) then $\mu \overset{\Delta}{=} S/M$ is the mean service rate.

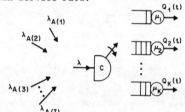

Figure 1: Controlling Packet Flow Out of a Node

C represents a controller who administers the dispatching of packets upon their arrival. The packets are typed according to the nature of the options the controller has available for their disposition, however, all types have the same mean length. Some types are a priori committed to be sent next to specified servers while others have options. For example a type {2,3,7} packet is one that the controller can dispatch to server 2, 3, or 7. The $\{A(i)\}_1^I$ are nonempty subsets of $1,2,\ldots K$ used to distinguish types. The $\lambda_{A(i)}$'s convey the arrival rates of independent Poisson packet arrival processes of each type. We will be concerned with comparing state insensitive (static) control C_{stat} with state sensitive (dynamic) control C_{dynam}. The state of the system is represented by the vector of birth-death processes $Q(t) = (Q_1(t),Q_2(t),\ldots Q_K(t))$ which is the vector of queue sizes except that for convenience we include the customer in service in each $Q_k(t)$.

With static routing, packets are dispatched amongst options in a proportionate way. The apportionment is implemented via a mechanism that is tantamount to throwing a biased die whose facets correspond to the alternatives. Static controllers are known to be analyzable from a classical queueing theory standpoint. The biases are state independent but probabilities of the facets can be chosen to minimize average delay. The static controller can therefore be viewed as having I dice, one for each type of packet. When a packet arrives he observes what sort of packet it is and then throws the corresponding die to determine which of the feasible alternatives to take. For such a static policy the queue inputs are independent Poissons. Thus the queues are independent parallel M/M/1 queues and the average system delay is well known. It is easy to show that the delay function is convex in the dice probabilities. Hence given the $\{\lambda_{A(i)}\}_1^I$, and the $\{\mu_k\}_1^K$, the selection of the optimum dice is a convex program. This sort of observation is the basis for numerical studies as in [4]. An analytical determination of the optimum dice can be extraordinarily difficult since a Lagrange multiplier formulation leads to a problem of finding the roots of a polynomial in many variables.

In contrast there are state sensitive controllers for which the number of preceding packets still to be serviced by each server influence the control. The dynamic controllers that we shall explore here are variations of the one which dispatches a packet to the queue among the alternatives for which the expected delay is the smallest. From a classical queueing theory standpoint these dynamic routing problems subsume problems that have been long recognized to be intractable.

2.2 The Heavy Traffic Perspective

Concerning the search for a mathematical setting in which questions regarding the comparative performances of static versus dynamic controllers can be addressed, one might be led to conclude that while classical queueing theory comes closest to providing the appropriate theory it unfortunately falls far short of the mark. Now, however, this ostensive intractability of dynamic routing problems is not viewed as unfortunate since the difficult circumstances encouraged on the one hand a deeper consideration of what the right question to ask is, and on the other hand an open search for new approaches.

It is fair to say that practical considerations dictate that the inquiry should be along the lines of investigating what if anything do dynamic policies offer in terms of enhancing a network's ability to resist performance degradation as it nears overload. After all, under nominal operating conditions the stochastic nature of demand requires that a commercial computer network function with substantial spare service capability. However, if a node or link fails or if some customers suddenly begin to become much more active than was anticipated, then one (or some) of the nodes will be driven toward overload and performance will

degrade. In practice flow control would be instituted to stem the degradation at
the expense of lost or blocked packets. Such crises are a crucial test of routing
policies and it is this possibility of an overload situation that prompts us to
compare dynamic and static strategies.

With this motivation we pose the mathematical question of determining
the ratio a of the average delay of the optimum static policy compared to that of
the dynamic policy in the limit as the input arrival rates increase and drive the
system toward overload.

We shall see that a heavy traffic diffusion theory is a suitable method
for addressing this degradation question. Using diffusion we shall analyze two
specific examples selected as the simplest vehicles for probing the effects of
a) distinct but intersecting sets of alternatives and b) differing service rates.
The solutions lead us to speculate that

$$a = \left(\sum_{k=1}^{K} \sqrt{\mu_k} \right)^2 \Bigg/ \sum_{k=1}^{K} \mu_k$$

expresses the limiting ratio for wide variety of examples. Indeed, the above expression represents the solutions obtained here and in the class of examples
treated in [3] where the diffusion approach to dynamic routing problems was first
employed.

The methodology proceeds along the following lines. For both C_{dynam}
and C_{stat} a vector process relating to packet delays on outgoing nodal links is
identified. In each case the multivariate equilibrium distribution would abstract
the relevant performance characteristics but this distribution is far out of
reach. In a central limit spirit we employ a positive integer parameter n which
is used in three ways; it dilates the time scale by a factor of n, it contracts
state space by a factor $n^{-1/2}$ and it brings the incoming packet flow precariously
close to the nodes ability to handle it by an amount proportional to $n^{-1/2}$. As
n→∞ we identify a diffusion (continuous path Markov process) with the heavily
loaded scaled processes. It is easy to find the equilibrium distribution for the
limiting diffusion $q(t) = \left(q_1(t),\ q_2(t),\ldots q_K(t) \right)$ where $q_k(t)$ is associated with
the limit of $\dfrac{Q_k(nt)}{\sqrt{n}}$.

The $q_k(t)$ are mathematically meaningful processes whose properties we
can explore, but what value do they have for comparing C_{dynam} and C_{stat}? The
point is that we associate a $q(t)$ process to each control by applying identical
scalings to both. We have already motivated the heavy loading aspect of the
scaling. The speeding of time is harmless as it leaves state occupancy statistics

invariant since it merely runs the processes faster. The third part of the normalization, the contraction of state space cancels out of any comparison (ratio) of statistics of $Q^{dynam}/\sqrt{n}$ and $Q^{stat}/\sqrt{n}$. So it is enough to compare $Q^{dynam}(nt)/\sqrt{n}$ and $Q^{stat}(nt)/\sqrt{n}$. We shall do so in the limit ($n \to \infty$) where it is most convenient.

          The equilibrium distribution for a (vector) diffusion is described by an elliptic partial differential equation called the Fokker-Planck (FP) [1]. The positiveness of delay is represented by certain boundary conditions. Now that sounds like the equilibrium distribution for C_{dynam} should be very difficult to express. However, here the Fokker-Planck reduces to the simple ordinary differential equation $\dot{y} = y$. The collapse of the FP to an ordinary differential equation occurs as follows. With experience one learns that the dynamically controlled diffusions we are dealing with are highly singular. The singularity leads to the condensatation of the equilibrium mass of the diffusion to a line and it is this condensation that leads to a one dimensional FP. Physically this corresponds to the guiding principle that wise dynamic policies are those that equalize, in the near term, the service delays corresponding to the various options. The attempt at equalization for the true vector of delays is manifest as true equality of "scaled" delay components in the diffusion process.

3.0 <u>EXAMPLE WITH LINKED SET OF ALTERNATIVES</u>

          Here we explore the case $K = 3$, $\{\mu_k = \mu\}_1^3$ with the types $\{1\}$, $\{2\}$, $\{3\}$, $\{1,2\}$ and $\{2,3\}$. We assume that the heavy traffic limit is such that $\lambda_{\{1,2\}}$ does not degenerate to a vanishingly small amount of traffic on either queue 1 or 2 (similarly for $\lambda_{\{2,3\}}$ on queues 2 and 3). We shall see that we can specify a dynamic control attaining $a = 3$. The situation is depicted in the figure below.

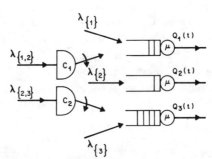

Figure 2: Three Controlled Queues in Parallel with
           Alternatives Including the Linked Sets
           $\{1,2\}$ and $\{2,3\}$

          When dealing with a few queues as we shall do in this example and the next it is convenient to simplify the notation. So sometimes we write λ_i for $\lambda_{\{i\}}$, λ' for $\lambda_{\{1,2\}}$ and λ'' for $\lambda_{\{2,3\}}$.

It is interesting to see some ways in which the system in Figure 2 can be driven into overload. Assume that $\mu = 1$ and $\{\lambda_i = .15\}_1^3$, and $\lambda' = .90$. Suppose λ'' is increased with the other rates held fixed. More and more of the λ' traffic will be directed to queue 1 to make room on the second queue for λ''. So just by increasing λ'' all three queues are driven into overload. For a second example $\mu = 1$, $\lambda_2 = \lambda_3 = .15$ and $\lambda' = \lambda'' = .9$. Now let λ_1 increase. This will force more and more of the λ' traffic onto queue 2 which in turn will cause the λ'' traffic to flood node 3. In this second example all three nodes are driven toward overload by increasing λ_1. If we change the second example by setting $\lambda'' = .65$ then increase of λ_1 drives only nodes 1 and 2 into saturation.

The first step is to present a dynamic control and prove that for it $q_1 = q_2 = q_3$. To do this, we assume $\lambda_1 = \lambda_2 = \lambda_3 < \mu$. Now the equality of the λ_i may seem to lose generality, however, the controllers have the ability to effect this so long as the traffic is sufficiently heavy. Our objective is to show that with dynamic control $a = 3$ is possible so if we can attain $a = 3$ performance while devoting a portion of the switchable traffic to equalizing the λ_i's then we have lost nothing by proceeding with $\lambda_1 = \lambda_2 = \lambda_3$. For the equalized arrangement we notice $\lambda' \to \lambda''$ as the traffic is increased. Let $\lim \lambda' = \lim \lambda'' = \lambda$.

Next we specify C_1 and C_2 in detail. Basically the controllers dispatch to the shorter queue. There are two exceptions. If $Q_3 > Q_2 > Q_1$, C_2 leaves a residual $\alpha\lambda'' \sim \alpha\lambda$ on Q3. If $Q_1 > Q_2 > Q_3$ then C_1 leaves a residual $\alpha\lambda' \sim \alpha\lambda$ on Q_1.

We shall prove that $q_1 = q_2 = q_3$ by showing $q_1 = q_2$ and $q_2 = q_3$. We begin by analyzing $Q_1 - Q_2$ and $Q_3 - Q_2$. Under the prescribed controls the resultant force fields for $Q_1 - Q_2$ and $Q_3 - Q_2$ point to the zero state. We shall also see that for α small enough the force magnitudes are bounded away from zero at all nonzero states. By symmetry it is enough to consider $Q_1 - Q_2$. There are dynamical changes occurring when a departure process for Q_i ($i = 1$ or 2) turns off and on depending on whether Q_i is zero or not. Below we list all possible regions affecting arrival processes only. On the right the resultant of the arrival forces is shown. The heavy traffic λ representation of λ' and λ'' is used. (We recommend [2] for a treatment of the connection of queueing theory with random walks.)

I. $Q_1 - Q_2 > 0$ holds along with one of the following:

    A. $Q_3 > Q_1 > Q_2$ $\overset{\bullet}{\circ}$ $\overset{2\lambda}{\longleftarrow}$

    B. $Q_3 = Q_1 > Q_2$ $\overset{\bullet}{\circ}$ $\overset{2\lambda}{\longleftarrow}$

    C. $Q_1 > Q_3 > Q_2$ $\overset{\bullet}{\circ}$ $\overset{2\lambda}{\longleftarrow}$

    D. $Q_1 > Q_2 = Q_3$ $\overset{\bullet}{\circ}$ $\overset{\frac{3}{2}\lambda}{\longleftarrow}$

    E. $Q_1 > Q_2 > Q_3$ $\overset{\bullet}{\circ}$ $\overset{(1-2\alpha)\lambda}{\longleftarrow}$

II. $Q_2 - Q_1 > 0$

    A. $Q_3 > Q_2 > Q_1$ $\xrightarrow{\alpha\lambda}$ $\overset{\bullet}{\circ}$

    B. $Q_3 = Q_2 > Q_1$ $\xrightarrow{\lambda/2}$ $\overset{\bullet}{\circ}$

    C. $Q_2 > Q_3 > Q_1$ $\xrightarrow{\lambda}$ $\overset{\bullet}{\circ}$

    D. $Q_2 > Q_1 = Q_3$ $\xrightarrow{\lambda}$ $\overset{\bullet}{\circ}$

    E. $Q_2 > Q_1 > Q_3$ $\xrightarrow{\lambda}$ $\overset{\bullet}{\circ}$

      The missing departure components of the force field cancel each other when $Q_1Q_2 \neq 0$ and otherwise can only strenghten the pull to zero. The net force field for $Q_1 - Q_2$ is stronger than the field for the walk whose dynamics are represented by the weakest component of the central force field for $Q_1 - Q_2$ namely $\min(\alpha\lambda, 1-2\alpha\lambda)$. So long as α is uniformly bounded the relative time* spent in a symmetrical neighborhood of zero is more than for the weak field walk. This remains true in the limit $(\lambda' + \lambda'' \uparrow 3\mu - \lambda_1 - \lambda_2 - \lambda_3)$ since as $n \to \infty$ the weak equilibrium mass condenses at the point zero (the upward arrow means convergence from below). The same consideration is true of $q_2 - q_3$. This motivates $q_1 = q_2 = q_3$.

      Since $q_1(t) = q_2(t) = q_3(t)$ we look at the sum process $s(t) \overset{\Delta}{=} q_1(t) + q_2(t) + q_3(t)$. The differential mean and variance are easily computed so

$$ds(t) = -\Delta dt + \sqrt{\lambda'' + \lambda' + \lambda_1 + \lambda_2 + \lambda_3 + 3\mu}\; dW_t$$

where W_t is a standard Wiener process. The FP is

$$\Delta \frac{\partial p}{\partial s} + \frac{\lambda'' + \lambda' + \lambda_1 + \lambda_2 + \lambda_3 + 3\mu}{2} \frac{\partial^2 p}{\partial s} = 0$$

which has the solution $\dfrac{2\Delta}{\lambda'' + \lambda' + \lambda_1 + \lambda_2 + \lambda_3} \exp\left\{ -\dfrac{2\Delta s}{\lambda'' + \lambda' + \lambda_1 + \lambda_2 + \lambda_3} \right\}$

---

* Instead of bothering to guarantee existence of the relative time we can employ the lim inf in the definition of relative time and avoid the issue. So the relative time that a stochastic process $N(t)$ spends in an interval I is

defined as $\underset{T \to \infty}{\underline{\lim}} \displaystyle\int_{\{t : N(t) \in I, 0 \le t \le T\}} dt.$

Since $q_i = s/3$, $i = 1,2,3$ we get

$$p(q_i) = \frac{6\Delta}{\lambda'' + \lambda' + \lambda_1 + \lambda_2 + \lambda_3} \exp\left\{\frac{-6\Delta q_i}{\lambda'' + \lambda' + \lambda_1 + \lambda_2 + \lambda_3}\right\} \quad i = 1,2,3.$$

Thus

$$E\{q_i\} = \frac{\lambda'' + \lambda' + \lambda_1 + \lambda_2 + \lambda_3}{6\delta} \quad \text{and} \quad \text{Var}\{q_i\} = [E\{q_i\}]^2 .$$

The average delay cannot be improved by any other controller since the $s(t)$ process has the same stochastic differential equation as that for the diffusion model for an M/M/3 system; so $a = 3$.

4.0 EXAMPLE WITH DIFFERING SERVICE RATES

Next we consider the packet queueing system depicted below:

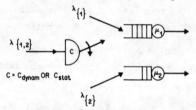

Figure 3: System with Two Parallel Outgoing
Trunks of Different Speeds

Here C_{dynam} dispatches switchable traffic to wherever the expected departure time is smaller. A new arrival on the $\lambda_{\{1,2\}}$ stream is therefore assigned to trunk j where j attains $\min_{i=1,2} \frac{Q_i(t)}{\mu_i}$. In the event of a tie for the minimum, a biased coin flipped so that the arrival is assigned to the i-th trunk with probability $\mu_i/(\mu_1+\mu_2)$.

The fact that μ_1 may not be equal to μ_2 causes complications in that the optimum coin for C_{stat} must be found and a substantial modification of the C_{dynam} analysis is called for since the analysis of [3] no longer applies.

The notion of stable relative time will prove useful. We say a random process $N(t)$ has a stable relative time if given any ε one can find a finite interval $I(\varepsilon)$ such that $\lim_{T\to\infty} T^{-1} \int_T d\tau > 1-\varepsilon$ where $T = \{t:N(t)\epsilon I(\varepsilon), 0 \le t \le T\}$. For convenience we use λ for $\lambda_{\{1,2\}}$ and λ_i for $\lambda_{\{i\}}(i = 1,2)$. Recall that the behavior of $Q(t)$ in heavy traffic is investigated by introducing a positive integer index n and defining $q^n(t) \triangleq \left(\dfrac{Q_1(nt)}{\sqrt{n}}, \dfrac{Q_2(nt)}{\sqrt{n}} \right)$. Moreover, the input corresponding to

$q^n(t)$ is also parameterized by n in such a way that $\lim\limits_{n\to\infty}[\mu_1 + \mu_2 - (\lambda+\lambda_1+\lambda_2)]\sqrt{n} = \Delta$

where Δ is a positive constant and $\lambda = \lambda(n)$, $\lambda_1 = \lambda_1(n)$, $\lambda_2 = \lambda_2(n)$ are nondecreasing and positive sequences.

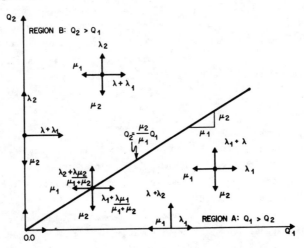

Figure 4:   Dynamics of the $\left(Q_1(t), Q_2(t)\right)$ walk (Disregard the dynamics on $Q_2 = \dfrac{\mu_2}{\mu_1} Q_1$ if this line and the lattice of positive integer pairs are disjoint).

The dynamics of this two dimensional random walk are depicted in detail in Figure 4 above. We shall show that as $n\to\infty$ the amount of probability mass of $q^n(t)$ that resides outside any open strip containing the line ℓ (the two boundary lines of the strip are parallel to ℓ) tends to zero. We employ $q(t) = (q_1(t), q_2(t))$ to convey the limiting behavior of $q^n(t)$.

To prove the accumulation of mass look at $R(t) \triangleq \dfrac{Q_1}{\mu_1} - \dfrac{Q_2}{\mu_2}$. The dynamics of this walk are represented in Figure 5.

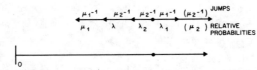

Figure 5:   The Walk Dynamics for R(t) when R(t) > 0.
Parenthesized Terms are Missing if $Q_2(t) = 0$.

The terms below the arrows represent the relative force encouraging a change of the amount indicated above the arrows. The dynamics at zero are of no consequence to the proof. Notice in region A it is possible for the μ_2 force to turn off; namely when $Q_2(t) = 0$. Similarly in B μ_1 can turn off.

Let $R^+(t) = \max\left(0, R(t)\right)$. We shall see that $R^+(t)$ has stable relative time so long as n is large enough. As in [3] the desultory departure forces thwart a straightforward determination of the equilibrium mass for $R^+(t)$. Moreover, the argument of [3] does not work because of general state space we are accommodating. Notice if μ_1 and μ_2 are noncomeasurable the range of the walk is a dense set.

To get the accumulation of mass we compare the positive $R^+(t)$ to a standard queueing process [2] with transitions described by

$$B_n = \left(B_{n-1} - D_n\right)^+ + A_n.$$

Renewal theory [2] assures us that a downward drift provides a stable relative time. The innovation (i.e., the change occurring between successive values of the subscript) for the queueing process, $A_n - D_n$, is the innovation for $Q_1(t) - \dfrac{\mu_1}{\mu_2} Q_2(t)$ with the μ_2 departures turned on.

When n is large the mean of the innovation is negative. To see this evaluate the expected value of the innovation in Figure 5 to get $i = \lambda_1 - (\lambda + \lambda_2)(\mu_1/\mu_2)$. The above term is negative for sufficiently large n since

$$(\lambda + \lambda_2) < \mu_1 + \mu_2 - \lambda_1,$$

and so $i \to \lambda_1 \left[1 + \dfrac{\mu_1}{\mu_2}\right] - \mu_1 \left[1 + \dfrac{\mu_1}{\mu_2}\right] < 0$ since $\lambda_1 < \mu_1$.

Not only is the drift negative but the drift is bounded away from zero for sufficiently large n. Stability now follows. The possible noncomeasurability of μ_1 and μ_2 and the consequent everywhere denseness of the walk do not thwart the argument. To see this we stress that renewal theory provides stability of uniformly restorative queueing walks [2]. Now $R^+(t)$ is not a queueing walk, however, a simple comparison shows that since the associated queueing process has stable relative time, $R^+(t)$ certainly has. Similarly $R^-(t) = \min\left(0, R(t)\right)$ has stable relative time and therefore so does $R(t)$. So given any $\varepsilon > 0$ for n sufficiently large $\left[\dfrac{Q_1(nt)}{\mu_1} - \dfrac{Q_2(nt)}{\mu_2}\right] \Big/ \sqrt{n}$ spends $(1-\varepsilon)$ 100 percent of its relative time within an ε neighborhood of zero. The conclusion is that as $n \to \infty$ the process

$$q_1^n(t) - \dfrac{\mu_1}{\mu_2} q_2^n(t) \to 0.$$

Let $s(t)$ correspond to the sum $q_1(t) + q_2(t)$ and $s^n(t) \triangleq q_1^n(t) + q_2^n(t)$. Conditional on the event that both $q_1^n(t)$ and $q_2^n(t)$ are positive.

$$E\{ds^n(t)\} = (\lambda_1 + \lambda_2 + \lambda - (\mu_1 + \mu_2)) \sqrt{n} \to -\Delta$$

$$E\{[ds^n(t)]^2\} = \lambda_1 + \lambda_2 + \lambda + \mu_1 + \mu_2 \to 2(\mu_1 + \mu_2).$$

In the limit as $n \to \infty$ both $q_1(t)$ and $q_2(t)$ are positive for almost all t. With this motivation we associate a diffusion with $s(t)$ characterized by $ds(t) = -\Delta dt + 2(\mu_1 + \mu_2)dW_t$. Moreover $s(t) > 0$ for almost all t. The FP is

$$\Delta \frac{\partial p}{\partial s} + (\mu_1 + \mu_2) \frac{\partial^2 p}{\partial p^2} = 0$$

So $p(q_1) = \Delta \mu^{-1} \exp(-\Delta \cdot q_1/\mu_1)$ and $p(q_2) = \Delta \mu^{-1} \exp(-\Delta \cdot q_2/\mu_2)$ and $E\{q_i\} = \mu_i \Delta$ (i = 1,2). By Little's theorem the expected delay is Δ^{-1} regardless. If we constrain μ_1 and μ_2 so that $\mu_1 + \mu_2 = \mu$ we note that the expected delay is independent of how the service rates are allocated. A diffusion analysis of the following two server queue also yields Δ^{-1} for the mean delay.

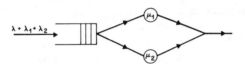

Figure 6:   Two Server Queue

4.1 The Coin Bias for C_{stat} and the Resulting a

The question remains as to what advantage this dynamic control offers over the optimum static control. The static controller uses a biased coin to make his decisions on the λ traffic. We shall determine the optimum coin bias. Let θ_1 be the probability of λ packet going to server 1 and $\theta_2 = 1 - \theta$, of going to server 2. With C_{stat} then the system is representable as two uncoupled M/M/1 queues (see [5] for basic queueing results).

Figure 7:   System with C_{stat} Control Represented as a Pair
of Uncoupled M/M/1 Queues

Recall that the formula for average time in system for an M/M/1 queue is $\mu^{-1}(1 - \lambda/\mu)^{-1}$. For the bifurcated arrangement shown above we have two such queues with a probability of $\dfrac{\lambda_k + \theta_k \lambda}{\lambda_1 + \lambda_2 + \lambda}$ of a system arrival going to one of the two. So the system delay is

$$D = \sum_1^2 \frac{\lambda_k + \theta_k \lambda}{\lambda_1 + \lambda_2 + \lambda} \frac{1}{\mu_k} \frac{1}{1 - \frac{(\lambda_k + \theta_k \lambda)}{\mu_k}}, \quad \left(\theta_1 + \theta_2 = 1\right).$$

For optimum bifurcation notice $\theta_i = \dfrac{\mu_i - \lambda_i}{\mu_1 + \mu_2 - \lambda_1 - \lambda_2}$ as $\lambda \nearrow \mu_1 + \mu_2 - \lambda_1 - \lambda_2$ otherwise on some subsequence $\{n_\ell\}_1^\infty$ one of the queues will possess $\rho_i \geq 1$ which cannot be associated with an optimal approach. The expression is convex in θ_1 as a check of second derivative with respect to θ_1 will demonstrate. In what follows assume $\theta_1(\lambda)$ and $\theta_2(\lambda)$ are set to minimize D.

The advantage of the dynamic over the static control is thus given by

$$a = \lim_{\lambda \nearrow} \sum_1^2 \left[1 - \frac{(\theta_k(\lambda)\lambda + \lambda_k)}{\mu_k}\right]^{-1} \frac{1}{\mu_1 + \mu_2 - \lambda_1 - \lambda_2 - \lambda} \quad (*)$$

First we determine $\theta_1(\lambda) = \theta$ when $\lambda_1 = \lambda_2 = 0$. To attain $\min[(1 - \theta\lambda/\mu_1)^{-1} + (1 - (1-\theta)\lambda/\mu_2)^{-1}]$ we take the partial with respect to θ and equate to zero to obtain $\dfrac{\theta^2 \lambda^2}{\mu_1^2 \mu_1^2}(\mu_1 - \mu_2) + 2\dfrac{\theta\lambda}{\mu_1 \mu_2}(2 - \lambda/\mu_2) + (1 - \lambda/\mu_2)^2 \dfrac{1}{\mu_1} - \dfrac{1}{\mu_2} = 0$. Assuming, without loss of generality that $\mu_1 > \mu_2$, we get

$$\theta_\pm = \frac{\mu_1}{(\mu_1 - \mu_2)\lambda}\left[(\lambda - 2\mu_2) \pm (\mu_2 + \mu_1 - \lambda)\sqrt{\frac{\mu_2}{\mu_1}}\right].$$

The three possible cases are given below. The first case does not require the above analysis but the remaining cases rely on the above formulas for θ.

<u>Case I</u>: $\lambda_1 = \lambda_2 = 0$, $\mu_1 = \mu_2 = \mu$.

Here we find $\theta \equiv 1/2$ independent of λ. Substituting θ and solving for a we get $a = 2$.

<u>Case II</u>. $\lambda_1 = \lambda_2 = 0$, $\mu_1 > \mu_2$

Substituting $\theta_\pm$ into $(*)$ we get two possibilities for a, namely,

$$\lim_{\lambda\nearrow}(\mu_1-\mu_2)\frac{(\mu_1+\mu_2-\lambda)}{\mu_1+\mu_2}\left\{\left[(\mu_1+\mu_2-\lambda)\mp\sqrt{\mu_2/\mu_1}(\mu_1+\mu_2-\lambda)\right]^{-1}\right.$$

$$\left.+\left[(\lambda-\mu_1-\mu_2)\pm\sqrt{\frac{\mu_1}{\mu_2}}(\mu_2\,\mu_1-\lambda)\right]^{-1}\right\}$$

So the optimum is

$$a=1+\frac{2\sqrt{\mu_1\mu_2}}{\mu_1+\mu_2}$$

Notice when $\mu_1=\mu_2=\mu$ we get $a=2$ checking Case I. When $\mu_2=0$ the controlled queue degenerates to M/M/1 and indeed $a=1$.

Case III. $\lambda_1\neq\lambda_2$, $\mu_1>\mu_2$

For sufficiently large λ in Case II the queue inputs exceed λ_1 and λ_2 respectively so this case gives the same answer as Case II namely

$$a=1+\frac{2\sqrt{\mu_1\mu_2}}{\mu_1+\mu_2}\ .$$

5.0 DISCUSSION

5.1 Conjecture

A formal diffusion analysis of the heavy traffic advantage of an M/M/K system with service rates $(\mu_1,\mu_2,\ldots,\mu_K)$ over the corresponding optimally bifurcated system with K independent M/M/1 queues with μ_k service rate for the k-th queue gives

$$a=\left(\sum_1^K\sqrt{\mu_k}\right)^2\bigg/\sum_1^K\mu_k.$$

This follows from a Lagrange multiplier argument and the result holds even if fixed committed packet streams $\{\lambda_k\}_1^K$ impinge on the K queues. In the examples worked here and in [3] the above expression gives the correct formula for the advantage. In other words for these examples the dynamic controller could asymptotically obtain M/M/K performance. These observations hint that a is the solution for a general class of input streams with alternatives $\{A(i)\}_{i=1}^I$ for which one can find a chain $A(i_1)$, $A(i_2)\ldots A(i_L)$ so that $A(i_\ell)\cap A(i_{\ell+1})\neq\emptyset$, $\ell=1,2,\ldots L-1$ and $\bigcup_1^L A(i_\ell)=\{1,2,\ldots K\}$. Of course the heavy traffic limit is assumed to be such that $\lambda_{A(i)}$ does not degenerate to a vanishingly small amount of traffic on any queue with index in $A(i)$ $(i = 1,2,\ldots I)$.

5.2 Applications

When a call is composed of many packets the virtual circuit concept implies each packet of a call takes the same route. A route commitment is made for all packets in a call at the start so the instantaneous state of a node plays no role in route selection, instead, average delays are meaningful. In practice optimal flows of various types of packets could be computed on the basis of delay measurements. These flows could be implemented by measuring existing flows and establishing new calls so as to move toward the ideal flow. The longer the calls, the more sluggish the system response. Thus C_{stat} would perform better than the virtual call control of a node.

With datagram transport, each packet is a separate entity and predecessor packets on the same call do not constrain the disposition of the current packet. Hence with a datagram service instantaneous response to the state of a node is possible, so C_{dynam} can be associated with datagram in the idealized situation we investigated.

Of course in actual implementations complicating aspects not treated here will enter the picture, such as the overhead penalties of call setup and termination packets (associated with virtual call) and supplementary addressing bits (associated with datagram service).

5.3 Cascading

While there is work to be done in terms of establishing the conjecture there is another dimension to generalization, namely, the treatment of networks of nodes that are dynamically controlled. Some extensions to cascaded structures have been undertaken by the author but will not be reported here.

6.0 ACKNOWLEDGMENT

The excellent numerical study discussed in [6] played a key role in stimulating the author's interest in looking deeper into the subject of controlling the inputs to parallel queues. Suggestions of J. A. Holtzman were very useful.

P.S. B. Gopinath and the author have established the conjectured result for a variety of new cases. It is planned to report these results in a forthcoming paper.

REFERENCES

[1] L. Arnold, (1974), "Stochastic Differential Equations," (Wiley-Interscience, New York).

[2] W. Feller, (1971), "An Introduction to Probability Theory and its Applications," Volume II, Chapter XII (John Wiley and Sons, New York).

[3] G. J. Foschini, and J. Salz, "A Basic Dynamic Routing Problem and Diffusion Approximation," IEEE Transactions on Communication Technology, to appear.

[4] H. Frank and W. Chou, (1971) "Routing in Computer Networks," Networks, Volume
     1, (John Wiley and Sons, New York, pp. 99-122).

[5] L. Kleinrock,(1975) Queueing Systems, Vol. I, (Wiley-Interscience, New York)

[6] A. Livne and R. R. Boorstyn, (June 1976) "On a Technique for Adaptive
     Routing," National Telecommunication Conference, November 1976, Dallas.
     While not included in the published proceedings the paper is drawn from
     A. Livne's Doctoral Dissertation "Techniques for Adaptive Routing,"
     Polytechnic Institute of New York.

COMPUTER PERFORMANCE, K.M. CHANDY AND M. REISER (EDS.)
NORTH HOLLAND PUBLISHING COMPANY, 1977

MODELING OF PACKET SWITCHING COMMUNICATION NETWORKS WITH FINITE BUFFER SIZE AT EACH NODE

J. Labetoulle and G. Pujolle
I.R.I.A. Laboria
Le Chesnay, France

In this paper we study packet switching networks with finite
storage capacity at each node. So far we do not know of any
method giving an analytical result to the problem of the
response time of such networks. We propose here a very fast,
thus very economical, numerical solution which gives the probabilities of saturation of each node, the mean response times
of the network and to know if the network can accept a given
load without saturation. This method is applied to the CYCLADES
network and the results are compared with simulations.

INTRODUCTION

All store-and-forward packet switching networks built until now have a finite storage capacity at each node. Until now, this choice has not been justified by convincing theoretical studies and has been frequently justified by considerations of
simplicity or by experience.

In this paper we study a model of store-and-forward packet switching networks in
which nodes will be of limited capacity. An approximate solution will be developed
to compute the expected response times and the stability conditions of the model.

Today, two types of service are proposed for the switching of packets : the virtual
circuit and the datagram service. The virtual circuit implies call procedures for
the setting of a circuit and deliverance procedures (ARPA or EPSS). In this case
we have an end traffic control, and our study will determine stability conditions.
Expected response times will be only very approximate due to the procedures of call
and deliverance.

The datagram service is a simple packet transmission service. There are neither
procedures of call or of deliverance, nor end-to-end traffic control. Each node of
the network carries out a control on the receipt of the packets. When there is an
error or a non-receipt, the preceding node retransmits. Here, a node -to-node protocol intervenes, which we assume very simple in our study : a negative acknowledgement which returns immediately at the preceding node. More sophisticated protocols will be studied later.

It is the behavior of such a network that we study in the sequel (CYCLADE/CIGALE,
EIN,...).

Till now, such systems have been modeled by networks of infinite capacity queues,
assuming that the overflow probabilities are negligible. The queueing delay at
each node with finite buffers size at low probability of overflow ($< 10^{-4}$) could

515

be approximated as the queueing delay at infinite buffer size as shown in [20].

To solve these models three types of methods exist :

1 - The classical Baskett, Chandy, Muntz and Palacios solution [1].

2 - Diffusion methods developped by Kobayashi [2] and Gelenbe [3], [4]. The method
    consists in representing the state of the system by a non discretized variable,
    or a vector. The equation which governs this variable is of a type found in
    classical problems of diffusion (heat for example).

3 - Iterative techniques based on heuristic considerations such as the method of
    Chandy et al. [5].

Recent studies of limited capacity networks have been made, but mainly for tandem
queueing systems: Pennotti and Schwartz [6], Rudin [7] for exponentially distributed service times, Rubin [8], Labetoulle and Pujolle [9] for constant service times
cases, Pujolle [10] for general service times.

Other studies compute the overflow probabilities at nodes : Lam [11], Schweitzer
and Lam [12], or determine stability conditions : Lavenberg [13], Schweitzer [14].

Here, we develop a numerical solution technique which includes most of these results. Applications to the seven node Cyclade network are given in the last section.

Description of the model

We consider a model with two levels (Figure 1) :

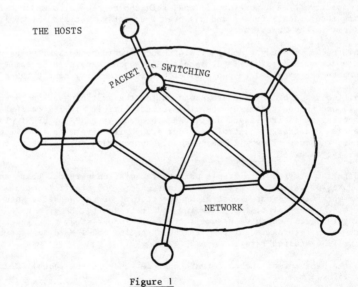

Figure 1

- <u>The store-and-forward packet switching itself</u>. A fixed routing is assumed, i.e. all the links used by a packet depend only on the departure and destination nodes. Two nodes are linked by at most one link and each link has its own storage capacity of M packets. Packets are sent in FIFO order. When a packet is transmitted from a node it can :

  - leave the network if the arrival node is the destination node

  - enter the queue of the next link

  - if this last queue is full, then it comes back to the preceding queue.

- <u>The hosts</u> : a host sends packets in the network and receives the packets leaving the network. We assume that the speed of the host is sufficiently high to avoid the rejection of packets when they arrive at their destination node. The packets received by a host to be sent in the network can be rejected if the buffers of the first following link are full. In this case the host keeps in its own buffer which must be sent again later. (See figures 1 and 2).

Therefore we model the host as :

- an infinite speed server when it is a receiver

- a set of infinite capacity queues when it is a sender.

<u>Remark</u> : It is possible to assume a network with limited capacity nodes (the total number of packets waiting at the node is limited). This case could be treated as an extension of our model with limited links.

Method of solution

We assume in this section that interarrival times from the outside and service times (retransmission times) are exponentially distributed.

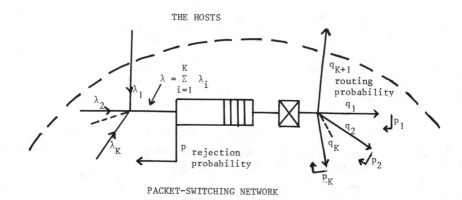

THE HOSTS

PACKET-SWITCHING NETWORK

<u>Figure 2</u>

It is obvious that the system precedingly described cannot be solved with an exact analytical method. We propose an approximate method based on the following idea : the arrival process to a queue of the network is the juxtaposition of several flows : (see figure 2)

- the flow from outside (the host)

- the flows coming from neighbouring nodes

because of limited capacity each flow cannot be govern with exponential distributions. However we shall assume that the superposition of these flows is Poisson. If we assume an infinite number of joined traffic, then the assumption of exponential distribution would be true. Moreover this assumption has been verified to be very good even for tandem queueing networks [15]. That proves the validity of our assumptions for this model.

We can equivalently consider an arriving flow $\lambda = \Sigma\lambda_i$ with packet recycling in case of saturation or a flow equal to $\lambda/(1-p)$ assuming packets are lost in case of saturation. (p is the probability of saturation).

In the same way, we may consider an equivalent server which is a function of routing probabilities (q_i, i=1,...,K+1) and of saturation probabilities (p_i) of the following queues. This equivalent server is approximated by considering that a packet leaving the station and going towards station j has the stationnary probability p_j of being rejected.

Let μ denote the service rate and let q_{K+1} denote the probability that a packet leaves the network.

This equivalent server has a service time distribution which is still exponential with rate $\tilde{\mu}$ where :

$$\tilde{\mu}^{-1} = \mu^{-1} \left(q_{K+1} + \sum_{j=1}^{K} \frac{q_j}{1-p_j} \right) \tag{1}$$

This formula becomes obvious if we consider the expected time to serve a customer going to queue j. This quantity is equal to :

$$\frac{1-p_j}{\mu} + \frac{2p_j(1-p_j)}{\mu} + \ldots + \frac{np_j^{n-1}(1-p_j)}{\mu} + \ldots = \frac{1}{\mu(1-p_j)}$$

The equivalent station is an M/M/1/N queue and the probability to have a customer rejected is equal to the probability that all the buffers are occupied, therefore :

$$p = \tilde{\rho}^M \frac{1-\tilde{\rho}}{1-\tilde{\rho}^{M+1}} \tag{2}$$

with $\tilde{\rho} = \frac{\lambda}{\mu(1-p)}$ \tag{3}

Notations and system of equations governing the model

We consider a network with K transmission links and for each of them, we define the following notations :

- A(i) represents the set of links arriving to the links i

- S(i) represents the set of links following the link i

- M_i is the maximal number of buffers of link i

- λ_i is the traffic rate arriving to link i

- $\lambda = \Sigma_1^K \lambda_i$ is the total arriving flow

- μ_i is the retransmission rate of link i (speed of the link)

- $\tilde{\rho}$ is the equivalent traffic intensity of link i : $\tilde{\rho}_i = \dfrac{\rho_i}{1-p_i}$

- p_i is the probability of rejection or the probability that the link is full

- λ_i^{ext} is the rate of customers arriving from outside of the network (the host)

- q_{ij} is the branching probability to link i

- $q_{i,K+1}$ is the probability to leave the network after link i

- ρ_i is the traffic intensity of link i : $\rho_i = \lambda_i/\tilde{\mu}_i$

and

$$\frac{1}{\tilde{\mu}_i} = \frac{1}{\mu_i} \left(q_{i,K+1} + \sum_{j=1}^{K} \frac{q_{ij}}{1-p_j} \right) \tag{4}$$

The model is governed by the following set of equations :

$$p_i = \tilde{\rho}_i^{M_i} \; \frac{1 - \tilde{\rho}_i}{1 - \tilde{\rho}_i^{M_i+1}} \qquad i = 1,\ldots,K \tag{5}$$

Conservation of flow

In this last system of equations we have :

- an equivalent server computed from the blocking probability

- an equivalent flow arriving at queue i, computed from external traffic flows.

This equivalent traffic flow will be the real flow only if the network is stable, in the sens of the ergodicity of queueing networks, i.e. if all the packets leave the network after a finite time.

Now, we shall prove that the steady state flows are the flows we use. Notice that

$$\lambda_i = \sum_{j=1}^{K} \tilde{\mu}_j(1-p_j(0))q_{ji} + \lambda_i^{ext} \quad , \quad 1 \leq i \leq K$$

where $p_j(0)$ is the stationary probability that server j is idle. We must prove that the λ_i, $1 \leq i \leq K$, also satisfy the equations

$$\lambda_i = \sum_{j=1}^{K} \lambda_j q_{ji} + \lambda_i^{ext}$$

which express the conservation of flow. It is sufficient to prove that

$$\tilde{\mu}_j(1-p_j(0)) = \lambda_j$$

where we have

$$p_j(0) = \frac{1 - \tilde{\rho}_j}{1 - \tilde{\rho}_j^{M_j+1}}$$

Therefore

$$\tilde{\mu}_j(1-p_j(0)) = \tilde{\mu}_j \, \tilde{\rho}_j \left(\frac{1-\tilde{\rho}_j^{M_j}}{1-\tilde{\rho}_j^{M_j+1}} \right) \tag{6}$$

and, using (5) in (6) we write

$$\tilde{\mu}_j(1-p_j(0)) = \tilde{\mu}_j \, \tilde{\rho}_j (1-p_j)$$

This completes the proof, since $\tilde{\rho}_j = \lambda_j/\tilde{\mu}_j(1-p_j)$.

The system will be ergodic if the queues in the hosts remain finite. In the following section, we study conditions under which the system (5) has a solution with $p_i < 1$, $\forall i$. We shall show that these conditions guarantee the ergodicity of the network.

Existence and uniqueness of the solution

First we must know if a solution to system (5) exists, different from the rivial solution $p_i = 1$, i. For this reason we begin to study the system of equations (2) and (3) :

$$(2) \quad p = \tilde{\rho}^M \frac{1-\tilde{\rho}}{1-\tilde{\rho}^{M+1}} \qquad\qquad (3) \quad \tilde{\rho} = \frac{\lambda}{\tilde{\mu}(1-p)}$$

or

$$1-p = \frac{1-\tilde{\rho}^M}{1-\tilde{\rho}^{M+1}} \qquad\qquad 1-p = \frac{\lambda}{\tilde{\mu} \, \tilde{\rho}}$$

Therefore a positive solution $\tilde{\rho}$ to the equation

$$\frac{\lambda}{\tilde{\mu} \, \tilde{\rho}} = \frac{1-\tilde{\rho}^M}{1-\tilde{\rho}^{M+1}}$$

gives a unique solution to the system (2), (3).

So, let us study the function $f(\tilde{\rho}) = \frac{\tilde{\rho}-\tilde{\rho}^{M+1}}{1-\tilde{\rho}^{M+1}}$. Notice that

$f(0) = 0$, $f(+\infty) = 1$. An elementary study of the function f shows that

$$f'(\tilde{\rho}) = \frac{1-(M+1)\tilde{\rho}^M + M\tilde{\rho}^{M+1}}{(1-\tilde{\rho}^{M+1})^2}$$

is always positive for $\tilde{\rho} \in [0, 1]$.

Consequently, the system (2), (3) has a unique solution with $0 < p < 1$ if and only if $\rho = \frac{\lambda}{\tilde{\mu}} < 1$.

If $\frac{\lambda}{\tilde{\mu}} \geq 1$, the only possible solution with $p \in [0, 1]$ is $p=1$. In this case, we see that the quantity $\tilde{\rho}$ becomes infinite.

The system (5) may be represented by a matrix system :

(7) $\vec{P} = \emptyset(\vec{P})$

where $\vec{P}$ is the vector with components p_i, $i = 1,...,K$ and $\emptyset$ is a vectorial function describe by (5).

The system (7) has at least one solution which is the vector $\vec{P} = \vec{1}$ or $p_i = 1$, $\forall i$.

Now, we can prove that if another solution exists for system (7), this solution is unique. Notice that $\emptyset$ is a monotone non-decreasing function for each component p_i i.e. the reduction of $\emptyset(\vec{P})$ at each component is a non-decreasing function. This property is obvious from the system (5). We use the classical notation $\vec{P}_1 < \vec{P}_2$ if the inequality is satisfied for all the components.

Let us consider the vectorial series :

$$\vec{P}^0 = \vec{0} \qquad (p_i^0 = 0 \text{ , } \forall i)$$
$$\vec{P}^{i+1} = \emptyset(\vec{P}^i) \tag{8}$$

The vector $\vec{0}$ not being solution of (7), we have $\vec{P}^1 > \vec{0}$. We deduce :

$\vec{P}^2 > \vec{P}^1$ because $\vec{P}^1 > \vec{P}^0$ and $\emptyset(\vec{P}^1) \geq \emptyset(\vec{P}^0)$

and by induction :

$$\vec{P}^{i+1} > \vec{P}^i$$

Each component p_j^i of $\vec{P}^i$, $i = 1,...,\infty$ represents a non-decreasing series, bounded from above by 1.

Therefore this series has a limit which satisfies $p_j = \emptyset_j \vec{P}^\infty$ and $\vec{P}^i$ has a limit $\vec{P}$ which satisfies $\vec{P} = \emptyset(\vec{P})$.

We can see that, $\forall \vec{P}'$ solution of (7), $\vec{P}'$ satisfies $\vec{P} \leq \vec{P}'$. In fact :
$\vec{P}^0 < \vec{P}' \rightarrow \vec{P}^1 = \emptyset(\vec{P}^0) < \vec{P}' = \emptyset(\vec{P}') \rightarrow \vec{P}^j < \vec{P}' \rightarrow \vec{P} \leq \vec{P}'$. So, if (7) has at least one solution, $\vec{P}$ may be called the smallest solution of (7). Now, we shall show that if $\vec{P} < \vec{1}$, then any other solution to (7) has at least one component equal to 1. If $\vec{P} < \vec{1}$, then $P_1' < 1$. The value p_1 is solution of equation (5) with $i = 1$, the other p_i's being the components of $\vec{P}$.

Therefore p_1 is a solution of (9) :

$$p_1 = (\frac{\rho_1}{1-p_1})^M \frac{1 - \frac{\rho_1}{1-p_1}}{1 - (\frac{\rho_1}{1-p_1})^{M+1}} = f_1(p_1) \tag{9}$$

where ρ_1 is a constant.

If $\vec{P}_2$ is a solution of (7) with a first component different from p_1 then :

$$\vec{P}_2 \geq \vec{Q}^0 = \{p_1 + \varepsilon, \ p_2, \ldots, p_K\} \tag{10}$$

$\vec{Q}^0$ is the same as the vector $\vec{P}$ except for the first component, which is increased by an ε sufficiently small to satisfy (10).

Let us consider the numerical series $\{p_1^i\}$ defined by : $p_1^0 = p_1 + \varepsilon$, $p_1^{i+1} = f_1(p_1^i)$.

This series defines a vectorial series $\{Q^i\}$ determined by : $Q^i = \{p^i, \ p_2, \ldots, p_K\}$.

The series $\{Q^i\}$ is an increasing series and it is obvious by induction that : $\vec{Q}^i \leq \vec{P}_2$. But equation (9) have only as solution p_1 and 1. Therefore, the first component of $\vec{P}_2$ equals 1.

We deduce that the system (7) possesses at most one solution $\vec{P}$ satisfying $\vec{P} < 1$.

Numerical computation

Equation (7) can be solved only by a numerical method. In fact, we use the method described in the preceding paragraph which consists in computing the series of vectors $\vec{P}^i$. We stop the iteration when : $||\vec{P}_{i+1} - \vec{P}_i|| < \varepsilon$. If at any step i, and for the queue j, we observe that $\rho_j = \lambda_j/\tilde{\mu}_j \geq 1$, then the only solution is $p_j = 1$. In this case we leave the domain of validity of the model.

When the saturation probabilities p_i are known, we may compute the expected number of customers in the queue,

$$N_i = \sum_{k=1}^{M_i} k. \ (\frac{\rho_i}{1-p_i})^k \ \frac{1 - \dfrac{\rho_i}{1-p_i}}{1 - (\dfrac{\rho_i}{1-p_i})^{M_i+1}}$$

and also the expected response time W_i : $W_i = \dfrac{N_i}{\lambda_i}$. Hence it is possible to compute the expected response time of any host-to-host path.

Study of the model outside its domain of validity

If the system is unstable, i.e. if the system (7) has no solution satisfying $\vec{P} < \vec{1}$, some queues in the hosts become infinite. It will be interesting in this case to know the behaviour of the network itself. The flow from a station to the following one cannot exceed the transmission rate of the links. Also, the fact that all the packets cannot be served modifies the probability q_{ij} to go to the queue j from i.

The throughput of a station is equal to its service rate multiplied by the probability that the server is busy. Therefore the throughput of station i is exactly $\mu_i(1-p_i(0))$. Let $\tilde{\lambda}_i$ denote the real arrival rate to station i, then

$$\tilde{\lambda}_i = \sum_{j \in A(i)} \mu_j q_{ji}^* \ (1-p_j(0)) \tag{12}$$

$$\frac{1}{\tilde{\mu}_i} = \frac{1}{\mu_i} \sum_{k \in S(i)} \frac{q_{ik}}{1-p_k} \tag{13}$$

$$\tilde{\rho}_i = \frac{\tilde{\lambda}_i}{\tilde{\mu}_i} \tag{14}$$

$$p_i = \tilde{\rho}_i^{M_i} \frac{1 - \tilde{\rho}_i}{1 - \tilde{\rho}_i^{M_i}} \tag{15}$$

$$p_i(0) = \frac{p_i}{\tilde{\rho}_i^{M_i}} \tag{16}$$

$$q_{ji}^* = \frac{q_{ji} \sum_{k \in S(A(i))} (1 - p_k)}{1 - p_i} \tag{17}$$

The iterative method of the previous section is used again, in which $p_i(0)$ and the q_{ij}^*'s intervene.

Extension to state-dependent service rates

In the case where the overhead is added to the transmission time, the service time can depend on the state. When the network is congested, the overhead is higher than when traffic is light. This is due, for instance, to the waiting time for acknowledgements.

Let $\mu_i(n)$ be the service rate when there are n customers in the queue. Let us take:

$$\frac{1}{\tilde{\mu}_i(n)} = \frac{1}{\mu_i(n)} \sum_{k \in S(i)} \frac{q_{ik}}{1 - p_k}$$

$$\rho_i(n) = \frac{\lambda_i}{\mu_i(n)} \quad \text{and} \quad \tilde{\rho}_i(n) = \frac{\lambda_i}{\tilde{\mu}_i(n)(1 - p_i)}$$

We obtain :
$$p_i = \frac{\prod_{n=1}^{M_i} \tilde{\rho}_i(n)}{1 + \tilde{\rho}_i(1) + \tilde{\rho}_i(1)\tilde{\rho}_i(2) + \ldots + \prod_{j=1}^{M_i} \tilde{\rho}_i(j)} \tag{18}$$

An iterative method may be used as in the previous section.

Extension of the model to diffusion processes

Up to this point, we have assumed that interarrival times in the network and service times were exponentially distributed. If we make no assumptions on these distributions, we do not know how to express in a simple way the probability of saturation of a finite capacity queue.

Approximations bu diffusion processes allow us to obtain that quantity in a simple manner. Let us consider a queue and let λ, μ, K_a, K_s denote arrival rate, service rate, squared coefficient of variation of interarrival times and service times, respectively. With diffusion approximations, the probability of saturation is given by [3, 10].

$$p = \frac{\rho(1-\rho)}{\hat{\beta}^{-(M-1)} - \rho^2} \quad \text{with } \rho = \frac{\lambda}{\mu} \quad \text{and } \hat{\beta} = e^{\frac{2(\rho-1)}{\rho Ka+Ks}} \tag{19}$$

As in the preceding model, we introduce the notions of equivalent flow and equivalent service. The limits of validity of the model will be as before and from now on, we shall assume that these conditions are satisfied. The following notations will be used :

$\tilde{K}a_i^{ext}$: squared coefficient of variation of arrival into queue i from the host if there is no feed-back

Ka_i^{ext} : squared coefficient of variation of arrival into queue i from the host in the case of feed-back

Ka_i : squared coefficient of variation of the equivalent flow arriving into queue i

Ks_i : squared coefficient of variation of service time at queue i

$\tilde{K}s_i$: squared coefficient of variation of the equivalent server.

Kobayashi [2] has established a formula giving the squared coefficient of variation of the arrival process in any station of a network. We shall use that formula in the sequel, assuming that the flow leaving a station is not regulated, but is lost. This with the condition to multiply the flow $1/(1-p_i)$. In that case, the formula becomes :

$$Ka_i = \frac{1}{\lambda_i} \{\tilde{K}a_i^{ext} \lambda_i^{ext} + \sum_{j \in A(i)} [(\tilde{K}s_j - 1) q_{ji} + 1] \lambda_j q_{ji}\}$$

or $\quad Ka_i = \tilde{K}a_i^{ext} + \frac{1}{\lambda_i} \sum_{j \in A(i)} [(\tilde{K}s_j-1)q_{ji} + 1 - \tilde{K}a_i^{ext}] \lambda_j q_{ji} \tag{20}$

$\tilde{K}a_i^{ext}$ can be expressed as a function of Ka_i^{ext} by :

$$\tilde{K}a_i^{ext} = P_i [Ka_i^{ext} - 1] + 1 \tag{21}$$

The squared coefficient of variation of service time at station i of a customer going to station j is : [10]

$$K_j^i = p_j + Ks_i(1-p_j) \quad \text{and its rate is :}$$

$$\nu_j^i = \mu_i(1-p_j)$$

The variance of the equivalent service time is :

$$var_i = \sum_{j \in S(i)} \frac{q_{ij}[K_j^i+1]}{(\nu_j^i)^2} - \frac{1}{\bar{\mu}_i}$$

Then we obtain the squared coefficient of variation of the equivalent service time at the station i as follows :

$$\tilde{K}s_i = -1 + \hat{\mu}_i^2 \sum_{j \in S(i)} \frac{q_{ij}[K_j^i + 1]}{\mu_i^2 (1-p_j)^2}$$

and finally substituting K_j^i by its value yields :

$$\tilde{K}s_i = -1 + \frac{Ks_j}{\sum\limits_{j \in S(i)} \frac{q_{ij}}{1-p_j}} + \frac{\sum\limits_{j \in S(i)} \frac{q_{ij}(1+p_j)}{(1-p_j)^2}}{\left[\sum\limits_{j \in S(i)} \frac{q_{ij}}{1-p_j}\right]^2} \tag{22}$$

Let us denote that :

$$\tilde{\rho}_i = \frac{\lambda_i}{(1-p_i)\tilde{\mu}_i} \tag{23}$$

$$\hat{\rho}_i = e^{-2 \frac{1 - \tilde{\rho}_i}{\tilde{\rho}_i Ka_i + \tilde{K}s_i}} \tag{24}$$

and the feed-back probability can be written :

$$p_i = \frac{\tilde{\rho}_i (1-\tilde{\rho}_i)}{\hat{\rho}_i^{-(M_i - 1)} - \tilde{\rho}_i^2} \tag{25}$$

Numerical computation

The system consisting of equations (20) to (25) for $i = 1,\ldots,K$ can by written in matrix form as :

$$\vec{P} = \emptyset(\vec{P}),$$

where P is the vector $(p_1,\ldots,p_K)$. The existence and unicity of the solution of this system may be proved as in the exponential case and are treated in the appendix 1.
$\vec{P} = \emptyset(\vec{P})$ has a non-trival solution $(\vec{P} = \vec{1})$ if $\rho_i = \frac{\lambda_i}{\mu_i} < 1$, $i = 1,\ldots,K$.

An iterative method, identical to that of the exponential case is used : if at some iteration there exists j such that $\rho_j \geq 1$ then the system is unstable. In that case, the behaviour of the network may be studied by a similar method as for the exponential case.

Let h denote the function, solution of the diffusion equation [3] for the G/G/1/N queue (equivalent to the closed two-server system with N customers). The expected number of packets in queue i is obtained by the integration of h between 0 and M_i. By removal of subscript i, we get :

$$N = \frac{\lambda_D(0)}{b(1-p)} \left[\frac{1}{\gamma} - \frac{1}{2}\right] + \frac{\lambda_D(0)}{b\gamma(1-p)} (M - 1 - \frac{1}{\gamma}) \hat{\rho}^{M-1} (1-\hat{\rho}^{-1}) \tag{26}$$

$$- \frac{\tilde{\mu}p}{b} \left[\frac{\hat{\rho}-1}{\gamma} (\frac{1}{\gamma} - M+1) + \frac{1}{\gamma} (M - \frac{1}{\gamma})\right] + \frac{\tilde{\mu}p}{2b} (2M - 1) + Mp$$

with

$$b = \frac{\lambda}{1-p} Ka + \tilde{\mu} \tilde{K}s, \quad a = \frac{\lambda}{1-p} - \tilde{\mu}, \quad \gamma = \frac{2b}{a}, \quad \tilde{\rho} = e^{\gamma},$$

$$p = \frac{\tilde{\rho}(1-\tilde{\rho})}{\tilde{\rho}^{-(M-1)}-\tilde{\rho}^2}, \quad p(0) = \frac{1-\tilde{\rho}}{1-\tilde{\rho}^2 \tilde{\rho}^{M-1}}.$$

The expected response time is obtained by Little's formula : $W = N/\lambda$.

Amelioration of the solution

An assumption that may be criticized in the previous model is the fact that a packet has always the same probability to be rejected independantly of the number of times it has been rejected. We can assume, and the simulations prove the validity of this assumption, that the probability of rejection for the first access is the probability of saturation of the next queue. For the second access and eventually the following ones the probability of rejection is certainly different.

Let us call r_{ij} the probability that a packet going from i to j will be rejected after a first rejection. We show in appendix 2 that under exponential and Poisson assumptions :

- r_{ij} is independent of the number of previous rejections
- r_{ij} is a function of $\tilde{\mu}_i$, $\tilde{\mu}_j$, λ_j, $\lambda_i q_{ij}$.

The equivalent service for a customer going from i to j can be represented by the scheme of figure 3.

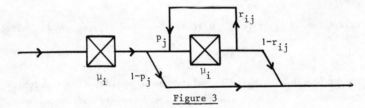

Figure 3

The new equivalent service has the following parameters :

$$\tilde{\mu}_i = \left[\frac{1}{\mu_i} \sum_{j=1}^{K+1} q_{ij} (1 + \frac{p_j}{1-r_{ij}}) \right]^{-1} \tag{27}$$

$$\tilde{K}s_i = -1 + \tilde{\mu}_i^2 \sum_j \frac{q_{ij}[K_i^j + 1]}{(\nu_i^j)^2} \tag{28}$$

with $K_i^j = p_j + Ks_i(1-p_j)$

$\nu_i^j = \mu_i / (1 + \frac{p_j}{1 - r_{ij}})$

The only assumption made here is that the value of r_{ij} is the same as in the exponential case. All numerecal results are obtained using formulas (27)(28). Let us note that the new equivalent service is not exponential for exponentially distributed service times.

Results and Conclusions

We apply the methods developped in previous section to compute the expected response time of the computer network Cyclade, with 7 nodes (Figure 4). We obtain a network with 23 queues. Sixteen of these queues denoted 1 through 16, are inside the store-end-forward packet switching network. We assume half-duplex links. The expected transmission time is shown by Figure 4. The transmission times corresponds to 4,8 and 9,6 kb/s links with an important overhead and with packets of 1000 bits. Packet routing is assumed fixed and is summarized in Table 1. The routes which are not indicated on Table 1 are chosen by the shortest path. Routing probabilities are computed from the routing data (given in Table 1 and in the text). We assume that external arrivals are identical at each host and equal to λ and that all the queues have the same buffer size of customers M. The seven hosts represented by seven infinite queues have a service rate equal to 8. We also assume that a packet arriving at a host from the outside of the network has equal probability of having any of the other six nodes as a final destination.

We have summarized in these tables (2 to 4) some results obtained with the above methodology. In these tables we compare the analytical results with simulations. Confidence intervals (95 %) of these simulations have been obtained using the technics described by Leroudier and Parent in [21].

Tables 2, 3 and 4 give the mean number in each queue (N), the probability of saturation of each buffer (P(M)) and the probability P(0) that each queue is empty under exponential assumptions. These tables compare the results obtained

    1 - by simulation

    2 - by the analytic method

    3 - by the classical BCMP method [1] assuming infinite buffers.

The parameters are

| Table 2 | M = 4 | $\lambda = 1$ | } | exponential service times |
| Table 3 | M = 4 | $\lambda = 1.5$ | } | |

In table 4 we present results obtained with Erlang 2 and Hyperexponential 2 service times.

We can conclude that our results are very accurate for exponential service times, even for heavy traffic. In tables 2, and 3 the analytical results are always within the confidence interval of the simulations. Table 4 shows the limit of this study. It seems that results are underevaluate for Erlang distributions and overevaluate for hyperexponential ones.

Results obtained by increasing M are the same as results found using BCMP [1] (from M = 20 results are exactly identical).

Comparison between infinite buffer models and finite buffer model shows very significant difference and it is surely not possible to model a finite buffer system with an infinite model.

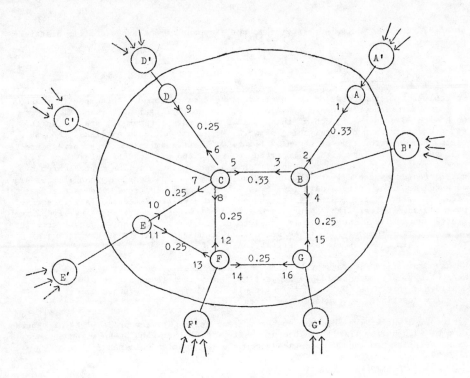

Figure 4

Source	Destination	Via
A'	F'	C
B'	F'	C
C'	G'	F
D'	G'	F
G'	C' , D'	B
F'	A' , B'	C

Table 1

Paramètres M = 4   λ = 1

	Simulation						Analytique			BCMP M=+∞
File	P(0)	±	P(M)	±	n̄	±	P(0)	P(M)	n̄	n̄
1	.684	.007	.011	0.002	.466	.018	0.677	0.015	.490	.428
2	.700	.005	.008	0.001	.425	.012	0.699	.009	.416	.428
3	.493	.008	.053	.004	.942	.027	.485	.051	.948	1.
4	.865	.004	.000	.000	.156	.006	.869			
5	.595	.006	.022	.002	.656	.017	.596	.021	.637	.667
6	.602	.008	.019	.003	.633	.019	.600	.020	.624	.667
7	.738	.006	.004	.001	.351	.012	.732	.006	.356	.464
8	.598	.008	.019	.003	.638	.020	.598	.021	.630	.667
9	.593	.008	.024	.003	.668	.024	.588	.027	.683	.667
10	.721	.006	.006	.001	.388	.013	.725	.008	.381	.364
11	.866	.004	.000	.000	.154	.006	.866	.001	.156	.154
12	.730	.007	.005	.001	.369	.014	.725	.008	.381	.364
13	.868	.005	.000	.000	.151	.006	.867	.001	.153	.154
14	.733	.006	.004	.001	.360	.012	.733	.006	.356	.364
15	.720	.008	.006	.001	.392	.016	.719	.009	.397	.364
16	.866	.005	.000	.000	.154	.007	.867	.001	.154	.154

Table 2

Paramètres M = 4   λ = 1.5

	Simulation						Analytique			BCMP M=+∞
File	P(0)	±	P(M)	±	n̄	±	P(0)	P(M)	n̄	n̄
1	.290	.018	.311	.028	1.995	.103	.297	.255	1.904	.818
2	.553	.007	.031	.003	.764	.021	.550	.030	.749	.818
3	.171	.010	.342	.016	2.376	.062	.165	.327	2.383	3.000
4	.797	.006	.003	.001	.263	.011	.800	.003	.250	.250
5	.386	.009	.101	.008	1.316	.038	.381	.093	1.291	1.5
6	.410	.009	.087	.007	1.213	.034	.400	.076	1.194	1.5
7	.602	.008	.023	.003	.641	.023	.600	.021	.629	.66
8	.395	.009	.100	.007	1.268	.038	.391	.086	1.247	1.5
9	.308	.012	.215	.017	1.745	.066	.318	.220	1.776	1.5
10	.531	.011	.055	.008	.883	.040	.544	.054	.866	.66
11	.793	.006	.002	.001	.263	.011	.795	.004	.266	.25
12	.542	.011	.050	.006	.835	.037	.544	.055	.869	.66
13	.799	.006	.002	.001	.255	.010	.800	.003	.249	.25
14	.597	.008	.021	.003	.649	.022	.600	.020	.629	.66
15	.414	.016	.157	.018	1.363	.076	.436	.137	1.324	.66
16	.799	.006	.003	.001	.261	.010	.800	.004	.262	.25

Table 3

Paramètres M = 4 λ = 1

File	Erlang 2			Hyper 2		
	simulation $\bar{n}$	$\pm$	Analytique $\bar{n}$	Simulation $\bar{n}$	$\pm$	Analytique $\bar{n}$
1	.334	.006	.302	.762	.049	.817
2	.375	.008	.308	.491	.019	.577
3	.756	.016	.671	1.230	.049	1.347
4	.143	.004	.115	.164	.009	0.220
5	.549	.010	.469	.788	.025	.889
6	.563	.013	.477	.713	.027	.826
7	.326	.008	.268	.432	.019	.492
8	.559	.013	.476	.750	.031	.857
9	.493	.010	.444	.872	.041	1.033
10	.305	.007	.260	.481	.024	.588
11	.138	.004	.114	.172	.009	.232
12	.302	.006	.260	.498	.028	.589
13	.146	.004	.114	.158	.008	.222
14	.325	.008	.264	.394	.016	.496
15	.301	.006	.263	.591	.042	.637
16	.140	.004	.114	.164	.010	.225

Table 4

We can estimate average network delay using Kleinrock's formula [16]. The average source-to-destination packet delay T is defined as follows :

$$T = \Sigma_{i=1}^{K} \lambda_i W_i / \quad \text{where} \quad = \lambda_j \lambda_j^{ext}.$$

In figure 5 we compare in two cases the source-to-destination packet delay with Ka = 1. and Ks = 1., for different values of the $\lambda_j^{ext'}$ s :

- end-to-end packet delay, response time of hosts included
- end-to-end packet delay, without response times of hosts.

We assume M = 4.

In figure 6 we compare the source-to-destination packet delay, with Ka = 1 and Ks = 1., for different values of the limited capacity M. We assume for each j = 1,...,7, λ_j^{ext} = 1.5.

The method developped in this paper may be applied to study the different mechanisms available for controlling flows in a network. Such list of mechanisms used to control flow may be found in Pouzin [18] or Chou and Gerla [19]. This new analytical tool can be still improved to include protocols, acknowledgements, etc...

APPENDIX 1

Proof of the uniqueness of the solution in the diffusion case

As in the exponential case, we show that the system with only one queue has an unique solution if $\rho = \lambda/\tilde{\mu} < 1$.

Our system of equations is the following :

$$p = \frac{\tilde{\rho}(1-\tilde{\rho})}{\tilde{\rho}^{-(M-1)} - \tilde{\rho}^2} \qquad (29)$$

$$\tilde{\rho} = \frac{\tilde{\rho}}{\tilde{\mu}(1-p)} = \frac{\rho}{1-p} \qquad (30)$$

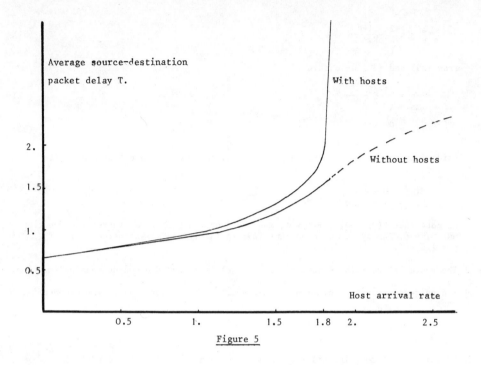

Figure 5

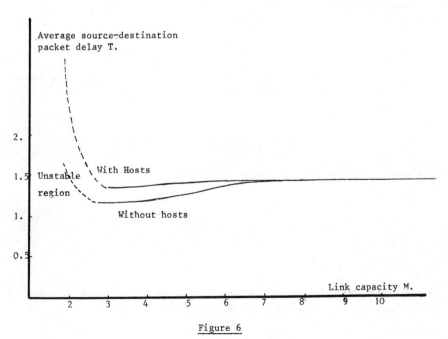

Figure 6

$$\hat{\rho} = e^{-2} \frac{1-\tilde{\rho}}{\tilde{\rho}Ka+Ks} \tag{31}$$

From (29) and (30) we obtain :

$$1-p = \frac{1-\tilde{\rho}\hat{\rho}^{M-1}}{1-\tilde{\rho}^2 \hat{\rho}^{M-1}} \tag{32}$$

$$1-p = \frac{\hat{\rho}}{\rho} . \tag{33}$$

Aside from the trivial solution p=1, ρ = +∞, there exists a solution only if

$$f(\tilde{\rho}) = \frac{\tilde{\rho} - \tilde{\rho}^2 \hat{\rho}^{M-1}}{1 - \tilde{\rho}^2 \hat{\rho}^{M-1}} = \frac{\lambda}{\tilde{\mu}}$$

We note that f(0) = 0, f(+∞) = 1, and the function f($\tilde{\rho}$) is an increasing function on [0, +∞[. The system of equations (29) to (31) possesses solutions only if $\rho = \lambda/\tilde{\mu} < 1$.

The vectorial function $\emptyset$ satisfying $\vec{P} = \emptyset(\vec{P})$ is a monotone non-decreasing function.

The uniqueness of the solution of this system may be proved as in the exponential case.

APPENDIX 2

Computation of coefficients r_{ij}

Let us consider the scheme of figure 7.

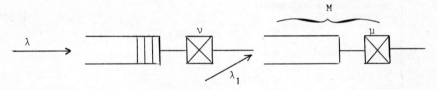

Figure 7

This scheme corresponds to the condition of queues i and j with

- $\lambda = \lambda_i q_{ij}$
- $\lambda_1 = \lambda_j - \lambda_i q_{ij}$
- $\nu = \mu_i$
- $\mu = \tilde{\mu}_j$

Let α_i = probability {after the next departure of service ν the second queue will be full knowing that there are i customers in the second queue}.

Obviously $r_{ij} = \alpha_M$.

The α_i must satisfy the following equations :

(1) $\qquad \alpha_0 = \dfrac{\lambda_1}{\nu+\lambda_1}\,\alpha_1$

$\vdots$

(i-1) $\qquad \alpha_i = \dfrac{\lambda_1}{\lambda_1+\nu+\mu}\,\alpha_{i+1} + \dfrac{\mu}{\lambda_1+\mu+\nu}\,\alpha_{i-1}$

$\vdots$

(M) $\qquad \alpha_{M-1} = \dfrac{\lambda_1}{\lambda_1+\nu+\mu}\,\alpha_M + \dfrac{\mu}{\lambda_1+\mu+\nu}\,\alpha_{M-2}$

(M+1) $\qquad \alpha_M = \dfrac{\nu}{\nu+\mu} + \dfrac{\mu}{\nu+\mu}\,\alpha_{M-1}$

To solve this system we can use a generating function satisfying equations (1) to (M) and use equation (M+1) as a normalizing equation.

Using $f(x) \quad \sum\limits_0^\infty \alpha_i\, x^i$, we obtain :

$$f(x) = [\lambda_1 - (\lambda_1 + \mu + \nu)x + \mu x^2] = \alpha_0\,[\lambda_1 - \mu x]$$

with ρ_1 and ρ_2 being the solutions of $\lambda_1 - (\lambda_1 + \mu + \nu)x + \mu x^2 = 0$ we obtain :

$$\frac{f(x)}{\alpha_0} = \frac{A}{\rho_1-x} + \frac{B}{\rho_2-x}$$

with

$$A = \frac{-\rho_1 + \dfrac{\lambda_1}{\mu}}{\rho_2 - \rho_1} \quad , \quad B = \frac{\rho_2 - \dfrac{\lambda_1}{\mu}}{\rho_2 - \rho_1}$$

This formula can be developped in a sum of power of x which gives α_M and α_{M-1} as function of α_0. α_0 is determined using equation (M+1). After computation we obtain:

$$\alpha_M = \left\{ \frac{\nu+\mu}{\nu} - \frac{\lambda_1}{\nu} \,\frac{(\rho_2^M - \rho_1^M) - (\rho_2^{M-1}-\rho_1^{M-1})}{(\rho_2^{M+1} - \rho_1^{M+1}) - (\rho_2^M - \rho_1^M)} \right\}^{-1}$$

and we have shown that $r_{ij} = \alpha_M$.

We can remark that if $\lambda_1 = 0$, then we obtain the classical result : $\alpha_M = \dfrac{\nu}{\nu+\mu}$;

REFERENCES

[1] Baskett F., Chandy K.M., Muntz R.R., Palacios F.G. - "Open, closed, and mixed networks of queues with different classes of customers" - J.ACM 22, 248, 1975.

[2] Kobayashi H. - "Application of the diffusion approximation to queueing networks" - J.ACM 21, 316-328, 1974.

[3] Gelenbe E. - "On approximate computer models" - J.ACM 22, 261-269, 1975.

[4] Gelenbe E. and Pujolle G. - "Approximation to a single queue in a network" - Acta Informatica 7, 123-136, 1976.

[5] Chandy K.M., Herzog U., Woo L. - "Approximate analysis of general queueing network" - IBM Research Report RC 4931, 1974.

[6] Pennotti M. and Schwartz M. - "Congestion control in store and forward tandem links" - IEEE Trans. on Com. 23, 1434-1443, 1975.

[7] Rudin H. - "An introduction to flow control" - IBM Research Report RZ 756, Zurich, 1976.

[8] Rubin I. - "Path delays in communication networks" - Appl. Math. Optimization 1, 1974.

[9] Labetoulle J. and Pujolle G. - "A study of queueing networks with deterministic service and applications to computer networks" - Acta Informatica 7, 183-195, 1976.

[10] Pujolle G. - "Ergodicity conditions and congestion control in computer networks" - IRIA/LABORIA Research Report 190, 1976.

[11] Lam S.S. - "Store-and-forward buffer requirements in a packet switching network" - IEEE Trans. on Com. 24, 394, 1976.

[12] Schweitzer P. and Lam S.S. - "Buffer overflow in a store-and-forward network node" - IBM Research Report RC 5759, Yorktown Heights, 1975.

[13] Lavenberg S.S. - "Stability and maximum departure rate of certain open queueing networks having finite capacity constraints" - IBM Research Report RJ 1625, San Jose, 1975.

[14] Schweitzer P. - "Maximum throughput in finite capacity open queueing networks" - IBM Research Report RC 5996, Yorktown Heights, 1976.

[15] Irland M. and Pujolle G. - "Models of tandem networks of queues motivated by packet switching" - IRIA Research Report - 1977.

[16] Kleinrock L. - "Communication nets-stochastic message flow and delays" - Mc Graw-Hill - New York, 1964.

[17] Reiser M. and Kobayashi H. - "Accuracy of the diffusion approximation for some queueing systems" - IBM J. Res. and Develop. 18, 2, 110-124, 1974.

[18] Pouzin L. - "Flow control in data networks - methods and tools" - International Conference on Computer Communications '- Toronto - Canada, 1976.

[19] Chou W. and Gerla M. - "A unified flow and congestion control model for packet networks" - International Conference on Computer Communications - Toronto - Canada, 1976.

[20] Chu W.W. - "Buffer behavior for poisson arrivals and multiple synchronous constant outputs" - IEEE Trans. on Com. 18, 530-534, 1970.

[21] Leroudier J. and Parent M. - "Discrete event simulation modelling of computer systems for performance evaluation" - Research Report IRIA/LABORIA 117, 1976.

COMPUTER PERFORMANCE, K.M. CHANDY AND M. REISER (EDS.)
NORTH HOLLAND PUBLISHING COMPANY, 1977

ROUTING UPDATES IN PACKET SWITCHED NETWORKS

J. M. Holtzman
Bell Telephone Laboratories
Holmdel, New Jersey, USA

Routing decisions in packet switched networks are
often based upon congestion updates passed around the network. There is a natural conflict in the selection of the
update period, T:

  i) Make T small to base decisions on recent information,
     and

 ii) Make T large to minimize the overhead associated
     with the updates.

This paper examines this conflict by means of an example of
periodic updating which is simple enough to yield to analysis
and transparent enough to provide some insight into what is
happening physically. The example is based on which of two
queues a traffic stream is to be routed to.

Two lower bounds for the mean queue size (at
either queue) are given. One lower bound is based on stationary queueing results; the other lower bound is based on a
transient analysis. The maximum of these two lower bounds
is another lower bound which, as a function of T, reflects
the above mentioned conflict in choosing T. In particular,
a minimizing value of T is displayed. The lower bounds are
also approximations for different ranges of T: one for small
T, the other for large T.

I. Introduction

Routing in packet switched networks is often accomplished by passing
updates of congestion information between nodes and selecting paths based on the
updates. There is a natural conflict in the selection of the update period:

  i) Make it small to base decisions on recent information, and

 ii) Make it large to minimize the overhead associated with the updates.

This paper examines this conflict.

To gain some insight into the problem, we consider a simple model chosen for both its admirable quality of being relatively easy to analyze and its transparency. The example is based on which of two queues a traffic stream is to be routed to. The numerical results turn out to be qualitatively consistent with phenomena already observed in some simulations of networks.

The model is described in Section II. Two lower bounds for the mean queue size (at either queue) are given in Section III. The maximum of the two lower bounds is another lower bound which, as a function of the update period T, reflects the above mentioned conflict in choosing T. It will be seen that oscillatory behavior plays a key role in interpreting the results. The possibility of oscillatory behavior with large T is fairly obvious and has been recognized before; we shall exploit this behavior in our analysis.

In Section IV, numerical results are given for the model. Section V contains some results on routing updates reported in the literature.

II.   The Model Studied

As mentioned in the Introduction, the model analyzed is simple but contains features we wish to highlight. It is illustrated in Figure 1.

A Poisson stream of data traffic with rate λ_d is to be routed to either one of two servers. Decisions are made every T seconds as to which server to route to, based on which server had the smallest queue at the beginning of the T-period (ties are resolved with a flip of a fair coin). All packets are routed to the chosen server for the entire T-period.

There is overhead as a result of updating the queue information every T seconds. This shall be simply modeled as an additional Poisson stream with rate $\lambda_u = k/T$ offered to each server. This grossly captures the update overhead effect as a function of T: k represents the amount of update information to be transmitted every T seconds.

All service times (for both the data and update packets) are mutually independent exponential random variables with mean μ^{-1}. It is assumed throughout that $\lambda_d + 2\lambda_u < 2\mu$.

One possible physical interpretation of Figure 1 is that the decision box is part of a switching node and S_1 and S_2 represent links on paths to a common destination, either output links at the node at which the decision is being made or links further away. The decision to route via S_1 or S_2 is updated every T seconds, e.g., by updating routing tables. The λ_u- streams represent update packets to accomplish node-to-node transfer of congestion information across the two links S_1 and S_2. They do not necessarily represent the congestion updates needed by the node making the routing decision in Figure 1. k represents the complexity of the congestion information transferred (e.g., related to routing table size).

Other representations of both the input process and the update overhead can be visualized (see, e.g., [9], where updates arrive deterministically, are given preemptive priority,[*] and have different service times from the data) but the above model suffices for our purposes here. Also note that a decision is made for the entire period of T seconds to route all packets one way as opposed to proportional routing (see, e.g., [11] or [7]) or routing by session, i.e., call (see, e.g., [11]).[†]

III. Analysis of the Model

Let x be the queue length at one of the servers (throughout we define queue to include the one in service). We shall derive two lower bounds for means of x, Ex_1 and Ex_2. The maximum of the two lower bounds is another lower bound which will be found to be informative when viewed as a function of T. The lower bounds are also approximations for different ranges of T: one for small T, the other for large T.

IIIA. First Lower Bound

The first lower bound, Ex_1, is simply 1/2 of the mean number of customers in the stationary solution of an M/M/2 delay system with input rate $\lambda_d + 2\lambda_u$ and mean service time μ^{-1}. This follows from the symmetry of S_1 and S_2 and the fact there can be no more customers in the M/M/2 system than the combined $S_1 - S_2$ system. This latter fact follows from the observation that the service (death) rate of this M/M/2 system is never less than the combined service system of S_1 and S_2 when both systems have the same number of customers. It may be seen from [5] that Ex_1 is an approximation for very small T,[††] which is equivalent to saying that for very small T, the expected waiting time for the minimum queue strategy approximately equals that of the M/M/2 queue.

IIIB. Second Lower Bound

Ex_2 is a lower bound for $\lambda_d > \mu$ and also an approximation for large T. It is instructive to motivate the development of Ex_2 by appeal to its approximation aspect. Thus, observe that for large T, the λ_d-stream will tend to be offered on an alternating basis to each server. That is, if the λ_d-stream is offered to one server for a T-period, its queue will build up while the other decays. Then the other server will have the minimum queue and be offered the λ_d-stream for the next T-period.

---

[*] Note that our assumption of updated queue information every T seconds corresponds to preemptively treating deterministic updates. Our first-come first-served queueing treatment of data and updates would give optimistic results for the queueing of data relative to priority treatment of updates. A further reference to update priorities is given in Section V.

[†] Also see [2] where the routing strategy can deterministically change between updates.

[††] The smallness of T is relative to saturating the system.

With this scenario, each server is offered an alternating Poisson stream with rates $\lambda_d + \lambda_u$ and λ_u. To derive a lower bound on the response to this input, we use the transient result for an M/M/1 system with offered rate λ (see, e.g., [4], p. 178):

$$E\{x(t)|x(0) = \ell\} = \ell + \lambda t - \mu \int_0^t [1 - p_{\ell 0}(\tau)]d\tau \,, \qquad \text{(III-1)}$$

where $x(t)$ is the number of customers in the M/M/1 system at time t and $p_{\ell 0}(t)$ is transition probability from state ℓ to the empty state. An obvious lower bound (neglecting the time in the empty state) is

$$E\{x(t)|x(0) = \ell\} \geq \ell + (\lambda-\mu)t \,. \qquad \text{(III-2)}$$

Another lower bound to (III-1) is

$$E\{x(t)|x(0) = \ell\} \geq f(\ell,t) \qquad \text{(III-3)}$$

where

$$f(\ell,t) = \frac{(\mu t)^\ell}{(\ell-1)!} e^{-\mu t}\left[\left(\frac{\ell}{\mu t} - 1\right)B(\ell-1,\mu t)^{-1} + 1\right] \qquad \text{(III-4)}$$

and $B(x,a)$ is the Erlang loss formula. (III-4) is an exact representation for $E\{x(t)|x(0) = \ell\}$ when $\lambda = 0$ (due to D. L. Jagerman and used for computational convenience).

With one of the servers offered an alternating Poisson stream with rates $\lambda_d + \lambda_u$ for $t\epsilon[0,T]$, $[2T,3T],\ldots$, and λ_u for $t\epsilon[T,2T]$, $[3T,4T],\ldots$, we then obtain the following periodic lower bound on $E\{x(t)\}$, the mean queue at that server:

$$E\{x(t)\} \geq (\rho_2-1)^{-1} + (\rho_2-1)\mu t - \frac{e^{-\left(1-\rho_2^{1/2}\right)^2\mu t}}{2\pi}\int_0^1 \frac{\sqrt{w(1-w)}\; e^{-4\rho_2^{1/2}w\mu t}}{\left\{w + \frac{\left[1-\rho_2^{1/2}\right]^2}{4\rho_2^{1/2}}\right\}^2} dw, t\epsilon[0,T] \qquad \text{(III-5a)}$$

$$E\{x(t)\} \geq \max\left\{y(T) + (\lambda_u-\mu)(t-T),\; f(y(T),(t-T))\right\}, \; t\epsilon[T,2T] \qquad \text{(III-5b)}$$

where $\rho_2 = (\lambda_d + \lambda_u)/\mu$, $y(T)$ is the right hand side of (III-5a) with $t = T$, and $f(y(T),t)$ is the function in (III-4), linearly interpolated between integers. The right hand side of (III-5a) is a lower bound since it is the exact solution when $x(0) = 0$ (see [1], p. 330). Thus, $E\{x(T)\} \geq y(T)$. The right-hand side of (III-5b) is a lower bound because it is a convex nondecreasing function which allows use of Jensen's inequality applied to $y(T)$.

Remark: A weaker, but easier to visualize, lower bound is the piecewise-linear build-up and decay function

$$E\{x(t)\} \geq (\lambda_d + \lambda_u - \mu)t \qquad\qquad t\epsilon[0,T]$$

$$E\{x(t)\} \geq [\lambda_d + \lambda_u - \mu)T - (\mu - \lambda_u)(t-T)]^+ \qquad t\epsilon[T,2T] \tag{III-6}$$

where $[x]^+ = \max(0,x)$.

The second lower bound, Ex_2, is taken here as the average of the right hand side of (III-5) evaluated at the end points of the T-periods (this is convenient for comparison with the simulation results of Section IV).

Observe that we have motivated Ex_2 as an approximation for large T and derived a lower bound for the resultant scenario of alternating offering of the λ_d-stream. However, it is also true that Ex_2 is a lower bound for all values of T. The following argument shows this. Because of the symmetry of the two servers, the λ_d-stream must be offered in the long run (as the number of T-periods $\to \infty$) an equal number of times to each server. It may be seen that alternating the λ_d-stream minimizes for any pattern of T-period decisions the lower bounds derived from (III-1) as (III-5) we derived from (III-1). Note that we are not saying that alternating is the best strategy for all T (which it clearly is not for small T) but that it minimizes over a class of lower bounds.

IIIC. Overall Lower Bound

With Ex_1 and Ex_2 both lower bounds, we have the following lower bound:

$$Ex_L = \max\{Ex_1, Ex_2\} \ .$$

Since Ex_1 is known to be an approximation for small T and Ex_2 would be expected to be a reasonable approximation for large $T(\lambda_d > \mu)$, Ex_L might be expected to also be a rough approximation for all T. Some simulation comparisons are shown in the next section.

IV. Numerical Results

Figures 2 and 3 show numerical results for Ex_1 and Ex_2 along with some simulation results, all plotted versus μT (the ratio of update period to mean

service time). In Figure 2, λ_d/μ = 1.2 and 1.8 for k = 1; in Figure 3, k = 1 and
4 for λ_d/μ = 1.5. Although the bounds are, as expected, weakest near the crossover, nevertheless the minimizing characteristics show up well.

Also shown in Figure 3 are the M/M/1 results which represent simple
approximations [$\rho/(1-\rho)$ with $\rho = (\lambda_d/2+\lambda_u)/\mu$]. The stationary queueing results
cannot, of course, indicate the minimizing values of μT since they monotonically
decrease with T. It is the oscillatory behavior which explains the curves for
large μT.

Note that randomly splitting the stream and using no updates at all
gives very good performance ($\rho/(1-\rho)$ with $\rho = \lambda_d/2\mu$) as compared to that shown in
Figures 2 and 3. However, that takes advantage of the symmetry in the example.
In more complicated situations, the success of a fixed pattern of routing with
no feedback depends on the asymmetries and on what is known about the traffic
rates.

V. Relation to Some Other Results

It is interesting to observe that in the simulation results reported in
[11], maximum capacity saved (as defined in [11]) occurs at about μT = 25 for a
variety of cases of routing on a packet basis (T$\approx$600, packet transmission time
= 25).* In [3], an update period is picked which corresponds to around μT = 50
but that decision was apparently not based merely on minimizing mean delay (see
p. 584). In [6], the update period is parametrically varied but looping plays
a role.

The ARPANET ratio of update period (0.64 sec under heavy loading) to
maximum size packet transmission time ($\approx$20 ms) is around 32 ([8]). More details
on the ARPANET routing updates are given in [10]. [10] investigates periodic
behavior in ARPANET with data with fixed interarrival times and periodic updates.
[10] also considers the relative priorities of data and updates as well as using
fixed routing with no updates at all for an ARPANET topology network with a uniform traffic matrix.

The results of Section III appear to be most directly related to the
simulation results of [11] where capacity saved is plotted as a function of T and
a minimum usually occurs at around μT = 25 (see the first paragraph in this
section). Further investigation would actually be required to pin down the
relationship of the results.

VI. Conclusion

The work reported here is clearly an early attempt to get a handle on
the update problem. In addition to the simplicity of the model, we have not

---

* The minimum does not show up in the mean delay results exhibited in [11] since
  the updating overhead effect is not included in those results; it is factored
  into the capacity results as a side calculation.

considered here proportional routing or routing by session, as mentioned in Section II, or the interactions of nodes and links, etc. However, the simplicity of the model has hopefully provided some insight into an aspect of the problem.

Acknowledgments

Very helpful discussions with H. Heffes and D. L. Jagerman, and the valuable assistance of D. D'Angelo, J. P. Darcy and R. H. Harris are gratefully acknowledged. H. Zucker brought my attention to Reference 1.

REFERENCES

1. Bailey, N. T. J., (1957), "Some Further Results in the Non-Equilibrium Theory of a Simple Queue," J. Roy. Stat. Soc., Ser, B, pp. 326-333.

2. Brown, C. W., (1975), "Adaptive Routing and Resource Allocation," Ph.D. (EE) Dissertation, Polytechnic Inst. of N.Y.

3. Cegrell, T., (1975), "A Routing Procedure for the TIDAS Message-Switching Network," IEEE Trans. on Commun. Vol. COM-23, No. 6, pp. 575-585.

4. Cohen, J. W., (1969), "The Single Server Queue," North Holland Pub. Co., Amsterdam.

5. Foschini, G. J., "On Heavy Traffic Diffusion Analysis and Dynamic Routing in Packet Switched Networks," presented at this Conference.

6. Fultz, G. L. and Kleinrock, L., (1971), "Adaptive Routing Techniques for Store-and-Forward Computer-Communication Networks," Proc. IEEE Int'l Conf. on Commun., pp. 39-1 to 39-8.

7. Gallager, R. G., (1977), "A Minimum Delay Routing Algorithm Using Distributed Communication," IEEE Trans. on Commun. Vol. COM-25, No. 1, pp. 73-85.

8. Kleinrock, L., (1976), "Queueing Systems, Vol. II: Computer Applications," John Wiley & Sons, N. Y.

9. Kleinrock, L. and Kamoun, F., (1976), "Data Communications through Large Packet Switching Networks," 8th Int'l. Teletraffic Congress, Melbourne, Australia.

10. Naylor, W. E., and Kleinrock, L., (1976), "On the Effect of Periodic Routing Updates in Packet-Switched Networks," Nat'l Telecommunications Ccnf., pp. 16.2-1 to 16.2-7.

11. Rudin, H., (1976) "On Routing and "Delta Routing": A Taxonomy & Performance Comparison of Techniques for Packet-Switched Networks," IEEE Trans. on Commun. Vol. COM-24, No. 1, pp. 43-59.

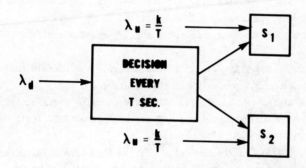

FIGURE 1 - 2 SERVER MODEL

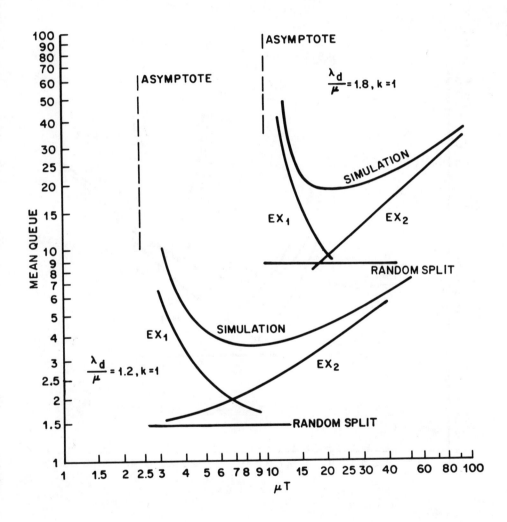

FIGURE 2 MEAN QUEUE VS $\mu T \left(\frac{\lambda_d}{\mu} = 1.2 \text{ AND } 1.8 \, ; \, k = 1 \right)$

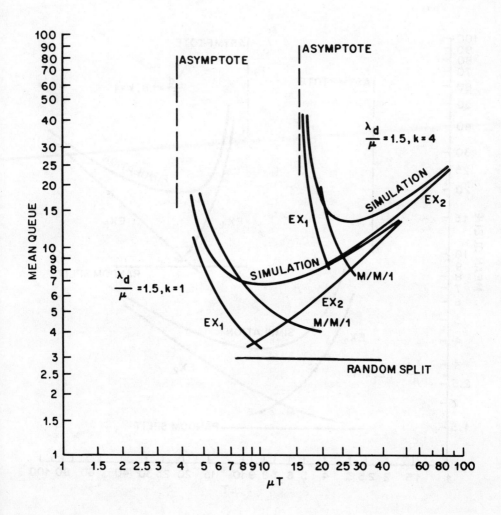

FIGURE 3   MEAN QUEUE VS $\mu T \left(\frac{\lambda_d}{\mu} = 1.5 ; k = 1 \text{ AND } 4 \right)$

COMPUTER PERFORMANCE, K.M. CHANDY AND M. REISER (EDS.)

NORTH HOLLAND PUBLISHING COMPANY, 1977

QUEUEING NETWORK MODELS OF COMPUTER SYSTEMS WITH LIMITED PARALLELISM IN SUBNETWORKS

T. W. Keller
Los Alamos Scientific Laboratory
Los Alamos, New Mexico, USA

The classic central server model of computer systems is extended by the introduction of "passive" resources to a model with more realistic I/O distributions. When the number of passive resources is less than the number of processors in the I/O sub-network of the model, the degree of parallelism obtainable in the subnetwork is restricted, with the result that I/O processes can block. Two computationally inexpensive decomposition techniques are presented which obtain approximate solutions to the model. The first has been applied by a number of authors [A1,C4,K2,W1], and makes the exponential assumption for a composite server approximating the properties of the subnetwork. The second, more accurate, method uses the results of Sauer [S1] to remove the exponential restriction on the composite server.

The solution methods are applied to an extended central server model of a CDC 6000 series computer system in which the passive resources are a pool of peripheral processors which limit the number of I/O processes which may be active. An investigation of the accuracy of both methods is made over a wide range of realistic model parameters. The central server model, ignoring passive resources, results in unacceptable error. The first approximation method when applied to the extended model results in adequate accuracy in most cases. The second method results in good accuracy for all cases.

INTRODUCTION

In this paper we develop a realistic model of computer systems which incorporates the competition of parallel I/O processes for the passive resource of I/O processors, and we formulate accurate and inexpensive solutions to the model. Previously developed solution methods were so computationally expensive that they discouraged evaluation of models of this complexity. Rapid and accurate solution methods were available only for much less realistic models. The last solution method we develop is an improvement over previous methods in that (1) it is significantly more accurate and (2) it is applicable to models with realistic service time distributions.

We first present a brief description of an existing computer I/O system with
characteristics which cannot be tractably modeled by exisiting techniques.
These characteristics are competition for I/O processors; namely peripheral
processors and channels. We next formulate a queueing network model incorporating peripheral processor activity. An approximate analytic method incorporating a technique for simplifying the passive resource queueing network
model is given, and the method is refined to include more realistic service
time distributions for the I/O devices. An extensive validation study shows
that the accuracy of the approximation method is good. Finally, the approximate solution method developed is shown to be applicable not only to the model
presented in this paper but also to a larger class of models of systems for
which the maximum level of parallelism in any subsystem is fixed.

DEFINITION

Passive Resource: A resource characterized by the manner in which it is
allocated and deallocated to processes by the system. The process holding
time is not an inherent characteristic of the resource, but is instead
determined by the holding times of associated "active" resources. By this
definition, a CPU is an "active" resource, while memory, channels, and
Control Data Corporation (CDC) peripheral processors are passive
resources.

STRUCTURE OF THE CDC 6000 SERIES COMPUTER I/O SYSTEM

We present the CDC 6000 series computer I/O subsystem as an example of a subsystem where contention for passive resources can result in serious performance
degradation. Although the modeling approach we take is general enough to be applied to many different systems, we will restrict ourselves at present to the
CDC architecture to illustrate the approach.

The I/O subsystem is composed of peripheral processors (PP's), channels, disks,
and drums. A PP is a programmable processor with its own memory and control,
and performs I/O functions. The PP's can access central memory independently
of the CPU which performs most of the numerical computation for the machine.
The 6000 series channels connect the PP's with external storage.

A user job executing in the CPU performs a read by posting an I/O request to
the Peripheral Program Monitor, which recognizes the request and assigns it to
a PP. If no PP is available, the request is placed in a first-come-first-
served (FCFS) queue from which PP's draw service requests. Once the I/O request is assigned a PP, the PP computes the disk sector address of the request
and queues (in FCFS order) for an I/O channel. After acquiring a channel, the
PP performs the read, transferring the data to a buffer in the PP's own memory.
The PP in turn transfers the data by blocks into the user job's central memory,
releases the channel, and posts a message to the user job that the I/O request
is satisfied. A write is handled similarly.

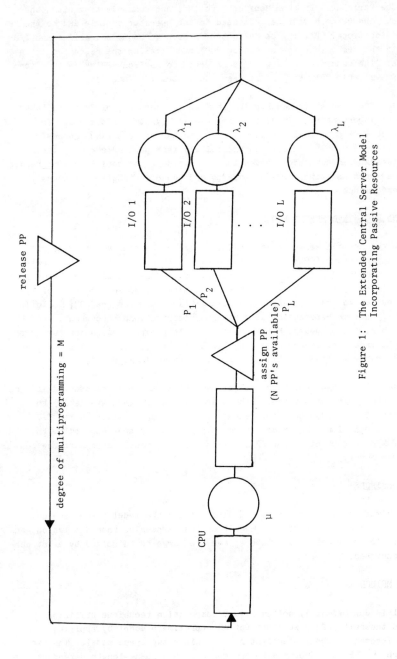

Figure 1: The Extended Central Server Model
Incorporating Passive Resources

PP's perform more than the above I/O functions to disks and drums. Other functions may include communicating with the operator through a CRT console, performing the Peripheral Program Monitor function, and communicating with other computers. One PP each must be dedicated to the operator console and to the PP Monitor. Additional PP's may be dedicated to computer communications and I/O drivers if the delay time introduced by FCFS queueing for the resources is intolerable. The remaining PP's will be referred to as "Pool PP's" as they form a pool of available PP's to perform user and system I/O functions.

It is clear from the above description that the number of pool PP's available can play an important role in determining overall system performance. If the number of pool PP's is small compared to the number of jobs simultaneously desiring I/O, then there exists the possibility that pool PP's can be the system bottleneck. In any case, contention between jobs for pool PP's will result in degraded response time for I/O requests and hence degredation of overall system performance.

THE EXTENDED CENTRAL SERVER MODEL

We extend the central server model [B2] to include the passive resource of peripheral processors (PP's). In this model I/O processing for a job consists of the assignment of a PP, then the entering of I/O queue i with branching probability p_i for a server which processes jobs with a mean service rate of λ_i. With no loss of generality we set the mean service rate for the CPU, μ, to 1. We initially assume exponential holding time distributions throughout. Let L be the number of I/O queues, M the degree of multiprogramming, N the number of PP's, P the vector of branching probabilities p_i (i=1,...,L) and λ the vector of service rates λ_i (i=1,...,L). The model is shown in Figure 1.

In this model PP's can be conceptualized as tokens; a job is refused admittance to an I/O queue without a token. Tokens are dispensed (when available) to a job awaiting I/O. A job does not release its token until it exits the I/O queue upon completion of service, at which point tokens are returned to the pool. If N$\geq$M no contention for PP's exists, and the model reduces to the central server model.

SOLUTION METHODS

Two approximate analytic techniques toward solving the model are presented. The methods are several orders of magnitude less expensive than simulation, and are tractable for models with state spaces too large to be solved by exact analytic techniques.

SOLUTION METHOD I

The model is approximately solved by a decomposition technique utilizing "Norton's theorem" [C2]. We construct an approximate model by applying Norton's Theorem to the I/O subsystem to obtain a two queue model. The two queues are the CPU and a composite I/O queue with a queue-length dependent service rate. The approximate model obeys local balance [C1] and is thus amenable

to product-form solution techniques. The ASQ program [K1] is used to solve the
approximate model. The solution algorithm is specified below.

Step 1. Construct the central server model corresponding to no contention
for a passive resource. Apply Norton's theorem to the I/O subsystem to
form an equivalent composite I/O queue with queue-length dependent service
rate T(m), m=1,...M, where M is the degree of multiprogramming.

Step 2. Redefine the I/O composite queue service rate T'(m), m=1,...,M
such that for N PP's, $N \leq M$,

$$T'(m) = \begin{cases} T(m) & m \leq N \\ T(N) & m > N \end{cases}$$

Step 3. Solve the resulting two queue model via ASQ.

Step 4. Stop.

For example, consider the central server model of Figure 2. We apply the restriction of two PP's for degree of multiprogramming three. Applying Step 1
(Figure 3) we obtain an I/O composite queue rate T(m), such that T(1)=.495,
T(2)=.657, and T(3)=.737. We apply Step 2 to redefine the I/O composite service rate in a two queue model as T'(1)=.495, T'(2)=T'(3)=.657, with the CPU
service rate unchanged. From Step 3 we obtain a CPU utilization of .566 .

This aproximation technique was developed independently (in sometimes very different forms) by Keller and Chandy [K2], Courtois [C4], and Williams and Bhandiwad [W1] for closed queueing network models ,and by Avi-Itzhak and Heyman
[A1] for open queueing network models. One reason for the concurrent development was undoubtedly the ease in which the intermediate queueing network models
could be solved by product-form techniques. Keller and Chandy presented the
approximation technique just discussed and gave an error estimate based on
simulation runs. Williams and Bhandiwad proposed the technique for general
subsystems of queueing network models but gave no quantitative error estimates.
Courtois models an interactive computer system by a closed queueing network
model in which the maximum number of jobs allowed to be active is fixed at a
constant, and the service rate for the degrees of multiprogramming greater than
the maximum is held fixed at the service rate for the maximum. Although the
subsystem considered by Courtois is different than that considered in this
work, the approximation principle is the same. Courtois does not consider the
error of his approximation in [C4] but refers the reader to [C5]. A systematic
validation of the technique is not presented. Similarly, an approximate open
network model by Avi-Itzhak and Heyman considers the entire machine as a subsystem of queues to be "condensed" into a single queue. Error bounds are obtained for only two cases of a simple two queue subsystem, that for which the
maximum number of jobs permitted in the subsystem is one, and that for which
there is no maximum. Exact analytic solutions for more realistic cases were
found intractable. The relative error for the simple cases analyzed is found
to be greatest when the arrival rate into the subsystem is nearly that of the

degree of multiprogramming: M = 3

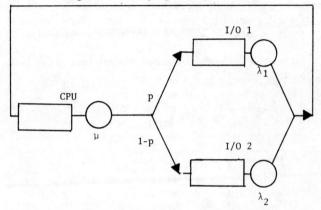

Service rates: μ = 1.0, λ_1 = .55, λ_2 = .45

Branching probability: p = .5

Figure 2:   Central Server Model

degree of multiprogramming: M = 1, 2, 3

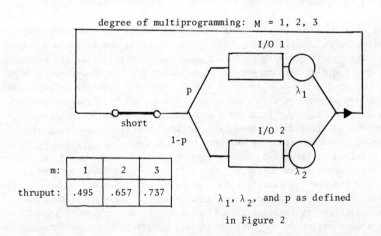

m:	1	2	3
thruput:	.495	.657	.737

λ_1, λ_2, and p as defined

in Figure 2

Figure 3:   Central Server Model
with shorted CPU

composite service rate (saturation).

Considerations stemming from [K2] led us to believe that the error of this technique could not automatically be dismissed as small for realistic models. This is verified in a later section. Thus a more accurate approximation method was developed and is next presented.

SOLUTION METHOD II

In contrast to the approximate model of the previous section, we will remove the exponential restriction on the I/O queues. The I/O service distributions will be characterized by first and second moments.The composite I/O service distribution will be characterized by its mean and coefficient of variation C_v. Again, we construct an approximate model by applying Norton's theorem to the I/O subsystem and limiting the maximum service rate. We make the admittedly false assumption that the initial model obeys local balance in order to obtain these rates. We then assign a coefficient of variation (other than 1) to the composite I/O queue and solve the reduced two queue network for the CPU utilization. We shall see that this solution method also results in greater accuracy for models with exponential I/O servers.

Note that we have introduced two important complexities into the problem of obaining an (approximate) solution. First, we must determine a C_v of the composite I/O queue. Second, we must solve a two queue model that does not obey local balance. Fortunately, Sauer [S1] attacks the second problem with excellent results.

In [S1] Sauer developes an algorithm for the solution of a two queue model with FCFS queueing disciplines and a generalized Erlang distribution for both queues. He shows that it is possible to formulate a generalized Erlang distribution for an arbitrary distribution with a differentiable Laplace transform such that the first two moments of the distributions agree. He uses his solution technique to obtain approximate solutions to central server models with non-exponential service distributions. The technique reduces the original model to a two queue model consisting of the CPU and a composite I/O with a service distribution representing an aggregate of all the individual I/O distributions. The first moments of the composite (queue-length dependent) distribution is obtained by applying Norton's theorem to the I/O subsystem. The composite coefficient of variation for the I/O subsystem is obtained by weighting each I/O C_v by its branching probability. Thus, while the mean composite service time is queue-length dependent, the composite C_v is not. The algorithm incorporates the recursive techniques put forward by Herzog, et al. in [H1]. We shall incorporate this algorithm into our approximate solution method and designate it algorithm S.

We now face the non-trivial problem of estimating an appropriate composite C_v. Let us first consider the case of exponential I/O queues for the extended central server model incorporating passive resources. For notational ease we will lump the parameters P, L, λ, and μ into the single parameter R. Thus M, N, and R completely specify the model. Now we note that for N=M the composite I/O coefficient of variation, $C(M,N,R)$, is 1. We note that for the case of N=1 the composite distribution is hyperexponential and it can be shown ([K4],p. 142) that

$$C(M,1,R) = w^2(\sum_{i=1}^{i=L} (p_i/\lambda_i^2))-1$$

(1)

where

$$w = (\sum_{i+1}^{i=L} p_i/\lambda_i)^{-1}$$

(2)

We observe that for this case $C(M,1,R)\geq 1$. Let us abbreviate $C(M,1,R)$ by simply C1. Now for models of interest with $1\leq N\leq M$, no such simple closed analytic form for $C(M,N,R)$ exists, since even the service time distribution for the composite queue is not well understood. However, it seems reasonable to assume that for the approximate model we are constructing an equivalent service time distribution (equivalence defined as resulting in the CPU utilization of the exact model) will posess a C_v which is monotonically decreasing from C1 to $C(M,M,R)$ as N increases from 1 to M. This implies a linear approximaion to the equivalent coefficient of variation would be in order, namely:

$$C(M,N,R) = \left(\frac{M-N}{M-1}\right)C1 + \left(\frac{N-1}{M-1}\right)C(M,M,R)$$

(3)

By taking appropriate derivatives of the generating function for the Erlang distribution of standard form ([K4], p. 144) we can obtain C1 for arbitrary I/O service distributions (so long as they have differentiable Laplace transforms). For example, for a model with two I/O queues with 2-stage Erlang hypoexponential distributions and mean service rates of λ_1, λ_2, branching probabilities p_1 and p_2, and equal mean holding times per stage, $C(M,1,R)$ is

$$\frac{3\rho^2}{2}\left(\frac{p_1}{\lambda_1^2} + \frac{p_2}{\lambda_2^2}\right)^{-1}$$

(4)

while for 3 stages it is

$$\frac{4\rho^2}{2}\left(\frac{p_1}{\lambda_1^2} + \frac{p_2}{\lambda_2^2}\right)^{-1}$$

(5)

We can thus determine $C(M,M,R)$ quite naturally for non-exponential I/O queues. Of course, for exponential I/O queues $C(M,M,R)$ is identically one.

From the above discussion we have all the information necessary to parameterize the approximate model which is solved by the following algorithm.

   Step 1. Construct the central server model (with exponential service times) corresponding to no contention for a passive resource. Apply Norton's theorem to the I/O subsystem to form an equivalent composite I/O

queue with service rate T(m), m=1,...,M, where M is the degree of multiprogramming. Use ASQ to solve the intermediate models.

Step 2. Redefine the I/O composite queue service rate T'(m), m=1,...,M
such that for N PP's, N≤M,

$$T'(m) = \begin{cases} T(m) & m \leq N \\ T(N) & m > N \end{cases}$$

Step 3. Determine C1, as defined.

Step 4. Estimate the C_v of the I/O composite queue when N=M by forming a
weighted sum of individual queues' coefficients of variation, where the
weight for queue i is the branching probability p_i. Denote this coefficient of variation by C(M,M,R).

Step 5. Set the coefficient of variation, C, for the composite queue to
the linear approximation (3).

Step 6. Use algorithm S to solve the two queue model parameterized in
Steps 2 and 5.

Step 7. Stop.

VALIDATION

In order to test the accuracy of the two approximation methods just presented,
a validation was performed against exact and simulation solutions for the extended central server model over a wide range of parameters. In this section
we present the structure of the model used in the validation, the parameter
space explored, the exact and simulation methods used, and the validation
results.

In order to keep the cases tractable to exact analytic techniques the number of
I/O queues is set to two. Both exponential and hypoexponential distributions
for the I/O servers are used. Distributions with two or three serial exponential stages characterized by the same mean service rate are used for the hypoexponential cases. The CPU service distribution is assumed exponential with
mean rate μ=1. Three variables are employed from which the P and λ of the test
cases are derived. The first is W, reflecting the total I/O work rate and defined by

$$W = (p_1/\lambda_1 + p_2/\lambda_2)^{-1} \tag{6}$$

while the second, A, reflects the balance between I/O queues and is defined by

$$A = (p_1\lambda_2)/(p_2\lambda_1) \tag{7}$$

while the third, B, is the ratio between I/O service rates;

$$B = \lambda_2 / \lambda_1 \tag{8}$$

W is allowed to range from .1 to 1, for when W exceeds .1 the CPU becomes saturated and the impact of contention for passive resources in the I/O subsystem
is minimal. For values of W≪1 the thruput of the system is so small as to be
relatively impervious to errors resulting from the approximation methods. A is
allowed to range from .1 to 1, the upper bound being chosen because if all other variables are held constant in the central server model, CPU thruput is symmetric about A=1. The lower bound is in consideration of realistic models of
I/O subsystems for which it is assumed that device workloads are balanced
within an order of magnitude. B is arbitrarily allowed to range from .1 to 1,
reflecting a device transfer rate imbalance not greater than an order of magnitude. M and N are drawn from the integer set [1,...,10] with the condition
that N<M. Although the number of I/O queues is set to 2, it is possible for
N>2 that all N jobs may be queued in a single I/O queue. The coefficient of
variation for the I/O queues ranges from $(3)^{-1/2}$ to 1 and is determined by the
number of exponential stages comprising the service distribution.

An extensive validation in the parameter space so defined was made for exponential I/O servers. Points in the space for hypoexponential I/O servers were
chosen by selecting all exponential I/O cases with error greater than 1% and
evaluating them with the number of exponential stages equal to 2, then 3.

System thruput, which for $\mu = 1$ is also the CPU utilization, was chosen as the
validation metric. Although other metrics could be used, thruput is the metric
most closely related to the system's capacity to do work, and we wish to consider the effect of pasive resource contention upon the system as a whole.

SOLUTION METHODS AND COSTS

Two methods for obtaining exact and near-exact solutions to the extended model
were used. For cases with less than 100 states a matrix technique was used
which is exact. For cases with larger numbers of states, an ASPOL [C3] simulation was coded for which the confidence interval techniques of Crane and
Iglehart [C6,C7] were employed. For all simulation results the CPU utilization
obtained is within ±.005 of the exact value with 90% confidence.

Costs (in time) of the various methods are measured in CDC 6600 CPU seconds and
do not include compilation and loading. The time for either approximation
technique was less than .05 seconds for all cases. The matrix method ranged in
cost from .05 to .4 seconds, depending upon the number of states. Simulation
runs varied from 8 to 195 seconds to obtain results of the desired accuracy for
cases with large numbers of states.

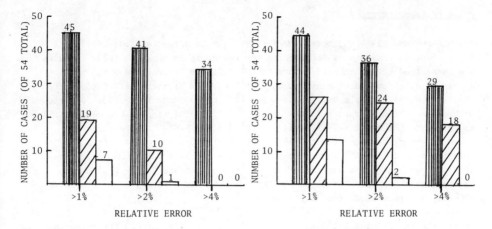

Figure 4: Exponential I/O Queues, W=.5   Figure 5: Exponential I/O Queues, W=1

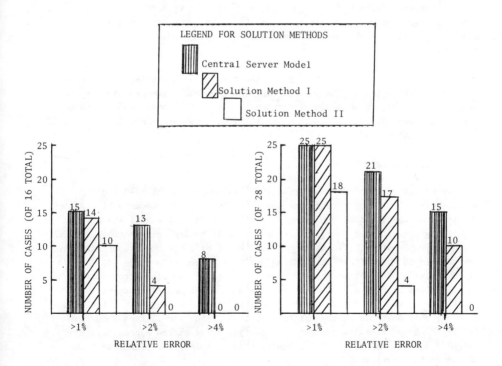

Figure 6: Hypoexponential I/O Queues, W=.5 . Figure 7: Hypoexponential I/O Queues,
                                                                    W=1

ERROR OF APPROXIMATIONS

Two hundred and six (206) models were solved in the parameter space defined.
For a complete analysis of the results the reader is referred to [K3]. Results
are summarized here. "Error" refers to the relative error between approximate
and exact solutions for the system thruput. For the exponential I/O cases the
classic central server model produced errors in the range [0,33.8%]. Solution
method I resulted in errors in the range [0,9.7%]. Solution method II resulted
in errors in the range [-2.5%,2.0%]. Figures 4 and 5 display the number of
cases by error magnitude for the 162 exponential I/O cases, as a function of
solution method. Data is partitioned upon W, since as W approaches 1 (saturation) the errors of the approximations in general increase. For W=.1 there
were no cases for which solution method I resulted in a relative error greater
than 1%, and thus no figure is presented.

Of the 162 exponential I/O cases, 44 resulted in relative errors for solution
method I greater than 1%, and thus were evaluated with hypoexponential I/O
queues by the procedure described earlier. For these hypoexponential I/O cases
the classic central server model produced errors in the range [-2.1%,16%].
Solution method I resulted in errors in the range [-2.9%,7.8%]. Solution
method II resulted in errors in the range [-2%,3%]. For W of .5 and 1.0 the
number of cases by error magnitude are displayed in Figures 6 and 7, respectively.

The relative accuracies of the solution methods can be evaluated by a glance at
the above error limits. The central server model, which ignores the passive
resource entirely, is accurate within 34%. The extended model when solved by
approximate solution method I, is accurate within 10%, while solution method II
is accurate within 5%.

SUMMARY AND APPLICATIONS

We have provided a tool for the analyst by developing an extended central
server model which incorporates the behavior of a passive resource by limiting
the level of parallelism in a subnetwork of the model. The motivation for
developing the extended model is that the classic central server model results
in unacceptable error. Two means of solving the extended model approximately
were developed. The first was independently developed by a number of authors
[A1,C4,K2,W1]. Validation against exact solutions showed the approximation to
be good (less than 5% error in thruput) in most cases and adequate (between 5%
and 8%) in a few. This approximation utilizes the same computation techniques
commonly used for solving the original central server model, thus incurring
little or no additional expense to the analyst. The second approximation
method requires some additional techniques but results in a significant improvement in accuracy.

The extended model finds a variety of applications. The computer system
designer faces the problem of how many I/O processors are required by the system. The operating systems analyst must decide how to best allocate the processors and when it is desirable to purchase additional processors. Simple

workload characteristics and device processing rates are sufficient to parameterize the extended central server model. The effect of varying the number of passive resources (I/O processors) for a large number of system configurations and workload characterizations is easily evaluated by the model. For example, the first approximation method was applied to a model [B1] of the University of Texas CDC 6400 interactive computer system to determine the benefit of increasing the number of peripheral processors. The model inexpensively revealed that additional processors only negligibly increased system thruput.

Buzen states in [B3] that the trend in I/O architecture has been toward increased parallelism. Knowledge of the effects upon performance of this parallelism is at this time qualitative and not quantitative for the reason that accurate methods easily modeling this parallelism are not available. The approximate solution methods discussed in this paper are a step toward providing this quantitative insight to the analyst.

ACKNOWLEDGEMENTS

This work was supported in part by National Science Foundation Grants GJ-1084 and DCR74-13302 while the author attended the University of Texas at Austin. Professor K. M. Chandy was responsible for many of the theories which are applied in this work. Professor J. C. Browne provided many useful insights into extending the applications of these results.

REFERENCES

[A1] B. Avi-Itzhak and D. P. Heyman, "Approximate Queueing Models for Multiprogrammed Computer Systems," Operations Research, Vol. 21, No. 6, pp. 1212-1231, 1973.

[B1] R. M. Brown, "An Analytic Model of a Large Scale Interactive System Including the Effects of Finite Main Memory," M.A. Thesis, Dept. of Computer Sciences, Univ. of Texas, Austin, Tx., 1974.

[B2] J. P. Buzen, "Queueing Network Models of Multiprogramming," Ph.D. Thesis, Harvard University, Cambridge, Mass., 1971.

[B3] J. P. Buzen "I/O Subsystem Architecture," Proc. IEEE, Vol. 63, No. 6, p. 871-878, June 1975.

[C1] K. M. Chandy, "The Analysis and Solutions for General Queueing Networks," Proc. 6th Annual Princeton Conf. Information Sciences and Systems, Princeton Univ., Princeton, N. J., March 1972.

[C2] K. M. Chandy, U. Herzog, and L. Woo, "Parametric Analysis of Queueing Network Models," IBM J. Res. Develop., Vol. 19, No. 1, p. 36, 1975.

[C3] Control Data Corporation, A Simulation Process-Oriented Language (ASPOL) Reference Manual, C.D.C. Special Support Division, Sunnyvale, Calif., 1972.

[C4] P. J. Courtois, "On the Near-Complete-Decomposability of Networks of
     Queues and of Stochastic Models of Multiprogramming Computing Systems,"
     Computer Science Dept. Rep. CMU-CS-72-111, Carnegie-Mellon Univ., Pitts-
     burgh, Pa., November 1971.

[C5] P. J. Courtois, "Error Analysis in Nearly Decomposable Stochastic Sys-
     tems," Econometrica, Vol. 43, No. 4, p. 691, July 1975.

[C6] M. A. Crane and D. I. Iglehart, "Simulating Stable Stochastic Systems, I:
     General Multiserver Queues," J. ACM, Vol. 21, p. 103, 1974.

[C7] M. A. Crane and D. I. Iglehart, "Simulating Stable Stochastic Systems, II:
     Markov Chains," J. ACM, Vol. 21, p. 114, 1974.

[H1] U. Herzog, L. Woo, and K. M. Chandy, "Solution of Queueing Problems by a
     Recursive Technique," IBM J. Res. Develop., Vol. 19., No. 3, pp. 295-300,
     May 1975.

[K1] T. W. Keller, ASQ Manual, Dept. of Computer Sciences Report TR-27, Univer-
     sity of Texas, Austin, Tx., 1973.

[K2] T. W. Keller and K. M. Chandy, "Computer Models with Constrained Parallel
     Processors," Proc. Sagamore Conference on Parallel Processing, 1974.

[K3] T. W. Keller, "Computer System Models with Passive Resources," Ph.D.
     Thesis, University of Texas, Austin, Tx., 1976.

[K4] L. Kleinrock, Queueing Systems, Vol. I: Theory, John Wiley and Sons, Inc.,
     New York, 1975.

[S1] C. H. Sauer, "Configuration of Computer Systems: An Approach Using Queue-
     ing Network Models," Ph.D. Thesis, University of Texas, Austin, Tx., 1975.

[W3] A. C. Williams and R. Bhandiwad, private communication.